BET
WITH THE
BEST

Published by
Daily Racing Form Press
100 Broadway, 7th Floor
New York, NY 10005

ISBN: 0-9700147-0-8

Library of Congress Control Number: 2001094502

Cover design by Chris Donofry
Text design by Serg Andreyev, Neuwirth & Associates, Inc.
Printed in the United States of America

ACKNOWLEDGEMENTS

THE GENERAL EDITOR of *Bet with the Best* was Victor Mather. The copy editor was Robin Foster. The manager of DRF Press is Dean Keppler.

Many thanks to *Daily Racing Form* employees Irwin Cohen, Chris Donofry, Elliott Eckstein, Charles Hayward, Laura Hubler, Mandy Minger, and Gary Nelson for their contributions.

TABLE OF CONTENTS

ACKNOWLEDGEMENTS   III

INTRODUCTION   V
AN OVERVIEW

1   BEYER   1
ON SIMULCASTING

2   BROHAMER   29
ON PACE

3   CRIST   61
ON VALUE

4   DAVIDOWITZ   75
ON BIAS, TRAINERS, AND KEY RACES

5   LITFIN   113
ON RECORD KEEPING

6   QUINN   137
ON CLASS

7   SHUBACK   171
ON EUROPEAN RACING

8   STICH   197
ON PEDIGREE

9   WATCHMAKER   215
ON STAKES RACES

ABOUT THE AUTHORS   247

INTRODUCTION
AN OVERVIEW

PERHAPS THERE ARE a few fans who discovered racing and the mysteries of past performances entirely on their own. Most of us, though, had a mentor: a parent, sibling, friend, or just a weather-beaten railbird who guided us on our initial steps to parimutuel glory. If we were very lucky, our mentor knew what he was talking about and taught us a few choice insights that still hold true in the modern, fast-paced simulcasting world.

Going to the races in the 21st century is more challenging than ever. A racetrack, simulcast parlor, or even a home computer can seem like a dizzying circus: Step right up and bet on Belmont, Calder, Lone Star, Yavapai Downs! Part-wheel that trifecta. Roll those doubles. Pick three! Pick four! What the heck, let's pick six! A handicapper is forgiven if, all too often, he wonders at the end of the day just where his expected juicy profit went.

But now imagine a day at the track with not one, but nine expert mentors, each patiently ready to guide you past danger to the far shores of profitability.

You open your *Daily Racing Form* and Tom Brohamer breaks down the race's pace while James Quinn assesses the field's relative class. Steve Davidowitz offers an insight on track bias, Lauren Stich finds the horse bred to handle the surface, Alan Shuback sifts through the inscrutable Europeans, and Mike Watchmaker tells you what to look for in stakes races. Steven Crist finds the best way to turn your opinion into an intelligent bet and Dave Litfin helps organize your thoughts into accurate records that will provide many more winners down the road. Andrew Beyer is on hand to provide the broader perspective on handicapping in the modern simulcast era.

And you don't even have to pick up their bar tab.

IF YOU'RE a handicapper who takes the sport seriously, you probably have read books and articles by many of these authors. The sport is constantly changing, however, and your opponents are getting better. If you don't keep up with those changes, you'll get left behind. This book is the first step into the 21st century for nine of the 20th century's leading handicappers. They have taken a new look at their specialties and applied their knowledge to racing as it is run today and likely to be run in the future.

Their insights will be indispensable for anyone who strives to bet with the best.

BEYER
ON SIMULCASTING
by Andrew Beyer

1

WHEN I WROTE *The Winning Horseplayer* in 1983, I observed that during the century there had been two profound revolutions affecting the way horseplayers bet. One was the elimination of bookmakers and their replacement by the parimutuel system. The other was the development of new forms of wagering—exactas, trifectas, pick sixes, and other exotica—to complement the traditional win, place, and show. Bettors who lived through each of these changes were forced to reexamine ideas that they had taken for granted all their lives.

I didn't expect to see another such revolution in my gambling lifetime, but the advent of full-card simulcasting has proved to be as dramatic a change as the game has even seen. For most of the history of racing, bettors have focused intensely on the races at their home track. Now horseplayers at many tracks can watch, and wager on, televised races from as many as 20 tracks around the country. Others stay at home and follow the action from coast to coast on television or on their computer via YouBet.

In every revolution, there is an old guard that resists and deplores the changes. I remember that in the early 1970's most veteran horseplayers decried the advent of exactas. The author Tom Ainslie wrote that exactas and trifectas should be of no interest to a serious student of the game. "They are," he declared, "strictly sucker bait." Of course, all players would eventually learn otherwise; the exotics created opportunities that never existed in the win-place-and-show era; jackpot bets such as the pick six generated payoffs that were inconceivable in the past. But it took time for many bettors to realize that the exotics were more than an evil temptation.

Similarly, when tracks in the United States began to offer full-card simulcasting in the mid-1990's, a horseplayer could easily have responded with the thought that this was a new form of sucker bait. I have always loved an abundance of betting action as much as any player, and—like most of my fellow habitues of the simulcast theater at Laurel Park—I was mesmerized by all the action on that wall of television screens. But I knew, too, how difficult it is to master the nuances of a single racetrack. When I play a race meeting in earnest, it's a demanding job. Each winter I go to Gulfstream Park and devote my total attention to the races there. I watch replays of every race—often scrutinizing a film several times—so that I can record trip notes for all the horses. I analyze each day's results to try to determine if any track bias existed. I study the methodology of all the major trainers, trying to learn their strengths and weaknesses. It's practically a full-time job to do all of this work for Gulfstream, yet the labor doesn't necessarily guarantee a winning result. How can a horseplayer possibly hope to succeed if he spreads his efforts thin while trying to pay attention to several tracks?

But after initially viewing the simulcast revolution with skepticism, another thought occurred to me. I realized that the mostly costly, frustrating race meetings I have experienced all had a common denominator. In 1994 I rented an apartment for the Saratoga season, and found myself trapped at a racetrack offering no promise. The racing secretary seemed to love small fields with odds-on favorites; a rainy month reduced the fields further and washed away most turf events. Sometimes fans found themselves sitting for 35 minutes between races, waiting for a four-horse field with no exacta wagering. Yet if you're stuck in Saratoga with nothing else to do, you're going to bet, and betting to alleviate the boredom turned out to be very expensive for me. I was so disgusted that I vowed I wouldn't be back to Saratoga until the next millennium, and I kept my promise. I had a similarly dismal season in Del Mar, where the steady diet of small fields—combined with the difficulty of battling the well-informed wise guys on the California circuit—gave rise to few good opportunities. But I was there, so I kept betting, and losing.

If I had been in a simulcast pavilion, scanning races across the nation, I would have dismissed the four-horse fields at Saratoga or the unpromising fare at Del Mar in an instant, turning my attention to some other track that offered more interest. Only because I was locked into betting poor races did I lose my money on them.

Unattractive meetings like Saratoga '94 arise all too frequently. Tracks across the country are plagued with horse shortages that give rise to unbettable small fields. Some race meetings are spoiled by bad weather. Sometimes a bettor will fret that larceny may be out of control at a certain track. The wondrous change made possible by the age of simulcasting is that nobody needs to be trapped. You're sick of seeing Russell Baze's mount at 2-5 in every race at Golden Gate Fields? No problem. There are dozens of other tracks that merit your interest.

MOST HORSEPLAYERS in the U.S. now have a wide choice of tracks to play, and it is a choice that deserves serious contemplation. But the first choice that any bettor should consider is his home track, for there is a definite home-court advantage in handicapping. The presentation of betting information on simulcasts, although it has improved since the infancy of the medium, is still flawed. A bettor depending on television for all his information will surely lose some wagers because he didn't know that a horse dumped his rider and ran off in the post parade; or that a sudden shower just before post time made the track wet-fast. A bettor at the track may have access to replay centers that make available the head-on shots of past races—an advantage usually denied to a simulcast player. And, of course, bettors at the track are more apt to hear scuttlebutt than simulcast customers. If a first-time starter in an upcoming leg of the pick three or the pick six is widely rumored to be a good thing, it's helpful to hear the whispers in advance.

Besides proximity to the live action, however, there are other factors that a horseplayer should consider in deciding where to focus his attention:

TAKEOUT

Many bettors are oblivious to the impact of takeout rates on their bottom line, but they would be more sensitized to this factor if they kept accurate records of their wagering (which every horseplayer ought to do anyway, for tax purposes). A player who churns

$1,000 a day through the betting windows and goes to the track five days a week is wagering roughly $300,000 a year. For every additional percentage point that the track takes from his wagering dollar, he loses $3,000. A couple of points can easily make the difference in winning and losing during the course of a year. When so many choices are available, it is crazy to try to fight the percentages and play tracks with exorbitant takeouts such as Philadelphia Park (30 percent on trifectas) and Hialeah (29 percent on pick threes) when tracks in California and Kentucky offer a better product with much lower takeout.

JUICE

I may be paranoid, but I believe racing is going through one of its periodic cycles when highly effective illegal drugs are in widespread use on many racing circuits. As a journalist, I can't prove it or declare this to be a fact. But as a gambler, I see signs of it everywhere. The game is difficult enough without having to wonder constantly who is getting what, and I'd prefer to avoid tracks where the problem seems to reach epidemic proportions.

Statistics in *Daily Racing Form* provide a barometer with which to gauge potential juice problems. Historically, even the greatest trainers rarely win more than 25 percent of their starts in a year. Bill Mott, arguably the best horseman in America, has a powerful stable and never runs horses where they don't belong, yet even in a year that he trained Cigar and earned the Eclipse Award, he won at only a 25 percent clip. If you scan racetracks around the country for the last two or three years, however, you'll find many where certain trainers are winning 30 or 35 percent of their races—or more. These are not horsemen like Mott, Shug McGaughey, or Dick Mandella having the best years of their lives. They are, in many cases, trainers who were virtual unknowns a couple years earlier. When a particular track is dominated by these miracle workers, I prefer to steer clear of it. Even if my suspicions are the unfounded delusions of a paranoid gambler, I know that these feelings will undermine my handicapping and betting.

POOL SIZE

The biggest bettors in the game, those who regularly put thousands of dollars on a single race, have limited choices of where to play. The high rollers almost always concentrate on the New York and Southern California tracks, plus Gulfstream Park in the winter, because these are among the few places where it is possible to make a monster bet without knocking the odds out of kilter. Bettors who want to take a shot at six- and seven-digit payoffs in the pick six are almost forced to follow California and New York, because these are the only places where big carryover jackpots are commonplace. However, the majority of players have more options. Obviously, they don't want to play tracks with minuscule betting pools, where even a $50 exacta wager will affect the payoffs. But there are many midlevel tracks—the places that handle $1 million a day or thereabouts—that offer reasonable moneymaking opportunities and have another inestimable advantage.

PARIMUTUEL COMPETITION

The essential nature of racetrack betting is very much like a poker game. You're competing against rival players at a table where the house takes a cut from every pot. Overcoming the house's take may be difficult, but your chances of success also depend on who is sitting at the table. If you're in Las Vegas, and the table is filled with local sharpies with names like Doc and Slim, you're in trouble. But if the table is occupied by a bunch of guys wearing convention badges saying they're from Toledo, you've got a shot. The principle is the same at the racetrack, although in the simulcast era your rivals may be sitting in front of a television monitor a thousand miles away and you can't tell for certain whether they are rubes or sharpies. But it is not difficult to make an educated guess.

Most of the savvy, high-rolling gamblers in the simulcast world concentrate on New York and California racing, plus Gulfstream Park, Churchill Downs, and Keeneland, because of the size of the betting pools and the availability of big jackpot wagers. Moreover, each of these circuits has a core of serious players who focus on the local track and know all of its nuances. Whenever I attempt to play California, I am struck by how well informed the local horseplayers are.

In the winter of 1999, as California started to offer full-card simulcasts from Gulfstream Park, I contacted my friend Jeff Siegel—the sharpest handicapper in the West—and suggested we consult on each day's card. I would phone him from Florida each day and give him my thoughts on the Gulfstream card; he'd brief me on Santa Anita. Siegel knew every angle and subtlety at his home track. Once he told me that he loved a horse who had raced one time in his career, six months ago, and lost by 20 lengths. On paper the animal looked hopeless, but Siegel knew that the colt had trained well for his debut and had been highly regarded; that he'd injured his shins in that race; that he'd now trained extremely well and had worked in company with an older horse.

This sounded like an esoteric and exciting opportunity—until the horse went off at 2-1. The California racing community is filled with wise guys like Siegel who know how all the horses are training and understand all the moves of all the trainers. When I bet into the California pools, I have the uneasy feeling that I am sitting at a poker table across from Doc and Slim, and I am wearing a convention badge on my lapel.

For the average horseplayer, there is no reason to take a seat at the toughest table in the casino when so many alternatives are available. Plenty of midlevel tracks offer good-quality racing without attracting the attention of the nation's wise guys—tracks on the level of Laurel and Pimlico, Delaware Park, Turfway Park, Remington, Lone Star, and so on. One statistic for a horseplayer to consult at these tracks is the percentage of a track's handle that comes from simulcast customers. If the majority of the money at a midlevel track is being wagered by the locals, a simulcast customer might be at a disadvantage playing against the home team. But some tracks have almost no smart local money in their pools. Prairie Meadows offers respectable racing that has been fueled by slot-machine revenue, and it may handle $1 million on a card. Yet as much as 90 percent of that total is wagered off-track, and I would guess that much of it comes from players leafing through simulcast programs, not even sure where Prairie Meadows is. (Altoona, Iowa, is the answer.) The average player will have a much better chance for success if he applies his attention to tracks like Prairie Meadows instead of bucking tough competition at places like Santa Anita.

IF I AM devoting my total concentration to a single racetrack, I will happily do battle against the other wise guys. The Gulfstream Park meeting is the major event of my gambling year, and I focus on it almost exclusively, whether I am sitting under the palm trees in Hallandale, Florida, or playing from the simulcast theater in the Laurel grandstand. My handicapping approach doesn't change in either case. I have tried, as well, to wage a war on two fronts simultaneously. One summer I decided to follow the races from Monmouth Park and Southern California. I wasn't sure that either place was going to offer bountiful opportunities, so I decided to double my possibilities by playing both. I taped the races from both circuits, and studied them each morning, making trip notes on a minimum of 18 races a day. I handicapped two cards a day in depth. By the end of the summer, my energy was depleted but my bankroll was no fatter. I concluded that I had been trying to do too much, that I was spending too much time in my preparation and that I didn't have the necessary mental sharpness when I was gambling. If it is dauntingly difficult to play two tracks in depth at the same time, how can a handicapper operate in the simulcast era with as many as a dozen tracks beckoning him? After much costly experimentation, I found an answer to this crucial question.

When full-card simulcasts were introduced at the Maryland tracks, I was initially as excited and distracted as a kid in a candy store. I flipped the pages of the *Daily Racing Form*, jumping from the past performances at Laurel to Belmont to Delaware to Philadelphia to Churchill Downs. I would refer to the Beyer Speed Figures, of course, and try to do a quick analysis of the race, but there wasn't time to do much else. Naturally, as I tried to bet on the basis of a superficial study, I was the sucker in the game. No horseplayer can win consistently by simply scanning the data in the past performances; anybody who thinks he can do so is delusional. If the average parimutuel takeout is 20 percent, a player has to be 20 percent smarter than the crowd just to break even. To beat the game it is essential to have an edge—to possess insights and information that rival bettors lack.

When I am concentrating on a single track, I attempt to gain such insights into every horse. I want to have notes on all the horses' trips and to know whether they raced over a track with a bias. In handicapping a race, I try to weigh the strengths and weaknesses of each horse. One horse earned a figure of 86 with an easy trip stalking the leaders; another earned an 80 racing near the rail on a day of an anti-rail track bias. I try to analyze the nuances of every race in a painstaking fashion. Yet when I reflect upon my most memorable wins, I am not sure that all of this in-depth study is necessary. Great scores are usually based on a single strong insight.

The biggest single-race win of my life came in the 1984 Belmont Stakes, after I observed that Swale and Pine Circle were parked impossibly wide at the Preakness on a day when the rail bias at Pimlico was extraordinarily strong. The two of them came back to run 1-2 in the Belmont Stakes and produce a $125.80 exacta. I made a memorable score on the 1988 Preakness after concluding that Risen Star was much the best horse in the Kentucky Derby despite his third-place finish; he was trying to rally eight wide into a slow pace set by the filly Winning Colors, and ran superbly under adverse conditions. But the race that best encapsulates the essential nature of the handicapping process—the quest for a key insight or piece of information that other bettors lack—was a bottom-level maiden race at Laurel on October 9, 1990. That was well before the dawn of the simulcasting era, but reflecting upon that race crystallized my philosophy of playing simulcasts.

The Maryland tracks then offered a jackpot wager called the double triple (known elsewhere as the twin trifecta), which required bettors to pick the first three finishers in two different races. The pool occasionally grew to dizzying levels. Earlier in the year, at Pimlico, it had surpassed $1 million, and on a memorable day I was one of the 10 winners holding a ticket worth $134,682. Now the pot was growing again, approaching the $200,000 mark, as Laurel carded races filled with bad maidens and first-time starters, events that were inscrutable to the best of handicappers. On October 9, the races were indecipherable on the surface, but the first half of the twin tri was filled with so many horrible horses that there seemed to be only three in the field who could run at all. They appeared likely to produce an obvious, short-priced result.

So I studied the fifth race harder, researching the first-time starters in the field. One of them was a horse named Lanahan, whose pedigree and workouts were thoroughly nondescript. But when I called up the record of his trainer on the computer, I felt a tinge of excitement as I stared at the data. Over the previous seven years, Lanahan's trainer, Marvin Kuhn, had won with 7 of 23 first-time starters—an impressive 30 percent. I researched the record of Lanahan's dam, a mare named Lady Pippin, and found that eight of her previous offspring had won races. In 1985 her daughter Fair Isis won as a first-time starter at Laurel at odds of 10-1. The trainer: Marvin Kuhn. In 1987 her son Sir Jace won as a first-time starter at Laurel at 9-1. The trainer: Marvin Kuhn.

After studying the rest of the race, I concluded that there were three logical contenders in the field. So I invested $1,296 in the twin trifecta, boxing the obvious favorites in the first leg and hoping to wind up with 24 live tickets for the second half—which is what happened. I was in the position to take the shot I wanted, making a four-horse box that included the 42-1 Lanahan.

I am not superstitious, but I took a position in front of the television monitor in Laurel's Sports Palace where I had rooted home my big win earlier in the year. I watched excitedly as two of my logical horses surged to take command of the race, and then the television camera panned back to a mass of horseflesh vying for third place. Five horses were abreast, but I thought I saw the distinct black silks worn by Lanahan's jockey narrowly in front of the pack. When the photo finish was developed, Lanahan's number went up in third place, and I had the only ticket on the double triple, worth $195,070.50.

The next day I wrote a column about the double triple in the *Washington Post*, and began it with a reflection upon the nature of handicapping:

"When I was a fledgling horseplayer, I often dreamed about discovering the Secret of Beating the Races—the system or the great truth that would enable me to win at the track. I would learn, of course, that there is no such big 'secret.' Modern-day horseplayers know all of the major factors that influence the outcome of races. The best we can hope to find are little secrets or insights: We might see a horse get into trouble that most other observers missed; we might detect a subtle bias in a racing surface; we might note that a particular trainer wins often with a particular pattern. Like prospectors for gold, we sift through a great mass of material in quest of an occasional nugget.

"On Monday morning, while sitting at my computer terminal, I found such a nugget. . . ."

It took me time, too much time, to relate this observation about the nature of handicapping to the challenges of the simulcast era. But when I did, I changed my whole approach to the modern racing game. I had always felt the need to know as much as I could about every horse in a race and to correlate that information before making a final betting decision, even though much of the information turned out to be irrelevant, and compiling it was enormously time consuming. Instead of gathering that great mass of material and hoping that a nugget would shine through, perhaps I should refine my search and look specifically for the nuggets. Find Swale parked wide on the rail-biased Pimlico track. Find Risen Star closing eight wide into a slow pace. Find Marvin Kuhn's astuteness with cheaply bred first-time starters. And then wait for the horses to be entered, or for the right situation to materialize.

Of course, there is nothing new about compiling a "horses-to-watch" list and waiting for the names to appear in the entries. But for most of the history of the game, attempting to follow and bet specific horses has been an exercise fraught with frustration. In *Picking Winners,* I related a tale of woe that still pains me to this day. During the winter of 1973, a heavy rain followed by a fast freeze created a phenomenal bias at now-defunct Bowie Race Course. A front-runner hugging the rail won virtually every race; horses who tried to make wide moves had no chance. As I reviewed the results during the period of this bias, I noted a horse named Right Risk who had gone off at 109-1 and made a powerful wide move before fading to finish sixth. Moreover, he had earned a giant speed figure—and this was an era when most bettors didn't have access to speed figures. A week later, he was entered at Bowie and listed at 30-1 in the morning line, and I went to the track confident that I was going to win a fortune. But when I arrived, I was disappointed to learn that he had been scratched, and I couldn't understand why. I found out two days later. I glanced at the race results and saw that Right Risk had been taken to Dover Downs, a little track in Delaware, and entered in a field where he was virtually unbeatable, based on his Bowie form. Not only did he pay $13.10 to win, but he was also the key to the "big exacta," a form of wagering requiring bettors to pick the top two finishers in two races. It would have been worth $35,297, and I am convinced I would have won it if I had only known that Right Risk was running. Almost every veteran horseplayer can relate a similar story, because it was once extremely difficult to keep tabs on horses who were being shipped from track to track. (And, of course, in the presimulcast era, it wasn't always easy to get a bet down, either.)

A young computer programmer named Miles Michelson, who was working on a contract basis for *Daily Racing Form,* solved this perennial problem one night in 1997. Michelson had noticed that YouBet, an on-line wagering operation, was offering a crude feature that allowed subscribers to track the whereabouts of up to five horses on major racing circuits. "I realized," he said, "that it wouldn't be difficult to do a similar feature on the DRF site using the entries data from around the country. So without asking anyone, I developed the first version of Stable Mail in a single night and included it on the entries section of the DRF site the following morning. That got me into a little bit of trouble the next day when people started asking questions about the service. But that quickly settled down as people understood the idea and came to like it."

Michelson's programming allowed a user to enter the name of any horse he wanted to follow. When that horse appeared in the entries at any track in the United States, Stable Mail would send the user an E-mail message notifying him: "Your horse, (Name), is entered in the seventh race at Belmont on July 9." There was no charge for the service. The system grew in popularity, and by the time Michelson left the *Form* at the end of 1999, Stable Mail was tracking more than 300,000 horses for some 35,000 individuals. When *Daily Racing Form* revamped its website in 2001, it made further improvements to the service, which has the capacity to track more than two million requests. The service is now called Horse Watch.

This is the crucial final ingredient for the simulcast-betting strategy that I now employ. The concept, in broad terms, is this:

- Find crucial nuggets of information about individual horses that might turn out to be decisive handicapping factors when they run next.
- Maintain a Horse Watch list of these promising horses.
- When one of these horses appears in the entries, handicap the race by focusing on him and judging whether he is worth a bet.

This is almost a complete reversal of the normal handicapping process. I used to believe in approaching a race with no preconceptions, weighing the pros and cons of each entrant, and determining which horse seemed the best. Now I analyze a race with the thought that I may want to bet a particular horse.

How do we mine the nuggets of information that are going to be the basis for this approach? Every horseplayer has his own favorite handicapping angles and factors that he thinks are most productive. I have believed—ever since I became aware of their existence in the early 1970's—that track biases give rise to more good betting opportunities than any other factor in the game. Sometimes the inside part of a track will seemingly be harder and faster than the rest of the racing strip, and the horse who pops to the lead on the rail will seize an insuperable advantage. Sometimes the inside part of a track may be disadvantageous, causing speed horses on the rail to wilt and allowing races to be dominated by stretch-runners who make wide late moves. Whenever such conditions arise, the perform-

ance of every horse is colored in some way by the bias. If a track is rail favoring and speed favoring, any good performance by a front-runner on the rail must be viewed with some skepticism. The bias probably helped him, and he isn't as good as he looks on paper. Conversely, a horse trounced while racing five wide may be forgiven for his loss. And a horse who managed to run creditably despite going very wide should be viewed as a strong candidate for a wager when he runs next. The knowledge that a bias existed on a given day is like a secret code for evaluating the horses who ran over that track. It is the source of dozens and dozens of potential nuggets. And it thus makes a highly effective tool for a simulcast-betting strategy.

When I am playing a single track intensively, I study films to detect any nuances in the condition of the racing strip. But when I am following several tracks at once, it isn't feasible to analyze all the films, so I rely heavily on the data in the official charts, which are published in *Daily Racing Form* and its *Simulcast Weekly*. I note the running style of each winner, and read the footnotes to learn whether the winners ran on or off the rail, as I try to determine whether the track favored a particular type of horse. Making such judgments based on the charts, I readily admit, is an exercise filled with peril, since chart callers can be inconsistent in their comments. Some are diligent about informing readers where different horses are positioned on the track, while others don't seem to have the word "rail" in their vocabulary. (If I have to make my own direct judgments about a bias, I will watch the track's race-replay show, assuming it is one of the many such shows available through DirecTV and other satellite providers.) However, if there are any uncertainties about the condition of the track, I will not use it as a basis for future wagers. When I am analyzing the charts from as many as half a dozen tracks, I expect to find enough clear-cut, strong biases that I don't have to deal with ambiguous situations.

The Maryland tracks are blessed with one of the best teams of chart callers in the U.S., and their footnotes dependably indicate where horses were positioned on the racing strip. Anyone who read the result charts for Laurel on February 12, 2000, would have a clear understanding of the track's bias.

FIRST RACE **1$\frac{1}{16}$ MILES. (1.41^{4}) CLAIMING. Purse $12,500 FOUR YEAR OLDS AND UPWARD, WHICH HAVE NEVER WON THREE RACES. Weight 122 lbs. Non–winners of two races at a mile or over since December 18 allowed, 3 lbs. One such race, 5 lbs. CLAIMING PRICE $14,500, for each $500 to $13,500 2 lbs. (Races where entered for $11,500 or less not considered). (Clear. 30.)**

Laurel

FEBRUARY 12, 2000

Value of Race: $12,500 Winner $7,125; second $2,625; third $1,375; fourth $750; fifth $375; sixth $250. Mutuel Pool $50,210.00 Exacta Pool $58,589.00 Trifecta Pool $36,275.00

Last Raced	Horse	M/Eqt.	A.Wt	PP	St	¼	½	¾	Str	Fin	Jockey	Cl'g Pr	Odds $1
26Jan00 ^{5}Lrl^{2}	Chief's Boy	Lbf	4 117	5	5	7	7	6^{4}	4^{3}	$1^{1\frac{1}{2}}$	Wilson R	14500	1.90
8Jan00 ^{4}Lrl^{3}	Snook	Lbf	4 117	1	3	1^{2}	$1^{1\frac{1}{2}}$	1^{hd}	1^{hd}	2^{hd}	Klinger C O	14500	a-*1.90
3Feb00 ^{3}Lrl^{2}	All Mighty John	Lb	7 115	2	2	$2^{\frac{1}{2}}$	2^{hd}	2^{hd}	2^{hd}	$3^{\frac{3}{4}}$	Johnston M T	14000	3.50
2Jan00 ^{5}Lrl^{7}	Brass Offering	Lb	4 117	6	4	3^{1}	3^{1}	3^{3}	3^{1}	$4^{2\frac{1}{4}}$	Dominguez R A	14500	a-1.90
29Dec99 ^{9}Lrl^{7}	Brilliant Verse	Lbf	5 117	4	7	$4^{\frac{1}{2}}$	4^{hd}	4^{1}	5^{1}	$5^{4\frac{1}{4}}$	Pino M G	14500	3.40
2Jan00 ^{5}Lrl^{8}	Biennale	L	6 117	3	1	5^{1}	5^{1}	$5^{1\frac{1}{2}}$	6^{10}	6^{15}	Verge M E	14500	15.80
3Feb00 ^{5}Lrl^{5}	One for Speedy	Lbf	4 114	7	6	$6^{1\frac{1}{2}}$	6^{hd}	7	7	7	Douglas F G	13500	31.20

***—Actual Betting Favorite.**
a–Coupled: Snook and Brass Offering.

OFF AT 12:15 Start Good. Won driving. Track fast.
TIME :25, :50, 1:15^{1}, 1:40^{2}, 1:46^{4} (:25.12, :50.01, 1:15.27, 1:40.51, 1:46.80)

$2 Mutuel Prices:				
	5–CHIEF'S BOY	5.80	3.00	2.20
	1–SNOOK (a-entry)		2.80	2.10
	2–ALL MIGHTY JOHN			2.40

$2 EXACTA 5–1 PAID $15.80 $2 TRIFECTA 5–1–2 PAID $32.40

Dk. b. or br. c, by Roanoke–Main Chance, by Elocutionist. Trainer Gaudet Edmond D. Bred by Bourne William T & Manfuso Robert T (Md).

CHIEF'S BOY raced under snug rating and towards the inside, angled five wide in upper stretch, ,closed nicely, took command late and drew clear under a drive. SNOOK sprinted clear early, set a slow pace along the inside, dueled in mid stretch and held well. ALL MIGHTY JOHN prompted the pace two wide, lodged a bid between rivals mid way on the final turn, dueled and was outfinished. BRASS OFFERING stalked the pace three wide, moved up three wide mid way on the final turn, pressed the issue and hung. BRILLIANT VERSE rated close up inside, angled four wide near the quarter pole and faded. BIENNALE raced off the rail and tired. ONE FOR SPEEDY raced four wide early and faltered.

Owners— 1, Gaudet Linda & Bailey Morris; 2, Englander Richard A; 3, Bassford Elaine L; 4, C & T Stable; 5, P T K Racing Ltd; 6, ORouke Donna; 7, Raszewski Joseph R

Trainers—1, Gaudet Edmond D; 2, Capuano Dale; 3, Leatherbury King T; 4, Capuano Dale; 5, Allen A Ferris III; 6, Tuminelli Joseph M; 7, Raszewski Joseph

Scratched— Tony Basich (2Jan00 ^{5}LRL^{5})

SECOND RACE **7 FURLONGS. (1.21^{2}) CLAIMING. Purse $23,000 FOUR YEAR OLDS AND UPWARD. Weight 122 lbs. Non–winners of two races since December 18 allowed, 3 lbs. A race, 5 lbs. CLAIMING PRICE $25,000, for each $2,500 to $20,000 2 lbs. (Races where entered for $18,500 or less not considered).**

Laurel

FEBRUARY 12, 2000

Value of Race: $23,000 Winner $13,110; second $4,830; third $2,530; fourth $1,380; fifth $690; sixth $460. Mutuel Pool $86,437.00 Exacta Pool $92,398.00 Trifecta Pool $63,169.00

Last Raced	Horse	M/Eqt.	A.Wt	PP	St	¼	½	Str	Fin	Jockey	Cl'g Pr	Odds $1
13Jan00 ^{7}Lrl^{2}	Glider Pilot	Lb	5 117	1	7	6^{1}	6^{2}	$4^{2\frac{1}{2}}$	$1^{1\frac{1}{2}}$	Wilson R	25000	1.20
13Jan00 ^{7}Lrl^{1}	Sonofaqueen	Lbf	6 119	7	1	$5^{\frac{1}{2}}$	5^{1}	2^{hd}	$2^{\frac{3}{4}}$	Juarez C	25000	3.70
9Jan00 ^{8}Pha^{1}	Spicy Award	Lf	5 117	5	3	$1^{\frac{1}{2}}$	$1^{\frac{1}{2}}$	$1^{\frac{1}{2}}$	$3^{3\frac{1}{2}}$	Pino M G	25000	3.80
13Jan00 ^{7}Lrl^{4}	Mount Defiance	L	5 115	2	4	3^{hd}	2^{1}	$3^{1\frac{1}{2}}$	$4^{1\frac{1}{4}}$	Johnston M T	22500	7.80
5Jan00 ^{7}Lrl^{4}	Endless Night	Lf	5 117	3	5	2^{hd}	3^{hd}	6^{hd}	$5^{\frac{1}{2}}$	Rocco J	25000	5.40
28Jan00 ^{6}Lrl^{2}	Allen Gorgeous	Lbf	7 117	6	2	$4^{2\frac{1}{2}}$	4^{hd}	5^{1}	$6^{\frac{3}{4}}$	Carstens D	25000	15.80
21Sep99 ^{7}Del^{6}	Mariatom	Lb	6 115	4	6	7	7	7	7	Goodwin N	22500	49.90

OFF AT 12:42 Start Good. Won driving. Track fast.
TIME :24, :47^{4}, 1:12^{2}, 1:24^{2} (:24.01, :47.96, 1:12.50, 1:24.46)

$2 Mutuel Prices:				
	1–GLIDER PILOT	4.40	2.60	2.20
	7–SONOFAQUEEN		3.20	2.40
	5–SPICY AWARD			2.40

$2 EXACTA 1–7 PAID $18.00 $2 TRIFECTA 1–7–5 PAID $42.80

Dk. b. or br. g, by Slew o' Gold–Glide Along, by Great Above. Trainer Dutrow Anthony W. Bred by Appleton Arthur I (Fla).

GLIDER PILOT wore a nasal strip, rated off the rail and behind foes on the turn, angled six wide into the lane, had his rider lose his whip in mid stretch then drew clear under steady pressure. SONOFAQUEEN was rated back after an alert start, raced five wide under a snug hold, lodged a bid in mid stretch and finished gamely. SPICY AWARD disputed the pace three wide, held a clear lead approaching the furlong marker then weakened late. MOUNT DEFIANCE saved ground forcing the pace and weakened late. ENDLESS NIGHT was sent up early between rivals, chased the issue two wide and faded. ALLEN GORGEOUS raced four wide forcing the pace and weakened. MARIATOM raced wide down the backstretch, angled to the inside on the turn and failed to respond.

Owners— 1, Federman Charlie; 2, Plaine Enterprises Inc; 3, Dipietro Teresa; 4, Germania Farms Inc; 5, Rouse Randolph D; 6, Clagett III Hal C; 7, Eubanks Daniel et al

Trainers—1, Dutrow Anthony W; 2, Costew John B; 3, Siravo Robert D; 4, Motion H Graham; 5, Casey James M; 6, Robb John J; 7, Eubanks Annette M

Sonofaqueen was claimed by Coast By Coast; trainer, Dutrow Anthony W.,
Endless Night was claimed by Leo Gasparini Racing Stable; trainer, Lake Scott A.

$2 Daily Double (5–1) Paid $18.80; Daily Double Pool $43,033.

THIRD RACE

Laurel

FEBRUARY 12, 2000

5½ FURLONGS. (1.02^{4}) CLAIMING. Purse $17,500 FOUR YEAR OLDS AND UPWARD. Weight 122 lbs. Non-winners of two races since December 18 allowed, 3 lbs. A race, 5 lbs. CLAIMING PRICE $18,500, for each $1,000 to $16,500 2 lbs. (Races where entered for $14,500 or less not considered).

Value of Race: $17,500 Winner $9,975; second $3,675; third $1,925; fourth $1,050; fifth $525; sixth $350. Mutuel Pool $101,851.00 Exacta Pool $140,180.00

Last Raced	Horse	M/Eqt.	A.	Wt	PP	St	¼	⅜	Str	Fin	Jockey	Cl'g Pr	Odds $1
13Jan00 ^{4}Lrl^{4}	Sell the Farm	L	6	117	3	3	2^{hd}	2^{1}	2^{4}	$1^{1\frac{3}{4}}$	Wilson R	18500	1.00
4Feb00 ^{8}Lrl^{7}	Wild Love Affair	Lb	5	119	2	4	$1^{\frac{1}{2}}$	$1^{1\frac{1}{2}}$	1^{2}	$2^{2\frac{3}{4}}$	Dominguez R A	18500	3.30
28Jan00 ^{6}Lrl^{3}	Swingin Verse	Lbf	5	117	1	6	6^{hd}	7	$4^{1\frac{1}{2}}$	$3^{\frac{1}{2}}$	Pino M G	18500	2.90
2Feb00 ^{8}Lrl^{7}	Passage East	Lb	7	117	4	2	$5^{1\frac{1}{2}}$	5^{2}	3^{1}	4^{nk}	Cortez A C	18500	13.60
13Jan00 ^{4}Lrl^{7}	One More Power	Lf	7	117	6	7	7	6^{hd}	5^{2}	$5^{8\frac{1}{2}}$	Douglas F G	18500	33.00
24Feb99 ^{6}Lrl^{3}	Mykanos	Lbf	4	117	7	1	4^{1}	$4^{\frac{1}{2}}$	6^{hd}	$6^{2\frac{3}{4}}$	Hutton G W	18500	35.00
28Jan00 ^{6}Lrl^{7}	Speed Freak	Lb	5	117	5	5	3^{3}	3^{4}	7	7	Frazier R L	18500	7.60

OFF AT 1:11 Start Good. Won driving. Track fast.

TIME :23, :46^{1}, :58^{3}, 1:04^{4} (:23.07, :46.30, :58.76, 1:04.82)

$2 Mutuel Prices:

5–SELL THE FARM	4.00	2.80	2.10
4–WILD LOVE AFFAIR		3.00	2.20
2–SWINGIN VERSE			2.20

$2 EXACTA 5–4 PAID $14.40

B. h, by Kipper Kelly–Needle Me On, by Executioner. Trainer Dutrow Anthony W. Bred by Stein Irma C (Fla).

SELL THE FARM wore a nasal strip, prompted the pace in the three path, closed under stout left handed pressure, drew even approaching the sixteenth pole then drew clear. WILD LOVE AFFAIR set the pace two wide, went well clear in upper stretch, was collared a sixteenth out and gave way grudgingly. SWINGIN VERSE saved ground throughout and finished willingly. PASSAGE EAST saved ground on the turn, eased out in upper stretch and finished willingly. ONE MORE POWER lacked speed, raced five wide into the lane and finished with interest. MYKANOS bore out leaving the gate, raced wide on the turn and failed to menace. SPEED FREAK forced the pace four wide and tired in upper stretch.

Owners— 1, Coast By Coast; 2, Team 26; 3, DLS Thoroughbreds Inc; 4, Dunromin Racing Stable; 5, Bender Sondra D; 6, Heft Arnold A; 7, Englander Richard A

Trainers—1, Dutrow Anthony W; 2, Wolfendale Howard E; 3, Allen A Ferris III; 4, O'Brien Maura C; 5, Murray Lawrence E; 6, Robb John J; 7, Capuano Dale

Sell the Farm was claimed by J B Square Inc; trainer, Runco Jeff C.,

Swingin Verse was claimed by Conner John D; trainer, Conner John D.

Scratched— Paco's Friend (29Jan00 ^{8}LRL^{4}), Oopster (28Jan00 ^{6}LRL^{5})

$2 Twin Trifecta (5–4–2) Paid $17.40; Twin Trifecta Pool $15,183.

FOURTH RACE

Laurel

FEBRUARY 12, 2000

$1\frac{3}{16}$ MILES. (1.54^{3}) OPTIONAL CLAIMING. Purse $32,000 FOUR YEAR OLDS AND UPWARD, WHICH HAVE NEVER WON THREE RACES OTHER THAN MAIDEN, CLAIMING, STARTER, OR HUNT MEET, OR CLAIMING $35,000–$30,000. Weight 122 lbs. Non-winners of two races at a mile or over since December 18 allowed, 3 lbs. One such race, 5 lbs. CLAIMING PRICE $35,000, for each $2,500 to $30,000 2 lbs. (Races where entered for $25,000 or less not considered).

Value of Race: $32,000 Winner $18,240; second $6,720; third $3,520; fourth $1,920; fifth $960; sixth $640. Mutuel Pool $76,076.00 Exacta Pool $87,100.00 Trifecta Pool $49,211.00

Last Raced	Horse	M/Eqt.	A.	Wt	PP	St	¼	½	¾	Str	Fin	Jockey	Cl'g Pr	Odds $1
2Feb00 ^{6}Lrl^{1}	Over To You	Lf	6	117	5	6	5^{hd}	5^{5}	5^{7}	$1^{\frac{1}{2}}$	1^{2}	Wilson R	35000	2.10
12Jan00 ^{8}Lrl^{2}	Mister Business	Lb	5	117	2	1	2^{2}	$2^{3\frac{1}{2}}$	2^{3}	$2^{2\frac{1}{2}}$	$2^{1\frac{3}{4}}$	Rocco J		6.80
5Jan00 ^{7}Lrl^{1}	Spartan Mission	Lb	5	119	1	2	3^{1}	$3^{\frac{1}{2}}$	$3^{3\frac{1}{2}}$	$3^{\frac{1}{2}}$	$3^{2\frac{1}{2}}$	Pino M G		1.90
13Jan00 ^{9}Lrl^{1}	Diplomat	Lb	5	113	6	4	1^{3}	1^{2}	1^{2}	4^{10}	4^{11}	Cortez A C	30000	3.10
20Apr99 ^{6}Del^{4}	Allpoints Bulletin	Lbf	5	117	3	3	6	6	6	$5^{2\frac{1}{2}}$	$5^{9\frac{1}{4}}$	Frazier R L		11.00
29Dec99 ^{4}Lrl^{1}	Game Two	L	5	117	4	5	$4^{3\frac{1}{2}}$	4^{4}	4^{1}	6	6	Johnston M T		10.10

OFF AT 1:37 Start Good. Won driving. Track fast.

TIME :24^{1}, :48^{1}, 1:12^{3}, 1:37^{4}, 1:56^{3} (:24.34, :48.25, 1:12.77, 1:37.92, 1:56.66)

$2 Mutuel Prices:

5–OVER TO YOU	6.20	3.60	2.60
2–MISTER BUSINESS		5.40	3.00
1–SPARTAN MISSION			2.20

$2 EXACTA 5–2 PAID $42.00 $2 TRIFECTA 5–2–1 PAID $58.80

Ch. g, by Rubiano–Overnight, by Mr. Leader. Trainer Wolfendale Howard E. Bred by Nuckols Charles Jr & Sons (Ky).

OVER TO YOU settled off the rail, steadily advanced three wide entering the lane, went to command near mid stretch, lugged in when clear a sixteenth out and was kept to a drive. MISTER BUSINESS prompted the pace two wide, went to a short lead near the quarter pole, steadied behind the winner at the sixteenth pole and held well. SPARTAN MISSION rated towards the inside, swung out four wide in upper stretch and rallied mildly. DIPLOMAT sprinted clear, set the pace along the inside, was headed approaching the quarter pole and weakened in mid stretch. ALLPOINTS BULLETIN was outrun. GAME TWO faltered. An objection by the rider of MISTER BUSINESS against the winner for alleged interference near the sixteenth pole was disallowed.

Owners— 1, Cole Robert L Jr; 2, Salomone Mark E; 3, DLS Thoroughbreds Inc; 4, Mucho Hombre Stable; 5, Porter II Richard C; 6, Little L F

Trainers—1, Wolfendale Howard E; 2, Trimmer Richard K; 3, Allen A Ferris III; 4, Albert Linda L; 5, Servis John C; 6, Delp Gerald C

Over To You was claimed by DLS Thoroughbreds Inc; trainer, Allen A Ferris III.

$2 Pick Three (1–3/5–5) Paid $26.00; Pick Three Pool $11,350.

FIFTH RACE
Laurel
FEBRUARY 12, 2000

6 FURLONGS. (1.08) MAIDEN SPECIAL WEIGHT. Purse $25,000 MAIDENS, FOUR YEAR OLDS AND UPWARD. Weight 122 lbs.

Value of Race: $25,000 Winner $14,250; second $5,250; third $2,750; fourth $1,500; fifth $750; sixth $500. Mutuel Pool $78,125.00 Exacta Pool $77,761.00 Trifecta Pool $46,156.00 Superfecta Pool $9,849.00

Last Raced	Horse	M/Eqt. A.Wt	PP	St	$\frac{1}{4}$	$\frac{1}{2}$	Str	Fin	Jockey	Odds $1
14Jan00 5Lrl2	Street Talk	Lbf 4 122	7	2	$5\frac{1}{2}$	4hd	2hd	11	Martinez S B	1.20
24Apr99 7Pim4	Hound Deer	Lb 4 122	4	4	$4\frac{1}{2}$	32	1hd	$2\frac{1}{3}$	Johnston M T	3.90
29Jan00 2Lrl2	Tracy's Marc	Lf 4 122	8	5	$6\frac{2}{1}$	64	$5\frac{1}{2}$	31	Goodwin N	8.10
28May99 7Pim6	Got to Be There	Lbf 4 122	2	6	22	2hd	3hd	4no	Rosenthal M E	11.80
14Jan00 5Lrl5	Quiet Gratitude	Lb 4 122	1	3	1hd	$1\frac{1}{2}$	$4\frac{3}{1}$	$5\frac{3}{3}$	Gerardo R	3.40
23May99 3Del7	Bob Dew	4 122	3	8	3hd	$5\frac{1}{1}$	67	65	Dominguez R A	31.90
17Dec99 5Lrl11	Plaefare Lad	Lbf 4 122	6	7	74	$7\frac{4}{1}$	$7\frac{3}{1}$	$7\frac{3}{1}$	Douglas F G	33.20
18Aug99 9Lrl8	Hey Hi-IRE	Lbf 4 112	5	1	8	8	8	8	Kravets J5	11.30

OFF AT 2:07 Start Good. Won driving. Track fast.
TIME :23, :464, :592, 1:12 (:23.16, :46.95, :59.40, 1:12.05)

$2 Mutuel Prices:

7-STREET TALK	4.40	3.20	2.60
4-HOUND DEER		4.80	3.80
8-TRACY'S MARC			3.20

$2 EXACTA 7–4 PAID $18.20 $2 TRIFECTA 7–4–8 PAID $66.40 $1 SUPERFECTA 7–4–8–2 PAID $141.50

Dk. b. or br. c, by Capote–Sing and Swing, by Dixieland Band. Trainer Gaudet Edmond D. Bred by Kinghaven Farms Ltd (Ont-C).

STREET TALK was bumped in the run into the turn, steadily advanced four wide into the lane, drew even past the furlong marker then was clear late under a drive. HOUND DEER came out early and bumped the winner, stalked the pace three wide, moved to a short lead in upper stretch, maintained the lead to the eighth pole and continued willingly. TRACY'S MARC angled the rail nearing the turn, was under urging on the turn, angled wide for the drive and finished well. GOT TO BE THERE disputed the pace two wide and weakened late. QUIET GRATITUDE rushed to the front, set a pressured pace along the inside and weakened late. BOB DEW saved ground in a forward position and weakened in mid stretch. PLAEFARE LAD broke slowly, raced wide and was outrun. HEY HI (IRE) raced wide and was outrun.

Owners— 1, Gaudet Linda & Bailey Morris; 2, Eppler Mary E; 3, Kushner Herbert W; 4, McGinnes Cynthia R; 5, Harris William R; 6, Vickers Arthur E; 7, Sams William D; 8, Kleemann Sandi L

Trainers— 1, Gaudet Edmond D; 2, Eppler Mary E; 3, Heil Nancy B; 4, Wilson Gregory L; 5, Bailes W Robert; 6, Jackson Bruce C; 7, Sams William D; 8, Marino Phil

---

$3 Twin Trifecta (7–4–8) Paid $805.80

SIXTH RACE
Laurel
FEBRUARY 12, 2000

$1\frac{1}{16}$ MILES. (1.414) ALLOWANCE. Purse $26,000 FILLIES THREE YEARS OLD, WHICH HAVE NEVER WON A RACE OTHER THAN MAIDEN, CLAIMING, OR STARTER OR WHICH HAVE NEVER WON TWO RACES. Weight 120 lbs. Non–winners of a race other than claiming at a mile or over since December 18 allowed, 3 lbs. Such a race since November 18, 5 lbs.

Value of Race: $25,480 Winner $14,820; second $5,460; third $2,860; fourth $1,560; fifth $780. Mutuel Pool $80,054.00 Exacta Pool $75,896.00 Trifecta Pool $44,929.00

Last Raced	Horse	M/Eqt. A.Wt	PP	St	$\frac{1}{4}$	$\frac{1}{2}$	$\frac{3}{4}$	Str	Fin	Jockey	Odds $1
28Jan00 7Lrl3	Sudenlylastsummer	L 3 115	6	1	$5\frac{1}{2}$	57	$45\frac{1}{2}$	31	1no	Younker M	5.60
28Jan00 7Lrl2	Prized Stamp	Lb 3 115	5	6	4hd	2hd	$21\frac{1}{2}$	1hd	2no	Frazier R L	1.10
27Jan00 5Lrl1	Midnight Nell	Lb 3 115	4	2	1hd	$1\frac{1}{2}$	11	22	$35\frac{1}{2}$	Dominguez R A	9.80
23Jan00 1Lrl1	Ticket To Tokyo	Lb 3 115	3	3	2hd	32	3hd	412	410	Wilson R	2.90
3Feb00 4Lrl1	Somewhat Special	L 3 115	2	4	$31\frac{1}{2}$	4hd	525	5	5	Goodwin N	12.80
5Feb00 8Lrl6	Northern Gambler	L 3 115	1	5	6	6	6	—	—	Hutton G W	4.90

Northern Gambler: Pulled up;

OFF AT 2:34 Start Good. Won driving. Track fast.
TIME :251, :494, 1:144, 1:403, 1:471 (:25.26, :49.80, 1:14.91, 1:40.70, 1:47.34)

$2 Mutuel Prices:

7-SUDENLYLASTSUMMER	13.20	4.80	4.00
5-PRIZED STAMP		3.00	2.60
4-MIDNIGHT NELL			3.00

$2 EXACTA 7–5 PAID $38.60 $2 TRIFECTA 7–5–4 PAID $193.00

B. f, (May), by Rinka Das–Sally Lunn, by Cyane. Trainer Fisher Janon III. Bred by Corbett Farm & William Beatson (Md).

SUDENLYLASTSUMMER raced four wide throughout, closed determinedly and was up in the final jumps. PRIZED STAMP steadied behind rivals on the first turn, prompted the pace three wide, went to a short lead in mid stretch, dueled and finished gamely. MIDNIGHT NELL, three wide the first turn, gained command in early backstretch, set the pace in the two path, dueled in the lane and just missed in a sharp effort. TICKET TO TOKYO went to a brief early lead, stalked the pace inside down the backstretch and final turn then weakened in mid stretch. SOMEWHAT SPECIAL was hustled along off the rail and dropped back. NORTHERN GAMBLER wore a nasal strip, steadied around the first turn, her rider had his saddle slip in the run down the backstretch and was pulled up.

Owners— 1, Corbett Farm; 2, Sorokolit William; 3, Cole Robert L Jr; 4, Appleton Arthur I; 5, Rag Time Stables; 6, T R M Stable

Trainers— 1, Fisher Janon III; 2, Capuano Dale; 3, Wolfendale Howard E; 4, Camac Robert W; 5, Eubanks Annette M; 6, Beck Michael T

Scratched— Real Concern (13Jan00 8LRL2)

SEVENTH RACE
Laurel
FEBRUARY 12, 2000

6 FURLONGS. (1.08) MAIDEN CLAIMING. Purse $10,500 MAIDENS, FOUR YEAR OLDS AND UPWARD. Weight 122 lbs. CLAIMING PRICE $14,500, for each $500 to $13,500 2 lbs.

Value of Race: $10,500 Winner $5,985; second $2,205; third $1,155; fourth $630; fifth $315; sixth $210. Mutuel Pool $79,983.00 Exacta Pool $91,092.00 Trifecta Pool $60,318.00

Last Raced	Horse	M/Eqt. A.Wt	PP	St	1/4	1/2	Str	Fin	Jockey	Cl'g Pr	Odds $1
27Jan00 1Lrl3	Seven Sundays	Lb 4 122	2	5	3½	3½	2hd	1³½	Unsihuay E J	14500	10.70
7Jan00 9Lrl7	Chouette	Lb 4 118	3	3	1²	1²	1½	2nk	Verge M E	13500	a-0.60
10Nov99 6Lrl5	Bagman	L 4 118	1	4	2⁵½	2²½	3²½	3¾	Douglas F G	13500	4.20
27Jan00 1Lrl4	First Pilot	Lb 4 118	4	6	5hd	4⁴	4⁴	4²¼	Cortez A C	13500	11.50
	Australian Gold	Lbf 4 118	8	1	6²½	5¹½	5¹½	5¾	Pino M G	13500	a-0.60
27Jan00 1Lrl6	Hear the Bull	L 4 118	5	8	7hd	7¹½	6⁴	6⁷½	Goodwin N	13500	10.80
7Jan00 9Lrl6	Cooper's Encounter	Lf 4 122	7	2	4¹	6¹	7¹½	7nk	Cullum W	14500	9.10
2Feb00 1Lrl3	Thisracalsready	Lf 6 122	6	7	8	8	8	8	Stisted J	14500	14.60

a–Coupled: Chouette and Australian Gold.

OFF AT 3:03 Start Good. Won driving. Track fast.

TIME :22³, :47, :59³, 1:12² (:22.76, :47.03, :59.72, 1:12.41)

$2 Mutuel Prices:	3–SEVEN SUNDAYS	23.40	4.80	2.60
	1–CHOUETTE (a–entry)		2.40	2.10
	2–BAGMAN			2.60

$2 EXACTA 3–1 PAID $53.20 $2 TRIFECTA 3–1–2 PAID $127.60

B. c, by Becker–Count Seven, by Little Current. Trainer Ambrogi Leo J. Bred by Ambrogi Leo J (Md).

SEVEN SUNDAYS was hustled along towards the inside on the turn, angled out approaching the quarter pole, lodged a four wide bid to the lead near the sixteenth pole and drew clear under a drive. CHOUETTE quickly went clear, set the pace along the inside, drifted out late and held well for the place. BAGMAN chased the pace two wide, was floated out some in deep stretch and hung. FIRST PILOT settled towards the inside, angled five wide in upper stretch and rallied mildly. AUSTRALIAN GOLD raced off the rail and had some late interest. HEAR THE BULL raced wide and failed to menace. COOPER'S ENCOUNTER saved ground into the stretch and weakened. THISRACALSREADY was outrun.

Owners— 1, Sun Burst Stable; 2, Reynolds David P; 3, Carter Joseph W Sr; 4, Ayres Fountain Spring Farm; 5, Reynolds David P; 6, James Hibbert; 7, Ridgely Mary Anne & Tammaro III Joh; 8, Dunromin Racing Stable

Trainers—1, Ambrogi Leo J; 2, Alfano Ronald A; 3, Green Ernest E; 4, Ayres Joseph W; 5, Jenkins Rodney; 6, Keefe Timothy L; 7, Tammaro John J III; 8, O'Brien Maura C

EIGHTH RACE
Laurel
FEBRUARY 12, 2000

1¹⁄₁₆ MILES. (1.41⁴) ALLOWANCE. Purse $26,000 FILLIES THREE YEARS OLD, WHICH HAVE NEVER WON A RACE OTHER THAN MAIDEN, CLAIMING, OR STARTER OR WHICH HAVE NEVER WON TWO RACES. Weight 120 lbs. Non-winners of a race other than claiming at a mile or over since December 18 allowed, 3 lbs. Such a race since November 18, 5 lbs.

Value of Race: $26,000 Winner $14,820; second $5,460; third $2,860; fourth $1,560; fifth $780; sixth $520. Mutuel Pool $70,560.00 Exacta Pool $75,265.00 Trifecta Pool $49,134.00

Last Raced	Horse	M/Eqt. A.Wt	PP	St	1/4	1/2	3/4	Str	Fin	Jockey	Odds $1
14Jan00 1Lrl1	Crafty Paces	Lbf 3 115	7	7	6³	6¹	4¹½	3⁵	1½	Delgado A	8.60
28Jan00 7Lrl7	Jan Luck	Lf 3 115	4	5	3¹	2¹	2²	1hd	2³	Hutton G W	6.80
5Jan00 6Lrl1	Cherokee Float	L 3 120	6	1	1²	1¹½	1¹½	2¹½	3¹½	Dominguez R A	0.90
3Feb00 4Lrl4	Reefme Darling	Lb 3 115	3	6	7	7	7	4³	4⁶½	Stisted J	30.40
14Jan00 7Lrl5	No Bettor Love	Lb 3 115	5	2	5³	4hd	3hd	5²	5²¼	Pino M G	4.30
13Jan00 1Lrl1	Round Of Shots	L 3 115	2	3	2½	3hd	6hd	6½	6²½	Verge M E	23.80
29Jan00 6Lrl3	Lying Eyes	L 3 115	1	4	4½	5³	5¹	7	7	Martinez S B	4.00

OFF AT 3:31 Start Good. Won driving. Track fast.

TIME :24⁴, :50¹, 1:16¹, 1:41², 1:47³ (:24.96, :50.36, 1:16.22, 1:41.43, 1:47.60)

$2 Mutuel Prices:	7–CRAFTY PACES	19.20	8.00	3.40
	4–JAN LUCK		7.20	4.40
	6–CHEROKEE FLOAT			2.60

$2 EXACTA 7–4 PAID $135.00 $2 TRIFECTA 7–4–6 PAID $400.80

Dk. b. or br. f, (Apr), by Ameri Valay–Pretty Paces, by Thirty Eight Paces. Trainer Sweeney Ronald M. Bred by Mr & Mrs Charles N Bassford (Ky).

CRAFTY PACES settled off the rail, circled five wide into the lane, closed gamely under stout left handed pressure and wore down JAN LUCK in the final yards. JAN LUCK was bumped entering the first turn, stalked the pace three wide, went to a short lead nearing mid stretch, drifted out late and gave way grudgingly. CHEROKEE FLOAT came in some soon after the start, was sent three wide around the first turn to take command, set the pace off the inside, was collared in upper stretch and weakened. REEFME DARLING steadied early, saved ground and lacked the needed response. NO BETTOR LOVE was in tight soon after the start, rated close up while three wide, was roused on the final turn and weakened. ROUND OF SHOTS stalked the pace between rivals, raced five wide in upper stretch and weakened. LYING EYES checked twice from the seven furlong marker to the six and a half furlong pole, stalked the pace inside and tired nearing the lane.

Owners— 1, Bassford Elaine L; 2, Jones Janice M; 3, Bender Sondra D; 4, Wilkins F B; 5, P T K Racing Ltd; 6, Pocock Stables; 7, Walleye Stable

Trainers—1, Sweeney Ronald M; 2, Morrison George E; 3, Murray Lawrence E; 4, Wilkins F Bryan; 5, Allen A Ferris III; 6, Boniface J William; 7, Campitelli Francis P

NINTH RACE

Laurel

FEBRUARY 12, 2000

$1\frac{3}{16}$ MILES. (1.54^3) 15th Running of THE HARRISON E. JOHNSON MEMORIAL. Purse $75,000. 4-year-olds and upward. By subscription of $100 each which should accompany the nomination. $350 to pass the entry box. $350 additional to start with 60% to the winner, 20% to second, 11% to third, 6% to fourth, and 3% to fifth. Supplemental nominations of $750 each will be accepted by usual time of entry with all other fees due as noted. Weight, 122 lbs. Non-winners of two races of $60,000 at one mile or over since July 1,1999, allowed 3 lbs. Of such a race since then, 5 lbs. Of such a race of $25,000 since then, 7 lbs. (Maiden and claiming races not considered in estimating allowances). Starters to be named through the entry box by the usual time of closing. Nominations closed Saturday, January 29, 2000.

Value of Race: $75,000 Winner $45,000; second $15,000; third $8,250; fourth $4,500; fifth $2,250. Mutuel Pool $90,380.00 Exacta Pool $83,127.00 Trifecta Pool $57,626.00 Superfecta Pool $10,405.00

Last Raced	Horse	M/Eqt.	A.	Wt	PP	St	¼	½	¾	Str	Fin	Jockey	Odds $1
1Jan00 ^{9}Lrl^{2}	S W Clarence	Lbf	6	117	3	1	$1^{1\frac{1}{2}}$	1^{1}	1^{1}	1^{4}	$1^{3\frac{1}{4}}$	Wilson R	2.90
31Dec99 ^{9}Lrl^{1}	Thunder Flash	L	4	117	4	3	$4^{2\frac{1}{2}}$	$4^{\frac{1}{2}}$	$4^{\frac{1}{2}}$	2^{2}	$2^{\frac{3}{4}}$	Dominguez R A	2.80
16Jan00 ^{7}Lrl^{3}	Sly Joe	Lb	5	115	2	9	9	$8^{\frac{1}{2}}$	$8^{5\frac{1}{2}}$	3^{1}	3^{2}	Delgado A	30.20
29Dec99 ^{7}Lrl^{1}	He's My Buckaroo	Lb	4	115	5	8	7^{hd}	7^{3}	$7^{1\frac{1}{2}}$	$5^{1\frac{1}{2}}$	$4^{2\frac{1}{2}}$	Johnston M T	12.80
1Jan00 ^{9}Lrl^{3}	Copy Cat	L	7	117	9	6	3^{hd}	$3^{3\frac{1}{2}}$	3^{hd}	$4^{1\frac{1}{2}}$	$5^{2\frac{1}{2}}$	Madrid A Jr	21.60
22Jan00 ^{8}Lrl^{2}	Test Pilot	Lb	4	115	8	5	5^{2}	$6^{2\frac{1}{2}}$	$6^{1\frac{1}{2}}$	6^{5}	$6^{2\frac{3}{4}}$	Frazier R L	16.70
27Nov99 ^{9}Lrl^{1}	Perfect To A Tee	Lb	8	122	6	7	$6^{1\frac{1}{2}}$	5^{hd}	5^{hd}	$8^{\frac{1}{2}}$	$7^{3\frac{1}{4}}$	Cortez A C	2.70
25Nov99 ^{8}Lrl^{4}	Red Classic	Lbf	6	115	1	2	8^{3}	9	9	9	8^{nk}	Verge M E	52.40
18Dec99 ^{9}Lrl^{5}	Testafly	L	6	115	7	4	2^{1}	2^{1}	2^{1}	7^{hd}	9	Pino M G	3.90

OFF AT 3:59 Start Good. Won driving. Track fast.

TIME $:24^{1}$, $:48^{2}$, 1:13, $1:37^{3}$, $1:56^{1}$ (:24.33, :48.51, 1:13.17, 1:37.72, 1:56.30)

$2 Mutuel Prices:

4-S W CLARENCE	7.80	4.20	3.40
5-THUNDER FLASH		4.20	3.60
3-SLY JOE			7.80

$2 EXACTA 4-5 PAID $22.80 $2 TRIFECTA 4-5-3 PAID $350.80 $2 SUPERFECTA 4-5-3-6 PAID $1,114.60

B. g, by Iron-Babalinka, by Stonewalk. Trainer Lingenfelter Thomas H. Bred by Reveley Mr & Mrs Richard (Pa).

S W CLARENCE gained command at once, was well rated setting the pace just off the inside, widened in mid stretch and maintained a safe margin under a drive. THUNDER FLASH angled out entering the backstretch, moved closer the far turn, advanced three wide between rivals nearing the lane and flattened out late. SLY JOE settled well off the rail, circled five wide the final turn, raced on his left lead in the drive and rallied mildly. HE'S MY BUCKAROO was unhurried early off the inside, made a mild run four wide between horses entering the lane but lacked any solid late response. COPY CAT angled in early, stalked the pace towards the inside and weakened near the sixteenth pole. TEST PILOT angled in nearing the first turn, saved ground, moved a bit closer leaving the far turn and weakened. PERFECT TO A TEE raced four wide, was put to pressure entering the far turn and tired. RED CLASSIC was outrun. TESTAFLY prompted the pace outside the winner, was put to stiff pressure leaving the far turn, chased the pace to upper stretch and tired.

Owners— 1, Spring Water Farm; 2, Lageman William; 3, Owens Susan; 4, Rag Time Stables; 5, Deschenes Victor J; 6, Lovelace Terry D; 7, The Nonsequitur Stable; 8, Brushwood Stable; 9, Brown J D & Shannon Richard

Trainers— 1, Lingenfelter Thomas H; 2, Ritchey Tim F; 3, Pruitt Peggy E; 4, Eubanks Annette M; 5, Schnitzler Rita A; 6, Gruwell Bessie S; 7, Albert Linda L; 8, Lawrence James L II; 9, Capuano Dale

TENTH RACE

Laurel

FEBRUARY 12, 2000

$1\frac{1}{16}$ MILES. (1.41^4) MAIDEN SPECIAL WEIGHT. Purse $25,000 MAIDENS, FOUR YEAR OLDS AND UPWARD. Weight 122 lbs.

Value of Race: $25,000 Winner $14,250; second $5,250; third $2,750; fourth $1,500; fifth $750; sixth $500. Mutuel Pool $56,731.00 Exacta Pool $66,123.00 Trifecta Pool $49,333.00 Superfecta Pool $16,732.00

Last Raced	Horse	M/Eqt.	A.	Wt	PP	St	¼	½	¾	Str	Fin	Jockey	Odds $1
27Dec99 ^{7}Lrl^{5}	Lord Rutledge	Lb	4	122	4	1	$1^{1\frac{1}{2}}$	1^{4}	1^{10}	1^{10}	$1^{8\frac{3}{4}}$	Johnston M T	2.40
29Jan00 ^{2}Lrl^{5}	Honor Jet	L	4	122	1	8	$4^{\frac{1}{2}}$	4^{2}	2^{hd}	$2^{1\frac{1}{2}}$	$2^{\frac{3}{4}}$	Pino M G	2.10
26Jan00 ^{3}Lrl^{3}	Bold Crossing	Lb	4	122	2	4	5^{1}	$5^{\frac{1}{2}}$	$4^{1\frac{1}{2}}$	3^{2}	$3^{3\frac{3}{4}}$	Douglas F G	4.90
29Jan00 ^{2}Lrl^{4}	Khan	Lb	4	122	3	3	6^{2}	6^{hd}	5^{hd}	5^{1}	$4^{\frac{1}{2}}$	Madrid A Jr	19.70
26Jan00 ^{3}Lrl^{5}	Jeezohflip	Lbf	4	122	6	6	7^{3}	7^{7}	6^{5}	4^{hd}	$5^{1\frac{1}{4}}$	Maysonett F	27.90
26Jan00 ^{3}Lrl^{2}	Mani's Flier	bf	4	122	7	9	9	$8^{3\frac{1}{2}}$	8^{10}	7^{15}	$6^{6\frac{1}{4}}$	Goodwin N	5.30
15Jan00 ^{4}Pha^{2}	Dog Doctor	Lb	4	122	5	2	2^{hd}	3^{5}	$3^{\frac{1}{2}}$	$6^{\frac{1}{2}}$	$7^{16\frac{1}{2}}$	Frazier R L	6.50
14May99 ^{12}Pim^{9}	Alongcametheprince	Lf	7	117	8	7	$8^{2\frac{1}{2}}$	9	9	9	$8^{3\frac{1}{4}}$	Rivera J^{5}	45.80
28Oct99 ^{1}Lrl^{6}	El Serrucho	Lb	4	122	9	5	3^{5}	2^{hd}	7^{hd}	$8^{2\frac{1}{2}}$	9	Rosenthal M E	29.80

OFF AT 4:26 Start Good. Won driving. Track fast.

TIME $:23^{1}$, $:46^{4}$, $1:12^{1}$, 1:39, 1:46 (:23.36, :46.87, 1:12.31, 1:39.00, 1:46.01)

$2 Mutuel Prices:

4-LORD RUTLEDGE	6.80	3.00	2.80
1-HONOR JET		3.20	2.60
2-BOLD CROSSING			3.20

$2 EXACTA 4-1 PAID $15.80 $2 TRIFECTA 4-1-2 PAID $77.40 $2 SUPERFECTA 4-1-2-3 PAID $301.90

B. c, by Broad Brush-Ms. Rutledge, by Lord Gaylord. Trainer Motion H Graham. Bred by Rutledge Farm (Ky).

LORD RUTLEDGE quickly went clear, set the pace well off the rail, opened up around the final turn and was much the best while being kept to a drive. HONOR JET was hustled along off the rail down the backstretch, advanced between rivals leaving the three furlong marker and held the place. BOLD CROSSING settled in mid pack early, circled four wide around the final turn and flattened out. KHAN raced towards the inside and lacked a response. JEEZOHFLIP came out leaving the gate bumping MANI'S FLIER and was outrun. MANI'S FLIER was knocked off stride leaving the gate and failed to recover. DOG DOCTOR saved ground and tired. ALONGCAMETHEPRINCE was outrun. EL SERRUCHO was rushed to contention, stalked the pace three wide to the far turn and faltered.

Owners— 1, Greenberg Herman; 2, Bryant Magalen O; 3, Sams William D; 4, Keil Steven D; 5, Yourman Robert E; 6, Weiss Frank R; 7, Harroff John C; 8, Tanzell Michael; 9, Quantum Racing Inc

Trainers— 1, Motion H Graham; 2, Voss Katharine M; 3, Sams William D; 4, Keil Steven D; 5, Peacock Roy M Jr; 6, Belmonte Rocco J; 7, Eppler Mary E; 8, Tanzell Michael; 9, Graham Robin L

$2 Daily Double (4-4) Paid $35.80; Daily Double Pool $16,066.

Laurel Park Attendance: Unavailable Mutuel Pool: Unavailable

The winner of the first race, Chief's Boy, rallied from last place and "angled five wide." In the second race, Glider Pilot came from next-to-last place and "angled six wide." In the third race, Sell the Farm "prompted the pace in the three-path." Over to You rallied from next-to-last place to win the fourth. In the seventh and eighth races, odds-on favorites opened clear leads and faded. The only front-running winners came in the last two races; one was "just off the inside" and the other "well off the rail." The preponderance of evidence suggests that the rail was bad on February 12 at Laurel, and that speed horses on the inside were at a distinct disadvantage.

Therefore, any horse who had a rail trip on that day—particularly one who battled for the lead along the inside—would have hidden form that might be the key to a future betting opportunity. Any horse who ran well on the rail might merit an almost automatic wager the next time he was entered. So I studied the charts to find the horses who had significant against-the-bias trips and merited inclusion in my Horse Watch list.

In the first race, Snook broke from post position 1 and set an unpressured pace before finishing second; even on a biased track, I am unimpressed by horses who take a clear lead, benefit from a slow pace, and lose. But the inside-speed horse in the second race certainly deserved attention. Mount Defiance broke from post 2 and engaged in a four-horse fight for the lead with the horses in posts 3, 5, and 6. (The footnotes confirm that he was the innermost horse in the battle: "Mount Defiance saved ground forcing the pace. . . .") His name goes into Horse Watch. In the fifth race, Quiet Gratitude dueled for the lead after breaking from post 1, while Bob Dew was close; he "saved ground in a forward position," according to the footnotes. In the sixth race, Ticket to Tokyo was involved in an early battle: he "went to a brief early lead [and] stalked the pace inside."

This day of racing underscores the reason that I consider biases to be a uniquely productive source of betting opportunities. Other handicapping factors may yield high-quality bets, too, but they come along one at a time, sometimes very slowly. But uncovering one bias at Laurel on February 12 yielded a mother lode of future wagers. And it turned out to be a very productive lode:

Mount Defiance won his next start, paying $6.40.

Bob Dew improved sharply to win his next race and paid $9.

Ticket to Tokyo came back to win as the favorite.

Cooper's Encounter, who "saved ground into the stretch" in the seventh race, won his next start and paid $28. Chouette, the pacesetter in the same event, came back after a layoff to pay $15.

Copy Cat, who ran in the ninth race and "stalked the pace toward the inside," won his next start, as did Test Pilot, who had "angled in nearing the first turn [and] saved ground."

Of course, I don't bet blindly or automatically on such horses. The value of my horses-to-watch list is that it gives me a starting point from which to analyze and attack a full-card simulcasting menu. Instead of trying to deal with as many as 200 races on a full simulcast menu, I am able to focus on a manageable number of events in which some of my Horse Watch horses are entered. I can approach each of those races with a potentially valuable nugget of information, an insight into a horse's performance that could be a crucial handicapping factor, but one that the average player might not possess. I will handicap these races in depth, trying to determine whether my horse fits this race and figures to win. This exercise involves all the usual elements of Handicapping 101, but I am most conscious of the following issues:

Do my horse's speed figures indicate that he has an edge, or is at least competitive, in this field?

Will the likely pace profile of the race help or hinder my horse?

Does my horse know how to win? (Sometimes, after putting a horse on my Horse Watch list on the basis of a single good effort, I will encounter a set of past performances showing a career record of 1 for 40.)

ALTHOUGH I usually don't pay much attention to Philadelphia Park for various reasons—for one thing, the too-high takeout—I detected a strong bad-rail bias there on December 7, 1999, and entered a few horses from the card on my Horse Watch list. In a field that produced a solid speed figure, the third-place finisher, I Am Me R. G., elicited a comment that read: "Saved ground, edged closer leaving turn, weakened." The mare appeared in the Philly entries eight days later. Even though I didn't know a great deal about Philadelphia Park, my one nugget of information made me conclude that I had found a standout.

6 Philadelphia Park

ⒻClm 10000(10–8)

5½ Furlongs (1:023) CLAIMING. Purse $9,500 (plus $3,500 State Bred) FOR FILLIES AND MARES THREE YEARS OLD AND UPWARD. Three-year-olds. 120 lbs.; Older. 122 lbs.; Non-winners of two races since October 19 allowed 3 lbs.; a race since then 5 lbs.; Claiming Price $10,000; for each $1,000 to $8,000 2 lbs. (Races where entered for $7,500 or less not considered).

START 5½ FURLONGS FINISH

1 Smithereens (GB)

Own: Plumstead Stables $10,000
BLACK A S (336 74 44 45 .22) 1999:(963 192 .20)

Ch. m. 6
Sire: Primo Dominie*GB (Dominion*GB)
Dam: Splintering*GB (Sharpo*GB)
Br: Kennard Mrs R B (GB)
Tr: Seeger Robert J(141 16 16 24 .11) 99:(570 88 .15)

L 119

Life	48	12	3	7	$118,397	D.Fst	30	10	2	3	$83,526 80
1999	13	4	0	1	$26,935	Wet	8	2	0	2	$29,855 81
1998	16	4	0	4	$49,804	Turf	10	0	1	2	$5,016 38
Pha	17	7	0	4	$61,030	Dist	12	5	0	0	$47,762 81

20Nov99–7Pha fst 5f :222 :461 :591 3↑ⒻClm 14000(14–12) 49 5 2 1½ 12 11 54½ Simpson R5 L 112 fb *1.70 79–12 Jollytrix108½ Reef Club117½ Fair And Square1172½ Pace, gave way 7
24Oct99–7Pha fst 5½f :214 :452 :584 1:054 3↑ⒻClm 10000(10–8) 69 4 2 13½ 13 12½ 11¼ Simpson R5 L 112 fb *1.90 85–15 Smithereens1121¼ Saucy Dottie115½ **No Jeans**1173½ Driving 9
26Sep99–5Pha fst 6f :213 :44 :563 1:10 3↑ⒻClm 10000(10–8) 79 8 1 11 · 12½ 12½ 2½ Simpson R5 L 112 fb 2.70 92–12 TopGunner119½ Ⓓ*Smithereens*1122½ **SturdyNiteLdy**1175½ Drifted out str. 8
Disqualified and placed third
25Aug99–5Del fst 5f :213 :45 :572 3↑ⒻClm 20000(25–20) 57 4 2 32½ 21½ 44½ 510½ Simpson R5 L 107 fb 10.20 87–08 AmricnTrsur1162¼ Cntnkrously1163¾ Sl'sHony1163¼ Well placed, gave way 10
2Aug99–5Del fst 6f :213 :444 :573 1:104 3↑ⒻClm 13500(13.5–11.5) 38 1 2 13 2½ 22½ 715¾ Santagata N L 116 fb *1.90 73–15 *AmricnTrsur*1162¾ BoldSurg1161¼ Unit'sTmm112¾ Rushed to lead, stoppd 7
6Jly99–3Pha fst 5f :221 :451 :574 3↑ⒻClm 10000 80 2 1 12 15 16 16 Simpson R5 L 112 fb *1.00 91–10 Smitherns1126 SunshinKt1171 Wtchin'ThStrs117hd Clear, not challenged 5
26Jun99–7Pha fst 6f :212 :433 :561 1:094 3↑ⒻClm 7500N2Y 77 3 1 11½ 14 15 16½ Simpson R7 L 110 fb 3.40 94–11 *Smithereens*1106½ Imperial Thanks1101¾ Twiceasweetheart11711 Driving 6
14Jun99–8Pha fm 5f Ⓣ :213 :451 :574 3↑ⒻClm 8000(10–8) 20 7 2 2½ 2½ 78 1016 Simpson R7 L 106 fb 9.80 75–09 Sweet Hunter1191½ *Miss Jetaway*119¾ Sweet Poison117¾ Outside, tired 10
16May99–1Del fst 5½f :214 :454 :582 1:05 4↑ⒻClm 13500(13.5–11.5) 26 3 4 2hd 31½ 811 817½ Capanas S L 116 fb 5.70 76–13 DixieGlitter1193¾ MsStarDuster1121¾ Mddie'sFlyer1141¾ Vied inside, tired 8
1May99–5Pha fst 5½f :22 :45 :573 1:041 3↑ⒻClm 14000(14–12) 45 4 6 33 31½ 54½ 59 Capanas S L 119 fb 4.20 84–09 *Starlite Cruisin*1223¼ Imperial Thanks112½ Ivor's Pass1172½ Tired 6
WORKS: Dec9 Pha 3f fst :382 B *10/15*

2 First Preference

Own: Simpson Debbie $10,000
MADRIGAL R JR (201 22 33 18 .11) 1999:(681 79 .12)

Ch. m. 6
Sire: Orbit Dancer (Northern Dancer) $2,500
Dam: Noblelenia (Vaguely Noble*GB)
Br: Huntsinger Larry S & Tyner Harold (Tex)
Tr: Simpson Deborah M(2 1 1 0 .50) 99:(9 1 .11)

L 117

Life	38	11	4	4	$106,637	D.Fst	31	11	3	3	$101,226 79
1999	13	4	0	1	$36,280	Wet	4	0	1	1	$4,190 55
1998	12	5	0	1	$48,828	Turf	3	0	0	0	$1,221 69
Pha	0	0	0	0	$0	Dist	2	0	0	0	$750 55

11Nov99–2Lrl fst 6½f :23 :471 1:12 1:182 3↑ⒻClm 13500(14.5–13.5) 34 8 1 41¼ 52½ 913 920 Reynolds L C L 114 f 16.20 68–19 *D.D.Mcn*1171½ AmericnTresure1173¾ Effervscnc1173 Stalked off rail,tired 9
26Oct99–3Del fst 6f :214 :451 :584 1:113 3↑ⒻClm 15500(17.5–15.5) 54 9 1 35 43 73½ 78 Colton R E L 114 f 8.30 77–12 Gllslss116hd Whtsweethert1161¾ ClosdCption116nk Was through after half 10
27Sep99–8Del fst 6f :224 :461 :583 1:112 3↑ⒻClm 16500(17.5–15.5) 77 4 1 1hd 2hd 2½ 32 Colton R E L 114 f 3.40 84–17 Beauty's Bid122hd Fortunate Kate1162 First Preference1141 Vied, faded 7
19Sep99–9Del fst 6f :22 :453 :581 1:11 3↑ⒻClm c-(10–8) 79 6 1 1hd 11 14½ 16¾ Colton R E L 116 f *1.40 88–12 First Preference1166¾ Lusty Girl1195 Miss Marshall112½ Clearly best 6
Claimed from Springton Farm for $10,000, Siravo Robert D Trainer
21Aug99–8Del fst 6f :222 :462 :591 1:121 3↑ⒻClm c-(7.5–6.5) 62 2 2 1hd 1½ 13 16 Frazier R L L 119 f *1.30 82–16 *First Preference*1196 Power Angel1161 Ila Vow1092¼ Pace, drew off 6
Claimed from S J B Stable Jr for $7,500, Passero Frank A Jr Trainer
11Aug99–4Del fst 5½f :22 :461 :59 1:052 3↑ⒻClm c-(7.5–6.5) 55 1 2 2½ 31½ 31 24¾ Martin C W L 119 f *2.70 86–10 *Top Gunner*1164¾ Ⓓ*FirstPreference*1192 Heff'sToy1162 Steadied, angled 9
Claimed from Springton Farm for $7,500, Siravo Robert D Trainer Disqualified and placed 4th
2Aug99–5Del fst 6f :213 :444 :573 1:104 3↑ⒻClm 12500(13.5–11.5) 66 6 1 35 33½ 43½ 44¾ Colton R E L 114 f 5.90 84–15 *AmericnTresur*1162¾ BoldSurg1161½ Unit'sTmmi112¾ Middle move, empty 7
17Jly99–8Del fst 1 1/16 :224 :462 1:112 1:451 3↑ⒻClm 16500(17.5–15.5) 48 6 2 21 21 39 615¾ McCarthy M J L 114 f 4.50 65–18 *Retail Sales*1166 Curved1161½ No Compassion114¾ Stalked, tired 6
29Jun99–9Del fst 6f :223 :461 :59 1:114 3↑ⒻClm c-(7.5–6.5) 68 3 4 11 1hd 1½ 12¼ Colton R E L 116 f *2.00 84–13 FrstPrfrnc1162¼ MssMrshll116¾ ExclsvCrmony116no Dueled, drew off late 7
Claimed from S J B Stable Jr for $7,500, Passero Frank A Jr Trainer
12Jun99–1Del fst 6f :221 :463 :592 1:123 4↑ⒻClm 5000N1Y 67 3 3 22 2½ 12½ 13½ Colton R E L 120 5.10 80–15 *First Preference*1203½ *Bold Surge*1202½ Stormin Jezabel120¾ Ridden out 9
WORKS: Nov7 Del 4f fst :522 B *8/8*

4 Super Attraction

Own: Diamante Racing Stable $10,000
ESTRADA E A (28 2 2 3 .07) 1999:(333 37 .11)

Ch. f. 4 FTMMAY97 $7,000
Sire: Superoyale (Raise a Native) $1,000
Dam: Dusty's Rain (Master Hand)
Br: Asmussen Equine Inv (Tex)
Tr: Gonzalez Andrea(10 1 0 2 .10) 99:(97 9 .09)

L 117

Life	25	5	5	3	$61,270	D.Fst	20	5	3	3	$56,180 69
1999	13	2	3	0	$17,810	Wet	5	0	2	0	$5,090 67
1998	12	3	2	3	$43,460	Turf	0	0	0	0	$0 –
Pha	22	5	4	3	$56,770	Dist	5	3	0	0	$25,980 67

28Nov99–3Pha gd 6f :222 :461 :591 1:122 3↑ⒻClm c-(7.5–6.5) 40 2 3 33 55½ 44 47¼ Glasser T P L 119 b 4.90 74–19 Magnifier1192½ Bold Surge117½ Haley's Alright1174¼ Steadied 3/8 pole 6
Claimed from Heavenly Acres Farm for $7,500, Saville Donald P Trainer
15Nov99–7Pha fst 5½f :223 :463 :591 1:06 3↑ⒻClm 7500N2Y 64 8 2 1hd 12½ 15 15¾ Glasser T P L 117 b 5.50 84–20 Super Attraction1175¾ ***Cha Cha Hedy***117hd Soul Of Aly1121¼ Kept to task 10
2Nov99–8Pha my 6f :221 :452 :58 1:111 3↑ⒻClm 7500N2Y 60 1 1 2hd 21 23 26 Glasser T P L 117 b 5.40 81–17 *Slew'sDBoss*1176 *SuperAttrction*117nk GreenBdger1175 Inside, no match 6
19Oct99–1Pha fst 6f :222 :46 :59 1:123 3↑ⒻClm 4000N1Y 51 4 2 1hd 11 12½ 12½ Glasser T P L 122 b 6.20 80–13 Super Attraction1222½ Unlikely Angel122½ Moon Bright112hd Driving 6
13Oct99–4Pha fst 6f :221 :453 :583 1:112 3↑ⒻClm 7500N2Y 39 7 3 3nk 41¼ 75½ 711½ Glasser T P L 117 b 30.40 74–14 **I Am Me R. G.**117½ Bay Of Ireland1171½ Green Badger1171¼ Outside, tired 8
26Sep99–5Pha fst 6f :213 :44 :563 1:10 3↑ⒻClm 10000(10–8) –0 4 8 823 827 837 855¾ Molina V H L 117 b 7.20 37–12 TopGunner119½ Ⓓ***Smitherns***1122½ **SturdyNitLdy**1175½ Fell back st. outrun 8
26Jun99–8Del fst 6f :221 :454 :583 1:113 3↑ⒻClm 17500(17.5–15.5) 56 7 2 41½ 21 45½ 68 Alvarado R Jr L 116 b 7.70 77–16 *Beauty's Bid*116hd Bright Thunder1194 No Compassion1141½ Bid, faded 7
12Jun99–2Del fst 6f :222 :463 :592 1:121 3↑ⒻClm 17500(17.5–15.5) 62 2 2 11 2hd 2½ 23¾ Alvarado R Jr L 116 b 9.50 78–15 ScrletTess1193¾ SuperAttrction116½ SmuriStr116hd Lead inside, gave way 7
9May99–4Pha fst 7f :222 :452 1:121 1:26 3↑ⒻClm 18000(18–16) 19 4 2 32½ 45 67½ 622 Cole A L 117 b 4.20 55–17 *Starlite Cruisin*1194 Smarten's Ida113½ Reef Club1171 Tired 6
18Apr99–6Pha gd 6f :223 :46 :582 1:111 4↑ⒻClm 18000(18–16) 67 6 1 1hd 1½ 3½ 21 Diaz S L 117 b 2.90 86–15 Juniper Tree1171 Super Attraction117hd **I Am Me R. G.**1153¼ Good effort 6

5 I Am Me R. G.

Own: Maurizio Mario $10,000
UNSIHUAY A (213 24 29 30 .11) 1999:(699 79 .11)

Ch. m. 8
Sire: I Am the Game (Lord Gaylord) $500
Dam: Rebekah Grace (Thirty Eight Paces)
Br: Chaney Richard H (Md)
Tr: Day Diane(55 5 6 7 .09) 99:(141 15 .11)

L 117

Life	67	14	12	11	$235,497	D.Fst	55	12	10	8	$200,967	90
1999	17	2	5	4	$28,215	Wet	10	1	2	3	$22,560	81
1998	8	3	0	0	$26,760	Turf	2	1	0	0	$11,970	90
Pha	24	6	6	6	$65,505	Dist	6	1	2	0	$18,044	73

7Dec99-6Pha my 6f :221 :46 :583 1:114 3↑ Ⓕ Clm 10000(10-8) 69 1 6 43 32½ 22 33 Unsihuay A L 117 fb 3.20 81-19 Top Gunner1172½ **Scat Singer**113½ I Am Me R. G.1171¾ Inside, weakened 6
23Nov99-9Pha fst 6f :221 :452 :58 1:104 3↑ Ⓕ Clm 10000(10-8) 70 7 2 63¾ 62½ 42 2nk Unsihuay A L 117 fb 9.50 89-18 RoyalCone110nk IAmMeR.G.1175 **SaturdayNiteLady**112½ Closed willingly 7
7Nov99-6Pha fst 7f :23 :47 1:131 1:254 3↑ Ⓕ Clm 12000(14-12) 35 6 7 52 2½ 88¼ 1017½ Unsihuay A L 114 fb 9.40 61-24 *Beautiful Baby*1193½ *Olga Int*114nk Royal Cone113hd Faltered 10
Previously trained by Robbins Charles R
13Oct99-4Pha fst 6f :221 :453 :583 1:112 3↑ Ⓕ Clm 7500N2Y 68 4 6 61½ 51½ 52½ 1½ Castanon J G L 117 fb 3.60 86-14 IAmMeR.G.117½ BayOfIreland1171¼ GreenBadger1171¼ Brutal trip, in time 8
5Oct99-4Pha my 5½f :222 :46 :582 1:044 3↑ Ⓕ Clm 7500N2Y 73 5 5 43½ 43½ 32 21¼ Simpson R5 L 112 fb 2.60 89-16 Soul Of Aly1121¼ *I Am Me R. G.*1123 High Shine1173½ 3 wide turn, late run 7
19Sep99-9Del fst 6f :22 :453 :581 1:11 3↑ Ⓕ Clm 10000(10-8) 48 3 6 64 21 36½ 412¼ Castanon J L • L 116 f 2.60 76-12 **FirstPreference**1166¾ LustyGirl1195 MissMrshll112½ 4 wide move, empty 6
7Sep99-5Pha sly 7f :214 :444 1:102 1:242 3↑ Ⓕ Clm 10000(10-8) 57 2 3 34 24 37 49¾ Cole A L 117 fb 3.20 75-20 *TopGunner*1173½ RoyalCone1195 BrickervilleBer1171¼ Between foes, tired 6
8Aug99-4Pha gd 6f :22 :452 :581 1:112 3↑ Ⓕ Clm 10000 67 6 1 45 42½ 43 21¾ Flores J L L 119 fb 3.20 84-17 Magnifier1171¾ IAmMeR.G.119¾ Watchin'TheStars1171¼ Angled in, rallied 7
4Jly99-7Pha fst 6f :223 :461 :584 1:112 3↑ Ⓕ Clm 13000(14-12) 32 5 4 51¾ 64¼ 79½ 713 Cole A L 116 fb 3.30 73-11 Juniper Tree117hd Soul Of Aly1171 **Saturday Nite Lady**1176½ 3 wide turn 7
19Jun99-7Pha fst 7f :223 :451 1:103 1:234 3↑ Ⓕ Clm 10000 70 2 7 72¼ 31½ 11½ 14 Cole A L 117 b 4.90 88-13 I Am Me R. G.1174 Miss Monmouth1101½ Flag Furled117½ Drew off 8

6 Saturday Nite Lady

Own: Labe Paul E Sr $10,000
SIMPSON R (300 50 44 43 .17) 1999:(766 118 .15)

B. m. 5
Sire: Beyond the Mint (Key to the Mint) $500
Dam: Lead Article (Dr. Do Much)
Br: Labe Paul E (Pa)
Tr: Lake Scott A(145 35 29 24 .24) 99:(570 158 .28)

L 112⁵

Life	28	5	5	5	$68,780	D.Fst	25	5	5	5	$68,780	76
1999	6	0	1	2	$6,992	Wet	3	0	0	0	$0	28
1998	14	5	1	2	$49,986	Turf	0	0	0	0	$0	–
Pha	13	1	2	4	$25,652	Dist	5	0	0	1	$2,790	41

23Nov99-9Pha fst 6f :221 :452 :58 1:104 3↑ Ⓕ Clm 10000(10-8) 58 4 6 3nk 2hd 31½ 35¼ Simpson R5 L 112 b 4.50 84-18 RoylCone110nk **IAmMR.G.**1175 SturdyNitLdy112½ Prompted pace, faded 7
9Oct99-5Pen fst 6f :214 :452 :581 1:12 3↑ Ⓕ Clm 10000(10-9) 13 7 4 32 23 59½ 720 Flores J L L 116 b *.70 64-15 *NzChnce*1142 *MidniteBlizzrd*116½ IDremofjniD.1112¼ Tired upper stretch 7
26Sep99-5Pha fst 6f :213 :44 :563 1:10 3↑ Ⓕ Clm 10000(10-8) 72 1 3 31½ 22½ 22½ 33 Flores J L L 117 b 5.90 90-12 TopGunner119½ D ***Smitherens***1122½ SturdyNitLdy1175½ Checked deep str. 8
Placed second through disqualification.
15Aug99-7Pen gd 6f :214 :451 :572 1:103 3↑ Ⓕ Alw 17380N$Y 28 2 6 32 43½ 510 923½ Flores J L L 115 b 10.80 67-12 Six Sense1165½ *Laura's Lucky Leaf*1072 Beachfront Rental1131½ Faded 9
27Jly99-7Pha fst 6½f :222 :453 1:104 1:172 3↑ Ⓕ Clm 18000(18-16) 62 2 5 22 2½ 23 46¾ Flores J L L 117 b *1.90 78-18 Fieldes Reward1173¼ *MystiqueFlight*1151¼ SoulOfAly1172¼ Eased out, tired 6
4Jly99-7Pha fst 6f :223 :461 :584 1:112 3↑ Ⓕ Clm 14000(14-12) 62 7 1 11 1hd 11 31 Flores J L L 117 fb *2.00 85-11 Juniper Tree117hd Soul Of Aly1171 Saturday Nite Lady1176½ Weakened 7
5Dec98-7Pen fst 6f :223 :461 :583 1:114 3↑ Ⓕ Clm 16000(16-14) 75 4 2 2½ 2hd 1hd 21 Potts C L L 116 b *1.60 84-22 Scary Ann1161 SaturdayNiteLady1162¼ LadyPickpocket1154¼ Just missed 6
13Nov98-9Pen fst 6f :221 :453 :582 1:121 3↑ Ⓕ Clm 20000(20-18) 62 6 2 31 31 3½ 31¾ Appleby D L Jr L 116 b 4.10 81-18 Jolene's Finality1181¼ ShadyClara116½ SaturdayNiteLady1161¼ Weakened 7
18Oct98-7Pha fst 6f :214 :444 :573 1:11 3↑ Ⓕ Clm 14000(14-12) 76 8 2 55 33½ 11½ 11½ Alvarado R Jr L 119 b 5.70 87-10 SaturdayNiteLady1191½ RSassyLady1171¼ *ConservativeMove*108¾ Driving 9
26Sep98-9Pen fst 6f :214 :45 :573 1:11 3↑ Ⓕ Clm 20000(20-18) 48 4 4 32 32½ 46 511½ Pena R D L 121 b 3.60 77-19 Jolene'sFinality1162½ SnppyCopeln1145 TkeTheCity1133 Weakened late 7
WORKS: Nov20 Pha 5f fst 1:032 B *8/10*

8 Cha Cha Hedy

Own: Kamikaze Stable $9,000
CASTANON J L (29 2 5 4 .07) 1999:(659 70 .11)

Ch. m. 5
Sire: Bucky Raj (Rajab)
Dam: Cachagua (Pretense)
Br: Longo Isidore Sam (Cal)
Tr: Reeder Donald S(126 18 20 20 .14) 99:(456 80 .18)

L 115

Life	51	5	8	5	$112,497	D.Fst	42	3	6	5	$87,177	81
1999	16	2	4	2	$34,135	Wet	6	2	2	0	$24,600	70
1998	17	2	1	3	$24,220	Turf	3	0	0	0	$720	62
Pha	10	3	2	1	$25,505	Dist	5	0	3	1	$8,340	67

26Nov99-6Pha sly 7f :22 :44 1:104 1:244 3↑ Ⓕ Clm 7500N2Y 70 7 2 2½ 1½ 12½ 14 Black A S L 117 b *2.20 83-16 Cha Cha Hedy1174 Green Badger1171 Soul Of Aly1147¾ In hand late 7
15Nov99-7Pha fst 5½f :223 :463 :591 1:06 3↑ Ⓕ Clm 7500N2Y 48 4 5 41¼ 22½ 25 25¾ Black A S L 117 *1.30 78-20 **Super Attraction**1175¾ *Cha Cha Hedy*117hd Soul Of Aly1121¼ No match 10
24Oct99-2Pha fst 5½f :221 :461 :584 1:05 3↑ Ⓕ Clm 7500N2Y 63 6 6 74 53½ 44½ 21¾ Cole A L 117 b 3.50 87-15 Smart Flow1171¾ Cha Cha Hedy1171½ High Shine1171¼ Pinched, rallied 9
16Oct99-10Pha sf 5f Ⓣ :231 :472 1:002 3↑ Ⓕ Clm 14000(15-13) 61 3 7 62¼ 64 65 63½ Cole A L 116 b 19.50 74-22 Explosive Rhythm1171¼ Miss Jetaway112nk **No Jeans**113¾ No factor 9
3Oct99-7Pha fst 1 :23 :462 1:12 1:382 3↑ Ⓕ Clm 14000(14-12) 47 7 1 2hd 21 611 817½ Black A S L 117 b 8.00 69-13 *Out Burst*1177¾ Royal Cone1124½ Shooting Fire1141¼ Tired 10
18Sep99-5Pha fst 7f :222 :452 1:102 1:233 3↑ Ⓕ Clm 14000(14-12) 63 1 4 21 21½ 33 34 Cole A L 119 b 3.10 85-13 Angel's Angel1121½ StarliteCruisin1172½ ChaChaHedy1195½ Inside, no rally 7
29Aug99-5Del fst 6f :214 :444 :571 1:094 3↑ Ⓕ Alw 33600N2X 40 7 1 41¼ 66¼ 611 617¼ Madrigal R Jr L 120 b 14.70 77-07 *Tropical Punch*115nk Rills1132 Zippy1171 Thru early 7
18Aug99-6Del fst 6f :22 :452 :582 1:114 3↑ Ⓕ Alw 33000N2X 77 3 4 31 44 32 2hd McCarthy M J L 122 b 6.10 84-16 H. F. Brimstone117hd Cha Cha Hedy122¾ Rills1139½ Rail, willingly 5
27Jly99-8Pha fst 6f :22 :453 :583 1:112 3↑ Ⓕ Alw 18990N2X 47 5 2 22 33 45½ 59¾ Madrigal R Jr L 122 b 5.40 76-18 Star One One1121¾ Quick 'n Smart111nk Intriga1133½ Outside, tierd 6
20Jly99-9Pha gd 6½f :22 :443 1:102 1:171 3↑ Ⓕ Alw 17935N1X 65 11 1 12 11½ 11½ 12¼ Madrigal R Jr L 117 b 5.50 86-09 Cha Cha Hedy1172¼ Count The Bells117¾ *Manhattan Vice*117¾ Drew off 12

9 No Jeans

Own: Bencardino Nina $8,000
FLORES L (312 58 40 40 .19) 1999:(544 93 .17)

Dk. b or br f. 4 FTMDEC95 $3,000
Sire: Norquestor (Conquistador Cielo)
Dam: Go Jean (Bold Ambition)
Br: Schipper Gerrit J (Md)
Tr: McCaslin John S(71 19 7 11 .27) 99:(197 53 .27)

L 108⁵

Life	14	6	1	3	$41,745	D.Fst	9	3	1	2	$20,325	64
1999	11	5	1	3	$36,945	Wet	4	3	0	0	$20,100	67
1998	3	1	0	0	$4,800	Turf	1	0	0	1	$1,320	67
Pha	12	6	1	2	$40,125	Dist	8	5	1	1	$33,325	67

11Dec99-5Pha my 5½f :221 :462 :593 1:062 3↑ Ⓕ Clm 6500(7.5-6.5) 65 6 1 12 12 13½ 11¼ Flores L5 L 108 b *1.50 82-19 No Jeans1081¼ Haley's Alright117hd Leading Lena1123 Off rail, hard drive 6
26Nov99-5Pha sly 5½f :213 :452 :583 1:054 3↑ Ⓕ Clm 5000 66 3 1 11½ 14 16 16¾ Flores L5 L 112 b *.80 85-16 *No Jeans*1126¾ Twiceasweetheart1172½ Cuban's Beauty117no Mild drive 5
13Nov99-5Pha fst 5f :224 :461 :593 3↑ Ⓕ Alw 5000s 58 3 2 21 21½ 22½ 45¼ Espindola M A L 119 b 3.20 77-19 Ourlittlemry1172 *TopGunnr*1191 ChnsonDSolil1222¼ Two wide, weakened 5
24Oct99-7Pha fst 5½f :214 :452 :584 1:054 3↑ Ⓕ Clm 10000(10-8) 64 8 1 23½ 23 22½ 31¾ McCormick M L L 117 b 3.00 83-15 **Smithereens**1121¼ Saucy Dottie115½ No Jeans1173½ Stalked, weakened 9
16Oct99-10Pha sf 5f Ⓣ :231 :472 1:002 3↑ Ⓕ Clm 13000(15-13) 67 2 3 1½ 11½ 12 31½ McCormick M L L 113 b 4.90 76-22 Explosive Rhythm1171¼ Miss Jetaway112nk No Jeans113¾ Faltered 9
3Jly99-7Pha my 5½f :22 :45 :573 1:043 3↑ Ⓕ Alw 17000N1X 67 3 6 1hd 1½ 11½ 1½ McCormick M L L 117 b 5.40 91-14 No Jeans117½ Miss Cowtown117nk Miss Sullivan1154¼ Driving 7
20Jun99-6Del sly 6f :213 :444 :573 1:104 3↑ Ⓕ Alw 32200N1X 63 9 4 21½ 21½ 45½ 69 McCormick M L L 118 b 12.40 80-18 *Quite Revealing*1182½ Whatasweetheart1182½ *Tropical Punch*114½ Tired 9
7Jun99-7Pha fst 5½f :214 :451 :583 1:054 3↑ Ⓕ Clm 15000(15-13)N3L 60 1 4 12 14½ 14½ 11¼ McCormick M L L 119 b *1.30 85-17 No Jeans1191¼ Close Approach117hd Shift Shape1191¾ Driving 6
9May99-2Pha fst 7f :223 :462 1:124 1:263 3↑ Ⓕ Clm 15000(15-13)N3L 51 8 5 21 4½ 21½ 33½ McCormick M L L 119 b 2.40 71-17 Lime Lake1193¼ Madam Bimbi116hd *No Jeans*1191½ Rough trip, poor ride 8
1May99-10Pha fst 6f :221 :451 :574 1:11 3↑ Ⓕ Clm 13000(15-13)N2L 64 7 4 3½ 1hd 12½ 14 McCormick M L L 113 b 5.00 88-09 No Jeans1134 *Shift Shape*1171¼ *Miss Buckaroo*1171¾ Drew off 8
WORKS: Oct8 Pha 4f fst :484 B *5/20*

I Am Me R. G. had earned a Beyer Speed Figure of 69 in her December 7 effort. Only one of her six rivals had a better last-race figure—Cha Cha Hedy had just run a 70, her best effort in months. Since I Am Me R. G. had earned her number running against a strong bias, and presumably figured to be much better than a 69 under normal circumstances, she had a clear edge over this field.

The probable pace of the race appeared to give I Am Me R. G. a further edge. Smithereens was a one-dimensional front-runner. So too was Super Attraction. So too was No Jeans. There was almost certainly going to be a hot pace in this race, benefiting the stretch-running style of I Am Me R. G. The mare was a dependable performer, with a career record of 12 for 55 on a fast track. In this small field, a price of 2-1 looked like a bargain, and I took it.

SIXTH RACE
Philadelphia
DECEMBER 19, 1999

5½ FURLONGS. (1.02³) CLAIMING. Purse $9,500 (plus $3,500 State Bred) FOR FILLIES AND MARES THREE YEARS OLD AND UPWARD. Three-year-olds. 120 lbs.; Older. 122 lbs.; Non-winners of two races since October 19 allowed 3 lbs.; a race since then 5 lbs.; Claiming Price $10,000; for each $1,000 to $8,000 2 lbs. (Races where entered for $7,500 or less not considered).

Value of Race: $9,500 Winner $5,700; second $1,900; third $1,045; fourth $570; fifth $285. Mutuel Pool $32,135.00 Exacta Pool $32,384.00 Trifecta Pool $17,352.00

Last Raced	Horse	M/Eqt. A.Wt	PP	St	¼	⅜	Str	Fin	Jockey	Cl'g Pr	Odds $1
7Dec99 6Pha3	I Am Me R. G.	Lbf 8 117	4	4	4¹	3²	22½	1²	Unsihuay A	10000	2.00
20Nov99 7Pha5	Smithereens-GB	Lbf 6 119	1	1	11½	11½	1½	2³¾	Black A S	10000	1.60
28Nov99 3Pha4	Super Attraction	Lb 4 117	3	7	7	7	6²	3no	Estrada E A	10000	22.80
11Nov99 2Lrl9	First Preference	Lf 6 117	2	3	3¹	4²	4²	4hd	Madrigal R Jr	10000	12.60
11Dec99 5Pha1	No Jeans	Lbf 4 109	7	2	2²	21½	3²	5½	Flores L5	8000	4.70
23Nov99 9Pha3	Saturday Nite Lady	Lb 5 112	5	5	5½	5²	5¹	66½	Simpson R5	10000	10.10
26Nov99 6Pha1	Cha Cha Hedy	Lb 5 115	6	6	6⁸	6⁴	7	7	Castanon J L	9000	6.80

OFF AT 2:37 Start Good. Won driving. Track fast.
TIME :21³, :45, :57³, 1:04² (:21.60, :45.07, :57.76, 1:04.49)

$2 Mutuel Prices:

5–I AM ME R. G.	6.00	3.20	3.00
1–SMITHEREENS–GB		3.20	2.80
4–SUPER ATTRACTION			5.00

$2 EXACTA 5-1 PAID $25.80 $2 TRIFECTA 5-1-4 PAID $185.40

Ch. m, by I Am the Game–Rebekah Grace, by Thirty Eight Paces. Trainer Day Diane. Bred by Chaney Richard H (Md).

I AM ME R. G. raced off rail, took the lead near sixteenth marker, edged clear. SMITHEREENS (GB) set pace just off rail, was no match late. SUPER ATTRACTION broke slowly, failed to menace. FIRST PREFERENCE saved ground just off pace, tired. NO JEANS prompted outside, tired. SATURDAY NITE LADY failed to menace. CHA CHA HEDY failed to threaten.

Owners— 1, Maurizio Mario; 2, Plumstead Stables; 3, Diamante Racing Stable; 4, Simpson Debbie; 5, Bencardino Nina; 6, Labe Paul E Sr; 7, Kamikaze Stable

Trainers— 1, Day Diane; 2, Seeger Robert J; 3, Gonzalez Andrea; 4, Simpson Deborah M; 5, McCaslin John S; 6, Lake Scott A; 7, Reeder Donald S

First Preference was claimed by Rap-A-Tap Stable; trainer, Vega Richard.

Scratched— Scat Singer (7Dec99 6PHA2), Kiss Pudding (15Nov99 7PHA7)

Readers familiar with my previous books will know that I have always advocated an aggressive approach to wagering, one that emphasizes exotic wagers and a go-for-the-big-score philosophy. When I am intensely following a single track, such as Gulfstream Park, I rarely bet to win unless I love a horse at a big price. Playing a 2-1 shot would be beneath my dignity, no matter how strong my convictions. But I have modified my preferred approach when I am following several tracks in the simulcast arena. I realize that I cannot know all the nuances in a race at Philadelphia Park, and it usually takes in-depth knowledge to uncover the obscure longshot who will sneak into third place and create a juicy trifecta. I might be able to convert my knowledge about a horse like I Am Me R. G. into a solid win bet, but trying to come up with winning exotic combinations is likely to be futile. So my betting strategy is relatively conservative and straightforward—though this does not rule out the possibility of big payoffs and big scores.

I started playing simulcasts in earnest in 1997, the year that the precursor to Horse Watch was created. This also happened to be a year when I was suffering from a mystery disease that seriously limited my physical mobility and left me with little to do but direct my mental energy into handicapping. I was intensely focused, but I didn't have the energy to go to the track often, so I patiently looked for ideal spots. I was a handicapping version of Tommy the Pinball Wizard, who didn't have any distractions, couldn't hear any buzzers and bells. During the course of the illness, I compiled a winning percentage and a return on investment that I have never achieved before and will probably never achieve again, and my stunning results during this period convinced me forever that my new approach to simulcasting was the right one.

In the fall of 1997 the race meeting at Keeneland was characterized (as it so often is) by a powerful rail-favoring bias. Unfortunately, the race charts from Kentucky are often vague in describing which horses were on the rail and which were wide, but I was able to see the race replays via satellite TV. Although I didn't do exhaustive trip handicapping, I did note the names of horses who made notable wide moves and listed them in Horse Watch. After Keeneland closed, most of the horses moved to Churchill Downs, and three of the names on my Horse Watch list appeared on the November 12 card. One of them, Colonel Vann, had earned a competitive figure after a wide trip from post 11 at Keeneland; he won and paid $58. The next horse finished second at 27-1. My third horse, Mr. Barrymore, was entered in the ninth race.

Information Hiway
Own: Humphrey G Watts
DAY P (63 17 9 .27) 1997:(1125 237 .21)

Ch. g. 7
Sire: Forty Niner (Mr. Prospector)
Dam: Dream Deal(Sharpen Up*GB)
Br: Firman Pamela H & Humphrey G Watts (Ky)
Tr: Arnold George R II (5 1 0 0 .20) 97:(232 41 .18)

Lifetime Record:	4	1	0	1	$28,504						
1997	4	1	0	1	$28,504	Turf	0	0	0	0	
1996	0	M	0	0		Wet	1	0	0	0	$1,092
CD	3	0	0	1	$5,312	Dist	1	1	0	0	$23,192

29Oct97-7CD fst 6f :212 :453 :582 1:12 3↑ Alw 33060N1X 73 5 6 53 43¼ 5¾ 6½ Martinez W L 113 2.90 82-18 *Not A Role Model*114nk Matlab114hd Forty Ninth Street116¾ 7
Steadied between foes 1-16, angled out, no late response
8Jun97-7CD my 1 1/16 :233 :483 1:133 1:443 3↑ Alw 44800N1X 80 2 55½ 63¾ 54½ 57¼ 57½ Arguello F A Jr L 112 12.00 80-13 Tricon1164 Flyfisher1162¼ De Guerin1201 Evenly, no rally 11
16May97-6CD fst 6½f :224 :462 1:114 1:18 Alw 40040N2L 80 4 5 21 31 31½ 34 Perret C L 121 5.20 84-10 *CraftyOne*1212 StrightNorth1212 InformtionHiwy1211½ No late response 7
25Apr97-3Kee fst *7f :222 :452 1:12 1:292 Md Sp Wt 36k 75 2 6 1hd 1hd 12½ 1¾ Gryder A T L 119 5.50 82-16 Information Hiway119¾ Air Power119½ Bust The Dust1192½ 12
Dueled, driving, lasted
WORKOUTS: Nov8 CD 4f gd :504 B *12/25* Oct28 CD 3f my :382 Bg *14/17* Oct24 CD 5f fst 1:023 B *12/36* Oct 12 Bel5f fst 1:06 B *29/29* Oct6 Bel 5f fst 1:031 B *15/19* Sep30 Bel 4f fst :491 B *18/49*

He Met a Lassie
Own: Kelly Thomas J
HEBERT T J (6 1 0 1 .17) 1997:(566 75 .13)

Ch. g. 7
Sire: Lac Ouimet (Pleasant Colony) $4,000
Dam: Jeanne's Lassie(Northern Fling)
Br: Kelly Thomas J (Ky)
Tr: Larry Kelly (8 1 0 3 .13) 97:(157 13 .08)

Lifetime Record:	4	1	2	0	$9,750						
1997	4	1	2	0	$9,750	Turf	0	0	0	0	
1996	0	M	0	0		Wet	1	0	1	0	$2,200
CD	0	0	0	0		Dist	0	0	0	0	

31Oct97-10Hoo fst 6f :214 :442 :562 1:092 3↑ Alw 16600N1X 78 7 3 2½ 2½ 2hd 2nk Hebert T J LB 113 fb 3.90 90-13 MedicineRiver115nk HeMetALassie113no Volumizer1172 Sharp try outside 8
7Oct97-5Haw fst 6f :221 :451 :574 1:104 3↑ Md 10000 67 4 2 1½ 12 11½ 14½ Fires E L 118 fb *1.90 88-15 He Met A Lassie1184½ *Jackson Lake*122no *Sherlock*1181 Driving 9
5Sep97-5AP fst 5½f :23 :464 :591 1:06 3↑ Md 25000 (25-20) 10 2 5 42½ 42 48 522½ Fires E L 118 b *.60 71-16 Shomrim's Royalty1167¼ Hi Sugar11412 Groovy Cannon1182¼ Off slowly 5
Previously trained by Kelly Timothy D
6Mar97-1Aqu wf 6f ⊡ :222 :462 :583 1:112 Md 25000 60 5 8 88¼ 43 25 23 Nelson D 118 13.10 86-11 *CllMeSocil*1133 HeMetALssie11810 TheQuibblr113¾ Poor brk, rallied wde 8
WORKOUTS: Oct26 CD 4f sly :51 B *21/36* Oct17 CD 3f fst :393 B *14/14* Sep23 AP 3f gd :37 B 2/7 Sep16 AP 5f fst 1:04 B *15/29* •Aug23 AP 4f fst :472 Hg *1/35* Aug16 AP 4f fst :522 B *28/33*

Ataki
Own: Paulson Allen E
TORRES F C (86 9 7 .10) 1997:(1175 180 .15)

B. h. 7
Sire: Strawberry Road*Aus (Whiskey Road)
Dam: Cruella(Tyrant)
Br: Paulson Allen E (Ky)
Tr: Romans Jerry L (18 0 1 2 .00) 97:(239 40 .17)

Lifetime Record:	6	1	2	2	$31,155						
1997	6	1	2	2	$31,155	Turf	1	0	1	0	$2,970
1996	0	M	0	0		Wet	0	0	0	0	
CD	1	0	0	1	$4,060	Dist	1	0	1	0	$2,970

29Oct97-4CD fst 6f :213 :453 :581 1:113 3↑ Alw 30160N1X 74 2 3 64¾ 64½ 55½ 33¼ Torres F C L 118 2.50 82-18 Texas Topper1133 Doppler Effect108nk Ataki1181 Slight gain 8
12Oct97-6Kee fst 6f :221 :454 :573 1:094 3↑ Alw 41000N1X 74 5 2 43 31½ 43 47½ Torres F C L 116 2.50 84-13 Dancing Outlaw1164½ Vermilion1131 Flatirons1142 Tired 7
2Oct97-5TP fst 6½f :223 :454 1:112 1:174 3↑ Md Sp Wt 25k 85 3 6 43 41¾ 12½ 18 Torres F C L 120 1.90 82-19 Ataki1208 Call Me Mr. Vain1204 Apollo Beach122nk Ridden out 11
Previously trained by Gomez Frank
18Aug97-5Crc fm 1 1/16 Ⓣ :233 :483 1:123 1:432 3↑ Md Sp Wt 16k 82 1 51¾ 53½ 44½ 22 2½ Coa E M 117 *.90 81-18 Windy Premier117½ *Ataki*1175 Made The Grade117no Rallied 10
2Aug97-9Crc fst 7f :233 :473 1:123 1:254 3↑ Md Sp Wt 19k 76 8 5 42 46 33½ 21 Coa E M 118 *.70 79-23 *Henriques*1181 Ataki1182½ Made The Grade1183¾ Rallied 10
19Jly97-3Crc fst 6f :22 :454 :59 1:131 3↑ Md Sp Wt 16k 74 6 5 55 49 34 31½ Homeister R B Jr 117 6.60 79-18 True Devil117¾ Demi Dinner117¾ Ataki1171¼ Late rally 9
WORKOUTS: •Sep12 CD 3f fst :362 B *1/16* Aug27 Crc 4f fst :49 B *2/31* Aug16 Crc 4f fst :493 B *16/79*

Dr. Shea
Own: Zahler James
ARGUELLO F A JR (37 2 5 4 .05) 1997:(763 58 .08)

B. h. 7
Sire: Well Decorated (Raja Baba) $5,000
Dam: Shave(Blade)
Br: Nuckols Alfred H Jr (Ky)
Tr: Flint Bernard S (20 2 5 .10) 97:(523 88 .17)

Lifetime Record:	10	1	2	0	$23,628						
1997	8	1	2	0	$23,076	Turf	1	0	0	0	
1996	2	M	0	0	$552	Wet	3	0	0	0	$552
CD	3	0	0	0	$552	Dist	0	0	0	0	$23,192

31Oct97-10Hoo fst 6f :214 :442 :562 1:092 3↑ Alw 16600N1X 73 4 7 811 812 66½ 42¼ Cox D W LB 113 6.30 88-13 Medicine River115nk **He Met A Lassie**113no Volumizer1172 Full of run 8
8May97-2CD sly 1 1/16 :243 :492 1:144 1:472 3↑ Clm 17500N2L 65 9 43 43½ 53¾ 610 610¾ Day P L 108 *1.40 63-22 Summer Shower1083½ Sun Magic113¾ Great Siege1202 9
Six wide trip, flattened out
27Apr97-7CD sly 1 1/16 :233 :48 1:134 1:472 Alw 41600N2L 40 4 56 53½ 78½ 714 625½ Hebert T J L 121 27.80 48-25 Rojo Dinero1214 Vermilion1215 Swipe1181 7
Exchanged bumps 5/8's pole, tired
6Apr97-8Kee fm 1 Ⓣ :223 :47 1:122 1:362 Transylvania71k 37 6 612 611 66½ 69¾ 623 Torres F C L 112 15.90 63-14 Near The Bank118hd Daylight Savings1142½ Song For James1131½ 6
6-wide stretch, never close
19Mar97-8TP fst 1 :213 :444 1:10 1:353 Alw 23770N1X 78 4 58 56 21½ 21 22 Torres F C L 118 2.90 90-16 Blair1182 Dr. Shea1185 Catty King1187 Bid, second best 6
21Feb97-9TP fst 1 :223 :46 1:104 1:372 Presidents49k 68 4 34 64¼ 67 610 611¾ Cox D W L 115 *2.50 71-21 Famously Free115¾ Won For The Road1151½ Miswaki Bandit1136 Tired 6
13Feb97-7TP fr 1 :232 :47 1:113 1:38 Md Sp Wt 23k 68 1 11½ 11½ 11 11 11 Cox D W L 121 4.20 80-21 Dr. Shea1211 Pourmeacoolone1211 Drennon Springs1142 Pace, driving 12
3Jan97-5TP fst 1 :23 :471 1:134 1:41 Md 30000 (30-20) 59 1 41¾ 31½ 21½ 11½ 2½ Spieth S L 121 *2.10 64-30 SongForJmes121½ *Dr.She*1211½ QuestionOfGold1174 Led outside stretch 12
21Dec96-6TP fst 6f :214 :443 :57 1:10 Md Sp Wt 23k 51 5 9 85¼ 711 79¾ 79¼ Spieth S L 122 10.50 84-10 Sodfather1222½ Drennon Springs1151 *Willowbrook Lane*122hd No factor 12
17Nov96-3CD wf 6f :214 :454 :584 1:124 Md 30000 (30-20) 53 1 6 43½ 45½ 46 54 Day P L 120 3.90 75-16 Rock City1202 King Walker118hd Green Fire1201½ Inside, weakened 11
WORKOUTS: Oct23 CD 5f fst 1:042 Bg*22/32* Oct9 CD 5f fst 1:043 B *14/22* Sep27 CD 4f fst :491 *6/26* Sep21 CD 4f fst :52B *6/28* Sep15 CD 3f fst :37 B *3/13* Sep6 CD 3f fst :37B *2/6*

Mr. Barrymore

Own: Jebb Stables

KUTZ D (37 3 5 5 .08) 1997:(455 50 .11)

Ch. g. 8

Sire: Rare Performer (Mr. Prospector)

Dam: Disco Jan(Torsion)

Br: Jebb Stables & Wafare Farm (Ky)

Tr: Bindner Walter M Jr (10 1 3 1 .10) 97:(149 22 .15)

Lifetime Record: 12 1 2 5 $30,964

1997	9	1	2	4	$25,609	Turf	2	0	0	1	$2,590
1996	3	M	0	1	$5,355	Wet	2	0	1	1	$7,020
CD	2	0	0	2	$4,180	Dist	2	0	0	0	$949

18Oct97- 6Kee fst 7f :221 :45 1:103 1:231 3+ Alw 41000N1X 69 7 3 52¾ 52¼ 56½ 510¼ Castillo O O5 L 108 f 14.80 79 - 11 ***Red Riser***1161¼ Trumps Clown1133 Andersonville1134 No rally 8

26Sep97- 6AP fm *1 Ⓣ :234 :481 1:131 1:374 3+ Alw 21000N1X 78 9 2½ 1hd 2hd 2½ 61½ Deegan J C L 116 10.20 84 - 14 DwnlessTim111nk DHFightOrFlight119 DH***Pourmcoolon***114¾ Weakened 11

19Sep97- 7TP fst 1 :224 :46 1:111 1:38 3+ Alw 28330N1X 80 6 2hd 1hd 2½ 34½ 34 Morgan M R L 116 f 8.30 76 - 29 Midway Magistrate1121½ Mc Clyde1152½ Mr. Barrymore116½ 8
Came out bumped start, bid, weakened

26Aug97- 8EIP hd 1 1/16 Ⓣ :24 :471 1:104 1:403 3+ Alw 23840N2L 75 1 12 11 1½ 11 32½ Morgan M R L 113 f 6.50 94 - 05 White King1132½ Runaway Affair112hd Mr. Barrymore113¾ Could not last 9

19Aug97- 8EIP sly 1 ⊗ :241 :473 1:124 1:38 3+ Alw 25900N2L 84 1 1½ 1½ 21 21 2nk Morgan M R L 114 f 5.80 87 - 16 SimonLordLovt113nk Mr.Brrymor1146 ***MidwyMgistrt***10811 Pace, good try 7
Hand timed by Daily Racing From

29Jly97- 5EIP fst 1 :24 :474 1:134 1:40 3+ Md 30000 (30-25) 73 1 42½ 32½ 2½ 11 16½ Castillo O O5 L 117 f *1.40 77 - 30 Mr. Barrymore1176½ Maria's Orbit1126 Our Bart1162 7
Came out bumped start, drew off, hand urging

6Jly97-12EIP fst 6f :23 :461 :583 1:112 3+ Md 30000 (30-25) 73 8 9 98 78¼ 65¾ 21 Johnson P A L 122 5.00 90 - 09 Tortfesor1171 ***Mr.Brrymore***1221 ***MedicineRivr***117¾ 6-wide bid, 2nd best 10

15Jun97- 3CD fst 6f :212 :461 :584 1:113 3+ Md 30000 (30-20) 65 7 8 86½ 74¾ 55 33 Johnson P A L 121 4.30 82 - 12 Company Clown113½ Bowl Bid1122½ Mr. Barrymore1211 12
6-wide stretch, mild gain

8May97- 7CD my 6f :214 :461 :59 1:122 3+ Md 30000 (30-20) 68 3 10 42½ 45 35½ 35½ Johnson P A L 122 4.40 75 - 21 Leave One's Mark1225 ***Stand Back***112½ Mr. Barrymore1221 11
Bumped, squeezed start, drifted out briefly 3/16

13Oct96- 4Kee fst *7f :231 :461 1:113 1:28 3+ Md Sp Wt 37k 43 1 4 21 31 59½ 621 Woods C R Jr L 119 f 5.80 68 - 20 ***Sierra Grande***1196 Storm Of The Night1194 Omaha Beach119hd 9
Came out bumped start, tired

WORKOUTS: Nov6 CD 5f fst 1:013 B *4/36* **Sep15 CD 5f fst 1:044 B** *33/36* **Sep9 CD 4f fst :52 B** *34/38* **Aug13 CD 4f gd :53 B** *24/26*

Devil Power

Own: Castle Rock Racing Stable

MARTINEZ W (83 4 9 7 .05) 1997:(1309 215 .16)

Ch. h. 7

Sire: Devil's Bag (Halo) $15,000

Dam: Pyramid Power(Upper Nile)

Br: Larry Millison Inc (Ky)

Tr: Gothard Akiko (3 1 0 0 .33) 97:(133 22 .17)

Lifetime Record: 4 1 1 0 $28,632

1997	4	1	1	0	$28,632	Turf	0	0	0	0	
1996	0	M	0	0		Wet	0	0	0	0	
CD	1	0	0	0		Dist	1	1	0	0	$23,192

22Oct97- 1Kee fst 7f :222 :452 1:12 1:252 3+ Md Sp Wt 36k 76 6 4 31 31½ 21 12½ Martinez W L 119 10.20 78 - 14 Devil Power1192½ Apollo Beach1223 Heart Tempo1192 Steady drive 10

2Oct97- 5TP fst 6½f :223 :454 1:112 1:174 3+ Md Sp Wt 25k 54 6 2 1½ 2hd 43 613¼ Troilo W D L 120 *1.70 69 - 19 **Ataki**1208 Call Me Mr. Vain1204 Apollo Beach122nk 11
Ducked out, bumped start, dueled, tired

20Sep97- 6TP fst 6f :222 :46 :581 1:104 3+ Md Sp Wt 26k 84 5 3 32 22 21½ 21 Troilo W D L 119 5.90 86 - 17 Motel Romeo1191 Devil Power1199 Stone Hinge119nk Bid, 2nd best, hung 11

16May97- 4CD fst 6f :213 :452 :574 1:104 3+ Md Sp Wt 36k 56 3 6 2hd 43¼ 69 713 D'Amico A J L 112 19.90 76 - 10 ***Copper Canyon***1122 ***Drennon Springs***113¾ Carson City Too1125 11
Drifted in start, dueled, tired

WORKOUTS: Aug31 TP 5f fst 1:03 B*6/6*

Charming Halo

Own: Sisk James T

ESPINOSA LE (18 1 2 1 .06) 1997:(227 13 .06)

Ch. g. 9

Sire: Sunny's Halo (Halo) $4,000

Dam: Hoverclubber(North Flight)

Br: Maggard James Paul (Ky)

Tr: Woodard Joe (1 1 0 0 1.00) 97:(14 2 .14)

Lifetime Record: 36 6 6 4 $51,972

1997	16	3	4	3	$33,208	Turf	0	0	0	0	
1996	8	1	1	1	$6,227	Wet	6	1	0	1	$10,366
CD	4	1	1	0	$12,700	Dist	4	1	1	0	$9,816

26Oct97- 9CD sly 6½f :23 :47 1:134 1:204 3+ Clm 12000 (13.5-11.5) 78 3 9 66 53¾ 22 13 Espinosa L E5 L 108 b 24.80 74 - 21 CharmingHalo1083 Inverlochy1173 AllApproved1141½ Rallied 4-wide, dvg 12

18Oct97-10Hoo fst 5½f :22 :452 :572 1:04 3+ Clm 10000 71 7 6 93¾ 98¾ 64¾ 21 Espinosa L E5 LB 112 b 19.30 90 - 16 It's Your Call1171 ***Charming Halo***112¾ Uwana Prop119hd Too late outside 10

4Oct97-11Hoo fst 6f :221 :451 :574 1:102 3+ Alw 5000s 72 5 9 1014 109 58 36¼ Leeds D L LB 117 b 10.10 79 - 18 Shamanuu1225 Pro Irish1171¼ Charming Halo117½ 5 wd into ln, rallied 10

12Sep97- 9Hoo fst 1 :231 :461 1:11 1:37 3+ Hcp 5000s 58 7 75½ 76 65½ 75½ 86¾ Leeds D L LB 116 b 8.00 78 - 13 EruditeLedr1131¾ K.T.TwntyTwo1151 NorthOfMrs1121¾ No threat outside 10

14Aug97- 5EIP fst 7f :221 :452 1:104 1:234 3+ Alw 5000s 55 2 4 55½ 55½ 67 613½ Espinosa L E7 L 112 b 4.70 80 - 12 Inverlochy1132 ***Manhattan Knight***1133¼ ***Ft. Bent***113nk No factor 6

29Jly97- 2EIP fst 5½f :224 :462 :582 1:044 3+ Alw 7500s 76 6 3 45½ 45½ 33½ 32¾ Espinosa L E7 L 112 b 5.70 92 - 13 Ruled Off1192 Baby Goodbye113¾ Charming Halo112½ No gain late, rail 6

20Jly97- 7EIP fst 5½f :221 :452 :573 1:041 3+ Alw 5000s 75 1 7 89 89 68 22½ Espinosa L E10 L 109 b 5.20 95 - 09 ***Ruled Off***1132½ Charming Halo1091½ Powerful Headache1082 8
Circled 7-wide stretch, 2nd best

4Jly97-11EIP fst 7f :23 :463 1:122 1:252 3+ Clm 7000 (8-7) 75 2 11 127½ 1110 67 11¼ Espinosa L E5 L 108 b 6.40 86 - 15 Charming Halo1081¼ Jack's Big Mac113hd Felluga1142 12
Seven wide stretch, closed fast, driving

27Jun97- 2CD fst 7f :231 :463 1:113 1:242 4+ Clm 6250 76 8 4 3½ 21 22 23 Espinosa L E5 L 108 b 18.20 83 - 12 ***You're The Man***1133 ***Charming Halo***1086 ***Colony Sound***112½ 11
Bumped start, stalked, second best

14Jun97- 2CD sly 7f :23 :471 1:131 1:264 4+ Clm c-5000 30 5 4 32½ 54½ 816 919½ Torres F C L 112 fb *2.50 54 - 19 Desert Corral112no Reno Mac1121½ Reynosa1074 Gave way 9
Claimed from Cramer Jeffrey D for $5,000, Dunne Leonard Trainer 1997(as of 06/14): (31 4 4 3 0.13)

The Preformer

Own: David L Muench Racing Stable INC

PECK B D (32 0 4 1 .00) 1997:(467 47 .10)

B. g. 7

Sire: Star de Naskra (Naskra) $10,000

Dam: American Storm(Affirmed)

Br: Margaux Stud Inc & Merrill Dan (Ky)

Tr: Muench David L (1 0 0 0 .00) 97:(2 0 .00)

Lifetime Record: 13 2 3 0 $19.260

1997	10	2	2	0	$16,660	Turf	1	0	0	0
1996	3	M	1	0	$2,600	Wet	0	0	0	0
CD	1	0	0	0	$600	Dist	1	0	0	0

28Oct97- 9CD fst 6f :222 :463 :584 1:114 3+ Clm 17500 (17.5-15) 75 10 4 54½ 31½ 44 54 Peck B D L 114 b 24.70 80 - 17 Groovy Ryder117nk ***Surpass***1213 Sudden Fling112nk Flattened out 11

18Oct97- 6Kee fst 7f :221 :45 1:103 1:231 3+ Alw 41000N1X 50 4 1 3nk 3nk 710 818¾ Albarado R J L 111 b 28.70 70 - 11 ***Red Riser***1161¼ Trumps Clown1133 Andersonville1134 Pressed, gave way 8

18Sep97- 4AP fst 6f :223 :46 :583 1:113 3+ Clm c-16000N3L 69 2 2 3½ 41 42 21¼ Gomez G K L 115 b *.90 84 - 20 ***Vilnius***1151¼ The Preformer1152 River Gulch119¾ 2nd best 8
Claimed from Calabrese Frank C for $16,000, McGehee Britt A Trainer 1997(as of 09/18): (95 23 15 17 0.24)

31Aug97- 3AP fst 6½f :23 :461 1:12 1:184 3+ Clm 16000N3L 76 2 2 1hd 11 2hd 2½ Gomez G K L 117 b *1.20 82 - 20 GelicHills114½ ThePreformer1174½ Iruntheshow113¾ Inside, couldn't last 11

13Aug97- 9AP gd 1 ⊗ :233 :471 1:123 1:38 Alw 21000N1X 61 6 41¾ 42½ 51¾ 47½ 412½ Razo E Jr L 116 b 6.20 73 - 15 Knightly Alarm1165½ D'affaires116no Go See Mervin1167 No rally 7

24Jly97- 5AP fst 1 :23 :461 1:111 1:37 3+ Clm 20000N2L 74 1 31½ 32½ 42 21½ 1½ Gomez G K L 114 b 1.80 91 - 08 The Preformer114½ Prairie Affair1179 Shadow Mountain1091¾ Driving 7

WORKOUTS: ●Nov9 CDT 5f fst 1:022 B *1/4* **Nov4 CDT 4f fst :51 B** *9/9* **Oct 24 Kee 4f fst :491 B** *2/15* **Oct14 Kee 3f sly :393 B** *7/7* **Oct8 Ke 4f fst :49 B** *4/17* **Aug 25 AP4f fst :482 B** *5/39*

```
Der Teufel                                  Dk. b or br g. 7                                      Lifetime Record:   15  1  1  3   $36,157
Own: Morsches Paul J Jr                     Sire: Devil's Bag (Halo) $15,000                      1997  8 1 1 1  $25,767 | Turf 1 0 0 0
WOODS C R JR (61 4 5 5 .07) 1997:(534 65 .12)  Dam: Fiji Fan(Danzig)                              1996  7 M 0 2  $10,390 | Wet  4 0 0 0  $6,758
                                            Br: Morsches Lumber Co (Ky)                           CD    6 0 0 3  $13,592 | Dist 1 0 0 0  $858
                                            Tr: Penrod Steven C (8 1 1 2 .13) 97:(136 21 .15)

2Nov97-6CD my 7½f :22 :45 1:112 1:322 3+ Alw 40600N1X    92 1 1 1013 1014 55½ 3nk Woods C R Jr L 112 b 31.70 83-19 Secreto Play113hd Trumps Clown113no Der Teufel112½  6-wide bid, hung 12
24Oct97-5Kee sly 1⅛ :473 1:122 1:39 1:522 3+ Alw 42508N1X  46 7 43½ 56 68 816 828¾ Perret C L 115 b 19.30 45-19 Turned To Gold1183 Keats And Yeats113½ Andiron110½  Gave way 8
10Oct97-9Kee fm 1 1/16 (T) :222 :461 1:104 1:42 3+ Alw 41032N1X  6210 54½ 63 64¼ 67½ 712½ Perret C L 113 b 22.50 80-06 He's A Tough Cat1133½ Orleans Road113hd Song For James1141½  Tired 10
7Sep97-9TP fst 1 1/16 :23 :464 1:122 1:461 3+ Alw 28900N1X  76 4 44 44 42½ 75¾ 67¾ Castillo O O L 112 b 12.30 66-35 Dubai Dust1133 Top Seed113nk Nan And Kev1121  Tired 9
22Aug97-9EIP fst 6½f :224 :46 1:111 1:173 Alw 25390N1X  72 4 6 64½ 54 42¼ 54 Johnson J M L 113 b 6.70 83-12 Moonlight Guy114½ Trumps Clown1083 Medicine River113hd  7
     Bumped start, flattened out
16Feb97-11GP fst 1⅛ (X) :463 1:122 1:393 1:531 Alw 31000N1X  52 5 66½ 66½ 55½ 98½ 814¼ Smith M E L 120 b *1.40 57-21 Hamilton Creek117½ One Wild Lad117nk Taragongroom117½  Gave way 9
25Jan97-7GP fst 1 1/16 :24 :472 1:113 1:452 Md Sp Wt 27k  86 3 12 11½ 14 14 11¾ Smith M E L 120 b 2.10 80-18 Der Teufel1201¾ Dixie's Home1208 Thunder Reef120nk  Ridden out 8
4Jan97-2GP fst 1 1/16 :233 :471 1:114 1:452 Md Sp Wt 28k  73 9 41½ 1hd 14 14 23½ Smith M E L 120 b 8.60 76-19 Jack Flash1203½ Der Teufel1202½ Peace Quest1205  No match 11
26Nov96-5CD fst 1 1/16 :24 :483 1:142 1:474 Md Sp Wt 33k  6710116½105½ 42½ 31½ 56 Borel C H 119 b 8.00 66-26 Oak Level1191¼ Stop Watch1194 Lord Mac Lean119no  12
     Brushed 1/8 pole, flattened out
12Nov96-5CD fst 1 :231 :47 1:121 1:38 Md Sp Wt 36k  66 5 63¾ 41 41¾ 31½ 33½ Borel C H 121 b 8.40 79-21 Rojo Dinero1211½ Coast Of Mane1212 Der Teufel1211½  No late response 12
WORKOUTS: Oct6 CD 4f fst :492 B 20//39 Oct1 CD 4f fst :511 B 18/27 Sep26 CD 4f fst :492 B 10/31 Sep19 CD 4f fst :50 B 13/26 Aug19 CD 4f fst :49 B 3/27 Aug14 CD 5f fst 1:014 B 4/16
```

```
Herat Attack                                B. g. 7                                               Lifetime Record:   3  1  1  0   $13,200
Own: Franks John                            Sire: Herat (Northern Dancer) $1,000                  1997  3 1 0 0  $13,200 | Turf 0 0 0 0
BOREL CH (92 23 10 12 .25) 1997:(1215 210 .17)  Dam: Hagley's Miss(Hagley)                        1996  0 M 0 0          | Wet  1 0 0 0
                                            Br: Franks John (Fla)                                 CD    0 0 0 0          | Dist 0 0 0 0
                                            Tr: Barnett Bobby C (22 5 1 3 .23) 97:(531 94 .18)

27Apr97-8LS my 6f :222 :461 :584 1:113 Alw 22000N2L  47 4 1 41¼ 52¾ 119½ 1213 Gonzalez C V L 122 13.70 — — Omarfairleygreen122nk FrenchJoseph122½ TulsTime122¾  Forward, faded 14
26Mar97-10P fst 1 :23 :464 1:124 1:393 Alw 25000N1X  44 7 31½ 52½ 76 611 616¾ Gonzalez C V L 118 8.50 64-23 BttleMountin115nk FrenchJoseph1135 BoleroTyp1121½  Four wide 1st turn 8
15Mar97-5OP fst 6f :214 :46 :59 1:121 Md Sp Wt 22k  6611 4 32 3nk 11 11½ Gonzalez C V L 119 8.80 80-15 Herat Attack1191½ Eastern Mint1191 Astronaut119½  Stayed clear late 12
WORKOUTS: Nov4 CDT 6f fst 1:172 B 5/7 Oct28 CDT 5f gd 1:044 B 16/16 Oct20 CDT 5f fst 1:032 B 5/13 Oct10LaD 5f fst 1:003 H 2/21 Oct3 CD 4f fst :504 H 6/12 Sep28 LaD 7f fst 1:35 H 4/4
```

```
Captain Easy                                Dk. b or br h. 7                                      Lifetime Record:   5  1  2  0   $33,500
Own: Dogwood Stables                        Sire: Easy Goer (Alydar)                              1997  5 1 2 0  $33,500 | Turf 0 0 0 0
SELLERS SJ (63 12 13 12 .19) 1997:(1319 268 .20)  Dam: Collins(Majestic Light)                    1996  0 M 0 0          | Wet  2 1 0 0  $20,400
                                            Br: Frances A Genter Stable Inc (Ky)                  CD    0 0 0 0          | Dist 2 1 1 0  $27,200
                                            Tr: Stewart Dallas (6 2 0 2 .33) 97:(14 4 .29)

25Sep96-3Bel sly 7f :221 :452 1:102 1:231 Md Sp Wt 34k  89 3 2 12 12½ 11 12¾ Chavez J F 116 b 2.50 85-15 Captain Easy1162¾ My Manizales11612 Averred116hd  Roused 1/8 pl, clear 7
2Sep96-2Sar fst 7f :224 :461 1:112 1:244 Md Sp Wt 34k  68 7 4 21½ 2hd 31½ 21¾ Chavez J F 116 b 6.60e 80-11 Pavanputra1161¾ Captain Easy1161½ Jack Flash116hd  Held well 12
17Aug96-2Sar wf 6½f :222 :454 1:102 1:164 Md Sp Wt 34k  53 3 8 86¾ 85½ 65½ 613¾ Smith M E 117 4.70 77-07 Stormin Fever1172 Jail Rock1172½ Doppler117¾  Check, brk slw, tired 9
29Jly96-2Sar fst 6f :222 :462 :584 1:112 Md Sp Wt 34k  51 7 6 95 85 76½ 610¾ Smith M E 119 *1.00 73-12 Haint1191 Snow Birdie1192 Crown Ambassador1195¼  12
     Steadied backstretch, wide turn
4Jly96-2Bel fst 5½f :223 :461 :581 1:042 Md Sp Wt 31k  80 1 6 79½ 75 33½ 2¾ Smith M E 116 14.20 96-11 D'nang116¾ Captain Easy1162 Mellifont1162  Rallied five wide 9
WORKOUTS: Nov3CD 5f my 1:011 B2/19 Oct27CD 5f sly 1:023 B 2/14 Oct 20CD 5f fst 1:024 Bg 6/20 Oct14 CD 5f my 1:032 B 5/10 Oct8 CD 4f fst :48 H 1/32 Oct2 CD 4f fst :502 B 14/29
```

The footnotes in the chart of his previous start said simply that "Mr. Barrymore had no rally." But he had broken from post 7 in a field of eight over an extremely biased Keeneland strip, and he had tried to make a wide move on the turn before he faded and lost by 10 lengths. That defeat was surely forgivable. In Mr. Barrymore's two previous dirt races, he had earned figures of 80 and 84—which made him solidly competitive in this field. Indeed, both of those numbers were superior to the last-race figure of every other entrant in the race except for Der Teufel. That rival had a figure of 92 in his last start, but he earned that number on a muddy track, rallying after a very fast early pace had taken a toll on the leaders. None of his other races in the previous nine months was good enough to beat Mr. Barrymore. I made a solid win bet on Mr. Barrymore, and a small exacta box with Der Teufel as protection.

NINTH RACE
Churchill
NOVEMBER 12, 1997

7 FURLONGS. (1.21¹) ALLOWANCE. Purse $41,600 (includes $11,600 KTDF Supplement). 3–year–olds and upward, which have not won a race other than maiden, claiming, starter or maiden stakes or have never won two races. Weights: 3–year–olds, 119 lbs. Older, 121 lbs. Non–winners of $14,260 since July 30, allowed 3 lbs. $11,780 since April 15, 5 lbs. $8,990 since November 30, 7 lbs. (Races where entered for $30,000 or less not considered in allowances).

Value of Race: $41,600 Winner $26,140; second $8,320; third $4,160; fourth $2,080; fifth $900. Mutuel Pool $183,384.00 Exacta Pool $187,953.00 Trifecta Pool $194,008.00 Superfecta Pool $85,132.00 Odd/Even Pool $208.00 Roulette Pool $91.00

Last Raced	Horse	M/Eqt. A.Wt	PP	St	¼	½	Str	Fin	Jockey	Odds $1
18Oct97 6Kee5	Mr. Barrymore	Lf 4 114	5	8	8hd	5hd	1½	11½	Kutz D	16.60
26Oct97 9CD1	Charming Halo	Lb 5 107	7	7	4hd	62	42½	2nk	Espinosa L E7	23.20
22Oct97 1Kee1	Devil Power	L 3 119	6	2	3½	4hd	3hd	32½	Martinez W	12.00
28Oct97 9CD5	The Preformer	Lb 3 112	8	6	6hd	3½	2hd	43	Peck B D	90.80
29Oct97 4CD3	Ataki	L 3 119	3	3	5hd	7½	51	51	Albarado R J	4.90
29Oct97 7CD6	Information Hiway	L 3 116	1	9	92	101	9½	61	Day P	1.40
2Nov97 6CD3	Der Teufel	Lb 3 114	9	1	11	8½	71	7nk	Woods C R Jr	11.80
31Oct97 10Hoo2	He Met a Lassie	Lbf 3 112	2	11	7½	11	11	8nk	Hebert T J	36.50
31Oct97 10Hoo4	Dr. Shea	L 3 114	4	10	10hd	92	10½	91½	Miller S E	50.30
25Sep96 3Bel1	Captain Easy	Lb 3 113	11	4	11½	1hd	61	10hd	Sellers S J	2.70
27Apr97 8LS12	Herat Attack	L 3 114	10	5	2hd	21	8hd	11	Borel C H	22.40

OFF AT 5:00 Start Good. Won driving. Time, :23¹, :47¹, 1:12², 1:24⁴ Track fast.

$2 Mutuel Prices:

5–MR. BARRYMORE	35.20	15.20	7.80
7–CHARMING HALO		17.60	7.80
6–DEVIL POWER			7.60

$2 EXACTA 5–7 PAID $402.60 $2 TRIFECTA 5–7–6 PAID $6,414.00 $1 SUPERFECTA 5–7–6–8 PAID $17,239.20 $1 ODD/EVEN ODD PAID $1.10 $1 ROULETTE 18 PAID $5.60

Ch. c, by Rare Performer–Disco Jan, by Torsion. Trainer Bindner Walter M Jr. Bred by Jebb Stable & Wafare Farm (Ky).

MR. BARRYMORE, never far back, raced five wide, continued in that position into the stretch and was hard ridden in the drive. CHARMING HALO, within easy striking distance, followed the winner from the outside into the stretch and wasn't good enough. DEVIL POWER, always well placed, loomed boldly from the rail but lacked the needed response. THE PREFORMER stalked the leaders early while in hand, made a bold run four wide to reach the front briefly between calls in the upper stretch, then flattened out. ATAKI, within easy striking distance throughout, had no rally. INFORMATION HIWAY drifted out at the start bothering HE MET A LASSIE, then failed to seriously menace. DER TEUFEL passed tired ones. HE MET A LASSIE, forced out at the start, was never close and nine wide in the lane. DR. SHEA was outrun. CAPTAIN EASY sprinted clear early, moved inside, made the pace for a half and gave way. HERAT ATTACK pressed the pace outside of CAPTAIN EASY the opening half and gave way.

Owners— 1, Jebb Stable; 2, Sisk James T; 3, Castle Rock Racing Stable; 4, David L Muench Racing Stable Inc; 5, Paulson Allen E; 6, Humphrey G Watts Jr; 7, Morsches Paul J Jr; 8, Kelly Thomas J; 9, Zahler James; 10, Dogwood Stable; 11, Franks John

Trainers— 1, Bindner Walter M Jr; 2, Woodard Joe; 3, Gothard Akiko; 4, Muench David L; 5, Romans Jerry L; 6, Arnold George R II; 7, Penrod Steven C; 8, Kelly Larry; 9, Flint Bernard S; 10, Stewart Dallas; 11, Barnett Bobby C

Overweight: Captain Easy (1).

$2 Pick Three (4–4–5) 3 Correct Paid $690.40; Pick Three Pool $28,987. $2 Late Daily Double (4–5) Paid $77.40; Late Daily Double Pool $94,780.

Churchill Downs Attendance: 5,299 Total Mutuel Pool: $743,125 Off–track Total Mutuel Pool: $4,346,443 Grand Total Mutuel Pool: $5,089,568

The $35.20 payoff on Mr. Barrymore, coupled with the earlier $58 payoff on Colonel Vann, made November 12 the acme of my year. And I had made each of these scores on the basis of a single nugget of information—knowledge that a horse had raced against the bias—rather than an in-depth command of the entire race. I was permanently convinced that I had found the road to success in the brave new world of simulcasting.

I have emphasized—and, in fact, overemphasized—the use of track bias as a tool in simulcast betting, because it is my tool of choice. But there are as many ways to create productive horses-to-watch lists as there are handicapping factors.

One potentially effective approach can be employed strictly through study of result charts: A handicapper can study the charts looking for races run with an extremely fast, competitive pace that would ordinarily compromise the chances of a front-running type. Such races may be readily identified when the running lines in the chart show that three or four horses were battling head-and-head for the early lead. A more sophisticated way to identify extreme pace situations is to use pace "pars," which indicate the average fractional times expected to accompany a given final time at a given track. These are available in an annual publication, "Par Times," by Gordon Pine (Cynthia Publishing, 11314 Ventura Blvd. #524, Studio City, CA 91604, phone 323-876-7325). A $1\frac{1}{16}$-mile race run in 1:45 at Lone Star Park would typically be run with fractions of $47\frac{2}{5}$ seconds and 1:12. If a handicapper encountered a Lone Star route race with fractions of 46 seconds, $1:10\frac{4}{5}$, and a final time of 1:45, he would know that the pace of the race was exceptionally fast (and, presumably, destructive to the horses racing near it). After identifying a race with a very fast pace, the handicapper should note the names of horses who were involved in a speed duel, particularly those who managed to run creditably in spite of it, and enter the names in his Horse Watch list. When these horses are entered again, the handicapper should analyze the race to determine its probable pace scenario. If a horse coming out of a race with a destructive pace now finds himself in a field with relatively little speed, he may be an outstanding bet—the type that can return a large parimutuel payoff.

Trainer patterns offer tremendous potential for betting in the age of simulcasts. There is so much statistical information now available that any handicapper can pore over data and identify trainers who show a solid win percentage and a positive return on investment in specific situations. Because I am wary that some stats may be based on limited samples or skewed by an aberrant large payoff, I prefer to identify productive trainers by my own observation of races in which they maneuvered their horses shrewdly and successfully. When a trainer wins a race and I conclude, "What a sharp move!" that's a man I want to follow. I'd like to know every time Marvin Kuhn saddles a first-time starter. I'd like to know every time Eddie Plesa Sr. stretches a horse in distance after giving him a one-mile workout. I'd like to know every time Christophe Clement saddles a European import making his first start in the U.S.

Although I am not a pedigree handicapper, I'd like to be able to spot certain exceptional situations involving bloodlines—such as the turf debut of a horse by Polish Numbers or Red Ransom.

Locating such plays used to require ancient methods—leafing through the pages of *Daily Racing Form*, scanning the past performances, and trying to spot interesting trainers or pedigrees. For a simulcast bettor following many tracks, this is not an efficient plan of attack. But the handicapping world is changing—again. *Daily Racing Form*'s Watches now allow users to specify different parameters, not just horses' names, and the service will continue to expand and improve. You can now track trainers on various circuits, specific race types, and pick-six carryovers.

Full-card simulcasting has already changed the nature of the racing game and the handicapping process, but the revolution has barely begun. With the aid of technology, horseplayers will be able to play multiple tracks using sophisticated methods that were once unimaginable.

BROHAMER
ON PACE
by Tom Brohamer

2

IN *MODERN PACE HANDICAPPING,* revised in 2000, I spent much time with energy distribution, track profiles, and track models. These are the tools of the pace handicapper. The best use of pace and speed figures depends on the proper utilization of these tools. But accurate pace figures are exceedingly difficult to create and often tricky to apply. Horse races are won by living creatures, who are subject to some of the same aches and pains suffered by their human counterparts. They are remarkably consistent considering their fragile physiology, but form cycles do exist, as do simple "bad days at the office."

Pace figures often fluctuate wildly and are greatly influenced by riding strategy and individual race matchups. Within a single race card, the handicapper must often cope with raw pace figures that approach opposite extremes of fast and slow. These extremes often contradict the basic trend for the day. The problem is tricky but not unsolvable. With experience, the handicapper will be able to resolve these apparent inconsistencies, although not always to full satisfaction.

Inexperienced handicappers generally fall into a pattern of overdependence on figures. They often miss the real crux of the situation: the matchup within the individual race. Popular Oklahoma handicapper Jim Bradshaw used to simplify the problem with the following: "Hell, boy, it ain't nothing but a horse race; just figure out who's gonna lead and who's gonna chase."

There is much wisdom in Jim's words. The basic concept of pace handicapping is to identify the early pace of the race and what it will cost the leaders in terms of energy. The handicapper next considers the pressers and closers and their chances within the framework of that pace. Pace figures are invaluable when used by competent handicappers, but they will never replace a careful analysis of pace based on running styles.

Horses will conform to their preferred running styles. They will not conform to the handicapper's sense of order based on a set of contrived numbers. The pace stalker with the best early-pace (second-call) figure will not take the lead unless past history shows a willingness to do so. Front-runners will lead, pressers will press, and closers will take back and come on late. That is the nature of the game. It is our task to determine where each runner will be positioned during the race and whether that position is favorable to the horse's winning chances.

In this chapter we will:

1) learn to identify horses' preferred running styles,
2) create a reliable format for pace analysis, and
3) adopt an objective technique for quantifying running positions based on early-speed ability. The first call of the race will be our main consideration.

THE BASIC RUNNING STYLES: ESP

There are three basic running styles with which we will concern ourselves:

1) Early-pace runners, which we will designate as "E" for "early." These are horses that, in order to perform at their best, must lead the field during the early stages of the race. It is important to understand that we will be examining races in which the horse performed at his very best. He will have won, or very nearly won, those races. Races in which the horse did not run to his best efforts are discarded in favor of races that offered the best chances of victory.

2) Pace pressers or stalkers will be labeled "P" for "presser." These are runners that press the pace from a length or two behind and maintain that pressure throughout.

3) Sustained runners, or "S" types, position themselves in the rear third of their fields and then sustain a late run to the wire. In order to win their races, they must depend upon a breakdown of the early-pace and presser scenarios. In most races, at most tracks, pure closers are the least desirable win bets.

Let's examine each style, and combinations of styles, separately.

EARLY PACE: "E"

The most important part of the pace scenario is the analysis of early pace. A disproportionate number of races are won on, or near, the lead, therefore much care should go into the labeling of early-pace horses. A horse designated as "early" will figure in every possible pace scenario. Lone front-runners are one of the best bets in racing. If several are able to contend for the lead, a pace duel probably ensues, and the off-pace runners gain the spotlight. Early-pace runners with pace figures that indicate that they cannot gain the early lead should be considered noncontenders.

An early-pace horse, an "E," is a runner whose very best races are on the lead. The "E" horse is habitually on the lead, or within a length of the leader while attempting to lead. Wins and near misses are accomplished *only* in that manner. The "E" horse that can also press the pace and still run effectively will be designated as both "E" and "P" (presser). We will cover that runner shortly. First let's consider the following:

1) The lone front-runner in a race is *always* a threat to win. Unless the horse is a confirmed quitter, he is in position to dictate the pace of the

race and the relative positions of every other competitor. Betting on these horses is one of the most solid plays in racing.

2) Races with two evenly matched front-runners may not produce the pace duel expected. The potential duel often results in both jockeys falling into a rhythm, each carefully measuring the other for a subsequent late effort. This potential pace duel often results in a 1-2 finish by the "E" runners, usually to the consternation of the inexperienced pace analyst. Add a third "E" runner to the scenario, however, and a duel is almost a certainty.
3) An expected pace duel may still result in a wire-to-wire win by one of the competitors. Some horses seem to thrive on hard-earned competitive victories. This "bulldog" runner can never be discarded and must always figure in the betting of the race.
4) Some races with multiple front-runners contain one runner that can be identified as "speed of the speed." This type will relegate the other "E" horses to noncontenders. Confirmed "E" types unable to gain the lead should not figure in the betting decision.

2 Gold Coast Type

Own: Savoy Stable $25,000

ROJAS J (38 4 3 4 .11) 2000:(226 28 .12)

Ch. c. 4 KEESEP97 $95,000
Sire: Geiger Counter (Mr. Prospector)
Dam: Sunset Strait (Naskra)
Br: Vinery & Walden Ben P (Ky)
Tr: O'Connell Kathleen(63 5 11 13 .08) 2000:(315 35 .11)

L 116

Life	9	3	1	3	$66,270	D.Fst	9	3	1	3	$66,270	97
2000	1	0	0	0	$180	Wet	0	0	0	0	$0	–
1999	5	2	0	2	$42,430	Turf	0	0	0	0	$0	–
GP	1	0	0	0	$180	Dist	5	2	0	1	$37,575	97

1May00-3GP	fst	6f	:224	:461	:582	1:103	4↑	Clm 50000(50-40)	56	5	5	52¼	54½	67	614	Toribio A R	L116	8.10	72-16	Fast Departure119½ Boodle B1166¼ I'm Impressed1161¼	Stumbled start	6
Previously trained by Catalano Wayne M																						
27Jun99-7Haw	fst	6½f	:224	:452	1:102	1:171		FullofDrive45k	78	2	2	1½	2½	21	34	Baird E T	L119	*1.80	82-15	Eejay117½ Stone Cool Cat1173½ Gold Coast Type119½	Weakened	6
18Jun99-7Haw	fst	6f	:22	:451	:572	1:103	3↑	Alw 37316N3X	71	6	7	815	816	88¾	66½	Guidry M	L114	*1.40	82-18	He Be Irish1172¾ *Night Time Gold*1171 Nice N' Salty1171	Showed little	8
19Apr99-8Haw	fst	6f	:221	:45	:564	1:092	3↑	Alw 29000N2X	88	1	8	1½	1hd	1½	12¾	Guidry M	L114	*.60	95-07	Gold Coast Type1142¾ Frigidoon1175¼ Honky Dory117nk	Driving	9
27Mar99-1Haw	fst	6f	:221	:452	:572	1:092		Alw 27000N1X	97	3	2	2½	1½	12	16½	Guidry M	L115	*1.30	95-14	*Gold Coast Type*1156½ Gadasky115no End Sweep Too1154¾	Driving	6
6Mar99-7FG	fst	6f	:213	:451	:571	1:101		Alw 34500N1X	85	4	3	31½	53½	32	31½	Ardoin R	L119	5.50	91-10	DeepGold1191½ MagicWorld119no *GoldCostType*119½	Rail trip, missed 2nd	7
12Aug98-1Haw	fst	5½f	:222	:461	:581	1:043		Alw 26000N2L	75	3	1	31½	31½	32½	33	Baird E T	115	3.50	104-13	Over Fan1131 Faultless Appeal1152 Gold CoastType1153	Drifted stretch	7
27Jun98-1Spt	fst	5f	:223	:464		:593		Md Sp Wt 26k	64	1	1	11	1½	15	17¼	Baird E T	120	*1.30	— —	GoldCoastType1207¼ PrairieBeau1202 ChiefMeadowlake120¾	Ridden out	6
10Jun98-3Spt	fst	5f	:224	:472		:594		Md Sp Wt 35k	47	4	3	31½	31	2hd	21½	Romero S P	120	4.60	— —	Plumbline1201½ *Gold Coast Type*1203 Chief Meadowlake1201	2nd best	8

WORKS: May9 Crc 6f fst 1:174 B *1/1* Apr17 Crc 5f fst 1:03 B *13/23* Apr8 Crc 6f fst 1:173 B *7/8* ●Mar25 OTC 5f fst 1:013 B *1/5* ●Mar4 OTC 4f fst :484 B *1/7*

Gold Coast Type (E) is an example of a one-dimensional front-runner. His three wins were accomplished only on the lead. He is also capable of dueling for the lead and continuing on to win, but he is ineffective when relegated to the role of presser. He should be considered a noncontender in races in which he does not figure to gain the early lead.

PACE PRESSERS AND EARLY/PRESSERS: "P" AND "E/P"

Pace pressers or "P," are often difficult to label. These stalkers position themselves one to three lengths off the leaders and then come on in the second and third fractions. They do not run from the back of the pack and are usually positioned third or fourth in the early going. When the pace of a race puts them in the back third of the field, these runners are forced out of their preferred style and become nonfactors.

What often makes them difficult to label is their close resemblance to other styles. There is usually a race or two in a presser's past performances in which he looks like a front-runner or closer, but the predominant style will be close to the pace. Pressers able to gain their preferred position are the most reliable horses at any racetrack. Although they can burn out by chasing too fast a pace, they are *relatively* immune to the early pace of the race. Except in certain matchups they are usually quick enough to maintain contact with the leaders. They usually run their race and must be considered for the win or an in-the-money performance.

Horses able to either lead or press the pace with equal ability represent the ideal betting situation. The ability to take the lead in a paceless race or to settle just off the lead of the dedicated "E" types is the perfect combination of running styles. Horses equally adept at either style are easily the most bettable of runners. This type tends to accumulate high win percentages. When in form, they can be counted upon for their best efforts. Cigar, Skip Away, and Silver Charm are recent high-profile examples of "E/P" types.

Abby Girl
Own: Herold Stephan G
NAKATANI C S (42 8 11 6 .19) 2000:(401 91 .23)

Ch. f. 3 (Feb) SARAUG98 $75,000
Sire: Meadowlake (Hold Your Peace) $25,000
Dam: Like an Explosion (Explodent)
Br: Wakefield Farm (Ky)
Tr: Dollase Craig(3 1 0 0 .33) 2000:(54 17 .31)

L 119

Life	6	3	2	1	$208,170	D.Fst	5	2	2	1	$183,330 98
2000	1	1	0	0	$47,700	Wet	0	0	0	0	$0 –
1999	5	2	2	1	$160,470	Turf	1	1	0	0	$24,840 80
Hol	2	0	1	1	$65,630	Dist	1	0	1	0	$20,000 86

16Apr00-3SA	fst	$6\frac{1}{2}$f	:22^2 :45^1 1:09^1 1:15^2	ⒻSanta Paula79k	**98**	4	3	$3^{1\frac{1}{2}}$	$3^{1\frac{1}{2}}$	$1^{\frac{1}{2}}$	$1^{1\frac{3}{4}}$	Nakatani C S	LB 116 n	1.80	91–11	AbbyGirl116$^{1\frac{3}{4}}$ MintlyFresh114$^{\frac{1}{2}}$ **ClssicOlympio**118$^{4\frac{1}{2}}$	3wd bid,inched clear	5
19Dec99-8Hol	fst	$1\frac{1}{16}$	:23^2 :46^3 1:11 1:43^2	ⒻHol Starlet-G1	**86**	5	3	$3^{1\frac{1}{2}}$	$3^{\frac{1}{2}}$	$3^{3\frac{1}{2}}$	3^8	Nakatani C S	LB 120	5.60	75–17	*Surfside*120^7 She's Classy120^1 *Abby Girl*120$^{5\frac{1}{2}}$	Pulled,bid 3wd,held 3d	5
14Nov99-8Hol	fst	7f	:22^3 :45^2 1:09^3 1:22^1	ⒻMoccasin100k	**86**	3	6	$2^{\frac{1}{2}}$	2^1	2^1	2^3	Nakatani C S	LB 117	*.60	88–12	**Classic Olympio**119^3 Abby Girl117$^{6\frac{1}{2}}$ BoldFeat118$^{6\frac{1}{2}}$	Pulled,stalked,2d best	6
9Oct99-8SA	fst	1	:23 :46^3 1:10^4 1:36	ⒻOak Leaf-G1	**92**	1	1	1^1	1^{hd}	2^1	$2^{1\frac{1}{4}}$	McCarron C J	LB 118	3.30	90–11	Chilukki118$^{1\frac{1}{4}}$ Abby Girl118$^{4\frac{1}{4}}$ Spain118$^{\frac{1}{2}}$	Rail,altered path 1/16	5
26Aug99-3Dmr	fst	$5\frac{1}{2}$f	:21^4 :45^1 :57^2 1:03^4	ⒻAlw 50000N1X	**95**	5	1	$3^{1\frac{1}{2}}$	3^{nk}	$1^{4\frac{1}{2}}$	1^8	Nakatani C S	LB 117	*.50	94–12	Abby Girl117^8 Kimme A Star114$^{4\frac{1}{2}}$ Desert End116^{no}	Rid.out,in hand late	5
19Jly99-7Hol	fm	$5\frac{1}{2}$f Ⓣ	:22^2 :45^2 :57^2 1:03^3	ⒻMd Sp Wt 41k	**80**	3	6	4^2	3^1	1^1	1^4	Nakatani C S	LB 118	*2.00	86–12	*Abby Girl*118^4 Minor Details118$^{1\frac{1}{2}}$ Blair's Favorite118$^{\frac{3}{4}}$	Bit tight 3/8	10

WORKS: May14 Hol Ⓣ 5f fm 1:00^4 H (d) *3/13* May7 Hol Ⓣ 5f fm 1:01^3 H (d) *3/10* Apr30 Hol 3f fst :36 H *3/12* Apr9 Hol 4f fst :48^2 Hg *4/45* ● Apr2 SA Ⓣ 5f fm 1:00^2 B (d) *1/5* Mar27 Hol 6f fst 1:13 H *2/11*

Abby Girl (P) is the quintessential "P" horse. In each of her three wins, she stalked the pace before moving to the lead at the stretch call. She clearly prefers her role as presser in shorter races and is less effective on the lead at longer distances.

Classic Olympio
Own: VHW Stables
SOLIS A (34 7 4 5 .21) 2000:(343 57 .17)

Dk. b or br f. 3 (Feb) KEENOV97 $27,000
Sire: Olympio (Naskra) $7,500
Dam: Palm Beach Dewey (Talc)
Br: Greg Peach (Ky)
Tr: McAnally Ronald(16 1 4 1 .06) 2000:(135 20 .15)

Ⓛ 122

Life	10	4	4	1	$254,115	**D.Fst**	8	3	3	1	$186,645	98
2000	4	1	2	1	$98,210	**Wet**	1	1	0	0	$45,540	90
1999	6	3	2	0	$155,905	**Turf**	1	0	1	0	$21,930	87
Hol	2	1	0	0	$67,605	**Dist**	2	1	1	0	$81,200	93

16Apr00-3SA	fst	6½f		:22^{2}	:45^{1}	1:09^{1}	1:15^{2}	ⒻSanta Paula79k	**93**	5	1	2^{hd}	2^{hd}	2½	3$^{2\frac{1}{4}}$	Solis A	B 118	*.80	89-11	**Abby Girl**116$^{1\frac{3}{4}}$ Mintly Fresh114$^{\frac{1}{2}}$ ClassicOlympio118$^{4\frac{1}{2}}$	Dueled,outfinished	5
3Mar00-7SA	fm	*6½f	Ⓣ	:22^{1}	:44^{1}	1:07^{3}	1:13^{4}	ⒻLa Habra109k	**87**	1	6	4$^{1\frac{1}{4}}$	3^{1}	2$^{2\frac{1}{2}}$	2$^{1\frac{1}{2}}$	Solis A	B 120	*1.50	87-11	SquallCity118$^{1\frac{1}{2}}$ ClssicOlympio120^{nk} MinorDetils118^{2}	Stalked,bid,held 2nd	8
10Feb00-7SA	wf	6½f	⊗	:22	:45	1:10^{1}	1:16^{4}	ⒻStrmyBtVlid76k	**90**	1	4	2^{1}	1$^{\frac{1}{2}}$	1$^{1\frac{1}{2}}$	1^{4}	Solis A	B 121	*.30	84-14	ClssicOlympio121^{4} Purgtory117^{6} GilddDiblo121^{8}	Insde,strong hand ride	5
23Jan00-8SA	fst	7f		:22	:44^{3}	1:10^{1}	1:23^{1}	ⒻSanta Ynez-G2	**86**	2	1	4$^{1\frac{3}{4}}$	4^{2}	2^{hd}	2$^{1\frac{1}{4}}$	Solis A	B 121	2.40	88-15	PnnyBlus118$^{1\frac{1}{4}}$ *ClssicOlympio*121^{8} MnImogn117$^{3\frac{1}{2}}$	Bulled btwn,outkicked	5
19Dec99-8Hol	fst	1$\frac{1}{16}$		:23^{2}	:46^{3}	1:11	1:43^{2}	ⒻHol Starlet-G1	**71**	2	4	4^{3}	4^{4}	4$^{8\frac{1}{2}}$	5$^{16\frac{1}{2}}$	Solis A	B 120	3.00	66-17	*Surfside*120^{7} She's Classy120^{1} ***Abby Girl***120$^{5\frac{1}{2}}$	Pulled,steadied 7-1/2	5
14Nov99-8Hol	fst	7f		:22^{3}	:45^{2}	1:09^{3}	1:22^{1}	ⒻMoccasin100k	**93**	6	1	1$^{\frac{1}{2}}$	1^{1}	1^{1}	1^{3}	Solis A	B 119	1.90	91-12	Classic Olympio119^{3} **Abby Girl**117$^{6\frac{1}{2}}$ Bold Feat118$^{6\frac{1}{2}}$	Inside, kicked clear	6
20Oct99-7SA	fst	6f		:21^{2}	:44^{3}	:57	1:09^{3}	ⒻAnoakia78k	**88**	3	1	3$^{\frac{1}{2}}$	3^{nk}	2$^{\frac{1}{2}}$	1$^{\frac{1}{2}}$	Solis A	B 115	*.60	92-10	*ClassicOlympio*115$^{\frac{1}{2}}$ She'sClassy117^{3} BoldFet117$^{2\frac{1}{2}}$	3 wide, determinedly	6
29Sep99-4SA	fst	5½f		:21^{4}	:44^{3}	:56^{3}	1:03	ⒻMd Sp Wt 38k	**98**	3	3	1^{hd}	1^{2}	1^{6}	1^{7}	Solis A	B 120	*.70	94-16	*ClsscOlympo*120^{7} PrdPlymkr120$^{3\frac{1}{2}}$ *HtCmmnctr*120$^{1\frac{1}{2}}$	Bobbled strt,rid. out	8
22Aug99-6Dmr	fst	5½f		:22	:45^{3}	:58^{1}	1:04^{3}	ⒻMd Sp Wt 54k	**75**	10	2	1^{hd}	2^{hd}	1^{hd}	2$^{2\frac{1}{2}}$	Solis A	B 118	*.90	87-13	SimplyFntstic118$^{2\frac{1}{2}}$ *ClssicOlympo*118^{4} ArlMtng118^{9}	Bumped 1/8,2nd best	10
2Aug99-6Dmr	fst	5½f		:21^{4}	:45^{3}	:58^{2}	1:05^{1}	ⒻMd Sp Wt 46k	**77**	2	6	2^{2}	2$^{2\frac{1}{2}}$	2$^{2\frac{1}{2}}$	2^{nk}	Solis A	B 118	*2.00	87-18	All Of Us118^{nk} ClassicOlympio118^{8} GoSpeedyJo118^{1}	Closed steadily late	9

WORKS: May13 Hol 6f fst 1:15^{1} H *9/15* **May7 Hol 5f fst 1:00^{2} H** *6/41* **May1 Hol 4f fst :49^{1} H** *18/33* **Apr24 SA 4f fst :49^{1} H** *16/28* **Apr10 SA 5f fst 1:04 H** *46/48* **Mar30 SA 5f fst 1:01 H** *16/28*

Classic Olympio (E/P) is an excellent example of a horse capable of leading or pressing the pace. She is equally adept at both styles and is a threat every time she takes the track.

SUSTAINED PACE (CLOSERS): "S"

A horse labeled "sustained" or "S" is the opposite of the "E" horse. This one runs on late in the race, often after the issue has been decided. He is habitually in the last third of the field at the first call, and then attempts to win by catching the leaders in the final fraction. First-call beaten lengths can be deceiving. This runner is often within three or four lengths at the first call, but usually against slow fractions. *Position* is the deciding factor in determining running style, not velocity. When labeling these horses, compare the horse's running positions to the number of horses in the fields. Evaluate position at the *first call* of his races, not at the pre-stretch call. Closers fit two basic molds:

1) Those that remain in the rear of the field and depend on a single late run in the final fraction of the race. These are the least dependable runners at any track, at any time. Only a superior runner will overcome the inevitable deficit left in the final stages. These horses only win with a complete breakdown of the early and presser scenarios. They typically accumulate box scores that show more seconds than wins and more thirds than second-place finishes.
2) Those that can move forwardly during the middle fraction of a race. These should have enough midrace speed to reach a contending position at the pre-stretch or second call. This type of closer is more dependable and usually holds his own in terms of win percentage.

Box of Jewels
Own: Ostrager Barry R
$10,000
FLORES D R (38 4 5 2 .11) 2000:(379 53 .14)

B. m. 5
Sire: Half a Year (Riverman) $2,000
Dam: Golden Jewel Box (Slew o' Gold)
Br: Mabee Mr & Mrs John C (Cal)
Tr: Cerin Vladimir(15 2 2 2 .13) 2000:(118 24 .20)

L 116

Life 41 5 8 9 $100,480 D.Fst 35 4 7 8 $78,895 77
2000 5 2 1 1 $21,400 Wet 5 1 1 1 $20,535 70
1999 16 1 3 6 $31,300 Turf 1 0 0 0 $1,050 49
Hol 4 0 1 0 $3,780 Dist 3 1 0 1 $10,200 75

9Apr00-1SA fst 6f :214 :451 :581 1:114 4↑ (F)Clm c-(12.5-10.5) 71 2 2 46½ 49 47 21 Valdivia J Jr LB 118 b 2.20 79-21 Halo Missy1181 Box Of Jewels118no Gold Medallion1182 Best stride late 5
Claimed from Baker & Baker for $12,500, Lloyd Kim Trainer
23Mar00-2SA fst 6f :22 :454 :583 1:113 4↑ (F)Clm 16000(16-14) 68 4 6 68½ 66 55 34 Baze T C5 LB 113 b 7.40 77-18 John's Hope120½ Light UpTheYear1203½ BoxOfJewels113no Split foes 1/16 7
24Feb00-4SA my 6f :22 :454 :583 1:112 4↑ (F)[S]Clm c-10000 66 4 3 54 43½ 31½ 1no Desormeaux K J LB 119 b *1.00 82-21 BoxOfJewels119no MissMillie117¾ RendisPrimvr1113½ Bit wide,up at wire 9
Claimed from Ostrager Barry R for $10,000, Cerin Vladimir Trainer
23Jan00-1SA fst 6f :221 :454 :582 1:114 4↑ (F)Clm 10000 68 1 9 95½ 88¾ 65 11½ Desormeaux K J LB 118 b 3.30 80-15 *BoxOfJwls*1181½ RndisPrimvr111½ FlyingHostss120½ 5wd into lane,rallied 9
6Jan00-8SA fst 7f :224 :46 1:112 1:25 4↑ (F)Clm 10000 58 1 9 42 63 88¾ 85¼ Valenzuela F H LB 120 b 3.80 75-18 Maestra Mia118½ Aunt Polly1181½ **Sisterbull**118nk Rail trip,steadied 1/4 12
20Nov99-9Hol fst 6f :221 :454 :584 1:122 3↑ (F)Clm 16000(16-14) 61 7 8 911 1012 89¼ 45 Valenzuela F H LB 118 b 10.30 70-18 John's Hope1181 *Countess Moon*1181½ **Kristen**1182½ Improved position 10
8Nov99-3SA fst 6½f :214 :442 1:102 1:172 3↑ (F)Clm 12500(12.5-10.5) 75 1 4 42½ 35 34 11 Valenzuela F H LB 118 b 3.20 81-13 Box Of Jewels1181 Zealous Devil1201½ *Fibber's Star*1182 Closed willingly 7
22Oct99-3SA fst 5½f :22 :452 :581 1:044 3↑ (F)[S]Clm c-10000 61 1 8 42½ 74½ 64¾ 32¼ Valdivia J Jr LB 118 b 4.00 83-11 Morell'sLove1221¼ JVivendi1161 *BoxOfJewels*118½ Saved ground,late 3rd 10
Claimed from Marshall Ronnie W for $10,000, Gonzalez Felix Trainer
29Sep99-3SA fst 7f :222 :452 1:11 1:244 3↑ (F)Clm 12500(12.5-10.5) 66 2 4 3nk 2hd 2hd 41 Valdivia J Jr LB 118 b 18.40 80-16 Muschi118hd Halo Missy118½ Synister Move116nk Dueled, outfinished 9
10Sep99-9Fpx fst 6½f :23 :471 1:112 1:172 3↑ (F)Clm 12500(12.5-10.5) 66 5 2 32 31 32 32¼ Espinoza V LB 116 b 4.10 91-09 *Maestra Mia*116¾ Little Itch1161½ Box Of Jewels1161½ Stalked,held third 6
1Sep99-1Dmr fst 6f :22 :452 :573 1:102 3↑ (F)[S]Clm c-10000 59 2 5 55½ 66 45½ 29 Ramsammy E LB 119 b 2.10 79-11 EncoreExpress1199 BoxOfJewels1194½ WhtAPriz119¾ 4 wide into stretch 7
Claimed from Blake & Three Kings Racing for $10,000, Mitchell Mike Trainer
16Aug99-1Dmr fst 6f :214 :444 :573 1:104 3↑ (F)[S]Clm 10000 76 3 5 45¼ 36 35½ 23½ Ramsammy E LB 119 b 4.30 82-14 *Morell'sLove*1193½ BoxOfJwls1194½ **Jodi'sLovDov**1192½ Bid 2w, closed well 8
WORKS: May14 Hol 4f fst :502 H *30/35* Apr27 Hol 4f fst :50 H *23/38* Mar17 SA 5f fst 1:013 H *25/47*

Box of Jewels (S) is a prototypical example of the first type of closer. Her box score of 41-5-8-9 speaks volumes for the unreliable nature of this type of runner. Note the predominance of seconds and thirds compared to wins. She simply leaves too much to accomplish in the final fractions of her races.

3 Memory Tap
Own: Stellar Racing Stables
JOHNSTON M T (221 45 42 38 .20) 2000:(561 106 .19)

B. c. 4 KEESEP97 $11,000
Sire: Pleasant Tap (Pleasant Colony) $12,500
Dam: Remember the Day (Settlement Day)
Br: Pin Oak Stud Inc (Ky)
Tr: Smith Hamilton A(38 11 6 3 .29) 2000:(136 39 .29)

L 115

Life 24 6 6 6 $209,515 D.Fst 18 5 4 4 $162,755 102
2000 6 3 2 0 $98,520 Wet 5 1 2 2 $46,460 80
1999 12 3 2 2 $85,845 Turf 1 0 0 0 $300 62
Pim 2 1 0 0 $45,000 Dist 8 4 2 1 $131,040 102

15Apr00-10Pim fst 6f :223 :452 :58 1:103 3↑ Fire Plug75k 102 6 5 68½ 68 54 13½ Johnston M T L 119 fb 4.40 93-15 MemoryTp1193½ **Dr.Mx**115no ChngingOthgurd1194 Swng out 1/8,riddn out 6
15Mar00-8Lrl fst 6f :221 :451 :572 1:093 4↑ OClm 50000(50-45)N 97 3 6 54½ 54½ 31½ 12½ Johnston M T L 117 fb 7.70 94-15 *MemoryTp*1172½ Mt.Lurel117½ SomeProspect116nk Bmpd,4wd mve,drv clr 6
26Feb00-8Lrl fst 7f :234 :47 1:112 1:233 4↑ OClm 50000(50-45)N 91 2 5 31 2hd 3nk 44¼ Johnston M T L 119 fb 2.50 85-22 ChronicleS.1141½ RaireStndrd114nk MyProblem1172½ Rail,dueled,gave way 6
10Feb00-8Lrl fst 6½f :223 :454 1:101 1:161 4↑ OClm 50000(50-45)N 92 4 6 65¼ 45 11 21 Johnston M T L 119 fb 4.60 97-16 VonGroovy1151 MmoryTp1195¾ CldNClcltng119nk Bmpd st,4wd mv,game 7
16Jan00-8Lrl fst 6f :214 :452 :573 1:10 4↑ OClm 35000(35-30)N 95 6 7 65½ 43½ 41½ 11 Johnston M T L 117 fb *3.20 92-15 MmryTp1171 MnstrOfDcrm1171½ SmPrspct117¾ Swung out 1/8,rddn out 8
2Jan00-8Lrl fst 6f :221 :451 :573 1:101 4↑ OClm 35000(35-30)N 98 2 5 53½ 55 42½ 2½ Johnston M T L 117 fb 9.90 90-17 ColdNClculting117½ *MemoryTp*117hd MinistrOfDcorm117hd Rallied inside 6
12Dec99-8Lrl fst 7f :224 :454 1:103 1:232 3↑ OClm 35000(35-30)N 88 5 2 1½ 1hd 2hd 3½ Dunkelberger T L L 114 fb 17.20 89-16 Ruby Hill117hd Glider Pilot119½ Memory Tap1142¾ Dueled 2w,grudgingly 7
17Nov99-8Lrl fst 7f :233 :471 1:121 1:243 3↑ OClm 35000(35-30)N 71 9 6 3½ 32 77¾ 88½ Frazier R L L 114 fb 33.00 75-21 GldrPlot117no LghtUpThTown1173¼ JsnShrp1171¼ Drifted wide, weakened 12
21Aug99-7Lrl fst 1⅛ ⊗ :48 1:13 1:382 1:502 3↑ Alw 31000N3X 76 8 5 43 52½ 44 511½ Bartram B E L 114 fb *2.30 74-18 ColonlChrs11710 Brthr'sAngl117½ Sn'sPrspctr119nk Wide turns, gave way 8
5Aug99-8Lrl fst 6f :224 :461 :582 1:111 3↑ Alw 31000N3X 74 5 7 74½ 34 36 44½ Reynolds L C L 113 fb 2.00 82-19 CllForllo1172¾ ColdNClcltng117hd Tom'sRvng1141½ 3-4wd,mild mv,flattned 7
WORKS: May16 Lrl 4f fst :473 H *2/14* ●May9 Lrl 5f fst 1:00 H *1/12* May3 Lrl 5f fst 1:02 B *7/18* Apr26 Lrl 4f fst :49 B *5/15* Apr12 Lrl 4f fst :492 B *7/22* Apr5 Lrl 5f fst 1:014 H *2/9*

Memory Tap (S) is at the opposite end of the spectrum. This is a terrific closer who nearly always enters contention by the stretch call. Note his box score compared to the previous example, especially at his favored six-furlong distance. His on-pace performance at seven furlongs should not be considered when evaluating probable performance at six furlongs. He is an "S" type and not a combination of running styles.

10 Apprehend
Own: Lindsay Ricky
STERLING L J JR (10 1 1 2 .10) 2000:(164 18 .11)

Ch. g. 5
Sire: Corporate Report (Private Account) $3,000
Dam: Sweet Talkin Sue (Northjet*Ire)
Br: Logsdon Gary S (Ky)
Tr: Lindsay Rick(1 0 0 0 .00) 2000:(69 9 .13)

L 119

Life	18	4	1	3	$38,667	D.Fst	16	4	1	2	$37,307	81
2000	3	0	0	1	$2,380	Wet	2	0	0	1	$1,360	53
1999	12	4	1	2	$35,362	Turf	0	0	0	0	$0	–
AP	0	0	0	0	$0	Dist	0	0	0	0	$0	–

16Apr00-7Spt	fst	$1\frac{1}{16}$	$:24^{2}$	$:49^{2}$	$1:14^{3}$	$1:46^{1}$	3↑ Clm c-(12.5-10.5)	**76**	6	8	$8^{7\frac{1}{2}}$	$8^{4\frac{1}{2}}$	$7^{5\frac{1}{2}}$	6^{5}	Silva C H	L116 b	4.90	82-17	Classic Fit116^{2} Future Crown116$^{1\frac{1}{4}}$ Cowboy Jo119^{1}	Outrun	8
Claimed from Tassone Bruce & Slager Michael L for $12,500, Slager Mike Trainer																					
4Apr00-5Spt	fst	1	$:24^{1}$	$:48^{2}$	$1:13^{3}$	$1:40^{3}$	3↑ Clm c-10000	**70**	4	6	$6^{5\frac{3}{4}}$	$5^{5\frac{3}{4}}$	4^{6}	$3^{2\frac{1}{2}}$	MacIas G	L116 b	2.60	74-33	Future Crown116^{nk} *Gold Zenith*116$^{2\frac{1}{4}}$ Apprehend116^{1}	Belatedly	7
Claimed from Wexler Stables for $10,000, Vinci Charles J Trainer																					
5Mar00-8Spt	fst	1	$:24^{4}$	$:49^{2}$	$1:15^{3}$	$1:41^{2}$	3↑ Alw 29232N1X	**62**	5	10	$9^{9\frac{3}{4}}$	$9^{7\frac{3}{4}}$	4^{6}	5^{11}	Valovich C J	L119 b	6.20	62-27	*Grand Play*119^{8} Beware The Ides119^{1} Rance119$^{1\frac{3}{4}}$	Flattened out	10
7Nov99-9Haw	fst	$1\frac{1}{16}$	$:23^{2}$	$:46^{4}$	1:12	$1:44^{1}$	3↑ Clm 10000	**81**	4	8	8^{11}	8^{11}	$5^{\frac{3}{4}}$	1^{1}	Zimmerman R	L119 b	8.80	92-19	Apprehend119^{1} DevonshireDrive114$^{\frac{1}{2}}$ ClssicFit107$^{1\frac{1}{4}}$	Split horses driving	9
21Oct99-1Haw	fst	$1\frac{1}{16}$	:23	:47	$1:12^{2}$	$1:46^{1}$	3↑ Clm 10000N3L	**70**	3	5	3^{3}	$2^{1\frac{1}{2}}$	1^{hd}	$1^{3\frac{1}{2}}$	Zimmerman R	L117 b	3.70	82-22	*Apprehend*117$^{3\frac{1}{2}}$ Rendezvous Man117^{15} Ten Wins117$^{8\frac{3}{4}}$	Driving	6
11Aug99-6Haw	fst	$1\frac{1}{16}$	$:23^{2}$	$:47^{3}$	$1:12^{3}$	$1:46^{1}$	3↑ Clm 10000N3L	**62**	1	7	$8^{4\frac{3}{4}}$	$9^{6\frac{1}{4}}$	6^{8}	$3^{6\frac{1}{2}}$	Sterling L J Jr	L117 b	14.70	75-28	Dear Demetri114$^{5\frac{1}{2}}$ Rematch114^{1} *Apprehend*117$^{\frac{1}{2}}$	Belatedly	10
14Jly99-7Haw	fst	1^{70}	$:24^{2}$	$:48^{2}$	$1:14^{1}$	$1:44^{1}$	3↑ Clm 10000N3L	**53**	7	4	$5^{3\frac{1}{2}}$	4^{3}	$4^{7\frac{1}{2}}$	$4^{12\frac{1}{2}}$	Zimmerman R	L117 b	4.00	65-30	Prairie Affair114$^{3\frac{1}{4}}$ *Dear Demetri*114^{6} E Z Drum Beat114$^{3\frac{1}{4}}$	No rally	8
28May99-10CD	fst	$1\frac{1}{16}$	$:24^{1}$	:48	$1:12^{3}$	$1:45^{2}$	4↑ Clm c-(7.5-6.5)	**52**	7	4	4^{4}	$5^{4\frac{3}{4}}$	8^{11}	8^{19}	Albarado R J	L120 b	4.50	64-18	OkSpringsAce116$^{2\frac{3}{4}}$ JunglePryer116^{hd} Clrk'sCrusde116$^{\frac{1}{2}}$	Wide early, tired	10
Claimed from Viar Charles O for $7,500, Morse Randy L Trainer																					
25Apr99-2CD	fst	$1\frac{1}{16}$	$:23^{4}$	$:48^{2}$	$1:14^{2}$	$1:47^{3}$	3↑ Clm 12500N2L	**77**	10	4	$4^{2\frac{1}{2}}$	2^{2}	2^{1}	1no	Day P	L123 b	*2.50	72-26	Apprehend123^{no} Max My Man120^{nk} *Tat Can Sell*120$^{1\frac{1}{2}}$	4 wide 1st turn	10
7Apr99-8OP	fst	1	$:23^{1}$	$:46^{3}$	$1:11^{4}$	$1:39^{2}$	3↑ Clm 20000(25-20)N2L	**51**	9	5	$6^{6\frac{1}{2}}$	$6^{6\frac{1}{2}}$	7^{10}	7^{11}	Murphy B G	L119 b	*2.00	71-23	Rosoro113$^{1\frac{1}{4}}$ I'mMagicToo113^{1} WrongWayBttle116$^{2\frac{1}{4}}$	Four wide first turn	12
21Mar99-2OP	fst	1	$:22^{4}$	$:47^{1}$	$1:12^{3}$	$1:39^{1}$	3↑ Clm 20000(25-20)N2L	**71**	6	6	$4^{4\frac{1}{2}}$	$3^{2\frac{1}{2}}$	$2^{3\frac{1}{2}}$	$2^{1\frac{1}{4}}$	Murphy B G	L119 b	10.90	82-13	Friendly Cop118$^{1\frac{1}{4}}$ Apprehend119$^{3\frac{1}{2}}$ *Rosoro*114$^{\frac{1}{2}}$	Getting to winner	10
24Feb99-3OP	fst	$1\frac{1}{16}$	$:23^{3}$	$:48^{1}$	$1:14^{1}$	1:47	3↑ Md 20000	**70**	3	3	3^{1}	2^{hd}	$1^{1\frac{1}{2}}$	$1^{5\frac{3}{4}}$	Murphy B G	L123 b	*2.00	69-28	Apprhnd123$^{5\frac{3}{4}}$ WldAndStrkng113^{3} BoundToRn115^{1}	Stalked, drove clear	12

WORKS: May11 Haw 4f fst $:48^{3}$ B *4/28* Apr29 Haw 4f fst $:51^{2}$ B *17/32*

Apprehend (S/P) is a combination of two running styles, presser and closer. His four wins have been accomplished from both positions and he has to be considered in two of the three probable pace scenarios. When in form, he appears equally adept at both running styles.

Argolid
Own: Allen William M
$12,500
PINCAY L JR (67 10 15 11 .15) 2000:(390 69 .18)

Dk. b or br g. 9
Sire: Saros*GB (Sassafras*Fr)
Dam: Procne (Acroterion)
Br: Ridder Thoroughbred Stable (Cal)
Tr: Acosta Kenneth D(3 1 1 0 .33) 2000:(14 2 .14)

L 118

Life	51	11	8	8	$450,241	D.Fst	46	11	8	7	$442,965	107
2000	5	1	1	0	$13,860	Wet	3	0	0	1	$3,610	80
1999	10	2	1	2	$23,970	Turf	2	0	0	0	$3,666	92
Hol	13	4	2	3	$181,877	Dist	10	2	4	1	$82,370	102

28Apr00-8Hol	fst	6f	$:22^{2}$	$:45^{3}$	$:57^{4}$	$1:10^{2}$	4↑ Clm 12500(12.5-10.5)	**87**	8	4	2^{1}	$2^{\frac{1}{2}}$	$1^{\frac{1}{2}}$	1^{nk}	Pincay L Jr	LB117 f	3.10	85-16	Argolid117^{nk} Go Not Whoa111$^{1\frac{1}{2}}$ *Joshua Knight*117$^{\frac{1}{2}}$	Stalked,bid,led,drvng	8
7Apr00-4SA	fst	6f	$:21^{4}$	:45	$:57^{2}$	1:10	4↑ Clm 10000	**90**	5	4	1^{hd}	1^{hd}	$1^{\frac{1}{2}}$	2no	Pincay L Jr	LB118 f	5.70	89-12	Gallahad118^{no} *Argolid*118no Asilmottamrich118^{5}	Dueled,gamely,missed	8
23Mar00-6SA	fst	$6\frac{1}{2}$f	:22	$:45^{3}$	$1:12^{1}$	$1:19^{2}$	4↑ [S]Clm 10000	**50**	5	7	$8^{4\frac{1}{2}}$	$9^{7\frac{1}{2}}$	$9^{8\frac{3}{4}}$	7^{6}	Valenzuela F H	LB118 f	3.60	65-18	Brown'sChmpion118^{no} IntrpidKing118$^{2\frac{1}{2}}$ Twcthfun113^{nk}	Tight 5/16,wkened	12
11Feb00-5SA	my	6f	:22	$:45^{1}$	$:57^{1}$	$1:09^{4}$	4↑ [S]Clm 10000	**63**	6	7	$5^{2\frac{1}{2}}$	$5^{4\frac{1}{4}}$	5^{8}	5^{10}	Valenzuela F H	LB119 f	5.40	80-16	*JetSetSwinger*117^{3} TizMighty117$^{2\frac{1}{2}}$ Cndlotto119$^{1\frac{1}{2}}$	4wd btwn foes,wkened	8
14Jan00-2SA	fst	$1\frac{1}{16}$	$:22^{4}$	$:46^{3}$	$1:11^{3}$	$1:45^{1}$	4↑ [S]Clm 10000	**—**	1	8	$8^{6\frac{3}{4}}$	$8^{8\frac{3}{4}}$	9^{13}	—	Valenzuela F H	LB118 f	*1.70	— 20	*RomnCzzn*118$^{2\frac{1}{2}}$ EvndrsChllng118^{2} Notsosntly116^{nk}	Off in air,wide,eased	9
29Dec99-3SA	fst	6f	:22	$:45^{1}$	$:57^{2}$	$1:10^{1}$	3↑ [S]Clm 10000	**90**	7	5	$6^{2\frac{3}{4}}$	$5^{2\frac{1}{4}}$	$3^{2\frac{1}{2}}$	1no	Valenzuela F H	LB118 f	*2.20	89-15	Argolid118^{no} Copelan's Eagle118^{1} Gudarian118^{hd}	Stalked 3wd,up at wire	10
18Dec99-5Hol	fst	7f	$:22^{1}$	$:44^{4}$	$1:09^{4}$	$1:23^{1}$	3↑ [S]Clm 10000(10-9)	**90**	6	3	3^{1}	$3^{2\frac{1}{2}}$	2^{2}	2^{hd}	Valenzuela F H	LB120	3.60	86-14	Prototype122^{hd} *Argolid*120^{7} Ceetoit120^{1}	4wd into lane,gamely	7
14Nov99-9Hol	fst	$6\frac{1}{2}$f	$:22^{1}$	:46	$1:11^{2}$	$1:17^{3}$	3↑ [S]Clm 10000(10-9)	**75**	6	6	$5^{2\frac{3}{4}}$	$6^{2\frac{3}{4}}$	4^{2}	$3^{3\frac{3}{4}}$	Valenzuela F H	LB120 f	5.40	79-12	*Prototype*120$^{\frac{3}{4}}$ Copelan's Eagle118^{3} Argolid120$^{\frac{3}{4}}$	5 wide into stretch	10
28Oct99-1SA	fst	7f	:23	$:45^{3}$	$1:10^{2}$	$1:23^{3}$	3↑ [S]Clm 10000	**83**	6	2	2^{hd}	2^{2}	$2^{\frac{1}{2}}$	1^{1}	Valenzuela F H	LB118 f	*1.80	87-15	Argolid118^{1} Worthy Find111$^{\frac{1}{2}}$ Gudarian118$^{2\frac{1}{2}}$	Re-rallied, driving	7
9Oct99-2SA	fst	6f	:22	$:44^{4}$	$:57^{1}$	$1:09^{4}$	3↑ Clm 12500(12.5-10.5)	**75**	6	1	3^{nk}	3^{1}	$4^{2\frac{1}{2}}$	$4^{3\frac{1}{2}}$	Valenzuela F H	LB118 f	10.90	87-08	SycmorSprings118^{1} *AyrHoyMnn*118^{2} Indombl118$^{\frac{1}{2}}$	Vied btwn,weakened	8
21Jly99-1LS	fst	$6\frac{1}{2}$f	$:22^{4}$	$:45^{2}$	$1:10^{1}$	$1:16^{4}$	3↑ Clm c-(10-9)	**57**	6	3	1^{hd}	3^{nk}	$6^{4\frac{3}{4}}$	6^{6}	Lambert C T	L116	*1.70	80-10	All Sams Jazz122^{1} *Lowflyinduck*116^{hd} Hot Apple Pie115$^{\frac{1}{2}}$	Dropped back	7
Claimed from Lewis Charles R for $10,000, Keen Dallas E Trainer																					
16Jun99-4LS	gd	1	$:23^{3}$	:47	$1:12^{4}$	$1:40^{1}$	3↑ Clm 20000(20-18)	**68**	1	3	$3^{2\frac{1}{2}}$	$4^{2\frac{1}{2}}$	5^{5}	$5^{11\frac{1}{4}}$	Lambert C T	L116 f	2.40	60-37	Galileo116$^{\frac{3}{4}}$ *Vilnius*116$^{5\frac{1}{2}}$ Vitapointe116$^{3\frac{1}{4}}$	Tired late	7

WORKS: ●Mar19 Hol 5f fst $:59^{3}$ H *1/20*

Argolid (E/S/P) is the rare horse that can win from virtually any early running position. He has recorded solid Beyer Speed Figures as an "E," a "P," and as a midpack "S." I cannot envision a win as a deep closer, but he is versatile enough to win from any other position. He must be considered in all three pace scenarios before deciding his probable position.

A RELIABLE FORMAT FOR PACE ANALYSIS

After running styles have been determined, the handicapper is best served by segmenting the race into its component parts. In my handicapping classes I recommend creating three lists of contenders and evaluating each separately. Runners with dual designations are considered in each group in which they appear.

1) The early-pace ("E") scenario will have the greatest effect on the overall result. It must be determined which runners will try for the lead and which of these can actually succeed in gaining that lead. The handicapper must then evaluate the cost of gaining the lead and the likely result of the effort. "E" horses unable to contend for the lead should then be discarded. Survivors of the early-pace matchup are then evaluated in light of the effort they are likely to expend.

2) The pressers ("P") scenario. Once the early pace has been determined, the pressers should be evaluated considering that probable pace. "P" types will have first run at the leaders and loom important in every scenario. Which of the "P" runners are capable of pressing today's pace and still having something left for the final stages? Which figure to burn out by chasing an uncomfortably fast early pace? Which of the pressers will be relegated to closers by virtue of the number of runners in front of them at the first call? Pressers that have shown no inclination to also act effectively as closers can now be safely eliminated. "S/P" runners must also be evaluated in the sustained pace analysis.

3) The closers ("S") scenario. Is there a probable meltdown in today's early-pace scenario? Is the presser scenario unlikely to produce the winner? Which of these late runners figures best on speed figures? My preference is to use this final scenario as a last resort. If the answers to the first two questions are "yes," then the winner may be in the third of our three scenarios. That is especially true when the closer shows a profile with a solid win percentage. If "E" or "P" types remain strong possibilities, I will disfavor late-running contenders. Price, however, is still the main consideration. If a *viable* closer seems grossly overlaid in relation to his overall chances, or the prevailing bias is in his favor, I will make the play. Otherwise the bet will almost certainly be on the forwardly placed runners.

SEPARATING THE CONTENDERS

Now that we have a basic format for analysis, it is time to take it to the next level. The purpose of analyzing each scenario is to weed out the contenders from the pretenders. Accurate pace figures are invaluable in this process, but they do not show the entire picture.

Pace figures are generally based on second call (pre-stretch) times and do not reflect the early positions of the runners. It is entirely possible for pace pressers to possess better early-pace figures than do the "E" types, but those figures do not tell the entire story. The second call of the race occurs after nearly two-thirds of the race has been completed. Pressers and closers have already made moves on the turn and may have gained favorable positions for the stretch run. But what about the earliest stage of the race?

It is during the first quarter-mile in a sprint, and the first half-mile in a route, that winning positions are established. Virtually every runner has a favored position from which he is able to launch his most effective performance. Pressers that cannot gain a preferred position by the first call are stuck in a role in which they perform at less than 100 percent. Midpack closers may be shuffled back into a deep-closing position or "E" horses may be unable to gain the lead. Horses unable to gain their favored positions seldom record their best efforts. That is the nature of the game and that is why we will continue to lose more bets than we win. The goal is to be right often enough to record adequate profits.

To that end, Jim Cramer, a Las Vegas handicapper and researcher, provided a clever solution to the problem of running positions. Jim expanded on the ideas in my book *Modern Pace Handicapping* by providing a simple methodology designed to quantify the analyses of the three pace scenarios. He starts with the usual first-call times recorded by each competitor. He then assigns numerical values based on probable position at the first call. For example, when three "E" horses are in the analysis they will quite likely be labeled E1, E2, and E3. E1 should be on the lead with the other two chasing early. It is also likely that a "P" could split these runners early, thus gaining a label of P2 or P3. The close-up position of a presser in the earliest stages seriously damages all but an E1's chances. The following examples use a loose interpretation of Jim's enhancements to my earlier material. My thanks to Jim for the basic ideas.

It will become clear early on that certain types tend to produce more than their fair share of winners. E1's, P1's, P2's, and S3-4's will tend to outperform their counterparts unable to gain position.

1 Fire Spark PP - 2
Own: Shaw II Charles R $25,000
ALBARADO R J (37 5 1 6 .14) 2000:(617 129 .21)

Ch. g. 6
Sire: Devil's Bag (Halo) $25,000
Dam: Flash Prancer (Mr. Prospector)
Br: Due Process Stable Inc (Ky)
Tr: Drury Thomas Jr(1 0 0 0 .00) 2000:(24 3 .13)

Nasal Strip ON L 117

Life	39	8	3	9	$164,853	D.Fst	34	7	2	9	$140,573 91
2000	6	1	1	1	$19,010	Wet	4	1	1	0	$23,980 93
1999	18	2	2	5	$67,190	Turf	1	0	0	0	$300 70
CD	0	0	0	0	$0	Dist	24	4	3	7	$104,428 93

1May00- 8Spt my 6f :222 :461 :58 1:104 3↑ OClm 32000N 73 1 9 97 911 88¾ 77 Guidry M L 116 fb 4.80 85 - 15 Wilbur1192 Hula Bird1161 *Fortuoso*1192 Showed little 9
26Mar00- 9TP fst 1 :223 :454 1:11 1:37 4↑ Alw 34400N3X 85 5 3 33 41 42½ 34 Deegan J C L 115 fb 6.50 83 - 23 Regency Tower1212 Silks1152 Fire Spark115½ 3 wide bid, tired 5
9Mar00- 6GP fst 6f :22 :45 :573 1:103 4↑ Clm c-(32-30) 86 7 2 65¼ 55½ 64¾ 2¾ Migliore R L 117 fb 5.40 85 - 18 Artic Alert117¾ Fire Spark117½ Roguish Prince1171¼ 3 wide turn, gaining 7
Claimed from Old Coach Farm for $32,000, Gorham Michael E Trainer
13Feb00- 6GP fst 7f :213 :441 1:094 1:23 4↑ Clm 32000(32-30) 73 4 6 55¼ 55 44 46¼ Elliott S L 117 fb 10.60 79 - 16 Derivative117½ Luke'sWy1172½ ExplodeN'Win1173¼ Lacked late response 12
17Jan00-11GP fst 1 1/16 :232 :472 1:124 1:46 4↑ Clm 32000(32-30) 74 6 3 32 52½ 66 56¾ Elliott S L 117 fb 5.80 71 - 21 Viewtoakill117no OnlyWhenILaugh117¾ AllExtr1191¼ Saved ground, tired 10
3Jan00- 1GP fst 7f :23 :454 1:104 1:233 4↑ Clm 25000(25-22.5) 90 2 5 1hd 11½ 13 14¾ Elliott S L 117 fb 3.90 82 - 16 Fire Spark1174¾ Runaway Risque117½ One Nigeria1121 On rail, drew clear 9
20Dec99-10Crc fst 1 :241 :483 1:132 1:392 3↑ Alw 25000N3X 52 7 2 2hd 31 711 822¼ Elliott S L 119 fb 26.80 68 - 12 Whr'sTylor1152¼ *BlzngGns*117½ Throwthbooktm115¾ Forced pace, faded 8
18Nov99- 9Aqu fst 1 :224 :45 1:092 1:353 3↑ Clm 35000(35-30) 78 3 5 43¼ 62¾ 63½ 95¾ Bravo J L 120 fb 16.90 84 - 15 Love Sedona1182¼ Felarof115¾ Raisor's Edge118¾ Chased inside, tired 12
27Oct99- 7Med fst 1 :232 :464 1:113 1:372 3↑ Alw 28050N2X 80 4 4 52½ 41¾ 2½ 1nk Bravo J L 118 fb *1.40 88 - 12 Fire Spark118nk Marketchase1182¼ Russian Sword118nk Driving 7
3Oct99- 6Del fst 1 1/16 :233 :47 1:12 1:45 3↑ Alw 33900N2X 86 8 4 32½ 2hd 1hd 3½ Dominguez R A L 118 fb 10.90 81 - 15 Cold Cat114no Italian Pride114½ *Fire Spark*1182½ 3 wide bid, not enough 8
20Sep99- 6Del fst 6f :222 :453 :574 1:092 3↑ Alw 33600N2X 79 7 7 51½ 3½ 33 38 Dominguez R A L 118 fb 8.10 88 - 11 A Huevo1155¼ Yavapai1142¾ Fire Spark1185¼ Bid 3 wide turn, faded 7
27Aug99- 8Lrl fst 7f :224 :453 1:101 1:224 3↑ Alw 28000N2X 80 4 2 31½ 22½ 43 33 Dominguez R A L 117 fb 2.50 90 - 13 Glider Pilot1171¼ Foundation1101¾ [D]Fire Spark117nk 2pth btw,lug in 3/16 7
Disqualified and placed 6th
WORKS: Apr23 Kee 4f fst :513 B *20/20*

1a Mr. Pickled Gap PP - 8
Own: Fox Run Stable $25,000
COURT J K (35 4 2 5 .11) 2000:(432 74 .17)

Ch. h. 6
Sire: Pancho Villa (Secretariat) $2,500
Dam: Bundler (Raise a Native)
Br: Lotz Nicholas M (Ky)
Tr: Bell Michael H(2 1 0 1 .50) 2000:(15 4 .27)

L 117

Life	45	7	9	7	$188,859	D.Fst	33	5	6	3	$113,663 96
2000	3	0	0	1	$3,075	Wet	10	2	3	3	$71,086 91
1999	13	3	2	0	$52,283	Turf	2	0	0	1	$4,110 87
CD	11	1	2	3	$54,390	Dist	23	5	4	4	$108,577 96

11Apr00- 8Spt fst 6f :222 :454 :581 1:104 3↑ OClm 32000N 80 5 6 98 710 65¾ 63¾ Guidry M L 116 b 4.50 88 - 16 Coach Hicks1161 Rocket Code1161½ B L's Sweep1161 No factor 10
Previously trained by Drury Thomas Jr
22Mar00- 8TP fst 6½f :223 :453 1:101 1:164 4↑ Clm 40000(40-30) 78 7 4 712 79 74¾ 52¼ Torres F C L 116 b 3.10 89 - 08 Cuprite1161 Green Beret1121 *Nikama*116hd 4-6 wide trip 7
Previously trained by Bell Michael H
28Jan00- 7FG sly 6f :214 :453 :58 1:112 4↑ Clm 35000(35-30) 80 3 8 811 810 76 31½ Melancon G L 117 fb 4.90 85 - 14 Barnum1171½ Silent Six114no Mr. Pickled Gap1171 Late gain 5-wide 8
30Dec99- 9FG fst 6f :22 :452 :573 1:101 3↑ Alw 34000N3X 80 4 7 710 711 65½ 65½ Melancon G L 117 fb 6.30 87 - 15 Robahush1153 R. B Spirit115½ Echo Canyon1171 Always back 8
19Dec99- 8FG gd *5½f Ⓣ :221 :46 :583 1:05 3↑ Alw 34000N3X 87 1 11 1112 1113 810 54 Melancon G L 117 fb 8.60 91 - 05 GrandHope1151½ ThanksFrnks115½ Ruth'sRocket1171 Passed tiring foes 11
26Nov99-12CD gd 6½f :222 :453 1:104 1:173 3↑ Clm 40000(40-30) 91 10 6 88 85¾ 54 21¾ Court J K L 116 fb 4.00 87 - 09 Super Marfalous1161¾ Mr. Pickled Gap116nk *He Be Irish*1111 Five wide bid 10
5Nov99- 9Haw fst 6f :213 :443 :571 1:101 3↑ Alw 34452N3X 80 7 9 913 1017 96½ 51½ Guidry M L 114 fb *1.60 90 - 15 [D]JaguarProspect114nk Ain'tNoYnk115¾ JcqueRock114hd Blocked stretch 10
7Oct99- 9TP fst 6f :214 :443 :571 1:102 3↑ Clm 40000(40-30) 93 3 5 68¼ 611 44½ 1½ Court J K L 116 7.20 89 - 21 Mr.PickldGp116½ WinnngRqust122nk *CurThJnx*114¾ Finished well on rail 7
10Sep99- 8TP fst 6f :221 :454 :582 1:112 3↑ Clm c-(25-20) 92 5 4 67½ 42½ 2hd 11 Borel C H L 116 b 2.90 84 - 24 *Mr. Pickled Gap*1161 Mr Bert1164 Serotonin1163½ 3 wide run, driving 6
Claimed from Bearden Wayne & England David P for $25,000, Bearden Wayne Trainer
22Jly99- 7EIP fst 6f :23 :461 :583 1:114 3↑ Clm 40000(40-30) 84 6 3 3nk 21 43½ 53¾ Court J K L 116 b 13.00 85 - 19 Tricky1161¼ *Saratoga Summer*109no Full Retail1141¼ Empty in drive 6
8Jly99- 7EIP fst 6f :232 :464 :591 1:12 3↑ Clm 25000(25-20) 81 2 5 69 68¼ 56½ 42¼ Johnson P A L 116 b 3.30 86 - 16 FullRetail1221½ *Donpickedthisone*116no ByeByeBoker116¾ Best stride late 6
20Jun99- 6CD fst 6½f :23 :454 1:102 1:163 4↑ Clm 40000(40-30) 71 4 5 1hd 42½ 66½ 911¼ D'Amico A J L 118 b 61.50 83 - 07 WillowbrookLane1204 *AcceleratedTime*1162¼ Calca116no Used early, tired 12
WORKS: Apr29 CD 4f fst :49 B *10/40* Apr5 CD 3f fst :39 B *19/19*

2 Cool Academy PP - 1
Own: Bearden Wayne & England David P $25,000
HEBERT T J (28 0 1 2 .00) 2000:(91 11 .12)

Ch. g. 5
Sire: Academy Award (Secretariat) $1,500
Dam: Discontent (Foolish Tanner)
Br: Johnson Mike (Ky)
Tr: Bearden Wayne (—) 2000:(85 13 .15)

L 123

Life	25	7	5	2	$101,654	D.Fst	17	4	4	2	$50,939 90
2000	6	4	1	0	$42,620	Wet	6	3	0	0	$43,135 93
1999	5	0	1	0	$2,865	Turf	2	0	1	0	$7,580 70
CD	0	0	0	0	$0	Dist	11	6	2	1	$69,414 93

27Apr00- 2Kee fst 6f :211 :441 :562 1:09 4↑ Clm 50000 72 10 5 1011 1015 1013 910¼ Hebert T J L 116 14.10 85 - 09 Felon1163 Pearl D'azur111no Mckendree1161¼ Outrun 10
13Apr00- 9Kee fst 6f :214 :453 :58 1:102 4↑ Clm 25000 90 1 1 2hd 2½ 11 12½ Hebert T J L 120 4.90 88 - 10 Cool Academy1202½ *Fallen Halo*1161½ **BarefootMan**116¾ Dueled, clear late 10
19Mar00- 6TP sly 6f :22 :443 :57 1:094 4↑ Clm 25000(25-20) 93 4 2 2½ 2½ 2½ 1nk Zuniga J E L 116 2.10 92 - 12 *Cool Academy*116nk Ingenius1169 Ja May Ka111hd Bumped rival start 5
3Mar00- 7TP fst 6f :221 :452 :581 1:112 4↑ Clm 17500(17.5-15) 78 3 2 21 21½ 11 1nk Zuniga J E L 116 f 2.30 84 - 18 *CoolAcademy*116nk ByeByeBoker1192 WinterWonderlnd1162 Held sway 7
13Jan00- 7TP fst 6f :221 :453 :574 1:094 4↑ Clm 17500(17.5-15) 87 5 1 32 11 1½ 2no Kutz D L 116 5.60 92 - 16 Bye Bye Boker116no *Cool Academy*1165 My DearWatson1141½ Outfinished 7
6Jan00- 4TP fst 6f :221 :451 :573 1:101 4↑ Clm c-(10-9) 78 6 5 66 74¼ 2hd 11 Johnston J A L 116 12.70 90 - 12 Cool Academy1161 *Squamish*116no Minisplit1142 4 wide run turn 7
Claimed from Johnson Mike B for $10,000, Powers James M Trainer
3Dec99- 6TP fst 6f :22 :45 :572 1:101 3↑ Clm 13500(13.5-11.5) 53 3 4 42½ 78 713 711½ Johnston J A L 116 8.40 78 - 10 Wild And Regal1162 Go Wild Red109½ *Over Fan*1102½ Inside, faded 8
6Nov99- 8Tdn fst 1 :233 :473 1:131 1:393 3↑ Clm 18000(18-16) 54 7 5 714 75½ 76¾ 712 Rivera H Jr L 116 6.60 73 - 23 Turk1163 Court Savvy1141¼ Brent's Michael1161½ No threat 8
21Oct99- 3Kee fst 7f :221 :451 1:102 1:231 3↑ Clm 15000 66 1 6 64 85½ 78 68¾ Johnston J A L 116 25.00 77 - 11 *KngrooKing*116hd EditorilSlm116hd WinterWondrlnd1201 No rally, evenly 12
2Oct99- 3TP fst 6½f :233 :471 1:123 1:191 3↑ Clm 13500(13.5-11.5) 70 6 1 62¾ 51¾ 3nk 21½ Johnston J A L 116 4.00 76 - 16 WinterWonderland1161½ CoolAcademy116nk Fan'sChoice116¾ 6 wide turn 7
13May99- 6RD fst 5½f :221 :45 :584 1:053 3↑ Clm 35000 72 1 5 64¾ 59 58½ 69½ Johnston J A LB 116 17.30 86 - 21 *Winning Request*1164 Banjo1162½ *Serotonin*122nk No factor 7
19Dec98- 8TP wf 6½f :223 :45 1:091 1:154 3↑ Alw 30915NC 74 1 2 1hd 3½ 68½ 611¼ Johnston J A L 115 33.00 81 - 16 Human Missile1222½ Lumberman121½ Danny Seth121¾ Inside, gave way 6
WORKS: Feb17 TP 4f fst :50 B *18/31*

3 Bold Naskra PP - 3
Own: Motley Crew II $25,000
SELLERS S J (44 7 7 3 .16) 2000:(431 64 .15)

Dk. b or br h. 5
Sire: Bold Ruckus (Boldnesian)
Dam: Femme de Naskra (Star de Naskra)
Br: Austin Bob & Buchman Dan (Okla)
Tr: McGee Paul J(8 0 0 0 .00) 2000:(80 18 .23)

L 117

Life	27	4	7	3	$87,686	D.Fst	22	3	5	3	$66,375 88
2000	5	0	2	1	$9,100	Wet	4	1	2	0	$21,150 87
1999	15	2	4	1	$34,488	Turf	1	0	0	0	$161 71
CD	3	0	0	0	$2,100	Dist	14	3	5	2	$66,208 88

2Apr00- 8TP sly 6½f :223 :454 1:111 1:181 4↑ Clm 25000(25-20) 85 6 4 1hd 2hd 1hd 2no Vitek J J L 116 b 2.80 84 - 18 Nikama116no Bold Naskra1162½ Bye Bye Boker1166 Dueled, outgamed 6
16Mar00- 8TP sly 6f :22 :443 :57 1:10 4↑ Alw 32400N2X 79 5 3 44¼ 44¼ 44 62¾ Zimmerman R L 116 b 3.80 88 - 14 Del B. Groovy1161 Offer116hd Double Salty1161 5 wide turn 6
20Feb00- 7TP my 6f :221 :45 :572 1:102 4↑ Clm 25000(25-20) 87 6 3 1½ 2hd 2½ 2nk Torres F C L 116 b 2.20 89 - 16 *Del B. Groovy*116nk Bold Naskra116¾ *Donpickedthisone*1166 Outfinished 8
28Jan00- 8TP fst 6½f :231 :461 1:112 1:181 4↑ Clm 40000(40-30) 67 6 4 31½ 31½ 54½ 58½ Laviolette B S L 116 b 4.90 75 - 22 Double Salty1163 Felon1162 Garcon Rouge1191½ Three wide, tired 6
8Jan00- 7TP fst 6f :22 :45 :571 1:093 4↑ Alw 28210N2X 88 8 1 3nk 31 3nk 3¾ Laviolette B S L 116 b 6.60 92 - 11 American Pass116½ Pretty Music116nk Bold Naskra116nk Held stubbornly 9
17Dec99- 6TP fst 5½f :221 :46 :581 1:044 3↑ Clm 25000(25-20) 81 6 2 42½ 22 1hd 12 Laviolette B S L 116 b 2.80 101 - 12 Bold Naskra1162 River Wisdom116no *Pro Cat*1161 4 wide 3/8 pole 7
25Nov99- 4CD fst 6½f :23 :461 1:103 1:164 3↑ Clm 25000(25-20) 76 6 4 31½ 3½ 31½ 45¾ Martinez W L 117 b 7.70 87 - 13 *Calca*1171 Zeke's Rib1174¼ Columbia Gorge117½ Flattened out late 8
4Nov99- 6CD fst 6f :212 :45 :573 1:11 3↑ Clm c-(17.5-15) 73 4 5 34 31½ 42 45½ Court J K L 117 b 7.20 82 - 15 HitThRoof1122¼ *Donpickdthison*117½ LuckySwp1172¾ 3 wide, nothing left 9
Claimed from Mcmahan Arvel & Bowman J W for $17,500, Foley Dravo G Trainer
3Oct99-10TP fst 6f :221 :452 :58 1:102 3↑ Clm 15000(15-10)N3L 82 3 6 1hd 11½ 13 14 Hebert T J L 116 b *3.00 89 - 18 BoldNaskra1164 Badasiwantabe116hd BlticDesire1164½ Off inside, driving 9
15Sep99- 2TP fst 1 :231 :471 1:133 1:411 3↑ Clm 20000(30-20)N3L 66 8 5 36 44½ 57 68½ Court J K L 112 13.40 57 - 36 Brave Noble1162½ Flagwave1132½ *Johnbill*119½ 4 wide, weakened 10
19Aug99- 8EIP fst 6f :23 :464 :592 1:124 3↑ Clm 17500(17.5-15)N3L 71 1 1 2½ 1½ 13 22½ Court J K L 116 *.90 81 - 19 Tourist Trap1112½ Bold Naskra1161¼ Hope It's ABonus1163½ Could not last 8
11Aug99- 7EIP fst 6½f :223 :461 1:114 1:182 3↑ Clm 25000(25-20) 75 1 5 32 32 42½ 45½ Court J K L 116 15.60 78 - 18 Prosong1223 You Look Good114no My Dear Watson1162½ Empty inside 9
WORKS: May5 CDT 5f fst 1:024 B *9/15* Apr25 CDT 5f my 1:042 B *7/7* Apr16 CDT 5f fst 1:013 B *1/3* Mar31 CDT 3f fst :374 B *3/5* Mar4 CDT 5f fst 1:052 B *7/8* Feb15 CDT 5f fst 1:05 B *5/7*

4 Barefoot Man
PP - 4
Own: Donamire Farm $25,000
JOHNSTON J A (2 0 0 0 .00) 2000:(275 31 .11)

Dk. b or br h. 5
Sire: Air Forbes Won (Bold Forbes) $2,500
Dam: Straight Edition (Going Straight)
Br: Donamire Farm (Ky)
Tr: Ball Katherine(1 0 0 0 .00) 2000:(26 5 .19)

L 117

Life	14	2	2	3	$54,723	D.Fst	13	2	2	2	$51,153	92
2000	3	0	0	2	$5,420	Wet	1	0	0	1	$3,570	78
1999	4	0	0	1	$4,355	Turf	0	0	0	0	$0	–
CD	1	0	0	0	$0	Dist	6	2	1	2	$44,931	92

13Apr00- 9Kee fst 6f :214 :453 :58 1:102 4↑ Clm 25000 80 2 2 1hd 1½ 21 34 Johnston J A L 116 fb 18.60 84 – 10 Cool Academy120¾ Fallen Halo1161½ Barefoot Man116¾ Pace, weakened 10
2Mar00- 9TP fst 6½f :222 :451 1:101 1:164 4↑ Alw 32400N2X 83 6 1 1hd 1½ 41 44½ Johnston J A L 116 fb 29.50 86 – 15 Voltage116½ Double Salty1163 Offer1161 3 wide, tired latge 7
16Jan00- 3TP fst 6f :222 :453 :58 1:111 4↑ Clm 30000 (30–20)N3L 74 2 2 1hd 1hd 1hd 3nk Kutz D L 116 fb 2.70 85 – 16 MyBuddyMB111hd President'sDcr116hd BrfootMn1162 Off inside, gamely 6
27Dec99- 8TP fst 5½f :224 :463 :592 1:061 3↑ Alw 27600N2X 70 4 7 73¾ 75¼ 79 86½ Kutz D L 116 fb 17.00 87 – 17 Skeptic110no American Pass115hd Pretty Music115nk 3 wide, tired 8
25Mar99- 9TP fst 6½f :222 :452 1:11 1:173 3↑ Alw 35030N2X 71 3 10 88 75¾ 64½ 54½ Kutz D L 116 fb 10.90 82 – 19 FleetCrossing1161 BttleRdy116nk RivrWisdom116½ Squeezed back st, 5w 10
27Feb99- 7TP sly 6½f :221 :45 1:102 1:171 4↑ Alw 35700N2X 78 6 3 31 3½ 35 33½ Kutz D L 119 fb 9.50 84 – 15 Pro Cat1163 Crafty Hombre116½ Barefoot Man119½ 3 wide, evenly drive 7
29Jan99- 9TP fst 1 :221 :46 1:121 1:384 4↑ Alw 29800N2X 69 8 2 11 2hd 66 714¼ Kutz D L 112 fb 6.60 64 – 29 WitinOnGlenn115nk ChiefWrHwk1156 FrostedMorn115no Off inside, tired 9
30Dec98- 9TP fst 6f :223 :461 :584 1:114 3↑ Alw 26700N2X 76 5 6 41½ 55½ 47¼ 47 Torres F C L 118 fb 4.30 75 – 27 HandsomeTurk1163 GoWildRed1162 Ragin'Rven1152 Flattened out late 9
3Dec98- 8TP fst 6f :222 :461 :584 1:114 3↑ Alw 24500N1X 74 2 5 2hd 2hd 12 11 Kutz D L 118 fb 3.70 82 – 21 Barefoot Man1181 Ingenius1151 Sinjar118nk Inside, driving 11
28Oct98- 5Kee fst *7f :223 :451 1:11 1:274 3↑ Alw 36930N2L 59 6 3 1hd 2½ 53½ 59 Kutz D L 113 b 3.80 81 – 11 Triple Deed112no Allen's Oop1132 Cuprite1165½ In bit tight 3/16 pole 9
18Oct98- 5Kee fst 6f :214 :452 :574 1:10 3↑ Alw 44000N1X 92 7 1 1hd 1hd 2½ 22½ Kutz D L 113 b 14.90 88 – 07 Rock Tunnel1182½ Barefoot Man1134 Dix CaratD'or110½ Dueled, 2nd best 7
9Oct98- 1TP fst 6f :222 :462 :591 1:121 3↑ Md Sp Wt 24k 69 10 3 3nk 1½ 12 11 Kutz D L 120 b *2.50 80 – 22 Barefoot Man1201 Bijensky1208 Thejazzman120½ 4 wide turn, driving 10
WORKS: May3 Kee 4f fst :493 B 7/20 Apr10 Kee 3f fst :383 B 17/17 Apr5 Kee 6f fst 1:15 B 2/3 Mar31 Kee 4f fst :493 B 8/19

5 Bucking the Tide
PP - 5
Own: Lenihan Patricia & Richard $25,000
ST JULIEN M (38 3 8 3 .08) 2000:(419 56 .13)

B. g. 4 FTKOCT97 $11,200
Sire: Buckhar (Dahar) $1,500
Dam: Rosie Rio (Rio Carmelo*Fr)
Br: Camps Mr & Mrs David (Ky)
Tr: Bindner Walter M Jr(3 0 1 0 .00) 2000:(50 3 .06)

L 117

Life	20	2	3	3	$68,953	D.Fst	9	1	0	0	$21,806	74
2000	4	0	0	2	$8,218	Wet	3	0	1	0	$6,085	87
1999	12	2	3	1	$58,590	Turf	8	1	2	3	$41,062	89
CD	0	0	0	0	$0	Dist	6	0	1	0	$9,445	87

1Apr00- 8TP fst 1 1/16 :232 :471 1:114 1:442 4↑ Alw 32600N2X 69 4 4 31½ 51¾ 83¼ 88¾ Martinez W L 115 b 9.10 72 – 27 Strike Reality1151½ Komba1152 Offer112no 4wide bid, tired 8
4Mar00- 9FG fm *5½f Ⓣ :22 :452 :573 1:034 4↑ Clm c-25000 83 7 4 43½ 44½ 32 32 Sellers S J L 117 b *2.00 99 — BrvPncho1171½ DistinctvMr.B117½ BuckngThTd1173½ Inside, out finished 7
Claimed from Calabrese Frank C for $25,000, Catalano Wayne M Trainer
5Feb00-10FG fm *7½f Ⓣ :251 :492 1:144 1:331 4↑ Alw 32000N2X 83 8 3 85 85½ 63½ 42½ Albarado R J L 117 b 6.30 87 – 10 FlowingSnds1171 Fortunefivehundred117hd Tlkmistr1191½ 5-w, mild rally 9
14Jan00- 7FG fm *1 Ⓣ :241 :484 1:142 1:39 4↑ Alw 32000N2X 82 4 4 42 21 21 34½ Albarado R J L 117 b 9.90 86 – 08 Cat Scan1173½ Artistic Star1171 Bucking TheTide1171 Bid, no match late 10
12Dec99- 9FG fm *1 1/16 Ⓣ :241 :49 1:133 1:451 3↑ Alw 32000N2X 89 8 2 22 21 2½ 32 Melancon G L 114 b 18.60 93 – 09 In Case Of Fire1141 Warhead1141 BuckingTheTide1143 Bid, no late kick 8
28Nov99- 7FG fm *1 Ⓣ :242 :483 1:131 1:383 3↑ Alw 32000N2X 81 4 2 53½ 43 34½ 42½ St Julien M L 114 b 7.20 91 – 06 Broke Spoke117hd Sunset Boy111no Flying Avie1142 No rally 9
7Oct99- 9Haw gd 1 1/16 Ⓣ :231 :472 1:122 1:444 Clm 25000 (25–20) 78 8 7 63½ 54 31½ 2¾ Meier R L 117 b 2.50 80 – 19 SuprmCommndr117¾ BucknqThTd117½ Snuggln'Mn119nk Wide first turn 10
5Sep99- 9Haw fm 1 Ⓣ :234 :472 1:114 1:361 Clm 25000 (25–20) 75 2 9 87¼ 76½ 44½ 22 Meier R L 117 b *1.30 84 – 14 Stormy Sonata1142 Bucking The Tide117¾ Hamouse1101½ Second best 12
11Aug99- 8Haw fst 6½f :223 :46 1:104 1:171 Alw 30800N2X 45 8 3 54½ 76 711 619¼ Houghton T D L 117 b 14.60 67 – 16 SeOfTrnquility1146¾ Mckendr114½ EndSwpToo1192¼ Middle of pack, tired 8
29Jun99- 3Haw gd *1 1/16 Ⓣ :223 :474 1:132 1:454 Alw 29000N1X 75 4 4 32 32½ 21½ 11¼ Meier R L 115 b 3.30 83 – 17 BuckingTheTide1151¼ MCSquared115¾ VlidAssembly1151½ Pinballed start 10
28May99- 3Haw fst 6f :212 :443 :572 1:104 Alw 29000N1X 74 5 3 34 33 22½ 41¼ Guidry M L 117 b *1.10 87 – 13 Hey Hank115hd Valid Assembly1151¼ Cat Springs115no Flattened out 6
27Apr99- 1Haw wf 6f :223 :461 :574 1:094 Clm 50000N2L 87 4 2 21½ 2½ 2½ 21½ Pedroza M A L 120 b 3.00 91 – 07 ScholarlyType1151½ BuckingTheTide1206¾ VlidAssembly115nk Outfinished 6
WORKS: May5 CD 4f fst :50 B 34/56 Apr19 CD 4f fst :502 B 35/54 Apr13 CD 4f fst :49 B 15/36 Mar28 CD 4f fst :53 B 20/20 Mar15 FG 4f fst :502 B 25/55 Feb28 FG 3f fst :38 B 9/14

6 Bydeed
PP - 6
Own: Victory Stables Ltd $25,000
DAY P (48 13 7 6 .27) 2000:(414 76 .18)

Ch. c. 4 OBSMAR98 $200,000
Sire: Shadeed (Nijinsky II) $5,000
Dam: Gala Gold Digger (Rollicking)
Br: Glade Valley Farms Inc (Md)
Tr: Whiting Lynn S (—) 2000:(47 9 .19)

L 119

Life	16	2	4	4	$60,638	D.Fst	14	2	4	3	$57,138	91
2000	5	1	1	1	$12,135	Wet	0	0	0	0	$0	–
1999	11	1	3	3	$48,503	Turf	2	0	0	1	$3,500	72
CD	1	0	0	0	$0	Dist	8	1	3	3	$28,927	91

9Apr00- 8OP fst 6f :214 :453 :58 1:103 3↑ Clm 30000 (30–25)N2L 78 3 3 1hd 1hd 1½ 13½ Doocy T T L 119 f *.80 89 – 11 Bydeed1193½ Lake Livingston1191½ Runaway Isle1221 Vied, drove clear 8
29Mar00- 8OP fst 1 :231 :47 1:121 1:383 4↑ Alw 26700N1X 61 3 3 43 33½ 610 610½ Nuesch D L 115 f 4.90 76 – 22 Seattlecity1151¾ Speculation1133 Penwest1162½ Fought rider early 9
17Mar00- 3OP fst 6f :22 :461 :582 1:103 3↑ Clm 30000 (30–25)N2L 79 4 5 42½ 42½ 22½ 22½ Nuesch D L 120 f 3.20 86 – 16 I'am Cured1202½ Bydeed1203½ Thejurysstillout1112 Restrained, clear 2nd 7
5Mar00- 5OP fst 6f :22 :453 :581 1:104 3↑ Clm 25000 (25–20)N2L 77 3 3 31½ 31 3½ 3no Nuesch D L 123 f *1.90 88 – 16 DH Millenium Mltdown114 DH BigGold118no Bydd123¾ Between foes late 6
Previously trained by Hudson James C
9Jan00- 7Hou fst 6f :22 :453 :581 1:114 4↑ Alw 12500N1X 65 1 7 62½ 62¾ 32½ 54 Beasley J A5 L 112 *1.20 83 – 15 Clicker1171 Working Well117½ Isle Bingo122¾ Tired 7
Previously trained by Asmussen Steven M
30Oct99- 5Kee fst 7f :221 :451 1:11 1:24 3↑ Alw 49000N1X 42 12 3 83½ 99 811 816½ Albarado R J L 116 5.50 66 – 15 Hall Pass1201½ Don's Diamond1142½ Why So Quiet114nk No factor 12
11Sep99- 9Haw fst 6f :222 :462 :583 1:111 3↑ Alw 28600N1X 74 4 5 32 31 32 33¼ Meche D J L 114 *2.50 83 – 17 Pretty Music1191½ Lively Alliance1122 Bydeed114¾ No winning bid 10
19Aug99- 7Haw fst 6f :222 :453 :58 1:103 Alw 28600N1X 67 6 6 44½ 44 3½ 33½ Meche D J L 117 2.40 86 – 17 Chilly A.1172½ Valid Assembly114¾ Bydeed1171 Mild rally 6
28Jly99- 9Haw fm 1 1/16 Ⓣ :224 :471 1:123 1:441 3↑ Alw 28600N1X 43 10 4 42½ 53 1010 1116½ Murphy B G L 114 3.10 67 – 19 Maneland1141 Regreta114¾ Babalover1141½ Fractious in gate 12
10Jun99- 7CD fm 1 Ⓣ :242 :474 1:123 1:373 Alw 42920N1X 72 7 1 1½ 2½ 24 36 Peck B D L 118 4.20 75 – 16 Morluc1184¾ Known Tune1181½ Bydeed1181½ Dueled, outside,tired 8
23May99- 8CD fst 6½f :223 :452 1:103 1:17 Alw 35275N1X 68 5 7 1hd 11 43 79¼ Albarado R J L 121 b 10.00 83 – 09 Always Believe1213 VictoryPlace1212¼ Kutsa1181¾ Bumped,steadied start 9
7Apr99- 2Kee fst *7f :223 :45 1:101 1:27 Md Sp Wt 37k 87 8 1 12 11½ 11 1nk Albarado R J L 119 b 3.10 92 – 10 Bydeed119nk Sailor's Warning1194 Early Report1193 Ducked in start 10
WORKS: Apr22 CD 5f fst 1:04 B 34/39 ●Feb28 OP 4f fst :474 H 1/32 Feb13 Hou 4f fst :512 B 34/52

7 Fleet Crossing
PP - 7
Own: Levine Earl $25,000
MARTINEZ S JR (—) 2000:(9 0 .00)

Ch. g. 5
Sire: Afleet (Mr. Prospector)
Dam: Rivers to Cross (Riverman)
Br: Levine Earl (Ky)
Tr: Levine Earl(2 0 0 0 .00) 2000:(34 0 .00)

L 117

Life	39	3	2	2	$101,427	D.Fst	28	2	2	1	$73,197	83
2000	8	0	0	1	$7,546	Wet	10	1	0	1	$28,046	87
1999	11	1	0	1	$26,368	Turf	1	0	0	0	$184	38
CD	13	1	1	0	$39,653	Dist	14	0	0	1	$5,826	75

22Apr00- 4Kee fst 1 1/16 :242 :474 1:12 1:434 4↑ Alw 65000N3X 80 5 3 34½ 45 46 410 Martinez S Jr L 117 b 41.80 76 – 15 TheGroomIsRed1162½ MkeYourMrk1163 StrikeRlity1164½ Empty in drive 6
2Apr00- 8TP sly 6½f :223 :454 1:111 1:181 4↑ Clm 25000 (25–20) 65 2 1 42 34½ 48½ 48½ Cooksey P J L 116 b 9.60 75 – 18 Nikama116no Bold Naskra1162½ Bye Bye Boker1166 Empty in drive 6
16Mar00- 9TP sly 1 :214 :444 1:103 1:371 3↑ Alw 34400N3X 47 3 1 1hd 32 49½ 520½ Fortner J L L 112 b 13.00 65 – 26 Farma'sBest1151 PrisAcdemy1185 Jody'sPlymte1152½ Suicidal fractions 6
4Mar00- 8TP fst 6½f :231 :462 1:111 1:18 4↑ Clm 25000 (25–20) 76 3 5 31 32½ 35½ 36½ Fortner J L L 116 fb 15.40 78 – 20 Donpickedthisone1165 Green Beret1161½ Fleet Crossing1161 No bid 6
20Feb00- 7TP my 6f :221 :45 :572 1:102 4↑ Clm 25000 (25–20) 54 5 7 75½ 710 713 713 Kuntzweiler G L 116 b 18.60 76 – 16 DelB.Groovy116nk BoldNskr116¾ Donpickdthison1166 No menace, 3 wide 8
9Feb00- 8TP fst 6f :22 :451 :58 1:113 4↑ Clm 25000 (25–20) 66 8 3 31 31 33 62¾ Thompson T J L 116 fb 33.50 80 – 19 Fraterno116½ Ingenius113no Personal Note111½ 3 wide, held well 8
2Feb00- 9TP fst 1 :224 :46 1:11 1:381 4↑ Alw 32200N3X 34 7 7 611 715 823 831 Sunseri J J L 116 fb 33.90 50 – 33 Johnbill11511 Texastoothpick115nk Dead Serious1153 No factor 8
15Jan00- 6TP fst 6f :222 :452 :573 1:10 4↑ Clm 40000 (40–30) 67 5 4 43½ 44 55½ 56½ Zimmerman R L 116 b 64.00 84 – 11 D Danny Seth116nk Nikama116nk Garcon Rouge1224½ Bumped, forced in 6
Placed 4th through disqualification.
28Nov99- 8TP fst 1 :233 :472 1:124 1:392 3↑ Alw 27240N3X 15 5 4 4½ 68 621 638½ Ramos J7 L 109 b 62.50 36 – 31 Dabney Carr1162 Strubinger1144 Jake The Flake1143 4 wide, stopped 6
14Nov99- 3CD fst 6½f :224 :461 1:111 1:174 3↑ Clm 17500 (17.5–15) 30 7 7 84¾ 87¾ 813 822¼ Court J K L 117 b 43.80 65 – 14 Kangaroo King121hd Kenneth1171½ Zeke's Rib1124 No factor,6wide 8
5Nov99-10CD fst 6½f :221 :452 1:104 1:172 3↑ Clm 25000 (25–20) 46 8 11 1114 1212 1213 1119¼ Ramos J7 L 110 b 109.40 70 – 14 D Willowbrook Lane118¾ Charlie Chan1195 Texas Topper117¾ Outrun 12
9Oct99-10Hoo my 6f :222 :452 :572 1:10 3↑ Clm 20000 74 2 8 78 711 47½ 38½ Thompson T J LB 117 f 22.20 78 – 22 Smooth Weave1173¼ Taylor's Day1175½ Fleet Crossing1171 Mild rally, late 8
WORKS: ●Mar29 TP 4f fst :49 B 1/10 ●Mar14 TP 3f fst :352 B 1/8

COOL ACADEMY: "E/P." $22^2/_5$ estimated time at the first call.

Despite an awful last race, this gelding is a serious threat at the $25,000 claiming level. He shows some flexibility in his running style, but current evidence suggests he is best served on the pace. He can also press the pace successfully, so he warrants an "E/P" designation. His Beyer figures before his last race are the top recent numbers in the field. When in form, he can probably reach the first quarter-mile in about $22^2/_5$ seconds. His $21^4/_5$ quarter at Keeneland is not confirmed by any other race and may have simply reflected a faster surface. (Comparative par times show Keeneland to be approximately three lengths faster at the first quarter-mile than Turfway Park.)

FIRE SPARK: "S." 23 estimated time at the first call.

This 6-year-old's best races are from the rear of his fields, so he warrants an "S" label. His September race at Delaware shows a close-up position early, but the basic consideration is position in relation to the rest of the field. He was fifth in that seven-horse field, so he had to catch the leaders from behind. He paid the price for being that close to a six-furlong pace by backing up badly through the stretch. Early position in longer races does not count; we are only considering the approximate distance of today's race. He does have several Beyer figures that would make him a factor, so he has to be considered in this race. The preponderance of thirds in his box score is typical of late runners and that makes him a risky win bet.

BOLD NASKRA: "E." $22^1/_5$ estimated time at the first call.

Excluding his effort at $5^1/_2$ furlongs, his very best races are on, or dueling for, the lead. He can stand heat but will be a shaky play if another horse is capable of 22 seconds or better. His Beyer figures are a strong fit and he gets a switch to a top rider. He is trained by a 23 percent trainer and has worked during his brief freshener. If he is able to gain his preferred position, he will be a strong contender for the win.

BAREFOOT MAN: "E." $22^2/_5$ estimated time at the first call.

This is another "E" runner, but his recent Beyer figures do not measure up to the top contenders. He should reach the first call about the same time as Cool Academy, but he has already lost to that horse from that same position. He will also have to contend with Bold Naskra, who figures faster at the first call and considerably faster at the pace or second call.

BUCKING THE TIDE: "S." 23 estimated time at the first call.

Most of his recent races have been around two turns. That will not help his early speed. His best sprints are as a presser, but the recent routes will almost certainly place him in the rear of the field. He will be an "S" in this race, which will take him out of his preferred stalking position.

BYDEED: "E." 22 $\frac{2}{5}$ estimated time at the first call.

Bydeed is a lightweight in the Beyer Speed Figure department. He will need a perfect pace scenario to be a serious threat. Both of his wins were on the lead, but that seems unlikely in here. The 21$\frac{4}{5}$ quarter at Oaklawn contradicts all of his other performances. Consider the bulk of his races, not the exception. I suggest downgrading that near miss in March. That race was against nonwinners of two races lifetime, and those are much easier than seasoned claiming winners. Focus on his wins; most of his off-pace races have resulted in nonthreatening finishes. The presence of Pat Day guarantees an underlay on a front-runner that figures not to gain the early lead. He may also be seriously outclassed.

FLEET CROSSING: "X." 23+ estimated time at the first call.

This is a dreadful horse without any current form or specific running style. Designate these runners as "X" and then estimate first-call position.

MR. PICKLED GAP: "S." 24+ estimated time at the first call.

Mr. Pickled Gap is a deep closer and he figures to be far off today's probable pace. He is coupled in the wagering with Fire Spark, and they have been jointly bet to favoritism here. He does win races, but he will need help in the early/presser scenarios to win in this spot. His record at Churchill Downs reflects his tendency to fall far off the early pace before launching a late bid. I strongly recommend playing against this type of favorite.

THE COMPETITORS:

Bold Naskra	"E"	22 $\frac{1}{5}$
Bydeed	"E"	22 $\frac{2}{5}$
Barefoot Man	"E"	22 $\frac{2}{5}$
Cool Academy	"E/P"	22 $\frac{2}{5}$
Fire Spark	"S"	23
Bucking the Tide	"S"	23

Fleet Crossing	"X"	23+
Mr. Pickled Gap	"S"	24+

THE PACE ANALYSIS:

EARLY PACE:

Bold Naskra

Bydeed

Barefoot Man

Cool Academy

Bold Naskra is capable of gaining the early lead, thus securing his favored position. He should be assigned an E1 label as the dominant front-runner. He has shown he can duel and win, which makes him especially dangerous. E1's win more than their fair share of races.

By virtue of his strong inclination to try for the lead, Barefoot Man warrants the label of E2. He should have plenty of company early and will probably not survive if relegated to the role of pace presser. E2's win a fair share of races, but not with the additional competition Barefoot Man will face from Bydeed and Cool Academy.

Bydeed does not generally manage the lead and Cool Academy is usually content to settle close-up early. This makes the separation difficult. No matter, this is a fairly loose framework and not an exact science. I would label Bydeed as an E3, and Cool Academy the same position, an E/P3. You will learn early on with this procedure that an E3 is seldom a winner, while P3's win more than their fair share.

EARLY PACE:

Bold Naskra	E1
Barefoot Man	E2
Bydeed	E3
Cool Academy	E/P3

PRESSERS:

Cool Academy	E/P3

This is nearly an ideal spot for Cool Academy. He is the only presser in the race and two of the "E's" are exceedingly vulnerable on pace and speed figures. He will have first run at the leaders and should defeat the two main "S" types. Cool Academy will have to get past Bold Naskra to win, but he is very tough and wins a high percentage of his races.

SUSTAINED PACE:

Fire Spark	S5
Bucking the Tide	S6
Mr. Pickled Gap	S8

Fire Spark is often forwardly placed in his races, while Bucking the Tide has been routing on the turf in most of his recent races. We should expect Fire Spark to gain a better early position. Fleet Crossing will probably be running seventh in the early going while Mr. Pickled Gap will certainly occupy his normal position behind the entire field.

THE FINAL ANALYSIS

This procedure takes much less time in actual practice than it does to explain. It takes only a few minutes to accomplish, but provides a valuable structure for the analysis of pace. The methodology is remarkably accurate, and you will probably gain a whole new perspective on the subject. It is not, however, bulletproof. Because of varying distances and surfaces, it is strictly a "ballpark" estimate of probable positions. The error rate should be more than acceptable and the bottom line should remain healthy. The remaining step is to set an acceptable price line before stepping up to the betting windows.

THE VIABLE CONTENDERS, IN ORDER OF THEIR EXPECTED WIN PROBABILITY:

Bold Naskra	E1
Cool Academy	E/P3
Fire Spark	S5

Patterns will become clear after using this methodology for only a short while. Experience will teach the reader to favor certain configurations. The most favorable is an E1 with the necessary speed figures to survive the matchup. In this example, Bold Naskra has a decided edge and is probably worth a play at 5-2 or better. Cool Academy's configuration is also highly desirable. He looms the second-most-probable winner. Both runners survive the paper matchup and need only perform on the track. I would accept 3-1 or better on this horse. Fire Spark's S5 rating is not hopeless, but he will have much to accomplish in the late going. S3's and S4's are winning patterns, but only when the early matchup disfavors the more favorably positioned runners. If Fire Spark should go off as a serious overlay, I might be inclined to bet him. Fire Spark and Mr. Pickled Gap are logical for the minor awards, but neither is a high probability for the win. The other runners do not survive the matchup and are not bettable at any price.

FIFTH RACE
Churchill
MAY 10, 2000

6 FURLONGS. (1.08³) CLAIMING. Purse $28,000 FOR FOUR YEAR OLDS AND UPWARD. Weight 123 lbs. Non–winners of two races since March 1 allowed, 2 lbs. Two races since February 2, 4 lbs. A race since April 5, 6 lbs. CLAIMING PRICE $25,000, for each $1,000 to $20,000 1 lb. (Races for $17,500 or less not considered).

Value of Race: $28,000 Winner $17,360; second $5,600; third $2,800; fourth $1,400; fifth $840.   Mutuel Pool $221,217.00 Exacta Pool $167,997.00   Trifecta Pool $150,041.00

Last Raced	Horse	M/Eqt. A.Wt	PP	St	¼	½	Str	Fin	Jockey	Cl'g Pr	Odds $1
2Apr00 8TP2	Bold Naskra	Lb 5 117	2	1	1½	1¹	1²	1¹	Sellers S J	25000	3.30
27Apr00 2Kee9	Cool Academy	L 5 123	1	3	3hd	3¹	2³	2³	Hebert T J	25000	3.40
11Apr00 8Spt6	Mr. Pickled Gap	Lb 6 117	7	5	7	5¹	3hd	3¹	Court J K	25000	2.50
13Apr00 9Kee3	Barefoot Man	Lbf 5 117	3	6	4hd	4³	5²	4²½	Johnston J A	25000	9.60
9Apr00 8OP1	Bydeed	Lf 4 119	5	7	2½	2hd	4hd	5³	Day P	25000	2.90
1Apr00 8TP8	Bucking the Tide	Lb 4 117	4	2	6²	6²	6⁵	6⁶	St Julien M	25000	11.60
22Apr00 4Kee4	Fleet Crossing	Lb 5 117	6	4	5¹½	7	7	7	Cooksey P J	25000	28.30

OFF AT 5:00 Start Good. Won driving. Track fast.
TIME :21³, :45¹, :57¹, 1:10² (:21.72, :45.25, :57.29, 1:10.55)

$2 Mutuel Prices:

3–BOLD NASKRA	8.60	4.40	3.00
2–COOL ACADEMY		4.40	3.20
1A–MR. PICKLED GAP			2.80

$2 EXACTA 3–2 PAID $37.20 $2 TRIFECTA 3–2–1 PAID $110.40

Dk. b. or br. h, by Bold Ruckus–Femme de Naskra, by Star de Naskra. Trainer McGee Paul J. Bred by Austin Bob & Buchman Dan (Okla).

BOLD NASKRA drifted out at the start while gaining the lead and bumped BAREFOOT MAN, made all the pace while in the three path and was kept to his task to hold COOL ACADEMY safe. The latter, never far back and saving ground throughout, loomed inside the winner for the drive and wasn't good enough. MR. PICKLED GAP, outsprinted for a half, made a run five wide entering the stretch, came out farther in the stretch run but lacked a final response. BAREFOOT MAN, bumped at the start, raced in a striking position in behind the leaders until the stretch, came out four wide for the drive and failed to respond. BYDEED pressed the winner from the outside into the stretch and tired. BUCKING THE TIDE wasn't a factor despite saving ground. FLEET CROSSING was finished early.

Owners— 1, Motley Crew II Motley Michael et al; 2, Bearden Wayne & England David P; 3, Fox Run Stable; 4, Donamire Farm; 5, Victory Stables Ltd; 6, Lenihan Patricia & Richard; 7, Levine Earl

Trainers—1, McGee Paul J; 2, Bearden Wayne; 3, Bell Michael H; 4, Ball Katherine; 5, Whiting Lynn S; 6, Bindner Walter M Jr; 7, Levine Earl

Cool Academy was claimed by Michael S Bramer & Steven L Morguel; trainer, Morguelan Steven L.,
Mr. Pickled Gap was claimed by Gange Paul A; trainer, Smith Jere R Jr.,
Bucking the Tide was claimed by James B Seidel & Randy Smith; trainer, Montano Angel.
Scratched— Fire Spark (1May00 8SPT7)

$2 Pick Three (4–4/9–3) Paid $111.20; Pick Three Pool $30,765.

Prenuptual Deal
Own: Vreeland James R
DELAHOUSSAYE E (235 32 32 42 .14) 2000:(222 29 .13)

Ch. c. 4 FTFCAL98 $40,000
Sire: Tactical Advantage (Forty Niner) $12,500
Dam: Groom's Swing (Rumaway Groom)
Br: Marablue Farm (Fla)
Tr: Palma Hector O(18 4 3 1 .22) 2000:(16 4 .25)

L 120

Life	5	2	1	1	$82,400	D.Fst	5	2	1	1	$82,400 97
2000	1	1	0	0	$31,800	Wet	0	0	0	0	$0 –
1999	1	0	0	1	$6,000	Turf	0	0	0	0	$0 –
SA	3	1	1	1	$45,200	Dist	2	1	1	0	$29,600 90

1Apr00-2SA fst 7f :22 :442 1:093 1:223 4+ Alw 54855N1X 97 6 7 2hd 4½ 12 12½ Delahoussaye E LB 118 3.30 92-14 PrenuptulDel1182½ VeryCerleon1184 GenrllyOn1181½ Dueled wide,cleared 7
15Apr99-6SA fst 7f :22 :45 1:091 1:214 Alw 50000N1X 90 5 2 54½ 53 33 37½ Stevens G L B 120 3.50 88-14 NationalSaint1202½ *Luftikus*1215 *PrenuptulDel*1203 4wd bid,tied up after 5
20Oct98-7SA fst 6f :212 :443 :563 1:093 Alw 37000N1X 90 1 2 14½ 2hd 2hd 21½ Delahoussaye E B 117 2.20 90-13 *Exploit*1171½ Prenuptual Deal117nk Out In Front1171½ Speed, held place 5
9Sep98-8Dmr fst 7f :214 :442 1:094 1:23 Del Mar Fty-G2 78 7 1 1½ 21½ 54½ 48 Delahoussaye E B 116 7.40 77-17 WorldlyMnner1195 DringGenerl1192½ WkiAmericn114½ Dueled,weakened 7
8Aug98-6Dmr fst 6f :22 :451 :574 1:11 Md Sp Wt 37k 84 4 7 1½ 11 11 13 Meza R Q B 118 5.80 84-15 PrenuptulDel1183 GroundEffct1181 NorthrnAvnu1184 Off slow,steadied 9
WORKS: Apr12 SA 4f fst :471 H *6/45* Mar28 SA 4f fst :474 H *6/30* Mar21 SA 7f fst 1:271 H *2/5* ●Mar14 SA 6f fst 1:123 H *1/9* Mar7 SA 5f gd 1:012 H *19/85* Feb26 SA 5f gd 1:003 H *24/169*

Treasureathend
Own: Stull Debra & Tom
$62,500
VALDIVIA J JR (188 12 21 15 .06) 2000:(180 11 .06)

B. c. 4 KEESEP97 $20,000
Sire: Geiger Counter (Mr. Prospector)
Dam: Dead End (Cox's Ridge)
Br: Upson Downs Farm (Ky)
Tr: Wilson James R II(14 1 1 1 .07) 2000:(18 1 .06)

L 118

Life	4	2	0	1	$44,350	D.Fst	3	2	0	1	$44,350 69
1999	1	0	0	0	$0	Wet	0	0	0	0	$0 –
1998	3	2	0	1	$44,350	Turf	1	0	0	0	$0 66
SA	0	0	0	0	$0	Dist	2	2	0	0	$38,350 65

14Jly99-5Hol fm 5½f ⓣ :214 :443 :561 1:022 Clm c-(62.5-55)N3L 66 7 2 83 63½ 95 87 Puglisi I L LB 116 f 19.60 85-08 Shipwrecked1161¾ CrusadingPro117½ Dillionire1181 Wide trip,weakened 9
Claimed from James Jason & Paul Mamakos for $62,500, Mamakos Jason Trainer
10Oct98-10Fno fst 6f :214 :443 :571 1:103 RonCloud Mem49k 60 5 4 54½ 3nk 12 13 Puglisi I L LB 118 4.50 86-09 Tresurethnd1183 LndCtchr118nk DnzigCommndr1184 Late rally, drew off 8
11Sep98-11Fpx fst 6½f :222 :46 1:111 1:172 Beau Brummel48k 69 3 2 31½ 31½ 33 35½ Espinoza V LB 114 4.10 87-11 BelmontShore1162 *Eagleton*1143½ *Tresurethend*1146 Pulled early, no bid 5
20Aug98-5Dmr fst 6f :214 :452 :584 1:121 Md 32000 (32-28) 65 5 4 47½ 34½ 11 18 Meza R Q LB 118 f 5.00 78-14 Treasureathend1188 *DnzigCommnder*1182½ Foreverme118½ Clear,drving 8
WORKS: Apr12 SLR 4f fst :464 H *1/1* Mar31 SLR 7f fst 1:282 H *1/2* ●Mar25 SLR 6f fst 1:133 H *1/4* Mar16 SLR 6f fst 1:14 H *1/1* Mar11 SLR 5f fst 1:001 H *5/13* Mar2 SLR 5f fst 1:021 H *5/5*

Windstrike
Own: Thom Tom A
$62,500
SOLIS A (288 49 50 51 .17) 2000:(276 47 .17)

Ch. h. 6
Sire: Retsina Run (Windy Sands) $1,000
Dam: Wind Warning (Don B.)
Br: Harper Jerry R (Cal)
Tr: West Ted H(76 12 8 11 .16) 2000:(78 12 .15)

L 118

Life	30	5	5	9	$198,454	D.Fst	21	2	4	9	$127,664 98
2000	4	1	1	0	$51,510	Wet	7	3	1	0	$70,790 98
1999	15	1	3	7	$65,040	Turf	2	0	0	0	$0 85
SA	7	2	1	0	$65,560	Dist	16	3	4	4	$111,610 98

25Mar00-3SA fst 6f :211 :44 :571 1:094 4+ Clm c-(50-45) 98 2 7 610 610 63¾ 4½ Berrio O A LB 120 n 2.60 90-12 *Venus Genus*118hd **Island Caper**118nk Grady120hd Off bit slow,5wd bid 7
Claimed from Acker Lindo & Verrati for $50,000, Spawr Bill Trainer
8Mar00-5SA sly 6½f :214 :443 1:094 1:161 4+ OClm 62500 97 2 3 63¾ 64½ 32 23½ Pincay L Jr LB 120 n 3.40 83-23 BeumsDVnis1183½ Windstrik1201½ OutstndingHro1181½ 5 wide into stretch 7
12Feb00-5SA my 6½f ⊗ :214 :444 1:093 1:162 4+ Clm 62500 (62.5-55) 93 7 1 42¾ 41¾ 12 11 Pedroza M A LB 117 3.30 86-13 Windstrike1171 Court Costs1171½ Riot116½ 4wd bid,clear,dvng 7
15Jan00-6SA fm *6½f ⓣ :213 :424 1:06 1:121 4+ Ⓢ SensatnlStrH112k 81 4 7 73 89½ 1012 119¼ Pincay L Jr LB 117 23.70 87-06 Spinlssjllyfsh1162 ExMrksThCop1172 Indhom118no Pulled,steadied early 11
26Dec99-7SA fst 6½f :221 :45 1:09 1:152 3+ OClm 62500 87 2 4 42 54½ 54 46¼ Pincay L Jr LB 118 10.40 84-08 Lake William1192½ Haflinger1172½ *CapeCanaveral*1171½ 5 wide into stretch 8
4Dec99-8Hol fst 7f :222 :451 1:101 1:23 3+ OClm 62500 93 3 4 53 65 32 31 Pincay L Jr LB 117 11.50 86-17 *Spinelessjellyfish*117½ StraightMn116½ Windstrike1172 Closed willingly 7
30Oct99-1SA fst 5½f :221 :451 :57 1:032 3+ Ⓢ CalCpStrSprH50k 85 3 5 42 53½ 55 53¼ Pincay L Jr LB 120 *1.50 89-05 Irrelevant118no Skol115hd **Lucky Hostage**1171½ Failed to respond 5
21Sep99-11Fpx fst 6½f :222 :452 1:092 1:153 3+ Gov's Cup H48k 95 1 2 32½ 42¾ 43½ 32 Espinoza V LB 116 2.30 100-08 Emailit1191½ Devoted Pirate116½ Windstrike1161½ Inside to 2nd turn 5
14Sep99-11Fpx fst 6f :214 :444 :572 1:094 3+ Aprisa H50k 93 6 9 810 96¾ 64¾ 3nk Espinoza V LB 115 5.60 98-07 *Emailit*118no F J's Pace114nk Windstrike1151½ Off bit slow,late bid 9
22Aug99-7Dmr fst 6f :221 :45 :571 1:093 3+ OClm c-62500 97 4 1 53½ 43½ 33 31½ Pedroza M A LB 119 4.90 90-13 **Rahy'sQuackerjack**1191 Vldour119½ Windstrike1196 Tight 4-1/2,fin. well 5
Claimed from Berg & Featherstone for $62,500, Truman Eddie Trainer
WORKS: Apr16 SA 5f fst 1:001 H *11/62* Apr10 SA 4f fst :493 H *20/29* Apr2 SA 3f fst :38 H *16/19* Mar19 SA 3f fst :354 H *4/23* Feb5 SA 4f fst :511 H *39/41*

Let's Go Surfing
Own: Arrias Fred & Donn Ron
$62,500
PINCAY L JR (307 53 36 37 .17) 2000:(300 53 .18)

B. g. 5
Sire: Cutlass Reality (Cutlass) $2,000
Dam: Lace Bikini (Splendid Courage)
Br: Harris Farms Inc (Cal)
Tr: Spawr Bill(88 24 9 13 .27) 2000:(83 23 .28)

L 118

Life	18	6	3	1	$177,000	D.Fst	16	5	3	1	$161,160 111
2000	2	1	1	0	$51,000	Wet	1	1	0	0	$15,840 82
1999	14	5	1	1	$122,400	Turf	1	0	0	0	$0 55
SA	8	3	2	0	$122,080	Dist	14	5	3	1	$163,800 111

5Feb00-3SA fst 6f :211 :44 :563 1:094 4+ OClm 62500N 98 1 3 1hd 1hd 11 21½ Flores D R LB 120 *.90 89-14 **LovAllThWy**1181½ Lt'sGoSurfing120¾ ThToyMn1181½ Inside duel,held 2nd 5
1Jan00-7SA fst 6f :212 :443 :564 1:092 4+ Alw 60250N1X 106 7 1 11 11 11 12½ Pincay L Jr LB 122 *.50 92-12 LtsGSrfn1222½ FlsPrspctr1214½ WstOfThPcs119no Gamely,strong handling 7
30Oct99-7SA fst 6f :211 :434 :554 1:082 3+ Ⓢ CalCupSprntH150k 111 3 5 2hd 2½ 2½ 21½ Almeida G F LB 113 7.10 97-05 LovThtRd1181½ *Lt'sGoSurfng*1131 Chmp'sStr1171 Dueled,led late,caught 9
7Oct99-6SA fst 6f :21 :432 :554 1:084 3+ Ⓢ Alw 44000N1X 103 6 5 2hd 2hd 11½ 14½ Almeida G F LB 118 4.60 96-08 Let's Go Surfing1184½ Little Memin1181 Tzigane118no Drew clear, driving 12
24Sep99-11Fpx fst 6f :221 :452 :572 1:092 3+ Clm c-(20-18) 100 7 6 11 14 13½ 15 Almeida G F LB 116 *2.60 100-13 *Let's Go Surfing*1165 *Chief Arias*1164 Ketchem1164 Inside, ridden out 7
Claimed from Baker David W for $20,000, Baker D Wayne Trainer
11Sep99-10Fpx fst 7f :214 :454 1:103 1:23 3+ Clm c-(16-14) 89 7 6 2hd 2hd 1hd 1hd Almeida G F LB 116 f 3.20 101-08 Lt'sGSrfng116hd HdwnB.Gd1162 *ATchOfGry*1161 Inched away,held game 9
Claimed from Aldabbagh Omar for $16,000, Aguirre Paul G Trainer
13Aug99-5Dmr fst 6½f :214 :444 1:103 1:164 3+ Clm c-(20-18) 70 1 2 1hd 1hd 2½ 77 Valdivia J Jr LB 119 b 14.10 80-12 MgnfcntMrks119hd CrstlCrctt1192 ATchOfGr1193 Inside duel,weakened 9
Claimed from Edlund Susan & Lidstrom Beverly for $20,000, Baker D Wayne Trainer
25Jly99-9Dmr fst 6f :214 :442 :564 1:092 3+ Ⓢ Alw 50000N1X 66 6 2 104½ 87¼ 87¼ 711¾ Valdivia J Jr LB 119 b 31.90 81-08 Spinelessjellyfish117nk Tzigane1192 Sky Jack1175 Broke out,bumped 10
20Jun99-5Hol fst 6f :214 :444 :564 1:093 3+ Ⓢ Alw 46000N1X 80 3 5 42½ 52¾ 43½ 55 Valdivia J Jr LB 117 b 30.60 84-11 B J's Dream116¾ Blowin Easy1173½ Lesters Boy116hd No late bid 9
31May99-7Hol fst 6f :22 :45 :563 1:092 3+ Ⓢ Alw 46000N1X 89 8 2 53 31½ 21½ 32½ Valdivia J Jr LB 117 b 59.80 87-08 *Guillermo*1151½ B J's Dream1121 Let's Go Surfing1171 4 wide to turn 9
WORKS: Apr19 SA 4f gd :513 H *22/23* Apr14 SA 6f fst 1:15 B *10/14* Apr8 SA 5f fst 1:013 H *18/29* Apr1 SA 4f fst :50 B *20/21* Mar23 SA 3f fst :363 H *10/25* Jan22 SA 5f fst 1:012 H *23/56*

Lucky Hostage
Own: Lewis Terry E
ESPINOZA V (318 57 45 38 .18) 2000:(312 58 .19)

B. g. 5
Sire: Saros*GB (Sassafras*Fr)
Dam: Lady Hostage (Hostage)
Br: Lewis Terry (Cal)
Tr: Dolan John K(43 8 12 7 .19) 2000:(38 5 .13)

L 118

Life	16	4	4	4	$137,568	D.Fst	14	4	3	3	$122,968 94
2000	3	0	1	2	$19,760	Wet	1	0	1	0	$8,600 90
1999	10	4	2	2	$112,368	Turf	1	0	0	1	$6,000 88
SA	6	1	3	2	$40,560	Dist	5	3	0	0	$63,660 90

18Mar00-6SA fm *6½f ⓣ :221 :441 1:064 1:13 4+ Clm 62500 (62.5-55) 88 5 2 1½ 2hd 22 32 Dettori L LB 118 fb 5.00 91-07 ShikhAbndon1181 FindOurStr1181 LuckyHostg118no Early foot, held 3rd 8
16Feb00-5SA wf 7f :224 :45 1:10 1:224 4+ Clm 50000 (50-45) 90 1 3 1hd 1hd 2hd 2nk Desormeaux K J LB 117 fb *2.60 91-12 Grady117nk LuckyHostge1175 *SheikhAbndon*1161½ Led again,caught wire 5
5Jan00-5SA fst 6½f :222 :451 1:091 1:152 4+ Clm 50000 (50-45) 90 4 2 1hd 1hd 21 33¼ Desormeaux K J LB 118 fb 3.50 87-13 **Rhy'sQckrjck**1181 LstMngoInprs1182½ LckyHostg1182½ Dueled, weakened 7
27Nov99-8GG fst 6f :214 :444 :563 1:09 3+ OClm 40000N 84 2 4 1½ 1hd 31½ 75¼ Atkinson P LB 117 fb *2.70 90-14 Horse Camp1173 On The Rocks117hd Skol117¾ Dueled off rail, wknd 10
30Oct99-1SA fst 5½f :221 :451 :57 1:032 3+ Ⓢ CalCpStrSprH50k 94 4 4 21 21½ 22 3nk Desormeaux K J LB 117 fb 2.10 92-05 Irrelevant118no Skol115hd Lucky Hostage1171½ Late bid btwn foes 5
26Sep99-10Fpx fst 6½f :211 :45 1:102 1:17 3+ Alw 48688N1X 86 6 3 2hd 2hd 1hd 1½ Espinoza V LB 122 fb *2.00 95-05 LuckyHostage122½ ColonelKelly1161 Stephnie'sJet1191 Dueled, gamely 9
28Aug99-7Dmr fst 6f :214 :444 :573 1:103 3+ Ⓢ Alw 50000N1X 90 1 7 1hd 1hd 2hd 1hd Desormeaux K J LB 119 fb 10.30 87-14 *LuckyHostge*119hd Tzign1191¾ *ThMorrisMonro*1182 Inside,headed,gamely 8
9Aug99-6Dmr fst 6f :22 :444 :572 1:102 3+ Alw 40000s 87 5 4 1hd 2hd 1½ 1½ Desormeaux K J LB 119 fb 2.10 88-12 *Lucky Hostage*119½ Dunson1214½ What Say You115½ Gamely,chilly ride 8
18Jly99-9Hol fst 7½f :221 :444 1:093 1:283 3+ Alw 40000s 88 2 4 21½ 2hd 2hd 2½ Desormeaux K J LB 118 fb 10.70 87-11 GoldnRomr116½ *LckyHstg*1182 NtvTwStppr1172 Stalked,bid,outkicked 9
28May99-6GG fst 1⅛ :224 :46 1:104 1:431 3+ Alw 25000s 58 2 2 2hd 1hd 56½ 514½ Baze R A LB 122 fb *2.20 71-14 McNichols1225 OvertimeMgic1222½ *DimondRport*1155 Dueled 2w, empty 9
WORKS: Apr11 SA 5f fst 1:004 H *14/30* Apr1 SA 4f fst :492 B *15/21* Mar13 SA 5f fst 1:01 B *18/44* Mar7 SA 4f gd :50 H *54/83* Feb27 SA 4f fst :484 H *18/63* Feb6 SA 5f fst 1:003 H *11/46*

Norcielo
Own: Tarabilla Farms LLC
DESORMEAUX K J (312 69 52 53 .22) 2000:(291 64 .22)

B. g. 4 NORSEP97 $12,000
Sire: Norquestor (Conquistador Cielo) $5,000
Dam: Lady of Perth (Lord Gaylord)
Br: Pipes Kevin G (Ky)
Tr: Dolan John K(43 8 12 7 .19) 2000:(38 5 .13)

L 118

Life	25	8	2	4	$176,520	D.Fst	17	5 2 3	$122,400	99
2000	3	2	0	0	$53,400	Wet	5	3 0 0	$48,600	111
1999	17	6	2	3	$121,070	Turf	3	0 0 1	$5,520	86
SA	4	4	0	0	$96,600	Dist	11	5 1 1	$81,270	99

25Mar00-2SA fm *6½f ⓣ :231 :453 1:081 1:142 4↑ OClm 80000N 86 8 3 12 2hd 2hd 82 Espinoza V LB 120 f 3.40 84-14 Macward120nk DH Concurrent118 DH Dunhill118¾ Pulled,dueled,wkened 8
13Feb00-3SA wf 6½f :214 :44 1:082 1:144 4↑ Alw 50750N1X 111 3 3 1½ 11 11½ 12 Desormeaux K J LB 117 f 2.90 94-13 Norcielo1172 *Freedom Crest*1174 *Diamant*1198 Off rail to lane,held 6
6Jan00-5SA fst 6½f :212 :441 1:092 1:161 4 Clm c-(40-35) 95 6 8 69 66 3½ 11¾ Delahoussaye E LB 117 2.50 87-18 *Norcielo*1171¾ *Too Costly*117nk Valley Don1161 Inside rally 10
Claimed from Lanning Curt & Lila for $40,000, Moger Ed Jr Trainer
12Dec99-4Hol fst 7f :221 :444 1:091 1:223 3↑ OClm 40000N 73 4 6 55½ 43½ 56½ 612½ Flores D R LB 116 2.70 76-12 *WakiAmerican*1162 BoldCapital1221½ VeryCaerleon1201 Rail trip,no rally 7
20Nov99-6Hol fst 6f :222 :453 :574 1:10 3↑ Alw 35175N1X 99 1 8 89 77 62¾ 23 Delahoussaye E LB 116 4.60 84-18 *LakeWilliam*1183 Norcielo116nk VeryCerleon1202 Came out lane,late 2nd 8
31Oct99-8SA fst 6½f :214 :443 1:092 1:154 Clm 50000 (50-45) 91 1 9 84¾ 52½ 2hd 12½ Delahoussaye E LB 117 3.00 89-09 Norcielo1172½ *Musical Sweep*119½ EnzoTheBaker1182½ Split foes,rail rally 9
17Oct99-5SA fst 6f :211 :442 :57 1:094 Clm 40000 (40-35) 91 3 8 87¾ 76½ 32½ 12 Delahoussaye E LB 117 6.70 91-11 *Norcielo*1172 Waki American1172 Select Few1182½ Wide rally, handily 8
26Sep99-11Fpx fst 7f :22 :46 1:111 1:234 Clm 25000 (25-22.5) 77 5 9 73¾ 74½ 21 22½ Valenzuela F H LB 117 4.00 94-05 Sydney's Olympics1142½ *Norcielo*1172½ Celestino C M1142 Squeezed start 9
10Sep99-5BM fst 6f :223 :452 :571 1:093 Alw 33200N1X 70 3 5 62¾ 54 57 411 Castanon A L LB 118 9.30 80-13 Blue Tune1189 Is It True Mex118½ Fog City Willy1181½ 2w trn, no rally 6
11Aug99-8Bmf fst 5½f :213 :45 :574 1:043 Alw 37530N1X — 2 6 — — — — Castro J M LB 118 5.20 — 11 Fra Cadfael1181 War Devil118no Slew's Comet1181½ Stmbld start, lost jck 6
WORKS: Apr10 SA 5f fst 1:00 H 8/48 Mar21 SA 3f fst :372 B 12/14 Mar13 SA 5f fst 1:001 H 9/44 ●Mar7 SA tr.t 4f gd :49 H 1/7 Feb26 SA 4f gd :481 B 16/103 Feb2 SA 4f fst :481 B 17/62

Love All the Way
Own: Cossey Ernest
$62,500
BLACK C A (139 10 16 18 .07) 2000:(136 10 .07)

Dk. b or br g. 5
Sire: Majesterian (Pleasant Colony) $1,000
Dam: Lovewillfindaway (George Navonod)
Br: Coal Creek Farm (Wash)
Tr: Carava Jack(95 12 16 10 .13) 2000:(95 12 .13)

L 118

Life	24	6	2	4	$153,830	D.Fst	21	6 1 4	$136,955	104
2000	3	1	1	1	$51,800	Wet	3	0 1 0	$16,875	102
1999	10	2	1	1	$72,660	Turf	0	0 0 0	$0	–
SA	6	2	1	1	$84,440	Dist	8	4 0 3	$81,570	104

15Mar00-7SA fst 6f :212 :44 :562 1:091 4↑ OClm 125000N 92 6 6 68 66½ 64½ 34½ Delahoussaye E LB 118 b *1.90 88-14 FullMoonMdness1202 Apremont1182½ LovAllThWy118no Wide 1/4, rallied 6
21Feb00-1SA wf 6½f ⊗ :212 :433 1:083 1:152 4↑ Clm 100000 (100-85) 102 1 5 512 58½ 46½ 22½ Black C A LB 118 b 5.20 89-17 *WakiAmericn*1182½ LoveAllTheWy118¾ FJ'sPce1185½ Off bit slow,late 2nd 5
5Feb00-3SA fst 6f :211 :44 :563 1:094 4↑ OClm 62500 101 4 5 513 59 55 11½ Delahoussaye E LB 118 b 9.20 90-14 LovAllThWy1181½ **Lt'sGoSurfing**120¾ ThToyMn1181½ Off slow,rallied lane 5
26Dec99-7SA fst 6½f :221 :45 1:09 1:152 3↑ OClm c-62500 87 3 7 86 89¾ 76½ 56¾ Pedroza M A LB 118 b 12.60 84-08 Lake William1192½ Haflinger1172½ *Cape Canaveral*1171½ Steadied early 8
Claimed from Warrior Stable & Ruden Barry for $62,500, Molina Mark S Trainer
17Nov99-7Hol fst 6½f :222 :45 1:103 1:171 3↑ OClm 125000 86 4 5 511 512 58 54 Black C A LB 120 b 18.30 81-24 Your Halo1191 Early Pioneer119hd *Freespool*1151½ Angled in,no threat 5
23Oct99-3SA fst 1 :224 :46 1:102 1:353 3↑ OClm 100000N 90 4 5 55½ 43 46 48 Black C A LB 118 b 8.90 85-17 Crows1183½ Pleasant Drive1182 Sei1182½ Off bit slow,no rally 6
9Oct99-3SA fst 6f :212 :44 :56 1:083 3↑ OClm 62500N 104 2 5 77¾ 64½ 32½ 1¾ Black C A LB 118 b 12.50 97-08 LovAllThWy118¾ *FJ'sPc*1181½ RoundboutRock1182½ Split foes 1/4,gamely 7
Previously trained by Folting Christy V
21Sep99-11Fpx fst 6½f :222 :452 1:092 1:153 3↑ Gov's Cup H48k 92 2 5 55 54¾ 55½ 43½ Black C A LB 116 b 6.40 98-08 Emailit1191½ Devoted Pirate116½ **Windstrike**1161½ Wide 4-1/2,mild bid 5
5Sep99-7Dmr fst 7f :222 :444 1:093 1:222 3↑ OClm 62500N 89 7 8 912 912 76½ 43½ Enriquez I D LB 119 b 13.20 87-09 Son'sCorona119½ **Rahy'sQuckerjck**123hd ShotMd1193 Squeezed bit start 9
Previously trained by Molina Mark S
7Aug99-9EmDsly 6½f :221 :441 1:082 1:15 3↑ Governor's H60k 88 6 9 912 811 55½ 42½ Ventura H LB 118 b *3.10 96-12 Handy N Bold1151½ HorseCamp113¾ FindOurStar115hd Far back, late rally 9
WORKS: Apr17 SA 4f fst :49 H 19/37 Apr10 SA 5f fst 1:023 H 41/48 Apr3 SA 5f fst 1:011 H 23/35 Mar27 SA 4f fst :474 H 4/41 Mar7 SA 4f gd :492 H 35/83 Jan29 SA 4f fst :50 H 33/51

Island Caper
Own: La Canada Stables LLC & Rehanek
$62,500
PEDROZA M A (231 33 26 25 .14) 2000:(218 33 .15)

Dk. b or br g. 7
Sire: Beau Genius (Bold Ruckus) $6,000
Dam: Maui Caper (No Robbery)
Br: Buster W R & Martin D L (Ky)
Tr: Carava Jack(95 12 16 10 .13) 2000:(95 12 .13)

L 118

Life	24	7	5	0	$159,135	D.Fst	22	6 4 0	$137,535	99
2000	3	1	2	0	$37,800	Wet	2	1 1 0	$21,600	92
1999	7	1	1	0	$33,180	Turf	0	0 0 0	$0	–
SA	12	3	2	0	$77,340	Dist	15	6 2 0	$113,915	99

25Mar00-3SA fst 6f :211 :44 :571 1:094 4↑ Clm 50000 (50-45) 99 4 1 23 26 21 2hd Pedroza M A LB 118 n 7.10 90-12 *Venus Genus*118hd Island Caper118nk Grady120hd Hustled,bid,missed 7
4Mar00-10SA gd 6½f :223 :46 1:101 1:163 4↑ Clm 40000 (40-35) 92 6 1 11 1hd 2hd 2no Pedroza M A LB 118 n 6.20 85-10 **Bienfeo**118no Island Caper118½ *Venus Genus*1181 Dueled,game btwn late 7
5Feb00-4SA fst 6f :214 :451 :572 1:10 4↑ Clm 32000 (32-28) 97 6 1 1hd 2hd 11½ 1½ Pedroza M A LB 117 22.80 89-14 Island Caper117½ **Bienfeo**115nk Emailit1172 Dueled, held on gamely 9
26Dec99-3SA fst 6½f :213 :443 1:083 1:15 3↑ Clm c-(32-28) 72 2 2 43½ 67 510 415¼ Solis A LB 117 4.60 77-08 Sing Because1178 Grady117½ Klinsman1177 Came out,no rally 7
Claimed from Dryer Fellows & Smith for $32,000, Stute Warren Trainer
21Nov99-7Hol fst 6½f :224 :464 1:113 1:174 3↑ Clm 32000 (32-28) 91 6 2 2½ 1hd 3½ 44 Delahoussaye E LB 118 22.30 78-26 Bold Capital1181 Nor'easter1181½ *Sing Because*1181½ Dueled, weakened 9
24Jun99-3Hol fst 6f :213 :442 :563 1:09 4↑ Clm 40000 (40-35) 63 5 3 54½ 79½ 77½ 712¾ Delahoussaye E LB 116 5.90 79-11 *Dynamic Deed*116nk **Windstrike**1174 *Path ToPower*1161 Threw head start 7
3Jun99-4Hol fst 6f :221 :444 :574 1:094 4↑ Clm 32000 (32-28) 89 6 1 3nk 2hd 1hd 2½ Solis A LB 116 3.30 87-13 Strategist116½ Island Caper1162 Free World1165 3 wide,worn down late 6
10Apr99-1SA fst 6f :214 :442 :563 1:093 4↑ Clm 40000 (40-35) 56 2 7 77 715 615 617 Delahoussaye E LB 118 4.00 75-15 ColdNCalculating1181½ PathToPower1185 Jdl1214½ Off slw,lugged out 3/8 7
20Feb99-3SA fst 6f :213 :443 :564 1:091 4↑ Clm 50000 (50-45) 87 5 3 35 44½ 54½ 53½ Delahoussaye E LB 118 3.80 90-13 Hilltown118nk Destiny's Venture118hd Rotsaluck1102½ Broke akwardly 6
30Jan99-3SA fst 6f :214 :45 :571 1:10 4↑ Clm 40000 (40-35) 86 2 2 2hd 2hd 2hd 1½ Delahoussaye E LB 118 4.30 90-07 Island Caper118½ Mc Fig118½ Sir Nibbles1181½ Dueled btwn foes,game 6
WORKS: Apr13 SA 5f fst 1:02 H 20/29 Apr6 SA 4f fst :493 H 16/23 ●Mar16 SA 4f fst :473 H 1/32 Feb26 SA 5f gd 1:011 H 46/169 Jan29 SA 4f fst :49 H 18/51 Jan22 SA 6f fst 1:153 H 26/33

Rahy's Quackerjack
Own: Warren Benjamin C
ENRIQUEZ I D (207 10 16 17 .05) 2000:(196 11 .06)

B. h. 5
Sire: Rahy (Blushing Groom*Fr) $40,000
Dam: Brett's Quack (Quack)
Br: Whitney Mrs C V (Ky)
Tr: Wickliffe Montie G(4 0 0 1 .00) 2000:(4 0 .00)

L 118

Life	22	5	3	2	$161,664	D.Fst	14	5 1 1	$139,900	106
2000	3	1	0	0	$26,940	Wet	1	0 0 0	$1,140	85
1999	13	2	3	2	$101,584	Turf	7	0 2 1	$20,624	93
SA	6	2	0	0	$44,560	Dist	6	2 0 0	$49,020	101

8Mar00-5SA sly 6½f :214 :443 1:094 1:161 4↑ OClm 62500N 85 5 5 3nk 31½ 54 58½ Enriquez I D LB 118 11.10 78-23 BeumesDVnis1183½ **Windstrik**1201½ OutstndingHro1181½ 3 wide, weakened 7
15Jan00-4SA fm *6½f ⓣ :221 :441 1:07 1:13 4↑ Clm c-(62.5-55) 80 9 2 21 22 42½ 74¾ Nakatani C S LB 118 5.20 87-06 FJ'sPace1181½ SheikhAbndon117½ OneMnArmy118½ Stalked btwn,no bid 11
Claimed from Premier Stables for $62,500, Baffert Bob Trainer
5Jan00-5SA fst 6½f :222 :451 1:091 1:152 4↑ Clm c-(50-45) 98 5 1 2hd 2hd 11 11 Nakatani C S LB 118 *1.30 91-13 Rh'sQckrjck1181 LstMngInprs1182½ **LckHstg**1182½ 3 wide turn,led,gamely 7
Claimed from Wahlgren Family Trust for $50,000, Mitchell Mike Trainer
18Dec99-6Hol fm 5½f ⓣ :222 :451 :57 1:024 3↑ OClm 62500 90 4 5 51¾ 41½ 2½ 21½ Nakatani C S LB 118 6.50 88-11 Srigor1181½ DH DevotdPirt118 DH *Rhy'sQuckrjck*118½ Inside bid,willingly 9
26Nov99-7Hol fm 5½f ⓣ :22 :443 :562 1:022 3↑ OClm 80000 85 2 8 76 73¾ 43½ 32¾ Pincay L Jr LB 118 4.70 89-07 HookCall118nk D TryJory1182½ Rahy'sQuackerjck1181 Off bit slow,rallied 8
Placed second through disqualification.
14Nov99-3Hol fst 6½f :221 :45 1:091 1:152 3↑ OClm 62500N 94 1 6 42 2½ 1hd 31½ Stevens G L LB 118 3.10 93-12 MellowFellow118½ RilMn118¾ Rhy'sQuckrjck1183 Off bit slw,led,caught 6
9Oct99-3SA fst 6f :212 :44 :56 1:083 3↑ OClm 62500N 92 4 4 43½ 43½ 42½ 44¾ Valenzuela P A LB 122 2.70 92-08 **LoveAllTheWy**118¾ *FJ'sPc*1181½ RoundboutRock1182½ 4 wide into stretch 7
5Sep99-7Dmr fst 7f :222 :444 1:093 1:222 3↑ OClm 62500N 96 5 4 2½ 2hd 2hd 2½ Nakatani C S LB 123 *1.50 90-09 Son's Corona119½ Rahy'sQuackerjack123hd ShotMd1193 Dueled,willingly 9
30Aug99-7Dmr fst 6½f :222 :444 1:092 1:154 3↑ Alw 52250N1X 106 5 4 2hd 11 11 12 Nakatani C S LB 119 3.50 92-16 Rhy'sQckrjck1192 ImprssvGrds1184 BottlOfRm1232 Inside duel,cleared 9
22Aug99-7Dmr fst 6f :221 :45 :571 1:093 3↑ OClm 62500 101 1 2 21½ 21 11 11 Nakatani C S LB 119 3.80 92-13 *Rhy'sQuckerjck*1191 Vldour119½ **Windstrike**1196 Stalked,bid,held game 5
WORKS: Apr19 SA 3f gd :353 H 2/19 Apr9 SA 5f fst 1:012 H 25/53 Apr2 SA 6f fst 1:141 H 13/17 Mar20 SA 5f fst 1:02 H 24/39 Feb27 SA 5f fst 1:03 H 53/60 Jan29 Fpx 4f fst :504 H 17/25

Blade Prospector (Brz)
Own: Raza Stable
BERRIO O A (131 15 8 15 .11) 2000:(124 14 .11)

Dk. b or br h. 5
Sire: Music Prospector (Crafty Prospector)
Dam: Met Blade*Brz (Restless Jet)
Br: Haras Rosa do Sul (Brz)
Tr: Avila A C(53 9 9 6 .17) 2000:(53 10 .19)

118

Life	11	6	1	0	$21,590	D.Fst	5	4	0	0	$13,504	–
1999	7	3	1	0	$13,166	Wet	3	1	1	0	$4,180	–
1998	4	3	0	0	$8,424	Turf	3	1	0	0	$3,906	–
SA	0	0	0	0	$0	Dist	0	0	0	0	$0	–

Previously trained by M R Campos

12Sep99♦ Cdad Jardim(Brz)	fst *1	LH 1:34^{1} 4↑	Classico Dante Marchione(Lstd) Stk 8900	17¼	Duarte L	132	–	Blade Prospector132 7¼ Krajicek132 Coubertain132	14
13Aug99♦ Gavea(Brz)	gd *1	LH 1:39 3↑	Classico Breno Caldas (Listed) Stk 11500	47¾	Duarte L	130	–	Pit Club136 Rio do Prata130 Gallaway Blue126	15
24Jly99♦ Cdad Jardim(Brz)	fst *6½f	LH 1:14^{2} 3↑	Allowance Race Alw 5500	114¼	Duarte L	123	–	Blade Prospector123^{14} Cartoon119 Amor Por Inteiro123	7
2May99♦ Cdad Jardim(Brz)	sly *1	LH 1:36^{3} 3↑	Cl Renato Junqueira Netto(Lst) Stk 10100	2^{nk}	Duarte L	128	–	Recalque128^{nk} Blade Prospector128 Tenpins132	6
10Apr99♦ Cdad Jardim(Brz)	sly *1	LH 1:35^{1} 3↑	Allowance Race Alw 3600	12½	Duarte L	119	–	Blade Prospector119 2½ Recalque119 Tenpins130	8
7Mar99♦ Gavea(Brz)	fm *1	Ⓣ LH 1:34	GP Estado do Rio de Janeiro-G1 Stk 28200	16^{22}		123	–	Funtastic123 Beijoqueiro123 Smoky Salmon123	18
10Jan99♦ Cdad Jardim(Brz)	fst *1¼	LH 2:06^{3} 3↑	Classico Piratininga-G2 Stk 37100	56¾		121	–	Jaitness130 Gran Ricci130 Aquecido130	14
28Nov98♦ Cdad Jardim(Brz)	fst *7f	LH 1:25	Allowance Race Alw 5000	1^{8}		123	–	Blade Prospector123^{8} Recalque117 Surreal123	9
22Oct98♦ Cdad Jardim(Brz)	fst *6½f	LH 1:17^{2}	Allowance Race Alw 5100	16½		123	–	Blade Prospector123 6½ Bebebar123 Runner Fighter123	7
28Jun98♦ Cdad Jardim(Brz)	gd *1	Ⓣ LH 1:36^{2}	Qlfr for Adhemar Almeida Prado Alw 8700	12^{16}		121	–	Limao121 Arrogant Rider121 Beautiful Dancer121	12

WORKS: Apr10 SA 5f fst :58^{1} H *2/48* Apr2 SA 3f fst :36^{4} H *11/19* ●Mar11 SA 6f gd 1:12^{3} H *1/18* Mar3 SA 7f fst 1:30 H *8/9* Feb25 SA 6f my 1:13^{1} H (d)*3/11* Feb19 SA 6f fst 1:13^{1} H *2/25*

Bienfeo
Own: Equils James W & Marcia S
$62,500
NAKATANI C S (322 72 60 47 .22) 2000:(317 72 .23)

B. g. 8
Sire: Video Ranger (Cox's Ridge) $3,500
Dam: Zonar (Barachois)
Br: Cho Myung Kwon (Cal)
Tr: Hess R B Jr(102 21 14 14 .21) 2000:(95 20 .21)

L 118

Life	49	8	8	6	$260,396	D.Fst	38	6	7	5	$183,221	102
2000	5	2	1	1	$74,920	Wet	7	2	1	1	$75,950	97
1999	9	2	2	0	$44,355	Turf	4	0	0	0	$1,225	91
SA	19	5	4	2	$161,790	Dist	18	3	4	3	$105,526	102

30Mar00–5SA fst 7f	:22^{3} :45^{2} 1:09^{3} 1:22^{3} 4↑ ⓈOClm c-40000	97	3 2	5^{2} 4^{3}	4^{2} 3^{1}	Berrio O A	LB 122	2.70	91–14	Wild NGolden111¾ MargedsDitto118^{nk} Bienfeo122 1¼	4wd into lane,late bid	8
Claimed from Lemalu Stables for $40,000, Avila A C Trainer												
4Mar00–10SA gd 6½f	:22^{3} :46 1:10^{1} 1:16^{3} 4↑ Clm 35000 (40–35)	92	5 3	4^{2}½ 4^{2}	3^{1}½ 1no	Berrio O A	LB 118	*2.10	85–10	Bienfeo118^{no} **Island Caper**118½ *Venus Genus*118^{1}	4wd bid,just up	7
21Feb00–1SA wf 6½f ⊗	:21^{2} :43^{3} 1:08^{3} 1:15^{2} 4↑ Clm 85000 (100–85)	87	5 2	4^{5}½ 3^{5}	3^{5}½ 4^{8}½	Berrio O A	LB 115	4.50	82–17	*WkiAmericn*118 2¼ **LoveAllTheWy**118¾ FJ'sPce118 5½	Lacked late response	5
13Feb00–1SA wf 6½f	:21^{4} :44^{4} 1:09^{2} 1:16 4↑ ⓈOClm 40000	97	3 3	4^{5} 4^{2}	3^{1} 1^{2}½	Berrio O A	LB 118	4.10	88–13	Bienfeo118 2½ Chikalis118^{hd} Stephanie's Jet118^{2}	4 wide turn,rallied	5
5Feb00–4SA fst 6f	:21^{4} :45^{1} :57^{2} 1:10 4↑ Clm 28000 (32–28)	96	3 7	8^{8}¼ 6^{5}	5^{3}¾ 2½	Berrio O A	LB 115	9.30	88–14	**Island Caper**117½ *Bienfeo*115^{nk} Emailit117^{2}	Split turn,late bid	9
11Dec99–1Hol fst 6f	:22 :45^{1} :57^{4} 1:10^{1} 3↑ Clm c-(16–14)	93	5 1	3^{3} 3^{2}½	2^{1}½ 2^{nk}	Pedroza M A	LB 118	3.30	86–20	Strategist118^{nk} Bienfeo118 2½ *Star's Wild*118^{7}	Bid btwn,willingly	6
Claimed from Lakeforest Stable for $16,000, Carava Jack Trainer												
24Oct99–5SA fst 6½f	:21^{4} :44^{3} 1:09^{3} 1:16^{1} 3↑ Clm 32000 (32–28)	84	9 1	6^{3}¾ 7^{4}¼	5^{3}½ 5^{4}½	Solis A	LB 118	9.00	82–14	Paramour118^{hd} Tower Full118 1½ Grady118^{1}	4 wide turn	9
23Sep99–1BM fst 6f	:22^{4} :45^{3} :57^{2} 1:09^{3} 3↑ Clm c-(32–30)	75	1 5	4^{3} 4^{6}	5^{5}½ 5^{8}	Baze R A	LB 117	2.30	83–15	Integrated Disc117 5½ Ole Moses119^{nk} Mr Ice Age117^{nk}	Inside, no rally	5
Claimed from Sangara K K for $32,000, Arterburn Lonnie Trainer												
15Sep99–7BM fst 6f	:22^{2} :45^{2} :57^{3} 1:10^{4} 3↑ Clm c-(25–22.5)	90	5 2	5^{3}½ 4^{1}¼	1^{hd} 1½	Castro J M	LB 119	*1.90	85–19	Bienfeo119½ All A Con117^{3} Linear115^{no}	Fanned 5w trn, drvng	6
Claimed from Ocean View Stable & Dennis Kanakari for $25,000, Hess R B Trainer Previously trained by Hess R B Jr												
14Aug99–10Dmr fst 6f	:21^{4} :44^{4} :57^{1} 1:10 3↑ Clm 32000 (32–28)	77	7 5	7^{4}½ 7^{6}¾	6^{5}¾ 7^{7}½	Antley C W	LB 119	5.10	83–13	Grady119½ F J's Pace119^{no} *Shot Md*119^{hd}	Steadied 3-1/2 & 3/8	11

WORKS: Apr14 SA 4f fst :49^{1} H *16/32* Mar23 SA 4f fst :46^{3} H *2/33* Jan28 SA 5f gd 1:03^{3} H *37/89*

The eighth race at Santa Anita on April 21, 2000 (PPs are listed above) is a much more complex example of the value to be gained from a logical structure to pace analysis. This is not a simple race. It is, however, readily segmented into the three pace scenarios. It should be immediately apparent that there is a wealth of early speed present in the race. But what is the quality of that speed? What are the chances of multiple early-pace horses surviving the matchups? Will the closers have an adequate pace at which to run? By answering these questions, the reader should be able to develop a reasonable betting strategy.

PRENUPTUAL DEAL: "E." 22 estimated time at the first call.

This developing 4-year-old seems to thrive on the lead. He has been most effective when he can run the first quarter in about 22 seconds. Both wins were on-pace efforts after a relatively slow quarter-mile time. His chances in this field depend upon sharing the lead through a comfortable first fraction. Prenuptual Deal's last race was his best ever and it was after a lengthy layoff. He is a perfect candidate for the dreaded "bounce."

TREASUREATHEND: "X." 23 estimated time at the first call.

This is a weak horse and he is coming off an extended layoff. When compared to other runners in the race, his Beyer Speed Figures are downright dreadful. Both his wins were off-pace efforts. His presence in this race is inexplicable and he rates an "X" for no chance.

WINDSTRIKE: "S." 22⅘ estimated time at the first call.

Windstrike is a decent closer with the ability to rally from far off the early pace. He is clearly better on a wet track and owns a poor 21-2-4-9 record on dry surfaces. This is a typical box score for many of these "S" types. He has several Beyer figures that fit this class level, but his overall record is a turnoff.

LET'S GO SURFING: "E." 21⅕ estimated time at the first call.

This is a talented front-runner who has managed to gain the lead in all of his recent races. He has shown he can still record lofty Beyer figures after dueling on the lead through a 21⅕ quarter-mile. His presence in this race does not bode well for the other "E" runners. Nor will it favor pressers, who, by definition, depend on being close-up to the pace. However, there are several negatives:

1) After a high-figure placing in the Cal Cup Sprint, and two strong allowance races, he is being risked for a claiming price for the first time since the claim.
2) A gap in training from February 5, 2000 to March 23, 2000 is cause for alarm. It is reasonable to assume that he is not quite the horse he was before the layoff.
3) He will be a certain underlay in the betting, especially in light of the possible negatives.

To the horse's credit, trainer Bill Spawr does not drop him to a ridiculously low claiming price. There must be some life left in this 5-year-old gelding.

LUCKY HOSTAGE: "E/P." 21⅘ estimated time at the first call.

Lucky Hostage is a hard-trying sprinter who is most comfortable on the lead. He has shown some ability to press the pace, but his wins have been on the lead. He can stand heat, but the probable pace of Let's Go Surfing should not be to his liking. Except for one race at 5½ furlongs, his Beyer figures are woefully lacking when compared to most of these runners.

NORCIELO: "S." 23 estimated time at the first call.

Norcielo managed the lead on a wet-fast track and then freaked to a best-ever Beyer figure. His probable position in this race is difficult to determine because of his recent on-pace races. The bulk of the data shows him to be an "S" type, and we should base the analysis on that probability. He wins races and represents the type of closer that should be preferred. His record at Santa Anita is remarkable and he has several Beyer figures that fit with these.

LOVE ALL THE WAY: "S." 23⅗ estimated time at the first call.

One thing of which we can be certain: He will be last in the early stages. However, that does not matter to this late-running sprinter, especially when we examine his triple-digit Beyers and his record at today's distance. Apparently, Love All the Way would run over broken glass if it were required. We have two quality closers to analyze in the three pace scenarios.

ISLAND CAPER: "E." 21⅘ estimated time at the first call.

His last race aside, this 7-year-old wants a share of the lead for his best effort. The last race may have been an aberrant performance and the finish merely illusionary. The 25⅘ final quarter, after a freakishly fast early pace, served to bring most of the field together at the wire. Island Caper ran on evenly and may have been simply dragged along to the finish. That does not appear to be a winning style for this horse.

RAHY'S QUACKERJACK: "E/P." 22⅖ estimated time at the first call.

Rahy's Quackerjack has declined rapidly since leaving the barn of top claiming trainer Mike Mitchell. He is an E/P but he needs a slow pace for his best efforts. He will not get a slow first quarter in this race.

BLADE PROSPECTOR: "X." No estimated time at the first call.

This 5-year-old import presents a minor problem to the analysis. Although he was a capable sprinter in his native Brazil, he has never raced at this exact distance. Class may be an issue, as should running style. His workout line shows a gap from March 11 to April 2. Experience has taught me to ignore these imports when sprinting. Most handicappers would be well served by the same policy.

BIENFEO: "S." 23 estimated time at the first call.

Although he has several races that border on the "presser" label, Bienfeo has always had several horses in front of him at the first call. His wins have been from the rear of his fields, and to label him as an "S/P" could be a costly mistake when it's time to analyze the pressers' scenario.

Let's sort the competition by probable first-call position:

THE COMPETITORS:

Let's Go Surfing	"E1"	$21\frac{1}{5}$
Lucky Hostage	"E/P2"	$21\frac{4}{5}$
Island Caper	"E2"	$21\frac{4}{5}$
Prenuptial Deal	"E4"	22
Rahy's Quackerjack	"E/P5"	$22\frac{2}{5}$
Windstrike	"S6"	$22\frac{4}{5}$
Norcielo	"S7"	23
Bienfeo	"S7"	23
Treasureathend	"X9"	23
Love All the Way	"S10"	$23\frac{3}{5}$
Blade Prospector	"X"	??

THE PACE ANALYSIS

We will take them one at a time, but there is no question as to the probable leader, Let's Go Surfing. Unless he regresses severely, he will be the one to catch and is the one to use as the measuring stick for this race. Other on-pace runners figure to pay dearly for that privilege.

EARLY PACE:

Let's Go Surfing	"E1"	$21\frac{1}{5}$
Lucky Hostage	"E/P2"	$21\frac{4}{5}$
Island Caper	"E2"	$21\frac{4}{5}$
Prenuptial Deal	"E4"	22
Rahy's Quackerjack	"E/P5"	$22\frac{2}{5}$

Let's Go Surfing will almost certainly gain the lead and, unless physical problems or a poor start should hamper him, he should be around until the very end. The probable first-quarter time should be about 21⅕. The other on-pace runners will have to duplicate that time and then hope to survive.

The other early runners and their probable chances:

1) Lucky Hostage is an "E/P2" runner and will have to duplicate his early speed at Fairplex to gain his customary position. That particular "bull-ring" requires brilliantly fast first quarters to gain position into the turn. This makes the effort misleading when compared to races around one turn. It also resulted in one of his poorer speed figures. He may try to challenge this field early, but his Beyer figures do not compare favorably to the other main contenders. His best efforts have been on the pace, and an early effort here will cost him dearly in the late stages. The handicapper is best served by eliminating this runner from any betting considerations.

2) Island Caper is an "E2" without a prayer of gaining the early lead. His last race aside, he is an "E" horse with virtually no chance in this matchup. He is a noncontender.

3) Prenuptual Deal is an "E4," which is nearly always a losing position. It will become readily apparent that this position for an "E" horse is one of the worst profiles possible. He is lightly raced, so perhaps he'll rate behind the early speed. Only a big price on the board should tempt the player to bet him to do something he has never successfully accomplished.

4) Rahy's Quackerjack is an "E/P5," which is also a terrible position for this type of runner. His usual 22⅖ quarter-mile will relegate him to the unfamiliar role of closer, something for which he has shown no previous inclination.

At this point in the analysis it is prudent to eliminate all of the early runners except Let's Go Surfing. You will occasionally err in calculating these positions, but in the majority of races you will have accurately estimated the probable early pace.

THE PRESSERS:

This race is begging for a presser capable of successfully pressing a sub-21⅘ quarter. Lucky Hostage and Rahy's Quackerjack have shown the ability to press and win, but neither survived the early-pace analysis. Neither horse has successfully pressed the type of pace this race should produce. The closers figure to run past them late.

THE CLOSERS:

In the first example we had legitimate threats from both the early and presser groups. It would have been foolhardy to support an "S" runner in that race. When the early and presser groups produce the top contenders, it is usually prudent for the player to stay within that framework. The winner will most often come from those groups. Closers, without a significant class advantage, will generally have too much to do in the final stages. However, when those scenarios fail to survive close scrutiny, the closers will have a big say in the outcome.

In this example, the closers should have a relatively easy time overhauling the casualties from the other two scenarios. Only Let's Go Surfing remains a serious threat, but his probable price and possible form flaws should direct the thoughtful player in another direction. If a high-percentage closer can be found, and the price is fair, the bet should come from that scenario.

THE CLOSERS:

Windstrike	"S6"	$22\frac{4}{5}$
Norcielo	"S7"	23
Bienfeo	"S7"	23
Love All the Way	"S10"	$23\frac{3}{5}$

1) Windstrike has a decent late run but his ability to win on a dry track is a major question mark. He has several competitive Beyer figures but none resulted in a win. Windstrike is the type of low-percentage closer that I caution the reader to avoid in nearly all situations.

2) Norcielo is the opposite of Windstrike. He wins a high percentage of his races, loves this distance, and is undefeated at Santa Anita. With the exception of one freakishly high figure on a wet-fast track, his winning Beyer figures are several lengths below the other main contenders. He is a threat, but only if Let's Go Surfing and Love All the Way do not run to their capabilities.

3) Bienfeo should also be running at the end, but he appears to be a cut below this class level. The possible pace does favor a strong race and his Beyer figures do not compare favorably to the main contenders.

4) Love All the Way is a deep closer but he still manages to win more than his fair share of races. This is his perfect distance and he regularly records triple-digit Beyer figures. He is the high-figure closer and he deserves much respect.

THE FINAL ANALYSIS:

THE VIABLE CONTENDERS, IN ORDER OF THEIR EXPECTED WIN PROBABILITY:

Let's Go Surfing	"E1"
Love All the Way	"S10"
Norcielo	"S7"

Let's Go Surfing, and his "E1" label, offers the ideal long-term win probability. At his best, he is capable of racing the other early-speed types into defeat while still recording a triple-digit Beyer Speed Figure. At a fair price, and without any serious form questions, he should be the play. But the price will *not* be fair and there are some possible form defects. A "P" type would be the ideal play, but none is to be found in here. There are, however, two very good closers: Norcielo and Love All the Way.

Love All the Way is a deep closer but he possesses the class and winning spirit lacking in most late runners. When confronted with a fast pace, he manages triple-digit speed figures. He should get that pace today. He is the second-most-probable winner and is bettable at a fair price. An acceptable price depends upon personal style and will vary with each player. I would accept 4-1 on Love All the Way.

Norcielo may be a cut below the other two main contenders, but he does fit today's class level and probable pace scenario. He is the third-most-likely winner and is bettable at 5-1 or higher (see race chart, opposite).

A FEW FINAL THOUGHTS

Route Races

Races beyond 7½ furlongs are handled in nearly the same manner as sprints. Pace styles and positions are equally important in these longer races. Horses unable to gain their favored positions are still highly vulnerable and should be eliminated from most betting decisions. The handicapper should also be aware of the following points:

EIGHTH RACE

Santa Anita

APRIL 21, 2000

6 FURLONGS. (1.07¹) OPTIONAL CLAIMING. Purse $57,000 (plus $14,250 State Bred) FOR FOUR-YEAR-OLDS AND UPWARD WHICH ARE NON-WINNERS OF EITHER $3,000 TWICE OTHER THAN MAIDEN, CLAIMING, STARTER OR NON-WINNERS OF THREE OR CLAIMING PRICE OF $62,500. 122 lbs. Non-Winners of two races since February 19 allowed 2 lbs.; of a race other thanmaiden since then, 4 lbs. (Horses eligible only to the above allowance conditions are preferred). (Winner races when entered for $50,000 or less not considered).

Value of Race: $59,850 Winner $34,200; second $14,250; third $6,840; fourth $3,420; fifth $1,140.   Mutuel Pool $439,725.00 Exacta Pool $266,365.00 Quinella Pool $37,250.00 Trifecta Pool $331,656.00

Last Raced	Horse	M/Eqt. A.Wt	PP	St	¼	½	Str	Fin	Jockey	Cl'g Pr	Odds $1
15Mar00 7SA³	Love All the Way	LBb 5 118	7	10	9½	8½	6½	1½	Black C A	62500	5.70
5Feb00 3SA²	Let's Go Surfing	LB 5 118	4	5	1½	1½	11	2no	Pincay L Jr	62500	2.00
25Mar00 2SA⁸	Norcielo	LBf 4 118	6	6	4hd	3hd	3hd	3½	Desormeaux K J		3.20
12Sep99 CJ¹	Blade Prospector-BR	LB 5 118	10	4	5hd	42	42½	4½	Berrio O A		10.90
1Apr00 2SA¹	Prenuptual Deal	LB 4 120	1	8	73	62	5hd	51	Delahoussaye E		6.10
18Mar00 6SA³	Lucky Hostage	LBbf 5 118	5	7	2½	2½	2hd	6hd	Espinoza V		45.20
25Mar00 3SA⁴	Windstrike	LB 6 118	3	9	10²	10²	7½	75	Solis A	62500	9.30
8Mar00 5SA⁵	Rahy's Quackerjack	LB 5 118	9	3	82	92	9½	8½	Enriquez I D		49.40
14Jly99 5Hol⁸	Treasureathend	LB 4 118	2	11	11	11	10¹	9½	Valdivia J Jr	62500	92.60
30Mar00 5SA³	Bienfeo	LB 8 118	11	2	6½	51	82	10½	Nakatani C S	62500	16.60
25Mar00 3SA²	Island Caper	LB 7 118	8	1	3½	71	11	11	Pedroza M A	62500	24.50

OFF AT 6:35 Start Good. Won driving. Track fast.

TIME :21², :44¹, :56³, 1:09² (:21.53, :44.38, :56.73, 1:09.48)

$2 Mutuel Prices:

7–LOVE ALL THE WAY	13.40	5.40	3.20
4–LET'S GO SURFING		3.40	2.60
6–NORCIELO			3.40

$1 EXACTA 7–4 PAID $17.50 $2 QUINELLA 4–7 PAID $16.80 $1 TRIFECTA 7–4–6 PAID $77.10

Dk. b. or br. g, by Majesterian–Lovewillfindaway, by George Navonod. Trainer Carava Jack. Bred by Coal Creek Farm (Wash).

LOVE ALL THE WAY settled outside, angled in and moved up on the turn, then surged late under urging between rivals to get up. LET'S GO SURFING had good early speed and dueled inside, inched away in midstretch but was caught late. NORCIELO was close up off the rail on the backstretch, came three deep into the stretch and went willingly to the wire. BLADE PROSPECTOR (BRZ) had good position wide between horses on the backstretch, continued outside on the turn and four wide into the stretch and also went on well to the end. PRENUPTUAL DEAL a bit crowded after the start, was sent along inside, came out for the stretch and put in a late bid. LUCKY HOSTAGE dueled outside the runner-up to the stretch, continued on well past midstretch but weakened late. WINDSTRIKE broke in a bit, was unhurried a bit off the rail to the stretch and improved position inside. RAHY'S QUACKERJACK was allowed to settle outside, went five wide on the turn and into the stretch and did not rally. TREASUREATHEND was a bit crowded early, saved ground without early speed and failed to menace. BIENFEO was well placed four wide on the backstretch, dropped back on the turn and weakened. ISLAND CAPER was sent along three deep early, stalked the pace between horses on the backstretch, also dropped back on the turn and weakened.

Owners— 1, Cossey Ernest; 2, Arrias Fred & Donn Ron; 3, Tarabilla Farms Inc; 4, Raza Stable; 5, Vreeland James R; 6, Lewis Terry E; 7, Thom Tom A; 8, Warren Benjamin C; 9, Stull Debra & Tom; 10, Equils James W & Marcia S; 11, La Canada Stables LLC & Rehanek

Trainers—1, Carava Jack; 2, Spawr Bill; 3, Dolan John K; 4, Avila A C; 5, Palma Hector O; 6, Dolan John K; 7, West Ted H; 8, Wickliffe Montie G; 9, Wilson James R II; 10, Hess R B Jr; 11, Carava Jack

1) The projected early speed at the first call is estimated at the end of a half-mile. Typical times range from around 46 to 49 seconds. Turf races will have a greater range of first-call times and will be less reliable.

2) Rating tactics have a much greater effect on longer races, thus making the estimate of time and position more difficult and less reliable. A poorly judged ride can skewer the entire analysis. The possible rewards of the system remain, but the reader should be aware that more mistakes will be made in route races.

3) Many routers are more flexible in their running styles. It will often be necessary to include a single horse in all three pace scenarios. This is especially true in turf racing.

Turf Racing:

The principles in this chapter also apply for turf racing, but with three additional points:

1) Quantifying running positions is exceedingly more difficult. Rating tactics, more than track speed, dictates the early running times. First-call times are sometimes painfully slow. The player often watches in horror as a jockey strangles a free-running front-runner. In my opinion, that strategy only serves to bring the closers into play earlier and often sacrifices the best chances of the early runners.

2) Most horses show wide variations in the first-call times of their races. When running on the turf, "patience" is the name of the game and times can fluctuate wildly.

3) The "E-P-S" labels are still effective, but the player is best served by estimating each runner's probable position from his customary position, rather than from any projected times. Recorded running times are less reliable and may be far off the mark.

COMPARATIVE PAR TIMES

The handicapper faces a race at $1\frac{1}{16}$ miles with the following three equal class "E" runners:

Horse A is from Lone Star and can run his top race after a first half in $47\frac{4}{5}$.
Horse B hails from Laurel and is comfortable on a first fraction of $48\frac{1}{5}$.
Horse C ships from Monmouth and can handle a first call of $47\frac{1}{5}$.
Which of these three runners figures as "E1" in the paper race? This is, of course, a trick question. *All three horses* should be given an "E1" label and a pace duel should ensue. The times listed above are the normal (par) first-call times for midlevel claiming races over these surfaces. The thoughtful handicapper must be aware of the idiosyncrasies of each track on his or her circuit. The player must also understand the feeder tracks from which horses ship into the local circuit. Consider the following sprint scenario from Churchill Downs:

Horse A is from a Churchill race at six furlongs and has effective 21⅘ early speed. Horse B's race was also at Churchill, but at the distance of 6½ furlongs. His estimated first-call time is 22⅘.

ANOTHER TRICK question: Will "A" be the "E1" in this early-pace scenario? The two horses actually have equivalent first quarter-mile times. The disparity in early speed between "A" and "B" is merely illusionary. The midlevel claiming pars for six and 6½ furlongs at Churchill Downs reveal a difference of five lengths at the first call. The positioning of the timer at Churchill explains this disparity, but the "why" is unimportant. Lack of awareness of this inconsistency can cause gross miscalculations when analyzing an early-pace scenario.

I recommend the reader spend enough time with results charts to determine the approximate times recorded by midlevel claiming horses on local and feeder tracks. The same goal can be accomplished with a careful examination of local past performances. There are also several sources that can provide comparative par times for most of the tracks in the United States. I strongly advise obtaining a set of these pars.

Sound Of The West
Own: Peace John H
DAVIS R G (159 21 22 20 .13) 2000:(438 58 .13)

B. f. 3 (Apr)
Sire: West by West (Gone West) $12,500
Dam: Burst of Sound (Stop the Music)
Br: Sporting Life Stables Inc (Ky)
Tr: Arnold George R II(35 4 3 6 .11) 2000:(191 26 .14)

L 121

Life	4	1	1	1	$38,570	D.Fst	3	0	1	1	$13,370 75
2000	4	1	1	1	$38,570	Wet	0	0	0	0	$0 –
1999	0	M	0	0	$0	Turf	1	1	0	0	$25,200 80
Bel	1	0	0	1	$4,620	Dist	0	0	0	0	$0 –

21Jun00-5Bel fm 1¼ Ⓣ :482 1:123 1:371 2:02 3↑ ⒻMd Sp Wt 42k 80 7 8 98½ 64 42 1nk Davis R G L116 3.80 81-18 SndOfThWst116nk MssClssActn1232¾ Rlphr1161¼ Quick move second turn 9
8Jun00-3Bel fst 1 1/16 ⊗ :23 :461 1:111 1:432 3↑ ⒻMd Sp Wt 42k 75 2 9 63¼ 63¼ 43½ 33 Davis R G L116 6.90e 77-21 BowlOfEmrlds116¾ *A.O.L.Hys*1162¼ *SndOfThWst*1163 Rated, good finish 11
20Apr00-6Aqu fst 1 :231 :464 1:111 1:354 ⒻMd Sp Wt 42k 62 2 5 54¼ 56 57½ 26¾ Davis R G L120 4.10 82-11 RosieDooley1206¾ SoundOfTheWst1201½ SndAngl115½ Going well rail late 5
12Mar00-2GP fst 7f :223 :454 1:113 1:244 ⒻMd Sp Wt 35k 50 5 10 64¾ 78½ 712 713½ Coa E M 121 14.50 62-20 Sunny Laugh1212 Irving's Baby1212¾ Jill's Zi Zi1212 Bmpd, checked start 10
WORKS: Jly15 Bel 5f gd 1:07 B (d) *2/3* Jly9 Bel 5f fst 1:013 B *13/25* Jly2 Bel 5f fst 1:05 B *16/16* Jun4 Bel 4f fst :513 B *40/44* May25 Bel 5f gd 1:032 B *13/15* May15 Bel 5f fst 1:012 B *10/19*

Zoftig
Own: Glencrest Stable & Walts-David St
ST JULIEN M (3 0 0 0 .00) 2000:(688 89 .13)

Gr/ro f. 3 (Apr) KEESEP98 $50,000
Sire: Cozzene (Caro*Ire) $40,000
Dam: Mrs. Marcos (Private Account)
Br: Glencrest Farm LLC (Ky)
Tr: Doyle Michael J (—) 2000:(159 17 .11)

Blinkers ON
L 121

Life	8	3	2	1	$401,024	D.Fst	4	2	0	1	$242,374 86
2000	7	2	2	1	$384,224	Wet	1	0	1	0	$110,050 92
1999	1	1	0	0	$16,800	Turf	3	1	1	0	$48,600 86
Bel	0	0	0	0	$0	Dist	0	0	0	0	$0 –

24Jun00-8AP sf 1⅛ Ⓣ :482 1:132 1:40 1:522 ⒻPucker Up-G3 86 3 4 62 62½ 54¼ 21½ St Julien M L118 5.10 73-22 Solvig1211½ Zoftig118hd Impending Bear118¾ Second best 6
22May00-8WO fst 1 1/16 :224 :47 1:13 1:482 ⒻSelene-G1 83 2 8 77¾ 54½ 2hd 11 St Julien M L116 *1.05 65-36 Zoftig1161 North Lake Jane116½ Inspired Kiss1184¾ Driving inside 8
5May00-9CD fst 1⅛ :461 1:111 1:373 1:501 ⒻKy Oaks-G1 82 2 11 98½ 95¾ 66 511¼ St Julien M L121 8.00 74-10 ***Secret Status***1216¾ Rings A Chime1211¼ *Classy Cara*1212½ Mild inside gain 14
8Apr00-8Kee gd 1 1/16 :231 :463 1:11 1:442 ⒻAshland-G1 92 5 4 46½ 43½ 32 2no St Julien M L116 7.90 83-23 Rings A Chime116no Zoftig1164 Circle Of Life1168 Angled out, hung 6
11Mar00-6FG fst 1 1/16 :233 :472 1:123 1:444 ⒻFG Oaks-G3 86 1 9 87½ 89½ 55 33¼ St Julien M L121 42.80 84-20 Shawnee Country1212 Eden Lodge1211¼ Zoftig1211 Good late energy 9
14Feb00-8FG fst 1 1/16 ⊗ :233 :471 1:122 1:454 ⒻAlw 30000N1X 81 5 7 75½ 55 1½ 12½ Emigh C A L119 3.50 82-19 Zoftig1192½ Zenith119nk Zakalachee1162 4-w 2nd turn, clear 8
16Jan00-6FG fm *1 Ⓣ :242 :493 1:153 1:401 ⒻAlw 30000N1X 74 8 12 74¾ 94¾ 65½ 43¼ Emigh C A L119 3.20 82-12 Ever After1192½ Evrobi119½ Azireprice119nk Late interest 12
31Dec99-6FG fm *5½f Ⓣ :223 :463 :59 1:051 ⒻMd Sp Wt 28k 76 11 9 97½ 97½ 42½ 1no Emigh C A L119 3.20 94-02 Zoftig119no AboveTheOdds1193 DeherOfThDog119hd 5-w, up final strides 12
WORKS: Jly17 Bel 5f fst 1:01 B *3/33* Jly11 WO 4f fst :501 B *6/12* Jun18 WO 5f fst 1:031 B *26/37* Jun11 WO tr.tⓉ 5f fm 1:013 H *23/24* ●May19 WO 3f gd :35 H *1/7* Apr29 CD 5f fst 1:022 B *26/46*

Polly Jo
Own: Birsh Philip S
VELAZQUEZ J R (246 40 38 35 .16) 2000:(714 115 .16)

Ch. f. 3 (Feb)
Sire: Virginia Rapids (Riverman) $5,000
Dam: T. N. T. Lady (Irish Tower)
Br: Philip S Birsh (NY)
Tr: Dickinson Michael W(12 7 3 1 .58) 2000:(65 25 .38)

L 121

Life	4	1	2	1	$47,640	D.Fst	3	1	2	0	$42,800 68
2000	4	1	2	1	$47,640	Wet	0	0	0	0	$0 –
1999	0	M	0	0	$0	Turf	1	0	0	1	$4,840 84
Bel	2	0	2	0	$17,600	Dist	0	0	0	0	$0 –

24Jun00-7Bel fm 1 1/16 Ⓣ :233 :471 1:112 1:411 3↑ ⒻⓈAlw 44000N1X 84 9 5 51½ 51¼ 32 3½ Bailey J D L115 2.95 86-15 Bid's Femme115hd Pearly White115nk Polly Jo1152¼ Game finish outside 10
1Jun00-9Bel fst 1 :241 :484 1:133 1:394 3↑ ⒻⓈAlw 44000N1X 68 6 6 41 3½ 3½ 22¼ Bailey J D L117f *1.20 64-28 Anthenin'sLegcy1132¼ PollyJo117hd PerlyWhit1153 Rated 4 wide, got 2nd 6
12May00-7Bel fst 1 1/16 :233 :474 1:124 1:453 3↑ ⒻⓈAlw 44000N1X 63 4 1 2½ 1hd 1½ 2¾ Bailey J D L115f *.40 68-24 *Doublecomet*114¾ PollyJo1151½ WinByDcision1151¾ Vied outside, gamely 8
13Apr00-5Aqu fst 1 :224 :453 1:111 1:38 3↑ ⒻⓈMd Sp Wt 42k 68 2 1 2hd 1½ 14½ 15½ Castillo H Jr L114f 3.00 78-22 Polly Jo1145½ Bellebottom Blues1148¼ Proprietress1221 Pace, ridden out 9
WORKS: Jly20 Tap 3f fst :38 B *1/1* Jly14 Tap 5f fst 1:071 B *1/1* Jly10 Tap 5f fst 1:071 B *1/1* Jly5 Tap Ⓣ 4f gd :501 B *2/3* ●Jun20 Tap Ⓣ 4f fm :49 B *1/4* Jun14 Tap 5f fst 1:012 B *2/4*

Miss Chief

Own: Laurin Stable
BAILEY J D (158 61 37 16 .39) 2000:(490 139 .28)

Ch. f. 3 (May)
Sire: Chief's Crown (Danzig)
Dam: Country Stage (Country Light)
Br: Roger Laurin (Ky)
Tr: Mott William I(80 20 12 12 .25) 2000:(378 93 .25)

L 121

Life	7	2	0	2	$89,377	D.Fst	1	1	0	0	$24,600	64
2000	6	1	0	2	$64,777	Wet	0	0	0	0	$0	–
1999	1	1	0	0	$24,600	Turf	6	1	0	2	$64,777	82
Bel	0	0	0	0	$0	Dist	0	0	0	0	$0	–

22Jun00-9CD fm 1⅛ Ⓣ :474 1:122 1:373 1:501 ⒻAlw 51200N2X 80 8 4 43 42 51½ 52 St Julien M L 121 *1.40 83-18 MegansBluff121½ Secretsinthesky1211 FortyGrn118hd Flattened out,lane 8
4Jun00-9CD fm 11/16 Ⓣ :232 :472 1:113 1:424 ⒻRegret-G3 82 7 9 98½ 87½ 54 33½ St Julien M L 115 11.30 87-08 Solvig1221 Trip1172½ Miss Chief1151¾ 4wide bid, mild gain 9
22Apr00-7Kee fm 1⅛ Ⓣ :472 1:114 1:37 1:494 ⒻPalisades110k 81 6 7 74 75 54 32½ Smith M E L 116 8.10 81-16 Velvet Morning116hd Solvig1232½ Miss Chief1162 Inside,no late gain 8
8Apr00-9Kee yl 1⅛ Ⓣ :493 1:142 1:40 1:524 ⒻAlw 55160N1X 80 7 6 31 32 21½ 11½ Smith M E L 120 5.40 69-23 MissChief1201½ SymphonicLady1184½ SwiftlyClssic1182 3wide, stiff drive 9
10Mar00-11GP fm *1 1/16 Ⓣ :234 :484 1:131 1:44 + ⒻAlw 37000N1X 69 8 3 31½ 32 63½ 65¾ Smith M E 118 8.70 79-17 LdyCrystl1181¾ SouthernIvy1181 FlmesInThSnd1181¾ Chased 3 wide, tired 9
16Feb00-10GP fm *1 1/16 Ⓣ :231 :483 1:13 1:44 ⒻAlw 34000N1X 64 1 3 42 76½ 812 78½ Bailey J D 118 *1.90 74-15 Mi Moochie118hd Lady Crystal118¾ Engage1132¾ Early foot, tired 10
22Aug99-1Sar fst 7f ⊗ :224 :462 1:123 1:261 ⒻMd Sp Wt 41k 64 1 7 66½ 56½ 44½ 1½ Bailey J D 116 3.65 74-16 Miss Chief116½ Stateliness1162¾ Domain116½ Hesitated start,got up 7
WORKS: Jly18 Bel 5f fst 1:021 B 12/19 Jly3 CD 4f fst :504 B 29/36 Jun20 CD 4f fst :491 B 32/86 Jun14 CD 4f fst :501 B 20/40 Jun1 CD Ⓣ 4f fm :523 B (d)5/6 May25 CD Ⓣ 5f fm 1:033 B (d)8/18

Jostle

Own: Fox Hill Farms Inc
SMITH M E (172 22 20 28 .13) 2000:(660 103 .16)

Dk. b or br f. 3 (Mar)
Sire: Brocco (Kris S.) $15,000
Dam: Moon Drone (Drone)
Br: Prestonwood Farm Inc (Ky)
Tr: Servis John C(1 0 1 0 .00) 2000:(88 14 .16)

L 121

Life	10	5	3	0	$458,170	D.Fst	7	3	2	0	$196,350	98
2000	5	1	2	0	$195,570	Wet	3	2	1	0	$261,820	93
1999	5	4	1	0	$262,600	Turf	0	0	0	0	$0	–
Bel	1	0	1	0	$50,000	Dist	0	0	0	0	$0	–

1Jly00-8Bel fst 1⅛ :453 1:094 1:352 1:48 ⒻMotherGoose-G1 98 6 1 1hd 2hd 1½ 22¼ Smith M E L 121 fb 18.00 89-09 Secret Status1212¼ Jostle1211½ Finder's Fee1213¾ Vied outside, gamely 7
19May00-11Pim my 1⅛ :461 1:11 1:381 1:522 ⒻBlackEydSsn-G2 93 5 3 22½ 2hd 11½ 12¼ Desormeaux K J L 122 fb 5.90 77-22 Jostle1222¼ March Magic1225½ Impending Bear122no Circled,clear,driving 7
21Apr00-8Aqu sly 1 :23 :461 1:111 1:363 ⒻComely-G3 90 5 2 21 1½ 1½ 21 Prado E S L 121 fb 5.10 84-24 March Magic1141 Jostle1211¾ Finder's Fee1212¾ Prompted pace, gamely 6
11Mar00-6FG fst 1 1/16 :233 :472 1:123 1:444 ⒻFG Oaks-G3 46 8 6 65 42½ 817 726½ Elliott S L 121 b 15.20 60-20 Shawnee Country1212 Eden Lodge1211½ Zoftig1211 Wide trip, no factor 9
19Feb00-9FG fst 1 1/16 :24 :474 1:122 1:45 ⒻDavona Dale-G3 79 6 9 63½ 65¾ 78½ 57¼ Martinez W L 122 b 6.00 79-19 ShawneeCountry122½ Chilukki1221 HumbleClerk1224¾ Passed tiring foes 9
27Nov99-6Aqu my 1⅛ :47 1:113 1:38 1:512 ⒻDemoiselle-G2 82 3 2 21½ 1hd 11½ 1hd Elliott S L 121 fb 8.00 79-11 Jostle121hd March Magic1121¾ Shawnee Country1213¾ Dug in, hard drive 8
7Nov99-9Lrl fst 1⅛ :483 1:133 1:39 1:52 ⒻSelima-G3 81 5 3 21 21 1hd 14½ Elliott S L 119 b 2.40 78-22 Jostle1194½ Dawn Princess119nk Class1198 3-4wd,rzd 5/16,drv clr 6
16Oct99-7Del fst 1 1/16 :234 :48 1:124 1:461 ⒻPollyDrmmond101k 77 1 7 51¾ 31½ 2½ 11 Elliott S L 114 b 2.70 76-24 Jostle1141 Disco Darlin'114nk High Code1133 Dueled,clear late 9
18Aug99-5Mth fst 1 :231 :48 1:132 1:39 ⒻMd Sp Wt 28k 68 5 2 2½ 11 16 18½ Elliott S 117 b *.90 79-18 Jostle1178½ Logan's Press Card117¾ Blushing Broad1174¾ Drew off nicely 7
2Aug99-1Del fst 6f :22 :46 :591 1:121 ⒻMd Sp Wt 30k 52 5 9 98½ 89¼ 45 23 Colton R E 118 b 8.90 79-15 Kthie'sSibiling1183 Jostle1182¾ CstingCinm1182 Steady advance 2nd bst 9
WORKS: Jly15 Pha 5f sly :584 B 2/4 ●Jun26 Pha 5f fst 1:003 B 1/5 Jun13 Pha 6f sly 1:161 B 1/1 Jun6 Pha 6f my 1:162 B 1/1 May3 Pha 5f fst 1:014 B 3/8

Resort

Own: Phipps Ogden M
PRADO E S (310 44 51 56 .14) 2000:(926 144 .16)

Dk. b or br f. 3 (Feb)
Sire: Pleasant Colony (His Majesty) $75,000
Dam: Extravagant Woman (Alydar)
Br: Phipps Ogden Mills (Ky)
Tr: McGaughey Claude III(49 16 8 4 .33) 2000:(134 36 .27)

L 121

Life	8	4	0	1	$117,110	D.Fst	6	3	0	0	$86,200	92
2000	6	3	0	0	$88,000	Wet	2	1	0	1	$30,910	70
1999	2	1	0	1	$29,110	Turf	0	0	0	0	$0	–
Bel	3	2	0	1	$60,910	Dist	0	0	0	0	$0	–

8Jly00-3Bel fst 1 1/16 :24 :474 1:121 1:433 3↑ ⒻAlw 48000N3X 84 6 4 42 31½ 2hd 1½ Prado E S L 117 *.80 79-21 Resort117½ RhinestoneDewey1163½ RumPunch1211½ Game on rail, driving 6
11Jun00-6Bel fst 1 1/16 :234 :48 1:14 1:46 3↑ ⒻAlw 46000N2X 92 1 6 52¾ 62 1½ 11½ Prado E S L 114 3.15 67-29 Resort1141½ Royal Fair1215½ Back In Action114½ Circled field, driving 6
7May00-7Del fst 170 :233 :47 1:114 1:431 ⒻGo For Wand76k 84 7 8 79 67½ 66½ 43½ Castillo H Jr L 116 4.70 82-22 Sincerely116½ Valleydar116¾ Weekend Kaper1162 Long drive, closed 10
19Apr00-6Aqu my 1⅛ :493 1:144 1:392 1:514 3↑ ⒻAlw 44000N1X 70 2 4 47 31½ 1½ 13½ Prado E S L 113 3.45 78-16 Resort1133½ PlentyOfLuck120½ AuthenticCller1099 3W move, ridden out 5
16Mar00-8GP fst 1 1/16 :24 :48 1:124 1:453 ⒻAlw 38000N1X 67 9 8 75 54 78½ 68¼ Bailey J D L 118 3.70 72-19 Parish Land1212¾ Cautious Cat1181½ Engage1181¾ Flattened out 9
9Jan00-8GP fst 7f :22 :444 1:102 1:24 ⒻAlw 32000N2L 67 5 10 95½ 74½ 55½ 67¾ Bailey J D 121 8.50 72-13 Sincerely1212 Welcome Surprise1211¾ During The Race1212½ No factor 10
17Nov99-4Aqu fst 7f :233 :471 1:134 1:261 ⒻMd Sp Wt 41k 66 7 5 51¾ 3nk 11 14½ Bailey J D 119 *.75 71-20 Resort1194½ Timely Rhythm1197¾ Sybil S.119nk 3 wide move, driving 9
21Oct99-2Bel my 6f :221 :454 :574 1:102 ⒻMd Sp Wt 41k 65 8 7 79 53½ 34½ 34 Bailey J D 118 11.90 85-15 Proposal118¾ Numerous Ambition1183½ Resort1185½ Split rivals, gamely 8
WORKS: Jly17 Bel 4f fst :473 H 2/57 Jly3 Bel 4f fst :492 B 20/35 Jun25 Bel 3f fst :36 H 2/27 Jun6 Bel 4f gd :493 B 6/21 Jun2 Bel 3f fst :38 B 7/13 May24 Bel 3f sly :373 B (d)3/4

Secret Status

Own: Elkins J A & Farish W S & Webber T
DAY P (9 2 1 2 .22) 2000:(698 151 .22)

Ch. f. 3 (Feb)
Sire: A.P. Indy (Seattle Slew) $150,000
Dam: Private Status (Alydar)
Br: Elkins J & Farish W S & Webber W T Jr (Ky)
Tr: Howard Neil J(7 1 2 1 .14) 2000:(114 18 .16)

L 121

Life	10	6	0	3	$711,163	D.Fst	10	6	0	3	$711,163	102
2000	6	5	0	1	$654,296	Wet	0	0	0	0	$0	–
1999	4	1	0	2	$56,867	Turf	0	0	0	0	$0	–
Bel	3	1	0	1	$155,740	Dist	0	0	0	0	$0	–

1Jly00-8Bel fst 1⅛ :453 1:094 1:352 1:48 ⒻMotherGoose-G1 102 3 4 55½ 53½ 2½ 12¼ Day P L 121 *.70 91-09 Secret Status1212¼ Jostle1211½ Finder's Fee1213¾ Came wide, driving 7
5May00-9CD fst 1⅛ :461 1:111 1:373 1:501 ⒻKy Oaks-G1 100 4 13 11 11 85½ 11 16¾ Day P L 121 4.90 85-10 SecretStatus1216¾ RingsAChime1211½ ClassyCr1212½ 5wide trip,ridden out 14
19Mar00-10Tam fst 1 1/16 :234 :481 1:133 1:45 ⒻFla Oaks-G3 82 1 1 1½ 2½ 1hd 1nk Day P L 118 *.70 96-04 Secret Status118nk March Magic1141½ Musical1116½ Dueled, gamely 8
20Feb00-10GP fst 170 :231 :463 1:104 1:401 ⒻDavona Dale-G2 92 6 9 88 75¾ 47½ 37 Day P 114 *1.60 88-10 CshRun1187 RegllyAppeling116no SecrtSttus114½ Swung out, missed 2nd 9
2Feb00-3GP fst 1 1/16 :242 :481 1:123 1:433 ⒻAlw 34000N2X 91 1 3 33 2½ 12 15½ Day P 121 *.70 90-12 Secret Status1215½ Bejoyfulandrejoyce1183¾ Laurel Light1211½ Ridden out 5
9Jan00-11GP fst 1 1/16 :233 :474 1:131 1:452 ⒻAlw 32000N2L 87 7 4 41¾ 2hd 12 11¾ Bailey J D 121 *.80 81-21 Secret Status1211¾ Misk1185 Gold Chalice1214½ 3 wide, driving 9
27Nov99-9CD fst 1 1/16 :241 :481 1:131 1:451 ⒻGolden Rod-G3 79 2 7 73¾ 53½ 53½ 32¾ Martinez W 111 9.60 81-22 HumbleClerk1191¾ CashRun1221 SecretStatus1111¼ Bumped start, rallied 9
15Oct99-2Kee fst 1 1/16 :231 :463 1:114 1:434 ⒻMd Sp Wt 46k 74 2 2 23 21½ 12 17 Day P 118 *.50 89-09 SecretSttus1187 TimeToGlitter118no JneRection1181½ Stalked, ridden out 12
26Sep99-6Bel fst 7f :224 :461 1:104 1:233 ⒻMd Sp Wt 41k 63 7 2 82½ 84¾ 610 511½ Smith M E 118 *2.00 72-15 MtlchPss1188½ WeddingWeknd1181½ Rochll'sTrms118½ Wide trip, no rally 9
12Sep99-7Bel fst 6f :221 :454 :58 1:104 ⒻMd Sp Wt 41k 72 5 5 68 54½ 35 33½ Day P 118 19.10 84-14 Emily's Angel1183 Proposal118nk Secret Status1189 Game finish on rail 8
WORKS: Jly17 Bel 6f fst 1:13 B 1/3 Jly9 Bel 4f fst :501 B 37/54 ●Jun26 Bel 5f fst :594 B 1/14 Jun16 Bel 6f fst 1:141 B 2/5 Jun8 CD 5f fst 1:03 B 16/21 Jun2 CD 5f fst 1:01 B 11/24

Let's take one last look at this procedure for pace analysis. The Coaching Club American Oaks is one of our most important Grade 1 races for 3-year-old fillies. This prestigious race, run at $1\frac{1}{2}$ miles, requires a top effort from a top filly. It is seldom won by a fluke performance. In the 2000 edition, Secret Status was hammered to 2-5 by the New York and simulcast bettors. She was a multiple Grade 1 winner, but the price and the probable pace of the race were strong reasons to play against her. Without belaboring the analysis, which filly figured as "E1" on a pace that should have been perfectly suited to her chances? Jostle possessed the only competitive Beyer figures *and* she held the coveted position of "E1" in a race mostly filled with "S" runners.

I said earlier that "E1's" present the ideal betting opportunities, especially when the Beyer Speed Figures are competitive. The $1\frac{1}{2}$-mile distance was the biggest question as to whether or not the play should be made. While it is true that pace figures are not as reliable at marathon distances, *pace analysis* is exceedingly important. Early-pace runners able to secure position are just as effective as they are at middle distances. Perhaps even more so.

Middle-distance closers tend to lose that explosive finish as the furlongs increase. Every runner in the race is tired. Passing even-paced horses in the final stages is difficult, even for the highest-class horses. An "E1" on a comfortable pace is as great a danger in a marathon as she is in shorter races. Jostle was unquestionably the correct play in this race. Secret Status's connections could obviously read *Daily Racing Form* and elected to use her earlier than she prefers. The result of playing into Jostle's best game was a weakening third at 2-5. Ouch! I sincerely hope the reader leaves this chapter with a resolve to play horses like Jostle whenever the price warrants.

EIGHTH RACE

Belmont

JULY 22, 2000

1½ MILES. (2.24) 84th Running of THE COACHING CLUB AMERICAN OAKS. Grade I. Purse $350,000. (Up To $45,900 NYSBFOA) FILLIES, THREE YEARS OLD. 3rd Leg of THE TRIPLE TIARA. By subscription of $350 each, which should accompany the nomination; $1,500 to pass the entry box and $2,000 to start. The purse to be divided 60% to the winner, 20% to second, 11% to third, 6% to fourth and 3% to fifth. 121 lbs. Starters to be named at the closing time of entries. Trophies will be presented to the winning owner, trainer and jockey. Closed Saturday, July 8th with 16 Nominations.

Value of Race: $350,000 Winner $210,000; second $70,000; third $38,500; fourth $21,000; fifth $10,500. Mutuel Pool $864,443.00 Exacta Pool $585,508.00 Trifecta Pool $485,657.00

Last Raced	Horse	M/Eqt. A.Wt	PP	¼	½	1	1¼	Str	Fin	Jockey	Odds $1
1a00 8Bel2	Jostle	Lbf 3 121	5	1^1	1^1	1	1$	1^1	1^3	Smith M E	2.85
8a00 3Bel1	Resort	L 3 121	6	7	7	3$	2^2	2^2	2^L	Prado E S	12.70
1a00 8Bel1	Secret Status	L 3 121	7	2$	2	2	3^1	3^1	3^2	Day P	0.45
21d00 5Bel1	Sound Of The West	L 3 121	1	4	5	6$	5^3	5^8	4^2	Davis R G	54.75
24d00 7Bel3	Polly Jo	Lf 3 121	3	3	3	4	4^3	4^2	5^{11}	Velazquez J R	54.50
24d00 8AP2	Zoftig	Lb 3 121	2	6^1	6	7	6^5	6^8	6^{11}	St Julien M	10.60
22d00 9CD5	Miss Chief	L 3 121	4	5	4	5^1	7	7	7	Bailey J D	17.50

OFF AT 4:50 Start Good. Won driving. Track fast.

TIME :24, :49^1, 1:15, 1:41, 2:05^1, 2:29^4 (:24.09, :49.20, 1:15.09, 1:41.01, 2:05.31, 2:29.99)

$2 Mutuel Prices:

5–JOSTLE		7.70	6.20	2.10
6–RESORT			12.20	2.10
7–SECRET STATUS				2.10

$2 EXACTA 5–6 PAID $83.50 $2 TRIFECTA 5–6–7 PAID $134.50

Dk. b. or br. f, (Mar), by Brocco–Moon Drone, by Drone. Trainer Servis John C. Bred by Prestonwood Farm Inc (Ky).

JOSTLE quickly showed in front, controlled the pace while in hand, turned back a bid from RESORT on the second turn, dug in gamely and drew clear under a drive. RESORT was rated along early, put in a quick three wide move leaving the backstretch, could not stay with the winner in the final furlong but continued on gamely to earn the place award. SECRET STATUS raced with the pace from the outside and had no response when roused. SOUND OF THE WEST was rated along inside and had no rally. POLLY JO was rated along inside, chased around the second turn and tired inside in the stretch. ZOFTIG had no response when roused. MISS CHIEF raced outside and tired.

Owners— 1, Fox Hill Farms Inc; 2, Phipps Ogden M; 3, Farish W S Elkins J A & Webber T J; 4, Peace John H; 5, Birsh Philip S; 6, Glencrest Stable & Walts-David Stab; 7, Laurin Stable

Trainers— 1, Servis John C; 2, McGaughey Claude III; 3, Howard Neil J; 4, Arnold George R II; 5, Dickinson Michael W; 6, Doyle Michael J; 7, Mott William I

$2 Pick Three (3–1–5) Paid $104.00; Pick Three Pool $264,759.
$2 Pick Six (4–6–10–3–1–5) 6
Correct Paid $4,719.00; Pick Six Pool $117,459. $2 Pick Six (4–6–10–3–1–5) 5
Correct Paid $86.00

CRIST
ON VALUE
by Steven Crist

A TYPICAL LIBERAL-ARTS education sets a graduate loose upon the world with a tremendous amount of knowledge he will never need or use again and some gaping holes about actually functioning in society. He may know the abbreviations for the periodic table of elements and the names of the leading Renaissance poets, but have no idea how to make a cup of coffee or write a business letter.

A similar situation exists for the American horseplayer, self-taught through handicapping literature and days of hard knocks at the old horse park. He has vast amounts of handicapping data swimming through his head—names, dates, running lines, speed figures, pedigrees, trainer patterns and angles—all devoted to the goal of discovering the likeliest winners of horse races. When it comes time to go to the betting windows, however, nearly every one of these well-informed enthusiasts almost immediately surrenders his edge. He is like the chemistry scholar who knows the molecular structure of the coffee bean but has no idea how much water to put into the percolator. Each is unable to convert his knowledge into something useful and pleasurable—a steaming cup of java, or a consistent profit on racetrack bets.

This is not to suggest that universities should stop teaching chemistry or literature, or that horseplayers should not continue to develop and enhance their skills as selectors. Like a liberal-arts education, the study of horses and how they perform is a worthy pleasure in itself, and in the case of handicapping, the world's savviest bettor cannot win with bad opinions. The point is that pure handicapping is only the first half of the battle in winning at the races.

Most horseplayers intuitively know this, but don't do much about it except complain. How often have you or a fellow trackgoer opined that you're a pretty good handicapper but you really need to work on your betting strategies or your so-called money management? This is sometimes an exercise in denial for people who are in fact bad handicappers, but it is probably true for many who can select winners as well as anyone.

The problem with this line of thinking is that it suggests betting is some small component of the game, which is like pretending that putting is a minor part of championship golf. In fact, if you handicap well and bet poorly, you've failed. It's as useless as crushing your tee shots while three-putting every green.

Turning your enthusiasm for racing and proficiency at handicapping into profitable betting requires an entirely new way of thinking about playing the races. It would take a far longer treatise than this chapter to explore fully the mathematics and mechanics of racetrack betting, and the strategies available to optimize one's wagering through different types of bets. Instead, the purpose here is to raise three fundamental concepts that may help the serious handicapper to focus on profit rather than prediction, making money instead of just picking winners: probability and odds; handicapping the competition; and using multiple bets to improve your prices.

PROBABILITY AND ODDS

Forget for a moment everything you know about parimutuel betting and pretend that horse racing is set up like sports betting or a game of blackjack: If you pick the winning horse, the track doubles your bet. Every winner, regardless of how many people bet on him, pays $4.

Now ask yourself two questions: 1) Do you want to play? 2) How would you handicap and bet differently from the way you do now?

Most horseplayers will realize after a moment of thought that the correct answer to the first question is yes. It might not be a great deal of fun, but you could sit around and wait for mismatches, races in which one horse is so clearly superior to the competition that anyone could fairly agree that he has a better than 50 percent chance of winning the race. You would never bet a horse you honestly believed had less than a 50 percent chance of winning.

If you could find 50 races in which you discovered a horse with a legitimate 70 percent chance of winning, you would invest $100—50 $2 bets—and get a $4 payoff on 35 of those 50 races for a return of $140. A $140 return on a $100 investment is a 40 percent profit, and you could quit your day job and spend the rest of your life refining your criteria for horses with a 70 percent chance of winning.

Racing unfortunately does not work this way. Horses that everyone perceives as having a 70 percent chance of winning pay substantially less than $4 because the odds are determined by the amount of money actually bet on each horse, and because track takeout and breakage further depress the payout.

It's worth examining the mechanics of this situation. Let's look at a $1,000 win pool on a hypothetical four-horse race in which every contestant attracts an amount of betting that accurately reflects his chance of winning:

HORSE	WINNING CHANCE	$ BET
A	50 percent	$500
B	30 percent	$300
C	15 percent	$150
D	5 percent	$ 50

Now, what will these horses actually pay to win? Based on the percentages, most horseplayers would guess about 1-1 ($4), 5-2 ($7), 6-1 ($14), and 20-1 ($42). In fact, the payouts are significantly lower.

Let's say this race is being run in Kentucky, with a 16 percent takeout and breakage that rounds payoffs down to the nearest 20-cent increment. That leaves only $840 of the original $1,000 pool to split up among the winning ticket-holders. (The other $160 goes to pay the race purses, maintain the track, and fatten the coffers of the Bluegrass State.) So Horse A does not pay $4, but $3.36, which is rounded down to $3.20. Horse

B does not pay $7, but $5.60. Horse C returns $11.20 instead of $14, and the long-shot returns $33.60 instead of $42.

In each of these cases, the actual return is lower than what is required to break even, much less show a profit, over time. If you bet horses who win 50 percent of the time and pay $3.20, you will lose 20 percent of your investment.

The point of this exercise is to illustrate that even a horse with a very high likelihood of winning can be either a very good or a very bad bet, and the difference between the two is determined by only one thing: the odds. A horseplayer cannot remind himself of this simple truth too often, and it can be reduced to the following equation:

Value = Probability x Price

This equation applies to every type of horse and bet you will ever make. A horse with a 50 percent probability of victory is a good bet at better than even money (also known as an overlay) and a bad bet at less (a.k.a. an underlay). A 10-1 shot to whom you take a fancy is a wonderful overlay if he has a 15 percent chance of victory and a horrendous underlay if his true chance is only 5 percent. There are winning $50 exacta payoffs that are generous gifts and $50 exacta payouts where you made a terrible bet.

Now ask yourself honestly: Do you really think this way when you're handicapping? Or do you find horses you "like" and hope for the best on price? Most honest players will admit they follow the latter path.

This is the way we all have been conditioned to think: Find the winner, then bet. Know your horses and the money will take care of itself. Stare at the past performances long enough and the winner will jump off the page.

The problem is that we're asking the wrong question. The issue is not which horse in the race is the most likely winner, but which horse or horses are offering odds that exceed their actual chances of victory.

This may sound elementary, and many players may think they are following this principle, but few actually do. Under this mindset, everything but the odds fades from view. There is no such thing as "liking" a horse to win a race, only an attractive discrepancy between his chances and his price. It is not enough to lose enthusiasm when the horse you liked is odds-on or to get excited if his price drifts up. You must have a clear sense of what price every horse should be, and be prepared to discard your plans and seize new opportunities depending solely on the tote board.

If you begin espousing this approach, you are sure to suffer abuse from your fellow horseplayers. When one of them asks you who you like in a race and you say, "I think the 4 is a bigger price than he should be," the likely response is, "So what? Who do you *like*?" Your cronies are apt to tell you that you should be betting on horses, not on prices, and after an inevitable stretch of watching some of their underlays win, you will begin to doubt yourself.

Sticking to your guns is easier said than done, but it is the only way to win in the long run. The horseplayer who wants to show a profit must adopt a cold-blooded and unsentimental approach to the game that is at variance with both the "sporting" impulse to be loyal to your favorite horses and the egotistical impulse to stick with your initial selection at any price. This approach requires the confidence and Zen-like temperament to endure watching victories at unacceptably low prices by such horses.

Two prominent races run during the spring of 2001 illustrate the principle of seeking overlays and being flexible in your approach.

My handicapping of the 2001 Kentucky Derby led me to the opinion that the race was most likely to be won by one of the three quality closers in the field of 17—Point Given, Dollar Bill, or Monarchos. I allotted only a combined 45 percent chance to the other 14 horses in the race and split up the 55 percent likelihood of victory by my three choices at 25 percent for Point Given and 15 percent each for Dollar Bill and Monarchos.

I now faced two totally unrelated decisions: Whom to "pick" in *Daily Racing Form* as my selections for the race, and then which horse to back on Derby Day.

If the Derby were being run at Utopia Downs and each of the 17 entrants were paying off at odds of 16-1, I would simply have picked the likeliest winner, which to my mind was Point Given. However, at probable odds of 2-1, I would be recommending a fundamentally bad bet—tripling your money on a horse with a 25 percent chance of victory only gets you to 75 percent, or a 25 percent loss. So I knew I would have to pick one of my other two, both of whom figured to be at least the 5-1 needed to make them square bets. With Monarchos listed at 6-1 and Dollar Bill at 10-1 on the early lines, I selected the superior value and picked the race Dollar Bill-Monarchos-Point Given.

By post time two days later, however, I invoked the handicapper's prerogative of changing his mind when it comes time to wager. The following table shows the probability I had allotted to each starter, the odds necessary to receive fair value, and the actual odds at post time:

HORSE	PROBABILITY	REQ. ODDS	ACTUAL ODDS
Point Given	25 percent	3-1	9-5
Dollar Bill	15 percent	6-1	6-1
Monarchos	15 percent	6-1	10-1
Millennium Wind	8 percent	12-1	9-1
Congaree	8 percent	12-1	7-1

HORSE	PROBABILITY	REQ. ODDS	ACTUAL ODDS
Balto Star	4 percent	24-1	8-1
Fifty Stars	4 percent	24-1	40-1
Jamaican Rum	4 percent	24-1	20-1
A P Valentine	4 percent	24-1	19-1
Thunder Blitz	4 percent	24-1	25-1
Express Tour	4 percent	24-1	18-1
Each of 6 others	<1 percent	>100-1	From 35-1 to 102-1

Point Given was still the likeliest winner in my mind, but 9-5 was still an unacceptable return for a horse with a 25 percent chance of victory. To nearly everyone's surprise, Dollar Bill had been bet down to 6-1 and Monarchos had floated to 10-1. Dollar Bill now offered no real value relative to my assessment of his actual chances, but Monarchos was offering well above the return I thought was fair, as was Fifty Stars. My lack of regard or appreciation for Invisible Ink, the eventual runner-up, cost me all my multi-horse bets on the race, but win bets on Monarchos and Fifty Stars saved the day.

Thirteen days later at Pimlico, an uninspiring five-filly Black-Eyed Susan Stakes caught my interest because there were only two legitimate contenders and I thought one of them might be severely overbet. Two Item Limit had the superior speed figures and experience to be a worthy odds-on favorite, but I thought there was a scenario under which Tap Dance, the second choice, might end up very loose on the lead. While Two Item Limit was the better filly, she might lag too far back off slow fractions and fall short at the end. I made Two Item Limit 60 percent to win the race, giving a 35 percent chance to Tap Dance and the remaining 5 percent to their three over-matched opponents. Odds of 2-1 or better on Tap Dance would make her playable.

Unfortunately, everyone else seemed to have had the same idea about Tap Dance waltzing to the lead. With five minutes to post, both fillies were even money, and I felt neither remorse nor disloyalty as I went to the window to make the only logical bet: Two Item Limit to win, which she did at $4.40. Betting 6-5 shots to win is not my usual style, but I saw no other way to play the race and was convinced I was receiving outstanding value.

When I first began playing the races, I probably would have bet on both Dollar Bill and Tap Dance instead of Monarchos and Two Item Limit, out of loyalty to my initial selections and the sense that you "should" bet on the horses you initially like.

The success of these two plays, though, was ultimately based upon the probability of victory I had assigned to each winner. I cannot argue in good conscience that Two Item Limit had precisely a 60 percent chance of victory as opposed to 57 or 63 percent, and I doubt that such calibration is in fact achievable. It is, however, possible through experience to get close enough that if you demand sufficient value to cover the margin of error, you should outperform the competition—your fellow horseplayers.

THE COMPETITION

One of the great romantic myths of racing is that the players are a merry band of brothers united in their quest to smoke out the winner of each race. This is the case at the blackjack table, where everyone is playing against the house and all the players win when the dealer busts out. At the racetrack, however, every bettor is playing only against the other bettors. The house takes its cut off the top and has no financial interest in how the remaining money is carved up.

If every horseplayer but you were a certifiable idiot, betting at random on names and colors, you would win every day. Conversely, if the only people betting into the pool were the small number of professionals who make a living this way, your chances for long-term victory would be slim.

Either way, what would make you a loser or a winner would not be a change in the number of winners you bet, but solely the odds that these horses would return. To put this another way: Your opportunity for profit at the racetrack consists entirely of mistakes that your competition makes in assessing each horse's probability of winning.

In that first happy scenario, where the escaped lunatics are betting at random, you would win because you would bet on high-probability horses at fat odds. Every horse in a seven-horse field would be 5-1 (after takeout) and you would just bet on those with a better than 20 percent chance of winning. Playing purely against the pros, every horse would be bet in accordance with his true chances, and takeout would reduce each return below an acceptable price. You would be taking the worst of it every time.

Reality combines these two situations, since both nitwits and sharpies populate the betting pools every day. Has the balance shifted? There has been much carping in recent years that the game has become much tougher, or even "too tough." The game almost surely was easier 50 years ago when takeout was lower and track attendance was much higher, due primarily to racing's near-monopoly on legalized gambling. Unfortunately, the hordes of fabled two-dollar bettors of that era have mostly been seduced away by the jackpots of state lotteries and slot machines, and the industry has raised takeout to compensate for lost business.

Does that mean today's player faces nothing but higher vigorish and the remaining sharpies? Not at all. I firmly believe that, in general, the nitwits still outnumber the sharpies. More importantly, most sharpies aren't as sharp as they think, and even the winning sharpies make plenty of egregious mistakes on individual races. As long as the volume of ill-informed money exceeds the takeout, there can be a positive expectation for the true sharpshooter who waits for the competition to make mistakes.

How do we identify, and thus attack, this ill-informed money? There is no such thing as a bet that cannot possibly win, since every horse has a theoretical, if infinitesimal, chance of winning any race, if only because every single opponent theoretically could fall down. What defines sucker money is not the horse selected, but the acceptance of odds on that horse that are substantially out of line with its chances of winning.

For an example, let's return to the 2001 Kentucky Derby. Balto Star to win is not necessarily a bad proposition. However, Balto Star at 8-1 is a horrendous proposition. A one-dimensional front-runner does win the Derby about once every eight or 10 years, but never when there is a glut of other high-quality speed in the race. So perhaps Balto Star is a legitimate 8-1 shot in a vacuum. For Balto Star to have won this Derby, however, Songandaprayer and Keats both would have had to take back off the lead. Even if you thought there was a 50 percent chance that each of them would be taken back, that makes it only 25 percent that both would, so you have to apply that against Balto Star's 8-1 in a vacuum and now he's more like 32-1. My assigning him a 4 percent chance of victory may have been overly generous.

At 8-1, however, Balto Star was eating up over 10 percent of the win pool, better than half the takeout. Eliminating him alone still left you better than 95 percent likely to win while cutting the takeout to 6 percent. Tossing others with even more microscopic scenarios for victory—Songandaprayer, Keats, Talk Is Money—would have allowed you to have a positive expectation on the race.

There are races run every day in which a similar strategy can be employed. Knowing that a single 5-1 shot in fact has a true chance closer to 50-1 wipes out the entire takeout on a race. An intense dislike of a 3-1 shot can be an extremely powerful tool and the entire motivation for playing a particular race.

There are also plenty of races in which your competition will make no actionable mistakes. Everyone seems to be at about the right price, and there is no compelling reason to jump into the pool. It is worth remembering that the whole is better than the sum of its parts: The betting public's post-time favorite wins more often than any individual public handicapper, and over time first choices win more than second choices, which win more than third choices, and so on down the line. There is no shame in passing a race because you just don't see any value in it. Nor should you force yourself to play a race in which you have no confidence in your own odds line. That doesn't mean you have to sit on your hands—$1 boxes for action were made to fill the spaces between races where you have a legitimate edge or opinion.

Players who have never undertaken a value-based approach to handicapping will almost surely find it useful to begin making their own true-odds lines. It is cumbersome at first, but over time it becomes second nature, to the point where it can be done in your head and becomes the way you instinctively approach every race. However you choose to handicap horses is work that you do before the betting opens. As soon as those first prices go up on the board, you are looking for discrepancies between your odds and those set by your opponents.

Of course, it's tempting to anticipate those discrepancies by comparing your personal line with the early ones published in *Daily Racing Form*, which are made by either a DRF handicapper or the track's morning-linemaker. No mortal can resist a peek, but these early lines are widely misunderstood and misused—yet another opportunity for you to take an advantage.

A *Daily Racing Form* line is made 48 hours before a race. (A Saturday DRF is printed Thursday night so that you can buy it Friday and do your homework the night before the races.) It is a sincere effort to predict how the race will be bet, but because of the required printing window, it cannot incorporate early or late scratches, jockey changes, and prevailing track or weather conditions.

A track's morning line has even more pitfalls. It is typically prepared by a track employee in the racing office or simulcasting department whose primary skill in life may not be oddsmaking and whose agenda is different from yours. Tracks want to advertise their races as being competitive rather than mismatches, which is why horses we all know are going to be 3-5 are routinely listed at 6-5 on the morning line. Similarly, nearly every race card features several horses who are legitimately 99-1, but few morning-line prices exceed 30-1. Racing offices do not want to offend the horsemen filling their cards by saying their horses have virtually no chance.

Given all that, it is astounding how many horseplayers believe there is some magical significance to the morning line and to any discrepancies between it and the actual betting. If a horse is 4-1 on the morning line and 2-1 in the actual betting, plenty of your competitors will decide that this horse is a "good thing," the focus of an international betting coup orchestrated by the mysterious "they" who "know." If the same horse is instead 8-1 as post time approaches, the same conspiracy theorists will pronounce the horse "dead on the board." In fact, in either case, all that has happened is that the linemaker, an overworked and fallible human being like the rest of us, made a bad guess about how much the public would fancy a particular horse.

It is this sort of flawed thinking among your parimutuel opponents that creates incorrect prices on the board and thus opportunities for you. If some horses in a race are being overbet, that means that the prices are too high on the other horses and this is where you should be looking.

Is your competition offering you enough value to make this a profitable undertaking? Without discussing or judging anyone's method of handicapping, the answer is surely yes. There are enough people betting virtually at random, not even consulting complete past performances, to cover the takeout. Even among your well-informed opponents, the vast majority are betting with little consideration for the mathematics of value, which means that at least half the time they are betting on underlays and thus jacking up the prices on the overlays.

It's not an easy game, but you're not playing against "the game." You're betting against the other bettors. It doesn't matter if they pick as many winners as you do, or even more, if you are betting only when the price is right.

USING MULTIPLE BETS TO IMPROVE YOUR PRICES

Despite facing higher takeout and fewer casual opponents, the 21st-century horseplayer has a tremendous opportunity that his counterpart of 50 years ago did not enjoy: the ability to bet a race in a dizzying array of options beyond win, place, and show. Nearly every race in America now offers both multi-horse bets—the exacta, trifecta, and superfecta— and also is part of at least one multi-race bet—a daily double, pick three, four, or six.

For the purposes of this discussion of value betting, we will not attempt to examine the mechanics and optimal strategies for each of these wagers, an exercise that would require an entire volume. Instead, the question is how multiple wagers can give the value-oriented horseplayer an additional opportunity for profit.

Many old-timers and other curmudgeons dismiss all multiple bets as some newfangled work of the devil and begin and end their argument by pointing to the higher takeout on these wagers. A typical takeout structure is New York's, where one-horse (win, place, and show) bets are subject to a 15 percent takeout, two-horse bets (daily doubles and exactas) face a 20 percent bite, and all wagers involving three or more horses or races are hit with a 25 percent takeout. No matter how you slice it, say the defenders of straight betting, over time you will do better playing against a 15 percent takeout than a 20 or 25 percent takeout. Isn't that a fundamental of value betting? Isn't choosing to play into a 25 instead of a 15 percent takeout the equivalent of getting $7.50 on a horse who should pay $8.50?

There are two good answers to this cranky argument. The first and most important is that a higher takeout is meaningless if the greater opportunity for profit exceeds the difference in the toll. Would you rather make a pre-takeout 35 percent profit and give back 25 percent for a 10 percent profit, or make 16 percent and give back 15?

The second answer is that multi-race bets allow a player to spread the effect of takeout over several races, so that he is actually facing a smaller bite per race than if he played them separately. Consider the difference between making win bets on three consecutive races and playing a pick three. In the first case, you are taxed 15 percent three consecutive times so your original dollar is sliced first to 85 cents, then to 72 cents, and finally to 61 cents. Playing those same three races via the pick three devalues your dollar just once, to 75 cents.

Wrapping your mind around this idea leads to an appreciation of the value opportunity in multiple betting. If you are playing a second or third race or horse at a reduced takeout, you are getting better odds on that additional race or horse than you normally could. This is why, over time, multi-race payoffs are higher than an equivalent parlay of the individual winners would be.

Let's look at the simplest version of how this works, a daily double. Suppose that in each of the two races, there is a horse paying exactly 2-1 who you think is actually 50 percent likely to win. If you parlay the two horses with $100 win bets, your $100 turns into $300 after the first race, and $900 after the second horse wins. Not bad—an $800 return, and 8-1 on a proposition you believed was 3-1 (50 percent times 50 percent).

But what will the daily double of these two horses pay? At a 15 percent takeout, each 2-1 horse has 28.3 percent of the win pool on him, meaning he will pay $6 to win. Assuming that these horses are bet the same way in the double pool, that means 28.3 percent of all tickets have the first winner, but out of *those* tickets, only 28.3 percent combine him with the second winner. Multiply those two probabilities, and it means that only 8 percent of the daily-double pool is bet on the winning combination.

At a 20 percent takeout, a double that accounts for 8 percent of the pool returns $20, and your $100 double gets you $1,000 instead of the $900 you would get for parlaying the same two horses—despite betting into a pool with a higher takeout. In effect, you are getting a $20 mutuel instead of an $18 mutuel.

This may not seem like a thrilling difference, but a 10 percent increase in payoff is enough to make many a chronic loser into a chronic winner. Moreover, the difference increases in pick threes and fours as you add more races, and can often be far more than 10 percent. Add a third 2-1 winner to the example above and the $18 parlay becomes a $54 three-horse parlay. The $20 double, however, even with a 25 percent takeout, becomes a $66 pick three.

What is happening here is the powerful, hidden effect of reducing takeout and thus getting "free" odds on additional horses or races. Now take this to the next logical step:

If you are getting inflated odds on one part of the bet, you can now tolerate getting only even odds, or even slightly unfavorable odds, on the other. This can make an otherwise unplayable race or races attractive.

An obvious example of this is the race with a heavy favorite you can neither bet nor beat. Let's say you think a 9-10 favorite in a four-horse field has a 50 percent chance of winning. He is actually being slightly underbet by the public, because if 50 percent of the pool were on him, he would pay $3.40, not $3.80. So there is a "mistake" being made by the public—a horse with a 50 percent chance of winning is attracting only 44 percent of the pool—but it is a mistake you cannot capitalize upon because the take-out eats up your edge.

However, by using this horse in the first leg of a multi-race bet or the top half of an exacta, you can realize the value of the gap. Only 44 percent of the exacta tickets will have this horse on top, and only 44 percent of the doubles or pick threes will have this horse winning the first leg.

Let's use the same race to see how a multiple pool can present a value opportunity that otherwise would not exist. Suppose that of our favorite's three opponents, you think two of them are inseparable but the third is badly overmatched. The public, however, gives the horse you despise nearly the same chance as the other two. Here is how the win pool and odds on the race might look:

HORSE	PROBABILITY	REQ. ODDS	ACTUAL ODDS
A	50 percent	1-1	4-5 (44 % of pool)
B	22 percent	7-2	3-1 (19% of pool)
C	22 percent	7-2	3-1 (19% of pool)
D	6 percent	16-1	7-2 (18% of pool)

Every single win bet in the race is unplayable because all the odds are below your acceptable price for value. Thirty years ago, you would have been obliged to pass the race or make a bad bet. But in the world of the multiple, what about making two exactas, A-B and A-C? If your assessment of their chances is correct, what are your chances of collecting and what will your return be?

To understand the mathematics of exacta odds, it is helpful to think of an exacta as if it were a daily double. The first race is the four-horse race that includes the favorite you are using on top. The second race is a three-horse race for second. Since you believe Horse A has a 50 percent chance of winning, you are 50 percent to "win the first race." Since horses B and C account for 44 of the remaining 50 percent, together they are 88 percent to win the "second race" for second place. So if your probabilities are correct, you are now 44 percent (50 percent x 88 percent) to have an A-B or A-C exacta come in.

What should these exactas pay? Here is where you take advantage of the otherwise unexploitable differences between your assessment of probability and the actual betting. Horse A is on top of only 44 percent of the exactas, not 50 percent. Eliminate him from the race for second and increase the other horses' percentages of the pool to add up to 100. If they were 19, 19, and 18 percent of the original remaining 56 percent, those numbers now increase to 34, 34, and 32 percent. Here's your second edge: While you think B and C have a combined 88 percent chance of running second to A, the pool has them at only 68 percent.

So the A-B and A-C exactas account for only 44 percent x 34 percent of the pool, roughly 15 percent. At a 20 percent takeout, the A-B and A-C exactas would each return $10.60.

If you bet $4 to win on Horse A and he wins 50 percent of the time, you collect $3.80 for every $4 you bet. If you bet the A-B and A-C exactas, you win only 44 percent of the time but when you do, you collect $10.60. This translates, over 100 plays, to a $20 loss on the win bet and a $66 profit on the exacta, a 5 percent loss as opposed to a 16.5 percent profit. What made the difference? Only your unspectacular assessment that the longest shot in the field had a 12 percent rather than 32 percent chance of finishing second.

An important side note: This example made an assumption, for simplicity's sake, that horseplayers should not routinely make about exactas. We took it as a given here that horses B, C, and D had the same comparative chance to finish second to Horse A as they did to win the race. There is a fruitful line of thought that this is often not the case, for reasons of pace or consistency. An erratic front-runner who can win when he breaks well and sets a moderate pace may have a 20 percent chance of winning but a much smaller chance of ever finishing second, since he stops badly when challenged early. Conversely, a chronic early lagger may clunk up for second far more often than he ever wins.

These kinds of horses present additional opportunities because they are rarely bet proportionately to these different likelihoods in the exacta and trifecta pools. So many players insist on wasting their money with lazy betting techniques such as wheels and boxes that they overuse these horses in the wrong positions. A horse who is only 5 percent to win a race but perhaps 15 percent to run second is a terrible win bet at 10-1 but a great horse to use underneath in exactas if he is being bet there at the same rate.

Several of the examples in this chapter were chosen or constructed for their relative simplicity in illustrating a concept rather than for their real-world popularity. There are not many recreational horseplayers who find it sufficiently challenging or rewarding to turn $4 into $10.60 44 percent of the time. (Perhaps more of them should, if only to finance their sexier parimutuel undertakings.)

The same principles of value betting, however, apply regardless of the complexity or size of mutuels you are chasing. To summarize:

1. Recognize the difference between picking horses and making wagers in which you have an edge. The only path to consistent profit is to exploit the discrepancy between the true likelihood of an outcome and the odds being offered.

2. You are playing against only the other bettors at the track, not against the game or the house. Although they do a pretty good job on the whole, your opponents make more than enough mistakes for you to win.

3. Multiple bets can make apparently valueless races highly playable, and can multiply the existing value in a race because of the opportunity to capitalize on more than one discrepancy on the board.

If all of this seems too calculating and joyless, by all means feel free to forget about it and enjoy yourself at the races betting horses you fancy regardless of their price. You'll have plenty of company, and the rest of us could use your money.

DAVIDOWITZ

ON BIAS, TRAINERS, AND KEY RACES

by Steve Davidowitz

I HAVE BEEN PLAYING the horses for more than 40 years. I guess that makes me about the same age as some of the players I used to see regularly in the Aqueduct grandstand when I was just starting out, people who graciously taught me the ropes. In those days, the racing season in New York started in mid-March and ended in late November or early December. While most players made a few bets on races in Florida or California during the winter, using local bookmakers, we all approached the return of live racing in the spring with renewed vigor and enthusiasm.

In this modern era of wall-to-wall, 365-day racing schedules and unlimited simulcasting, it is ironic that I have naturally gravitated back toward a nine-month betting season that begins with a major Kentucky Derby prep stakes in early February and ends a week or so after the Breeders' Cup in early November.

While I probably need the extended break to protect my sanity, I am firmly convinced that my personal nine-month betting season contributes as much to a profitable year as any special research, for two crucial reasons: 1) The timing and variety of my schedule gives me something to look forward to as each portion of the racing season runs its course. It spikes my enthusiasm; it keeps me from getting burned out. 2) I can plan serious betting attacks on familiar tracks, tracks with recognizable track biases, tracks with familiar trainers who have discernible, reliable patterns of performance, tracks with ample opportunities to evaluate new 2-year-olds, emerging 3-year-olds, and other division leaders that inevitably show up in simulcast races, or on the circuits I plan to visit.

Simulcasting, in fact, has changed everything. Today, it is possible to focus on any racing circuit at any time of year. It is becoming increasingly possible to do the same at home, armed with a satellite dish, a telephone, and/or a home computer.

I am quite selective in choosing my preferred tracks and betting venues, even to the point of eliminating some that could be quite profitable if I could stand them. For instance, I learned to stay away from Aqueduct during its winter meet ever since going there on three different days in the late 1970's, catching three of the nastiest colds of my life. *Forgetaboutit!*

I happily give up winters at Aqueduct, even though the inner dirt racing surface frequently produces easy-to-spot, inside-speed-favoring biases that reduce the art of handicapping to finding the speed horse most likely to get a ground-saving trip.

Even with such local knowledge, I do not believe I would win serious money at Aqueduct. The racing puts me to sleep and the bleak winter environment does not inspire anything close to my best work.

To me, the inherent esthetics and comfort of a racetrack or betting parlor are almost as important as the quality of racing and its readability. I know for an absolute certainty that I make better handicapping decisions, better betting decisions, when I am in an interesting, positive environment and feeling up for the chase.

In the 1970's, I regularly and painfully played Keystone Racetrack (Philadelphia Park) because I covered the track for Philadelphia-based newspapers. But it was agonizing to walk the grandstand and see hundreds of disgruntled players treading on the discarded clutter of the slushy, muddy grandstand floor. It was equally disheartening to see the same parade of horses taking turns beating one another, often with inexplicable reversals of form.

I used to love Penn National Racecourse, an unpretentious track in the Amish hills of central Pennsylvania, before a horsemen's dispute with management in the late 1990's led to a significant horse exodus and was followed by an unrelated, but equally damaging, race-fixing scandal involving a handful of jockeys subsequently banned from the track.

Beyond these two troubling events, many of the track's most loyal customers, including me, felt completely disconnected from Penn National when management announced in March 2001 that it was eliminating the intriguing "World Series of Handicapping," the granddaddy of all handicapping tournaments, a $200,000 contest that brilliantly tested handicapping *and* wagering ability.

Although I prefer to build my racing year around tracks and racing dates that feature championship-quality sport, there has to be room to include well-appointed, well-run tracks of lesser quality where the sizes of the fields themselves can create lucrative betting opportunities—especially in exactas and trifectas. In 2000, for instance, I visited Canterbury Park during the summer and played Ellis Park simulcasts into early August. Both tracks offered more than a few betting opportunities that were hard to pass up, especially on the turf.

Canterbury's turf course (which I observed firsthand from 1985-90 as a columnist for the *Minneapolis Star Tribune*) remains one of the best-banked, fairest turf courses in America. On a well-banked course like that it is often possible to find sharp contenders in outer post positions at better odds than they deserve.

In the summer of 2000, Ellis Park's turf course featured a pronounced front-running track bias that went against the grain of the prevailing view that most turf courses favor stretch-running types. It is an axiom of my handicapping that any track tendency that goes against the grain of conventional wisdom is an opportunity for potential value plays. Thus, I plan to keep an eye out for plays at both tracks in the future.

EVALUATING AND USING TRACK BIAS

Question: If you are in the grandstand of your favorite track on a sunny day and you see three front-running horses win the first three races, what do you conclude?

If you say the track is kind to speed, you probably are right; most American tracks are kind to speed. But, if you automatically conclude that the track is *biased*, unfairly influencing the outcome of races, you probably are wrong.

A true bias occurs only when horses in the race are given a clear, unfair advantage or are noticeably hindered from doing their best. In some cases a true bias even helps horses do something they would not be capable of doing on their own.

The trick to spotting a truly meaningful track bias is to prepare properly for your day at the track. Know in advance which horses *should* show speed and which ones seem to need a while to get into their best stride. Bring to each race the knowledge of a potential speed duel, or a fast or slow pace. Know in advance what you expect to see in each race and make your track-bias judgments accordingly.

For instance, if three generally faint-hearted speed horses go head and head in fast fractions and two of them are still fighting it out at the wire, with the third horse only a length away, you probably do not need any further evidence to conclude that a "speed bias" is in play. Faint-hearted speedballs that battle themselves into suicidal fractions are not supposed to stick around for the finish.

If you see two races in a row like that, my suggestion is to bet the third race as if there were a mountain of evidence that a strong speed bias exists. Don't wait for everybody else to catch on. Don't wait for the prices on all speed horses on the card to be overbet. Take the risk; adjust your handicapping. Be among the first on your block to buy into the concept. Play with the probable bias. In most cases, the mutuel prices will more than compensate for the risk of being wrong.

Each year when I come out of my self-imposed winter hibernation with a two-week trip to Gulfstream Park in Hallandale, Florida, or Santa Anita Park in Arcadia, California, or Fair Grounds in New Orleans, Louisiana, I expect to encounter racing surfaces that are relatively easy to read.

If I go to Fair Grounds, I will be returning to a track that I spent two full years studying in the 1960's and have revisited every few years since. This historic track, which has been on the upswing since the Krantz family rebuilt the burned-out antique grandstand in the mid-1990's, now offers one of the best meets in the country. Purses have doubled and there are larger-than-usual fields in most races, courtesy of extensive simulcasting and slot machines at the track and its satellite OTB locations.

Best of all, Fair Grounds' racing surface includes a stretch run of 1,346 feet, one of the longest in American racing. This provides a natural forum for stretch-running types and stalkers who save ground on the turns, but wait until the top of the stretch to launch their most effective rallies. This may not qualify as a true track bias, but it is relatively rare in today's age of cookie-cutter, speed-favoring racing surfaces. Moreover, the opportunities for closers are occasionally accentuated by a slower, deeper rail path in the stretch, which can appear after an unexpected rainfall.

In fact, despite a generally quick-drying racing surface that usually produces a smooth and relatively fast rail path, the "rally-wide" track bias has been seen at Fair Grounds a few times each meet since my earliest handicapping adventures in New Orleans.

Back in the 1960's, the rally-wide tendency was so pronounced that I needed to coin the term *track bias* to describe the way the track was influencing results to Jimmy Durante, the raspy-voiced entertainer who let me use his front-row box seats when he was out of town. All I had to do was mark Jimmy's program when he brought friends to the track. The year was 1964 and I was 22.

In those days, the outside paths remained the best place to be for most of the meet. That was because Fair Grounds did not have the benefit of modern track maintenance to assist in the drainage process. The track—like the rest of New Orleans—was built over underground streams, a condition so unusual that it still forces the residents to inter their dead above the ground.

Although much has changed in recent years to mute the stretch-running bias, the combination of the naturally heavy water table in the New Orleans soil and the humid Gulf Coast climate ensures that Fair Grounds' racing surface will rarely get dry enough to be pasteboard-hard and superfast, even in long periods of sunny weather. It also opens the door to an occasional return of the rally-wide bias that was so prevalent decades ago.

In the 1960's, the betting public had no idea that early speed on the rail was a disadvantage in Fair Grounds' sprint races. Nor did they realize that early speed was a major asset—as it still is—in two-turn routes up to $1\frac{1}{16}$ miles where the starting gate is positioned close to the clubhouse turn. To this day, the betting public has trouble identifying true contenders at any track that presents shifting or multiple biases.

Spotting a track bias is not as easy as many people assume. As indicated earlier, a pair of front-running winners early on a racing card does not automatically translate into a bias favoring front-running speed. Yet, despite that caveat, it is not that difficult to predict a reoccurring bias in advance. The trick is to know something about the geometry of the track and the way rain can affect the racing surface. It also pays to know what will occur when a rain-splattered track is drying out and what countermeasures the track-maintenance crew may employ to protect the racing surface from inclement weather. To properly evaluate the power of track bias in handicapping, a good player must become familiar with what happens to a track during and after a rainstorm as well as how the track itself responds to special grooming before and after a rainstorm.

For instance, when rain is in the forecast, most tracks will follow a set procedure designed to keep the moisture from seeping deep into the track cushion. This cushion usually consists of three to four inches of topsoil and serves as a shock absorber to the horses running at full speed.

In preparing for rain, the track-maintenance crew will "seal" the surface by rolling it repeatedly with heavy machinery to compress the cushion. This will temporarily squeeze excess water and air holes out of the topsoil, pack it down, and boost drainage off the top. It also will nullify any rally-wide bias while accenting the traditional emphasis on early speed so customary in American racing.

When rain falls on a sealed surface, horses with good early speed just skip along on the lead, losing less energy than usual, making it more difficult for stretch-running types to be effective. When such a wet surface begins to dry out, some moisture inevitably seeps into the topsoil, softening it up. When this occurs there is every chance that the front-running tendency will be muted. For a while, at least—perhaps only a few races, perhaps a full day—an outside-lane bias and/or a rally-wide bias may assert itself.

At Monmouth Park, a jewel of a track on the Jersey shore about 50 miles from New York, rain can arrive unexpectedly from almost any direction. When it does, an alert New Jersey player should anticipate that a dead rail path may be in play as soon as the drying-out process begins. The tilt of the track toward the inner rail guarantees that excess water will drain in that direction, leaving it deeper and slower than the rest of the track.

A similar, slower rail path used to occur regularly at Fair Grounds, but not since the track completely rebuilt its racing surface to accelerate its drainage properties. This reconstruction has virtually reversed Fair Grounds' tendency for a slower rail path except on days following sustained downpours.

Keep in mind that a change in the weather at most tracks is a signal for a change in the prevailing track bias, or the first sign that a bias is going to occur.

At Keeneland in Lexington, Kentucky, for instance, rain is about the only thing that can stop this high-class track from its tendency toward one of the most powerful rail biases in the game. This is especially true during the spring meet, when the majority of races on dry-track days are won by horses who control the pace along the inside, or make their strongest moves along the rail in the stretch. While the tendency toward rail runners might be muted briefly after a rainstorm, the bias is sure to return in all its glory within a day of dry weather.

On the other hand, Belmont Park tends to produce a slower, deeper rail path than most tracks. This is primarily due to the way the surface is maintained and the degree of sand purposely mixed in with clay and other organic materials that make up Belmont's unusual main track.

Indeed, a rainfall at Belmont may turn the sandy track into a smooth, beachlike strip quite favorable to front-runners, but the rail usually will remain deeper and slower than the rest of the surface until special track maintenance is employed to shift the topsoil away from the rail. Rain or no rain, this shifting of sand tends to occur sometime in late June or early July, as the track begins to bake and become inherently faster under the hotter summer weather. In the fall, after the annual 6½-week Saratoga meet, the slower rail path will reappear like magic when racing returns to Belmont.

At the majority of North American tracks, dry, hot weather tends to accentuate "speed-favoring" tendencies. This includes venerable Saratoga, which has a long history of strong track biases depending upon the prevailing weather. During the 2000 Saratoga meet, for instance, a series of rainstorms during the first three weeks reversed the previous years' tendency toward speed and produced some of the strongest rally-wide biases I've seen in some time.

Here is a day's worth of Saratoga result charts from the 2000 meeting when the rally-wide bias on dirt was in full play. The date was September 2, Hopeful Stakes Day. There had been a light overnight rain, and heavy rain would fall immediately after the Hopeful.

Besides examining the result charts for winners and contenders who made their best gains while kept three or four wide on the main track, it is just as important to note which horses deserved extra credit for good efforts on the slower rail path, as well as those who could have been forgiven for relatively weak performances against the grain of the track.

FIRST RACE
Saratoga
SEPTEMBER 2, 2000

1 1/16 MILES. (Inner Turf)(1.39⁴) MAIDEN SPECIAL WEIGHT. Purse $42,000. (Up To $8,148 NYSBFOA). For Maiden Fillies and Mares Three Years Old And Upward. Three Year Olds 117 lbs.; Older 122 lbs. (Non–starters for a claiming price less than $40,000 in the last three starts preferred). (Clear. 76.)

Value of Race: $42,000 Winner $25,200; second $8,400; third $4,620; fourth $2,520; fifth $1,260. Mutuel Pool $440,713.00 Exacta Pool $508,235.00 Trifecta Pool $273,863.00

Last Raced	Horse	M/Eqt.	A.Wt	PP	St	1/4	1/2	3/4	Str	Fin	Jockey	Odds $1
8Jly00 9Bel⁸	Belle Eternelle	L	3 117	6	2	3hd	4 1½	3hd	3½	1nk	Samyn J L	3.50
17Aug00 7Sar⁶	Sweetest Secret	L	3 117	2	3	8½	8 1½	4½	2hd	21	Chavez J F	1.20
18Aug00 1Sar¹⁰	Coming Out	L	3 117	7	6	1½	1½	1½	11½	31¾	Sellers S J	8.40
21Jly00 4Bel⁷	Lianda		3 117	9	9	6 2½	5hd	6½	76	4no	Gryder A T	28.25
24Aug00 5Sar⁶	Queenofeverything	b	3 117	3	5	5hd	6½	7½	5hd	5½	Prado E S	b-18.60
18Aug00 1Sar⁹	Morning Call	L	3 117	8	7	2½	2½	2½	41	6no	Day P	9.20
1Jly00 1Bel¹⁰	Miss Kuruklata	L	4 122	10	8	4 2½	3hd	5hd	6hd	74¾	Luzzi M J	b-18.60
17Aug00 7Sar³	Breaking Story	L	3 117	5	1	7 1½	7½	82	83	82	Santos J A	6.50
	Double Dagger	L	3 117	1	10	10	10	10	10	91	Smith M E	15.40
13Jly00 4Bel⁴	Lucy Does The Hula	Lb	3 117	4	4	9 12	9 10	95	92	10	Espinoza J L	34.50

b–Coupled: Queenofeverything and Miss Kuruklata.

OFF AT 1:01 Start Good. Won driving. Course firm.
TIME :23¹, :47¹, 1:12½, 1:36⁴, 1:42⁴ (:23.36, :47.37, 1:12.26, 1:36.84, 1:42.95)

$2 Mutuel Prices:

6–BELLE ETERNELLE	9.00	3.70	2.80
3–SWEETEST SECRET		2.70	2.30
8–COMING OUT			3.60

$2 EXACTA 6–3 PAID $19.60 $2 TRIFECTA 6–3–8 PAID $135.00

Dk. b. or br. f, (May), by St. Jovite–Etoile Eternelle, by Timeless Moment. Trainer Voss Thomas H. Bred by Virginia Kraft Payson (Ky).

BELLE ETERNELLE raced close up inside while in hand, angled out in upper stretch, dug in gamely while between rivals and prevailed under a drive. SWEETEST SECRET was outrun early, rallied four wide on the second turn and finished gamely outside. COMING OUT quickly showed in front, set the pace under pressure and stayed on gamely along the inside through the stretch. LIANDA chased the pace from the outside and stayed on well to the finish. QUEENOFEVERYTHING was bumped after the start and raced inside. MORNING CALL pressed the pace from the outside and tired in the final furlong. MISS KURUKLATA chased outside and tired. BREAKING STORY had no response when roused. DOUBLE DAGGER raced greenly and had no rally. LUCY DOES THE HULA was bumped after the start and tired.

Owners— 1, Payson Virginia K; 2, Oxley John C; 3, Hughes B W; 4, Leigh Gerald W; 5, Rich Meadow Farm; 6, Colton Richard C Jr; 7, Vangelatos Peter; 8, Humphrey G W Jr; 9, Hunter Barbara; 10, Pont Street Stable

Trainers— 1, Voss Thomas H; 2, Ward John T Jr; 3, Reinstedler Anthony; 4, Clement Christophe; 5, Sciacca Gary; 6, Mott William I; 7, Sciacca Gary; 8, Arnold George R II; 9, Skiffington Thomas J; 10, Carroll Del W II

Scratched— Willing Heart (28Nov99 3AQU¹¹), Purrfect Punch (11Jly00 4DEL³), Misty Springs (23Jun00 7BEL⁵), Decadent Designer (8Jly00 9BEL²), Miss Prized (18Aug00 1SAR¹¹), Shagadellic (13Jly00 4BEL²), Slipping (17Aug00 4SAR³)

SECOND RACE
Saratoga
SEPTEMBER 2, 2000

1⅛ MILES. (Turf)(1.45^{2}) CLAIMING. Purse $35,500. (Up To $6,887 NYSBFOA). For Fillies and Mares Four Years Old And Upward. Weight 122 lbs. Non-winners of two races at a mile or over on the turf since July 12 allowed, 2 lbs. A race at a mile or over since then, 4 lbs. CLAIMING PRICE $45,000, for each $5,000 to $35,000 1 lbs. (Races where entered for $30,000 or less not considered). (Winners preferred).

Value of Race: $35,500 Winner $21,300; second $7,100; third $3,905; fourth $2,130; fifth $1,065. Mutuel Pool $547,859.00 Exacta Pool $565,231.00 Quinella Pool $77,270.00 Trifecta Pool $377,167.00

Last Raced	Horse	M/Eqt.	A.Wt	PP	St	¼	½	¾	Str	Fin	Jockey	Cl'g Pr	Odds $1
27Jly00 ^{5}Sar^{2}	Maggie May's Sword	Lf	4 117	12	10	2½	2½	2½	1^{1}	1¾	Prado E S	40000	7.40
20Aug00 ^{1}Sar^{2}	After You	L	5 117	3	3	$8^{2\frac{1}{2}}$	8^{1}	8^{2}	4½	$2^{1\frac{1}{4}}$	Pitty C D	40000	11.80
18Jun00 ^{2}Mth^{4}	Show My Gal	L	5 118	10	5	4^{1}	4^{2}	$4^{1\frac{1}{2}}$	3½	3½	Gryder A T	45000	5.70
21Aug00 ^{2}Sar^{7}	Lauren's Hot Dance	L	4 119	11	11	12	12	12	8½	4^{nk}	Sellers S J	40000	22.20
9Aug00 ^{4}Sar^{4}	Simona-CH	Lb	6 118	9	12	$11^{4\frac{1}{2}}$	$11^{5\frac{1}{2}}$	$11^{1\frac{1}{2}}$	10½	5no	Davis R G	45000	9.50
21Jun00 ^{7}Bel^{6}	Rose Esther	Lb	4 118	7	4	1^{1}	$1^{1\frac{1}{2}}$	1½	2^{hd}	$6^{1\frac{1}{4}}$	Smith M E	45000	f-20.30
19Aug00 ^{1}Sar^{1}	All Net Joe	b	4 116	8	6	$6^{1\frac{1}{2}}$	$6^{1\frac{1}{2}}$	$6^{1\frac{1}{2}}$	5½	7½	Chavez J F	35000	14.90
20Aug00 ^{1}Sar^{1}	Sweet Scarlet	L	6 120	2	1	5½	5½	5^{hd}	6^{hd}	8^{hd}	Decarlo C P	45000	5.70
27Jly00 ^{5}Sar^{5}	Shebakayskittycat	L	5 117	6	9	7^{hd}	7^{hd}	7^{hd}	9^{hd}	9^{nk}	Luzzi M J	40000	5.80
20Aug00 ^{1}Sar^{4}	Bail Money	Lb	4 116	4	8	10^{5}	$10^{2\frac{1}{2}}$	9½	$11^{2\frac{1}{2}}$	$10^{1\frac{1}{4}}$	Day P	35000	3.75
9Aug00 ^{4}Sar^{7}	Belawan	L	7 116	5	7	9½	9½	10½	12	$11^{2\frac{1}{2}}$	St Julien M	35000	29.50
19Jly00 ^{5}Bel^{8}	Mariquita's Secret	L	4 118	1	2	3^{1}	3½	3½	7^{hd}	12	Ebina M	45000	19.70

f-Mutuel Field: Rose Esther.

OFF AT 1:33 Start Good. Won driving. Course firm.
TIME :22^{3}, :46^{2}, 1:10^{4}, 1:34^{2}, 1:47^{3} (:22.79, :46.55, 1:10.87, 1:34.49, 1:47.62)

$2 Mutuel Prices:				
	11-MAGGIE MAY'S SWORD	16.80	9.50	6.90
	4-AFTER YOU		12.00	7.80
	9-SHOW MY GAL			4.80

$2 EXACTA 11-4 PAID $193.00 $2 QUINELLA 4-11 PAID $115.50 $2 TRIFECTA 11-4-9 PAID $952.00

B. f, by Sword Dance*Ire-Little Cris Cross, by Apalachee. Trainer Morrison John. Bred by Curtin Cheryl A (Fla).

MAGGIE MAY'S SWORD raced with the pace from the outside, responded when roused, drew clear in the stretch and was driving under the wire. AFTER YOU was rated along inside, rallied inside turning for home and finished gamely. SHOW MY GAL chased the pace from the outside and stayed on gamely to the finish. LAUREN'S HOT DANCE was outrun early, raced inside and had some traffic problems along the inside in the stretch. SIMONA (CHI) raced wide and finished well outside. ROSE ESTHER quickly showed in front, set the pace and tired in the final furlong. ALL NET JOE chased the pace, came wide for the drive and had no rally. SWEET SCARLET was rated inside, came wide into the stretch and had no rally. SHEBAKAYSKITTYCAT raced wide and had no response when roused. BAIL MONEY was rated along inside and was taken up sharply when in tight in the stretch. BELAWAN had no rally. MARIQUITA'S SECRET showed speed along the inside and tired in the stretch.

Owners— 1, Tucker Jeffrey; 2, Gerrity Joseph W Jr; 3, Sunny Meadow Farm; 4, West Point Stable Wolfe Steven & Br; 5, Augustin Stable; 6, Bomze Richard M; 7, Thor John; 8, Yorkes Arthur & Leuci Patrick; 9, Cruguet Jean & Miron Julie; 10, Backer William M; 11, Lichtefeld Paul A & Stewart Jack D; 12, Gabrielle Farm & Laneve Nickolas S

Trainers—1, Morrison John; 2, Hernandez Ramon M; 3, Friedman Mitchell; 4, Contessa Gary C; 5, Sheppard Jonathan E; 6, O'Brien Leo; 7, Sciacca Gary; 8, Reynolds Patrick L; 9, Cruguet Jean; 10, Tagg Barclay; 11, Romans Dale; 12, Dutrow Richard E Jr

Maggie May's Sword was claimed by Acclaimed Raysing Stable; trainer, Iwinski Allen.

Scratched— Stone Ends (27Aug00 ^{1}SAR^{5}), Kerry Offaly (16Aug00 ^{10}SAR^{5}), Sign Of Courage (29Jun00 ^{3}BEL^{4})

$2 Daily Double (6-11) Paid $99.50; Daily Double Pool $516,611.

THIRD RACE
Saratoga
SEPTEMBER 2, 2000

6 FURLONGS. (1.08) MAIDEN CLAIMING. Purse $31,000 (Up To $6,014 NYSBFOA) For Maiden Two Year Olds. Weight 119 lbs. CLAIMING PRICE $75,000, for each $5,000 to $65,000 1 lbs.

Value of Race: $31,000 Winner $18,600; second $6,200; third $3,410; fourth $1,860; fifth $930. Mutuel Pool $558,310.00 Exacta Pool $614,026.00 Trifecta Pool $375,360.00

Last Raced	Horse	M/Eqt. A.Wt	PP	St	1/4	1/2	Str	Fin	Jockey	Cl'g Pr	Odds $1
16Jly00 2Bel5	Friday's A Comin'	Lb	2 119	3	5	21	1$\frac{1}{2}$	13$\frac{1}{2}$	14$\frac{1}{2}$	Smith M E	75000	8.10
	Max Patch		2 119	5	11	73	63	5$\frac{1}{2}$	2nk	Chavez J F	75000	14.30
	Special Saint	L	2 119	10	7	3$\frac{1}{2}$	3$\frac{1}{2}$	2$\frac{1}{2}$	32	Bailey J D	75000	3.00
14Aug00 4Sar2	Sweat Equity		2 119	4	3	4hd	5$\frac{2}{1}$	6$\frac{5}{2}$	42$\frac{1}{2}$	Day P	75000	3.85
14Aug00 4Sar4	Storm's Lining	Lb	2 117	11	1	1$\frac{1}{2}$	21$\frac{1}{2}$	4$\frac{1}{2}$	5nk	Sellers S J	65000	21.70
14Aug00 4Sar3	Wind In The Sky	L	2 119	6	2	5$\frac{2}{1}$	41$\frac{1}{2}$	3hd	62$\frac{1}{2}$	Davis R G	75000	8.00
	Carson City Carl		2 117	7	10	103	9$\frac{1}{2}$	7$\frac{1}{2}$	71$\frac{1}{4}$	Luzzi M J	65000	21.20
3Aug00 2Sar4	Classic Endeavor	b	2 119	1	6	8$\frac{1}{2}$	7hd	8hd	8nk	Migliore R	65000	2.65
16Jly00 2Bel7	Inscrutable	b	2 117	9	8	11	8$\frac{1}{2}$	93$\frac{1}{2}$	94$\frac{1}{2}$	Prado E S	65000	30.50
3Aug00 2Sar9	Pauls Hardworker	Lb	2 117	8	9	9hd	10$\frac{1}{2}$	1010	23$\frac{1}{4}$	Samyn J L	65000	60.75
10Aug00 6Sar6	Cabot Trail	L	2 119	2	4	6$\frac{1}{2}$	11	11	11	Gryder A T	75000	18.30

OFF AT 2:06 Start Good. Won driving. Track fast.
TIME :22⁴, :46¹, :58³, 1:12¹ (:22.82, :46.23, :58.75, 1:12.24)

$2 Mutuel Prices:				
	3–FRIDAY'S A COMIN'	18.20	11.40	7.40
	5–MAX PATCH		14.40	8.10
	10–SPECIAL SAINT			4.30

$2 EXACTA 3–5 PAID $292.00 $2 TRIFECTA 3–5–10 PAID $1,462.00

Ch. c, (Apr), by Wheaton–Tudor Guest, by Medieval Man. Trainer Tagg Barclay. Bred by Jacks or Better Farm Inc (Fla).

FRIDAY'S A COMIN' showed good speed while under wraps, angled to the outside on the backstretch, swept to the front on the turn and drew away under a drive. MAX PATCH was hustled along early and rallied outside to get the place spot. SPECIAL SAINT showed speed from the outside, raced wide and had no rally. SWEAT EQUITY showed speed along the inside and had no rally. STORM'S LINING tired after a half mile. WIND IN THE SKY chased inside and tired in the stretch. CARSON CITY CARL raced four wide and tired. CLASSIC ENDEAVOR was outrun. INSCRUTABLE stumbled at the start and had no rally. PAULS HARDWORKER was outrun. CABOT TRAIL tired after showing brief speed.

Owners— 1, My Monarch Stable; 2, Rich Meadow Farm; 3, Vanderhyde Thomas; 4, Ramsey Kenneth L & Sarah K; 5, Mitchell Robert S; 6, Roberts Bea & Robert H; 7, Carl Massero; 8, Team Five Star Stable; 9, John Tatta & December Hill Farm; 10, Sigel Marshall E; 11, Vegso Peter

Trainers—1, Tagg Barclay; 2, Sciacca Gary; 3, Stewart Dallas; 4, Simon Charles; 5, Morse Randy L; 6, Hough Stanley M; 7, Schettino Dominick A; 8, Galluscio Dominic G; 9, Hennig Mark; 10, Donk David; 11, Jolley Leroy

Special Saint was claimed by Sampson Steve; trainer, Reynolds Patrick L.,
Sweat Equity was claimed by Hemlock Hills Farm; trainer, Domino Carl J.,
Classic Endeavor was claimed by Schwartz Herbert T; trainer, Schwartz Scott M.
Scratched— Fairest Riches

$2 Pick Three (6–11–3) Paid $1,147.00; Pick Three Pool $128,491.

FOURTH RACE
Saratoga
SEPTEMBER 2, 2000

6½ FURLONGS. (1.14²) ALLOWANCE. Purse $45,000. (Up To $8,730 NYSBFOA). For Three Year Olds And Upward Which Have Never Won Two Races Other Than Maiden, Claiming, Starter, Or Restricted Or Which Have Never Won Three Races. Three Year Olds 119 lbs.; Older 123 lbs. Non–winners of $25,000 other than restricted since June 30 allowed, 2 lbs. (Races where entered for $60,000 or less not considered in allowances.)

Value of Race: $45,000 Winner $27,000; second $9,000; third $4,950; fourth $2,700; fifth $1,350. Mutuel Pool $509,620.00 Exacta Pool $538,866.00 Quinella Pool $48,808.00 Trifecta Pool $316,946.00

Last Raced	Horse	M/Eqt. A.Wt	PP	St	1/4	1/2	Str	Fin	Jockey	Odds $1
22Apr00 9Kee5	Rollin With Nolan	L	3 117	3	5	56	2hd	25$\frac{1}{2}$	1no	Bailey J D	0.75
16Aug00 7Sar1	Rich In Glory	Lf	3 119	6	1	31	1$\frac{1}{2}$	1hd	23$\frac{1}{2}$	Luzzi M J	2.75
17Jun00 7Bel7	Peeping Tom	Lb	3 117	2	6	6	6	3$\frac{1}{2}$	33$\frac{3}{4}$	Bridgmohan S X	10.40
26Jly00 8Sar3	Actin Time	Lb	4 121	5	2	41$\frac{1}{2}$	4hd	43$\frac{1}{2}$	410$\frac{1}{2}$	Prado E S	7.50
11Aug00 7Sar4	Bulling	Lb	3 117	1	3	1hd	32	52$\frac{1}{2}$	54	Rojas R I	9.50
30Jly00 4Sar6	Irish Dawn	Lf	3 117	4	4	2hd	51$\frac{1}{2}$	6	6	St Julien M	20.80

OFF AT 2:37 Start Good For All But ROLLIN WITH NOLAN Won driving. Track fast.
TIME :22¹, :45⁴, 1:10, 1:16² (:22.31, :45.83, 1:10.09, 1:16.46)

$2 Mutuel Prices:				
	3–ROLLIN WITH NOLAN	3.50	2.40	2.20
	6–RICH IN GLORY		2.80	2.30
	2–PEEPING TOM			2.80

$2 EXACTA 3–6 PAID $8.00 $2 QUINELLA 3–6 PAID $5.20 $2 TRIFECTA 3–6–2 PAID $28.60

Ch. c, (May), by Summer Squall–Pi Phi Hi D, by Sauce Boat. Trainer Zito Nicholas P. Bred by John T L Jones Jr & Bud Boschert (Ky).

ROLLIN WITH NOLAN stumbled badly at the start but recovered quickly, rallied three wide, dug in determinedly in the stretch and got the nod after a prolonged drive. RICH IN GLORY contested the pace from the outside, dug in gamely along the inside in the stretch and fought it out to the finish, just missing. PEEPING TOM broke slowly, raced wide and finished well outside. ACTIN TIME raced close up while in hand, was steadied on the turn and had no rally. BULLING ducked out at the start, contested the pace along the inside and tired in the stretch. IRISH DAWN showed speed while between rivals, was steadied on the turn and tired.

Owners— 1, Ramsey Kenneth L & Sarah K; 2, Timber Bay Farm; 3, Flatbird Stable; 4, Scattaglia Luis L; 5, Hobeau Farm; 6, McKee Stables

Trainers—1, Zito Nicholas P; 2, Schettino Dominick A; 3, Reynolds Patrick L; 4, Frankel Robert; 5, Jerkens H Allen; 6, Romans Dale

$2 Pick Three (11–3–3) Paid $373.50; Pick Three Pool $119,654.

FIFTH RACE **7 FURLONGS. (1.20^{3}) MAIDEN SPECIAL WEIGHT. Purse $41,000 (Up To $7,954 NYSBFOA) For Maiden Fillies and Mares Three Years Old And Upward. Three Year Olds 118 lbs.; Older 121 lbs.**

Saratoga

SEPTEMBER 2, 2000

Value of Race: $41,000 Winner $24,600; second $8,200; third $4,510; fourth $2,460; fifth $1,230. Mutuel Pool $747,513.00 Exacta Pool $769,590.00 Trifecta Pool $557,453.00

Last Raced	Horse	M/Eqt.	A.Wt	PP	St	¼	½	Str	Fin	Jockey	Odds $1
11Aug00 ^{6}Sar^{2}	Regent Gold	Lb	3 118	1	7	6^{3}	6^{5}	3^{1}	1^{hd}	Day P	2.25
18Aug00 ^{1}Sar^{5}	Fort Ann	L	3 118	8	3	$5^{\frac{1}{2}}$	$3^{\frac{1}{2}}$	1^{1}	$2^{2\frac{3}{4}}$	Perret C	7.40
18Aug00 ^{1}Sar^{3}	Mt. Bonsi	Lb	3 118	5	5	8^{hd}	$8^{\frac{1}{2}}$	$4^{\frac{1}{2}}$	$3^{2\frac{3}{4}}$	Chavez J F	2.85
13Feb00 ^{11}GP^{9}	Your Sweetness	L	3 118	3	4	$2^{2\frac{1}{2}}$	1^{hd}	$2^{\frac{1}{2}}$	$4^{\frac{1}{2}}$	Migliore R	4.50
11Aug00 ^{6}Sar^{6}	Flying Tassie	L	3 118	6	6	4^{hd}	$5^{2\frac{1}{2}}$	$5^{2\frac{1}{2}}$	$5^{1\frac{1}{2}}$	Leon F	24.00
4Aug00 ^{5}Sar^{8}	Sybil S.	Lb	3 118	4	9	9	$7^{\frac{1}{2}}$	7^{1}	$6^{1\frac{3}{4}}$	Bridgmohan S X	46.75
11Aug00 ^{6}Sar^{7}	Sweet Vale	L	3 118	7	2	$3^{\frac{1}{2}}$	$4^{\frac{1}{2}}$	$6^{\frac{1}{2}}$	$7^{7\frac{3}{4}}$	Bailey J D	9.10
18Aug00 ^{1}Sar^{2}	Kristi's Sunshine	Lb	3 118	2	8	$1^{\frac{1}{2}}$	$2^{\frac{1}{2}}$	8^{10}	$8^{9\frac{3}{4}}$	Smith M E	6.60
7Jan00 ^{2}Aqu^{2}	August	Lbf	3 118	9	1	7^{hd}	9	9	9	Pezua J M	37.50

OFF AT 3:12 Start Good. Won driving. Track fast.

TIME :22^{2}, :46, 1:11^{2}, 1:25 (:22.47, :46.00, 1:11.59, 1:25.13)

$2 Mutuel Prices:				
	1–REGENT GOLD	6.50	3.70	2.50
	8–FORT ANN		6.20	3.40
	5–MT. BONSI			2.80

$2 EXACTA 1–8 PAID $57.50 $2 TRIFECTA 1–8–5 PAID $141.00

Ch. f, (Mar), by Seeking the Gold–In My Cap, by Vice Regent. Trainer Lukas D Wayne. Bred by Hermitage Farm LLC (Ky).

REGENT GOLD raced close up inside early, dropped back on the turn, rallied five wide approaching the stretch, finished determinedly from the outside and was along late, driving. FORT ANN raced close up outside, rallied three wide on the turn, drew clear in midstretch and continued on gamely but could not resist the winner. MT. BONSI raced inside and finished well. YOUR SWEETNESS contested the pace from the outside and tired in the stretch. FLYING TASSIE chased along the inside and tired. SYBIL S. had no response when roused. SWEET VALE chased outside and tired. KRISTI'S SUNSHINE contested the pace along the inside and tired. AUGUST tired.

Owners— 1, Padua Stable & Sanan Anne; 2, Coppola Albert P; 3, Bryant Joseph D; 4, The Thoroughbred Corporation; 5, Peace John H; 6, Sigel Marshall E; 7, Melnyk Eugene; 8, Hicks Judy B; 9, Southbelle Stable

Trainers—1, Lukas D Wayne; 2, Vestal Peter M; 3, Bond Harold James; 4, Kimmel John C; 5, Arnold George R II; 6, Donk David; 7, Pletcher Todd A; 8, Romans Dale; 9, Stabile Anthony A

$2 Pick Three (11–3–1) Paid $209.50; Pick Three Pool $158,536.

SIXTH RACE **6 FURLONGS. (1.08) ALLOWANCE. Purse $43,000 For Three Year Olds And Upward, foaled in New York State and approved by the New York State–Bred Registry Which Have Never Won A Race Other Than Maiden, Claiming, Or Starter. Three Year Olds 119 lbs.; Older 122 lbs. Non–winners of $24,000 since July 1 allowed, 2 lbs. (Races where entered for $35,000 or less not considered in allowances).**

Saratoga

SEPTEMBER 2, 2000

Value of Race: $43,000 Winner $25,800; second $8,600; third $4,730; fourth $2,580; fifth $1,290. Mutuel Pool $763,034.00 Exacta Pool $814,163.00 Trifecta Pool $609,985.00

Last Raced	Horse	M/Eqt.	A.Wt	PP	St	¼	½	Str	Fin	Jockey	Odds $1
13Aug00 ^{9}Sar^{2}	John Paul Too	L	3 117	10	2	$3^{\frac{1}{2}}$	3^{2}	1^{hd}	$1^{3\frac{1}{2}}$	Migliore R	1.15
13Aug00 ^{9}Sar^{3}	Son	f	3 119	6	3	$2^{\frac{1}{2}}$	$2^{\frac{1}{2}}$	$2^{\frac{1}{2}}$	$2^{\frac{3}{4}}$	Davis R G	3.85
19Aug00 ^{3}Sar^{5}	Smooth Talc	L	3 117	11	1	$8^{3\frac{1}{2}}$	$7^{\frac{1}{2}}$	$7^{\frac{1}{2}}$	3^{2}	Smith M E	24.75
24Jun00 ^{3}CD^{6}	Rainy Day Blues	L	3 117	3	10	7^{hd}	$6^{\frac{1}{2}}$	6^{hd}	$4^{\frac{1}{2}}$	Day P	7.40
13Aug00 ^{9}Sar^{4}	Wahoo	Lbf	4 120	1	4	$1^{\frac{1}{2}}$	1^{hd}	$3^{4\frac{1}{2}}$	$5^{\frac{1}{2}}$	Gryder A T	9.10
5Aug00 ^{5}Sar^{8}	Mr Smartypants	Lb	4 120	7	9	9^{5}	9^{5}	8^{1}	6^{1}	Chavez J F	21.30
8Jun00 ^{6}Bel^{6}	Dancing Lou	L	3 117	5	8	6^{hd}	8^{2}	9^{7}	$7^{2\frac{1}{4}}$	Luzzi M J	16.10
28Jly00 ^{7}Mth^{5}	Houstand	L	4 120	8	6	5^{3}	4^{hd}	4^{hd}	$8^{\frac{1}{2}}$	Bridgmohan S X	23.70
19Aug00 ^{3}Sar^{4}	Monologue	Lbf	3 117	4	5	4^{hd}	5^{2}	$5^{\frac{1}{2}}$	9^{4}	Sellers S J	5.50
9Jan00 ^{2}Aqu^{3}	Forever Man	Lf	3 117	9	7	10^{5}	10^{3}	10^{8}	$10^{12\frac{3}{4}}$	Pezua J M	70.00
13Aug00 ^{9}Sar^{9}	G Gordon	Lb	7 120	2	11	11	11	11	11	Rojas R I	121.25

OFF AT 3:46 Start Good. Won driving. Track fast.

TIME :22^{3}, :46, :58^{2}, 1:11^{1} (:22.75, :46.14, :58.52, 1:11.36)

$2 Mutuel Prices:				
	11–JOHN PAUL TOO	4.30	2.80	2.50
	6–SON		3.80	3.30
	12–SMOOTH TALC			6.30

$2 EXACTA 11–6 PAID $13.40 $2 TRIFECTA 11–6–12 PAID $126.50

Dk. b. or br. c, (Jan), by Sea Hero–Lady She Is Too, by Two's a Plenty. Trainer Kimmel John C. Bred by Frank Stella (NY).

JOHN PAUL TOO raced close up outside, rallied three wide into the stretch and drew clear late, driving. SON contested the pace from the outside and continued on gamely to earn the place award. SMOOTH TALC raced four wide and was going well from the outside late. RAINY DAY BLUES came wide into the stretch and had no rally. WAHOO contested the pace along the inside and tired in the final furlong. MR SMARTYPANTS had no response when roused. DANCING LOU was hustled along outside and had no rally. HOUSTAND chased outside and tired. MONOLOGUE chased the pace along the inside and tired in the stretch. FOREVER MAN had no rally. G GORDON stumbled at the start and tired.

Owners— 1, Kimmel Caesar P Solondz Philip J &; 2, Nerud John A; 3, Double R Stable Kaufman Robert & Is; 4, Ramsey Kenneth L & Sarah K; 5, Hauman Eugene E; 6, Carrothers Margaret N & Parker Patr; 7, Pastore Richard S & Mazzilli Philip; 8, Baker Charlton; 9, Patti Gale A Lerner Harold Gross Ja; 10, Southbelle Stable; 11, Martino Phyllis

Trainers—1, Kimmel John C; 2, Jerkens James A; 3, Stoklosa Richard; 4, Simon Charles; 5, Hushion Michael E; 6, Hertler John O; 7, Picou James E; 8, Baker Charlton; 9, Patti Gale A; 10, Stabile Anthony A; 11, Martino Phyllis

Scratched— Unrelenting Desire (13Aug00 ^{9}SAR^{6}), Wild Bidder (19Aug00 ^{3}SAR^{6}), Electra Q Shun (19Aug00 ^{3}SAR^{3})

$2 Pick Three (3–1–11) Paid $36.60; Pick Three Pool $178,241.

SEVENTH RACE

Saratoga

SEPTEMBER 2, 2000

1⅜ MILES. (Inner Turf)(2.12) MAIDEN SPECIAL WEIGHT. Purse $42,000. (Up To $8,148 NYSBFOA). For Maiden Three Year Olds And Upward. Three Year Olds 117 lbs.; Older 122 lbs. (Non–starters for a claiming price less than $40,000 in the last three starts preferred).

Value of Race: $42,000 Winner $25,200; second $8,400; third $4,620; fourth $2,520; fifth $1,260. Mutuel Pool $686,800.00 Exacta Pool $660,938.00 Trifecta Pool $500,488.00

Last Raced	Horse	M/Eqt.	A.Wt	PP	¼	½	¾	1	Str	Fin	Jockey	Odds $1
16Aug00 4Sar2	R C Indy Go	Lb	4 122	7	5½	5hd	3½	2½	1hd	1½	Chavez J F	b-1.60
23Jly00 1Sar2	Rather Be	L	4 122	9	82	83	7hd	52½	41½	2½	Miller B	6.40
30Jly00 1Sar10	Discovery Ridge	Lb	5 122	3	25	1hd	13	1½	22½	3¾	Luzzi M J	37.25
13Aug00 1Mth4	Private Bound	Lb	3 117	2	6½	73	62½	42	56	4½	Santos J A	a-7.70
6Aug00 10Sar7	Regal Dynasty	Lb	4 122	10	72½	61½	43	32½	3½	510¼	Bailey J D	2.60
3Jun00 4Del7	Ham I Am	L	3 117	8	10	10	9hd	7hd	6½	63¼	Smith M E	9.70
6Aug00 10Sar4	Shoo Launch	L	3 117	1	45	41½	82	96	83½	72	Day P	6.10
15Jun00 Lch6	Favorite Seat	L	3 117	4	92	92	10	86	76	89¾	Migliore R	a-7.70
3Jly00 10Lrl9	Flashing	Lb	3 117	6	3½	3½	51	6hd	915	919	Prado E S	58.50
22Jly00 2Bel10	Wood And Plenty	Lb	3 117	5	1hd	27	21	10	10	10	Rojas R I	b-1.60

a–Coupled: Private Bound and Favorite Seat.
b–Coupled: R C Indy Go and Wood And Plenty.

OFF AT 4:16 Start Good. Won driving. Course firm.
TIME :23^{2}, :46^{3}, 1:12, 1:37^{1}, 2:02, 2:14^{4} (:23.51, :46.72, 1:12.01, 1:37.39, 2:02.11, 2:14.84)

$2 Mutuel Prices:

2B–R C INDY GO (b-entry)	5.20	3.30	2.60
9–RATHER BE		5.20	4.10
6–DISCOVERY RIDGE			7.70

$2 EXACTA 2–9 PAID $40.00 $2 TRIFECTA 2–9–6 PAID $562.00

B. c, by A.P. Indy–Hot Silver, by Nureyev. Trainer Bond Harold James. Bred by Skymarc Farm Inc (Ky).

R C INDY GO was rated along early, rallied outside on the second turn, dug in resolutely in the stretch and prevailed under a drive. RATHER BE was outrun early, rallied inside on the third turn and finished gamely. DISCOVERY RIDGE contested the pace along the inside and stayed on gamely to the finish. PRIVATE BOUND was rated along early, rallied wide on the final turn and stayed on well to the finish. REGAL DYNASTY raced wide on every turn and weakened in the stretch. HAM I AM put in a wide run on the final turn and tired in the stretch. SHOO LAUNCH, rated along early, was steadied on the backstretch the second time around and tired. FAVORITE SEAT raced inside and had no response when roused. FLASHING tired. WOOD AND PLENTY contested the pace from the outside and tired.

Owners— 1, Rudlein Stable & Clifton William L; 2, Hudson River Farms; 3, Morgan Elliott R and Kathleen & Lit; 4, Live Oak Plantation; 5, P E Nicholson G A Seelbinder & R Ni; 6, Gottlieb Roy D; 7, Mary Lou Whitney Stable; 8, Cobra Farm Inc; 9, Thayer Stella F; 10, Stable Alnoff

Trainers—1, Bond Harold James; 2, Sheppard Jonathan E; 3, Morgan Anne C; 4, Clement Christophe; 5, Toner James J; 6, Dickinson Michael W; 7, Zito Nicholas P; 8, Clement Christophe; 9, Connors Robert F; 10, Bond Harold James

Scratched— Swamp Wolf (19Aug00 10SAR4), Allan Prell (2Aug00 1SAR5), Papa's Boy (19Aug00 10SAR2), Tragic Kingdom (16Aug00 4SAR3) Leady (19Aug00 10SAR3), Man From Wicklow (19Aug00 10SAR11), Ariel Chief (25Aug00 6MTH4), Conveyor Belt (13Jly00 1BEL5), Vegas (4Jly00 5BEL4), Southern Classic (29Jun00 2BEL6)

$2 Pick Three (1–11–2) Paid $57.50; Pick Three Pool $152,921.

EIGHTH RACE

Saratoga

SEPTEMBER 2, 2000

1⅛ MILES. (Turf)(1.45^{2}) ALLOWANCE. Purse $55,000. (Up To $10,670 NYSBFOA). For Four Year Olds And Upward Which Have Not Won Either $17,905 Other Than Maiden, Claiming, Starter, Or Restricted At A Mile Or Over On The Turf In 2000 Or Which Have Never Won Four Races Other Than Maiden, Claiming, Starter, Or Restricted. Weight 123 lbs. Non–winners of $30,000 at a mile or over on the turf since October 1 allowed, 3 lbs. $35,000 at a mile or over in 1999–00, 5 lbs. $20,000 twice at a mile or over in 2000, 7 lbs. (Maiden, claiming, starter or restricted races not considered in allowances). (Preference by condition eligibility).

Value of Race: $55,000 Winner $33,000; second $11,000; third $6,050; fourth $3,300; fifth $1,650. Mutuel Pool $704,865.00 Exacta Pool $688,393.00 Trifecta Pool $542,843.00

Last Raced	Horse	M/Eqt.	A.Wt	PP	St	¼	½	¾	Str	Fin	Jockey	Odds $1
6Aug00 8Sar8	Indy Vidual	L	6 116	2	1	11½	11½	11½	13	12¾	Migliore R	5.50
19Aug00 7Sar1	A Little Luck	Lb	6 116	6	7	5½	5½	51½	2½	21¾	Gryder A T	6.60
16Aug00 8Sar6	Devil Ray	L	4 116	4	3	3½	3½	3½	32½	31¾	Samyn J L	25.75
4Jly00 9Bel6	Almutawakel-GB	L	5 120	5	5	2½	2½	2hd	4½	4no	Bailey J D	0.90
31Jly00 7Sar4	Just Listen	L	4 116	3	4	62½	62½	62½	51½	52	Ebina M	10.60
31Jly00 7Sar3	Tarquinius	Lb	4 116	1	2	7hd	8	7hd	73½	64	Prado E S	5.30
6Aug00 8Sar9	Sejm's Madness	Lb	4 116	7	6	4hd	4½	4hd	6½	7½	Davis R G	15.30
12Aug00 6Sar2	Phone the King	L	5 116	8	8	8	7hd	8	8	8	Espinoza J L	32.75

OFF AT 4:48 Start Good. Won driving. Course firm.
TIME :23^{3}, :47^{2}, 1:11, 1:33^{1}, 1:46 (:23.76, :47.57, 1:11.01, 1:33.39, 1:46.07)

$2 Mutuel Prices:

2–INDY VIDUAL	13.00	6.20	5.10
6–A LITTLE LUCK		6.00	4.30
4–DEVIL RAY			7.70

$2 EXACTA 2–6 PAID $65.50 $2 TRIFECTA 2–6–4 PAID $672.00

B. h, by A.P. Indy–I'm Splendid, by Our Native. Trainer Kimmel John C. Bred by Kimmel Caesar P (Ky).

INDY VIDUAL quickly opened a clear lead, set the pace and remained clear under a drive. A LITTLE LUCK raced inside and finished gamely to earn the place award. DEVIL RAY chased the pace along the inside and had no rally. ALMUTAWAKEL (GB) chased outside and tired. JUST LISTEN raced inside and had no response when roused. TARQUINIUS raced inside and had no rally. SEJM'S MADNESS raced wide and tired. PHONE THE KING was outrun.

Owners— 1, Kimmel Caesar P; 2, Crompton Kathleen; 3, McLeod Kelly; 4, Shadwell Stable; 5, Guez Marie Romaine & Guez D; 6, Stronach Stable; 7, Marbet Farm; 8, Pont Street Stable

Trainers—1, Kimmel John C; 2, Tagg Barclay; 3, Markgraf David; 4, Hennig Mark; 5, Cruguet Jean; 6, Orseno Joseph; 7, Plesa Edward Jr; 8, Carroll Del W II

Scratched— Truluck (6Aug00 8SAR7), Worthy Crane (30Aug00 7SAR5)

$2 Pick Three (11–2–2) Paid $60.50; Pick Three Pool $149,705.
$2 Pick Six (3–3–1–11–2–2) 6
Correct Paid $3,150.00; Pick Six Pool $140,019. $2 Pick Six (3–3–1–11–2–2) 5
Correct Paid $50.00

NINTH RACE
Saratoga
SEPTEMBER 2, 2000

7 FURLONGS. (1.20³) 96th Running of THE HOPEFUL. Grade I. Purse $200,000 (Up To $34,800 NYSBFOA). FOR TWO YEAR OLDS. By subscription of $200 each, which should accompany the nomination; $1,000 to pass the entry box and $1,000 to start. The purse to be divided 60% to the winner, 20% to second, 11% to third, 6% to fourth and 3% to fifth. 122 lbs. Trophies will be presented to the winning owner, trainer and jockey. Closed Saturday, August 19, with 30 Nominations.

Value of Race: $200,000 Winners $80,000 each; third $22,000; fourth $12,000; fifth $6,000. Mutuel Pool $879,264.00 Exacta Pool $684,613.00 Trifecta Pool $536,788.00

Last Raced	Horse	M/Eqt.	A.	Wt	PP	St	¼	½	Str	Fin	Jockey	Odds $1
27Jly00 9Sar2	DH Yonaguska	b	2	122	2	7	4½	1hd	11½	1	Bailey J D	3.55
16Aug00 9Sar1	DH City Zip	L	2	122	9	2	3hd	73	31½	1nk	Santos J A	1.40
26Jly00 6Sar1	Macho Uno		2	122	7	6	7½	6½	2hd	37¼	Prado E S	9.10
17Jly00 1Pha1	Saint Verre	L	2	122	8	4	5hd	4½	42	42¼	Smith M E	4.40
26Jly00 1Del1	What's Up Dog	f	2	122	10	9	11	11	6½	51½	Hershbell A	107.00
16Aug00 9Sar3	Standard Speed	L	2	122	1	10	102½	10hd	71½	63¼	Pitty C D	57.50
6Aug00 3Sar1	Evening Attire		2	122	3	11	9½	93	93½	7¾	Davis R G	7.60
16Jly00 8Cby1	One By The Knows	L	2	122	11	1	2½	3½	8½	81½	Sellers S J	18.20
16Aug00 9Sar4	Jacksrbetter		2	122	5	5	6hd	5hd	5hd	98¼	Gryder A T	40.25
16Aug00 9Sar7	Zone Judge	L	2	122	6	8	81½	8½	102	103¼	Chavez J F	28.75
19Aug00 9Mth3	T P Louie	Lf	2	122	4	3	1hd	2hd	11	11	Migliore R	66.00

DH—Dead Heat.

OFF AT 5:18 Start Good. Won driving. Track fast.
TIME :22³, :46¹, 1:11¹, 1:24² (:22.72, :46.21, 1:11.38, 1:24.52)

$2 Mutuel Prices:

2–DH YONAGUSKA	3.70	4.00	3.20
9–DH CITY ZIP	2.90	3.00	2.50
7–MACHO UNO			4.90

$2 EXACTA 2–9 PAID $12.00 $2 EXACTA 9–2 PAID $9.20 $2 TRIFECTA 2–9–7 PAID $53.00 $2 TRIFECTA 9–2–7 PAID $34.40

Yonaguska—Dk. b. or br. c, (Apr), by Cherokee Run–Marital Spook, by Silver Ghost. Trainer Lukas D Wayne. Bred by Edward P Evans (Ky).

City Zip—Ch. c, (Feb), by Carson City–Baby Zip, by Relaunch. Trainer Rice Linda. Bred by Stronach Stables (Ky).

YONAGUSKA contested the pace along the inside, drew clear when roused in upper stretch, took a clear lead past the eighth eighth pole then dug in gamely under a steady drive and held on to earn a dead heat for the win. CITY ZIP raced close up while in hand, dropped back on the turn, came six wide nearing the stretch and finished fast from the outside to be on even terms at the wire. MACHO UNO was hustled along outside, rallied five wide on the turn and dug in gamely while between rivals through the stretch. SAINT VERRE showed good speed from the outside, chased the pace while four wide and tired in the final furlong. WHAT'S UP DOG was hustled outside, raced four wide and had no rally. STANDARD SPEED was hustled along inside, raced on the rail and had no rally. EVENING ATTIRE broke slowly, was hustled outside, raced while and lugged in while racing greenly in the stretch. ONE BY THE KNOWS showed good speed from the outside, contested the pace while between rivals and tired in the stretch. JACKSRBETTER raced close up inside, had no response when roused and tired in the stretch. ZONE JUDGE was hustled inside and had no response when roused. T P LOUIE contested the pace along the inside and tired in the stretch.

Owners— 1, Tabor Michael B; 2, Charles R Thompson Carl Bowling & L; 3, Stronach Stable; 4, Allen Joseph; 5, McIngvale James; 6, Perez Robert; 7, Grant Mary & Joseph & Kelly Thomas; 8, Kenneth Troutt & Lisa Troutt; 9, Aiken Gary; 10, Roberts Bea & Robert H; 11, B & J Stable

Trainers—1, Lukas D Wayne; 2, Rice Linda; 3, Orseno Joseph; 4, McGaughey Claude III; 5, Wohlers Laura; 6, Russo Sal; 7, Kelly Timothy D; 8, Walden W Elliott; 9, Azpurua Manuel J; 10, Hough Stanley M; 11, Ciresa Martin E

Scratched— Scorpion (16Aug00 9SAR2)

$2 Pick Three (2–2–2) Paid $72.50; Pick Three Pool $167,239.
$2 Consolation Pick Three (2–2–9) Paid $45.00

Obviously, if a player is armed with the proper understanding of what happens to a racing surface as it progresses through rain-related cycles, he or she will be able to spot a bias more accurately and tailor serious bets to fit the prevailing tendencies. To this end, meet-long statistics can be dangerous, in that they can stress longer-term trends that may have nothing to do with the short-term trend (bias) you are handicapping into. This—the value of a winning short-term trend over any long-term trend—is one of the least appreciated and most powerful handicapping notions in the game. It is

TENTH RACE
Saratoga
SEPTEMBER 2, 2000

1 MILE. (Inner Turf)(1.33^3) ALLOWANCE. Purse $44,000. (Up To $8,536 NYSBFOA). For Three Year Olds And Upward Which Have Never Won A Race Other Than Maiden, Claiming, Or Starter Or Which Have Never Won Two Races. Three Year Olds 119 lbs.; Older 123 lbs. Non–winners of $25,000 at a mile or over since July 1 allowed, 2 lbs. (Races where entered for $50,000 or less not considered in allowances). (Preference by condition eligibility).

Value of Race: $44,000 Winner $26,400; second $8,800; third $4,840; fourth $2,640; fifth $1,320. Mutuel Pool $515,591.00 Exacta Pool $438,235.00 Trifecta Pool $353,806.00 Superfecta Pool $184,127.00

Last Raced	Horse	M/Eqt.	A.Wt	PP	St	¼	½	¾	Str	Fin	Jockey	Odds $1
6Nov99 8GP7	Brahms	Lb	3 117	6	7	6½	7½	7½	6½	11½	Day P	1.50
10Aug00 8Sar2	Quiet Quest	L	3 117	4	2	1½	1hd	1hd	1½	2nk	Chavez J F	3.25
19Aug00 4Sar4	River Bed	Lb	3 117	10	8	8^2	6½	5½	4½	3nk	Bailey J D	6.80
10Aug00 8Sar4	Polish Times	L	3 119	3	3	52½	51½	6½	2hd	41¼	Bridgmohan S X	10.00
6Aug00 4Sar3	Kolinor	Lb	3 119	1	1	3hd	4hd	4hd	3hd	5¾	Davis R G	8.20
6Aug00 4Sar6	Slewfrito	Lb	4 121	7	5	4hd	3hd	3½	5½	64½	Prado E S	12.90
19Aug00 4Sar11	El Temperamental	L	4 121	5	4	2½	2½	2hd	7^6	7½	Luzzi M J	f-42.50
11May00 8Bel6	Heavenly Show	Lb	4 121	9	9	91½	9½	8^2	8^2	83¼	Migliore R	31.00
26Jly00 5Sar9	Secret Friend-CH	L	4 121	8	6	7½	81½	9½	10	9¾	St Julien M	55.50
9Oct99 CRK1	Commanche Saddle-IR		3 117	2	10	10	10	10	9½	10	Sellers S J	12.30

f–Mutuel Field: El Temperamental.

OFF AT 5:41 Start Good. Won driving. Course good.
TIME :24^2, :48^2, 1:13^2, 1:37^3 (:24.58, :48.53, 1:13.52, 1:37.78)

$2 Mutuel Prices:				
	5–BRAHMS	5.00	3.10	2.60
	4–QUIET QUEST		3.60	2.50
	9–RIVER BED			3.10

$2 EXACTA 5–4 PAID $15.00 $2 TRIFECTA 5–4–9 PAID $55.20 $2 SUPERFECTA 5–4–9–3 PAID $243.50

Dk. b. or br. c, (Mar), by Danzig–Queena, by Mr. Prospector. Trainer Walden W Elliott. Bred by Hamilton Emory A (Ky).

BRAHMS was rated along inside, altered course to the outside in upper stretch, responded when roused and was clear under the wire, driving. QUIET QUEST contested the pace along the inside and stayed on gamely to the finish. RIVER BED was rated along outside, rallied four wide on the second turn and finished gamely outside. POLISH TIMES raced close up while between rivals and stayed on gamely through the stretch. KOLINOR raced close up inside while well in hand and had no rally. SLEWFRITO chased the pace while three wide and tired in the stretch. EL TEMPERAMENTAL contested the pace from the outside and tired in the stretch. HEAVENLY SHOW was steadied along the inside on the first turn and had no rally. SECRET FRIEND (CHI) had no response when roused. COMMANCHE SADDLE (IRE) broke slowly and raced inside.

Owners— 1, Van Meter II Thomas F; 2, Ritzenberg Mrs Grace E; 3, Snowden Diane & Guy B; 4, Bloom William & Georgallas James; 5, Englander Richard A; 6, Applegreen Farm; 7, Old Brookside Farm; 8, Brodsky Alan; 9, Canzone Peter J & Eloise Sr; 10, Padua Stables

Trainers—1, Walden W Elliott; 2, Turner William H Jr; 3, Mott William I; 4, Donk David; 5, Schosberg Richard; 6, Sciacca Gary; 7, Mueller Russell; 8, Hennig Mark; 9, Galluscio Dominic G; 10, Lukas D Wayne

Scratched— Knock Again (19Aug00 4SAR5), Slowhand (7Aug00 8SAR5), Past Due Account (19Aug00 4SAR9), Trumpster (19Aug00 4SAR6), Mateeghan (4Jly00 7BEL7), Carefree (23Aug00 8SAR2), Immediate Delivery (21Aug00 9SAR6), Banner Headline (29Jly00 1SAR8)

$2 Daily Double (2–5) Paid $15.00; Daily Double Pool $358,997.
$2 Daily Double (9–5) Paid $7.90 $2 Pick Three (2–2–5) Paid $109.00; Pick Three Pool $198,759.
$2 Consolation Pick Three (2–9–5) Paid $45.60

Saratoga Attendance: 18,373 Mutuel Pool: $3,111,247.00 ITW Mutuel Pool: $6,048,883.00 ISW Mutuel Pool: $10,526,808.00

such a potent factor that I can hardly do it justice here, except to repeatedly point out examples in different contexts where it will pay enormous dividends.

GOING TO SCHOOL AT GULFSTREAM PARK

If I bypass Fair Grounds and head to Florida for the Fountain of Youth Stakes at Gulfstream, I expect to encounter a dirt racing surface that is overly kind to front-running types, especially those who figure to get over to the inside rail. While this bias does not exist every racing day, or each year, it exists often enough to distort the results of many races in most Gulfstream seasons.

When a front-running rail bias is in full force, as it was during the 2000 Gulfstream meet, I refrain from making the obvious plays at short odds and concentrate on picking longshots that have a hint of speed for play in exactas and trifectas. Rarely will I take a serious plunge on a heavily bet favorite even if the bias is in that horse's favor. I will, however, *take negative note of bias-aided horses that failed to deliver and positive note of those that were forced to race wide and/or rallied mildly into the teeth of the extreme speed bias.* Down the road these horses will need to be upgraded, or given a free pass for the race they lost against the grain of the track. Often, these horses will become deserving plays on normal tracks.

Give a good trainer a horse that was able to run strongly against a biased track and there is an excellent chance the same horse will defeat better competition down the road. Conversely, a well-bet horse that failed to run a winning race while the bias was in his favor may have given you all the reason you need to downgrade him in his next start. The same thing goes for a horse that won a race *primarily* because he had the bias in his favor.

Indeed, the true power of track bias is not necessarily in the race you are handicapping, but in the potent tool it provides for evaluating winning and losing races in future past-performance lines.

Consider, for example, the performances of the relatively young 3-year-olds below who ran against the bias at Gulfstream. My notebook was filled with horses that made headway against the Gulfstream bias in February and March 2000.

Here are the early-season past performances of **Red Bullet,** an important winner of major stakes as a 3-year-old in 2000.

Red Bullet		Ch. c. 3 (Apr)	Life	2 2 0 0	$43,800	D.Fst	2 2 0 0	$43,800 94
Own: Stronach Stable		Sire: Unbridled (Fappiano)	2000	2 2 0 0	$43,800	Wet	0 0 0 0	$0 —
		Dam: Cargo (Caro*Ire)	1999	0 M 0 0	$0	Turf	0 0 0 0	$0 —
		Br: Stronach Frank H (Ky)				Dist	0 0 0 0	$0 —
		Tr: Orseno Joseph (—) 2000:(61 11 .18)	CD	0 0 0 0	$0			

5Feb00–9GP fst 7f   :222 :454 1:113 1:241   Alw 32000N1x   94 5 10 83½ 52 11 12½   Bailey J D   L 122   *1.30 79–26 Red Bullet122 2½ Chervy1226½ Admiral Perry119¾   Slow start, wide rally 10
8Jan00–6Aqu fst 6f ⊡:224 :461 :584 1:104   Md Sp Wt 41k   87 2 9 62½ 63½ 1hd 17   Bridgmohan S X   L 120   2.00 88–15 Red Bullet120⁷ Dream Boy113 1½ Timely Devil120²   Came wide, ridden out 9
WORKS: Feb21 AdS 5f gd 1:01⁴ H 1/1   Jan28 GP 5f fst 1:00³ H 5/28   Jan4 Bel tr.t 4f fst :52 B 24/25   Dec24 Bel tr.t 4f fst :51 B 66/117   Dec18 Bel tr.t 4f fst :50¹ B 53/76   Dec10 Bel tr.t 5f fst 1:01 Hg 10/54

Red Bullet, the eventual Preakness winner, foreshadowed his potential with his first two races. One was against the grain of the inside-speed-favoring Aqueduct inner track. The other was against the grain of the inside-speed-favoring Gulfstream Park strip.

The talented **Unshaded** was another top colt who flashed his future in graded stakes by also winning nicely from off the pace at Gulfstream. My guess is that you would have had no trouble predicting a stakes future for Red Bullet or Unshaded based upon their stretch-running, winning performances over speed-favoring surfaces early in their 3-year-old racing seasons. I can assure you that the scenario repeats itself year after year and extends to lower levels of competition.

Captain Red

Own: Celtic Pride Stable
NAKATANI C S (–) 2000:(477 108 .23)

B. c. 3 (Feb) SARAUG98 $100,000
Sire: Mr. Greeley (Gone West) $15,000
Dam: Mary Roland (Relaunch)
Br: Darlene Wahman (Ky)
Tr: Zito Nicholas P(27 9 1 4 .33) 2000:(173 26 .15)

L 116

Life	9	3	1	1	$82,210	D.Fst	6	2	0	1	$58,380 97
2000	6	3	0	1	$71,550	Wet	3	1	1	0	$23,830 77
1999	3	M	1	0	$10,660	Turf	0	0	0	0	$0 –
Bel	2	1	0	0	$28,230	Dist	4	2	0	0	$55,260 97

14May00-6Bel	fst	7f	$:22^1$ $:45^3$ $1:11^1$ $1:24^4$	3↑ Alw 45000N2X	**86**	2	3	1½	1½	14½	11	Gryder A T	L 116	*1.25	79–14	CaptainRed116[1] Storm'nEddy121½ Sam'sMiki114[5]	Speed inside, driving 6
2Apr00-9Aqu	fst	7f	$:22^2$ $:45$ $1:09^2$ $1:22^1$	3↑ Alw 43000N1X	**97**	7	3	1^2	1½	12½	12½	Gryder A T	L 114	3.70	89–19	*Captain Red*1142½ *Rockin' Ruby*1216½ Gilgamesh1231½	Pace, clear, driving 9
11Mar00-3GP	fst	6f	$:22^1$ $:45^2$ $:58$ $1:11$	Alw 37000N1X	**81**	4	1	21½	2½	42¾	43½	Nakatani C S	L 119 n	6.70	81–21	Graeme Hall119hd Canfield1191¼ Mahabarat122[2]	Bid turn, weakened 8
9Feb00-7GP	gd	6f	$:22^3$ $:46^3$ $:59$ $1:12^1$	Md 80000 (80-75)	**77**	10	1	21½	2½	2hd	1¾	Prado E S	L 122 n	4.10	78–26	Captain Red122¾ *Gustow Deeds*1222¼ Onerous122½	All out, prevailed 11
21Jan00-10GP	fst	6f	$:22^2$ $:46^3$ $:59^1$ $1:12$	Md 62500 (62.5-57.5)	**73**	7	8	73½	31½	21½	32½	Prado E S	L 122 n	3.30	76–23	Light Craft122[2] Brave Ghost122½ *Captain Red*1221¼	Bmpd, steadied start 12
8Jan00-3GP	fst	6f	$:21^3$ $:45^1$ $:58$ $1:11$	Md Sp Wt 30k	**63**	7	4	52¾	4^1	6^4	67½	Coa E M	L 122 n	6.70	77–18	Chervy1223¼ Jo Jo Pace122½ Gustow Deeds122hd	4 wide, tired 10
27Nov99-2Aqu	my	6f	$:21^4$ $:45^2$ $:57^3$ $1:10^2$	Md Sp Wt 41k	**62**	4	1	1^2	1hd	23½	2^9	Stevens G L	L 119 b	3.95	77–16	**Port Herman**119[9] Captain Red1191½ Alf109[2]	No match for winner 7
14Nov99-5Aqu	fst	7f	$:23^1$ $:46^3$ $1:11^4$ $1:24^1$	Md Sp Wt 41k	**63**	9	4	61½	51½	4^4	5^7	Prado E S	L 118	5.50	74–17	Ekundu118¾ Big E E1181¼ Call It Off118[4]	Chased, no response 11
11Oct99-7Bel	gd	7f	$:22^2$ $:45^2$ $1:09^3$ $1:22^2$	Md Sp Wt 41k	**52**	6	3	3^1	3^2	5^{10}	515½	Prado E S	118	15.80	74–13	Golden Brush1187¾ Trumpster1181½ Ansky1183½	Chased outside, tired 8

WORKS: Jun3 Sar tr.t 5f fst $1:03^3$ B *1/1* May27 Sar tr.t 5f fst $1:02^2$ B *4/9* May6 Bel 5f fst $1:00^1$ H *4/29* Apr22 Kee 4f fst $:48^3$ B *7/28* Apr15 Kee 5f fst $1:01^4$ B *10/28* Mar25 Kee 4f fst $:48^4$ B *2/14*

Captain Red hinted at above-average ability while struggling to close ground against the Gulfstream bias in two races in January. Finally, when he caught a relatively normal track after a rain shower on February 9, he won while showing improved speed and finishing ability—the sign of a sharp horse. Two starts later—on April 2, in New York—Captain Red was able to control the pace on a bias-free track to score by 2½ lengths at 3.70-1. Second-place finisher Rockin Ruby came back to win his next start to add to the power of this performance, which earned Captain Red his best Beyer Speed Figure. In Captain Red's next start at Belmont he cruised to victory over another field of older horses while setting a moderate pace.

TENTH RACE
Gulfstream
JANUARY 15, 2000

1$\frac{1}{16}$ MILES. (1.40^{1}) 11th Running of THE HOLY BULL. Grade III. Purse $100,000. 3–year–olds by subscription of $100 each which shall accompany the nomination, $1,000 to pass the entry box and $1,000 additional to start, with $100,000 guaranteed. The owner of the winner to receive $60,000, $20,000 to second, $11,000 to third, $6,000 to fourth and $3,000 to fifth. Weight, 122 lbs. Non–winners of $50,000 twice at a mile or over, allowed 3 lbs. $50,000 at one mile or over, 5 lbs. $50,000 or $35,000 at one mile or over, 8 lbs. $30,000 or $20,000 at one mile or over, 10 lbs. Starters to be named through the entry box by the usual time of closing. Horses finishing first, second or third, in the Holy Bull Stakes will automatically be nominated to the Florida Derby. Trophy to winning owner. This race will be limited to 14 starters, with also eligibles. (high weights preferred). Closed Wednesday, January 5.

Value of Race: $100,000 Winner $60,000; second $20,000; third $11,000; fourth $6,000; fifth $3,000. Mutuel Pool $497,701.00 Exacta Pool $378,711.00 Trifecta Pool $365,946.00

Last Raced	Horse	M/Eqt.	A.Wt	PP	St	¼	½	¾	Str	Fin	Jockey	Odds $1
20Dec99 ^{9}Crc^{1}	Hal's Hope		3 112	3	1	$1^{1\frac{1}{2}}$	$1^{2\frac{1}{2}}$	$1^{1\frac{1}{2}}$	$1^{2\frac{1}{2}}$	$1^{5\frac{1}{4}}$	Velez R I	40.20
26Dec99 ^{9}TP^{1}	Personal First	Lf	3 117	10	9	3^{hd}	2^{hd}	$2^{2\frac{1}{2}}$	2^{1}	$2^{1\frac{3}{4}}$	St Julien M	4.90
4Dec99 ^{7}Crc^{1}	Megacles	L	3 113	7	5	8^{3}	7^{hd}	5^{1}	3^{3}	$3^{1\frac{1}{2}}$	Smith M E	9.00
27Nov99 ^{11}CD^{10}	Nature	Lb	3 113	6	7	5^{hd}	4^{hd}	$3^{\frac{1}{2}}$	$4^{3\frac{1}{2}}$	$4^{\frac{1}{2}}$	Santos J A	50.80
3Dec99 ^{7}Lrl^{1}	Grundlefoot		3 112	4	4	10^{7}	10^{6}	11	5^{2}	$5^{2\frac{1}{2}}$	Chavez J F	20.70
27Nov99 ^{7}Aqu^{1}	Greenwood Lake	L	3 122	1	11	11	11	10^{hd}	6^{2}	$6^{7\frac{3}{4}}$	Samyn J L	1.30
18Dec99 ^{9}Hol^{3}	Cosine	Lb	3 114	11	8	$6^{3\frac{1}{2}}$	5^{1}	$4^{1\frac{1}{2}}$	$7^{3\frac{1}{2}}$	7^{1}	Bailey J D	4.70
1Jan00 ^{3}Crc^{1}	Painted Pistol	Lbf	3 113	2	3	9^{7}	9^{3}	9^{hd}	9^{4}	$8^{3\frac{1}{2}}$	Sellers S J	49.70
11Dec99 ^{11}Crc^{2}	Wayward Ways	L	3 112	8	6	2^{hd}	$6^{1\frac{1}{2}}$	6^{3}	$8^{1\frac{1}{2}}$	$9^{5\frac{1}{4}}$	Prado E S	5.10
25Nov99 ^{8}Aqu^{1}	High Note	Lb	3 114	9	10	7^{hd}	8^{3}	$7^{\frac{1}{2}}$	10^{5}	$10^{8\frac{1}{4}}$	Velazquez J R	82.50
11Dec99 ^{11}Crc^{6}	Fight For Ally	b	3 117	5	2	$4^{1\frac{1}{2}}$	$3^{\frac{1}{2}}$	8^{hd}	11	11	Douglas R R	55.60

OFF AT 5:05 Start Good. Won driving. Track fast.
TIME :23^{2}, :47^{3}, 1:12^{3}, 1:38, 1:44^{2} (:23.43, :47.61, 1:12.69, 1:38.07, 1:44.52)

$2 Mutuel Prices:				
	3–HAL'S HOPE	82.40	29.00	17.20
	10–PERSONAL FIRST		7.60	6.20
	7–MEGACLES			7.00

$2 EXACTA 3–10 PAID $477.00 $2 TRIFECTA 3–10–7 PAID $4,006.60

Dk. b. or br. c, (Mar), by Jolie's Halo–Mia's Hope, by Rexson's Hope. Trainer Rose Harold J. Bred by Harold Rose (Fla).

HAL'S HOPE made the pace along the inside, then responded to pressure in the drive and increased his margin to the wire. PERSONAL FIRST four wide around the first turn, stalked the pace into the stretch and proved second best while unable to stay with the winner. MEGACLES wearing a nasal strip, was reserved after being bumped at the start, then rallied along the inside around the far turn and outfinished the others. NATURE bumped at the start, steadied along the inside on the first turn, saved ground into the stretch and weakened. GRUNDLEFOOT outrun early, passed tired rivals. GREENWOOD LAKE wearing a nasal strip, dropped far back after breaking slowly, swung out to race six wide on the far turn and was never a threat. COSINE reserved off the pace, raced in contention three wide around the far turn and tired. PAINTED PISTOL unhurried early, raced five wide on the far turn while being outrun. WAYWARD WAYS showed speed around the first turn and faded. HIGH NOTE was no factor after breaking slowly. FIGHT FOR ALLY rank while chasing the pace around the first turn, stopped.

Owners— 1, H J Rose Trust; 2, Waldron D Killingworth L & Shively; 3, Rocking J B Stable & Fore Hearts; 4, Monroe Joyce & Roy K; 5, P L Fowler; 6, Dee Conway & F Dematies & J Cornacc; 7, Woodlynn Farm; 8, Willis Family Stables; 9, Dogwood Stable; 10, D F Flanagan; 11, Nolan Chris

Trainers—1 Rose Harold J; 2 Paulus David E; 3 Calascibetta Joseph; 4 McPeek Kenneth G; 5 Capuano Gary; 6 Zito Nicholas P;

TENTH RACE
Gulfstream
FEBRUARY 19, 2000

$1\frac{1}{16}$ MILES. (1.40[1]) 54th Running of THE FOUNTAIN OF YOUTH. Grade I. Purse $200,000 guaranteed. 3–year–olds. By subscription of $250 each which shall accompany the nomination, $2,000 to pass the entry box and $2,000 additional to start, with $200,000 guaranteed. The owner of the winner to receive $120,000, $40,000 to second, $22,000 to third, $12,000 of fourth, and $6,000 to fifth. Weight, 122 lbs. Non–winners of $75,000 twice at one mile or over, allowed 3 lbs. $75,000 at one mile or over, 5 lbs. $50,000 or $30,000 at one mile or over, 8 lbs. $30,000 or $25,000 at one mile or over, 10 lbs. Starters to be named through the entry box by the usual time of closing. Horses finishing first, second or third in the Fountain of Youth Stakes will automatically be nominated to the Florida Derby. Trophy to winning owner. This race will be limited to 14 starters, with also eligibles. (High weights preferred). Nominations closed Wednesday, February 9.

Value of Race: $200,000 Winner $120,000; second $40,000; third $22,000; fourth $12,000; fifth $6,000. Mutuel Pool $1,522,712.0 Exacta Pool $1,034,995.0 Trifecta Pool $929,135.00

Last Raced	Horse	M/Eqt. A.Wt	PP	St	¼	½	¾	Str	Fin	Jockey	Odds $1
30Jan00 7SA2	High Yield	Lb 3 117	4	3	1¹	1¹½	1hd	1¹	1³¼	Day P	2.40
15Jan00 10GP1	Hal's Hope	3 117	8	4	2¹½	2¹½	2³	2²½	2²½	Velez R I	10.30
7Nov99 4GP1	Elite Mercedes	L 3 117	10	8	3½	3²	3²½	3²½	3nk	Bailey J D	9.70
15Jan00 10GP6	Greenwood Lake	L 3 122	3	7	11	11	10¹	7hd	4¹¼	Nakatani C S	3.90
29Jan00 9GP3	American Bullet	L 3 114	6	6	7¹	8⁴	6²	5³	5½	Douglas R R	54.20
29Jan00 8GP1	Un Fino Vino	L 3 112	2	2	5¹	5¹½	4¹½	4½	6½	Chavez J F	8.80
13Nov99 7Haw1	Deputy Warlock	Lb 3 119	11	11	9⁵½	9⁸	9⁸	9⁴	7²	Smith M E	23.70
29Jan00 10GP1	Polish Miner	3 114	9	9	8⁴½	7hd	8¹½	8hd	8⁸	Velazquez J R	5.20
29Jan00 8GP2	Rupert Herd	b 3 113	7	10	10³	10⁴	11	11	9nk	Sellers S J	35.30
8Jan00 8Aqu2	Ben The Man	Lb 3 114	1	1	4³	4³	5⁴	6¹	10³¼	Prado E S	8.60
15Jan00 10GP2	Personal First	Lf 3 117	5	5	6³½	6⁵	7hd	10¹	11	St Julien M	18.70

OFF AT 5:17 Start Good. Won driving. Track fast.
TIME :23¹, :46, 1:09⁴, 1:35⁴, 1:42² (:23.25, :46.01, 1:09.88, 1:35.81, 1:42.56)

$2 Mutuel Prices:

4–HIGH YIELD	6.80	4.00	3.00
8–HAL'S HOPE		9.00	6.00
10–ELITE MERCEDES			6.00

$2 EXACTA 4–8 PAID $75.20 $2 TRIFECTA 4–8–10 PAID $450.40

Ch. c, (Mar), by Storm Cat–Scoop the Gold, by Forty Niner. Trainer Lukas D Wayne. Bred by Brushwood Stable (Pa).

HIGH YIELD wearing a nasal strip, outran HAL'S HOPE for the lead around the first turn, responded when challenged by that rival again approaching the end of the backstretch and drew off through the stretch under a strong hand ride. HAL'S HOPE bumped at the start, stalked the pace after being outrun for the lead, moved to challenge HIGH YIELD racing around the far turn but couldn't stay with that rival while proving second best. ELITE MERCEDES wearing a nasal strip, was forced out behind PERSONAL FIRST racing into the first turn, chased the pace three wide into the stretch and weakened. GREENWOOD LAKE far back early, saved ground into the stretch, angled out and closed willingly. AMERICAN BULLET bumped at the start, was reserved into the far turn, advanced into striking position entering the stretch, then lacked the needed late response. UN FINO VINO checked racing into the first turn forcing out PERSONAL FIRST, raced in striking position three wide around the far turn and failed to rally. DEPUTY WARLOCK allowed to settle, angled wide for the stretch run and failed to menace. POLISH MINER reserved early, angled wide in early stretch and failed to threaten. RUPERT HERD was no factor after being squeezed back at the start. BEN THE MAN wearing a nasal strip, chased the pace along the rail into the far turn and faded. PERSONAL FIRST bumped at the start, was forced out and steadied on the first turn, then was through after a half mile.

Owners— 1, R Lewis Mrs J Magnier & M Tabor Et; 2, Rose Family Stable Ltd; 3, Winstar Farm & P Wittmann; 4, Dee Conway & F Dematies & J Cornacc; 5, Robinson Jill E; 6, Sunny Meadow Farm; 7, Select Stable; 8, Phipps Ogden M; 9. Smith G A & Johnston W E: 10. Stronach Stable: 11. D Walderon L Killingworth & W Shive

TWELFTH RACE

Gulfstream

MARCH 11, 2000

1⅛ MILES. (1.46²) 49th Running of THE FLORIDA DERBY. Grade I. Purse $750,000. THREE YEAR OLDS. By subscription of $3,000 each which shall accompany the nomination, $6,000 to pass the entry box and $6,000 additional to start, with $750,000 guaranteed. The owner of the winner to receive $450,000 to first; $142,500 to second; $75,000 to third; $45,000 to fourth; $22,500 to fifth and $15,000 to sixth. Weight, 122 lbs. Horses finishing first, second or third in the Spectacular Bid Stakes, Holy Bull Stakes, Hutcheson Stakes, The Unbridled and/or the Fountain of Youth Stakes, will automatically be nominated to the Florida Derby. Florida Derby Trophy to winning owner. Closed March 1 with 3 nominations. Early nominations closed October 13, 1999.

Value of Race: $750,000 Winner $450,000; second $142,500; third $75,000; fourth $45,000; fifth $22,500; sixth $15,000.   Mutuel Pool $2,012,592.0 Exacta Pool $1,260,682.0   Trifecta Pool $1,179,265.0 Superfecta Pool $280,502.00

Last Raced	Horse	M/Eqt.	A.Wt	PP	St	¼	½	¾	Str	Fin	Jockey	Odds $1
19Feb00 10GP2	Hal's Hope	L	3 122	4	1	1½	1hd	1½	1hd	1hd	Velez R I	6.90
19Feb00 10GP1	High Yield	Lb	3 122	1	2	2hd	23½	24	27	210	Day P	1.00
19Feb00 3GP2	Tahkodha Hills	Lb	3 122	10	9	72	6hd	62	32½	32	Coa E M	57.40
4Mar00 11GP8	Settlement	Lb	3 122	8	10	10	10	10	7hd	41	Velazquez J R	69.60
12Feb00 9GP1	Postponed	L	3 122	3	4	95	99	95	4½	51¾	Santos J A	13.90
27Feb00 8GP5	Scottish Halo	Lb	3 122	2	7	8hd	8½	71½	84	6nk	Chavez J F	5.40
19Feb00 10GP7	Deputy Warlock	Lb	3 122	9	8	6hd	72	5hd	5½	7½	Smith M E	13.70
19Feb00 10GP3	Elite Mercedes	L	3 122	5	3	4hd	54	34	62	89½	Bailey J D	4.40
19Feb00 3GP1	Bare Outline	L	3 122	6	5	31½	3½	41	912	9	Nakatani C S	22.00
26Feb00 9Lrl2	Hades	Lbf	3 122	7	6	52	41	8hd	10	—	Migliore R	56.60

Hades:Eased;

OFF AT 5:46 Start Good For All But SCOTTISH HALO Won driving. Track fast.
TIME :23², :47, 1:10⁴, 1:37³, 1:51² (:23.49, :47.02, 1:10.86, 1:37.75, 1:51.49)

$2 Mutuel Prices:

4–HAL'S HOPE	15.80	5.20	3.60
1–HIGH YIELD		3.00	2.40
10–TAHKODHA HILLS			8.60

$2 EXACTA 4–1 PAID $34.20 $2 TRIFECTA 4–1–10 PAID $593.60 $2
SUPERFECTA 4–1–10–8 PAID $10,262.20

Dk. b. or br. c, (Mar), by Jolie's Halo–Mia's Hope, by Rexson's Hope. Trainer Rose Harold J. Bred by Harold Rose (Fla).

HAL'S HOPE outsprinted rivals for the early advantage, set the pace in hand while slightly off the rail along the backstretch, angled to the inside while extending his lead a bit midway on the turn, dug in when challenged in upper stretch, battled heads apart leaving the furlong marker then turned back HIGH YIELD under steady left hand urging. HIGH YIELD was in hand while saving ground into the first turn, forced the pace inside the winner along the backstretch, eased back slightly and moved to the outside nearing the five-sixteenths pole, closed the gap with the rider glancing back in upper stretch, drew along side the winner to challenge in midstretch, fought heads apart into deep stretch but could not get up. TAHKODHA HILLS was unhurried for six furlongs while slightly off the rail, moved around ELITE MERCEDES on the turn then rallied mildly along the inside to gain a share. SETTLEMENT broke slowly, trailed to the turn, advanced six wide into the stretch and passed only tiring horses. POSTPONED raced far back to the turn, swung six wide at the quarter pole and lacked a strong closing bid. SCOTTISH HALO stumbled at the start and failed to seriously threaten thereafter. DEPUTY WARLOCK saved ground to the turn and lacked a further response. ELITE MERCEDES steadied in tight between horses on the first turn, angled in entering the backstretch, made a mild move along the inside midway on the turn and steadily tired thereafter. BARE OUTLINE chased three wide to the turn and faded. HADES raced wide throughout and gave way after going six furlongs.

Owners— 1, Rose Family Stable; 2, R Lewis Mrs J Magnier & M Tabor Et; 3, Centaur Farms Inc; 4, Evans E P & Lewis L; 5, Vance Jeanne G; 6, Oxley John C; 7, Select Stable; 8, Winstar Farm & P Wittmann; 9, Condren William J; 10, Paraneck Stable

Trainers— 1, Rose Harold J; 2, Lukas D Wayne; 3, Ziadie Ralph; 4, Hennig Mark; 5, Schulhofer Flint S; 6, Rizzo Paul; 7, McPeek Kenneth G; 8, Walden W Elliott; 9, Zito Nicholas P; 10, Albertrani Louis

Hal's Hope won the Holy Bull Stakes at Gulfstream when he took the lead and the rail all the way around the track. **High Yield** beat Hal's Hope in the Fountain of Youth when the former had the rail path and the latter was forced to race in the two and three path. **Greenwood Lake,** the $1.30-1 betting choice in the Holy Bull and the $3.90-1 second choice in the Fountain of Youth, had no chance to win either race under the prevailing track conditions.

In the Florida Derby, Hal's Hope outdueled a pretty game High Yield when they swapped rail-running positions with five furlongs left to be run in the 1⅛-mile contest.

Given this evidence, there was little doubt in my mind that Hal's Hope would be seriously overbet in all subsequent starts, unless able to get a favorable track bias and an equally favorable inside running position. Likewise, when the equally one-dimensional High Yield battled so gamely in the two and three path to just miss beating Hal's Hope at Gulfstream, he became a major win play as the logical front-runner in the Blue Grass Stakes at Keeneland, a track that also can be prone to strong inside-speed biases in the spring, as noted earlier.

NINTH RACE
Keeneland
APRIL 15, 2000

1⅛ MILES. (1.46⁴) 76th Running of THE TOYOTA BLUE GRASS. Grade I. Purse $750,000 For three year olds. Weights. Colts and geldings, 123 lbs. Fillies, 118 lbs.

Value of Race: $750,000 Winner $465,000; second $150,000; third $75,000; fourth $37,500; fifth $22,500. Mutuel Pool $1,585,714.0 Exacta Pool $935,575.00 Trifecta Pool $730,956.00 Superfecta Pool $172,412.00

Last Raced	Horse	M/Eqt. A.Wt	PP	St	¼	½	¾	Str	Fin	Jockey	Odds $1
11Mar00 12GP2	High Yield	Lb 3 123	4	3	1½	1hd	1½	1hd	1hd	Day P	1.90
12Mar00 9FG2	More Than Ready	L 3 123	7	1	31	3hd	3hd	22½	23	Velazquez J R	4.80
19Mar00 11Tam1	Wheelaway	Lb 3 123	5	4	52	53½	52	42½	3½	Migliore R	9.00
25Mar00 9TP4	Deputy Warlock	L 3 123	2	7	75	75	75	53	41¼	Guidry M	20.30
11Mar00 12GP9	Bare Outline	Lb 3 123	3	6	43½	47	46	3hd	53	Coa E M	65.60
11Mar00 12GP4	Settlement	Lb 3 123	1	8	8	8	8	7½	63	St Julien M	67.30
12Mar00 9FG1	Mighty	3 123	8	5	65	66½	63½	6hd	74	Sellers S J	2.20
11Mar00 12GP1	Hal's Hope	L 3 123	6	2	21	21½	21½	8	8	Velez R I	3.80

OFF AT 4:26 Start Good. Won driving. Track fast.
TIME :231, :46, 1:094, 1:352, 1:483 (:23.34, :46.00, 1:09.97, 1:35.58, 1:48.79)

$2 Mutuel Prices:

4–HIGH YIELD	5.80	3.40	3.00
7–MORE THAN READY		5.00	4.60
5–WHEELAWAY			4.80

$2 EXACTA 4–7 PAID $33.20 $2 TRIFECTA 4–7–5 PAID $293.20 $2
SUPERFECTA 4–7–5–2 PAID $2,068.80

Ch. c, (Mar), by Storm Cat–Scoop the Gold, by Forty Niner. Trainer Lukas D Wayne. Bred by Brushwood Stable (Pa).

HIGH YIELD, astutely handled from the start, moved up inside HAL'S HOPE and MORE THAN READY to vie for the lead approaching the first turn, gained a slight advantage while relaxing nicely despite establishing solid fractions, shook off HAL'S HOPE approaching the stretch, was engaged immediately after from the outside by MORE THAN READY, was brushed repeatedly when that one leaned in at the three-sixteenths, then, under stout lefthanded encouragement, gamely held that one safe when brushed again in the late stages. MORE THAN READY, close up outside nearing the first turn, was eased in behind HIGH YIELD and HAL'S HOPE on the backstretch to save ground, moved rapidly from between HAL'S HOPE and BARE OUTLINE leaving the five-sixteenths pole to go after the winner, loomed boldly and hung while leaning in and brushing HIGH YIELD repeatedly through the drive. WHEELAWAY, unhurried while following the leaders four or five wide, continued in that manner to reach contention entering the stretch but couldn't muster the needed response. DEPUTY WARLOCK, outrun for seven furlongs while able to save ground, swung out seven wide for the drive and finished willingly. BARE OUTLINE drifted in at the start, hit the side of the gate and bobbled soon after, lost a bit of position and moved out to stalk the leaders four wide, remained a threat into the final furlong and flattened out. SETTLEMENT, outrun while saving ground, improved position while not a threat. MIGHTY drifted out at the start and brushed the side of the gate, was unhurried into the backstretch while four or five wide, saved ground around the second turn but failed to menace. HAL'S HOPE went up early to vie for the lead outside of HIGH YIELD, held on well until midway of the second turn, tired and wasn't abused in the drive.

Owners— 1, R & B Lewis M Tabor Mrs J Magnier E; 2, Scatuorchio James T; 3, Kimmel Caesar P & Solondz Philip J; 4, Select Stable; 5, Condren William J; 6, Edward P Evans & Lee Lewis; 7, Claiborne Farm & Dilschneider Adele; 8, Rose Family Stables Ltd Harold J Ro

Trainers— 1, Lukas D Wayne; 2, Pletcher Todd A; 3, Kimmel John C; 4, McPeek Kenneth G; 5, Zito Nicholas P; 6, Hennig Mark; 7, Brothers Frank L; 8, Rose Harold J

$2 Pick Three (4–5–4) Paid $556.40; Pick Three Pool $52,216.

While play for me usually is light at contemporary Gulfstream, I am ready to open both barrels as soon as the bias disappears, which occurred more often than usual in 2001 and for reasons no human on earth can fathom. But even when few bets materialize, I know my note taking and patience will pay off in future races at Keeneland, or Churchill Downs, or Belmont Park, where many Gulfstream horses will be headed later in the spring.

Throughout the 2000 Gulfstream meet, many horses earned inflated Beyer Speed Figures and inflated pace numbers while running on the inside part of the track. Do I have to tell you how often these horses were defeated at low odds in subsequent races on normal racing surfaces throughout the country? Do I need to tell you how much of an advantage it was to have a long list of horses that were helped or hurt by the prevailing Gulfstream bias?

There is no trick to using track bias in the 21st century, although you probably should use a home computer to catalog daily bias information at your favorite track(s). You also might consider Internet-based services to help you with track profiles, post-position surveys, and the like. But it is up to you to take accurate notes on performances against the prevailing bias. No long-term statistical survey will serve you as well, and I can guarantee there will be more missed readings of track bias by more people than your wallet can stand. Again, discipline yourself to take your own "bias" notes. A good performance against a legitimate bias should be every bit as meaningful as a good performance into the teeth of an unfavorable pace scenario or a major traffic problem.

Just visualize how many low-odds losers you can avoid by keeping track of bias notes. Or, how many longshot winners may suddenly be within reasonable reach. This is at the heart of building a winning game—knowing more than other players about why a horse ran so well or so poorly.

FROM HOLLYWOOD TO SANTA ANITA

If I decide to start my year at Santa Anita, a track that I do follow enough during my idle winter respite to bet pick-six carryovers, I will be accepting these negative facts:

Santa Anita is a very fast racing surface with a pronounced tendency toward inside speed at all main-track distances. Although the tendency rarely changes during extended dry periods, and offers little value as a price-getting handicapping factor, Santa Anita can offer many value plays if you shift your focus away from biases and toward trainer moves.

When it rains during the winter meet—and it usually rains a lot from late January to mid-February—the racing surface can develop erratic running lanes and may be difficult to assess from day to day. This is no fun for jockeys, trainers, or horseplayers, and is a condition that Santa Anita has tried to solve via numerous countermeasures, with minimal success.

Some astute trainers absolutely refuse to train or race their horses over the Santa Anita surface after the winter rains begin, and many keep their runners at Hollywood Park.

Another thing to keep in mind about Santa Anita is that workout times are inordinately fast and contribute less to the conditioning process than slower works over the deeper Hollywood Park racing surface. That does not mean you should throw out horses who work fast at Santa Anita, but it does mean that more than one or two fast Santa Anita works will be needed to move a horse forward, especially after a layoff.

Knowing the relationship between these two Southern California tracks will lead you to some interesting comparisons between horses that have been working steadily at Hollywood versus those that have trained at Santa Anita. In general, I give extra credit to absentees and first-time starters that are vanned in from Hollywood, and will automatically upgrade horses sent over by a handful of trainers who specialize in using the Hollywood Park racing strip to set up their absentees for wakeup races. Some will surprise you with their price-getting ability. One of the best at putting this potent angle into play is Hall of Famer Ron McAnally, who splits his stable between the two tracks and wins a much higher percentage with his Hollywood Park-based horses.

Again, reliable *trainers*, not track biases, provide the incentive to play Santa Anita. And, you might be surprised how often the most reliable trainer plays are not revealed by statistical studies, but by a simple comparison of individual past-performance profiles.

You should note that Beautiful Noise won her maiden race after a layoff and a series of Hollywood Park workouts in 1998 and repeated the pattern with her February 19 victory. The final workout before the February 19 victory did occur at Santa Anita, but in McAnally's approach to layoff types, that final work over the track sometimes is the finishing touch in a perfect game plan. (This same horse also won her next outing following a one-month respite, then finished second to multiple stakes winner Sweet Ludy following another six-week absence and won still another race after a similar six-week break and a series of Hollywood-based workouts!)

The stats say that trainer D. Wayne Lukas is an unprofitable play with his first-time starters. While this prevailing view is supported by reams of data, a pick-six or pick-three player should be careful before eliminating Lukas-trained first-timers. The tendency is contradicted by several winning first-time starters every year. In all but the rarest cases, each of these winning firsters has one common characteristic, or "tell," as poker players like to call it: a very sharp final workout at four or five furlongs (usually from the starting gate) to conclude a series of moderate works. Among the ready-set-go first-time-starter winners trained by Lukas in 1999 alone were Surfside, Commendable, Cash Run, and Exchange Rate.

Here is a perfect example of a sharp Lukas-trained first-time starter that won at a square mutuel during the final week of Del Mar in 2000.

Pristine	Dk. b or br f. 2 (Feb) KEESEP99 $1,100,000		Life	0 M 0 0	$0	D.Fst	0 0 0 0	$0	–
Own: Lewis Robert B & Beverly J	Sire: Gone West (Mr. Prospector) $125,000		2000	0 M 0 0	$0	Wet	0 0 0 0	$0	–
	Dam: Existentialist (Relaunch)		1999	0 M 0 0	$0	Turf	0 0 0 0	$0	–
	Br: Jamm Ltd & W Lazy T Ltd (Ky)	Ⓛ 118							
SOLIS A (134 18 25 13 .13) 2000:(655 106 .16)	Tr: Lukas D Wayne(18 1 1 1 .06) 2000:(557 83 .15)		Dmr	0 0 0 0	$0	Dist	0 0 0 0	$0	–

WORKS: Sep1 Dmr 5f fst :59² Hg7/59   Aug26 Dmr 5f fst 1:02 H 27/40   Aug13 Dmr 3f fst :35⁴ Hg3/28   Aug6 Dmr 4f fst :49² H 35/52   Jly22 SA 6f fst 1:15 H 11/17   Jly15 SA 4f fst :48¹ H 6/33
　　　Jly9 SA 5f fst :59⁴ Hg7/40   Jly1 SA 5f fst 1:01 H 18/40   Jun24 SA 5f fst 1:01³ H 20/31   Jun17 SA 4f fst :48¹ H 14/48   Jun10 SA 4f fst :49¹ H 25/42   Jun4 SA 3f fst :36² H 11/25

While trainers Bob Hess Jr. and Mike Mitchell are well regarded for their work with recent claims, Jack Carava gets less press, but is among the most productive trainers in the country with newly claimed stock. In the East, you might find comparable work with Edwin T. Broome on the New Jersey circuit and Richard Dutrow Jr.

Bob Baffert is so-o-o-o streaky and frequently overbet, but his ace in the hole, which signals his sharpest horses, is a crisp five- or six-furlong workout four, five, or six days before an allowance or stakes engagement. If his horses are stretching out to a middle distance, or stepping up in class, all the better. Or, if they are racing in a maiden or entry-level allowance race with blinkers and Lasix for the first time, you can bet I will have them on my pick-six tickets.

Baffert works many of his horses in company, and if you get up early enough during the Santa Anita meet for the good breakfast at "Clockers' Corner," you just might see for yourself which of his horses are more advanced. Some players I know bring their video cameras to Clockers' Corner, the better to evaluate these works, but if you prefer sleep, or are playing Santa Anita from a distance, you should check out *Racing*

Digest's workout report, filed by Bruno DeJulio, or the workout reports published on the Internet by Bob Selvin's National Turf organization. Both of these professional services provide useful information about horses working in company and are valuable aids to *Daily Racing Form* past performances in Southern California.

For example, when eventual Dubai World Cup winner Captain Steve was set to make his second career start in the same maiden race with another Baffert runner, the uncoupled Coldwater Canyon, the latter was 3-5 while the former was 3-1, despite extremely encouraging comments filed by DeJulio after the pair worked in company.

Said DeJulio, "Captain Steve caught up to Coldwater Canyon and was clearly best of the two."

Captain Steve won the maiden race; Coldwater Canyon was third, beaten 8½ lengths.

As most know, the Santa Anita turf courses are also interesting, especially the hillside turf course that features a slight right-hand turn on the downhill run from the starting gate, plus a strip of dirt that horses must cross over as they enter the homestretch. This unusual combination is tailor-made for "horses for courses." (Horses with proven form over this unusually configured course often return to top form in their first outing over it after a series of poor races on dirt, or following a lengthy absence.)

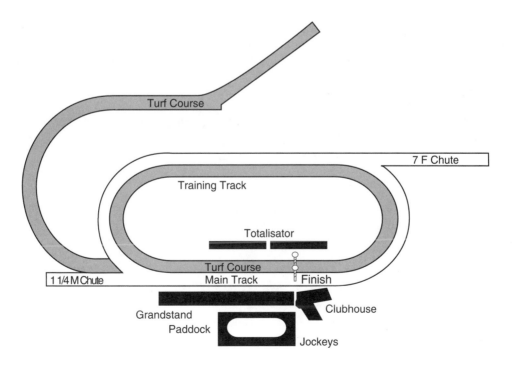

No matter where I choose to begin my year, I expect to build a foundation for the balance of the season. Actually, my season does not begin with a midwinter sojourn. It begins the previous summer at Del Mar and Saratoga, where I annually take notes on the top 2-year-olds who debut at both tracks.

At Santa Anita or Fair Grounds or Gulfstream in the winter, I expect to see some of the more accomplished 2-year-olds I saw the previous season. I also expect to see promising maidens in early- season maiden and allowance races as newly turned 3-year-olds.

A familiarity with breeding will help identify horses that should win 2-year-old sprints or longer races as the months go by. Likewise, a knowledge of trainers will help identify horses most likely to succeed or fail as they are placed in races they were bred to appreciate.

During the 2000 summer season, I made notes on more than five dozen 2-year-olds, accenting their exposed form, their trips, and their likely preferences for sprints, routes, turf, and/or wet tracks. I also included notes about their training regimens, how they looked in the post parades, and whether I thought they would be serious Kentucky Derby prospects if properly handled. This not only helped me catalog insights about these horses for future reference, but also added some depth to my knowledge of horses that raced against them when they reappeared in future maiden and allowance races.

Here are two such profiles of top 2-year-olds I saw in 2000, both of whom were injured before they returned to form late in the spring of 2001.

DEL MAR, July 26:

FLAME THROWER *graduated with very good overall speed and galloped out in a manner suggesting more in the tank. Baffert-trained, instantly reminded me of Silver Charm from a talent standpoint. Still learning, bred to handle a mile (his sire, Saint Ballado, sired Captain Bodgit). Acts and looks like a very good horse.*

SARATOGA, September 23, and BELMONT PARK, October 14:

A P VALENTINE, *flashed a large, well-proportioned body when third in maiden debut at Saratoga behind two sharp, experienced rivals and came back at Belmont to win as rider pleased with long, easy strides in 1:23 for seven furlongs. By A.P. Indy, trained by Derby ace Nick Zito, and has the talent to match. Worth a future-book bet before he competes in stakes and is the most talented 2-year-old I've seen in the East.*

As I move through my racing calendar, I bring with me an arsenal of trainer angles that have been uncovered in actual play. While I believe in statistical tendencies and appreciate the voluminous stacks of data compiled by various databases, I repeat my distrust for raw statistics that are not supported by tendencies I see first-hand. (Scientific types may scoff at my preference for anecdotal evidence, but it is my strong belief that good horseplayers should trust what their eyes and personal research reveal far more than cold statistics. That is because the astute human observer is much faster at spotting a change in trends. The following statistical anecdote should illustrate this point.)

Early in his American career, the Hall of Fame trainer Laz Barrera was pitiful at stretching horses out from a sprint to a route. A three-year study in the early 1970's showed that Barrera was zip for more than 50 attempts. Then along came Bold Forbes, the precociously fast colt that Barrera expertly managed to Kentucky Derby and Belmont Stakes victories in 1976. With that experience, Barrera instantly became a 25 percent ace with stretch-out types, but it took about five years before Barrera's run of victories in routes turned his negative sprint-to-route stats around.

"In Cuba, I never had that trouble," Barrera explained some years later. "I won long races all the time. But here the game was speed from the gate so I trained horses that way. I guess I needed a horse like Bold Forbes to remind me of what I used to do with nervous, very fast horses. I had Angel [Cordero] gallop him very slowly to calm him down, not train him for speed. He had plenty speed already. . . The horse helped make me see things differently. I was like a good baseball player in a slump. I needed to go back to fundamentals to relearn what I already knew."

The lesson applies as much to horseplayers who are having problems with their game. It also speaks to the point that trainer patterns, even those compiled over a significant period of time, can be turned upside down by a sharp horseman willing to experiment or learn from others.

Statistics might be all you need to single out James Toner as a longshot bomber in New York turf races. Stats also will bear out Hall of Famer P. G. Johnson's skill with first-time turf horses, or turf absentees. There is no question that statistical trends can help identify important tendencies that will lead you away from many losers and lead you toward many logical contenders. But statistics aside, I find it far more beneficial to line up a few recent past-performance profiles of a hot or cold trainer to observe exactly what I can trust in a betting situation.

For instance, Elliot Walden's stats with absentees suggest that he wins with about 20 percent of such attempts, a good ratio. A close inspection, however, will reveal that he wins more than 25 percent with his absentees in route races and/or stakes. Thus, by refining your statistics, you can show a flat-bet profit on Elliot Walden absentees in stakes beyond a mile. You also can be more selective—as in spotting Walden-trained horses that possess more talent than most and are being brought back to face seemingly tough competition.

Look below at License Fee. Walden is deadly with good horses coming back for a shot in a stakes at one mile or more.

License Fee
Own: WinStar Farm
DAY P (194 30 29 31 .15) 2000:(907 184 .20)

Ch. m. 5
Sire: Black Tie Affair*Ire (Miswaki)
Dam: Star Deputy (Deputy Minister)
Br: Pedigree Farms Inc (Ont-C)
Tr: Walden W Elliott(16 3 1 2 .19) 2000:(309 57 .18)

L 116

Life	34	13	4	5	$627,236	D.Fst	25	8	2	5	$319,981 101
2000	5	3	1	0	$247,895	Wet	3	2	0	0	$46,340 95
1999	14	3	1	4	$182,675	Turf	6	3	2	0	$260,915 100
Sar Ⓣ	1	1	0	0	$125,700	DistⓉ	0	0	0	0	$0 –

13Aug00- 8Sar	yl	1 1/16	[T]	:24^2 :48^4 1:12^3 1:43^2	3↑ ⒻBlstnSpaBCH-G3	99	7	1	11½	11½	12½	11½	Day P	L 116 b	3.20	85-15	License Fee1161½ **Pico Teneriffe**116nk **Hello Soso**114hd	Pace, clear, driving	7
15Jly00- 9Pha	yl	1 1/16	Ⓣ	:24^4 :49^3 1:14^1 1:44^4	3↑ ⒻDrJamesPnnyH100k	100	6	1	1½	11½	1^2	11½	Melancon L	L 116 b	*2.70	85-15	*License Fee*1161½ MysteriousMoll1161¾ Arty'svirginiagirl114½	Inside, drvg	7
29May00- 7LS	fm	1	Ⓣ	:25 :49^1 1:12^3 1:37^1	3↑ ⒻWinstar Dist200k	88	3	1	1hd	1½	31½	55¼	Sellers S J	L 114 bn	*2.10	76-19	Mumtaz113¾ Evening Promise117½ Really Polish1141¼	Speed, faded	9
7May00- 7Aqu	fm	1 1/16	Ⓣ	:23^3 :48^1 1:12^1 1:42^1	3↑ ⒻBeaugay H-G3	100	1	1	1½	1½	2hd	2½	Chavez J F	L 114 b	4.10	97-08	***Perfect Sting***119½ License Fee1141¼ **Fictitious**1143¼	Stayed on gamely rail	7
13Apr00- 6Kee	fm	1	Ⓣ	:23^1 :47 1:12 1:36^3	4↑ ⒻAlw 56713N1T	94	4	2	2^1	2hd	2½	1^3	Day P	L 116 bn	*1.30	89-10	LicenseFee116^3 Swimmingly1161½ GatherTheDy1161½	Pressed, ridden out	9
13Nov99- 9CD	fst	1		:22^2 :44^4 1:09^3 1:34^2	3↑ ⒻCD Distaff-G2	93	8	5	77¼	65½	55¼	48½	Day P	L 112 b	*3.00	89-16	Let1135¼ Roza Robata114no Dif A Dot1153¼	Seven wide, no rally	9
Previously trained by Hough Stanley M																			
22Oct99- 6Kee	fm	1	Ⓣ	:23^4 :46^3 1:10^4 1:34^4	3↑ ⒻBryanStation65k	93	5	3	33½	3^1	1½	21½	Albarado R J	L 117 b	4.80	96-06	*Pratella*1191½ License Fee1171½ White Beauty1171½	Stalked, second best	7
22Aug99- 8Sar	fst	7f		:22 :44^3 1:09^2 1:23	3↑ ⒻBallerina H-G1	96	10	1	5^2	63¼	52¾	53¼	Espinoza J L	L 113 b	33.75	87-16	Furlough114no *Bourbon Belle*1171½ [DH]*Catinca*121	Chased 5 wide,no rally	10
4Aug99- 9Sar	fst	6f		:21^4 :44^4 :56^4 1:09^2	3↑ ⒻHonrblMissH-G3	97	5	5	51½	5^4	56½	33¼	Espinoza J L	L 114 b	8.20e	91-11	BourbonBelle1163¼ GoldPrincess116hd LicenseFe114½	Gamely far outside	10
5Jly99- 8Mth	fst	1 1/16		:23 :46 1:10 1:41^3	3↑ ⒻMllyPtchBCH-G2	89	2	5	31½	3^1	58½	612¼	Bravo J	L 113 b	15.20	81-07	Heritage Of Gold1144¼ Harpia1163¼ *Tap To Music*116¾	Very wide trip	6
20Jun99- 8Bel	fst	6½f		:22^4 :45^3 1:09^4 1:16^2	3↑ ⒻVagrancy H-G3	92	1	2	4¾	51½	5^2	5^3	Bailey J D	L 114 b	2.35	87-17	[D]*HurricneBertie*114^1 GoldPrincss1141½ *DltMusic*113no	Rail trip, no punch	5
6Jun99- 3Bel	fst	7f		:22^2 :45^3 1:10^2 1:23^1	4↑ ⒻAlw 60000N$Y	101	2	3	2½	3nk	1hd	1½	Day P	L 119 b	2.95	86-11	License Fee119½ Snit119^6 *Gold Princess*1171¾	With pace 3w, driving	5

WORKS: Aug30 Sar tr.tⓉ 4f fm :49^1 B (d) *17/24* Aug8 Sar tr.t 4f gd :50 B *7/15* Jly29 Sar tr.t 4f fst :52^2 B *26/29* Jly10 CD 4f fst :50 B *18/24* Jly3 CD 5f fst 1:00^3 B *4/13* Jun20 CD Ⓣ 4f gd :49^2 B (d) *3/12*

Jerry Hollendorfer is a Northern California ace who gets hammered at the windows with nearly all of his starters, especially with Russell Baze assigned to ride. In other words, it is very difficult to make money betting on Hollendorfer-trained runners in Northern California, even though the stats overwhelmingly endorse his prowess. In Southern California, however, Hollendorfer is barely a 12 percent trainer, but serious money can be made playing his horses in one gilt-edged situation that persistently clicks at nearly 30 percent: Drop-down maiden claimers shipping in to Southern California, especially Del Mar, as the example below indicates.

Augmenter
Own: Halo Farms Hollendorfer & Magerman
DESORMEAUX K J (136 31 23 19 .23) 2000:(673 138 .21)

Dk. b or br c. 2 (Feb) BARMAY00 $30,000
Sire: High Brite (Best Turn) $5,000
Dam: Go Not A' Ramblin (Huguenot)
Br: David Newcomb (Cal)
Tr: Hollendorfer Jerry(19 3 3 1 .16) 2000:(588 125 .21)

L 115

Life	2	1	0	0	$13,200	D.Fst	2	1	0	0	$13,200 66
2000	2	1	0	0	$13,200	Wet	0	0	0	0	$0 –
1999	0	M	0	0	$0	Turf	0	0	0	0	$0 –
Dmr	1	1	0	0	$13,200	Dist	0	0	0	0	$0 –

31Jly00- 4Dmr	fst	5½f	:22^2 :46 :58^3 1:05^1	[S]Md 32000 (32-28)	66	7	3	1hd	1^4	14½	1^7	Pincay L Jr	LB 118	4.60	86-12	Augmenter118^7 El Chubbo113nk Really Free1181½	Drew off, ridden out	9
Previously trained by Schvaneveldt Blane																		
21Apr00- 2SA	fst	2f	:11^1 :21^2	Md Sp Wt 47k	—	8	10			8^5	75¾	Chavez H	B 120	47.10	92-11	Trailthefox120no *Breoni*1201½ *Kenny Mais*120½	Broke slowly	10

WORKS: Sep2 Dmr 5f fst 1:00 H *15/55* Aug25 Dmr 5f fst 1:01 H *27/51* Aug18 Dmr 4f fst :48^2 H *13/32* Aug6 Dmr 4f fst :51^2 H *50/52* Jly26 GG 5f fst 1:01^3 Hg *16/30* Jly19 GG 5f fst 1:01^3 H *20/31*

In general I am mostly interested in trainers that can win a high percentage with first-time starters, shippers, recent claims, horses stepping up in class, and most of all, with absentees. A reliable trainer who can prepare a horse to run sharply in such situations usually will deliver juicy parimutuel payoffs.

It takes real talent to get a horse ready for his career debut, or to judge when a fit horse is well spotted against tougher company. Likewise, there are thousands of horses claimed each year, but surprisingly few trainers know when another trainer's horse is undervalued and ready to beat better.

SHIPPING AWAY from home for a shot at a lucrative pot is another area where everything must be measured correctly, and there are precious few trainers on any circuit who do this with consistent success. Hall of Famers D.Wayne Lukas and Bobby Frankel are among the very best stakes-class "shipping" trainers in America, and I always take a close look at horses flown thousands of miles by Bob Baffert, Elliot Walden, or rising young star Tom Amoss.

Allen Goldberg and Allen Iwinski, based in New Jersey and Pennsylvania, respectively, are adept at shipping into New York and Maryland with sharp claiming stock. So is Maryland-based Barclay Tagg, who is at his best with turf horses.

The most rewarding trainer angle by far, however, involves the individual who specializes in bringing back sharp, well-placed horses after long rests. Consider the special skill Michael Dickinson needed to win the 1998 Breeders' Cup Mile with Da Hoss after a lengthy absence and a single prep race. Consider the degree of skill involved in picking out a target race weeks or months in advance and making all the right moves to get the horse into peak condition for the designated task. In some cases the horse involved may have been injured or forced to the sidelines due to illness, or will be making his first start for new connections. But in the hands of an ace, especially a low-profile ace, a fit absentee may offer considerable value in all wagering pools, especially in exotic pools where a live 10-1 shot can produce mammoth payoffs.

If it is my job to share reasons why trainer-pattern research remains one of the most fertile longshot-producing areas in all of handicapping, it is your job to find the trainers on your circuit that deliver a high percentage while employing their strongest winning moves. It also is your job to retain the flexibility of a good observer and avoid being seduced by long-term patterns that are being contradicted by clear-cut immediate evidence.

In the East, I expect absentee turf routers trained by Christophe Clement to be ready to fire their best race first time back from a layoff, and statistics will bear this out. But if Clement's first few starters at Gulfstream run poorly, I have found that his win percentage with absentees will remain low until he ships north.

Bill Mott, an acknowledged master with layoff types, is a consistent statistical star, worth about 25 percent winners in all situations. His layoff types are legendary on the East Coast. But close examination of Mott's absentees will find that he wins at a disproportionately higher rate with the fresh horses he ships in from the deep Payson Park training facility. Even in this obvious case, it pays to refine normal statistical trends. Because of the lower win percentage and paltry odds that usually attach themselves to Mott-trained absentees, I have even found it profitable to downgrade his absentees that do not train at Payson.

H. James Bond is another Eastern trainer who is deadly with absentees, and he's also one of the few trainers in America who regularly wins route races on the dirt or turf with first-time starters. Bond, like Clement and Mott, loves to use the Payson Park training track during the winter. Bond also is fond of using the relatively slow Saratoga training track to prepare his ready-to-run stock at Belmont Park. In other words, Bond willingly stables his horses hours away from Gulfstream Park in the winter and hours away from Belmont Park in the spring and fall in order to give them a peaceful routine and a deep, tiring surface to train over.

Out west, the list of trainers who can win with horses coming off layoffs is long and deep. Few perform more skillfully with this type than nationally prominent Dick Mandella, John Shirreffs, Julio Canani, Jenine Sahadi, and low-profile Simon Bray, a former Mott assistant who is razor-sharp with first-timers on the turf.

Bray has shown in a very short time that he is also among the best in the country with absentee routers. Below is a typical Bray past-performance profile. Candace in Paris was headed for a career in graded stakes before she died on the track.

Candace In Paris	B. f. 3 (Apr)		Life 1 1 0 0 $27,000	D.Fst 0 0 0 0	$0 –
Own: Paulson Madeleine A	Sire: Theatrical*Ire (Nureyev)		2000 1 1 0 0 $27,000	Wet 0 0 0 0	$0 –
	Dam: Vinista (Jade Hunter)		1999 0 M 0 0 $0	Turf 1 1 0 0	$27,000 90
	Br: Paulson Madeleine A (Ky)	119			
NAKATANI C S (11 4 0 2 .36) 2000:(610 141 .23)	Tr: Bray Simon (—) 2000:(50 12 .24)		Dmr ⓣ 0 0 0 0 $0	Dist ⓣ 1 1 0 0	$27,000 90

2Jly00–9Hol fm 1⅛ ⓣ :23¹ :46 1:10² 1:41¹ 3↑ ⑯Md Sp Wt 45k   90 5 4 31⁴ 2⁵ 13¼ 1⁸ Nakatani C S   B 116   *2.10 87–10 Candace In Paris116⁸ Setareh116¹ Reluctant Maggie116½   Ridden out 11
WORKS: Jly22 Hol 5f fst 1:00 H 4/35   Jun26 Hol 5f fst 1:01 Hg 15/36   Jun19 Hol 5f fst 1:01³ Hg 17/39   Jun12 Hol 5f fst 1:00³ H 12/43   Jun4 Hol 5f fst 1:00² H 9/41   May29 Hol 5f fst 1:00⁴ H 2/32

Sahadi is great with first-time starters, and they work fast. Moreover, she has a good touch with sprinters aiming for target races, as she demonstrated with Lit de Justice and Elmhurst in the 1996 and 1997 Breeders' Cup Sprint. Sahadi is at her absolute best with turf horses, however, especially the middle-distance types.

Canani excels with imports and acclimated Europeans off long layoffs in stakes. The same is true for Dick Mandella, named to the Hall of Fame in 2001. Mandella can train any horse in any situation, period.

Wally Dollase, one of my personal favorite trainers, is terrific with absentee types and very good at developing the young horse into a win machine. I do not play all of Dollase's horses blindly, but I eliminate very few of his starters in any betting situation.

Bobby Frankel, a certifiable turf ace, became a Hall of Famer by dominating at least one full meet each year on the Southern California circuit. When he's hot, Frankel can go on extended streaks of success with every kind of horse *except* first-time starters.

Neil Drysdale, another Hall of Famer, skillfully trained Fusaichi Pegasus to victory in the 2000 Kentucky Derby. He, too, is a layoff expert, especially with imports on the turf. So is Paco Gonzalez, who, like Mandella, is outstanding with all types of horses, including Derby-class 3-year-olds, although he has had none of consequence to work with since developing Free House in 1997.

Carla Gaines and Bob Baffert are among the best first-time-starter trainers in Southern California, but only Gaines gets fair and square prices. The stats also say that California-based Richard Matlow is an ace with first-timers in maiden sprints—but I rarely play the ones that have more than one fast work. Also, I expect to see that fast work buried two or three works back behind a couple of slow ones. The evidence behind the raw statistics says that Mr. Matlow likes to get a little price value with his most reliable winning technique.

Majestic Holiday		B. g. 3 (May)		Life	0 M 0 0	$0	D.Fst	0 0 0 0	$0 –
Own: Cavanagh Family Trust		Sire: Majestic Style (Nureyev)							
		Dam: Dreamer's Holiday (Tree of Knowledge)		2000	0 M 0 0	$0	Wet	0 0 0 0	$0 –
	$32,000	Br: Thomas M & Marguerite F Cavanagh Family Trust (Cal)	① 116	1999	0 M 0 0	$0	Turf	0 0 0 0	$0 –
GOMEZ G K (87 12 9 14 .14) 2000:(341 48 .14)		Tr: Matlow Richard P(7 3 1 0 .43) 2000:(9 3 .33)		Hol	0 0 0 0	$0	Dist	0 0 0 0	$0 –

WORKS: May25 Hol 6f fst 1:16¹ H 13/14 • May17 Hol 5f fst 1:01² H 10/34 • May10 Hol 5f fst 1:02³ H 27/42 • May3 Hol 5f fst 1:03⁴ H 24/35 • Apr24 Hol 4f fst :47³ Hg3/23 • Mar25 Hol 5f fst 1:02³ H 15/32
Mar18 Hol 4f fst :50¹ H 14/22 • Mar11 Hol 3f fst :36 H 2/17 • Jan6 Hol 3f fst :37² H 2/6

In the East, first-time starters from Ben Perkins Jr., Mike Hushion, and Stanley Hough are usually well meant, and the same is certainly true for Todd Pletcher. But Pletcher is equally potent with his second-out maidens that have run well, or flashed only a hint of speed, in their debuts. The latter group has been known to produce above-average prices.

When I get rolling into April, May, and June, I come armed with my Gulfstream trip notes and trainer patterns on the circuits I frequent, along with my list of notable 2-year-olds from the previous year and any follow-up notes I may have made. I also will add more notes on these and other newly turned 3-year-old maiden and allowance winners who have shown up in South Florida, Southern California, or Louisiana, where good horses are prepped for the Triple Crown chase.

I am not really looking for the Kentucky Derby winner, even though it is sometimes obvious which horses are the most likely contenders. Fusaichi Pegasus, for example, was very impressive in a February 2000 allowance race at Santa Anita. As for other notable

3-year-olds of the 2000 season, if you were at Gulfstream Park early in the year, you had to like the way the Carl Nafzger-trained Unshaded won two races over that surface.

When I begin playing the Keeneland-Churchill Downs circuit in late April and early May, I expect some Florida trainers, especially the ones who were not winning races in bunches at Gulfstream, to wake up at Keeneland. I expect this because I have seen the pattern often enough to take advantage. I also expect that Turfway Park claiming horses will fit perfectly in Keeneland claiming races, even though the prevailing prejudice of most Keeneland racegoers is to downgrade Turfway horses. Likewise, in recent seasons, numerous horses shipping in from Fair Grounds have had a hidden edge over those shipping in from Gulfstream. The improved quality of racing in New Orleans is a logical explanation for this trend, but the betting public has been slow to capitalize.

At Pimlico, I am truly lost, because the game is so difficult to penetrate for just a few days of play, even though I spent more than eight years living in Maryland and playing the local circuit during the 1970's, watching inside-speed biases dominate. Too much has changed in Maryland and the only races I consider for play are the stakes on the Black-Eyed Susan and Preakness cards.

To me, the racing season is like the major-league baseball season. It has a beginning, middle, and a championship final phase. My spring training takes place in the three winter meets I've described above. My regular season revolves around the Triple Crown prep races, including all those maiden and allowance races that feature hot-to-trot 3-year-olds. The Triple Crown racing cards usually offer outstanding wagering opportunities involving talented, well-trained horses in intriguing spots, scenarios that repeat themselves every year. Following this plan, I have had a series of successful seasons and have enjoyed many winning days on the undercards for all three Triple Crown races.

As I see it, the opportunity to structure a racing season around preferred races and race meets is far more sensible than an overdrawn racing schedule loaded with meaningless events and tiresome meets. By the time I get to Del Mar and then Saratoga in August, I am not only armed to the teeth with track-bias notes and trainer-pattern updates, but I am also ready to incorporate **key races** into my game.

THE KEY-RACE METHOD IN CONTEMPORARY HANDICAPPING

The first person I ever heard discuss the concept of "key races" was Jules Schanzer, a handicapper at the old *Morning Telegraph* who kept a book on winning 2-year-old maidens and wondered aloud if there was a "key" to any race that produced two or more next-out winning maidens. This was such a sound idea that I decided to augment *Daily Racing Form* result charts by putting a circle around the name of any horse that came out to win his next start. A little bit later I used this circle as a means to help uncover consistent winning patterns at difficult-to-read tracks, including Laurel, which had undergone a complete change of its racing surface prior to the 1972 meeting. Thus was born the research tool known as the key-race method, which I later expanded to help identify the inherent quality of maiden and allowance races.

The illustration below is a make-believe key race, which is presented merely to display all the possible notations I use to add valuable information to my result charts.

The marks you see between the date of the last race and the horse's name refer to the "class of race"—up, down, or same—that the first two finishers came from.

The notations I've added next to the horse's name refer to the class of the next race, and the date is noted after the horse's name.

The symbols are as follows:

$\wedge$ = up in class

$\vee$ = down in class

$\sim\sim$ = same class

A (circled) horse means that horse won his next race.

An <u>underlined</u> horse means that horse finished second in his next start.

A horse with **xx** means that the horse won or ran second two starts later, with an excusable race in between. I define an "excusable race" as a change from dirt to turf or vice versa and/or any race that offered a reasonable excuse for a bad performance, including a muddy track, severe traffic problems, or a ridiculously high placement in class.

If this hypothetical key race on page 106 were real, I would be looking for **Flashy Cat**, the front-runner who tired in the race after a tough three-wide speed duel. I also would be willing to give **Fast Delivery** a close look, even though his third-place finish was aided by the overall shape of the race.

EIGHTH RACE
Churchill
JUNE 25, 2000

1 1/16 MILES. (1.41³) ALLOWANCE. Purse $51,200 (includes $11,200 State Bred) FOR FILLIES AND MARES THREE YEARS OLD AND UPWARD WHICH HAVE NOT WON TWO RACES OTHER THAN MAIDEN, CLAIMING OR STARTER, OR THREE RACES. Three Year Olds 112 lbs.; Older 123 lbs. Non-winners of $18,290 twice since December 25 allowed,3 lbs. $14,570 twice since June 30, 5 lbs. $11,780 twice in 1999–2000, 7 lbs. (Races for $35,000 or less not considered in allowances).

Value of Race: $51,200 Winner $32,080; second $10,240; third $5,120; fourth $2,560; fifth $1,200. Mutuel Pool $272,209.00 Exacta Pool $220,002.00 Trifecta Pool $228,176.00

Last Raced	Horse	M/Eqt. A.Wt	PP	St	¼	½	¾	Str	Fin	Jockey	Odds $1
24May00 5CD7	Tutorial	Lf 4 116	3	5	8	7 1½	4½	1½	1 1¾	Sellers S J	3.60
26May00 6CD4	My Sweet Caroline	Lf 4 118	5	1	2 1	2hd	1hd	2hd	2hd	Torres F C	11.50
4Jun00 8CD1	Fast Delivery	Lf 3 109	4	8	5hd	6 2	5 1	4½	3 1¾	Martinez W	3.60
26May00 6CD3	Silver Chele	Lb 4 118	6	4	4 1½	5 1	3hd	5 6	4 1¾	Court J K	1.40
24May00 5CD9	Flashy Cat	L 5 116	2	2	1 1½	1hd	2 1	3 2	5 4¾	Hebert T J	16.40
27Apr00 5Kee3	Naughty Crown	L 4 113	7	6	6hd	4hd	6 1½	6 3	6 4¾	St Julien M	5.80
18May00 9CD9	Rocktheboat	Lbf 4 116	1	3	3½	3 1½	7 6	7 6	7 11¼	Borel C H	42.30
11Jun00 8CD5	Encourager's Guilt	Lb 4 116	8	7	7 2	8	8	8	8	D'Amico A J	19.10

OFF AT 4:10 Start Good. Won driving. Track fast.

TIME :23⁴, :47³, 1:12⁴, 1:38³, 1:45² (:23.86, :47.78, 1:12.83, 1:38.69, 1:45.51)

$2 Mutuel Prices:

3–TUTORIAL	9.20	5.20	4.20
5–MY SWEET CAROLINE		10.40	6.20
4–FAST DELIVERY			3.40

$2 EXACTA 3–5 PAID $102.40 $2 TRIFECTA 3–5–4 PAID $432.20

Ch. f, by Forty Niner–Fulbright Scholar, by Cox's Ridge. Trainer Arnold George R II. Bred by Mjaka I Stable (Ky).

TUTORIAL, unhurried into the backstretch, was taken five wide, edged closer on the second turn, made a sweeping run five abreast approaching the stretch, took over and edged clear late under strong handling. MY SWEET CAROLINE went up early to press pacesetting FLASHY CAT four wide, gained a slim lead on the second turn, then couldn't handle TUTORIAL in the drive. FAST DELIVERY, rated in behind the leaders early, raced three or four wide into the stretch, came out a bit farther for the drive and couldn't muster a serious response while improving position. SILVER CHELE, well placed from early on while stalking the leaders three or four wide, was empty when the test came. FLASHY CAT gained the lead early, raced three wide, made the pace for nearly six furlongs, lost the advantage to MY SWEET CAROLINE and weakened gradually the last eighth. NAUGHTY CROWN edged inside early, saved ground, advanced with the winner while inside that one approaching the stretch but was empty in the drive. ROCKTHEBOAT, in hand while saving ground from the beginning, faded in the drive. ENCOURAGER'S GUILT raced six wide much of the way and wasn't a factor.

Owners— 1, Humphrey G W Jr; 2, Considine Dan & Snowden Steve C; 3, Jacobs David & Andrea; 4, Esfahani Ray; 5, Montgomery Glenn & Sara; 6, Gainesway Stable Anthony R Beck; 7, Crawford Gerald & Kammeier Fred; 8, Six Pack Stable

Trainers— 1, Arnold George R II; 2, Connelly William R; 3, Moran Betty L; 4, Nafzger Carl A; 5, Montgomery Gary W; 6, O'Callaghan Niall M; 7, Barnett Bobby C; 8, Thompson Michael R

Obviously, the added information in my result charts takes some bookkeeping, but it is worth it. Whenever a chart contains more than one "winning" circle, it means those horses have come out of that race to win their next starts. This is enormously helpful in identifying relatively strong races, especially maiden races in which there is minimal information about the quality of competition. It also helps identify strong turf races for similar reasons.

THE METHODOLOGY was first published more than 20 years ago, in the original edition of my book *Betting Thoroughbreds*. In recent years, however, I have found key races to be more useful when I've added notations about second-place finishers and/or what kind of competition these horses actually face in their next starts. At the same time I resist calling a fast race, or a race with a hot pace, a potential key race. I do not need to label swiftly run races. I already know they were run in fast time. That label is sufficient to convey the point. I already know that a fast horse was in that race. What I need key races for is to identify subtle class differentials that are not usually identified by pure speed or pace clockings.

For more detailed information on how to construct a thorough set of key-race result charts, I suggest consulting the second revised edition of *Betting Thoroughbreds*, published by Dutton-Penguin USA and available through DRF Press in paperback.

While *Daily Racing Form* does italicize future winners from the three horses in the company line, which can be valuable information (see past performance below), I find that it also pays to look beyond the top three finishers.

Indeed, I have gained the most benefit from my key-race notations by searching through my catalog of result charts for horses that have either shown contending speed or finished better than two or more next-out winners or second-place finishers.

When I find a horse that has been involved in a true key race, I will not hesitate to include him in any exotic play, from the exacta to the pick six. By itself, my key-race method will point out many horses worthy of exotic play. To seriously pound such a horse in the win pool, however, I usually insist upon a winning trainer pattern, or a track bias, or a favorable pace scenario to complement the key-race info. Betting blindly on any one fact or factor is rarely a winning approach. Indeed, the simple, most significant impact of key-race information is to provide more insight into the quality of competition a given horse has been facing. There is no mysticism in this, but finding key races will lead to much better handicapping decisions.

The result chart below is a real-life key race as it occurred at Saratoga during the 1999 meet. There is nothing earth-shattering here, just a good bet in the making.

THIRD RACE 6 FURLONGS. (1.08) MAIDEN SPECIAL WEIGHT. Purse $40,000 (plus up to $7,760 NYSBFOA).

Saratoga
2-year-olds. Weight, 117 lbs.

AUGUST 16, 1999

Value of Race: $40,000 Winner $24,000; second $8,000; third $4,400; fourth $2,400; fifth $1,200. Mutuel Pool $428,891.00 Exacta Pool $550,375.00

Last Raced	Horse	M/Eqt. A.Wt	PP	St	1/4	1/2	Str	Fin	Jockey	Odds $1
28Jly99 4Sar2	Sykes Alive	Lb 2 117	2	1	1½	13	13½	14¼	Bailey J D	0.90
	Graeme Hall	2 117	4	5	33½	2hd	23½	29¼	Albarado R J	11.20
24Jly99 9Crc7	Tubrok	2 117	1	3	5	46	3½	33¾	Davis R G	10.60
	Traditionally	2 117	5	4	2hd	32½	412	416½	Smith M E	1.15
3Jly99 4Bel8	Deception Island	Lb 2 117	3	2	41½	5	5	5	Chavez J F	24.75

OFF AT 2:04 Start Good. Won ridden out. Track fast.

TIME :22², :45⁴, :58, 1:10⁴ (:22.43, :45.82, :58.16, 1:10.95)

$2 Mutuel Prices:				
	4-SYKES ALIVE	3.80	2.50	2.10
	1-GRAEME HALL		4.50	2.50
	2-TUBROK			2.80

$2 EXACTA 4-1 PAID $16.60

Ch. c, (Jan), by Silver Deputy–Malicious, by Risen Star. Trainer Lukas D Wayne. Bred by Hersey Farm Corporation (Ky).

SYKES ALIVE broke running, set the pace while in hand, drew away when roused and was ridden out to the finish. GRAEME HALL chased the pace along the inside, could not get to the winner but was easily best of the others. TUBROK, outrun early, came wide for the drive but lacked a rally. TRADITIONALLY came away in good order, raced with the pace while three wide and tired in the stretch. DECEPTION ISLAND stopped after showing brief speed.

Owners— 1, Cloverleaf Farm; 2, Eugene Melnyk & Laura Melnyk; 3, Buckram Oak Farm; 4, Phipps Ogden; 5, Farmer Tracy

Trainers— 1, Lukas D Wayne; 2, Pletcher Todd A; 3, Moubarak Mohammed; 4, McGaughey Claude III; 5, Zito Nicholas P

Scratched— Bookie, Kendall Point (11Jly99 4BEL6)

On September 5, 1999, toward the end of the Saratoga meet, **Graeme Hall** showed up in the second race—a maiden special weight contest similar to that on August 16—as a well-meant Todd Pletcher-trained second-time starter. When he won at 5-1, I put a circle around his name in my August 16 result chart. Less than two hours later, **Tubrok** appeared in another maiden race on the card and finished a very good second at 14-1 for trainer Mohammed Moubarak. So, I put a line under his name in the August 16 result chart. That night, I reviewed my result charts and noticed that **Traditionally** had raced with the pace alongside Graeme Hall in the August 16 maiden race and marked his name down for possible future consideration.

On September 18 at Belmont, Traditionally was entered back for the first time in a one-mile maiden race that he was perfectly bred to handle. Having Shug McGaughey for a trainer boosted my confidence, and having Jerry Bailey for a jockey encouraged me even more. Having upgraded Traditionally's maiden race by virtue of the performances of two of the few horses he faced in a small, above-average field, I bet him straight and was ecstatic to get $9.60 for my trouble.

For another good example of this concept, here is a note from a New York-based professional player, Ron Calderon, who has built a winning game around principles of track bias, trainer patterns, and key races on the New York circuit.

"On June 23, 2000, in the fourth race, I took full advantage of my key-race work," Calderon wrote. "Running in this race was Slowhand, coming out of the 9th race, on May 19, a maiden special weight race and a key race if there ever was one. What made me really love Slowhand was the fact that he was the only horse in the field coming out of a key race and the two winners from his May 19 race both had already come back to win in the maiden special weight class level. In the race I played him—on June 23—Slowhand was dropping into a maiden claimer.

"To summarize," continued Calderon, "we had a horse dropping in class after coming out of MSW key race, a race in which two horses had come back to win in MSW company!"

Calderon did not have to add that Slowhand won the fourth race at Belmont on June 23 at a fancy $31.80, but I confess to having missed that winner. I sometimes have trouble getting into Belmont in May and June because my early-season focus is diverted to the Triple Crown chase and West Coast racing for its lucrative pick-six pools. A few good plays inevitably slip through the cracks. But not all of them. I do see horses that made an impression on me in Florida or Kentucky at Belmont and can catch up very quickly when I begin to rebuild my whole New York season around two days—Met Mile Day and Belmont Stakes Day.

The Met Mile is one of my favorite races. Run about two months into my racing season and on the cusp of the summer seasons throughout the country, the Met annually reintroduces me to the best middle-distance horses and seven-furlong sprinters in America.

I saw Carry Back win this race, and Kelso, too. But my affection for the Met is not a nostalgic exercise. Every year there is a hot speedball and a strong nine-furlong horse and perhaps even a well-regarded California shipper in this race. In most years, there also will be a very good 3-year-old refugee from the Triple Crown chase. This kind of context is fundamental to good handicapping. Before you can evaluate the way a track is playing, or just how good a horse has to be to win an allowance or stakes race, you have to have some idea what the best horses on the grounds are capable of doing. You need standards of performance and you need to know which horses in each division can do what, and how fast. I love the Met because it is a great handicapping challenge and because I usually leave the race with a greater understanding of contemporary Belmont.

By the time the Belmont Stakes comes into focus, I will have seen most of the better 3-year-old colts and fillies in the land. I will have played races over biased and unbiased surfaces at Gulfstream, Fair Grounds, Keeneland, Churchill Downs, Santa Anita, and Hollywood Park. I will be loaded with bias notes, trainer-pattern updates, and horses to watch and avoid. I have had losing seasons, of course, but with my personal schedule and selected simulcast play, I build considerable momentum toward what I consider *the* meets of the year—Saratoga, Del Mar, and the fall meets that lead to the Breeders' Cup.

At Del Mar, purses are high and the quality of racing is not what it should be, a direct result of the oversaturation of racing throughout California. Still, there is no more pleasant place in America to play the horses, and the pick-six pools regularly hit $250,000 without carryovers. Single-day carryovers of $140,000 generate pools that approach $750,000.

I love to play Del Mar *and* Saratoga simultaneously because both tracks have readable track surfaces and a series of maiden races, allowance races, and stakes for 2-year-olds from the first day to the last. I love 2-year-old racing because there is money to be made in spotting the new stars before they become obvious, and Saratoga and Del Mar feature the best-bred, best-trained horses in the sport. As I said, I handicap better when I am turned on by my environment.

At Del Mar in 2000, the main track played fair until mid-August, when it suddenly became a front-running, inside-favoring surface that delivered many longshot winners to a crowd that seemed unprepared for that kind of radical bias. A good example was **Skimming**, winner of the Pacific Classic.

Trained by Bobby Frankel, Skimming had won the San Diego Handicap wire to wire when the racing surface was not particularly favorable to front-running types. Thus, he was an outstanding play at 9-2 odds when he looked to be the logical front-runner in the 1¼-mile Pacific Classic on a surface that had been dominated by inside-speed types for four straight days.

Skimming
Own: Juddmonte Farms Inc
GOMEZ G K (—) 2000:(595 86 .14)

B. c. 4
Sire: Nureyev (Northern Dancer) $125,000
Dam: Skimble (Lyphard)
Br: Juddmonte Farms (Ky)
Tr: Frankel Robert(2 0 0 1 .00) 2000:(253 70 .28)

L 126

Life	12	5	2	1	$926,601	**D.Fst**	7	5	0	1	$840,017 118
2000	8	5	1	1	$920,017	**Wet**	1	0	1	0	$80,000 109
1999	3	M	0	0	$0	**Turf**	4	0	1	0	$6,584 –
Bel	0	0	0	0	$0	**Dist**	1	0	1	0	$80,000 109

26Aug00-8Dmr	fst	1¼	$:45^{2}$ $1:09^{4}$ 1:35 $2:01^{1}$	3↑ PacificClsc-G1	**118**	5	1	1^{1}	$1^{1\frac{1}{2}}$	$1^{2\frac{1}{2}}$	1^{2}	Gomez G K	**LB** 124	4.70	95 – 14	Skimming124^{2} Tiznow$117^{1\frac{1}{4}}$ **Ecton Park**$124^{\frac{1}{2}}$	Inside,clear,driving 7
6Aug00-8Dmr	fst	$1\frac{1}{16}$	$:22^{3}$ $:45^{4}$ $1:09^{3}$ 1:41	3↑ San Diego H-G3	**113**	3	1	1^{1}	1^{3}	1^{6}	1^{8}	Gomez G K	**LB** 112	3.50	98 – 02	*Skimming*112^{8} PrimeTimber$116^{1\frac{1}{2}}$ NationlSint$117^{3\frac{1}{2}}$	Rail,drew off, driving 7
5Jly00-8PrM	gd	1⅛	$:46^{2}$ $1:10^{2}$ $1:35^{4}$ $1:48^{2}$	3↑ PrMCrnhskrH-G3	**109**	4	2	$2^{1\frac{1}{2}}$	2^{1}	1^{hd}	$2^{1\frac{1}{2}}$	Espinoza V	**LB** 111	8.10	89 – 15	Sir Bear$116^{1\frac{1}{2}}$ *Skimming*111^{hd} **Ecton Park**$117^{\frac{3}{4}}$	Stalked, led, held 2nd 5
8Jun00-3Hol	fst	$1\frac{1}{16}$	:24 $:47^{3}$ $1:11^{4}$ $1:42^{4}$	3↑ OClm 80000N	**103**	4	1	1^{2}	$1^{1\frac{1}{2}}$	1^{1}	1^{2}	Solis A	**LB** 120	1.30	86 – 14	Skimming120^{2} PtienceGm117^{4} LthlInstrumnt117^{7}	Rail,strong hand ride 5
13May00-8Hol	fst	$1\frac{1}{16}$	$:23^{2}$ $:46^{2}$ $1:10^{2}$ $1:41^{4}$	3↑ Mvn LeRoy H-G2	**103**	2	3	1^{hd}	$1^{\frac{1}{2}}$	$2^{\frac{1}{2}}$	3^{5}	Espinoza V	**LB** 111	8.30	86 – 17	Out Of Mind$116^{\frac{1}{2}}$ Early Pioneer$116^{4\frac{1}{2}}$ *Skimming*111^{2}	Pulld,led rail,held 3d 7
21Apr00-5SA	fst	1	:23 $:46^{3}$ $1:11^{1}$ 1:36	4↑ OClm 40000N	**100**	7	4	$4^{1\frac{1}{2}}$	3^{nk}	2^{hd}	1^{2}	Solis A	**LB** 118	5.90	91 – 12	Skimming118^{2} Kaiser So Say$118^{\frac{3}{4}}$ Brigade118^{3}	4wd move,stdy handling 10

Previously trained by Barry Hills

3Feb00◆Wolverhmptn(GB)	fst	$1\frac{1}{16}$	LH $1:50^{1}$	3↑ Bet Direct ITV Cndtns St(dirt) Alw 16200	4^{5}	Hills M	136	*1.25	King Priam129^{nk} Weet-A-Minute$132^{1\frac{1}{4}}$ Adelphi Boy$127^{3\frac{1}{2}}$ *Led to over 2f out,drifted right.late.Bled.Pantar 7th*	7
Timeform rating: 96										
11Jan00◆Wolverhmptn(GB)	fst	$1\frac{1}{16}$	LH $1:50^{3}$	4↑ Cowes Maiden Stakes (dirt) Maiden 7100	1^{3}	Hills M	126	*.50	Skimming126^{3} Sovereign Abbey121^{10} Nafith126^{5} *Pressed pace,led after 2f,clear over 1f out,handily*	10
Timeform rating: 73+										

Previously trained by Andre Fabre

1Oct99◆M-Laffitte(Fr)	sf	*1	Ⓣ RH 1:43	Prix de Manneville Hcp 32700	$8^{10\frac{3}{4}}$	Peslier O	124	6.00	Sabrinsky$129^{1\frac{1}{2}}$ Le Piemont112^{nk} Isigny113^{nk} *Wide in 5th,weakened 3f out.Alexandrino 7th*	9
12Sep99◆Longchamp(Fr)	gd	*1	Ⓣ RH $1:37^{2}$	Prix du Grand Palais Alw 28600	$6^{2\frac{3}{4}}$	Peslier O	126	4.00	Danzigaway$122^{\frac{1}{2}}$ Ground Speed122^{no} Mulhim$126^{1\frac{1}{2}}$ *Led to 1-1/2f out,gradually weakened*	11
Timeform rating: 94										
3Aug99◆Deauville(Fr)	sf	*1¼	Ⓣ RH $2:13^{1}$	Prix de Troarn Alw 22800	$6^{6\frac{1}{4}}$	Peslier O	130	*2.00	Tsar's Pride120^{4} Samirana$120^{\frac{1}{2}}$ Wanini Boy126^{hd} *Unhurried in 5th,lacked rally*	11
Timeform rating: 90										
19Oct98◆Deauville(Fr)	hy	*7f	Ⓣ Str $1:31^{1}$	Prix de Caen-EBF Alw 32900	2^{2}	Peslier O	121	*.70	Sabrinsky126^{2} Skimming121^{6} Goldeneye126^{15} *Unhurried in 3rd,dueled briefly 1-1/2f out,second best*	4

WORKS: Sep11 **Dmr 5f fst** **$1:02^{4}$ H** *32/41* Sep4 **Dmr 3f fst :36 H** *3/13* Aug21 **Dmr 5f fst $1:01^{4}$ H** *52/71* Aug15 **Dmr 5f fst 1:01 H** *30/55* Jly31 **Dmr 5f fst $1:01^{4}$ H** *41/59* Jly24 **Dmr 5f fst $1:01^{2}$ H** *19/39*

Meanwhile, the turf course, which took a steady pounding with no rain or relief, also played to speed horses throughout the meet. It isn't always like that at Del Mar. In some years, there is more moisture in the track, caused by the daily haze that rolls in from the Pacific Ocean during the morning hours. When the haze shows up for several days in succession, the main track tends to be favorable to rally-wide types, while the turf may reward ground-saving stretch-runners. Toward the end of the 2000 meet, when the humidity increased and daily morning haze blocked out the sun for several hours, the Del Mar racing surface lost its front-running bias and played to its rally-wide tendencies.

While I prefer rally-wide racetracks because they emphasize stamina over sheer speed, the prevailing track profile at Del Mar track can be spotted with minimum difficulty. Yet, these subtle shifts in humidity and track tendencies can be terribly confusing to many fans, especially the thousands of tourists or part-time players who visit Del Mar for a day or two.

Saratoga, my favorite racetrack in the world, has been a speed highway for most of the 1990's. But, as suggested earlier, this historic track is prone to switch to a rally-wide racing surface after any quantity of rain.

In 2000, Saratoga was hit with a ton of bad weather, which ensured a rally-wide track for most of the meet. This turned handicapping upside down for many players—even experienced ones—who had become accustomed to seeing a parade of front-running winners there. Many found it hard to adjust. All but a few players seemed slow to accept the track's rally-wide tendency, even though rail-bound horses kept stopping in race after race.

I can't think of a better situation to play the horses. I won't gloat. Let's just say that I hit at least one pick six that covered expenses for the summer and headed toward the Breeders' Cup in the fall with my rent paid for the year. I hope to do as well on my racing odyssey in future seasons. And I strongly recommend that players of all levels of skill build their own racing schedules along similar guidelines. Here's my tentative schedule for 2002:

FEBRUARY: Gulfstream, or Fair Grounds, or Santa Anita Park, with a side trip to Las Vegas for a handicapping tournament or two.

MARCH: Back into action with spot plays on the simulcast menu from the above three tracks. (I get seven racing channels, and I have a telephone-wagering account. When possible I also spend a few weeks each year in Lake Tahoe playing simulcasts at Caesar's Race Book.)

APRIL: Spot plays on the Keeneland simulcast menu when Gulfstream and Santa Anita close in mid-April. A possible trip to Oaklawn Park for the "Festival of the South," which features strong cards every day leading up to the Arkansas Derby, or a similar trip to Keeneland for Blue Grass Stakes Week. At the very least, if I remain at home in Connecticut, I will go to Aqueduct for the Wood Memorial. (Aqueduct's spring meet is light years more compelling than the winter session.)

MAY: Kentucky Derby Week at Churchill Downs; spot plays on Black-Eyed Susan Day and Preakness Day at Pimlico; Peter Pan Day and Met Mile Day at Belmont Park; spot plays on the Hollywood Park simulcast menu every day.

JUNE: Belmont Stakes Week; daily simulcasts from Churchill Downs and Hollywood Park.

JULY: Spot plays on the Hollywood Park, Belmont Park, and Ellis Park simulcast menu.

LATE JULY, AUGUST, AND EARLY SEPTEMBER: Two to three weeks at Del Mar and two to three weeks at Saratoga. Extensive simulcast play of Saratoga races while at Del Mar and vice versa. Also, Claiming Crown Day at Canterbury Park, Arlington Million Day, and some Ellis Park racing, mostly via simulcasts, plus a side trip to the Reno Flamingo Hilton Handicapping Tournament, a well-run competition in early August.

LATE SEPTEMBER: Super Derby Day at Louisiana Downs; spot plays on the Belmont Park simulcast menu every day. (I do not play Fairplex Park races after Del Mar closes.)

OCTOBER: Spot plays on the Belmont Park and Keeneland simulcast menu, especially Breeders' Cup Preview Days. Ditto for Hollywood Park and Oak Tree racing at Santa Anita.

NOVEMBER: Breeders' Cup Weekend; assorted spot plays for the next week or so on the nationwide simulcast menu featuring horses I have been following.

MID-NOVEMBER, DECEMBER, JANUARY TO MID-FEBRUARY: No action other than plays with betting partners into sizable Southern California pick-six carryovers and/or $1 million guaranteed pools.

LITFIN
ON RECORD KEEPING
by Dave Litfin

MY INTEREST IN horse racing began to take hold right around the time the Miracle Mets were wrapping up that memorable World Series. That's when I happened upon a copy of Tom Ainslie's just-published *Complete Guide to Thoroughbred Racing.*

That was a lucky break for me. Ainslie was scholarly and his comprehensive guide was also a fun and interesting read. A few months later, offtrack betting became a reality in my neighborhood, and that made placing a bet as easy as getting a slice of pizza. Which is not to say there weren't some bumps in the road along the way—like those days when I cut school and bet my lunch money unwisely, and wound up pizzaless and taking nourishment from Aqueduct's relish bins with a plastic spoon.

Many of the other authors in this collection quenched my thirst for knowledge through the years, and I rely on their insightful counsel and practical plans to this day. I've borrowed and molded their ideas to fit my needs, while adding new wrinkles here and there that get good results.

Results are the bottom line in my chosen profession.

The record-keeping techniques and procedures described throughout this chapter have, out of necessity, become second nature, almost like breathing. There is nothing mystical about these daily routines. No magical secret to beating the races is held within. They are very effective but they do require a fully developed attention span. The reward for such efforts will be solid and insightful opinions about the day-to-day dynamics at your circuit. Take from this array what you will, because no methodology works for all styles of play. My only guarantee is that several of the nuggets found here have the power to improve or fine-tune some part of your overall handicapping process.

If we should cross paths by the paddock area or on the backstretch on some summer Sunday at Saratoga, feel free to show your appreciation by buying me a hot dog. But please, hold the relish.

WHY KEEP RECORDS?

Spending the time required to get an edge at the track is work, and you've got to work smart, because your parimutuel competition is doing the same thing. (Then again, after 30-plus years at the track, I still find it hard to believe some of the incredibly misguided things I overhear, so the potential to make profits is most definitely there.)

Keeping fairly detailed up-to-date records is part of my job. But I like to cash tickets, too. I used to unearth lots of overlays by looking through stacks of yellowed *Daily Racing Forms* and coming up with hidden horses for courses, but thanks to improvements to the past performances in recent years, when a horse is a four-time winner from five starts at a given track, it's right there for everyone to see. So are Beyer Speed Figures, claiming-price brackets, allowance purses and conditions, claimed-from lines, workout rankings, and so forth.

But the first law of parimutuel wagering is that the value of information is inversely related to the degree of its use. In order to get a greater edge, we need to find ways of obtaining information that isn't circulating through the mainstream.

My method is to focus on knowing as much as possible about one circuit—in my case, New York—and to keep careful records. I use *DRF Simulcast Weekly* for evaluating shippers, and to keep up to speed with any obvious track biases at the major out-of-town tracks.

I need to be sure I'm betting into situations that offer value. By "value" I don't mean haphazard stabs in wide-open races on any ambulatory 8-1 shot that has a mane and a tail. Certainly, it is nice to find the occasional wolf in sheep's clothing, but the majority of them are just sheep. Legitimate 8-5 shots that go off at 3-1 are terrific value, and a steady diet of them will keep your bankroll well nourished.

To find value in the parimutuel forum you need a unique perspective. This is best achieved by developing frames of reference that are not readily available to John Q. Public.

What specifically makes a 3-1 shot in one race a good value, as opposed to the one in the next race that isn't?

7 Country Only

Own: Moreton & Marisol Binn Lessee Binn R
CASTILLO H JR (—) 2000:(158 26 .16)

B. c. 3 (Mar) OBSFEB99 $400,000
Sire: Carson City (Mr. Prospector) $35,000
Dam: Only Maisie (Stalwart)
Br: Copeland Dreabon (Ky)
Tr: Kimmel John C (—) 2000:(94 20 .21)

L 122

Life	7	3	1	1	$139,080	D.Fst	6	3	1	1	$136,680 100
2000	2	2	0	0	$98,460	Wet	1	0	0	0	$2,400 61
1999	5	1	1	1	$40,620	Turf	0	0	0	0	$0 –
FG	0	0	0	0	$0	Dist	3	3	0	0	$123,660 100

12Feb00-8Aqu	fst	1 1/16 [•]	:23^{3}	:47	1:11^{2}	1:43^{3}	Whirlaway82k	100	4	1	1^{hd}	1½	12½	15½	Castillo H Jr	L 122	*1.05	91–16	Country Only122^{5½} Hades114^{4} Button Raise115^{1}	Speed outside, driving	8
8Jan00-8Aqu	fst	170 [•]	:24	:48^{1}	1:12^{2}	1:41^{3}	Count Fleet81k	97	1	1	1^{1}	1½	12½	13¾	Castillo H Jr	L 114	3.70	93–15	*CountryOnly*114^{3¾} BenTheMan115^{3¾} MjorAdonis113½	Pace, clear, driving	7
18Dec99-4Aqu	fst	1 1/16 [•]	:22^{4}	:47	1:11^{4}	1:44^{4}	Md Sp Wt 42k	88	12	1	11½	1^{1}	12½	13½	Gryder A T	L 119	2.45	85–13	*Country Only*119^{3½} Prime Pine119^{6¼} *Big E E*119^{2¾}	Pace, clear, driving	12
20Nov99-6Aqu	fst	1	:22^{3}	:45^{1}	1:09^{3}	1:36^{1}	Md Sp Wt 42k	84	1	2	2½	21½	2^{hd}	2^{hd}	Gryder A T	L 118	2.55	87–15	Bare Outline118^{hd} *Country Only*118½ Perfect Cat118^{14}	Stayed on gamely	9
18Sep99-3Bel	fst	1	:23^{1}	:46^{2}	1:11^{1}	1:36^{1}	Md Sp Wt 42k	74	9	1	14½	1^{1}	22½	310¼	Gryder A T	L 117 b	16.70	73–14	Polish Miner117^{9¾} *Highest Praise*117½ Country Only117^{1}	Set pace, tired	9
28Aug99-4Sar	gd	6f	:21^{4}	:45^{1}	:58	1:11^{1}	Md Sp Wt 40k	61	3	3	1^{1}	2½	31½	4^{8}	Gryder A T	L 117 b	14.30	77–09	*Millencolin*117^{1} *Polish Miner*117^{6¼} *Alotabull*117¾	Vied inside, tired	10
7Aug99-6Sar	fst	6f	:22	:45^{3}	:57^{4}	1:10^{3}	Md Sp Wt 40k	42	4	10	96½	104½	7^{14}	618½	Gryder A T	L 117	14.30	69–13	*High Yield*117^{8¾} Polish Miner117^{2} Highest Praise117^{1¼}	Raced greenly	10

WORKS: ●Mar3 Bel tr.t 5f fst :58^{4} H *1/6* Feb24 Bel tr.t 5f fst 1:00^{3} B *3/23* ●Feb3 Bel tr.t 5f fst 1:00 B *1/19* ●Jan27 Bel tr.t 5f fst 1:00^{4} B *1/24* Jan20 Bel tr.t 5f fst 1:00^{3} H *3/51* Dec31 Bel tr.t 5f fst 1:02^{2} B *34/60*

As you scan the record of Country Only, what are some of the things that might have foreshadowed his successful jump to consecutive stakes wins directly off a maiden graduation?

Two things that stand out are the steadily improving line of Beyer Speed Figures and the fact that he is carrying his speed better on the front end since beginning his current form cycle on November 20 with blinkers off.

Those familiar with Aqueduct's inner track would also point out that the tight-turned configuration tends to favor horses with early speed, and that horses seldom win a two-turn route from post 12 as this one did. On race day for the Count Fleet, you might even have checked the post-position listings on *Daily Racing Form*'s "Track Facts" page and seen that Country Only had been the sole route winner from post 12 through the first month of the winter meet. In the Count Fleet he was breaking from the rail, which at two turns normally produces an easier trip than the extreme outside.

You would also have noted the trio of next-out winners italicized in the August 28 company line, and that the winner of his debut race had come back to win as well.

So was 7-2 on Country Only an overlay? More information would make it easier to tell, and manufacturing that info is the gist of what we're going to do here.

With a file of annotated result charts and a homemade "handicapper's notebook," which you will soon learn to compile, the picture becomes clearer. By consulting these handy reference sources you would also have known the following:

- The winner of Country Only's debut race, High Yield, came back to win the Grade 1 Hopeful.
- One of the three next-out winners italicized in Country Only's company line on August 28, Millencolin, next won the Kentucky Cup Juvenile at Turfway Park.
- In addition to that trio, four others from the August 28 maiden race who finished behind Country Only came back to win next time out.
- Country Only's 21.85-second first quarter August 28 ranked second-fastest of five sprints on the Travers undercard, surpassed only by the 21.67 run by Five Star Day in the Grade 1 King's Bishop.
- Country Only ran in the faster division of a split maiden-special-weight mile on September 18, a race won by a 4-5 shot in 1:36.34. The second division was run in 1:37.88.
- In that September 18 mile, Country Only set the pace against the grain of a strong bias that favored outside closers.
- Of the 40 one-mile races run on a fast main track at Aqueduct's recently concluded fall meet, the fractions of 45.25 and 1:09.64 pressed by Country Only in his November 20 comeback ranked third-fastest and second-fastest, respectively.
- Trainer John Kimmel's Strolling Belle had won a classified allowance on December 2, and had come back to take the Ladies Handicap on December 18. In the Ladies Handicap, Strolling Belle got a rider switch from Aaron Gryder to Heberto Castillo, the same switch Country Only was getting in the Count Fleet. Kimmel's Go Again Valid had won an allowance on December 19, and had come back on January 1 to win a division of the Interborough Handicap.

Considering this extra information, Country Only's odds of 7-2 in the Count Fleet begin to look good. And consider that 4-5 Ben the Man was exiting a route allowance win over the track that received a Beyer of 85, three points lower than Country Only's maiden win.

Coming up with this kind of background history isn't as time consuming as it initially seems once you get the hang of the routine. It takes about an hour daily to properly maintain a file of result charts and a handicapper's notebook for the circuit of your choice.

If the techniques you're about to digest sound intriguing, I suggest you give them a full-blown try at the beginning of the next meet you follow and continue it through to the end. You might be amazed at the things you'll discover as the days go by, and chances are you'll feel naked without these records at your disposal regularly.

THE RESULT CHARTS

For those who entertain any serious thought of playing this game for profit, spending time with the charts is a prerequisite for success. The charts are the essential building blocks of just about any research that might be required.

Let's go over some basic annotations.

Key Races

Here is the chart of Country Only's second career start. I have circled the next-out winners:

FOURTH RACE
Saratoga
AUGUST 28, 1999

6 FURLONGS. (1.08) MAIDEN SPECIAL WEIGHT. Purse $40,000 (plus up to $7,760 NYSBFOA). 2-year-olds. Weight, 117 lbs.

Value of Race: $40,000 Winner $24,000; second $8,000; third $4,400; fourth $2,400; fifth $1,200. Mutuel Pool $801,032.00 Exacta Pool $789,769.00 Quinella Pool $104,900.00 Trifecta Pool $605,650.00

Last Raced	Horse	M/Eqt. A.Wt	PP	St	¼	½	Str	Fin	Jockey	Odds $1
8Aug99 9ElP4	Millencolin	2 117	6	5	2½	1½	11	11	Day P	3.15
7Aug99 6Sar2	Polish Miner	2 117	5	2	4hd	52	2½	26¼	Bailey J D	2.10
	Alotabull	b 2 117	10	1	5hd	31½	52	3¾	Smith M E	6.50
7Aug99 6Sar6	Country Only	Lb 2 117	3	3	11	2hd	31	4½	Gryder A T	14.30
12Aug99 5Sar6	Holy Toledo	Lb 2 117	4	10	3hd	4hd	4hd	5½	Prado E S	10.90
14Aug99 5Sar3	Saint Joseph	2 117	1	8	8hd	93½	6hd	61	Chavez J F	4.50
	Great Future	2 117	9	7	7½	8hd	82	7nk	Davis R G	23.60
	Famous Again	L 2 117	2	4	98	71	7½	84½	Sellers S J	25.00
	Hotspur	2 117	7	9	10	10	10	9nk	Antley C W	18.40
	Cajun Concert	2 117	8	6	6½	6½	9½10		Velazquez J R	38.50

OFF AT 2:10 Start Good. Won driving. Track good.
TIME :21⁴, :45¹, :58, 1:11¹ (:21.85, :45.31, :58.19, 1:11.32)

$2 Mutuel Prices:

6–MILLENCOLIN	8.30	3.80	2.90
5–POLISH MINER		3.50	2.90
10–ALOTABULL			4.50

$2 EXACTA 6–5 PAID $24.20 $2 QUINELLA 5–6 PAID $11.00 $2 TRIFECTA
6–5–10 PAID $114.00

Ch. c, (May), by Dehere–Imaglee, by Grey Dawn II. Trainer Lukas D Wayne. Bred by Michael V Prentiss (Ky).

MILLENCOLIN raced with the pace from the start, took over and drew clear in upper stretch then dug in gamely and held off POLISH MINER for the win. POLISH MINER, close up early, was roused on the turn, came wide into the stretch and finished gamely despite racing greenly in the drive. ALOTABULL, hustled outside, chased the pace while three wide and tired in the stretch. COUNTRY ONLY showed good speed along the inside and faded in the final furlong. HOLY TOLEDO, hustled on the rail, chased the pace and tired in the stretch. SAINT JOSEPH, outrun early, raced inside and had no impact on the outcome. GREAT FUTURE chased outside and tired. FAMOUS AGAIN, put to the whip on the backstretch, raced three wide on the turn and had no response. HOTSPUR raced greenly. CAJUN CONCERT chased the pace while three wide and tired.

You can use arrows pointing up or down to indicate whether the horse came back to win with a rise or drop in class. Holy Toledo and Hotspur came back to win at Calder in the fall, hence the "Crc" notations. It's a good idea to scan each issue of *DRF Simulcast Weekly* for horses that ship out from your home track to win somewhere else, especially when you're following a meet like Saratoga, because horses scatter across the country when the meet is over, and you want to be aware of the ones who enjoy immediate success somewhere else.

Sometimes, as in the case of Cajun Concert, who came back to win a maiden race for a $75,000 claiming price, I'll note the conditions of the next-out win alongside the horse's name.

Millencolin might have merited two up arrows to signify his next-out stakes victory. I just wrote in "Ky Cup Juv." Use whatever symbols you're comfortable with, so long as they serve as a clear reminder when you need to refer to the chart weeks or months later.

Trips

Generally speaking, tough-trip horses tend to be grossly overbet. Often, a horse gets into trouble because he lacks the speed or athleticism to avoid it in the first place. I don't think it's an efficient use of time to watch replays over and over while feverishly scribbling notes about every little thing, because the really bad stuff winds up in the chart footnote anyway. I'm more impressed by the horse who can give his rider a push-button acceleration to avoid a traffic jam midway on the turn, or smoothly shift into another lane without breaking stride.

Some of the toughest trips don't involve any actual trouble, but have more to do with difficult pace scenarios or stressful positions. A horse that gets caught dueling between horses through taxing fractions is having a very stressful trip, even though the comment line may merely say "Tired."

An angle that consistently produces winners concerns the horse who wins a pace battle only to lose the war. Probably the most widely known example of this angle in recent years occurred in the 1997 running of the Santa Anita Derby:

A look at the positions, beaten lengths, and footnote comments reveals that Silver Charm locked into a speed duel with Sharp Cat through the first quarter while between rivals, and the battle raged until midstretch before Sharp Cat finally threw in the towel. Silver Charm came on again to narrowly miss catching Free House, who had been eased back off the duel to stalk in perfect striking position. Note that at the half-mile, Free House was third, 2½ lengths off the dueling leaders, and one length clear of the rest of the field.

SIXTH RACE
Santa Anita
APRIL 5, 1997

1⅛ MILES. (1.45^{4}) 60th Running of THE SANTA ANITA DERBY. Purse $750,000 Guaranteed. Grade I. 3-year-olds. By subscription of $300 each to accompany the nomination (early bird) on or before December 5. Early bird nominees to the Santa Anita Derby are automatically eligible to both the San Rafael and the San Felipe Stakes with nomination and starting fees waived to those two stakes. Late nominations closd Saturday, February 1, by payment of $3,000 each. Supplementary nominations are due at time of entry, Thursday, April 3, by payment of $20,000. All horses to pay $15,000 to start, with $750,000 guaranteed, of which $450,000 to first, $150,000 to second, $90,000 to third, $45,000 to fourth and $15,000 to fifth. Weight, 120 lbs. Starters to be named through the entry box by the closing time of entries. A trophy will be presented to the owner of the winner. The winner of the 1997 Santa Anita Oaks will be automatically eligible to the 1997 Santa Anita Derby with no fees. Late nominations closed Saturday February 1, $3,000 each, with 1. Supplementary nominations closed Thursday, April 3, $20,000 each. Closed Thursday, December 5, with 128 nominations.

Value of Race: $750,000 Winner $450,000; second $150,000; third $90,000; fourth $45,000; fifth $15,000. Mutuel Pool $1,811,804.40 Exacta Pool $1,009,667.00 Trifecta Pool $940,766.00 Quinella Pool $124,370.00

Last Raced	Horse	M/Eqt.	A.	Wt	PP	St	¼	½	¾	Str	Fin	Jockey	Odds $1
16Mar97 ^{7}SA^{1}	Free House	LB	3	120	4	2	$3^{1/2}$	3^{1}	$3^{1/2}$	3^{2}	1^{hd}	Desormeaux K J	a-7.30
16Mar97 ^{7}SA^{2}	Silver Charm	LB	3	120	3	3	2^{hd}	$2^{2\frac{1}{2}}$	$2^{2\frac{1}{2}}$	$1^{1/2}$	2^{2}	Stevens G L	2.10
2Mar97 ^{5}SA^{3}	Hello-IR	LB	3	120	2	5	6^{hd}	$6^{2\frac{1}{2}}$	$5^{1/2}$	$4^{1\frac{1}{2}}$	3no	McCarron C J	3.70
16Mar97 ^{7}SA^{6}	Steel Ruhlr	Bb	3	120	8	10	10	10	7^{3}	6^{4}	4^{3}	Blanc B	63.20
8Mar97 ^{8}BM^{3}	Carmen's Baby	LB	3	120	10	9	5^{4}	$4^{1/2}$	$4^{1\frac{1}{2}}$	5^{hd}	$5^{1/2}$	Almeida G F	62.00
9Mar97 ^{6}SA^{1}	Sharp Cat	LBb	3	115	1	1	1^{hd}	1^{hd}	1^{hd}	2^{hd}	$6^{3\frac{1}{2}}$	Nakatani C S	2.00
28Feb97 ^{7}SA^{1}	P. T. Indy	B	3	120	6	7	$8^{1/2}$	$8^{1\frac{1}{2}}$	$9^{1/2}$	8^{5}	$7^{4\frac{1}{2}}$	Davis R G	10.70
2Mar97 ^{5}SA^{4}	Bagshot	LBb	3	120	7	8	9^{4}	9^{1}	10	$9^{2\frac{1}{2}}$	$8^{1\frac{3}{4}}$	Garcia J A	a-7.30
15Mar97 ^{8}SA^{3}	Swiss Yodeler	LB	3	120	9	4	$4^{2\frac{1}{2}}$	5^{3}	$6^{4\frac{1}{2}}$	7^{hd}	9^{4}	Douglas R R	41.00
8Mar97 ^{7}SA^{1}	Classic Credential	LB	3	120	5	6	$7^{2\frac{1}{2}}$	$7^{2\frac{1}{2}}$	8^{1}	10	10	Solis A	14.40

a-Coupled: Free House and Bagshot.

OFF AT 2:47 Start Good. Won driving. Time, :22, :45, 1:09, 1:34^{2}, 1:47^{3} Track fast.

$2 Mutuel Prices:				
	1-FREE HOUSE (a-entry)	16.60	6.00	3.40
	4-SILVER CHARM		3.60	2.80
	3-HELLO-IR			3.40

$1 EXACTA 1-4 PAID $21.70 $1 TRIFECTA 1-4-3 PAID $90.50 $2 QUINELLA 1-4 PAID $18.20

Gr/ro c, (Mar), by Smokester-Fountain Lake, by Vigors. Trainer Gonzalez J Paco. Bred by McCaffery Trudy & Toffan John A (Cal).

FREE HOUSE forced the pace three deep on the first turn, settled behind the dueling leaders outside CARMEN'S BABY on the backstretch and off the rail on the second turn, bid three deep into the stretch, gained a short lead under urging past midstretch and gamely prevailed under pressure. SILVER CHARM dueled between rivals into the first turn, battled outside SHARP CAT on the backstretch and second turn, took a short advantage into the stretch and gamely came back on once headed to narrowly miss while inside the winner. HELLO was briefly fractious in the gate, came off the inside on the backstretch, moved up outside on the second turn and four wide into the stretch and went willingly to the wire. STEEL RUHLR settled off the rail, moved up outside into and on the second turn, swung out in upper stretch and finished well while lugging in late. CARMEN'S BABY angled in early, saved ground while not far back to the stretch, came out and weakened, then did not return to be unsaddled when lame and was vanned off. SHARP CAT pushed open the front of the gate before the start but did not come out, broke alertly and dueled inside SILVER CHARM to the stretch, respnded when initially headed but weakened in the final furlong. P. T. INDY bumped lightly at the start, settled off the rail while unhurried to the stretch and lacked a rally. BAGSHOT bumped lightly at the start, raced off the rail early, found the fence on the first turn, came out on the second turn and was not a threat. SWISS YODELER four wide into the first turn, continued outside CARMEN'S BABY on that turn and early on the backstretch, angled to the rail into the second turn and gave way. CLASSIC CREDENTIAL between rivals early, continued off the rail, found the inside for the second turn and also gave way. KING CRIMSON (6) WAS WITHDRAWN.

Owners— 1, McCaffery Trudy & Toffan John; 2, Lewis Beverly J & Robert B; 3, Kirkwood Al & Sandee; 4, Delaplane E Edward & Paula; 5, Markarian Edward & Noriega Robert; 6, The Thoroughbred Corp; 7, Folsom Robert S; 8, McCaffery Trudy & Toffan John; 9, Steinmann Heinz; 10, Cobra Farm Inc

Trainers—1, Gonzalez J Paco; 2, Baffert Bob; 3, McAnally Ronald; 4, Cardiel Fidel; 5, Lage Armando; 6, Lukas D Wayne; 7, Mandella Richard; 8, Gonzalez J Paco; 9, Harrington Mike; 10, Puype Mike

Scratched— King Crimson (16Mar97 ^{7}SA^{3})

Silver Charm had the much tougher trip, and came back to win the Kentucky Derby at 4-1.

A horse that wins the duel in a fast-paced race is usually a serious threat to win any subsequent outing when the pace scenario appears more favorable. Circle the running lines of pace-duel winners such as Silver Charm so that they stand out quickly.

The Fractions

One of the unfortunate things about a key race is that you don't know it's going to be a key race until two or three horses in the field have already come back to win. An unusually fast pace is one of the standard tip-offs to a potentially key race, and it's a good idea to underline noteworthy fractions in charts as they occur.

It's also a good habit to break down the individual segments for each race. Getting into this habit enables you to isolate unusually fast or slow segments, and to pick up horses who are moving into the fastest part of the pace.

In the A Phenomenon Handicap at Saratoga in August 1999, Yes It's True was coming off four consecutive graded-stakes wins at four different tracks, and was the 3-5 choice against six older sprinters. But the winner at a juicy 10-1 was Intidab, who was coming out of a loss at 1-2 in a four-other-than allowance.

Yes It's True didn't enjoy the kind of advantage one might expect of a 3-5 favorite. With the exception of an isolated 118 earned under optimal conditions on a gold rail at Pimlico on the Preakness undercard, Yes It's True had been running in the 103-106 range for most of the year.

Intidab had run 107's in his first two dirt sprints at Belmont, and a last-out 102 was better than it looked. Notice anything about the fractions (see chart, opposite)?

The first quarter of 22.94 seconds was comparatively slow, and Intidab was under rating tactics with just one horse behind him. (In the preceding race, also at six furlongs, maiden-claiming sprinters had opened with a 22.78 first quarter.)

The second quarter, run on the turn, went in 22.75, through which Intidab was four wide and gained 1½ lengths. Tactically speaking, he was having a very difficult trip, rallying wide on the turn during the fastest part of the race.

Intidab kept coming through a strong 23.64 final quarter, but had been the victim of overconfident handling and was left with too much to do. The final figure of 102 was more the function of a slow first quarter than anything else.

ONE OF the most underrated influences on results is wind, and this is especially true at Aqueduct, which is right next to John F. Kennedy International Airport and Jamaica

THIRD RACE
Belmont
JULY 14, 1999

6 FURLONGS. (1.07⁴) ALLOWANCE. Purse $48,000 (plus up to $9,312 NYSBFOA). 3-year-olds and upward which have not won four races other than maiden, claiming, starter or restricted. Weights: 3-year-olds, 118 lbs. Older, 123 lbs. Non-winners of $30,000 in 1999, allowed 2 lbs. $40,000 in 1998-99 or $25,000 twice in 1999, 4 lbs. $25,000 in 1999, 6 lbs. (Races where entered for $50,000 or less not considered in allowances).

Value of Race: $48,000 Winner $28,800; second $9,600; third $5,280; fourth $2,880; fifth $1,440. Mutuel Pool $246,142.00 Exacta Pool $345,307.00

Last Raced	Horse	M/Eqt. A.Wt	PP	St	¼	½	Str	Fin	Jockey	Odds $1
7Nov98 5Aqu9	Gray Raider	Lf 5 116	1	2	2½	2hd	21	1nk	Santos J A	13.20
5Jly99 3Bel1	Intidab	Lb 6 118	4	5	4½	4½	3½	21	Velazquez J R	0.55
16Jun99 2Bel1	Adverse	L 5 116	5	1	1½	1½	1½	3¾	Espinoza J L	3.55
17Oct98 9Bel6	Dice Dancer	Lf 4 120	3	4	5	5	4hd	45¼	Samyn J L	4.40
17Jun99 6Bel3	Jim's Mistake	Lb 5 120	2	3	3½	3½	5	5	Migliore R	12.40

OFF AT 2:02 Start Good. Won driving. Track fast.
TIME :22⁴, :45³, :57¹, 1:09¹ (:22.94, :45.69, :57.31, 1:09.33) 22.94 22.75 23.64

$2 Mutuel Prices:

1-GRAY RAIDER	28.40	6.30	2.10
4-INTIDAB		2.90	2.10
5-ADVERSE			2.10

$2 EXACTA 1-4 PAID $61.50

Gr. h, by Rubiano-Miss Creeker, by Red Ryder. Trainer Domino Carl J. Bred by Blackburn James (Ill).

GRAY RAIDER showed good speed while in hand, dug in gamely in the stretch and prevailed under a drive. INTIDAB, rated outside, advanced four wide on the turn and finished gamely from the outside. ADVERSE set the pace while in hand and weakened in the final furlong. DICE DANCER, unhurried early on, finished gamely inside. JIM'S MISTAKE chased three wide and tired in the stretch.

Bay. Aqueduct is surrounded by runways, water, and low-lying structures, so when the wind blows, there is nowhere to hide.

You can get a good idea of wind velocity by watching the infield flags. When the flagpole itself starts bending, as it did during day-long winds upward of 40 miles per hour at the Big A on April 8, 2000, it is a major factor to consider.

The wind can create speed-favoring conditions when there is a tailwind down the backstretch, especially in one-turn races out of the chute. The early leader gets blown along without expending much energy, and when the closers fan out to make their runs in the stretch, they are stymied by a headwind.

Those were the conditions on April 8, when Golden Missile ran second as the favorite in the Westchester Handicap (see chart page 122).

Yankee Victor was the sixth front-running winner of the afternoon. Of the eight one-turn races that day, Yankee Victor's first quarter in 23.19 had been the slowest; his half-mile of 45.53 was also pedestrian, considering that in the preceding race, Ruby Rubles had gone wire to wire in a $75,000 stakes for New York-breds after being blown through a half in 43.98. The slow pace gave Yankee Victor a tremendous advantage, and he remained clear while against the wind through a final quarter in 26.12 seconds.

Unless you knew about the strong wind-created bias and the slow pace, it was hard to know what to make of Golden Missile's nonthreatening second with a Beyer Speed Figure of 103 in the Westchester. But he had finished resolutely to slice nearly four

EIGHTH RACE

Aqueduct

APRIL 8, 2000

1 MILE. (1.32²) 72nd Running of THE WESTCHESTER HANDICAP. Grade III. Purse $100,000 (Up To $19,400 NYSBFOA) A HANDICAP FOR THREE YEAR OLDS AND UPWARD. By subscription of $100 each, which should accompany the nomination; $500 to pass the entry box; $500 to start, with $100,000 added. The added money and all fees to be divided 60% to the winner, 20% to second, 11% to third, 6% to fourth and 3% to fifth. Trophies will be presented to the winning owner, trainer and jockey. Closed Saturday, March 25, 2000 with 25 Nominations.

Value of Race: $110,000 Winner $66,000; second $22,000; third $12,100; fourth $6,600; fifth $3,300. Mutuel Pool $561,216.00 Exacta Pool $444,918.00 Trifecta Pool $354,237.00

Last Raced	Horse	M/Eqt. A.Wt	PP	St	¼	½	¾	Str	Fin	Jockey	Odds $1
11Mar00 11GP2	Yankee Victor	Lb 4 115	3	4	1½	1 1	1½	12½	13¾	Castillo H Jr	7.00
5Mar00 8FG5	Golden Missile	Lb 5 116	7	1	3hd	4hd	4½	3½	22	Gryder A T	1.15
18Mar00 8Aqu3	Watchman's Warning	Lbf 5 113	1	6	67	5hd	63½	42	3no	Velasquez Cornelio	15.80
4Mar00 4GP1	Western Expression	L 4 113	6	2	22½	21½	23½	25	42¾	Prado E S	4.30
26Feb00 10GP4	Best of Luck	Lb 4 115	2	7	7	7	7	7	53	Samyn J L	4.10
6Feb00 8Aqu2	Durmiente-CH	L 6 113	4	5	4hd	3½	3½	61	6nk	Bridgmohan S X	6.70
25Apr99 8Aqu3	Pasay	L 5 112	5	3	5½	68	5hd	5½	7	Espinoza J L	52.00

OFF AT 4:22 Start Good. Won driving. Track fast.
TIME :23, :45², 1:08¹, 1:34¹ (:23.19, :45.53, 1:08.25, 1:34.37)

WIND SLOW PACE

$2 Mutuel Prices:			
4-YANKEE VICTOR	16.00	5.70	4.20
8-GOLDEN MISSILE		3.10	2.50
1-WATCHMAN'S WARNING			4.10

$2 EXACTA 4–8 PAID $41.80 $2 TRIFECTA 4–8–1 PAID $290.50

Dk. b. or br. c, by Saint Ballado–Highest Carol, by Caro*Ire. Trainer Morales Carlos J. Bred by Lundock Rodney G (Fla).

YANKEE VICTOR quickly showed in front, set the pace along the inside while in hand, drew clear when roused in upper stretch and was driving under the wire. GOLDEN MISSILE was rated along three wide and rallied to earn the place. WATCHMAN'S WARNING was rated inside and finished well on the rail. WESTERN EXPRESSION attended the pace from the outside while in hand, tried the winner turning for home but proved no match for that rival and tired in the final furlong. BEST OF LUCK was hustled along on the backstretch, came wide for the drive and had no rally. DURMIENTE (CHI) was unhurried early, raced four wide on the turn and had no response when roused. PASAY raced between rivals and tired.

Owners— 1, Binn Moreton Enllomar Stable et al; 2, Stronach Stable; 3, Englander Richard A; 4, Flying Zee Stable; 5, Bohemia Stable; 6, La Marca Stable; 7, Lazy F Ranch

Trainers— 1, Morales Carlos J; 2, Orseno Joseph; 3, Schosberg Richard; 4, Serpe Philip M; 5, Jerkens H Allen; 6, Klesaris Robert P; 7, Penna Angel Jr

lengths off the winner's margin in the final furlong, and in view of the entire situation, and the fact that he had run Beyers of 115 or better in three of his five starts before the Westchester, odds of 9-2 were excellent value for a subsequent triumph in the Pimlico Special.

Let's review the procedures for marking charts:

- Circle horses who came back to win their next race, noting any pertinent class moves.
- Circle the running lines of horses who won pace duels.
- Compare fractional and final times at identical distances on the same day, underlining anything exceptional.
- Break down the race's fractions into individual segments.
- Note any changes in weather, wind direction and velocity, and/or changes in track surface, such as drying-out tracks that are harrowed for later races after being sealed earlier.

THE HANDICAPPER'S NOTEBOOK

Admittedly, this is an old-fashioned approach that would be laughed out of Silicon Valley. But it ain't broke, so why fix it?

The New York racing calendar consists of six different meetings: Aqueduct inner dirt (winter); Aqueduct spring; Belmont spring-summer; Saratoga; Belmont fall; and Aqueduct fall.

For each meet, I go to Wal-Mart and pick up a 1½-inch three-ring binder for about $1.79, along with some loose-leaf paper. I also need a good pair of scissors, some dividers, pens in black and red ink, and a big package of glue sticks. You might say that much of what I do, I learned in kindergarten.

The notebook is divided into three sections: Track profiles, trainers, and a betting log.

Track profiles

The track profile was the brainchild of Tom Brohamer, who wanted to know what kinds of running styles and energy expenditures were most successful at various distances. I've tailored the model somewhat to fit my needs.

For each winner at each distance on dirt and on turf (keeping each of the two turf courses at Belmont and Saratoga separate), I record the following data, using red ink only for wet tracks:

DATE	NAME	(FIELD SIZE)	POST	RUNNING LINE	MUTUEL	RACE FRACTIONS
7-28	Flying Kris	(6)	6	3-1½ 3-½ 3-hd 1-1¼	$5.00	21.62 45.07 1:11.58

At a glance, I see that on July 28, Flying Kris broke from the outside post in a field of six and stalked the pace from close range before edging clear in deep stretch. His low $5 mutuel says he had obvious merits, and the race fractions complete the array.

That's all there is to it. It can be an extremely beneficial habit to cultivate, because before long you will have developed a sort of "past performance" for the track, which can be as enlightening as ordinary horse past performances.

Most of the time there is no obvious all-encompassing bias, but there may be distinct trends at some distances. Early speed may be paramount at six furlongs but terrible at one mile, for example.

When a bias does manifest itself, keepers of track profiles are the first to know about its arrival, as well as its departure.

Inside biases generally go hand-in-hand with speed, and when closers dominate they usually do so on the outside. But during the first part of Saratoga's 1999 meet, an unusual and strong outside-speed bias was present. This was the six-furlong profile through the feature race on August 4, the Honorable Miss Handicap:

7-28	Flying Kris	(6)	6	3-1½ 3-½ 3-hd 1-1¼	$5.00	21.62 45.07 1:11.58
	Positive Gal	(10)	10	2-½ 2-hd 1-hd 1-¾	$4.80	21.94 45.22 1:10.13
	Magicalmysterycat	(7)	6	2-hd 1-hd 1-hd 1-¾	$9.20	21.71 45.19 1:10.91
7-29	Sense Of Boundary	(11)	8	3-1 2-hd 1-1½ 1-4¼	$50.50	22.13 45.31 1:10.59
	More Than Ready	(5)	4	2-hd 2-hd 1-7 1-9¾	$2.70	22.27 45.11 1:09.65
7-31	Country Hideaway	(7)	4	5-4 3-1 3-½ 1-nk	$6.10	21.86 45.39 1:10.20
	Uncle Abbie	(9)	8	1-½ 1-hd 1-½ 1-1	$5.30	22.16 46.13 1:11.48
	Sharcan	(9)	6	1-hd 1-½ 1-2½ 1-2¾	$17.20	21.88 44.89 1:10.21
8-1	Assinica	(10)	9	5-5 4-1 1-2½ 1-3¼	$58.00	21.67 45.57 1:11.84
	Katz Me If You Can	(9)	1	2-½ 2-½ 1-hd 1-3	$10.40	22.15 45.76 1:11.45
	Rare Rock	(7)	4	1-1 1-1½ 1-2 1-nk	$5.40	21.97 44.81 1:10.17
8-2	Informal Attire	(7)	6	2-1½ 1-½ 1-4½ 1-5	$17.80	21.95 45.34 1:10.20
	Shawnee Country	(7)	5	3-½ 2-hd 1-hd 1-1	$15.80	22.37 45.97 1:10.82
	Champagneforlisa	(11)	9	1-½ 1-½ 1-½ 1-3½	$7.50	21.98 45.46 1:11.36
8-4	Kings Command	(7)	7	2-hd 1-hd 1-1½ 1-1	$16.40	22.41 45.78 1:10.96
	Bourbon Belle	(10)	9	1-½ 1-hd 1-4½ 1-3¼	$11.00	21.88 44.85 1:09.53

Each of the first 16 winners had either led or been within one length of the lead after the initial half-mile, and the three inside posts combined were a woeful 1 for 48.

In the Honorable Miss, which was won by Bourbon Belle, the stone-cold closer Furlough had rallied along a deep rail right into the teeth of the bias. In her return on August 22, with the bias gone, Furlough's run from the clouds to win the Ballerina Handicap by a nose anchored a $228 pick three that turned out to be my biggest score of the season.

On August 5, the day after the Honorable Miss, the outside-speed bias was still holding, and it was a marvelous tool for separating contenders in a four-other-than allowance:

```
Lumberman                                    Ch. g. 4  KEEAPR97 $135,000                                    Life  20  6  2  1  $177,291 | D.Fst  15  6  1  1  $169,641  103
Own: Dogwood Stable                          Sire: Woodman (Mr. Prospector)                                 1999   4  1  1  0   $38,530 | Wet     3  0  1  0    $7,650   95
                                             Dam: She's the Mint (Key to the Mint)                L 114     1998  16  5  1  1  $138,761 | Turf    2  0  0  0        $0   76
                                             Br:  Downing C Gibson III (Ky)                                 Sar    3  3  0  0   $64,800 | Dist    6  4  0  0  $106,341   94
SELLERS S J (35 6 6 2 .17) 1999:(853 178 .21)  Tr: Stewart Dallas(8 1 1 1 .13) 99:(222 42 .19)

19Jun99-8CD   fst 1      :223 :452 1:101 1:351 3↑ Alw 58800N1m        97 4 2 21   2hd  21   24½  Hebert T J     L 123 b  4.20  89-16 Hanarsaan1234½ Lumberman1233 Powerful Goer1161              Bid, no match 6
 6Jun99-8CD   fst 1      :232 :463 1:11  1:35  4↑ Clm 75000(75-55)    103 7 1 11½  11   12½  14¾  Hebert T J     L 116 b  8.70  95-10 Lumberman1164¾ Double Affair113¾ One Mean Man1202¾        Steady drive 7
13May99-9CD   fm 1    Ⓣ :243 :482 1:122 1:363 3↑ Alw 49450N4X        76 4 4 41½  73½  88   812¼ Borel C H      L 115 b 19.50  74-16 Orleans Road1181¾ Jelly RollBump1183¾ Rivershade123¾   Inside, weakened 10
21Apr99-7Kee  fst 6½f    :222 :444 1:083 1:144 4↑ Alw 60000N$Y        85 2 2 42½  33½  32   56¼  Sellers S J    L 118 b  4.90  95-07 ThTrdr'sEcho1152½ HndsomTurk1231 HowlnWolf123¾       Inside, empty late 7
19Dec98-8TP   wf  6½f    :223 :45  1:091 1:154 3↑ Alw 30915NC         95 6 6 43   41½  32½  22½  Martinez W     L 121 b  3.90  89-16 Human Missile1222½ Lumberman121½ Danny Seth121¾         4 wide turn 6
26Nov98-8CD   gd 1 1/16 Ⓣ :244 :481 1:13 1:45 3↑ Alw 58080N$mY       66 6 3 3½   22   59½  715  Martinez W     L 108 b 14.50  64-21 Western Trader1163 Pavillon114¾ Hurrahy1148            3 wide, tired 10
 5Nov98-8CD   fst 1 1/16 :24  :474 1:124 1:443 3↑ Alw 45600N4X        91 2 1 1hd  41   36   39¼  Sellers S J    L 115 b 11.20  79-17 Oak Level1142½ Jelly Roll Bump1216¾ Lumberman115½       Inside, tired 6
17Oct98-6Kee  fst 7f     :222 :45  1:10  1:224 3↑ Alw 53375N3X        88 7 1 42½  64½  2hd  1¾   Sellers S J    L 116 b  1.90  91-05 Lumberman116¾ Hitech1111½ Sand Ridge1132                Driving 7
 3Oct98-6Hoo  sly 1 1/16 :213 :46  1:104 1:43     Indiana Dby314k     62 8 7 76¾  1013 1019 1027¾ Peck B D     LB 115 b  7.40e 62-28 One Bold Stroke122nk Dixie Dot Com1174¾ Da Devil1225½ Failed to menace 11
30Aug98-5Sar  fst 7f     :223 :451 1:094 1:23  3↑ Alw 39000N2X        94 2 2 42   42   3½   1¾   Velazquez J R  L 116 b  7.10  90-13 Lumberman116¾ Shawaf1182 Phone The King114no             7
   Speed inside in hand, altered course stretch, along in time
13Aug98-10Sar fst 7f     :222 :453 1:101 1:23  3↑ Alw 37000N1X        88 3 3 51½  42½  2hd  11¼  Sellers S J    L 114 b 11.30  90-15 Lumberman1141¼ Funny Toy119hd Wildfarel114¾    Came wide, clear late 9
30Jly98-4Sar  fst 6f     :221 :461  :59  1:12     Clm 50000(50-45)    81 2 7 61¾  4¾   3nk  14   Bailey J D     L 117 b  4.60  81-20 Lumbermn1174 Gmbino1131 LittleSoftSho1195½    Rough trip, found room 7
WORKS: Jly29 Sar 5f fst 1:012 B 10/29  Jly15 Kee 5f fst 1:033 B 7/10  May29 Kee 5f fst 1:002 B 5/11  ●May24 Kee 4f sly :482 B 1/6  May7 Kee 5f fst 1:01 B 5/23
```

```
Storm Punch                                  Gr. g. 4  FTMOCT96 $32,000                                     Life   9  4  2  2  $136,949 | D.Fst   9  4  2  2  $136,949   99
Own: Lazy Lane Farms Inc                     Sire: Two Punch (Mr. Prospector)                               1999   3  0  1  2   $51,140 | Wet     0  0  0  0        $0    -
                                             Dam: Too Fast to Catch (Nice Catch)                  L 114     1998   3  2  1  0   $38,160 | Turf    0  0  0  0        $0    -
                                             Br:  Hutchison Farm (Md)                                       Sar    0  0  0  0        $0 | Dist    2  1  0  0   $18,669   72
PRADO E S (28 1 4 3 .04) 1999:(1110 272 .25)   Tr: Motion H Graham(4 0 2 0 .00) 99:(242 50 .21)

17Jly99-9Lrl  fst 6f     :22  :444  :563 1:083 3↑ DeFrancsMem-G1      96 3 1 1hd  1½   1hd  33¾  Johnston M T   L 114 f 37.70  95-06 YsIt'sTru114¾ GoodAndTough1233 StormPnch114½        Dueled off rail, tired 6
 6Jun99-9Pim  fst 6f     :23  :454  :574 1:101 3↑ Chesapeake S100k    99 1 2 1hd  1½   11   31   Johnston M T   L 115 f  5.70  93-11 WrMCollct1221 JstCllMCrl115hd StormPnch115¾   Pace 2-path, weakened 5
13May99-8Pim  fst 6f     :231 :46   :574 1:101 3↑ OClm 60000(60-50)N  92 1 6 11   1hd  2hd  23   Prado E S      L 117    *1.40  91-15 Nimble1163 Storm Punch117hd ClashByNight114¾     Stp slw,rail,weakening 6
17Jly98-8Lrl  fst 6f     :223 :454  :574 1:101 3↑ Alw 30000N3X        88 5 1 11   1½   13   13¾  Prado E S      L 113    *1.00  91-14 Storm Punch1133¾ Fortuoso117½ Silver's Prospect111½             Driving 6
25Jun98-6Lrl  fst 7f     :223 :452 1:10  1:232    Alw 27000N3L        72 1 3 1½   1½   12   1¾   Prado E S      L 115     *.90  92-10 StormPnch115¾ It'sOnlyMony1153 RndmStr117no   Drifted out late,drvng 6
14May98-7Pim  fst 6f     :224 :453  :58  1:11  3↑ Alw 27000N2X        90 1 5 1hd  1hd  13   2¾   Johnston M T   L 114     1.70  89-12 Fortuoso117¾ Storm Punch114no Yaawright1178¼                  Gamely 6
 1Sep97-9Cnl  fst 7f     :222 :451 1:093 1:223    New Kent54k         59 4 3 1½   1½   31½  49½  Prado E S      L 120     *.80  — —   Victory Gallop1142 Unreal Madness1205 Luisita's Choice1142½     Gave way 6
 9Aug97-10Lrl fst 6f     :223 :462  :583 1:111    Primer54k           80 6 3 11   1½   12   11¾  Prado E S      L 113     *.60  88-15 Storm Punch1131¾ Luisita's Choice1144 Wild Explo1139            Ridden out 6
16Jly97-6Lrl  fst 5½f    :232 :471  :593 1:06     Md Sp Wt 20k        57 1 3 12   11½  12   13   Prado E S      L 120     *.90  86-15 Storm Punch1203 Essential120½ Brilliant Code1202¼                Handily 8
WORKS: ●Jly30 Lrl 5f fst :584 H 1/20  Jly11 Lrl 5f fst :593 B 2/18  ●Jly4 Lrl 5f fst :593 H 1/13  ●Jun20 Lrl 5f my 1:002 H 1/11  ●May30 Lrl 5f fst :59 H 1/6  ●May8 Lrl 5f fst :591 Hg 1/16
```

The first two betting choices were Lumberman, who was 5-2 and breaking from the rail, and Storm Punch, the 2-1 favorite, starting on the outside in a field of 10.

Post position was really at the heart of deciding which way to go. Only 11 seven-furlong races had been run at the meet, but it was obvious that the bias was just as prevalent out of the chute as it was at six furlongs, and perhaps even stronger. Horses breaking from posts 1 through 5 had managed just one win from 55 aggregate starts, so even though Lumberman had a 3-for-3 record at Saratoga, the track would be his enemy this time. Meanwhile, the two outside posts had already produced seven winners, which strongly favored Storm Punch.

Storm Punch broke on top (as so many horses from the outside had already done at the meet) and wired the field.

Lumberman was bogged down on the inside and faded to sixth. He came back to win his next start.

Distance-specific track profiles let you see at a glance if there is any bias in post positions or running styles, and the mutuel payoffs help to confirm or discredit the ebb and flow of these passing trends.

The fractional and final times can also be very useful, because it's nice to know when a horse has done something special.

Trainers

There are many statistical studies available about the performances of trainers in all conceivable categories, but here's the problem:

What do you suppose Bob Baffert's winning percentage is with gray second-time starters at Del Mar on Thursdays? It would take some doing to check this silly angle, but I'll bet you it's somewhere in the range of 15 to 20 percent, just like the vast majority of standard subsets.

As Mark Cramer wrote in *Kinky Handicapping*, ". . . too many computer printouts, too much information to sort will weigh down that part of the mind that should be liberated for agile thought. In the realm of trainers, there is so much overkill, that buried under mounds of stats, the horseplayer misses those one or two elegant bits of information that translate into a big score."

It's been my experience that specific knowledge about trainers' methods is needed to lay a strong foundation for worthwhile wagers. Finding these elegant bits of information is made easier by cutting out past performances of race winners and filing them away for future reference in my notebook, sorted by trainer. (While the introduction of trainer statistics in *Daily Racing Form*'s past-performance pages in the fall of 2000 was a great help, I feel that keeping my own records is still indispensable.) Underneath the past performances, I note the date, distance, class conditions, and the mutuel payoff.

Once this simple but effective procedure becomes part of your record-keeping routine, all sorts of patterns begin to emerge, creating a much sharper image of how trainers get their horses ready. I'm looking for methods that trainers use repeatedly in the long run, and for short-term patterns as well. Especially noteworthy are subtle insights as to how young horses are developed through workouts and race placement; which specific meets an outfit appears to shoot for; or what an outfit does with recent claims such as Madok.

Madok
Own: Lamarca Stables
$65,000
VELAZQUEZ J R (247 51 31 39 .21) 1999:(742 151 .20)

B. g. 5
Sire: Prospectors Gamble (Crafty Prospector)
Dam: Sing Sweet Syl (Singular)
Br: Whiting Ronald J (Fla)
Tr: Klesaris Robert P(30 6 4 3 .20) 99:(156 28 .18)

L 115

Life	**36**	**9**	**5**	**7**	**$207,424**	**D.Fst**	**33**	**9**	**4**	**7**	**$198,754** **101**
1999	**7**	**2**	**0**	**4**	**$60,970**	**Wet**	**2**	**0**	**1**	**0**	**$8,670** **92**
1998	**10**	**2**	**4**	**1**	**$74,970**	**Turf**	**1**	**0**	**0**	**0**	**$0** **26**
Bel	**8**	**3**	**0**	**3**	**$67,295**	**Dist**	**2**	**2**	**0**	**0**	**$45,000** **94**

11Jun99-3Bel	fst 1	:224	:454	1:103	1:361	4↑ Clm 75000(100-75)	**94**	3	4	43½	3½	11	1no	Velazquez J R	L 114 b	5.90	83-19	Mdok114no [D]ClshByNight114nk TejnoCouture1191¼	4w move,clear,held on	5
15May99-5Bel	fst 6f	:222	:452	:572	1:101	4↑ Clm c-(45-35)	**90**	1	8	88¼	73¾	54	32¼	Bridgmohan S X	L 117 b	6.30	88-12	*Adverse*1171 *Hit The Roof*1171¼ *Madok*117nk	Game finish outside	8
Claimed from Gumpster Stable for $45,000, Martin Carlos F Trainer																				
28Apr99-6Aqu	fst 6½f	:214	:442	1:091	1:154	4↑ Clm c-(35-30)	**90**	3	5	71¾	62¾	52½	32¼	Douglas R R	L 116 b	2.45	90-19	Sunny Side116¾ Gestalt1091½ Madok1162¼	Game finish outside	7
Claimed from Malakasa Farms for $35,000, Klesaris Robert P Trainer																				
31Mar99-3Aqu	fst 6f	:214	:441	:562	1:092	4↑ Alw 48000N4X	**77**	4	5	615	510	59½	58¼	Douglas R R	L 115 b	3.90	83-18	Simud1171¼ L. B. On Tour1154¼ *Baltimore Gray*1191¼	Steadied 1/2 mile pole	6
14Mar99-3Aqu	fst 6f	:224	:452	:57	1:091	4↑ Clm 55000(60-50)	**92**	5	1	31½	41¼	42	32¾	Douglas R R	L 115 b	2.25	89-13	Double Screen1131¾ *Simud*1191 Madok115nk	4w trip, good finish	6
3Feb99-6Aqu	fst 6f	[·] :224	:452	:572	1:094	4↑ Clm 55000(65-55)	**93**	4	3	44	44	43	31	Douglas R R	L 117 b	6.70	92-14	Simud117½ *Arromanches*112½ Madok117nk	Game finish outside	7
8Jan99-7Aqu	fst 6f	[·] :231	:463	:583	1:122	4↑ Clm 62500(65-60)	**94**	4	1	52½	53¼	52½	11♦	Diego I7	L 108 b	6.80	80-26	[DH]Madok108 [DH]Laredo1171 Hit The Roof110nk	Game finish outside	6
12Dec98-8Med	fst 6f	:213	:441	:562	1:094	3↑ OClm 45000(45-35)N	**80**	1	5	36½	510	56½	45¾	Diego I7	L 109 b	1.70	84-17	TrckyFrosty1162¾ BushysRwrd112¾ L.B.OnTor1182¼	Lacked late response	7
21Nov98-4Aqu	fst 6f	:222	:453	:573	1:102	3↑ Clm 50000(50-40)	**99**	11	1	41	31½	21½	2¾	Velazquez J R	L 117 b	4.10	86-17	Brutally Frank117¾ Madok1172¾ Distinctive Bid1153	Game finish outside	11
15Oct98-8Bel	fst 6f	:222	:451	:571	1:093	3↑ Alw 46000N4X	**64**	3	3	56	54¼	510	515½	Velazquez J R	L 116 b	7.90	78-15	Oro De Mexico1163 Holzmeister1161¼ *Wouldn't We All*120hd	Outrun	5
17Sep98-3Bel	fst 6f	:22	:451	:573	1:103	3↑ Clm c-(50-45)	**88**	4	3	11½	1hd	21½	32	Nakatani C S	L 118 b	*2.10	86-16	LeadingTheChrge1141¼ Arromnches118¾ Mdok118hd	Pace off rail, gamely	6
Claimed from Petronella Robert A for $50,000, Araya Rene A Trainer																				
3May98-7Aqu	fst 1⅜	:483	1:131	1:381	2:162	4↑ Alw ---s	**69**	3	4	46	57	515	525¾	Desormeaux K J	L 116 fb	3.65	53-20	Northface12413 Dustin's Dream1241¼ Kid From The Bronx1135½	Used up	7

WORKS: **Jun24 Bel 5f fst 1:024 B** *25/32*

Bob Klesaris had formerly trained Madok for Malakasa Farms. After losing him for $35,000 on April 28, 1999, he reclaimed the gelding for $45,000 next time out, which was a solid vote of confidence considering that the 5-year-old had won only once during the past 12 months. The new owner was La Marca Stable, and when they rested their new purchase for four weeks and brought him back for a higher price on June 11, they were reprising a pattern that had worked with two other 5-year-old males.

Sopran Fair
Own: Lamarca Stables
$32,500
ESPINOZA J L (173 26 24 24 .15) 1998:(691 58 .08)

B. h. 5
Sire: Carson City (Mr. Prospector) $35,000
Dam: Fair to All (Al Nasr*Fr)
Br: Azienda Agricola San Uberto in Cerrecchia SRL (Ky)
Tr: Klesaris Robert P(49 8 8 3 .16) 98:(335 70 .21)

L 115

Life	14	5	1	2	$50,813	D.Fst	7	3	1	1	$34,493	91
1999	1	1	0	0	$14,400	Wet	0	0	0	0	$0	–
1998	8	2	1	1	$17,497	Turf	7	2	0	1	$16,320	58
Aqu ⊡	2	1	1	0	$17,900	Dist	2	1	1	0	$17,900	91

22Jan99-9Aqu fst 170 ⊡ :231 :472 1:12 1:414 4↑ Clm 25/20000 **91** 7 1 1½ 1½ 13 11¼ Douglas R R L 115 6.80 89–14 Sopran Fair1151¼ Remember Cass119½ QuietCall1101 Pace, clear, held on 9
2Dec98-9Aqu fst 1 1/16 ⊡ :234 :481 1:13 1:454 3↑ Clm c-18/16000 **84** 4 1 11 11 12 2hd Diaz V5 L 110 5.90 76–28 StrongGy117hd *SoprnFr*1103½ KdFromThBrnx1172 Rated,dueled,outfinish 11
Claimed from Palm Harbor Stable for $17,000, Odintz Jeff Trainer
19Nov98-5Aqu fm 1⅛ Ⓣ :491 1:14 1:393 1:51 3↑ Clm 35/30000 **58** 4 1 1½ 1hd 126¼ 1213½ Teator P A L 117 11.00 76–16 *Demi's Bret*117½ The Quibbler1172½ Play After Dark117nk Set pace, tired 12
14Nov98-9Aqu fst 1 :23 :46 1:11 1:37 3↑ Clm c-12500 **90** 3 1 11½ 12½ 12½ 12¼ Teator P A L 117 2.95 84–16 SoprnFr1172¼ FortrssStrong11713 EdgcmbFlyr1193¾ Quickly clear,driving 9
Claimed from Ciampoli L for $12,500, Mott William I Trainer
29Oct98-9Aqu fst 6f :222 :461 :583 1:12 3↑ Clm 12500 **72** 8 2 2hd 22½ 44 75 Teator P A L 116 6.30 74–21 *Handel*111nk Tres1161½ Winwithwalker116nk Vied between, weakened 11
27Sep98-6Bel fst 1 :23 :462 1:11 1:354 3↑ Alw 45000N3X **52** 3 2 22½ 55 613 627 Teator P A 117 19.40 58–15 DeputyDiamond1129 **Felrof**1176 BckRingAl1174½ Chased inside, stopped 6
Previously trained by Luigi Camici
10Jun98♦ Capannelle(Ity) gd *1 ⓉRH 1:392 4↑ Premio Pelder Hcp 10900 11½ Mezzatesta V 135 9.90 Sopran Fair1351½ Guerrino1142½ Kovalsky136¾ 7 *Tracked leader,led 150y out,driving*
10Mar98♦ Capannelle(Ity) gd *7½f ⓉRH 1:304 4↑ Premio Sedan Hcp 12500 102½ Mezzatesta V 129 6.00 Chiara Gioffry118hd Pach Royal116¾ Miss Slip122hd 13 *Led to 1-1/2f out,met challeneges,weakened late*
24Feb98♦ Naples(Ity) sf *1¼ ⓉRH 2:114 4↑ Premio Sperlonga Alw 12700 37½ Mezzatesta V 121 3.90 Roma Caveau1213¾ Ui Togn1283¾ Sopran Fair1211½ 5 *Led to 1f out,weakened*
Previously trained by D Ferrero
21Dec97♦ Varese(Ity) fst *7½f LH Premio Madesimo (dirt) Alw 12900 34 Botti M 128 *.30 Via Oriani1241 Golden Refrein1283 Sopran Fair1283 5 *Tracked in 3rd,no rally.Time not taken*
16Nov97♦ Varese(Ity) fst *7½f LH Premio Castellanza (dirt) Alw 13200 15 Botti M 128 4.90 Sopran Fair1285 Classic Commanche1281½ Bac1285 7 *Led after 1f,drew clear 2f out.Time not taken*
20Apr97♦ San Siro(Ity) gd *5f ⓉStr :573 Premio Solaro Alw 26600 712¼ Dettori S 121 22.00 Hambye1221¼ Evensong1211¾ Thunderblack1183¼ 7 *Always outrun*

WORKS: Jan13 **Bel tr.t 5f fst 1:024 H** *2/19* Dec22 **Bel tr.t 3f fst :382 B** *14/17* Nov8 **Bel 4f fst :482 B** *5/16*

Sopran Fair was a $17,000 claim for La Marca Stable and Klesaris on December 2, 1998. After a few weeks' freshening, he had wired $25,000 stock at almost 7-1 to begin his 1999 season.

Durmiente (Chi)
Own: La Marca Stable
BAILEY J D (11 4 2 1 .36) 1999:(931 233 .25)

Ch. g. 5
Sire: The Great Shark (Storm Bird)
Dam: Doride*Chi (Balcones)
Br: Haras Porta Pia (Chi)
Tr: Klesaris Robert P(7 0 1 2 .00) 99:(234 39 .17)

L 112

Life	49	7	12	9	$156,451	D.Fst	34	5	10	6	$120,334	107
1999	10	4	1	1	$111,920	Wet	4	1	1	0	$28,900	97
1998	22	1	7	4	$26,544	Turf	11	1	1	3	$7,217	45
Aqu	0	0	0	0	$0	Dist	4	2	0	1	$42,700	97

14Oct99-8Bel fst 1 1/16 :231 :461 1:101 1:411 3↑ Alw 48000N3X **107** 5 2 2½ 1½ 17 18¼ Velazquez J R L 117 3.60 91–23 Durmint1178¼ **BstOfLuck**1146¼ **CrryMyColors**1131¾ When ready, ridden out 5
7Aug99-8Cby gd 1⅛ :463 1:111 1:381 1:503 3↑ Ⓡ Jewel150k **87** 9 8 52¼ 43 43 58½ Martinez W LB 120 2.20 87–07 OnBrckShy1205¾ HnstVntr1241¼ *CptnRpprtn*1201½ Between foes,flattened 14
2Jly99-9Mth fst 1 1/16 :234 :471 1:112 1:432 3↑ Alw 35000N3X **100** 3 3 2½ 21 2hd 2nk Castillo H Jr L 122 *1.00 84–36 *Key Lory*118nk Durmiente1228½ Gallapiat's Aussie1206 Gamely 5
5Jun99-3Bel fst 1½ :48 1:132 2:034 2:303 4↑ Hcp 50000s **98** 1 2 1hd 21½ 21½ 11¼ Bailey J D L 116 3.45 91–06 Durmint1161¼ GoldStrDputy1224¼ *Dustin'sDrm*1134¼ Speed,rail,came again 9
20May99-5Bel gd 1⅛ :454 1:10 1:35 1:473 4↑ Clm 45000 (50-40) **97** 2 2 2hd 2hd 12 12¾ Bailey J D L 115 8.80 93–22 *Durmiente*1152¾ Buddh'sDelight1174½ Gurnteed1171¼ Pressed pace, driving 6
17Apr99-3Kee fst 1⅛ :473 1:121 1:382 1:511 4↑ Clm c-25000 **85** 2 1 1hd 11 12½ 11½ Day P L 115 2.60 79–20 *Durmiente*1151½ *Wavering Warrior*1154½ Likeable Irish1151¼ Inside, driving 5
Claimed from Greene William S Farris Don & Glove for $25,000, Kohnhorst Richard B Trainer
3Apr99-9Kee yl 1½ Ⓣ :493 1:151 2:053 2:292 4↑ Alw 60000N3X **45** 8 1 2hd 109½ 1021 1028½ Campbell J5 L 109 59.50 65–09 Foreign Land114¾ Magest114hd *Keats And Yeats*1141 Pace, stopped 10
6Mar99-8OP fst 1 1/16 :224 :462 1:114 1:441 4↑ Alw 27000N2X **82** 8 4 55½ 44½ 47½ 48¼ Johnson J M L 116 10.60 75–18 Chief Three Sox1164 Dixie Road1222½ Da Devil1161¾ Evenly 10
24Feb99-7OP fst 1⅛ :472 1:121 1:382 1:511 4↑ Alw 35000N2Y **93** 7 2 2½ 2hd 2hd 3½ Lopez J L 114 19.60 80–28 Charley Gunn114½ RodAndStaff114hd Durmiente1142 Dueled, stubbornly 7
7Feb99-5OP fst 1 :222 :453 1:11 1:374 4↑ Alw 30000N3X **73** 8 6 811 75½ 55 47¾ Lopez J L 116 2.30 82–09 Rhonesquarterswish1161¾ Tlihin1165¼ DixieDoodle116¾ 4-wide both turns 8
10Nov98-9CD sly 1 1/16 :242 :481 1:134 1:47 3↑ Clm 25000 (25-20) **90** 3 8 79 42¾ 3nk 21 Romero R P L 117 26.70 75–25 Adax1171 Durmiente117no *Timolaus*11713 5wide bid, hung 10
Previously trained by Miguel Medina
3Oct98♦ Hipodromo(Chi) fst *1 3/16 LH 1:57 3↑ Criterium Mayores Hcp 48000 32↓ Rivera L 117 4.40 Mancuso130hd Minotauro de Creta1172 DH Chopito108 8 *Finished in DH for 3rd.A Galope Tendido (130) 6th*

WORKS: ●Nov6 **Bel tr.t 5f fst 1:003 H** *1/13* Oct7 **Bel tr.t 1 fst 1:413 H** *1/1* Sep9 **Bel tr.t 5f fst 1:021 B** *2/7*

Claimed for $25,000 by La Marca and Klesaris out of a win at Keeneland on April 17, Durmiente returned just over a month later to score for nearly twice his purchase price at 8-1. He then won a starter handicap at Belmont, and in the fall, off a freshening, he won a three-other-than allowance with a Beyer of 107.

Madok was offered at nearly 6-1 in a five-horse field, and like his predecessors, he won on the rise.

ONE OF the oldest angles in the books involves an entry in which one horse is "stepping" while the other is "prepping" for a future engagement, and basically kept out of his mate's way.

Jimmy Jerkens, the son of Hall of Fame trainer Allen Jerkens, employed this angle twice at Aqueduct's 2000 winter meet.

Funlovin	Dk. b or br f. 3 (Mar) SARPRE98 $25,000		Life	2 1 0 0	$24,600	D.Fst	2 1 0 0	$24,600	56
Own: John Confort & Albert Weis	Sire: Husband (Diesis*GB) $2,500		2000	2 1 0 0	$24,600	Wet	0 0 0 0	$0	–
	Dam: Somersetroad (Bold Navy)		1999	0 M 0 0	$0	Turf	0 0 0 0	$0	–
MONTALVO C (98 15 13 16 .15) 1999:(227 24 .11)	Br: John A Nerud Revocable Trust (NY)	116⁵							
	Tr: Jerkens James A(45 13 6 9 .29) 1999:(137 30 .22)		Aqu⬤	2 1 0 0	$24,600	Dist	2 1 0 0	$24,600	56

14Jan00–5Aqu fst 6f ⬤:23³ :48³ 1:02 1:15⁴ ⓈMd Sp Wt 41k   56 7 6 3½   1½   1³ 1² Rocco J S⁵   115 b   7.40 63–30 Funlovin115² PachiPachi120²½ SweetMtrirch120ⁿᵏ Speed outside, driving 10
6Jan00–2Aqu fst 6f ⬤:23 :46³ :59³ 1:12⁴ ⓈMd Sp Wt 41k   28 9 10 10³½ 107½ 9¹⁰ 7¹²½ Bridgmohan S X   120   3.45e 66–16 Key Oui120¹ Allison's Purse113⁴ Glorious Gift120½   Steadied turn 11
WORKS: Dec31 Bel tr.t 4f fst :50 B 53/99 Dec8 Bel tr.t 5f fst 1:04⁴ B 12/12 Nov30 Bel tr.t 4f fst :50² B 48/79

Funlovin, part of a 3-1 entry, steadied on the turn and was never close at any stage of her debut on January 6. A check of the chart showed that Funlovin "raced greenly while wide," and that her entrymate, Key Oui, had won the race.

Uncoupled second time out with blinkers added by Jerkens, Funlovin showed much more early speed to win by open lengths at 7-1.

Open Sesame	Ch. g. 3 (Apr) FTCFEB99 $125,000		Life	2 1 0 0	$24,600	D.Fst	2 1 0 0	$24,600	76
Own: Moore John & Susan	Sire: Phone Trick (Clever Trick) $30,000		2000	2 1 0 0	$24,600	Wet	0 0 0 0	$0	–
	Dam: Dancing Mahmoud (Topsider)		1999	0 M 0 0	$0	Turf	0 0 0 0	$0	–
SAMYN J L (—) 2000:(79 6 .08)	Br: Woodlynn Farm Inc (Ky)	121							
	Tr: Jerkens James A(4 2 1 1 .50) 2000:(56 20 .36)		Aqu	0 0 0 0	$0	Dist	0 0 0 0	$0	–

4Mar00–5Aqu fst 6f ⬤:23 :46¹ :58² 1:11   Md Sp Wt 41k   76 2 5 1ʰᵈ 1ʰᵈ 1½ 1³½ Castillo H Jr   120 14.00 87–15 OpenSesme120³½ PointOfAmric120⁵½ KnockAgin120¹½ Vied inside, driving 9
26Jan00–3Aqu fst 6f ⬤:24 :47³ :59³ 1:11⁴ Md Sp Wt 41k   19 8 2 7²½ 9¹¹ 9²⁰ 8²²½ Lopez C C   120   .55e 60–16 Iron Chancellor120⁷½ Juro120ⁿᵏ King Of War120⁴½ Greenly outside, tired 10
WORKS: Mar16 Bel tr.t 4f fst :48² B 15/52 Mar1 Bel tr.t 4f fst :50 B 22/46 Feb24 Bel tr.t 4f fst :50 B 36/54 Feb10 Bel tr.t 4f fst :48³ B 3/40 Jan20 Bel tr.t 4f fst :47³ H 2/73 Jan9 Bel tr.t 5f fst 1:01¹ B 9/33

Less than two weeks later, Jerkens sent out another entry in a maiden sprint. Iron Chancellor had just run a big race to finish second, and his obvious merits led to miserly 1-2 odds. He won easily by more than seven lengths, while his entrymate, Open Sesame, raced "greenly outside."

When Open Sesame came back uncoupled for his second start, I was waiting. Like Funlovin, he showed much more early speed, and drew off in deep stretch at a $30 number. The trainer pattern is clear.

I FOLLOW any trainer named Jerkens closely, and it's been apparent since Jimmy Jerkens went out on his own in the fall of 1997 that the apple didn't fall far from the tree. In 1998, his first full year, he went 35 for 185 (19 percent). In 1999 he improved to 22 percent wins with a 30-for-137 record. He finished out 2000 with a record of 59 for 211, winning at a 28 percent clip. Since a 33 percent success rate is regarded as the universal average of favorites, it behooves bettors to follow a guy who wins nearly as often, especially when he improves horses and wins with them at good prices.

Lager was claimed for $45,000 out of a win at Monmouth in late summer of 1998, but first time out for his new barn a month later he pulled up on the far turn, and didn't make it back to the races until the next Memorial Day Weekend, when he missed by a nose in an allowance route at Philadelphia Park. That taxing effort right off the bench seemed to knock him for a loop again, though, because he was off the board in his next three starts, and needed a drop to $25,000 claimers on October 1 to win for the first time in 13 months.

Lager disappeared again, but when he returned on Aqueduct's inner dirt five months later for new trainer Jimmy Jerkens, he seemed like a brand-new horse. Despite the long period of inactivity, Lager overcame the extreme outside post with a quick four-wide move in the two-turn route, and beat $35,000 claimers at 7-1. Two starts later, he won a classified allowance, and then Jerkens spotted him very aggressively in the Grade 3 Excelsior Handicap. Lager put up a furious finish to win by a nose at 29-1. Coming out on the short end of the photo was Best Of Luck, trained by Allen Jerkens.

A week after Lager's huge upset in the Excelsior, the younger Jerkens again demonstrated his prowess at improving new acquisitions first time back from a layoff, when the Cynthia Knight-owned Tippity Witch overcame a tough trip to win her N2X allowance by a neck at $21, earning a new top Beyer Speed Figure in the process.

Six days after Tippity Witch's score, Jerkens won with another freshened runner for Cynthia Knight. Crown Thy Good retained his propensity for slow starts, but rallied four wide to win a maiden race by six lengths at $12.60.

```
6 Crown Thy Good                                B. c. 4                                                        Life  9 1 1 1  $23,645 D.Fst  2 1 0 1  $15,530 68
Own: Cynthia Knight                             Sire: Chief's Crown (Danzig) $15,000                           2000  2 1 0 1  $15,530 Wet    0 0 0 0      $0  -
SANTAGATA N (14 0 1 3 .00) 2000:(454 68 .15)    Dam: Senora Tippy (El Gran Senor)                     L 120    1999  5 M 0 0     $315 Turf   7 0 1 0   $8,115 82
                                                Br: Knight Landon (Ky)                                         Mth(T) 0 0 0 0     $0 Dis(T) 5 0 1 0   $7,975 82
                                                Tr: Jerkens James A (—) 2000:(101 35 .35)
12May00-4Bel fst 1 :22⁴ :46 1:11³ 1:38² 3↑ Md 40000 (50-40)   68 9 87¾ 42 12½ 16¼ Castillo H Jr   L 119 b  5.30 73-24 Crown Thy Good1196¼ Just Tsu It116¾ Al Dor Rob119nk  Off slowly, 4 wide 9
Previously trained by Badgett William Jr
18Feb00-3GP fst 1 1/16 [illegible] 4 Md 25000 (25-22.5)   62 10 8 711 54 35½ 34 Migliore R   L 122 bn 5.10 75-22 TroblInLov120½ LgndryPnny1203½ CrownThyGd1223½  Slow st, best others 10
24Dec99-11Crc fm 1 1/16 (T) :23¹ :47⁴ 1:12¹ 1:43² 3↑ Md Sp Wt 17k   56 1 10 913 910 85½ 68¾ Chavez J F   L 120 b 11.10 71-13 Taking Sides1201¼ Spooning1203½ Exciteful120½  Hesitated start 10
24Oct99-10Bel sf 1 1/16 (T) :24³ :49¹ 1:14³ 1:46¹ 3↑ Md Sp Wt 42k   57 2 6 63¼ 75½ 714 715 Decarlo C P   L 117 b 28.75 46-41 Krato1174¼ Heavenly Show1176¾ E's Other Paddock1122¼  No response 10
3Oct99-1Bel fm 1 1/16 (T) :23 :47⁴ 1:11³ 1:41⁴ 3↑ Md Sp Wt 42k   66 2 10 96½ 108¾ 99¾ 88½ Decarlo C P   L 117 28.75 74-16 Sndngrvel1213¾ ReglDynsty1172 HevenOnSeven121¾  Came wide, no rally 10
24Jly99-5Bel fm 1 (T) :22⁴ :45³ 1:10 1:34³ 3↑ Md Sp Wt 41k   36 4 12 1220 1218 1120 1124½ Bailey J D   L 115 5.40 60-21 CretionSong1153 Rockin'Ruby121½ Sndngrvl1214¼  Knocked off stride st. 12
4Apr99-11Hia fm 1⅛ (T) 1:47⁴ Md Sp Wt 14k   51 5 11 813 77¾ 6†15 617 Turner T G   L 122 *1.90 74-08 TemptationBound1226 Untuttble122nk Stokosky1229¼  Bumped hard early 11
13Nov98-4Aqu gd 1 1/16 (T) :22³ :47² 1:12³ 1:43²   Md Sp Wt 39k   82 1 7 97¾ 84 56¾ 27 Decarlo C P   L 118 54.75 84-11 Swmp1187 CrownThyGood118hd WinningConnction118½  4w move, rallied 10
12Oct98-7Bel yl 1 1/16 (T) :24² :49 1:13⁴ 1:47³   Md Sp Wt 39k   38 2 12 96½ 1214 1119 916 Migliore R   L 118 10.10 38-38 Procopius1182½ Devil's Egg118nk Meteoric Rise118nk  Greenly between foes 12
WORKS: May27 Bel 6f fst 1:15 B 1/3  May9 Bel tr.t 4f fst :48³ B 6/29  Apr19 Bel 4f sly :50 B (d)2/3  Apr11 Bel tr.t 4f fst :50³ B 25/42  Mar31 Bel tr.t 4f fst :49¹ B 26/36
```

If trainer-pattern players believe good things come in threes, they should've been all over Dat You Miz Blue at 5-2 when she won by a pole June 7, also with a best-ever Beyer. I hope Ms. Knight gave her new trainer a bonus.

```
Dat You Miz Blue                                B. f. 3 (Feb)                                                  Life  7 4 2 0 $173,540 D.Fst  6 3 2 0 $145,340 90
Own: Knight Cynthia                             Sire: Cure the Blues (Stop the Music) $15,000                  2000  1 1 0 0  $28,200 Wet    1 1 0 0  $28,200 93
                                                Dam: Emma Loves Marie (Wild Again)                     113     1999  6 3 2 0 $145,340 Turf   0 0 0 0      $0  -
SMITH M E (124 18 13 23 .15) 2000:(611 99 .16)  Br: Landon Knight Stable (NY)                                  Bel   4 2 1 0  $81,140 Dist   3 2 1 0  $96,600 93
                                                Tr: Jerkens James A(32 7 5 3 .22) 2000:(122 39 .32)
7Jun00-8Bel gd 6f :21⁴ :44⁴ :57 1:09³ 3↑ (F)Alw 47000N3X   93 2 4 45 3nk 12½ 15¾ Smith M E   114 2.65 90-11 DatYouMizBlue1145¾ Wallen119nk FickleFnny1181¼  Wide move, ridden out 6
Previously trained by Badgett William Jr
14Nov99-6Aqu fst 6f :22² :46 :58¹ 1:11   (F)(R)N Y Stallion100k   83 1 4 2½ 12½ 110 113 Bailey J D   122 *.10 83-17 DtYouMizBlu12213 Impchbl114¾ CstingCnm1175½  When ready, ridden out 5
23Oct99-6Bel fst 1 :23⁴ :47³ 1:12¹ 1:37²   (F)(S)MaidOfThMist100k   78 3 1 11½ 1hd 21½ 23 Bailey J D   121 *.85 74-22 MddieMy1143 DtYouMizBlue1213¼ WintrDrms11410  Set pace,second best 7
6Oct99-8Bel fst 7f :23 :46³ 1:11³ 1:25¹   (F)(S)JosephAGimma54k   79 5 8 31½ 2hd 17 110¼ Bailey J D   114 *.40 76-20 DtYouMzBlu11410 CstngCnm114½ Bd'sFmm1191¼  Awkward start,drew off 8
19Sep99-5Bel fst 1 :22² :45 1:10 1:36³   (F)Matron-G1   60 3 5 61½ 61½ 67¼ 618¼ Prado E S   119 8.40 63-22 Findr'sF119¾ DrlingMyDrling1191¼ CirclOfLif1195¼  Stout restraint,4 wide 7
20Aug99-4Sar fst 6f :22² :46¹ :58 1:10²   (F)Alw 42000N1X   87 5 2 3½ 2hd 2½ 21½ Bailey J D   117 3.25 87-11 Surfside1171½ DatYouMizBlue1176¾ Marigalnte1172  Tried winner 1/4 pole 8
29Jly99-6Sar fst 5f :22³ :45³ :57³   (F)(S)Md Sp Wt 40k   90 6 5 11½ 12 110 114¼ Bailey J D   116 *.60 101-07 DtYouMizBlue11614 Rpunzell1162¼ WintrDrms1164¼  Drew away, ridden out 7
WORKS: Jun24 Bel 5f fst 1:00² B 7/36  Jun17 Bel tr.t 3f fst :37¹ B 8/24  ●Jun5 Bel tr.t 3f fst :35 H 1/19  Jun1 Bel 6f fst 1:15¹ B 2/3  May25 Bel tr.t 5f fst 1:01³ B 16/33  May17 Bel tr.t 5f fst 1:02 B 4/7
```

Studying trainers' methods can be a big key to unlocking the mysteries of maiden races, because in many instances there isn't much established form to evaluate. But you don't need years of experience with local trainers to play maiden races effectively, as long as you know what to look for.

One of your first preparatory steps in the handicapping process should be to consult the Beyer Pars, which are frequently published on *Daily Racing Form*'s "Track Facts" pages.

BEYER PARS

AT AQUEDUCT

Average winning Beyer Speed Figures by respective class levels:

OPEN CLAIMING	MALE	FEMALE
10,000-14,000	85	73
15,000-20,000	88	78
21,000-34,000	92	82
35,000-49,000	94	84
50,000-75,000	97	87

MAIDEN ALLOWANCE	MALE	FEMALE
Maiden Special	85	74
Allowance NW1x	92	80
Allowance NW2x	95	86
Allowance NW3x	100	92

In maiden races, the more horses that have already matched or exceeded par for the class, the tougher a spot it will be for a first-time starter. When none of the experienced runners has run to par, a first-timer from a good barn that's been live recently makes for one of the best betting opportunities in the game:

Pine Forest
Own: Spiegel Robert

Dk. b or br f. 3 (May)
Sire: Pine Bluff (Danzig) $25,000
Dam: Forest Majesty (His Majesty)
Br: Robert Spiegel (Ky)
Tr: Donk David(5 0 1 2 .00) 2000:(30 3 .10)

L 115

	Life	5 M 0 0	$4,920	D.Fst	4 0 0 0	$4,920	71
	2000	1 M 0 0	$2,460	Wet	1 0 0 0	$0	32
	1999	4 M 0 0	$2,460	Turf	0 0 0 0	$0	–
	Aqu	2 0 0 0	$2,460	Dist	1 0 0 0	$2,460	66

BRIDGMOHAN S X (129 16 11 25 .12) 2000:(398 49 .12)

13Apr00–6Aqu fst 6f :21³ :44² :56⁴ 1:10 3↑ⒻMd Sp Wt 41k 71 5 2 43½ 3³ 45 46½ Bridgmohan S X L 114 15.20 81–16 Field Of Dreams114no Atelier114⁴½ Guess What114¹½ Wide trip, no rally 7
10Nov99–3Aqu fst 6f :22² :46 :58² 1:11 ⒻMd Sp Wt 41k 34 1 5 1½ 42½ 51⁰ 62⁰ Bailey J D L 118 b 3.85 63–20 Away118¹¹ Totally Private118no Ostara118³½ Vied inside, tired 6
20Oct99–6Bel sly 1¹⁄₁₆ ⊗:22³ :46¹ 1:12 1:47 ⒻMd Sp Wt 42k 32 4 1 1hd 3¹ 49 61⁶½ Prado E S L 118 b 4.30 45–29 PenutGllery118¹½ WeddingWknd118³ FormlRcption118⁹½ Tired after 3/4s 11
26Sep99–6Bel fst 7f :22⁴ :46¹ 1:10⁴ 1:23³ ⒻMd Sp Wt 41k 66 6 3 2½ 3¹ 3⁶ 41⁰½ Velazquez J R L 118 6.50 74–15 MtlchPss117⁸½ WddngWknd118¹½ Rchll'sTrms118½ Chased 3 wide, no rally 9
29Aug99–4Sar fst 5½f :22¹ :46 :58³ 1:05³ ⒻMd Sp Wt 40k 48 5 7 7⁷ 77¾ 76½ 66¾ Velazquez J R 117 6.60 84–08 Lucky Livi117½ Mike's Way117²¼ All Spades117no Bumped st, alter course 9
WORKS: Apr2 Bel tr.t 6f fst 1:13¹ B 2/4 ●Mar25 Bel tr.t 5f fst 1:00² H 1/34 Mar16 Bel tr.t 5f fst 1:01³ B 13/37 Mar9 Bel tr.t 5f fst 1:01¹ B 3/17 Mar1 Bel tr.t 5f fst 1:02³ B 14/26 Feb23 Bel tr.t 4f fst :47⁴ H 2/49

Validcrown
Own: Liang Thomas

B. f. 3 (Apr)
Sire: Crown Pleasure (Foolish Pleasure)
Dam: Valid Funding (Valid Appeal)
Br: The Oaks Horse Farm Corp (Fla)
Tr: Skiffington Thomas J (—) 2000:(10 1 .10)

Ⓛ 115

	Life	1 M 0 0	$190	D.Fst	1 0 0 0	$190	23
	2000	1 M 0 0	$190	Wet	0 0 0 0	$0	–
	1999	0 M 0 0	$0	Turf	0 0 0 0	$0	–
	Aqu	0 0 0 0	$0	Dist	0 0 0 0	$0	–

LUZZI M J (121 12 26 12 .10) 2000:(382 43 .11)

17Feb00–1GP fst 6f :22³ :46 :58⁴ 1:12 ⒻMd 50000 (50–45) 23 8 2 2¹ 22½ 56½ 71³ Santos J A 121 4.40 66–17 FoxyRchl121¹³ RdRivrShowdown121⁴½ Znny'sDncr121hd Early foot, faded 8
WORKS: Apr25 Bel tr.t 4f fst :51¹ B 49/65 Apr13 Hia ⊕ 6f sf 1:15 B (d)2/3 Apr6 Hia ⊕ 5f fm 1:05 B (d)7/7 Mar23 Hia ⊕ 5f fm 1:03² B (d)6/11 Mar16 Hia ⊕ 4f fm :52² B (d)3/4 Mar7 Hia 4f fst :52 B 15/16

Lucky Dynamo
Own: Robinson J Mack
ROSARIO H L JR (124 19 11 15 .15) 2000:(134 19 .14)

Dk. b or br f. 3 (May)
Sire: Broad Brush (Ack Ack) $100,000
Dam: Beau Prospector (Mr. Prospector)
Br: J Mack Robinson (Ky)
Tr: Alexander Frank A(3 0 1 1 .00) 2000:(39 5 .13)

Ⓛ 108^7

Life	1	M	0	0	$300	D.Fst	1	0	0	0	$300	10
2000	1	M	0	0	$300	Wet	0	0	0	0	$0	–
1999	0	M	0	0	$0	Turf	0	0	0	0	$0	–
Aqu	0	0	0	0	$0	Dist	0	0	0	0	$0	–

6Feb00–7GP fst 6f :22^4 :46 :58^1 1:11^1 ⒻMd Sp Wt 30k **10** 7 7 9^{10} 9^{11} 8^{15} 7$^{26\frac{3}{4}}$ Smith M E 121 fb 9.30 56–15 *Laurica*121$^{4\frac{3}{4}}$ Our Recall121$^{4\frac{1}{4}}$ Rural Queen121$^{2\frac{3}{4}}$ Swerved, steadied str 9
WORKS: Apr25 Bel 5f fst 1:02^4 B *31/33* Apr15 Bel 5f fst 1:01^3 H *5/23* Apr7 Bel 4f fst :50 Bg*21/23* Mar30 GP 5f fst 1:01^2 B *3/10* Mar24 GP 4f fst :48 H *4/20* Mar18 GP 5f fst 1:01^4 H *5/12*

Kris Pit
Own: Celtic Pride Stable
PRADO E S (80 20 14 12 .25) 2000:(554 85 .15)

Ch. f. 3 (Mar) KEESEP98 $370,000
Sire: Kris S. (Roberto) $75,000
Dam: K. C. Super Pet (Gulch)
Br: Jaime S Carrion Trustee (Ky)
Tr: McGaughey Claude III(19 6 3 2 .32) 2000:(71 15 .21)

115

Life	0	M	0	0	$0	D.Fst	0	0	0	0	$0	–
2000	0	M	0	0	$0	Wet	0	0	0	0	$0	–
1999	0	M	0	0	$0	Turf	0	0	0	0	$0	–
Aqu	0	0	0	0	$0	Dist	0	0	0	0	$0	–

WORKS: Apr25 Bel 4f fst :48^2 H *12/70* ●Apr17 Bel 4f gd :49 Bg(d)*1/5* Apr13 Bel 3f fst :37^1 B *10/14* Apr8 Bel 4f fst :49^2 B *19/39* Apr2 Bel 3f fst :36^3 B *5/11* Mar22 GP 4f fst :52 B *37/39* Mar13 GP 4f fst :50^2 Bg*29/38* Mar9 Pay 4f fst :51^3 B *3/8* Mar4 Pay 4f fst :50^2 Bg*3/19* Feb28 Pay 4f fst :51 B *9/32* Feb21 Pay 4f fst :50^2 Bg*2/33* Feb14 Pay 4f fst :50^4 B *2/20*

Smiling Virginian
Own: Siegel Jan & Mace & Samantha
VELAZQUEZ J R (80 15 17 16 .19) 2000:(425 71 .17)

Ch. f. 3 (Jan) FTKJUL98 $50,000
Sire: Virginia Rapids (Riverman) $5,000
Dam: Mia Smiling (Smile)
Br: Frances A H Leidy (Md)
Tr: Dutrow Richard E Jr(36 11 7 10 .31) 2000:(98 24 .24)

115

Life	0	M	0	0	$0	D.Fst	0	0	0	0	$0	–
2000	0	M	0	0	$0	Wet	0	0	0	0	$0	–
1999	0	M	0	0	$0	Turf	0	0	0	0	$0	–
Aqu	0	0	0	0	$0	Dist	0	0	0	0	$0	–

WORKS: Apr26 Aqu 5f fst 1:01 H *2/5* ●Apr20 Aqu 5f fst 1:00^4 Hg*1/15* ●Mar30 Aqu 5f fst 1:00^1 B *1/9* Mar24 Aqu 5f fst 1:03 B *2/6* Mar16 SA 4f fst :48^2 H *7/32* Mar3 SA 6f fst 1:15^1 H *16/37* Feb26 SA 5f gd 1:01^1 H *46/169* Feb18 SA 4f gd :48^4 H *16/57* Feb13 SA 4f my :53 H (d)*34/42* Feb7 SA 4f fst :48 H *9/32*

Lela
Own: Humphrey G W Jr
SAMYN J L (33 3 6 4 .09) 2000:(114 10 .09)

Dk. b or br f. 3 (Jan) OBSAUG98 $62,000
Sire: Williamstown (Seattle Slew) $7,500
Dam: My Gidget (Liloy*Fr)
Br: Bradyleigh Farms Inc (Ky)
Tr: Arnold George R II(17 1 2 3 .06) 2000:(113 18 .16)

115

Life	1	M	0	0	$102	D.Fst	0	0	0	0	$0	–
2000	1	M	0	0	$102	Wet	1	0	0	0	$102	47
1999	0	M	0	0	$0	Turf	0	0	0	0	$0	–
Aqu	0	0	0	0	$0	Dist	0	0	0	0	$0	–

Entered 27Apr00– 5 AQU
16Mar00–6TP sly 1 :22^3 :46^2 1:12^1 1:39^3 ⒻMd Sp Wt 27k **47** 6 5 4$^{5\frac{1}{2}}$ 5^6 6$^{7\frac{1}{2}}$ 6$^{7\frac{1}{4}}$ Martinez W L 121 3.70 67–26 MoreThnHlf121^2 TurningPoint121^2 FreAndFoolish121^2 3 wide 2nd turn 10
WORKS: Apr20 Bel tr.t 4f fst :50^1 B *40/79* Apr14 Bel 4f fst :48^4 B *7/26* Mar29 CD 5f fst 1:01 B *7/17* Mar6 FG 5f fst 1:01^3 B *11/27* Feb27 FG 4f gd :48^1 B *2/36* Feb19 FG 5f fst 1:02 B *5/34*

Cherokee Canyon
Own: Aces Wild Stable & Kathy Jo Stable
CASTILLO H JR (75 13 11 9 .17) 2000:(239 39 .16)

B. f. 3 (May) OBSFEB99 $250,000
Sire: Cherokee Run (Runaway Groom) $20,000
Dam: Statue (Exclusive Native)
Br: Joe Mulholland (Ky)
Tr: Kimmel John C(23 5 4 5 .22) 2000:(138 28 .20)

L 115

Life	3	M	1	1	$10,675	D.Fst	3	0	1	1	$10,675	53
2000	2	M	1	1	$10,675	Wet	0	0	0	0	$0	–
1999	1	M	0	0	$0	Turf	0	0	0	0	$0	–
Aqu	1	0	1	0	$8,200	Dist	1	0	1	0	$8,200	53

25Mar00–5Aqu fst 7f :22^4 :46 1:11^4 1:25^4 ⒻMd Sp Wt 41k **53** 2 7 1$^{\frac{1}{2}}$ 1^{hd} 1^{hd} 2$^{2\frac{1}{4}}$ Migliore R L 119 b 5.70 69–19 Cat Cay119$^{2\frac{1}{4}}$ Cherokee Canyon119$^{3\frac{1}{4}}$ Seattle Joke119^{nk} Set pace, gamely 9
1Mar00–5Aqu fst 6f ⊡ :23 :46^2 :58^4 1:11^3 ⒻMd 50000(50-40) **45** 3 10 6$^{3\frac{1}{4}}$ 3^1 3$^{4\frac{1}{2}}$ 3^9 Castillo H Jr L 120 b *2.75 75–16 OtOfThBggy120$^{5\frac{1}{2}}$ DsrtD'or120$^{3\frac{1}{2}}$ ChrokCnyon120$^{\frac{3}{4}}$ Taken up start, 4 wide 10
30Jly99–4Sar fst 5½f :21^4 :45^4 :58^4 1:05^2 ⒻMd Sp Wt 40k **36** 5 8 7$^{2\frac{1}{4}}$ 5$^{3\frac{3}{4}}$ 7$^{4\frac{3}{4}}$ 10$^{13\frac{3}{4}}$ Prado E S L 116 5.40 77–18 TrumpMyHert116$^{2\frac{1}{4}}$ SltCreek111$^{4\frac{3}{4}}$ UnbridledVic116$^{\frac{1}{2}}$ Chased inside, tired 12
WORKS: ●Apr24 Bel tr.t 4f fst :46^2 H *1/9* Apr15 Bel tr.t 5f fst 1:00^3 H *2/21* Apr8 Bel tr.t 5f fst 1:00^3 H *4/28* Mar21 Bel tr.t 4f fst :49^1 B *9/23* Mar15 Bel tr.t 5f fst 1:01^3 H *6/17* Feb24 Bel tr.t 5f fst 1:02^2 B *12/23*

Syrah
Own: Schwartz Jonathan D
GRYDER A T (162 32 18 23 .20) 2000:(436 93 .21)

Dk. b or br f. 3 (May)
Sire: Cox's Ridge (Best Turn)
Dam: French Galaxy (Majestic Light)
Br: Eaglestone Farm Inc (Ky)
Tr: Hushion Michael E(30 11 1 3 .37) 2000:(81 23 .28)

Ⓛ 115

Life	0	M	0	0	$0	D.Fst	0	0	0	0	$0	–
2000	0	M	0	0	$0	Wet	0	0	0	0	$0	–
1999	0	M	0	0	$0	Turf	0	0	0	0	$0	–
Aqu	0	0	0	0	$0	Dist	0	0	0	0	$0	–

WORKS: Apr25 Bel tr.t 5f fst 1:03^4 B *18/22* Apr20 Bel 3f fst :36^4 Hg*4/34* Apr14 Bel 5f fst 1:01^2 H *4/14* Apr2 Bel tr.t 5f fst 1:03^1 B *17/19* ●Mar26 Bel tr.t 4f fst :46^4 H *1/26* Mar15 Bel tr.t 4f fst :49 B *18/46* Mar5 Bel tr.t 4f fst :50 B *18/37*

The average winning figure for females at this level is 74. Pine Forest was the only runner who had even been in the same area code as par, but at 8-5 she was no great bargain, especially since she might have been likely to "bounce" off a career-top figure earned first time back from a five-month layoff.

Second choice at 9-5 was Cherokee Canyon, which was hard to believe. She had already lost for a claiming tag, and came out of a second-place finish in a very slowly run race, in which she earned a figure 21 points below par.

Even allowing for the fact that young horses can improve by leaps and bounds on short notice, this looked like a good opportunity for a first-time starter with any ability whatsoever.

Kris Pit at 4-1 fit the bill. For that matter, so did the other new shooter, Syrah at 7-1.

Kris Pit, though, was a $370,000 yearling purchase by Celtic Pride Stable and she showed a deceptively good half-mile breeze on April 17: Her work from the gate and around the "dogs" (traffic cones placed out from the rail to protect the inside paths) was a full second faster than the next-best time at the distance, serving as a good advertisement for cutting out and saving the work tabs from your *Daily Racing Form*.

Another success story in a long-term pattern, Kris Pit, like the majority of Shug McGaughey's firsters over the years, did not race greenly and was not short on conditioning. She took control of the race with a quick four-wide move nearing midstretch to win going away.

THE BETTING LOG

My, this all sounds so easy, doesn't it? Once good record keeping starts snowballing, you'll have more information at your fingertips about the intricacies of your circuit than 99 percent of the crowd. Heck, after you read this whole book, you'll know as much as anybody alive.

Trouble is, a competitive race might contain half a dozen horses with some positive aspect or another. At other times, everyone looks simply awful. Rare is the race where one horse towers over the field and beckons sweetly at a big price.

You're going to have to make some close calls, take some risks, and develop a sense of when to leave a race alone, which is most of the time.

Your investments are not protected by the Federal Deposit Insurance Corporation. That's why they call it gambling.

It's not within my power to instill in you the magical keys to winning at the races, other than to say you should prepare as thoroughly as possible and strive to wager in a way that reflects your handicapping opinion as much as you can.

I happen to favor win betting (hedged with exacta and trifecta savers using my key horse underneath the likely spoilers) because repeated experience has convinced me that I lack the creative right-brained instincts required of the best exotic bettors.

Successful handicapping is much more than just good record keeping. It is an intuitive art that is difficult, if not impossible, to systematize. The irony is that most of us insist on trying to come up with workable systems to pick winners, but prefer to rely on intuition, impulse, and sometimes sheer idiocy when it comes to determining how much to bet.

That's doing things backward. No simple system will work for long, due to the nature of parimutuel wagering: If something works, people eventually start catching on, and mutuels are driven down to a point where it becomes a losing proposition.

But the fundamental mathematical principles of betting will not ever change. And still the vast majority of horseplayers go about their betting routines in the most haphazard ways, choosing to ignore the realities that are at the heart of turning consistent profits.

It's not within my power to make you a great bettor, but it's a relatively simple matter to show you how much to bet, so that if you have a good opinion you will not tap out before proving it to yourself.

You're going to have to come to grips with reality, though. The reality is that unless you catch lightning in a bottle by hitting a life-changing pick six on a $32 ticket, you can't quit your day job and play the races for a living. Not unless you are ready, willing, and able to bet obscenely large sums of money several times each day.

Let's assume that I'm sharp enough to overcome the parimutuel takeout and that I actually have a 20 percent edge with my best bets. Assuming I play the races 300 days a year and come up with three prime selections a day, I will bet 900 races.

Betting $20 a race, I would invest a total of $18,000, and a 20 percent advantage would produce an expected profit of $3,600, give or take. That won't quite cover three kids, two cars, and a mortgage, so I have to bet more.

If I want to make $36,000 a year at the windows with my 20 percent edge, I have to bet $180,000, or $200 a race.

If I want to make $72,000 (pretax dollars), I have to bet $400 an average of three times a day. That's $1,200 a day, sometimes more. Not including expenses.

How about it? Do you think you could bet $400 a race without it affecting your judgment, your nerves, and your heart rate? Could you swallow the head-bobbing, photo-finish zaps and the close-call disqualifications that are a big part of this game, and go on to the next race functioning as a normal human being?

What are you going to do when you're up to $800 a race, and that inevitable losing streak comes along?

Streaks

It would be nice if 33 percent winners meant that for every 10 bets, you cash somewhere between three and four times.

If only it worked that way!

But it doesn't. Take it from someone whose job is mass-producing winners for the public daily. Sometimes 33 percent winners in a series of 100 races involves a torrid 29-for-46 run followed immediately by an agonizing stretch where you go 4 for 54. Sound far-fetched? It happened to me at Aqueduct in the fall of 1999.

Sometimes you hit eight straight and feel omniscient, but the next day could just as easily bring the onset of a 30-race losing streak.

Streaks have the power to make or break the best gamblers on the planet, and you must prepare for their eventuality. This means that if you plan to win in the long run, even if it's just walking-around money for a few of life's little extras, you have to be careful out there.

Playing the Percentages

In *Thoroughbred Handicapping: State of the Art,* William Quirin ran computer simulations of the most widely known betting strategies, including traditional flat betting; fixed-percentage betting; Jim Quinn's Fixed Percentage—Minimum; James Selvidge's Base Bet Plus Square Root; and Tom Ainslie's Unit Wagering in Ratio to the Odds.

Each system was tested at 30.4 percent winners at an average mutuel of $7.50, and the sample included runs of up to 10 consecutive losing selections. The simulation involved 1,000 re-creations of a full season's worth of play, each time with the selections occurring in different order, and each system was tested at 1 percent, 2 percent, 3 percent, 4 percent, 5 percent, and 10 percent bets of a $1,000 bankroll.

To make a long story short, Quirin's simulations showed there was minimal risk of tapping out at 1 percent, and that tap-outs were quite common at 10 percent. The happy medium seemed to lie somewhere in the range of 4 to 5 percent.

That means if you wager in the $40-to-$50 range for your prime bets, you should have at least $1,000 in betting capital to see you through the hard times. If you've got a 20 percent edge and want to shoot for the $72,000 we talked about, that means you should have upward of $10,000 in reserve.

Whether you fancy win betting, exactas, pick threes, or a smorgasbord of every option on the menu, the first thing you need to do is establish a maximum bet based on your bankroll.

You must have a bankroll! Not half of the tax-refund check that's coming in a few weeks; not the money your brother-in-law owes you; and not the monthly payment for your kid's orthodontist.

It must be discretionary income that will not affect your life should you crash and burn. At the same time, your maximum bet should be sufficiently large enough, relative to your personal situation, to make you think twice about risking it.

For want of a better term, I use the "6-4-2" method:

- A couple of times a month, when I feel a horse has a 50 percent chance of winning and is going off at 2-1 or better, preferably at least 5-2, I will push the envelope and bet 6 percent of my bankroll. These are the heart-pounding ones where my palms are sweating as the field loads into the gate, and I need to take a few of those "relaxing/cleansing breaths" they teach in Lamaze classes.

- Normal prime bets, which occur on average once or twice daily, rate an exposure of 4 percent. These are usually midrange-odds horses anywhere from 3-1 to 6-1 in situations where I feel that there's no question of betting value.

- And since I'm human and like action, I allow myself up to three bets each day at the 2-percent level on angles, intuition (educated hunches), and horses who, should they win without me at boxcar odds of 8-1 or better, would make me feel like kicking my cat. I can only indulge myself in these action bets if I haven't already lost a 6-percent bet, or two 4-percent bets. When that happens, my action-bet privileges for the day are revoked.

I enter each wager in my betting log in much the same way I keep track profiles, noting the date and race number, the key horse(s), the amount bet, the result, and the newly adjusted bankroll.

Assuming a $1,000 bankroll, your bet range would be $60 for a max, $40 for a normal play, and $20 for live longshots.

Nobody says you have to be strictly a win bettor. A $40 play might entail $30 to win on your key horse along with a pair of $5 exacta savers underneath two other contenders, or that $40 might be earmarked for a pick-three play, and so on.

As long as you stay within your limits, your chances of tapping out are minimal if you have a good opinion, because you will be betting more during hot streaks and less during cold spells.

If your handicapping opinion isn't strong enough to generate a profit from flat bets or fixed percentage, there is no way in the long run to manipulate any kind of progressive betting scheme that will make it so.

It's not easy, but there are people who do win money at this game, even if most of them may never break the bank. With an investment of time and effort, there's nothing that says you can't become one of them.

QUINN
ON CLASS
by James Quinn

WHETHER HANDICAPPERS USE THE knowledge to identify contenders, to make selections, to guide eliminations, or to spot overlays that fit a race especially well, an understanding of race conditions is vital, perhaps indispensable, to success at the racetrack.

Players who appreciate the class demands of eligibility conditions can form mental images of the past performances of horses who are well suited to particular kinds of races. Just as importantly, they can visualize past-performance patterns that are not well suited.

In nonclaiming races, as a rule, horses ill suited to the class demands of the race are unlikely to win. Knowing this makes the handicapping process more efficient, and much more effective.

In any maiden claiming race, for example, practiced handicappers realize that the horses moving from an acceptable performance in a maiden special weight will be dropping significantly in class. Far fewer handicappers realize that a horse dropping in claiming price, accompanied by a high pace figure, will frequently be the next-best bet under maiden claiming conditions, and at much sweeter odds.

Fewer still will appreciate that speed handicapping is notoriously unreliable in maiden claiming races. Or that maiden claiming graduates with unusually high speed figures should be outclassed in any allowance race. Or that the same high-figure grads should be expected to lose in any open claiming race (versus winners) having a selling price equal to or greater than the maiden claiming price.

A few more provocative comments should whet the appetite for the broader discussion.

In maiden special weight races, three kinds of contenders dominate the winners' circles at all tracks, and only these three types should be backed. Only one of the types, well hidden, pays at higher odds than it should. Players willing to adhere to the guidelines that apply will be capable of winning 40 percent of the maiden races they play. Profits run surprisingly high.

In nonwinners allowance races, casual racegoers haven't a clue, but regular handicappers too often do not know how to take advantage of the ignorance. The races generally will be dominated by the younger, lightly raced, nicely bred horses that might be any kind or, at least, will be winding their way to the better races. That means 3-year-olds should usually be preferred to older horses, a fact often obscured by the very experts who should know better.

Within the stakes divisions, a clear, well-defined hierarchy exists. It's crucial to know that Grade 1 and Grade 2 stakes winners typically will defeat lower-grade stakes winners, although it has become more difficult than ever to identify the authentic Grade1/Grade 2 talent.

At lower levels of the stakes hierarchy, class matters more than speed and pace by a definite margin, but it's the interplay among those factors, as well as current form, that spells the ultimate difference, and represents the ultimate challenge of handicapping.

Under classified allowance conditions, it's important to appreciate when class should predominate and when class might be expected to disappoint. When class might disappoint, handicappers should prefer instead the horses in especially sharp form and particularly well suited to the distance, footing, and probable pace. That requires comprehensive handicapping.

In specialty races, such as starter handicaps, optional claiming races, and restricted claiming races, handicappers who can handle the class factor cleverly will have gained a precious edge. The guidelines will be few, but trusty.

And in the numerous claiming races where speed and pace routinely predominate over relative class, an important consideration will be rises and drops in claiming class, and whether each should be positive or negative.

Although the standard array of eligibility conditions and their class demands might be considered timeless, contemporary racing features a number of annoyingly confusing complications embedded in the conditions. Nonwinners allowance conditions, for example, now will admit not only horses who haven't won twice other than maiden or claiming races, but also will admit "nonwinners of three races," which means that winners of one allowance race plus a stakes race, or perhaps of two stakes races, might remain eligible.

Optional claiming races are intended to admit both nonclaiming and claiming horses at comparable class levels. Which should handicappers prefer, and when?

Starter races for maiden claiming graduates at a specified selling level or lower who have not yet won two races lifetime do not remotely resemble starter races for claiming horses who have started for a specified selling price since a specified date. These dissimilar starter races may look similar to the untrained eye.

In general, hybrid conditions intended to make as many horses as possible eligible to the same race to help fill fields have proved annoying and even misleading to practitioners, notably to bettors unaware of the role of eligibility conditions and how to interpret them.

Toward the end of the 2000 winter season, racing secretary Mike Harlow of Santa Anita, which was more desperate than most major tracks to fill nonclaiming fields, carded a classified allowance route that included an amazing array of eligibility conditions. The race was open to 4-year-olds and up that were:

a. nonwinners of $35,000 in first-place money since May 1, 1999, or
b. nonwinners three times other than maiden or claiming, or
c. nonwinners of four races lifetime, or
d. entered for a $100,00 claiming price.

Because in any nonclaiming race, handicappers should remain alert for horses that simply outclass the conditions and, therefore, perhaps outclass the opposition, it's convenient to arrange these eligibility conditions, from superior to lower-class.

By admitting nonwinners of $35,000 first money since May 1, 1999, 11 months ago, the classified conditions permitted trainer Bob Baffert to enter the multiple-graded-stakes winner Classic Cat, who had run poorly twice since the specified date (May 1, 1999) and not at all since September 29, 1999.

Six of 17 lifetime and winner of nearly $1.2 million, Classic Cat had been a three-time Grade 2 winner. He had won the Lexington Stakes (Grade 2), the Ohio Derby (Grade 2), the Remington Park Derby, and Santa Anita's San Bernardino Stakes (Grade 2), and he had defeated multiple Grade 1 winner Budroyale twice. He was made the 8-5 favorite, and if Classic Cat were intended to win this classified event, he should have won, probably easily.

In this classified spot, however, handicappers should have abandoned Classic Cat. Handicappers should steadfastly assume that multiple Grade 1/Grade 2 winners will not be well intended to win classified allowance races. The big shots inevitably will be warming up for bigger races and larger purses. Classic Cat unleashed a strong middle move in the race, assumed the lead briefly, and tired. He finished third, beaten two lengths in a textbook prep for a later graded stakes.

When graded-stakes stars are entered in classified allowances having a specified date more than 90 days ago, it's crucial to analyze the situation accurately. If they have run infrequently, or not at all, since the specified date, review their races immediately preceding the specified date—in this example, May 1, 1999.

If the horses show multiple Grade 1/Grade 2 victories during the most recent form cycle, assume they are not well intended to win a classified purse. But if they have won lower-order stakes, including Grade 3 stakes, they may be well intended indeed, and may whip the classified horses handily. The more recent the classy wins just before the specified date, the better.

The next-highest class level in this example, nonwinners three times other than maiden or claiming, is important. If the classier stakes winners are absent or, like Classic Cat, unintended, now the race is likely to be won by that younger, lightly raced, nicely bred kind moving through his nonwinners conditions.

The next level, nonwinners of four races lifetime, extends eligibility to European imports that are either relatively lightly raced and still unclassified, or simply superior to today's conditions. European imports typically will have won their first race in non-maiden races. They may have won three races other than maiden or claiming, as many as three listed/group stakes races, and still remain eligible for this classified purse. These horses may enjoy a definite class edge.

The lowest class level in the example, a $100,000 claiming price, invites higher-priced claiming horses to try to win a richer purse. The claiming horses tend to be older and they may have won stakes or graded stakes a few seasons ago. Or they may be 4-year-olds and 5-year-olds who never have reached graded-stakes status, but have won open stakes of lower value, other classified races, and several high-priced claiming races, and impressively, with strong combinations of speed and pace figures.

The claiming horses will be hard-knockers and consistent, and unless they are out-classed by a graded-stakes star or the lightly raced, improving kind that just possesses greater ability, they will be threats to win.

In the Santa Anita classified race, Classic Cat tired, and an ordinary-looking 5-year-old still eligible to nonwinners-three-times-other-than allowances rallied from last in the stretch at 7-1. The outcome was not especially predictable, at least by class evaluation. Yet numerous races will be predictable precisely by class evaluation. Specific selection-and-elimination guidelines follow.

MAIDEN RACES

We begin with maiden races for 3-year-olds and for 4-year-olds and up, where the performance patterns that should be expected to win are clear, limited, and rather obvious to the practiced eye and where handicappers who follow the recommended guidelines should expect to be clear and obvious winners.

More than any other kind, maiden races have been exposed for the child's play they can be, due to the advances conferred on handicappers by the information age. Professional speed figures such as the Beyer Speed Figures, which appear in *Daily Racing Form,* inform handicappers which of the experienced maidens can actually run par and faster than par.

Readily accessible trainer and sire stats indicate which of the first-time starters are likely to impress. Workouts are now ranked according to their relative speed, and local handicappers put them in broader context.

Although longshots do not upset many maiden races, and those that do are not espe-cially predictable, average odds on bettable maiden winners should settle at 5-2 or slightly higher, yielding rates of profit near 40 percent.

The key to consistent success with maidens is to restrict support to three types:

1) experienced maidens who have recently equaled or exceeded par
2) first-time starters who satisfy the acceptable standards of sire perform-ance, trainer performance, and workouts
3) second starters

Experienced maidens that have already equaled or exceeded par will be extremely difficult for first starters to defeat. It's foolish to trifle with these swift maidens. In a six-week handicapping program I delivered with partner Tom Brohamer at Del Mar in the 1990's, we encountered a dozen older maidens that had surpassed par. All 12 won. Participants in that program will hesitate to take par-and-faster maidens lightly.

On the other hand, experienced maidens that have not equaled par are easy pickings for numerous first starters and second starters. And a sucker bet among maidens is the horse who exceeded par a few races back, but has failed to follow that performance with better races.

Beyer Speed Pars are published intermittently for the various tracks in *Daily Racing Form,* and these should be consulted regularly. Below is a partial list of prominent tracks and the Beyer Speed Pars for maiden races open to 3-year-olds and older:

Aqueduct/Belmont Park/Saratoga	88
Aqueduct Inner	77
Santa Anita/Hollywood Park/Del Mar	88
Gulfstream Park	79
Calder	75
Churchill Downs/Keeneland	79
Turfway Park	67
Arlington Park/Hawthorne	75
Monmouth Park/The Meadowlands	74
Bay Meadows/Golden Gate Fields	79

In a majority of maiden fields the experienced runners will have finished slower than par. Now, the first starters and second starters can shine.

When evaluating first starters, rely upon these guidelines. The sire should win with 11 percent or more of his first-timers. The trainer should win with 11 percent or more of his first starters. Two workouts at four and five furlongs or longer should be sharp. Sharp means faster than 12 seconds per furlong up to five furlongs, faster than 1:13 at six furlongs, and faster than 1:27 at seven furlongs.

If the local track surfaces are considered deep and slow, add a second to the workout standards.

These performance standards can be considered liberal, and highly reliable. The 11 percent winners expected of sires and trainers corresponds to their percentages of starters. If trainers or sires amass 20 percent winners with first starters, award extra credit, notably if the experienced runners are below par.

It's not unusual for two of the trainer-sire-workout criteria to be positive, the third negative. If so, don't bet on the favorite or on low-priced contenders, but if the odds are 8-1 or thereabouts, at times the play makes sense, notably if the experienced runners have been dismal.

The most rewarding bet in maiden races involves second starters. If second starters possess talent, they should be expected to improve by three to five lengths. The improvement corresponds to eight to 13 points on the Beyer scale. Handicappers can, therefore, look longingly for second starters who have run within three lengths of the more experienced high-figure maidens in the field.

The public will overbet the more experienced high-figure maidens. The underbet second starters often will improve by several lengths and win at juicy mutuels. These bets can be considered among the shrewdest, most rewarding in modern racing.

More than occasionally, handicappers will be confronted with a dull maiden lineup having a second starter showing one dull line. What to do?

If other relevant factors look positive—sire, workouts, barn, jockey, low odds at debut—a bet at double-digit odds makes sense. The play will be more likely to succeed when the firsters leave much to be desired.

The same three criteria can apply in maiden dashes and six-furlong sprints for 2-year-olds. Except now, the trainer-sire win percentages should be raised to 15 percent, and at least one of the sharp workouts should have occurred out of the gate. Second starters in juvenile sprints can be expected to improve by five to seven lengths, which is reliably projected by adding 13 to 18 points to the Beyer Speed Figure.

Maidens on the turf must be treated distinctly. Here, too, the information age has rushed to the rescue. The crucial consideration is the pedigree of each first and second starter. Horses bred for grass run well on the grass. Tomlinson Turf Ratings, which appear in *Daily Racing Form*, provide handicappers with a useful tool in this area. Lee Tomlinson has rated more than 11,000 sires on their potency for turf racing. Be prepared to back any maiden with a rating of 280 or higher when he makes his first and second grass starts.

As Bill Quirin demonstrated 20 years ago, the attractiveness of grass pedigrees when evaluating inexperienced horses on the turf can be attributed to the generous mutuels so many of the horses return when they do win. Backing maidens having grass pedigrees at 5-2, even 5-1, gets handicappers nowhere. At double-digit odds, however, even 20-1 or higher, the properly bred maidens will win enough and pay enough to toss meaningful profits. The bets can key an unsteady supply of boxcar exotics as well.

Among experienced maidens on the turf, the best bets are off-the-pace runners who already have completed the final fractions of a grass route in under 12 seconds a furlong. Grass maidens who have done that will be found infrequently, but they also will be difficult to deny.

Another pleasant reality is that maidens who have run well in their first attempt on the grass typically will run even better the next time, especially if wheeled back within three weeks.

NONWINNERS ALLOWANCES

Although allowance races are uncharted, unfriendly territory for racing's casual audience, informed handicappers have greater incentive than ever to feel superior in these situations. Not only do they know the territory, but also new variations in the eligibility conditions have enhanced that advantage.

In Southern California, for instance, horses that have won one allowance race other than maiden or claiming (NW1X) limited to Cal-breds now can run back under the same NW1X conditions open to all comers. Numerous common Cal-bred winners will be outclassed in the open company, but some will possess a class edge.

When optional claiming conditions are juxtaposed with nonwinners allowance conditions, handicappers who realize which claiming classes correspond well, and not so well, to the allowance levels will not be confused. The accessibility of par times for all tracks allows handicappers to compare not only the claiming and nonclaiming class levels of local tracks, but also to make the same comparisons between claiming levels and nonclaiming classes at the several shipping tracks.

If the winner of a $32,000 claiming race for 4-year-olds and up at Fair Grounds ships to Gulfstream Park and is entered in a nonwinners-once-other-than, is the shipper outclassed, or does he fit snugly? The shipper probably belongs, but a $32,000 claiming shipper from Fair Grounds would be outclassed at Gulfstream Park in a nonwinners-twice allowance.

Dozens of variations on the theme can be answered quickly and accurately by handicappers in the know. A comparative table for 30 racetracks appearing in the nonwinners-of-two-other-than section below should assist in the comparisons.

Because the nonwinners allowance races have been carded primarily for still-developing, relatively inexperienced and unclassified horses, a sensible objective for handicappers is to identify the horses that might outclass the conditions.

If class standouts are missing, as they routinely will be, the objective is to identify the horses that fit the conditions well, and soon should be competing in better races. Horses well suited to the conditions may not win, but they are always contenders.

NONWINNERS ONCE OTHER THAN MAIDEN OR CLAIMING (NW1X)

The NW1X allowance race most likely will be won by a younger, lightly raced colt or filly of solid connections and decent breeding that already has impressed in a few attempts.

Thus, 3-year-olds should be preferable to those 4 and older throughout the core season, a position lost on too many public selectors and turf writers. During the winter, in races limited to horses 4 and up, the lightly raced, nicely bred, well-connected 4-year-olds should be preferable to those 5 and older. Handicappers should not often prefer 5-year-olds and up that have never won an allowance race.

Horses having few attempts should be strongly preferred to horses having numerous attempts. Horses that have run 15 times or thereabouts might be eliminated on that basis alone, and can be discounted in close calls in favor of horses having fewer than 10 starts. Any favorite or low-priced contender that has lost more than six NW1X allowance attempts is probably a poor bet.

Among the lightly raced contenders—recent maiden graduates, especially—high speed figures can be misleading. If the pace of the high-figure performance has been uncontested or slow, many younger horses will disappoint when the pace quickens, or toughens.

Alternately, if a young, lightly raced prospect in a NW1X has set, pressed, or stalked a rapid pace before losing, but has held well, and reveals a slightly lower speed figure, that horse will be dangerous against an ordinary pace.

In routes, and on the turf absolutely, European imports typically will possess a distinct class advantage against the local runners. The imports often will have beaten half the field or displayed good form in a listed or group stakes in Europe. They now may face chronic nonwinners-of-one allowance runners. If the class edge proves distinct, it does not matter that the imports have not raced in six months, or will be running at a new distance (marathoners aside), or on an unfamiliar surface. The class edge dominates in NW1X allowances. If the odds are fair, take the money.

The reliable selections and eliminations in NW1X allowances are:

COMMON SELECTIONS:

1) Lightly raced 3-year-olds and 4-year-olds having relatively few attempts and impressive performances
2) Maiden winners who have equaled par for the NW1X allowance level, provided they have contested a par pace or faster

3) European imports who have beaten half the field in a listed or group stakes of France, England, Ireland, Italy, or Germany

4) In 4-and-up races during winter, in the absence of the above, winners of claiming races at class levels comparable to the NW1X allowance level

COMMON ELIMINATIONS:

1) 4-and-up horses having more than 15 starts, or having lost more than six NW1X allowances

2) 5-and-up horses, unless they are lightly raced, exit a top barn, and have superior speed and pace credentials

3) Recent maiden winners that have subpar speed figures for the NW1X allowance level, or have won following a soft or slow pace

4) 4-and-up claiming horses who have not won or finished close recently at a claiming level equal to today's NW1X

5) Maiden claiming winners last out, no matter how fast the final time or how great the margin of victory

6) Horses who have been entered more than once in a 3-year-old claiming race, unless the most recent claiming races have resulted in unusually fast, impressive victories and no authentic allowance prospects have been entered

Handicappers who support the horses recommended to be eliminated are urged to alter the habit.

Charismatic notwithstanding, 3-year-old claiming horses of winter and spring are generally washouts, while the nonclaiming 3-year-olds constitute the cream of the crop. The class rise from 3-year-old claiming to 3-year-old allowance is steep. Either the early pace will prove too rapid or too hotly contested for 3-year-old claiming winners, or the needed late responses will prove too stiff.

During summer and fall, the situation changes. By now most of the classier 3-year-olds will have graduated from the NW1X allowances. In addition, owners and trainers will have become more realistic about the prospects of their ordinary and cheaper 3-year-olds. Inevitably, 3-year-old claiming horses will be entered too ambitiously high in the claiming ranks during winter and spring, but as the calendar unwinds, the youngsters will be lowered successively in class.

By fall, most 3-year-old claiming horses will be competing at their appropriate levels. A few of the high-priced winners now may win in NW1X allowances, whose brightest candidates will have been narrowed significantly.

The situation extends itself to the winter of the 4-year-old season in an intriguing way. Now the 4-and-up horses who have been competing regularly in the NW1X allowances, but losing, will be poor bargains. Consistent claiming horses 4 and older can step up and win convincingly—unless that lightly raced, impressively improving 4-year-old of good connections has been entered.

Anyone who has experienced the simulcasts from Gulfstream Park during January, February, and March has confronted not less than dozens of 4-and-up NW1X allowance races, a perplexing number of them at seven furlongs. The races can be puzzling, mainly because the majority of the horses have been chronic nonwinners of similar allowance races. Their records look dull, the Beyer Speed Figures dismissively low.

The antidote is to limit play to the lightly raced, improving 4-year-olds and to the hard-knocking claiming horses who do figure—mainly shippers from New York, Churchill Downs, and Fair Grounds.

These guidelines apply too to the optional claiming races that so many tracks now rely upon to fill the NW1X allowance fields. The fields will consist of diverse lineups of claiming and nonclaiming types. Horses not entered to be claimed warrant the first inspection. Only when the preferred allowance profiles are missing should the claiming horses be preferred.

Regarding the state-bred winners at the NW1X allowance level running back at the same level against open company: Whether this type of horse can be a contender depends upon the quality of the state-bred allowance performance. Rely on the speed figure. If the speed figure of the state-bred race has matched the NW1X par, and the early pace has been satisfactory, the state-bred winner may be a repeater. Not only has he already conquered the NW1X allowance condition, but also he has done it in style.

If, however, the state-bred speed figure looks weak, or the pace has been soft, the state-bred winner almost surely will be outclassed in open company.

The NW1X allowance appears on virtually every major race program. Handicappers must learn to analyze the races confidently and effectively. The variations, nuances, and apparent contradictions may be complicating. Yet the guidelines here apply persistently well. They should eliminate errors of the grossest sort, and will be entirely capable of tossing profits.

NONWINNERS TWICE OTHER THAN MAIDEN OR CLAIMING (NW2X)

For talented horses, the step up from nonwinners of one to nonwinners of two is small. The order of competition has not changed substantially, and younger, still-developing, impressively improving horses en route to stakes do not dwell for long at this interme-diate step.

Thus, similar performance profiles will be relevant much of the time. Prefer younger to older. Prefer lightly raced, nicely connected horses to horses that have been trying repeated-ly and failing. Prefer European imports exiting the classier races, even though they may be returning from lengthy layoffs and running on unfamiliar surfaces at unfamiliar distances.

If lightly raced winners of one allowance race show lofty speed figures, remember to notice whether the high figure resulted from a slow (soft) pace. That kind of NW2X allowance candidate will be vulnerable, and often a delight to bet against.

Yet, in one essential way, the nonwinners-twice allowance condition has been altered dramatically.

With the proliferation of big-ticket stakes, the driving force at every major and mid-size track in the nation, too many younger, lightly raced, impressively developing 3- and 4-year-olds will proceed from the initial allowance victory directly to stakes. Some will win, and most cannot. Of the stakes winners, most will try to win another stakes. Of the runners-up and close finishers, most will return to snatch a second allowance win, especially at tracks where allowance purses are fat.

In consequence, the composition of the NW2X field has been altered. The fields typically will contain a few lightly raced winners of one allowance race, a few lightly raced winners of one allowance race that have competed in stakes without winning, the usual chronic nonwinners of two allowance races, and various midlevel horses who have formerly won an allowance race and since have competed variously in claiming races, other NW2X races, and even in an occasional stakes.

Unless a class stickout can be found, the handicapping process should emphasize the tricky interplay between class and speed. A guiding principle holds that relative class should supersede speed, especially as the quality of the races improves.

Speed figures reflect speed. They may not reflect stamina and determination, the other attributes of class, not to mention the more complex interactions of speed, pace, form, stamina, and determination.

At the highest levels of the stakes hierarchy, for example, the Grade 1 and Grade 2 stakes, speed figures frequently do reflect the several attributes of class exceedingly well, because the class demands of the best races call into play all of the above.

At other levels of the nonclaiming division, the interplay between speed and class can be less reliable. High speed figures in lower-level allowance races can be unreli-able. Good performances in higher-level nonclaiming races may be equally unreliable, such as a close finish in a stakes race that has been low-rated on speed.

These class-speed dynamics can be on display at the nonwinners-twice allowance level. Review the past performances of the two main contenders in a NW2X allowance at Hollywood Park, May 21, 2000. The Beyer Speed par is 95.

Which horse do handicappers prefer?

Sea of Ice
Own: Nicoletti Paul & Mari Ann
FLORES D R (38 4 5 2 .11) 2000:(379 53 .14)

Dk. b or br f. 4
Sire: Iam the Iceman (Pirate's Bounty) $2,000
Dam: See and Believe (Believe It)
Br: Nicoletti Mari Ann & Paul (Cal)
Tr: Jones Martin F(10 1 1 2 .10) 2000:(46 6 .13)

L 116

Life	9	3	1	1	$109,412	D.Fst	6	3	1	1	$105,887	94
1999	8	3	0	1	$102,412	Wet	0	0	0	0	$0	–
1998	1	M	1	0	$7,000	Turf	3	0	0	0	$3,525	83
Hol	3	3	0	0	$92,700	Dist	3	2	0	1	$64,387	85

28Nov99-7GG	fst	6f	:214 :443 :564 1:09	3↑ ⒻOClm 40000N	83	3	11	97¼	52¾	31	34	Lopez A D	LB 116	*2.10	91-09	AffirmedJudgement1152½ *Greny*1161½ SeaOfIce116hd	Stmbld strt, bid,hung	11
4Nov99-7SA	fm	*6½f Ⓣ	:214 :442 1:071 1:132	3↑ ⒻAlw 47000N2X	77	7	6	88¾	87¼	109¾	86	Alvarado F T	LB 116	10.00	84-10	Honest Lady116½ *What's TheFuss*118hd AffirmedMiss120½	Wide into lane	11
7Oct99-7SA	fm	*6½f Ⓣ	:22 :434 1:07 1:13	3↑ ⒻAlw 47705N2X	83	1	6	31½	41¼	52¼	52½	Black C A	LB 117	13.80	90-08	ⒹExcite1181¾ ImprfctWorld116no BoxOfficGirl118no	Lacked room stretch	9
Placed 4th through disqualification.																		
19Aug99-7Dmr	fm	1 Ⓣ	:23 :464 1:104 1:354	ⒻPiedraFndtnH80k	68	1	2	31	41¾	64½	78½	Black C A	LB 116	15.20	79-10	Kits Peak115½ Dusty Heather1142 Winterwish116½	Saved ground to lane	8
25Jly99-5Dmr	fst	7f	:221 :444 1:092 1:22	ⒻⓈFleetTreat110k	72	6	2	2hd	31½	22½	711¼	Black C A	LB 121	*1.10	82-08	*Bright Magic*1163½ Sulaymondo1164 Kinky Kinky1162	Dueled, weakened	9
26Jun99-4Hol	fst	6½f	:22 :444 1:09 1:153	3↑ ⒻAlw 53130N1X	94	2	3	2½	21	2hd	12	Black C A	LB 116	5.40	93-08	Sea Of Ice1162 *Corissa's Whisper*1136 Maria Alana1141½	Steady handling	8
26May99-5Hol	fst	6f	:22 :452 :573 1:102	3↑ ⒻⓈAlw 50000N1X	85	3	3	21½	2hd	11	1½	Black C A	LB 118	2.70	85-12	*Sea Of Ice*118½ Queenie Z118nk Griselle120hd	Stalked,led,driving	6
30Apr99-7Hol	fst	6f	:212 :443 :57 1:101	3↑ ⒻⓈMd Sp Wt 47k	84	8	3	21½	31½	21	12	Black C A	LB 118	5.10	86-09	*Sea Of Ice*1182 *Ex Miss Fuzz*115hd Apollo'sMusic1162	Stalked,led,driving	12
16Oct98-6SA	fst	6½f	:213 :442 1:094 1:162	ⒻⓈMd Sp Wt 35k	67	2	4	24	28	26	26	Black C A	B 120	13.10	81-12	Ode To Élaine1206 *Sea Of Ice*120¾ Gaminee1201	Chased, held place	8

WORKS: May15 Hol 5f fst 1:05 H *35/35* May9 Hol 6f fst 1:144 H *2/8* May3 Hol 6f fst 1:15 H *12/23* Apr27 Hol 5f fst 1:024 H *22/39* ●Apr20 Hol 5f fst :591 H *1/45* Apr14 Hol 4f fst :481 H *3/36*

Tera Kitty
Own: Gleis Josephine T
NAKATANI C S (45 8 11 6 .18) 2000:(404 91 .23)

B. f. 4
Sire: Fly Till Dawn (Swing Till Dawn) $4,000
Dam: Terakat (Storm Cat)
Br: Gleis Josephine T (Ky)
Tr: Jory Ian P D(20 0 2 3 .00) 2000:(88 8 .09)

L 119

Life	13	4	3	1	$122,479	D.Fst	8	3	1	1	$85,479	93
2000	4	1	2	1	$65,439	Wet	1	0	1	0	$10,800	86
1999	9	3	1	0	$57,040	Turf	4	1	1	0	$26,200	93
Hol	3	1	0	0	$9,840	Dist	3	2	0	0	$26,400	89

31Mar00-5SA	fst	1 1/16	:231 :464 1:112 1:441	4↑ ⒻⓇSnta Lucia H80k	82	3	2	2½	2hd	2hd	33¼	Pincay L Jr	LB 117 n	*2.60	79-21	CahillConnection1151¼ CemMilhas1142 TerKitty1172	Inside duel,held 3rd	6
18Mar00-4SA	fst	1	:224 :462 1:112 1:371	4↑ ⒻOClm 40000N	93	3	1	11	2½	1½	12	Kinane M J	LB 118 n	*2.10	85-19	Tera Kitty1182 *Houdini's Honey*1181 Melo Note1186½	Battled back inside	8
25Feb00-2SA	my	1 1/16	:231 :462 1:104 1:432	4↑ ⒻOClm 40000N	86	3	1	12½	11½	2hd	2½	Pincay L Jr	LB 117	*.90	85-19	Sunley Seeker118½ *Tera Kitty*117no Wicked118½	Fought back btwn,game	5
28Jan00-3SA	fst	1	:223 :46 1:111 1:38	4↑ ⒻOClm 40000N	88	1	1	16	13½	11	2¾	Valenzuela P A	LB 118	3.10	80-21	ExbourneFree116¾ TeraKitty1188 Clearandconcise116nk	Worn down late	7
12Dec99-7Hol	fm	5½f Ⓣ	:22 :442 :562 1:03	3↑ ⒻAlw 41300N1X	76	8	4	53¼	76	96½	63¾	Pincay L Jr	LB 117	*2.50	85-10	New Focus1202 *Pleasing Nod*118½ Excessive Girl122½	Steadied 3/8	12
26Nov99-3Hol	fm	5½f Ⓣ	:214 :442 :561 1:022	3↑ ⒻAlw 40250N1X	93	2	6	2hd	2hd	2½	2hd	Pincay L Jr	LB 117	2.30	92-07	Cpote'sCper120hd TerKitty1171½ DrminNSchmin1181	Inside duel, gamely	8
10Nov99-3Hol	fm	5½f Ⓣ	:22 :444 :564 1:032	ⒻClm 50000 (50-45)	85	4	7	32	43½	41¼	11	Pincay L Jr	LB 118	4.90	87-12	Tera Kitty1181 SuccessInExcess120½ Harlan'sPleasure118½	Steadied 3/8	12
17Oct99-6SA	fm	*6½f Ⓣ	:214 :434 1:064 1:124	3↑ ⒻAlw 45320N1X	79	2	4	1hd	1hd	3½	75¾	Blanc B	LB 116	16.30	87-09	AffirmedMiss120½ *ThtrGossip*1181½ Sh'sGrnd120nk	Inside duel, weakened	12
30Aug99-5Dmr	fst	6½f	:22 :443 1:093 1:162	3↑ ⒻAlw 51500N1X	75	9	1	3½	54	56½	49½	Blanc B	LB 120	19.30	79-16	*Seth's Choice*1187 *Maria Alana*1162 Excessive Girl121½	4 wide turn	9
4Aug99-6Dmr	fst	6f	:22 :452 :574 1:102	3↑ ⒻAlw 40000s	89	3	3	1½	1hd	12	11	Blanc B	LB 114	19.60	88-15	TerKitty1141 *QuenOfWilshir*1163 RisA.Disy119no	Btwn foes to lane,game	9
Previously trained by Semkin Sam																		
11Jly99-7Hol	fst	6f	:22 :452 :574 1:101	3↑ ⒻAlw 40000s	54	6	3	52	64½	77¾	710¾	Espinoza V	LB 116	5.30	75-11	Whittle1163 The Wind Moria1123 Contessa Luso1141	Steadied 3/8	9
25Jun99-7Hol	fst	6½f	:214 :444 1:102 1:171	3↑ ⒻAlw 40000s	63	7	3	41¾	43	53¼	44	Espinoza V	LB 116	3.90	81-13	Sulaymondo117hd *Whittle*1162 Monica Luxury1142	4 wide, no rally	8

WORKS: May13 Hol 6f fst 1:132 H *3/15* May5 Hol 5f fst 1:002 H *6/45* Mar10 Hol 5f fst 1:003 H *9/39*

Because Tera Kitty's recent record has been sharp, and because last out she finished third by 3¼ lengths in a stakes, the Hollywood bettors backed her to even money in a six-horse NW2X race.

But Sea of Ice figured to win here and she won like much the best—by seven lengths at a paltry 5-2.

Tera Kitty was seriously overestimated. The stakes she exited was low-rated, her Beyer Speed Figure a weak 82, five lengths shy of par for the NW2X filly level at Hollywood Park. That should have offered a clue as to Tera Kitty's true status. Another telltale sign was the fact that Tera Kitty required seven attempts to surpass her NW1X conditions.

A third convincing clue came from Tera Kitty's two wins before the NW1X score—a $50,000 3-year-old claiming dash on the grass on November 10, 1999, and the $40,000 starter sprint for maiden claiming winners who had never won two races, on August 4, 1999, at Del Mar.

The record reflects an improving 4-year-old filly with humble beginnings and not a single sign of higher potential. Tera Kitty may take a second allowance purse someday, but she is no even-money shot in any contest in the nonclaiming division and her future looks limited to claiming company.

Sea of Ice won a maiden race on the second attempt. She immediately won a state-bred NW1X allowance sprint and next confirmed her higher potential by winning a NW1X allowance that was open to all comers, a performance four to five lengths faster.

Next she tackled stakes horses going short and long, on dirt and turf. Then the barn selected NW2X grass sprints, to no avail. The November 28, 1999 loss at Golden Gate Fields, when favored at 2-1, can be excused. Sea of Ice stumbled badly at the start.

The performance profile fits the NW2X allowance level well enough. The filly had breezed through the maiden and NW1X allowance levels in her first four attempts. Rated off the open NW1X allowance win on June 26, 1999, Sea of Ice looked best of today's six. Nine starts into her career, Sea of Ice remains lightly raced with a right to improve.

Sea of Ice and Tera Kitty are examples of horses that regularly fool handicappers in NW2X allowances. Review the past performances again, proceeding in-depth from the most recent race back to the beginning of each filly's career, moving up the PP's and marking the best races lifetime and interpreting the pattern of development.

Which filly looks best? I hope handicappers will agree the classier filly is probably Sea of Ice.

As a rule, when analyzing contenders in NW2X allowances, credit a good performance in a stakes, but be careful to evaluate the speed and pace figures recorded in the stakes. If the figures are weak, as in Tera Kitty's stakes third, withdraw the extra credit.

The diversity of horses who will compete under NW2X allowance conditions demands that handicappers appreciate the correspondence between claiming levels and allowance levels, not just at local tracks, but among the several tracks. Tough, consistent claiming winners can win under NW2X allowance conditions, as long as the claiming wins have occurred at comparable class levels, based upon studies of par times.

This table presents the comparable allowance levels and claiming classes for 30 racetracks. Review it carefully and use it as a handy reference tool.

Claiming Classes and Allowance Levels with Corresponding Par Times

TRACK	NW1X	NW2X	NW3X
Arlington	18,000	25,000	50,000
Hawthorne	14,000	18,000	30,000
Sportsman's	12,500	16,000	25,000

TRACK	NW1X	NW2X	NW3X
Churchill	25,000	40,000	75,000
Keeneland	15,000	25,000	35,000
Turfway	12,500	15,500	30,000
Fair Grounds	20,000	25,000	50,000
Lone Star	15,000	20,000	35,000
Louisiana	15,000	20,000	30,000
Oaklawn	25,000	35,000	50,000
Remington	12,500	16,000	35,000
Calder	25,000	32,000	40,000
Gulfstream	32,000	40,000	62,500
Hialeah	25,000	35,000	40,000
Tampa Bay	8,000	10,000	16,000
Laurel	18,500	25,000	50,000
Pimlico	18,500	25,000	40,000
Delaware	12,500	25,000	40,000
The Meadowlands	35,000	45,000	50,000
Monmouth	20,000	25,000	32,000
Philadelphia	7,500	15,000	25,000
Aqueduct	35,000	50,000	75,000
Belmont	50,000	60,000	100,000
Saratoga	50,000	60,000	100,000
Del Mar	40,000	50,000	100,000
Hollywood	40,000	50,000	100,000
Santa Anita	40,000	62,500	100,000
Bay Meadows	20,000	25,000	40,000
Emerald	20,000	32,000	50,000
Golden Gate	16,000	20,000	32,000

Source: 2000 Par Times, by Gordon Pine, Cynthia Publishing Company

The table reveals, for example, that $25,000 claiming shippers from Fair Grounds entered under NW2X allowance conditions would be acceptable at Louisiana Downs and might enjoy a class edge at Hawthorne, but would be outclassed at Churchill Downs. Simulcast handicappers who make such comparisons will not often be fooled when shippers make the switches from claiming to allowance, and vice versa.

As they can under NW1X conditions, 4-and-up claiming horses can shine under NW2X conditions during winter and spring when the allowance races are carded for horses 4 and up. Older nonwinners of two allowance races may be no great shakes. Consistent claiming winners at the comparable levels can whip these chronic non-winners, and they do.

The situation becomes notably ripe for claiming horses in races for fillies and mares. Wanting to breed the horses, numerous owners refuse to enter their fillies and mares for a claim, even though they obviously cannot compete effectively in the nonclaiming division.

Finally, European imports again enjoy a significant class advantage in NW2X allowances, provided they have finished within six lengths of the winners in listed or group stakes abroad. Discount the distance, footing, and recency; the class edge tells again. If imports have won ungraded, unlisted stakes in Europe, they sometimes can beat nonwinners of two allowance races in the States regardless. The best bets are multiple winners in Europe.

Because many United States NW2X allowances now contain the added clause "or nonwinners of three races," often European imports will have won two lower-level stakes *and* have finished well enough in group company. These horses hold a genuine class distinction in most NW2X races they contest.

Imports from South America, South Africa, and Australia can be treated distinctly. Because their stakes have been rated by local jurisdictions (not the international pattern committees), these imports should have competed regularly at the Group 1 level and should have won at least one of those races.

ADVANCED NONWINNERS ALLOWANCES

Allowance races for nonwinners three times or four times other than maiden or claiming are for the top horses in the division only. They qualify as the sport's dividing line. Winners at this level have exhibited high class.

After younger, still-developing horses have won two allowance races, the authentically gifted proceed to stakes. Unexceptional horses are destined to remain behind, and to reside ultimately in the claiming ranks.

In the modern game, handicappers analyzing a NW3X allowance field should look first for horses who already have impressed in a graded stakes. It's customary for the leading contenders in NW3X allowances to have won a stakes, especially if they are returning from lengthy layoffs or are being tested at a new distance or on a new footing.

The better the stakes credentials, the better. To make matters more concrete, consider that these class levels at Southern California tracks, as indicated by studies of par times, are all comparable: claimers $80,000 and higher, NW3X/NW4X, classified allowance, restricted stakes, and open stakes of $100,000 or less.

So horses that can cope well with the advanced nonwinners allowances can defeat classified horses, and several stakes horses, too. The broad conclusion should be starkly clear. Prefer the classier contenders. Good performances at par or faster in better races (stakes) are the first line of defense in the NW3X and 4X allowances.

Equally as important, common performances at the lower class levels do not qualify in NW3X allowances. The NW2X win should be impressive, fast, and convincing. If the speed figure was low, the pace soft, or the manner of victory unimpressive, discount the horse stepping up.

The main contender in a NW3X allowance is a colt or filly returning from a sharp, fast performance in an open or graded stakes, provided the probable pace, distance, and footing today will be comfortable. These provisions are crucial. If form appears in decline, or the pace may be bothersome, or the distance or footing may prove problematic, discount the drop in class.

Because these horses have finished well in the stakes, they will be overbet under NW3X conditions.

A second contender under NW3X conditions is the lightly raced colt or filly who has crushed maidens and has whipped NW1X and NW2X horses handily. In this context, speed and pace numbers become decisive. Standards should not be bent. The figures, early as well as late, must be firm. Keep the following Beyer Speed Pars in mind:

	SPRINT	ROUTE
Major tracks	103	99
Midsize tracks	96	92
(Fillies and Mares)	-5	-6

Any prospect unable to run within two to three lengths of the desired speed pars at the lower allowance levels, or at any claiming level, cannot be trusted in NW3X allowances. Claiming horses, to be sure, should have exceeded the NW3X pars in the claiming races, and the early pace should have been swift.

Because the NW3X conditions are never carded with claiming horses in mind, claimers never figure best unless the lightly raced improving types and stakes drop-downs are missing.

Several barns in charge of young, developing 3-year-olds often will combine the class rise to the NW3X level with a change in distance, footing, or running style. Handicappers should be dubious. Because the class rise is significant, the combined changes may place heavily bet horses in double jeopardy. Some extraordinary young-sters will come shining through at miserly odds, but too many others will not. If the distance or footing is new, the pedigree should support the change. Sprint-to-route will be accomplished readily by talented horses in NW1X/NW2X allowances, but not so easily at the NW3X level.

Dirt-to-turf, route-to-sprint, and track-to-track are more complicated transitions and might be treated as too complicated when moving up to NW3X. Favorable trainer stats do not rescue the situation frequently enough, and notably at low odds.

The NW3X and 4X allowances have become endangered species due to the emer-gence of so many stakes races everywhere; these allowance races do not fill. Fields that do go are depressingly small. The logical contenders will usually be bet to a fault. The advanced allowances are difficult to beat.

CLASSIFIED ALLOWANCES

Classified allowance races fall on a class continuum that ranges from minimally restricted to highly restricted. As the restrictions become more severe, form becomes more important and class less so. The minimally restricted race is not very restricted at all and bows to class. The highly restricted race bars most of the good horses on the grounds and bows to form.

Under minimally restricted conditions, horses that have not won a specified amount of first-place money, usually large, more than once for the past 90 days or longer, usu-ally longer, are permitted to enter. Stakes winners since the specified date remain eli-gible. Only multiple stakes winners since the specified date will be barred. Classier horses have the edge.

Under highly restricted conditions, horses that have not won a specified amount of first-place money once for 90 days or longer are permitted to enter. Recent stakes win-ners will be barred, and so might stakes winners for the past six to nine months. The horses at advantage in this spot are the less classy sorts in sharp form and particularly well suited to the distance, footing, and probable pace.

Under no circumstances should handicappers expect multiple Grade 1/Grade 2 stakes winners returning from lengthy layoffs to be primed to win a classified allowance race. Owners and trainers will prefer to win another top-grade stakes. An all-out effort to grab a minor purse is not happily indulged. The top-class horses may win regardless—they certainly possess the ability—but the odds will be miserly. Not well intended, too many of them will lose. Handicappers should anticipate that, and support the lower-level, higher-odds alternatives with confidence.

Classified allowance races at many major tracks are virtually extinct. Victimized by the proliferation of stakes, the classified fields do not fill. The glorious exception is Churchill Downs, which cards a ceaseless diversity of classified races, with full fields that challenge handicappers' best efforts.

Simulcast handicappers who judge themselves to be adept at the game should not miss Churchill Downs.

STAKES

Five- and six-horse fields apart, many stakes races offer handicappers who know how to penetrate them a surprising percentage of their liveliest, most reliable overlays. Although stakes might have been judged too competitive by traditional methods, a variety of relatively new information resources have leveled the playing field.

Every so often, a nonhandicapper breaks into print with sarcastic remarks regarding the unreliability of the gradings of stakes, not just in the United States, but worldwide. For handicappers of the simulcast era, however, the importance of the gradings cannot be overstated. That's because (a) Grade 1 and Grade 2 stakes continue to be far superior to any other kind; (b) Grade 3 and listed (open) stakes having purses of $100,000-added and greater remain superior to open stakes valued at less than $100,000 and to restricted stakes; and (c) stakes below Grade 2 can be distinguished fairly according to the size of the purse.

The key to understanding the stakes division is to imagine within each a hierarchy having a definite structure and order of competition. In descending order of importance, the class levels within the hierarchy are:

Grade 1/Grade 2

Grade 3 and listed, purses of $100,000 and up

Open, purses below $100,000

Restricted

Handicappers must first appreciate that Grade 1/Grade 2 stakes are significantly superior to Grade 3 stakes and any open stakes. Not a trifle superior—far superior. Winners of Grade 1 events collect not only the richest purses, but also millions in breeding value.

Winners of Grade 2 stakes accumulate breeding value as well, if not in Kentucky or Florida, at least in California, New York, Illinois, Texas, or elsewhere.

Winners of Grade 3 and listed (open) stakes accumulate no breeding value. Owners who spend millions for well-bred yearlings with nice conformation do so because they anticipate a harvest of millions more when the horses become successful sires. Trainers are motivated by breeding value, too, because they usually will be rewarded with a valuable share in a stallion they have "made" on the racetrack. Trainers can sell the share annually, or use it to breed a mare to the stud; they can then train or sell the resulting offspring.

The implications for effective handicapping stand out.

In a Grade 1 or Grade 2 stakes, the handicapping can begin—and often ends—with a studied glance down the class column of *Daily Racing Form,* intending to isolate the one, two, or three horses that have won *two or more Grade 1/Grade 2 stakes.*

Roughly 15 seasons ago, Grade 1 winners could be expected to trounce Grade 2 winners. No more. The general decline in the quality of the competition has meant the Grade 1/Grade 2 winners are more alike than dissimilar. Many contemporary Grade 1 fields are small, weak, or both, and the title has been inexorably cheapened. Numerous Grade 1 events of recent years have lost the Grade 1 distinction, including major preps for the Kentucky Derby, such as the Wood Memorial and the Arkansas Derby, as well as several time-honored flagship stakes in the 4-and-up handicap division.

One Grade 1 title, therefore, is no longer definitive. The Grade 2 title may be equally as precious. Handicappers must demand the 4-and-up stakes horses possess two Grade 1/Grade 2 titles.

Handicappers can remain flexible and, to a degree, lenient when the stakes remain limited to 3-year-olds. Now, one Grade 1/Grade 2 title should represent higher class, especially a Grade 1 win.

When Fusaichi Pegasus entered the gate for the 2000 Kentucky Derby, he was not yet a Grade 1 winner. Having won New York's Wood Memorial (Grade 2) and Santa Anita's San Felipe Stakes (Grade 2), Fusaichi Pegasus was a dual Grade 2 winner, which satisfies the standard for 3-year-olds performing at the highest echelons of the division. One Grade 2 would not have met the standard.

When the brilliant turf miler Lure, age 4, entered the gate at Santa Anita for the Breeders' Cup Mile of 1993, he had won exactly one Grade 1 event, the Breeders' Cup

Mile at Gulfstream Park in 1992. Lure had won a Grade 2 stakes, however, superseding the standard for evaluating 4-and-up stakes candidates.

The next step is important, and simple.

Among horses 4 years old and up that have won two or more Grade 1/Grade 2 events, check the Beyer Speed Figures, with emphasis on the latest victories. The 4-and-up Grade 1/Grade 2 Beyer par is 109. Speed figures recorded during the 4-year-old season or later should match that par, and preferably should exceed it. Truly top handicap horses will run three to five lengths faster than par, a Beyer 115 to 119. Exceptionally talented handicap horses will record Beyer figures of 120 and slightly higher, at least occasionally.

Multiple Grade 1/Grade 2 handicap horses who have exceeded the Beyer par qualify as the horses to beat on class. Class supersedes speed at the highest levels, to be sure, but class and speed will be strongly correlated among the leading stakes stars of each season, almost without exception. Slightly slower stakes horses, in particularly ripe form and well suited to the pace, distance, and footing, surely can defeat the cream of the crop at any specific moment, but more often the slightly slower horses will be defeated by the multiple Grade 1/Grade 2 winners that have earned the towering speed figures.

A caveat relates speed to distance in the Grade 1/Grade 2 events. At a mile and a quarter, whenever possible, rely upon the speed figures earned at that classic distance, and not at the middle distances.

Pace and pace figures will be unimportant in most Grade 1/Grade 2 stakes for 4-year-olds and up. Older handicap horses, by a wide majority, can equal or exceed the pace par, and still finish strongly. Unless the early pace looks to be inordinately slow or destructively fast, discount the pace factor. In Grade 1/Grade 2 stakes for 4-year-olds and up, class laughs at pace.

In graded stakes limited to 3-year-olds, however, and especially during the first nine months of the year, early pace can be critical, and the relation between speed and pace figures to be telltale. The basic relationship is highly symmetrical. As the pace figure improves, the speed figure declines, and vice versa. This has spelled the ruin of over-rated, still-developing 3-year-olds every season.

In Southern California years ago, for an exceptional illustration of the phenomenon, a colt named Split Run was sent off in the Santa Anita Derby (Grade 1) at even money. It was the colt's third start. In beating maidens going short, Split Run had run fast early and slow late, winning by a widening margin in unexceptional time. In beating NW1X colts going long, Split Run had run slow early and fast late, winning by another widening margin (10 lengths) with a superb speed figure.

In the Santa Anita Derby, Split Run was forced to press a rapid pace for the first six furlongs. When the late running began, he fell back badly, and finished up the track.

Eventually Split Run fashioned a fine career of stakes performances in Chicago on the grass. A good horse, Split Run never did win a Grade 1/Grade 2 stakes on the main track. He could not run fast early, and fast late.

When analyzing Grade 1/Grade 2 stakes, maybe the most underrated role of speed handicapping relates to the various division leaders in the new season. Division leaders 4 and up should maintain customary performance levels, and young 4-year-olds might improve by two to three lengths. Many will decline. If a leading stakes performer has declined by three lengths or more early in the next season, accept the deterioration at face value. As these horses will be overbet based upon past reputations, attractive overlays can be found.

When Southern California's Best Pal was a 4-year-old, he was the top handicap horse in the nation, absolutely. His best Beyer Speed Figures topped 120, and regularly surpassed 115. By age 5, Best Pal was not the same. His speed figures had dropped noticeably, to 110-119 and thereabouts. He continued to be overbet heavily.

At 6, Best Pal's numbers dropped again. He was bet down still. These former standouts must be discounted, and the alternatives backed with confidence. To be sure, once in a while, the jaded stars will put it all together again and demolish a Grade 1/Grade 2 field. When Best Pal was 7, he smashed the opposition in the Grade 2 San Antonio Handicap. He had lost a series of stakes before that, and he lost a series of stakes afterward, while overbet nearly every time.

Do not be fooled. As a rule, if Grade 1/Grade 2 horses have lost too many steps the next season, but continue to be heavily bet based on past lives, ignore the horses until they are lowered in class.

Below Grade 1/Grade 2 stakes, the purse is the lure. Grade 3 stakes and open stakes having purses of $100,000-added and greater are distinguished on class by the size of the purse and the performances of the winner and close runners-up. Credit the winners of the classiest stakes, notably any impressive Grade 1/Grade 2 drop-downs, but the handicapping must be comprehensive. The horses to beat may have exited the richest races, but the probable pace should be comfortable, the distance and footing suitable, and form should be intact, improving, or peaking. Peaking form would be especially attractive.

The consistent Grade 3 and open stakes winners 4 and up rising to the Grade 1/Grade 2 levels should be expected to lose, and usually do. Their chances improve to the extent that genuine Grade 1/Grade 2 horses are absent (which happens more frequently than ever), and if their own form is extra sharp.

Pace qualifies as a more salient factor than in Grade 1/Grade 2 circumstances. Although most Grade 3/listed horses can set, press, and stalk a rapid pace and finish well, a fast, contested early pace can weaken the horses that have engaged one another.

Recent runners-up and close finishers at the Grade 1/Grade 2 levels that drop into Grade 3 conditions are inevitably at an advantage, and often at surprisingly sweet odds, especially if they have won a Grade 1/Grade 2 event in the past. In a closely matched situation, emphasize the past six races, the branch of recent consistency. Pay particular attention to the speed figures of the good races, defined as an in-the-money finish or within three lengths.

In 3-and-up stakes races, impressive winners of one or two allowance races are not acceptable at the Grade 1/Grade 2 levels at short odds, but they may deliver in a Grade 3/listed situation, provided their combined speed and pace figures indicate they should be competitive. If impressively improving 3-year-olds or young 4-year-olds have won three allowance races in an abbreviated time, or two allowance races and an open stakes, having a purse of $100,000 or greater, they might be accepted in Grade 1/Grade 2 circumstances, provided (a) their speed and pace numbers are competitive; (b) the odds are fair to generous; and (c) the older, established runners look ordinary and worse.

It bears repeating once more that in any stakes limited to 3-year-olds, handicappers should be skeptical of success on the rise if the pace figures (fractional times) of the recent wins have been ordinary to slow, regardless of high speed figures. Encountering a faster pace while moving up in class defeats more nonclaiming 3-year-olds than any other factor.

In any graded/listed stakes at a mile and a quarter, pedigree plus performance makes a difference. Wherever possible, prefer to rate the horses based on their other races at a mile and a quarter. Performances at middle distances are not strongly correlated with performances at the classic distance, a phenomenon illustrated practically every year in the Kentucky Derby. Horses that can break track records at nine furlongs may finish up the course at 10 furlongs.

As for pedigree, Grade 1/Grade 2 contenders at a mile and a quarter had best possess a Dosage Index of 4.00 or lower. The controversy over Dosage notwithstanding, the evidence supporting its role in Grade 1 races at a mile and a quarter is, to my mind, overwhelming and undeniable. Approximately 40 percent of stakes winners of open stakes up to nine furlongs possess a Dosage Index greater than 4.00. But when stakes winners at a mile and a quarter are considered, only 5 percent possess a Dosage Index greater than 4.00

The two populations are significantly different. The method can be applied not only to the Kentucky Derby and the Belmont Stakes, but also to all Grade 1 stakes at a mile and a quarter.

OPEN STAKES having purses below $100,000-added are a separate category. These horses typically will be outclassed when they attempt to vault in class to open stakes of $150,000 and greater. Their fabulous consistency in the lower-order stakes does not serve them well enough when the stakes have been raised substantially.

On the East Coast at prominent tracks such as The Meadowlands, Monmouth Park, Laurel, Pimlico, Calder, and elsewhere, a number of amazingly consistent stakes winners in stakes having purses below $100,000-added will be found. The horses will have prevailed in these bargain stakes again and again. Their speed figures may be similarly consistently impressive. But when they jump up in class, they lose and regularly finish out of the money.

Finally, in Grade 1/Grade 2 sprints, the underestimated but likeliest winners frequently will be horses moving from Grade 1/Grade 2 victories or close finishes in routes, notoriously if the horses can display tactical speed. These horses will possess a powerful combination of speed and stamina that proves too powerful a punch for dyed-in-the-wool sprinters. I call these versatile horses the power sprinters.

If the race will be closely contested in the stretch, the power sprinters prevail. Because the distance appears too short, the power sprinters exhibit the added charm of paying more than they should.

SUCKER BETS

One of the most profound developments in modern racing concerns the Grade 1 stakes winner who is not authentic. When the original edition of *The Handicapper's Condition Book* was released (1981), I wrote that Grade 1 stakes winners were greatly superior to any other kind.

No longer.

Actually, the trend could be recognized more than a decade ago. Too many Grade 1/Grade 2 stakes winners have been mere impostors. The general decline in the competitive quality has meant that Grade 1/Grade 2 titles have been won because the opposition was slight and the fields were small, not because the winners were genuine.

The unfortunate trend has actually been beneficial to handicappers in the know. Consider the record of Puerto Madero below, an especially interesting illustration of the species.

Puerto Madero (Chi)
Own: Hubbard & Sutherland
PINCAY L JR (39 6 11 6 .15) 2000:(362 65 .18)

B. h. 6
Sire: Gallantsky (Nijinsky II)
Dam: Paty Game*Chi (Saratoga Game)
Br: Haras Santa Olga (Chi)
Tr: Mandella Richard(16 5 5 4 .31) 2000:(130 30 .23)

L 120

Life	22	11	3	2	$1,331,690	D.Fst	18	9	3	1	$1,180,021	115
2000	3	0	0	1	$420,000	Wet	4	2	0	1	$151,669	114
1999	4	1	0	1	$416,000	Turf	0	0	0	0	$0	–
Hol	5	2	1	1	$389,000	Dist	1	0	0	0	$0	87

25Mar00♦ NadAlSheba(UAE) fst *1¼ LH 1:59² 4↑ Dubai World Cup-G1 — 411½ Pincay L Jr 126 – Dubai Millennium126⁶ Behrens1265½ Public Purse126hd 13
Timeform rating: 119 Stk 6000000 — *Trailed to 3f out,finished well w/o threatening.Ecton Park 5th*
Previously trained by Mandella Richard

4Mar00-5SA	gd	1¼	:47² 1:12 1:36³ 2:01²	4↑ S Anita H-G1	**114**	5	8	88½	75¼	63¾	32¼	Pincay L Jr	LB 118 n	15.90	92-13	GenerlChllenge1211¼ Budroyle1221 PuertoMdero1181½	Wide rally,fin well	8
16Jan00-7SA	fst	1 1/16	:23 :46 1:09² 1:40⁴	4↑ S Pasqual H-G2	**87**	6	6	68½	610	613	616¼	Desormeaux K J	L 120	4.50	83-10	Dixie Dot Com1181½ *Budroyale*1221½ Six Below116nk	Off bit slow,outrun	6
27Jun99-5Hol	fst	1¼	:47 1:10² 1:34² 1:59³	3↑ HolGoldCup-G1	**103**	4	4	31½	31	43½	47¾	Desormeaux K J	L 124 b	4.10	89-03	Real Quiet124½ Budroyale124nk *Malek*1247	Stalked,weakened lane	4
29May99-8Hol	fst	1⅛	:46 1:09³ 1:34 1:46²	3↑ Californian-G2	**97**	7	6	68	68	35½	312½	Desormeaux K J	LB 122	*1.10	81-11	OldTrieste1167 *Budroyale*1205½ PuertoMadero1222	Angled in,best of rest	7
6Mar99-5SA	fst	1¼	:47² 1:11² 1:35² 2:00³	4↑ SantaAnitaH-G1	**103**	4	5	53¾	56¼	58½	510½	Desormeaux K J	LB 122	2.80	87-11	Free House123½ Event Of TheYear119½ SilverCharm1243	Chased, empty	6
30Jan99-10GP	fst	1⅛	:46³ 1:10² 1:35³ 1:48¹	3↑ Donn H-G1	**115**	6	5	42½	32	1½	12¾	Desormeaux K J	L 120	4.20	96-14	Puerto Madero1202¾ *Behrens*1132½ Silver Charm126nk	Well placed, driving	12
20Dec98-7Hol	fst	1⅛	:47⁴ 1:11² 1:36¹ 1:48²	3↑ NativeDivrH-G3	**112**	5	2	21	33	3½	12½	Desormeaux K J	L 121	*.70	84-16	*PuertoMadero*1212½ *MusicalGmbler*1171¼ RiverKeen1148½	Bid,clearly best	5
15Aug98-7Dmr	fst	1¼	:46 1:10¹ 1:34⁴ 2:00¹	3↑ PacificClsc-G1	**96**	5	7	86¾	79½	611	613¾	Desormeaux K J	L 124	*1.20e	83-11	Free House1244 Gentlemen1245 Pacificbounty124hd	No rally	9
28Jun98-7Hol	fst	1¼	:46² 1:09³ 1:34 2:00	3↑ HolGoldCup-G1	**114**	7	6	76¼	46	34	21¾	Desormeaux K J	L 124	1.70e	93-05	*Skip Away*1241¾ Puerto Madero1241 Gentlemen1243	Inside rally lane	8
30May98-9Suf	fst	1⅛	:46² 1:10¹ 1:34⁴ 1:47¹	3↑ Mass H-G3	**114**	4	5	44½	33½	23½	24¼	Desormeaux K J	LB 116	2.00	99-07	*SkipAway*1304¼ PuertoMadero1164¾ K.J.'sAppel1134	4 path 2nd, bid, wknd	5
30Apr98-5Hol	fst	7f	:22² :44⁴ 1:08³ 1:21³	4↑ Alw 55000N$Y	**98**	1	6	67½	67½	45½	1nk	Desormeaux K J	LB 120	*1.20	94-11	PuertoMadero120nk Kenzig116nk TheBarkingShrk1167½	Electrifying move	6

WORKS: May9 Hol 4f fst :46³ H *2/28* ●May3 Hol 6f fst 1:11⁴ H *1/23* ●Apr27 Hol 6f fst 1:11⁴ H *1/23* ●Apr21 Hol 4f fst :46³ H *1/38* ●Apr13 Hol 3f fst :36 H *1/13* Mar21 NAS 4f fst :49 B *3/4*

After finishing fourth to the brilliant Dubai Millenium in the Grade 1 Dubai World Cup, March 25, 2000, Puerto Madero was entered next in Hollywood Park's Grade 2 Mervyn LeRoy Handicap, where he was sent off at even money and finished last.

Puerto Madero had won the Grade 1 Donn Handicap at Gulfstream Park on January 30, 1999, defeating Behrens and Silver Charm in excellent time and manner, a lifetime best effort. At the time, Behrens's class was suspect and Silver Charm was jaded. When Puerto Madero failed to contend in ordinary time in his next two starts, the Donn performance also became suspect.

As a rule, horses 4 and up cannot be accepted as top-of-the-line unless they reveal two or more Grade 1/Grade 2 stakes wins. One is not enough.

In eight races following his special performance in the 1999 Donn Handicap, Puerto Madero did not win another race, and did not finish within two lengths of any winner.

CLASS ON THE GRASS

An increase in races for maidens and unclassified juveniles apart, turf races at the route typically are carded for the better horses on the grounds. At major tracks, even in the claiming division, only the higher-priced horses are invited to perform on the grass.

The implication for handicapping is elegantly simple. Of the numerous handicapping factors, it's primarily class on the grass. Form is typically positive. Speed figures can be wildly unreliable. Pace is significantly less meaningful. And trips are ridiculously overbet. More on that point momentarily.

Class becomes critical on the grass because the majority of the races will be decided in the late stages. Late speed, powered by deeper reserves of stamina and determination, is the trump. Late speed is best defined as the fractional time from the pace call (second call, six-furlong call) to the wire. The factor is so important, so decisive, so much of the time, that handicappers can generate profits on the turf if they will adhere closely to a single special guideline:

> Prefer horses who have finished fastest from the second call
> (six-furlong call) to the wire *at today's class level or higher*.

Keep these final fractions in mind: at a mile, faster than 24 seconds; at a mile and a sixteenth, faster than 30 seconds; at nine furlongs, faster than 36 seconds. Grass closers that can finish that fast will be difficult to hold off.

Many handicappers who become attuned to the importance of the final fraction on the turf become careless about the relative class at which the late speed has been demonstrated. Because turf routes are furiously contested throughout the late stages, with margins of victory small to minimal, the operative phrase "at today's class level or higher" should never be ignored. Those late drives depend ultimately upon the interaction of speed, stamina, and determination, the essential attributes of class. Speed is not enough. Stamina is not enough. Determination is not enough. It's the interaction of the three attributes that matters the most. Thus, the attention to class levels. As a rule, rises in class are more difficult to accomplish successfully on the turf than on the main track. The double jump in claiming class from $40,000 to $62,500, for example, may be accomplished frequently on the dirt. The same double jump is accomplished infrequently on the turf.

The calculation of late speed is done easily. Only the past performances of *Daily Racing Form* are needed. First, calculate the race's final fraction by subtracting the six-furlong time from the final time. Second, modify the calculation by the number of lengths gained (or lost) by the horse from the six-furlong call to the wire.

The 2000 Grade 3 Inglewood Handicap at Hollywood Park can serve as a sample race that illustrates virtually every important aspect of effective handicapping on the grass. A $100,000-added Grade 3 event, at a mile and a sixteenth for 3-year-olds and up, it attracted eight horses. The four whose records appear here were the main contenders. Review the records carefully. For each good race among the most recent six, calculate the final fractions of each contender.

Bonapartiste (Fr)
Own: Ecurie Fabien Ouaki
MCCARRON C J (22 6 6 2 .27) 2000:(223 45 .20)

Gr. h. 6
Sire: Kendor*Fr (Kenmare*Fr)
Dam: Fab's Melody (Devil's Bag)
Br: Ecurie Fabien Ouaki (Fr)
Tr: McAnally Ronald(16 1 4 1 .06) 2000:(135 20 .15)

L 118

Life 33 6 11 4 $674,519 D.Fst 0 0 0 0 $0 –
2000 4 0 3 1 $100,340 Wet 0 0 0 0 $0 –
1999 5 1 0 2 $90,390 Turf 33 6 11 4 $674,519 107
Hol Ⓣ 7 3 2 0 $160,330 Dist Ⓣ 0 0 0 0 $0 –

29Apr00-8Hol fm 1⅛ Ⓣ:49² 1:12¹ 1:35¹ 1:47 + 3↑ Fastness H-G3 100 4 3 2½ 21 2hd 2½ McCarron C J LB 119 *.70 93-10 Senure114 1½ Bonapartiste119² Hook Call114² Bid,outfinished 5
8Apr00-9SA fm 1⅛ Ⓣ:49² 1:12¹ 1:35⁴ 1:47⁴ 4↑ El Rincon H-G2 101 6 5 53½ 43½ 2hd 2nk McCarron C J LB 118 3.10 90-11 Falcon Flight114nk Bonapartiste118¹ Otavalo114¹ Inside bid,led,caught 7
18Mar00-8SA fm 1½ Ⓣ:50² 1:14² 2:02³ 2:26 4↑ SanLuisRey-G2 103 2 6 64 52½ 4¾ 31 Solis A LB 122 8.40 91-10 DrkMoondncer122no SinglEmpir122¹ Bonprtist122 2½ Wide, bid, weakened 6
19Feb00-4SA fm 1¼ Ⓣ:49 1:13² 1:37¹ 2:01⁴ 4↑ Ⓡ SanMarinoH81k 99 1 3 24 22 2hd 21 McCarron C J LB 120 *1.30 84-21 Majorien119¹ Bonapartiste120½ Easy Song116 2½ Game btwn foes late 7
29Dec99-5SA fm 1⅛ Ⓣ:47 1:10¹ 1:34 1:46¹ 3↑ Alw 70000N$mY 96 2 5 54 54½ 32 32½ McCarron C J LB 118 *1.50 95-02 *Foggy Day*117¹ The Fly116 1½ Bonapartiste118¹ Swung 4wd into lane 6
4Dec99-7Hol fm 1½ Ⓣ:49⁴ 1:14² 2:01⁴ 2:25⁴ 3↑ HolTurfCup-G1 78 2 3 31 31½ 78 717¾ McCarron C J LB 126 8.50 70-20 LazyLode126 1½ *PublicPurse*126² SingleEmpire126 2½ Pulled,rail,weakened 7
6Nov99-9GP gd 1½ Ⓣ:47 1:10³ 2:24³ 3↑ BC Turf-G1 101 4 7 107 87 55¾ 69¼ McCarron C J L 126 42.10 85-02 Daylami126 2½ *Royal Anthem*126² Buck's Boy126 1¼ Steadied 1st turn 14
1 1/4 fraction unavailable
30Oct99-7SA fm 1¼ Ⓣ:47³ 1:11³ 1:35¹ 1:59 3↑ OakTreeTfCh-G1 99 1 5 52¾ 42½ 42½ 34¼ McCarron C J LB 124 *2.20 89-09 Mash One124² Lazy Lode124 2½ Bonapartiste124nk Saved ground to 1/4 6
2May99-9Hol fm 1⅛ Ⓣ:47 1:10⁴ 1:34¹ 1:46² 3↑ Fastness H78k 106 1 5 43 52½ 63½ 1no McCarron C J LB 121 *1.00 96-14 Bonapartiste121no Alvo Certo117¾ *Native Desert*118 1½ Steadied 3/8 & 1/4 6
7Nov98-9CD fm 1½ Ⓣ:49¹ 1:13⁴ 2:03³ 2:28³ 3↑ BC Turf-G1 77 4 7 85½ 89 915 918 McCarron C J L 126 10.80 74-09 *Buck's Boy*126 1½ Yagli126 1¾ Dushyantor126no Steadied, rank early 13
4Oct98-7SA fm 1¼ Ⓣ:50 1:14² 1:38² 2:02 3↑ OakTreeTfCh-G1 107 1 3 32 21½ 2½ 2no McCarron C J LB 124 2.90 78-18 Military124no Bonapartiste124 3½ River Bay124 4½ Bid,gamely,just missed 5
5Sep98-4Dmr fm 1⅜ Ⓣ:48⁴ 1:14 1:38² 2:14 3↑ Del Mar H-G2 106 4 5 54 41¾ 2hd 1hd McCarron C J LB 115 3.10 98-05 Bonapartiste115hd River Bay123¹ *Military*116 1¼ 5-wide into lane,game 6

WORKS: May14 Hol Ⓣ 5f fm 1:02² H (d) *10/13* May7 Hol Ⓣ 4f fm :50¹ H (d)*2/4* Apr27 Hol Ⓣ 4f fm :48² B (d) *1/2* Apr21 SA Ⓣ 5f fm 1:02³ H (d)*4/4* Apr16 SA Ⓣ 4f fm :49¹ B (d)*4/5* ●Apr6 SA Ⓣ 4f fm :47⁴ H (d) *1/4*

Chullo (Arg)
Own: Bunge H & Montagna G
NAKATANI C S (45 8 11 6 .18) 2000:(404 91 .23)

Dk. b or br h. 6
Sire: Equalize (Northern Jove)
Dam: Que Ilusion*Arg (Cipayo*Arg)
Br: Haras San Pablo (Arg)
Tr: Mandella Richard(23 6 6 7 .26) 2000:(138 31 .22)

L 118

Life 10 6 1 1 $554,009 D.Fst 2 1 0 1 $106,619 –
2000 1 0 1 0 $40,000 Wet 1 0 1 0 $40,000 105
1999 1 0 0 0 $0 Turf 7 5 0 0 $407,390 99
Hol Ⓣ 1 0 0 0 $0 Dist Ⓣ 0 0 0 0 $0 –

5Mar00-5SA sly 1 ⊗:23³ :46² 1:10 1:36³ 4↑ Arcadia H-G2 105 5 2 31 21 22½ 2½ Nakatani C S LB 117 fn *1.40 87-20 *Commitisize*112½ Chullo117⁴ Sultry Substitute114 3½ Came back on late 6
13Jun99-9Hol fm 1 Ⓣ:23¹ :46 1:08⁴ 1:32⁴ 3↑ ShoemakrBCM-G2 99 5 3 32½ 74¼ 63½ 64½ McCarron C J LB 124 3.60 94-09 Silic124no Ladies Din124½ Hawksley Hill124nk Pulled,weakened 8
Previously trained by Eduardo Martinez Dehoz
14Mar98♦ San Isidro(Arg) fm *1¼Ⓣ LH 1:57² 3↑ GP Asoc Latinoamericano JCs-G1 Stk 270000 710½ Conti O F 120 *.90 Jimwaki132 1½ Sidon120³ Gabarito120½ 13
Tracked in 5th,weakened 2f out.Quari Bravo 4th,Mash One 6th
13Dec97♦ San Isidro(Arg) gd *1½Ⓣ LH 2:32¹ 3↑ Gran Premio Carlos Pellegrini-G1 Stk 320000 14½ Conti O F 119 *1.00 Chullo119 4½ Quari Bravo119 Bueno Bob119 13
Tracked in 4th,led 2f out,handily.Mario Eterno 4th,Jimwaki 5th
8Nov97♦ Hipodromo(Arg) fst *1⅝ LH 2:31³ Gran Premio Nacional(Arg Drby)-G1 Stk 136000 14 Conti O F 126 *1.00 Chullo126⁴ Lazy Lode126½ Intempestivo126½ 10
Close up,led 2f out,going away.Mario Eterno 4th,De Un Suspiro 5th
11Oct97♦ San Isidro(Arg) gd *1¼Ⓣ LH 1:59¹ Gran Premio Jockey Club-G1 Stk 142000 12½ Conti O F 123 *.65 Chullo123 2½ De Un Suspiro123 1½ Intempestivo123 1½ 11
Well placed in 3rd,led 1f out,ridden out.Lazy Lode 5th
7Sep97♦ Hipodromo(Arg) fst *1 LH 1:34² Polla de Potrillos(Arg2000Gns)-G1 Stk 71500 3nk Conti O F 123 *.65 Golfer123 Enrulao123 Chullo123 6
Tracked leaders,bid 1f out,failed
9Aug97♦ San Isidro(Arg) fm *1 Ⓣ LH 1:33¹ San Isidro 2000 Guineas-G1 Stk 71500 14½ Conti O F 123 *.85 Chullo123 4½ Handsome Halo123 Mr. Grillo123 12
Well placed in 3rd,led 2f out,drew clear.Mario Eterno 4th
5Jly97♦ San Isidro(Arg) fm *1 Ⓣ LH 1:33 Gran Criterium-G1 Stk 64000 16 Conti O F 123 3.15 Chullo123⁶ Bat Marsico123hd Mario Eterno123¹ 17
Led after 3f,handily.Nineth Sprout 4th
9May97♦ San Isidro(Arg) fm *7½f Ⓣ LH 1:29³ Cl JB Zubiaurre(Lst-1st-timrs) Stk 17000 16 Conti O F 121 *1.70 Chullo121⁶ Maviero Hei121 1½ Knighthood121nk 17
Tracked leaders,led 2f out,quickly clear.Carlacho 4th

WORKS: May17 Hol 4f fst :52⁴ H *35/37* May11 Hol Ⓣ 5f fm 1:03 H (d)*5/6* May7 Hol Ⓣ 4f fm :50¹ H (d)*2/4* Apr30 Hol Ⓣ 1 fm 1:43² H (d) *1/2* Apr25 SA 7f fst 1:26⁴ H *2/4* Apr20 SA Ⓣ 6f fm 1:15¹ H (d)*8/9*

Montemiro (Fr)
Own: Red Baron's Barn
ESPINOZA V (52 9 4 13 .17) 2000:(393 71 .18)

B. h. 6
Sire: Kris*GB (Sharpen Up*GB)
Dam: Mira Monte*GB (Baillamont)
Br: Petra Bloodstock Agency Ltd (Fr)
Tr: Vienna Darrell(6 0 0 2 .00) 2000:(69 16 .23)

L 113

Life 24 5 5 3 $192,695 D.Fst 0 0 0 0 $0 –
2000 1 0 0 0 $0 Wet 0 0 0 0 $0 –
1999 4 1 2 0 $69,812 Turf 24 5 5 3 $192,695 106
Hol Ⓣ 1 0 1 0 $30,000 Dist Ⓣ 3 2 0 0 $37,330 106

29Apr00-7GG fm 1 Ⓣ:24³ :47⁴ 1:10⁴ 1:35² 3↑ S F Mile H-G2 82 10 6 2½ 1hd 42 811½ Flores D R LB 116 3.50e 83-06 Ladies Din120hd Fighting Falcon116³ Self Feeder116¹ Bid 3w, empty 10
1Aug99-4Dmr fm 1⅛ Ⓣ:50¹ 1:14 1:37¹ 1:48³ 3↑ EddieReadH-G1 77 4 10 106¾ 106 1010 1014 Blanc B LB 112 9.50 78-10 Joe Who116nk Ladies Din119½ Bouccaneer115 1½ No speed, no rally 10
4Jly99-8Hol fm 1⅛ Ⓣ:48³ 1:12 1:35 1:47¹ + 3↑ American H-G2 100 5 5 53½ 53 51¾ 2nk Blanc B LB 112 3.20 91-13 *Takarian*114nk Montemiro112no Special Quest115no Late bid 4 wide 6
29May99-7GG fm 1⅛ Ⓣ:24 :48⁴ 1:12³ 1:43¹ + 3↑ SilveyvilleH50k 106 4 6 52½ 41½ 1½ 16 Lopez A D LB 116 4.70 92-14 Montemiro116⁶ DrmticGold120¾ WstCostWrrior115nk Quick rally, drvng 8
Previously trained by J De Choubersky
4Apr99♦ Longchamp(Fr) sf *1 Ⓣ RH 1:39 5↑ Prix des Gravilliers (Div 1) Hcp 42400 2nk Jarnet T 139 5.70 Celtic Exit116nk Montemiro139nk Army of One132¹ 18
Timeform rating: 103 *Led,clear over 1f out,dueled 70y out,couldn't last*
3Dec98♦ M-Laffitte(Fr) hy *1 Ⓣ Str 1:45³ 3↑ Prix Tantieme (Listed) Stk 46400 2nk Thulliez T 123 3.70 Bluebell Dancer120nk Montemiro123½ Matin de Printemps123½ 7
Timeform rating: 106 *Tracked in 4th,bid 1f out,gamely.Marrast 4th,Army of One 5th*
10Nov98♦ Saint-Cloud(Fr) hy *1 Ⓣ LH 1:50¹ 3↑ Prix de Saint-Denis (Div 1) Hcp 60200 22 Jarnet T 136 6.50 Symboletho126² Montemiro136² Army of One129nk 17
Timeform rating: 102 *Mid-pack,5th 3f out,2nd 1f out,chased winner home*
15Oct98♦ Longchamp(Fr) hy *1 Ⓣ RH 1:47³ 3↑ Prix du Ranelagh (Listed) Stk 44300 47 Jarnet T 126 *2.50 Banafsajee122 2½ Gallipoli126² Alips122 2½ 8
Timeform rating: 92 *Never a factor*
6Sep98♦ Longchamp(Fr) sf *1 Ⓣ RH 1:44² Prix Samos (Restricted) Alw 62100 32 Jarnet T 123 6.00 Dame Kiri120 1½ Timely Lady120½ Montemiro123² 6
Timeform rating: 99 *Missed break,trailed to 1f out,fnshd fast.Alips 4th,Gallipoli 6th*
28Jly98♦ Vichy(Fr) sf *1 Ⓣ RH 1:40² 4↑ Prix Jacques de Bremont (Lstd) Stk 43700 46½ Jarnet T 123 4.20 Keep Playing123¹ Gallipoli123 1½ Banafsajee120⁴ 6
Timeform rating: 91 *Chased in 6th,passed tired ones*
6Jun98♦ M-Laffitte(Fr) yl *1 Ⓣ Str 1:37⁴ 4↑ Prix du Chemin de Fer du Nord-G3 Stk 61000 58 Asmussen C B 123 7.50 Jim and Tonic127² Kaldou Star123 2½ Go Between123 1½ 6
Timeform rating: 92 *Led to 1f out,weakened*
23Apr98♦ Longchamp(Fr) hy *7f Ⓣ RH 1:25³ 4↑ Prix de l'Ile Saint-Louis Alw 26500 63¼ Peslier O 130 3.00 Bartex123hd King Country127hd Riviera127 1½ 9
Rated in 5th,lacked room 1-1/2f out,evenly late

WORKS: May16 SA 5f fst 1:02¹ H *17/27* May11 SA 4f fst :50³ H *21/31* May6 SA 3f fst :37 H *11/28* Apr25 SA 5f fst 1:01³ H *17/31* Apr20 SA Ⓣ 6f fm 1:13² H (d)*3/9* Apr15 SA Ⓣ 6f fm 1:14³ H (d) *1/1*

Central Lobby (Ire)
Own: Juddmonte Farms Inc
BLANC B (30 5 0 5 .17) 2000:(181 26 .14)

Ch. h. 5
Sire: Kenmare*Fr (Kalamoun*GB)
Dam: Style of Life (The Minstrel)
Br: Weld Mrs C L (Ire)
Tr: Frankel Robert(14 4 1 2 .29) 2000:(119 32 .27)

L 115

Life	17	4	5	4	$194,893	D.Fst	1	0	0	0	$0 77
2000	2	2	0	0	$73,800	Wet	0	0	0	0	$0 –
1999	9	1	3	2	$79,600	Turf	16	4	5	4	$194,893 105
Hol Ⓣ	1	0	1	0	$10,600	Dist Ⓣ	1	0	1	0	$4,782 –

9Apr00–7SA	fm	1	Ⓣ :23 :46^3 1:10 1:34	4↑ OClm 100000N	105	4	5	5^{7½}	5^{4½}	5^{2¼}	1^{½}	Blanc B	LB 118	2.30	89–11	Central Lobby118½ *Sardaukar*118^1 *Kaibo*118^1	4wd into lane,rallied	10
23Jan00–3SA	fm	1	Ⓣ :22^4 :46^4 1:10^1 1:34	4↑ Alw 58000N2X	105	3	6	6^{4¼}	6^{1½}	1^1	1^{2½}	Nakatani C S	LB 120	*1.40	89–13	*CentralLobby*120^{2½} ChelseaBrrcks118^1 Mirmr118^{2½}	Rail bid,stdy handling	8
26Dec99–5SA	fm	1	Ⓣ :23 :46^3 1:11^3 1:36	3↑ Alw 54000N1X	95	8	4	4^{2¼}	3^1	1^{1½}	1^3	Nakatani C S	LB 118	4.70	79–23	*Central Lobby*118^3 Aware122^{hd} Passinetti120^{1½}	3 wide bid, driving	11
16Oct99–2SA	fm *6½f		Ⓣ :21^3 :43^3 1:06^3 1:12^4	3↑ Alw 46420N1X	94	4	6	6^6	6^{3¾}	3^{nk}	3^{1¼}	Nakatani C S	LB 122	*1.50	92–09	Concurrnt118^1 *Spinlssjllyfish*120^{nk} *CntrlLobby*122^3	Rail trip,outfinished	8
2Oct99–5SA	fm	1⅛	Ⓣ :47^2 1:11^1 1:36 1:48^1	3↑ Alw 46000N1X	87	1	1	1^{1½}	1^1	1^{hd}	7^{3½}	Antley C W	LB 118 b	*2.00	85–10	*Santovito*116no *Daytime*116½ Boss Ego116^1	Inside,weakened late	11
22Aug99–5Dmr	fm	1	Ⓣ :23^1 :46^4 1:11 1:35^1	3↑ Alw 54810N1X	93	5	2	2^{1½}	2^{hd}	2^1	2^{1¾}	Desormeaux K J	LB 119 b	*1.70	89–11	GnStormn'normn121^{1¾} CntrlLobby119^{hd} *Mott*121^3	Stalked,bid,outkicked	9
24Jly99–4Dmr	fm	1	Ⓣ :23 :47^3 1:11^4 1:36	3↑ Alw 64800N1X	85	1	9	9^{7¾}	7^{4¾}	4^2	4^2	Desormeaux K J	LB 119 b	*1.30	85–08	The Smokster123^{1¾} Baxter Pass115^{hd} Calypso Poet119^{no}	Reared start	9
23May99–4Hol	fm	1	Ⓣ :23^2 :47^1 1:10^1 1:34^4	3↑ Alw 53265N1X	91	5	5	5^2	4^3	3^2	2^{hd}	Desormeaux K J	LB 118	3.50	89–11	Eastern Giant120^{hd} Central Lobby118^{2½} Faculty118½	Led late,caught	12
6May99–5Hol	fst	1$\frac{1}{16}$	:23^2 :46^2 1:10^1 1:42^4	3↑ OClm 40000N	77	7	2	3^4	4^{7½}	7^{12}	7^{13½}	Desormeaux K J	LB 118	2.60	72–18	CrowningStorm116^{hd} *MrgdsDncr*119^{6½} Surpriztom118^{1¼}	3 wide, weakened	7
21Mar99–6SA	fm	1	Ⓣ :23^4 :47^4 1:12^2 1:37	4↑ Alw 54810N1X	90	3	4	4^{3½}	3^1	3^{nk}	2^{1½}	Peslier O	LB 120	*.90	72–22	AKing'sPresenc120^{1½} CntrlLobby120^2 *Musgrv*120^1	Awkward start,pulled	8
26Feb99–4SA	fm	1	Ⓣ :23 :47^2 1:11^2 1:35^2	4↑ Alw 54000N1X	90	4	4	3^2	1^{hd}	2^{hd}	1^{½}	Desormeaux K J	LB 117	*.60	82–18	[D]CentrlLobby117½ KingTngo119^{1½} Cstleross117^{1¼}	Driftd ot deep stretch	10

Disqualified and placed third Previously trained by Andre Fabre

15Sep98 ♦ Saint-Cloud(Fr)	sf	*1½ Ⓣ LH 2:37^3	Prix du Lion d'Angers (Listed)	3^1	Jarnet T	128	*2.70	Ultimately Lucky128^{nk} Blushing Risk128¾ Central Lobby128^2	9
Timeform rating: 107			Stk 45800					*Trailed,sharp wide gain final frlng but never catching first two*	

WORKS: May13 Hol 6f fst 1:12^3 H *2/15* ●May4 Hol 5f fst :59^4 H *1/22* Apr27 Hol 5f fst 1:00^3 H *3/39* Apr20 Hol 4f fst :48^2 B *6/40* ●Apr1 Hol 6f fst 1:12^4 H *1/15* Mar25 Hol 5f fst 1:01^4 H *8/32*

EIGHTH RACE
Hollywood
MAY 21, 2000

1$\frac{1}{16}$ MILES. (Turf)(1.38^3) 60th Running of THE INGLEWOOD HANDICAP. Grade III. Purse $100,000 added. 3-year-olds and upward. By subscription of $100 each on or before May 10, 2000 or by supplementary nomination of $5,000 each by 3:00 pm Saturday, May 14, 2000. $1,000 additional to start, with $100,000 added. The added money and all fees to be divided 60% to the winner, 20% to second, 12% to third, 6% to fourth and 2% to fifth. Closed with 25 nominations.

Value of Race: $110,500 Winner $66,300; second $22,100; third $13,260; fourth $6,630; fifth $2,210. Mutuel Pool $427,396.00 Exacta Pool $227,661.00 Quinella Pool $32,154.00 Trifecta Pool $256,839.00 Superfecta Pool $105,320.00

Last Raced	Horse	M/Eqt.	A.Wt	PP	St	¼	½	¾	Str	Fin	Jockey	Odds $1
29Apr00 GG	Montemiro-FR	LB	6 113	5	7	7^{1½}	7^{½}	7^{hd}	5^{½}	1^{1¼}	Espinoza V	27.50
29Apr00 Hol	Bonapartiste-FR	LB	6 118	3	4	3^1	2^{½}	2^{1½}	1^1	2^{nk}	McCarron C J	3.10
25Mar00 NAS	Takarian-IR	LB	5 118	2	3	5^1	6^{½}	6^{1½}	2^{hd}	3^{½}	Black C A	17.20
29Apr00 GG^4	Adcat	LBb	5 115	1	6	8	8	8	6^{½}	4^{nk}	Solis A	10.90
5Mar00 ^{5}SA	Chullo-AR	LB	6 118	4	2	2^{hd}	4^{hd}	3^{hd}	4^{1½}	5^{½}	Nakatani C S	2.50
9Apr00 SA^1	Central Lobby-IR	LB	5 115	7	5	4^{½}	3^1	4^{hd}	8	6	Blanc B	2.20
8Apr00 ^{9}SA^5	Foggy Day-FR	LB	6 117	6	8	6^1	5^{½}	5^{hd}	7^1	7^3	Pincay L Jr	17.70
16Apr00 ^{9}LS^1	Commitisize	LB	5 116	8	1	1^1	1^1	1^{½}	3^{½}	8	Flores D R	7.10

OFF AT 4:38 Start Good. Won driving. Course firm.
TIME :24^1, :48^1, 1:11^1, 1:34^3, 1:40^3 (:24.25, :48.39, 1:11.26, 1:34.67, 1:40.71)

$2 Mutuel Prices:				
	5–MONTEMIRO–FR	57.00	20.00	10.40
	3–BONAPARTISTE–FR		4.40	3.20
	2–TAKARIAN–IR			9.20

$1 EXACTA 5–3 PAID $122.70 $2 QUINELLA 3–5 PAID $111.20 $1 TRIFECTA 5–3–2 PAID $949.10 $1 SUPERFECTA 5–3–2–1 PAID $3,655.00

B. h, by Kris*GB–Mira Monte*GB, by Baillamont. Trainer Vienna Darrell. Bred by Petra Bloodstock Agency Ltd (Fr).

MONTEMIRO (FR) pulled his way along toward the inside and was in a bit tight into the first turn, went outside a rival on the backstretch and second turn, waited off heels leaving that turn, split rivals and came out into the stretch and rallied under strong handling to prove best. BONAPARTISTE (FR) stalked the pace outside a rival, bid between horses into the second turn and outside the leader on that bend, took a short lead in upper stretch, inched away in midstretch but could not hold off the winner. TAKARIAN (IRE) was close up a bit off the rail then outside a rival on the backstretch, was briefly in a bit tight leaving the backstretch, split horses on the second turn, came out for the stretch and continued willingly to the wire. ADCAT saved ground unhurried early, continued a bit off the rail on the second turn and waited off heels a quarter mile out, came out some into the stretch and rallied late. CHULLO (ARG) was close up stalking the pace along the inside, came out a bit into the stretch, split horses in midstretch and was outfinished, then did not return to be unsaddled when lame and was vanned off. CENTRAL LOBBY (IRE) was well placed tracking the leader three deep, inched forward into the second turn, dropped back leaving that turn, steadied behind the winner into the stretch and lacked the needed response. FOGGY DAY (FR) off a bit slowly, pulled himself into a tight spot off heels and steadied into the first turn, continued outside, went up four wide nearing and on the second turn and into the stretch, then weakened. COMMITISIZE sped to the early lead, angled in on the first turn, set the pace inside, dueled inside the runner-up on the second turn and weakened in the stretch.

Owners— 1, Red Baron's Barn; 2, Ouaki Ecurie F; 3, Nichols Thomas L; 4, Gallagher's Stud Kimmel C P & Solon; 5, Bunge H & Montagna G; 6, Juddmonte Farms Inc; 7, Shugart Corporation Goldstein & Sil; 8, Pegram Michael E

Trainers— 1, Vienna Darrell; 2, McAnally Ronald; 3, Greely C Beau; 4, McAnally Ronald; 5, Mandella Richard; 6, Frankel Robert; 7, Silva Jose L; 8, Baffert Bob

$2 Daily Double (3–5) Paid $180.60; Daily Double Pool $32,699.
$1 Pick Three (3–3–5) Paid $486.90; Pick Three Pool $82,356.

Before inspecting the horses' records closely, look below at the final fractions recorded by each horse in his key races:

FINAL FRACTIONS

Bonapartiste	Apr 29	Gr.3	35	2nd by $1\frac{1}{2}$
	Apr 8	Gr.2	$34\frac{4}{5}$	2nd by a neck
Chullo	Jun 13	Gr.2	$24\frac{1}{5}$	6 by $4\frac{1}{2}$
Montemiro	Jul 4	Gr.2	$34\frac{3}{5}$	2nd by a neck
	May 29	Stk	$30\frac{1}{5}$	Won by 6
Central Lobby	Apr 9	NW3X	23	Won by a half
	Jan 23	NW2X	$23\frac{2}{5}$	Won by $2\frac{1}{2}$

Recheck the calculations of late speed. Half-lengths are rounded up or down to the nearest fifth (length). With practice, the calculations of late speed become simple and automatic.

An additional point. The Beyer Speed Par for a Grade 3 stakes going long is 105. Although in grass routes for 3-year-olds and up/4-year-olds and up, it's reassuring to note the contenders have equaled par, at least on occasion, and although each of the four contenders for this Grade 3 stakes has done that, speed fanciers must be flexible on the turf. The pace of grass routes can be inordinately slow. When that happens, final times will necessarily be slower than par, not because the horses are weak, but because the pace has been too slow.

This occurs routinely. If speed figures of good grass horses look suspiciously low, check the fractional times. If the fractions have been milk-wagon slow, forgive the final times and the corresponding speed figures.

Now to the four contenders in the Grade 3 Inglewood Handicap.

BONAPARTISTE: The final fractions of his most recent graded stakes have been uniformly strong, and Bonapartiste can obviously win the Inglewood Handicap. He also likes the Hollywood Park grass course. The connections are superb.

On the minus side, and this is pertinent because relative class is crucial in turf routes, Bonapartiste violates a basic guideline of class evaluation. When a horse repeatedly finishes close at similar class levels without winning, mark the horse down. Because the odds will be low and he so often finishes close without winning, Bonapartiste shapes up as a class handicapper's sucker bet. Horses such as Bonapartiste are best backed to finish second and third in the exotics, but not to win.

CHULLO: Chullo is a Chilean champion sent out by the Dick Mandella barn with a leading rider, Corey Nakatani, up. Class credentials aside, Chullo is an immediate toss-out on form. The point is important and readily recognized. Away since June 13, 1999, Chullo returned on March 5, 2000, and finished a close second in a Grade 2 stakes at Santa Anita. Chullo should have returned to the races within three to six weeks. Instead, he has been away 2½ months. Anytime a top horse returns from a long layoff and runs well, and then is absent again for too long a time, it's a highly negative pattern. At low odds, abandon these horses without mercy.

MONTEMIRO: Second at 4 in a listed stakes in France in December 1998, Montemiro's first two stakes in the States were outstanding, and in the Grade 2 American Handicap on July 4, 1999, at Hollywood Park, he was sent off at 3-1 and finished the final fraction in a strong 34⅗ seconds, losing by a neck. Dull in the 1999 Eddie Read at Del Mar, a Grade 1 event, Montemiro was sidelined for nine months. He returned on April 29 in the Grade 2 San Francisco Mile at Golden Gate Fields, a race he badly needed. A closer, Montemiro that day abandoned his style and ran well up front until the eighth pole. He drops from a Grade 2 stakes into the Grade 3 Inglewood Handicap. As class handicappers appreciate, the drop from Grade 2 to Grade 3 is frequently a significant drop-down. The connections—trainer Darrell Vienna and jockey Victor Espinoza—are excellent on grass, and Espinoza has been fashioning a breakthrough year.

Montemiro fits the late-speed and class requirements of the Inglewood and he should show improved form. Fair-value odds should be 5-1, 6-1, maybe 7-1.

CENTRAL LOBBY: Central Lobby paired par figures for today's Grade 3 stakes in his recent NW2X/NW3X victories for remarkable grass trainer Bobby Frankel. His final fractions of 23 flat and 23⅖ are very strong.

But Central Lobby is a well-traveled 5-year-old and he violates a fundamental class guideline for evaluating older turf horses. His strong final fractions did not occur *at today's class level or higher*. Younger 3-year-olds and lightly raced 4-year-olds excepted, strong finishes at lower levels do not translate well to the same strong finishes in graded stakes on the grass. The point cannot be overstated. Central Lobby did not figure to win the Grade 3 Inglewood Handicap, but disciples of Bobby Frankel on the turf, not sufficiently convinced of the importance of class on the grass, could be expected to overbet Central Lobby to a fault.

They did. The odds at post time were:

Bonapartiste	3-1
Chullo	5-2

| Montemiro | 27-1 |
| Central Lobby | 2-1 |

Handicappers who had approached the Grade 3 Inglewood following the guidelines promoted here, obviously not a majority, naturally would have backed the curiously underbet Montemiro. The outcome was sweet. Following a troubled trip, which featured traffic jams and found him repeatedly steadying on the far turn, the classy Montemiro sailed by the other contenders easily, and won going away.

Other than a disregard for class on the grass at today's class level or higher, the odds on Montemiro are difficult to explain. The outcome was no fluke.

The troubled trip Montemiro overhauled raises another and greatly underestimated tenet regarding routes on the grass. Trip handicapping is overplayed. More often than not, trip handicapping does not seriously apply. Steadying, checking, being blocked behind traffic, and racing extra wide are part and parcel of turf racing. The pace is slow and the turns are sharp.

The conventional trouble lines do not matter much. The real running begins inside the quarter pole, often in the upper stretch. The best horses level out at those critical junctures, and they rally to win. If a rallying closer takes up badly, or checks sharply, breaking stride, *after his late surge has begun,* that's trouble that matters and these horses deserve a place on the horses-to-watch lists.

Otherwise, discount trip handicapping on the turf. It's incidental, not fundamental.

If trips count less, jockeys count more on the turf. Patience, timing, and a strong finish are the decisive attributes. Whoop-de-do front-runners, and riders who use too much horse too soon, do not get home first.

In the 1970's in Southern California, jockey Fernando Toro won so many grass routes that he became famous as "Toro on the turf." Virtually without exception, every ride looked the same. Toro hugged the rail. He steadied and checked repeatedly in the middle and late stages, around the far turn, and into the upper stretch. Still, he normally found a clear path late, set down his charger, and won regardless.

An opposite style was displayed in the late 1970's and 1980's by the great Sandy Hawley. Hawley parked his horses on the far outside time after time, going extremely wide around the far turn and into the upper stretch. No less an expert than Bobby Frankel called Hawley the best grass rider ever. Trips aside, like Toro, Hawley saved his horses' energies, set them down late, and won.

Contemporary leaders Jerry Bailey in New York and Chris McCarron in Southern California look nothing short of tremendous on the grass, while guiding the turf cavalries of trainers Bill Mott and Ron McAnally, respectively.

Grass routes for maidens, stakes on grass for nonclaiming 3-year-olds, and other turf routes for developing 3's and 2's are entirely different. Now pedigree counts the most. Youngsters bred for the grass are likely to run well on the surface in their first and second attempts. Indisputable studies confirm the point, and so does practical experience. An expanding role for those timely Tomlinson Turf Ratings.

Not much more is germane to turf racing. A particularly profitable pattern, however, deserves a special notice. Any horse 3 and up that can dispense two powerful late moves in a grass route will be extremely difficult to deny *at the same class level or lower*. The horse not only will have completed the final fraction in 12 seconds or faster, but also will have completed the quarter-mile from four furlongs to six furlongs in under 24 seconds, as powerfully as 23 flat.

Hunt for these superior grass closers. The pair of late bursts will remain hidden to most racegoers. So the horses not only win more often than they should, but also they pay much more than they should, a la Montemiro.

CLAIMING RACES

Claiming races are the province of speed handicapping and pace analysis. The truest indication that a claiming horse might rise in class successfully is a speed figure at the lower level that equals par at the higher level. The best indication that a claiming horse might repeat a good performance is a pace analysis that reveals the claimer won't be ruined by a faster, more hotly contested early pace.

Class evaluation is strictly secondary.

Secondary does not mean irrelevant. Local circuits are characterized by class barriers in the claiming divisions, which savvy handicappers can exploit.

In Southern California, the rise from $25,000 to $32,000 may be one step, but it's a nasty step. The corresponding drop from $32,000 to $25,000 is larger than it looks. The apparently nondescript drop from $12,500 to $10,000 at Santa Anita and Del Mar is larger than it looks as well, since the $10,000 level at both plants is bottom-of-the-barrel and many of those fields are dismissively cheap.

As noted extensively in the treatment of the nonwinners allowance series, class evaluation applies forcibly whenever claiming horses switch to the allowances, and vice versa.

Under two circumstances, class evaluation in claiming races retains a basic charm. One is starter races. The second is conditioned (restricted) claimers.

Starter races are open to horses who have "started" for a specified claiming price during a specified time interval. Because these horses cannot be claimed, starter races become hideouts for claiming horses that actually are worth more than the starting price.

A reliable rule of thumb urges handicappers to double the starting price. Main contenders should have won against open company at those levels or higher. If a starter handicap invites horses that have started for a $25,000 tag during the past six months, the most likely winner will have beaten $50,000 claiming horses during that period.

Another strong horse in any starter race is the horse who already has won a similar starter race, especially in the recent past. The trainers have managed to get the horses eligible. Even though these horses might be competing effectively at higher claiming levels, they hold a class edge at the starter level, and their trainers will not lose them. Trainers like that.

When Bobby Frankel was a notoriously successful claiming trainer in the 1970's, he was amazingly adept at gaining eligibility to starter races with claiming horses that should have been running at loftier levels. Frankel once maneuvered an 8-year-old gelding named Strong Award into Southern California's $5,000 starter series when the old-timer might have been beating $25,000 open company instead. Frankel won eight consecutive $5,000 starter handicaps with the gelding.

Starter races have drifted into the background of the claiming game. Nowadays the notion of a starter series at the various claiming levels no longer exists. Yet the basic instinct of horsemen to get better horses eligible under cheaper claiming conditions does persist.

Conditioned (restricted) claiming races bar horses who have won multiple races lifetime at today's claiming class, or they bar horses that have won within a specified time interval, most frequently the current year.

An efficient approach to conditioned claiming events, which can become a bore to handicap in depth, eliminates all horses that already have lost more than one restricted claiming race at today's level or lower. It makes little sense to exercise patience with these types.

At times, horses who have been consistent winners recently at lower open claiming levels will move into a conditioned claimer at a higher level and prevail, but the most reliable prospects in conditioned claiming races will be drop-downs from higher open claiming levels, notably drop-downs having early speed. Claiming horses that possess early speed tend to become the multiple winners, and these have been barred from this condition.

The drop-downs from higher open company grab the advantage at the first or second calls and they waltz to victory. Horses that have been running on or near the front end in open company at today's restricted claiming level can do the same. The handicapping is quick and effective.

Handicappers can invoke class considerations at times to cope with the most difficult races of all, the claiming races limited to 3-year-olds. Three-year-old claiming horses are consistently inconsistent. Most will not repeat good races and peak efforts, making the conventional handicapping a dubious enterprise. Form reversals are legion.

The remedy can be elegantly elementary. During the first six to nine months of the year particularly, play in the 3-year-old claiming races can be limited to allowance droppers. Among the 3-year-olds, the claiming and nonclaiming horses populate two different worlds. One group has talent, the other has none.

Horses that have displayed even a hint of talent—early speed, a midrace move, beat half the field, a finish within six lengths, a superior pace figure (especially a superior pace figure)—in an allowance race will be a major threat in a 3-year-old claiming race.

To wrap on a pleasantly optimistic note, when horses drop from allowance to 3-year-old claiming, the odds can be mysteriously generous. Take the odds.

SHUBACK
ON EUROPEAN RACING

by Alan Shuback

IN RETROSPECT IT SEEMS like a tale out of the misty annals of ancient folklore: horses from England, France, Venezuela, and Australia, with form at tracks such as Longchamp, La Rinconada, and Flemington. The names of their riders were equally exotic—Smirke, Bustamente, Chancellier—and, to top it all off, the races were run on grass and started not from a gate, but from behind a tape.

What was one to make of it, this brainchild of John Schapiro at Laurel Racecourse called the

Washington, D.C., International? It looked to most observers like a novelty act, part of a carnival that would pass through the nation's capital once a year to break up the monotony of a dirt-racing diet.

In 1952, Schapiro, keen to bring an international flavor to American racing, hit on a formula that would be repeated in years to come with ever greater success at Atlantic City, Belmont Park, and Arlington Park, and later in such far-flung locales as Tokyo, Hong Kong, and Dubai.

Schapiro was decades ahead of his time. His realization that horses could be transported in relative comfort and in short order via air revolutionized horse racing. In creating the Washington, D.C., International, Schapiro not only laid the foundation for the Arlington Million, the Breeders' Cup, the Japan Cup, and the Dubai World Cup, but also ushered in the era of international racing, which has since become the driving force in both racing and breeding.

So the next time you sit puzzling over the form of some Irish-bred son of a Kentucky-bred stallion formerly trained in France by an Englishman, making his first American start at Santa Anita for an expatriate Chilean after having been sent to Australia for the W.S. Cox Plate, you can pin the blame on John Schapiro, the father of modern international racing in the United States.

LITTLE WAS known about foreign racehorses when they first began arriving in the United States. Not only were details of their performances sketchy, but also there was a decided lack of understanding of what was going on in other countries, even in England and France, which have always exported the majority of the foreign horses that have run in America.

Progress toward an informed estimation of foreign form has been long and slow, at times painfully so. Only on rare occasions were bettors able to gauge the true worth of an import and bet, or lay off, with any intelligence.

Not long ago, most handicappers routinely dismissed imported horses. This was a dual function of the meager information available and a provincial attitude on the part of many bettors that foreign-raced horses were simply inferior to their American counterparts, even if they were Kentucky-breds.

In the dark myself as to which imports were capable of performing well in America, I learned an important lesson on the subject during my first trip to England. What I discovered there in 1983 has stood me in good stead ever since.

I had seen a 3-year-old colt named Tolomeo finish second in the Sussex Stakes, a Group 1 mile at Goodwood, a race in which he suffered a troubled trip.

Earlier, Tolomeo had finished ninth in an Epsom Derby run in boglike conditions that suited only the winner, Teenoso. What's more, most British observers felt that the Derby's mile and a half was a quarter-mile too far for Tolomeo.

He would have won the one-mile St. James's Palace Stakes but for missing the break. As it was, he finished a fast-closing head behind Horage. Next, in the Eclipse Stakes, at 1¼ miles, he was outgamed by Solford and Muscatite when finishing third, beaten by only a neck.

Clearly, this was a Group 1 performer who was crying out for a distance between one mile and 1¼ miles. Moreover, his form suggested an aptitude for firm ground, so when his name appeared in the entries for the ten-furlong Arlington Million, I took a long look at his chances.

Tolomeo (Ire)			B. c. 3							Life	9	1	5	1	$92,525	–	D.Fst	0 0 0 0	$0	–
Own: D'Alessio Carlo			Sire: Lypheor*GB (Lyphard)							1983	6	0	3	1	$85,915	–	Wet(295)	0 0 0 0	$0	–
			Dam: Almagest*Ire(Dike)							1982	3	1	2	0	$6,610	–	Turf(270)	9 1 5 1	$92,525	–
			Br: Corduff Stud (Ire)							AP ⓣ	0	0	0	0	$0	–	Dist ⓣ	1 0 0 1	$15,480	–
			Tr: Cumani Luca M (—) (—)																	

27Jly83♦Goodwood(GB)	fm 1 ⓣRH 1:37³ 3♦	Sussex Stakes-G1		22½	Piggott L	122	2.75	Noalcoholic133²½ Tolomeo122ʰᵈ Wassl122¼	11
		Stk 135000						Rated wide in mid-pack,late gain into 2nd.Lomond 7th	
2Jly83♦Sandown(GB)	gd 1¼ ⓣRH 2:06² 3♦	Eclipse Stakes-G1		3ⁿᵏ	Starkey G	120	4.50	Solford120ʰᵈ Muscatite120ʰᵈ Tolomeo120ⁿᵏ	9
		Stk 172000						Tracked leaders,dueled late,gamely.Stanerra 4th,Time Charter 6th	
14Jun83♦Ascot(GB)	gd 1 ⓣRH 1:40	St James's Palace Stakes-G1		2ʰᵈ	Starkey G	126	6.00	Horage126ʰᵈ Tolomeo126⁶ Dunbeath126ⁿᵏ	7
		Stk 57000						Outrun early,lacked room 2f out,strong bid 1f out,just missed	
1Jun83♦Epsom(GB)	hy 1½ ⓣLH 2:49	Epsom Derby-G1		9²¹½	Dettori G	126	14.00	Teenoso126³ Carlingford Castle126³ Shearwalk126ⁿᵒ	21
		Stk 348000						Mid-pack,close up 5f out,angled in 4f out,soon weakened	
30Apr83♦Newmarket(GB)	gd 1 ⓣStr 1:43⁴	2000 Guineas Stakes-G1		2²	Dettori G	126	18.00	Lomond126² Tolomeo126½ Muscatite126½	16
		Stk 155000						Rated in mid-pack,lacked room 1-1/2f out,finished fast.Diesis 8th	
12Apr83♦Newmarket(GB)	yl 1 ⓣStr 1:47¹	Craven Stakes-G3		42³¼	Dettori G	119	2.75	Muscatite119ⁿᵏ Spanish Place119¹ Guns Of Navarone119¹½	5
		Stk 23000						Rated at rear,bid 2f out,faded final furlong.Lyphard's Special5th	
10oct82♦Newmarket(GB)	gd 7f ⓣStr 1:28²	Westley Maiden Stakes		1³	Piggott L	126	*.80	Tolomeo126³ The Minster126⁶ Hesham126¹	28
		Maiden 8400						Mid-pack,progress 3f out,led 1-1/2f out,drew clear.Petong 8th	
16Sep82♦Yarmouth(GB)	gd 7f ⓣStr 1:26⁴	Shadwell Maiden Stakes		2½	Guest R	126	3.50	Lord Protector126½ Tolomeo126½ Full Rainbow126½	12
		Maiden 2700						Trailed,progress halfway,bid 1f out,second best	
24Aug82♦Yarmouth(GB)	yl 7f ⓣStr 1:30³	Fee Farm Maiden Stakes		2½	Guest R	126	10.00	Polished Silver126½ Tolomeo126⁷ Swaledale126¹	10
		Maiden 2700						Towards rear,progress halfway,2nd over 1f out,held by winner	

And when New York City OTB displayed a price of 45-1 (he eventually went off at 47.50-1), I knew I was on to something. No matter that he would have to beat the great John Henry, who had won the inaugural running two years earlier. The British bookies were offering 8-1, a price much closer to his real value.

I was duly rewarded when Pat Eddery brought Tolomeo up the rail to surprise Chris McCarron and John Henry. I had made an important handicapping discovery, one that would pay off handsomely again and again: Cultivating a true understanding of foreign form would be an invaluable tool in betting European imports, especially their first time in America.

Tolomeo's extraordinary Million price (he was 38-1 at Arlington) was made possible by the limited foreign information that was available to American bettors in those days. This lack of data made overlays on first-time foreign starters commonplace throughout the 1980's. Many bettors, confused by the names of strange horses, jockeys, and race-tracks, found it easier just to disregard European invaders.

But bettors could not bear the full brunt of the blame. The past-performance data available to them at the time offered little clue as to the ability of foreign horses.

That problem was rectified in 1991, when *The Racing Times* debuted and offered the first expanded past-performances for foreign horses, giving each race two lines and featuring extensive trip notes. *The Racing Times* folded the next year and *Daily Racing Form* eventually adopted the enhanced foreign-race PP's in 1993.

By that time, foreign invaders had been winning so frequently there was no longer much value to be found in backing them blindly.

The American attitude toward foreign horses had changed from one of virtual dismissal to one of mindless adoration. European horses with little chance were being bet simply because they were European. Not much attention was paid to the quality of their form, or to the form of South American imports.

Given the atmosphere, it became even more essential to be selective, to focus on the contenders and eliminate the pretenders.

I would not have had a clue as to the potential of Tolomeo, or of his chances in the Arlington Million, unless I possessed a grasp of the quality of the races he had been running in, as well as the quality of the horses he had been running against. That kind of comprehension can only be gained through an understanding of two things: first, how racing in every country is set up—its schedule, its program of maidens, conditions races, handicaps, and stakes events; and second, more importantly, the true significance of foreign form, not as it relates to American form, but in and of itself.

That is something that is ever evolving and can only be comprehended fully by following racing in foreign countries on an almost daily basis. Yet it is the key to interpreting foreign form.

Most of the rest of this chapter is devoted to an analysis of the logistical setup in each of the world's major racing nations. The balance will offer a comparison of races at different levels throughout the world, with examples of particular foreign horses that have been successful in America. Once you understand the structure and context of European racing, you will be much more astute at evaluating the form of foreign-raced horses when they appear in the entries here.

TRAINING IN BRITAIN

Unlike North American Thoroughbreds, which are normally quartered and trained at the track where they do most of their racing, horses in Britain are trained at private "yards" throughout the country.

The two major training centers are at Newmarket, the headquarters of British racing, which also includes two racecourses, and at Lambourn, not far from Newbury Racecourse. Most of the best horses are trained at Newmarket, about 70 miles northeast of London; Lambourn, about 60 miles west of London, is also strong, but not quite as influential as Newmarket. This system means that horses travel to the races almost every time they run. On most occasions, the majority of British horses would be considered shippers by American standards. The same is true of almost all horses in Europe.

TRAINING IN FRANCE

Chantilly, the headquarters of French racing, is as idyllic a training center as can be found anywhere in the world. About 40 miles north of Paris, the training base at Chantilly is just a short ride from the elegant racecourse there, and is also convenient to the three Parisian tracks at Longchamp, Saint-Cloud, and Maisons-Laffitte.

There is a major training center at Maisons-Laffitte as well, but the bulk of the horses there are jumpers who do most of their racing at Auteuil in Paris and at nearby Enghien, north of Paris.

As much as 90 percent of the best racing in France is conducted on the Paris circuit (Longchamp, Chantilly, Saint-Cloud, Maisons-Laffitte, and Deauville).

Horses that run on the Parisian circuit, where there is never more than one meeting per day and rarely more than five meetings per week, cannot dodge the competition. No matter its age or sex, or the distance or class of the race in which it runs, a Parisian horse must meet at least some of the better horses in its division every time it competes.

For this reason, a Parisian horse will have more condition under its belt after three or four races than almost any horse in the world. Even lightly raced Parisian horses arrive in America ready to do battle.

TRAINING IN IRELAND

The Curragh, which means "the course" in ancient Celtic, is the headquarters of Irish racing. Its racetrack, 30 miles west of Dublin, is the home of all the Irish classics.

The setup of racing in Ireland is similar to that in Britain. Most of the best training yards are at The Curragh. The Irish, however, have always preferred jump racing, and while Irish flat racing at the top end is very good indeed, there is little depth to the game. A few trainers (Aidan O'Brien, Dermot Weld, Jim Bolger, and John Oxx) and owners (John Magnier, Michael Tabor, and the Aga Khan) dominate flat racing on the Emerald Isle.

Most of the Irish horses imported to America come from the lesser stables, or are simply rejects from the big yards. With a few notable exceptions, Irish imports tend to struggle in America.

TYPES OF EUROPEAN RACES

Throughout Europe, there is little variation in the way racing is structured in terms of class levels and competition, and most countries base their system on one that has been in place in Britain since the late 18th century.

One of the longest-lasting achievements of the British Empire was the spread of horse racing around the world. The British invented the Thoroughbred breed and laid down the rules of racing. They dominated the sport from its inception in the 1600's until well into the 20th century.

With British-based Mideast potentates like the Maktoum family of Dubai having injected massive amounts of money into racing, the game in Britain has been returned to a position of worldwide prominence in spite of the low levels of prize money.

And that brings us to the first lesson to be learned when interpreting foreign form: You cannot necessarily gauge the importance of a race by comparing its prize money to that of an American race. What matters is the inherent quality, and prize money can be misleading.

These are the types of races run in Europe: maiden races, claiming races, conditions races, handicaps, listed races, and group races. There are also subdivisions within each race type. In addition, a sprinkling of races are restricted to apprentice riders, amateur riders, and amateur female riders.

Maiden Races

Most open maiden races in Britain are worth between $7,000 and $14,000. Only a handful have a value greater than $20,000, and none goes higher than $26,000. The better maiden races are run at Newmarket, Ascot, and Newbury, as well as at York's August meeting and Goodwood's big meeting in late July/early August, but a good maiden may turn up at almost any track save the low-end establishments such as Bath, Carlisle, Catterick, and Folkstone, and the Scottish tracks at Hamilton and Musselburgh (Edinburgh).

In France, up to 90 percent of the best racing takes place on the Parisian circuit (Longchamp, Chantilly, Saint-Cloud, Maisons-Laffitte, and Deauville). At those tracks, the only true maiden races are restricted to first-time starters (designated in *Daily Racing Form* past performances as "MFT"—maiden first-timers).

There are other "virtual" maiden races that are written for horses that have never won a race, claiming races excepted, but it is extremely rare to see the winner of a claimer run in such an event.

In France, maidens, and even first-time starters, are much more likely to run in genuine allowance races. This custom has led to changes in the condition books at U.S. tracks where French imports are most likely to turn up in the entries.

For example, Southern California, New York, Kentucky, and Florida all now write a number of allowance races with conditions like the following: "have not won either $3,000 once other than maiden, claiming, or starter, or which have never won two races." The last condition is a concession to the numerous French imports that have achieved their first career victories in allowance races.

When handicapping such races, it is wise to distinguish between a French import whose first career win occurred in a true maiden race, whether it was an event for Parisian debutants or regular maidens in the provinces, and the probably superior runner who notched his first victory in an allowance race.

An even more important handicapping tool is to take note of horses that win first time out, especially on the Parisian circuit or at the best British and Irish tracks. That reveals an inherent talent. If such a horse arrives in America still lightly raced, its debut score should bear weight in your calculations.

In Britain there is another type of maiden race, called an auction maiden. This is a race restricted to horses that were sold at auction as yearlings or 2-year-olds and is less valuable than an open maiden event.

A subcategory of this sort of event is the median auction maiden race. This is restricted to horses that were sold at auction in a particular price range, and is even less valuable than an auction maiden.

In Ireland, maiden races are dominated by the big stables run by O'Brien, Weld, Bolger, and Oxx. Generally speaking there is a big class difference between horses trained by one of those four and most of the rest of Ireland's trainers. Horses from the less prestigious

Irish yards usually have to go to lesser tracks such as Roscommon, Listowel, or Tipperary to find a maiden victory. Afterward, they rarely amount to much on the flat.

(Something to remember is that all races in Britain are stakes races in the generic sense—that is, owners must put up an entry fee for every horse in every race they enter. This is the reason maiden races are called maiden stakes. The same rule applies to conditions races, claiming races, listed races, and group races, but only group races and listed races qualify as what we call stakes races in North America.)

Claiming Races

There are relatively few claiming events in Europe. Most horses go directly from maidens into handicaps, conditions races, or listed or group races.

Horses that have shown little ability in maidens sometimes wind up in claimers, where they may be joined by previously unraced horses that have failed to show much talent in the morning. The top claiming price of British claimers never exceeds $35,000, and even these are inferior to the weakest handicap races.

Some French claimers offer prices as high as $50,000, and in any given French claimer, the range of available prices is usually greater than in America or even Britain.

There are no claiming races run in Ireland.

The big difference between claimers in Europe and America is the manner in which horses are claimed. In Europe, the claim is not put in until after the race. Moreover, the claiming price for which a horse is entered is the minimum for which he may be claimed. If a prospective owner really wants a chance of getting the horse for which he is entering a claim, he must usually bid at least a few thousand pounds or francs higher than the claiming price to be sure of defeating other bidders.

Another form of British claiming race is a selling race. This is an event in which all runners are eligible to be claimed except the winner, who is auctioned off after the race. If no bids are taken on the winner, he remains with his current owner.

Horses that have run in claiming or selling races rarely appear in America. If they do, it is only because they have later improved dramatically. In Britain, this improvement as often as not has been made after a horse has been switched to all-weather (dirt) racing.

Conditions Races

There are generally five types of conditions races run in Britain. In order of importance these are: open conditions stakes, novice stakes, classified stakes, limited stakes, and auction stakes.

There are far fewer conditions races in Britain, or anywhere else in Europe, than there are allowance races in America. The concept of a horse "going through his conditions" is unknown in Europe, where allowance races are used as springboards between maiden and listed or group races, as get-well races for a group-race performer that has gone off form, or for a horse of listed- or group-race potential returning from a layoff.

Open conditions stakes in Britain are more valuable than maidens, but not nearly as rich as similar events in America. There are some conditions races worth as much as $30,000, but most fall in the $12,000 to $20,000 range.

Conditions races are usually written with weight penalties incurred by horses that have won a certain type of race since a certain date.

As with maiden events, most of the best conditions races are run at Ascot, Newmarket, Goodwood, Newbury, or York, but almost every track in the country runs a number of competitive races at this level.

Novice stakes in Britain are for horses aged either 2 or 3 who have not won more than two races, generally of the low-end conditions-race type.

Classified stakes are for horses that are rated within a certain range by the Jockey Club handicapper. Weights are determined by the number of victories a horse has scored at a certain level within a certain time frame.

Limited stakes are restricted to horses whose handicap rating does not exceed the rating specified in the conditions of the race. Auction stakes are similar to auction maidens except that they are usually written for winners only.

From time to time a trainer will run a horse in an open conditions race first time out if that horse has been working well in the morning. One reason for this ploy is the need to discover a horse's proper level as quickly as possible, preferably before the handicapper can load him up with weight.

In France, conditions races are either restricted or open. Restricted races are limited to horses that have been born or bred in France. Such races almost always include horses that have been bred in foreign countries but foaled in France.

On the Parisian circuit, where a majority of the French imports to America come from, the best allowances are worth 184,000 francs, which was worth just $25,000 in spring 2001.

As recently as October 1998, a 184,000-franc race would have been worth $33,900. As a general rule it is wise to be somewhat aware of European rates of exchange vis-a-vis the dollar, so that you can gauge the relative values of races.

IN AUGUST 2001, THESE EXCHANGE RATES WERE:

Britain: 1 pound = $1.421

Ireland: 1 pound = $1.139

France: 1 franc = $ .137

Germany: 1 mark = $ .459
Italy: 1 lira = $ .00046

Most restricted Parisian allowances are worth 160,000 francs. Low-end allowances in Paris, written for horses that have not won a race at a certain very low level since a certain date, are worth 140,000 francs.

Those open 184,000-franc allowance races are written with many conditions. The best are for horses that have never won a Group 1 nor been placed in a Group 2 since a certain date. Others might be for horses that have never won a listed race, nor been placed in a certain type of allowance since a certain date.

Allowance racing on the Parisian circuit is quite competitive at the top level. Only familiarity with the horses that are running at this level, including which horses have graduated from this level to go on to listed- or group-race success, will enable one to validly interpret their form.

Irish allowance races usually feature horses decidedly inferior to those that have graduated from maidens directly into listed-race company. Their value tends to range between $9,000 and $15,000, but they are not as good as their British or French counterparts.

Handicaps

In all European countries, virtually every horse is rated by the national Jockey Club handicapper weekly. Every Monday morning, an envelope appears in the mailbox of every trainer with that week's ratings. Those ratings determine what weight every horse entered in a handicap will carry.

Most European handicaps are restricted to horses falling within a given rating group. Every country uses a different numbering system for rating horses, but all are based on the British system.

In Britain, the best handicaps after open handicaps are for horses rated 0 to 110. Horses rated higher than 110 are usually listed- or group-race types and are ineligible for such races.

If a horse in a 0-110 handicap is rated 110, it will be assigned top weight of 140 pounds, and horses rated lower would be allowed one pound less for each point below 110. A horse rated 105 would carry 135 pounds, a horse rated 100 would carry 130 pounds, etc.

The same method, usually employing a different numbering system, is used throughout Europe, South America, Africa, Australia, New Zealand, and Asia. The United States and Canada are two of the few racing nations in the world that do not employ such a system, and that is one reason why weights for handicaps at the graded-race level in North America are so frequently controversial.

The top handicaps in Britain, such as the Royal Hunt Cup, the Wokingham, the Stewards' Cup, the Ebor, and the Cambridgeshire, can be worth up to $150,000, but they are only rarely as good as a listed race.

British handicaps, however, can generally be judged by their purses. The most valuable are just below listed-race quality. Those in the middle range ($50,000 to $75,000) are roughly equivalent to money allowances. Handicaps in the $25,000 to $50,000 range can be equated to anything from a $50,000 claiming race to an allowance for nonwinners of two.

Another type of handicap run in Britain is called a rated handicap. This type of race is limited to horses within a certain rating range—for example, 0-100—but the high weight is never more than 133 pounds and the bottom weight never less than 119 pounds, so that the weights are more compressed than in regular handicaps.

Nursery handicaps are races restricted to 2-year-olds.

In France, the best handicaps in Paris are "tierce" races. These are events on which huge amounts of money are wagered at offtrack betting shops throughout the country as a form of national lottery. Serious horseplayers as well as the general public try to predict which horses will finish in the first three (*tierce*), the first four (*quarte*), or the first five (*quinte*).

These events are usually worth about $45,000 but, like the best British handicaps, are only rarely as good as listed races. There are also lesser handicaps that can be worth as little as $16,000.

In Ireland, the system of handicaps is quite similar to that in Britain. The best of these are referred to as premier handicaps.

Relative Weights

No less an authority than Steve Cauthen once said, "Weight is relative." By that, he meant that horses carrying 130 pounds each in a race have the same chance against each other as if they were carrying 114 pounds each.

Again and again, horseplayers in the United States, when confronted with a runner that has been carrying a high weight in his last few starts in a foreign country (where the scale of weights is invariably higher), interpret a drop in weight in the horse's U.S. debut as weight off.

Not true. If a horse who carried 130 pounds in a European race was only giving a pound or two to his rivals, then he will be in the same boat in America if, when carrying 118 pounds, he is giving away the same one or two pounds.

Listed Races

Better than the best handicaps but still below the Group 1's, 2's, and 3's are listed races, the equivalent of the best ungraded stakes in North America.

The European Pattern Race Committee continuously reviews the three most recent runnings of all listed races, taking note of improvements or deteriorations in quality, so their status can be assumed with confidence. As is the case with conditions races, a good listed race can turn up at any British track, but the majority of the 133 listed contests run in Britain take place at the major venues. Their value varies, but most fall in the $30,000 to $45,000 range.

In France, two-thirds of the 121 listed races are run on the Parisian circuit. These are the best listed events in that country and are usually worth $35,000.

The best British and French listed races are equal or superior to many German or Italian Group 2's. Examples are the Winter Derby, the Predominate Stakes, the Glasgow Stakes, the European Free Handicap, the Oak Tree Stakes, the Acomb Stakes, the Sirenia Stakes, the Arc Trial, and the Dubai Duty Free Cup in Britain, and the Prix Djebel, Prix Imprudence, Prix La Fleche, Grand Handicap de Deauville, Prix de l'Avre, Prix de Reux, Prix du Cercle, Prix Ridgway, Criterium du EBF, Coupe du EBF, Prix de Lieurey, Grand Prix de Compiegne, Prix de Boulogne, Prix de Liancourt, Prix Charles Laffitte, and Prix Coronation in France.

Ireland runs 42 listed races: 18 at Leopardstown, 13 at The Curragh, three at Cork, two each at Gowran Park and Galway, and one each at Fairyhouse, Tralee, Naas, and Down Royal. Most are worth between $28,000 and $35,000.

Germany has 67 listed events on its schedule. They are spread rather democratically throughout the better German tracks at Baden-Baden, Hamburg, Dusseldorf, and Cologne, with Dortmund, Munich, Mulheim, and Hoppegarten, the track in Berlin that has been rehabilitated since German reunification, getting their share as well. A typical race is worth $20,000, but a few at major meetings like Baden-Baden range up to $45,000.

All of the best of Italy's listed races are divided between San Siro in Milan (22) and the Capannelle in Rome (17), with Pisa getting three (two in the winter and one in late autumn) and Turin, Naples, Florence, and Varese one each. Italian listed races range from $37,000 to $70,000. Despite these high purses, they are rarely as good as listed events in Britain, France, or Ireland.

While the better listed events in any country are run at the major tracks, which of them are good, bad, or indifferent in any given year ultimately becomes a matter of familiarizing oneself with racing in that country.

Group Races

A Group 1 race is generally a race of international status. Some, such as the classics (Derbies, Oaks, and Guineas), have greater historic importance for breeders.

Others, such as the King George VI and Queen Elizabeth Diamond Stakes, the Champion Stakes, the Irish Champion Stakes, the Queen Elizabeth II Stakes, the Grand Prix de Saint-Cloud, or the Prix de l'Arc de Triomphe, frequently supersede the classics in importance.

Here are the 10-year ratings (1991-2000) of all European Group 1 races, compiled by the International Classification Committee, the same organization that annually rates the leading European and North American horses.

BRITAIN

King George VI & Queen Elizabeth Diamond Stks	$1\frac{1}{2}$m	3+	131
* Epsom Derby	$1\frac{1}{2}$m	3yo	128
Queen Elizabeth II Stakes	1m	3+	127
Juddmonte International Stakes	$1\frac{5}{16}$m	3+	126
Eclipse Stakes	$1\frac{1}{4}$m	3+	126
St. James's Palace Stakes	1m	3yo	126
Coronation Cup	$1\frac{1}{2}$m	4+	125
Champion Stakes	$1\frac{1}{4}$m	3+	125
* 2000 Guineas Stakes	1m	3yo	125
Sussex Stakes	1m	3+	124
July Cup	6f	3+	123
Dewhurst Stakes	7f	2yo	122
* St. Leger Stakes	a $1\frac{13}{16}$m	3yo	122
Lockinge Stakes	1m	4+	121
Haydock Park Sprint Cup	6f	3+	121
* Epsom Oaks	$1\frac{1}{2}$m	3yo f	121
* 1000 Guineas Stakes	1m	3yo f	120
Nunthorpe Stakes	5f	2+	120
Ascot Gold Cup	$2\frac{1}{2}$m	4+	119
Middle Park Stakes	6f	2yo	119
Coronation Stakes	1m	3yo f	119
Yorkshire Oaks	$1\frac{1}{2}$m	3+ f&m	119
Racing Post Trophy	1m	2yo	119
Nassau Stakes	$1\frac{1}{4}$m	3+ f&m	117
Cheveley Park Stakes	6f	2yo f	115
Fillies Mile	1m	2yo f	113
		AVERAGE	(122.0)

FRANCE

Prix de l'Arc de Triomphe	$1\frac{1}{2}$m	3+	131
Grand Prix de Saint-Cloud	$1\frac{1}{2}$m	3+	127
* Prix du Jockey-Club			
(French Derby)	$1\frac{1}{2}$m	3yo	126
Prix du Moulin de Longchamp	1m	3+	125
Prix d'Ispahan	$1\frac{1}{8}$m	3+	123
Prix Jacques le Marois	1m	3+	123
Prix Ganay	$1\frac{5}{16}$m	4+	122
Prix de la Salamandre	7f	2yo	122
Grand Prix de Paris	$1\frac{1}{4}$m	3yo	121
* Poule d'Essai des Poulains			
(French 2000 Guineas)	1m	3yo c	121
Prix de l'Abbaye de Longchamp	5f	2+	121
Grand Criterium	1m	2yo c	120
Prix Morny	6f	2yo	120
Prix Lupin	$1\frac{1}{4}$m	3yo	119
Prix de la Foret	7f	3+	119
* Prix de Diane			
(French Oaks)	$1\frac{5}{16}$m	3yo f	119
Prix Vermeille	$1\frac{1}{2}$m	3yo f	119
Prix Jean Prat	$1\frac{1}{8}$m	3yo	118
* Poule d'Essai des Pouliches			
(French 1000 Guineas)	1m	3yo f	116
Prix Saint-Alary	$1\frac{1}{4}$m	3yo f	116
Prix Royal-Oak	$1\frac{15}{16}$m	3+	115
Criterium de Saint-Cloud	$1\frac{1}{4}$m	2yo	114
Prix Marcel Boussac	1m	2yo f	113
Prix du Cadran	$2\frac{1}{2}$m	4+	113
		AVERAGE	(120.1)

IRELAND

* Irish Derby	$1\frac{1}{2}$m	3yo	129
Irish Champion Stakes	$1\frac{1}{4}$m	3+	127
* Irish 2000 Guineas	1m	3yo	123
Irish St. Leger	$1\frac{3}{4}$m	3+	120
* Irish Oaks	$1\frac{1}{2}$m	3yo f	119

Tattersalls Gold Cup	1⁵⁄₁₆m	4+	119
*Irish 1000 Guineas	1m	3yo f	118
Heinz 57 Phoenix Stakes	6f	2yo	117
National Stakes	+7f	2yo	113
Moyglare Stud Stakes	1m	2yo f	113
		AVERAGE	(119.8)

+Previously run at 1 mile

GERMANY

Grosser Preis von Baden	1½m	3+	124
Bayerisches Zuchtrennen	1¼m	3+	120
Deutschland-Preis	1½m	3+	120
Europa-Preis	1½m	3+	120
*Deutsches Derby	1½m	3yo	118
Gelsenkirchen-Pokal	1½m	3+	118
		AVERAGE	(120.0)

ITALY

Gran Premio di Milano	1½m	3+	121
Gran Premio del Jockey Club	1½m	3+	119
Premio Roma	1¼m	3+	118
Gran Premio Presidente della Repubblica	1¼m	4+	118
Premio Vittorio di Capua	1m	3+	116
*Derby Italiano	1½m	3yo	115
*Oaks d'Italia	1³⁄₈m	3yo f	111
Gran Criterium	1m	2yo	111
		AVERAGE	(116.1)

*Classic races

Some races have been improving over the last decade, while others have been in decline. The most apparent shift in quality seems to be the decline of 3-year-old racing and the improvement of races for older horses. The Arc, the Grand Prix de Saint-Cloud, the Juddmonte International, the Eclipse Stakes, and the Irish Champion Stakes have had their ratings go up during the last five years, while the ratings of the Epsom Derby, the 2000 Guineas, the French Oaks, the French 1000 Guineas, the Irish Derby, and the Irish 1000 Guineas have all declined.

Group 2 races are generally contests of national importance that frequently serve as preps for Group 1 events, while Group 3 races rank a bit below those.

Over the years, I have found that it pays to be wary of European horses coming to the United States to begin a second phase of their careers if they have already been successful at the Group 1 level. I believe that this is because horses who have reached a peak of development under a training and racing regimen that is so different from that employed in North America may well dislike, or even resent, a change of scene. For example, User Friendly, King's Theatre, Quest For Fame, Jet Ski Lady, Sunshack, Dr Fong, Shake the Yoke, Gold Splash, Second Set, Saratoga Springs, Nicer, Sir Harry Lewis, Le Triton, Fragrant Mix, Jolypha, A Magicman, and Poliglote were all Group 1 winners in Europe during the last 10 years who failed to recapture their best form in America. In fact, most of these horses failed to win so much as a Group 3 after being transplanted to this side of the Atlantic.

The exceptions are far fewer: Dark Moondancer, Cudas, and Ryafan, who won a Group 1 in France at 2 but only a Group 2 in England at 3 before running off three straight Grade 1 victories in America.

This small group also includes Blushing John, who duplicated and even surpassed his winning French 2000 Guineas form after being switched to dirt in America, where he won the Santa Anita Handicap.

It should also be noted that, with the exception of Ryafan, the group of successful Group 1 imports all came from France, from where it seems we receive a more adaptable type of racehorse than we do from England or Ireland, although there are plenty of ex-French Group 1 winners who have failed in America.

This theory also applies to horses that have reached their peaks at the Group 2 or Group 3 level. Or at any level, for that matter.

One way to distinguish such horses is to look at their Timeform ratings. If those numbers do not show a general pattern of improvement, that horse may have already peaked. Also, beware of horses that have more than 10 or 12 starts in Europe when they arrive in the U.S. Lightly raced horses tend to improve, while horses that have been running in the same division for a season or more without distinguishing themselves may not have any more improvement in them.

Sometimes a horse reaches a peak of development after having won a maiden race. Such horses will never win stakes races, no matter what country or stable they come from.

One useful handicapping tool is being able to recognize when a horse has failed to "train on." Sometimes you will see a European horse who was a group or listed winner at 2, but who could not even break into the top three in any kind of a race at 3.

Such horses are likely to be offered at a bargain price for any prospective new

American owner, but they are no bargain once they reach these shores. Invariably, they fail to recapture their previous form in America just as surely as they had failed to do so in the old country.

HANDICAPPING TIPS

We have already discussed why it is that ex-French horses, especially those formerly trained on the Parisian circuit, tend to do somewhat better in America than imports from other countries.

Here are some other tips to use when calculating the chances of newcomers to these shores.

Timeform Ratings

In July 1999, *Daily Racing Form* introduced a valuable new feature to its foreign past performances: Timeform ratings.

Founded in 1947 by the legendary British handicapper and bettor Phil Bull, Timeform is the most widely respected ratings service in Europe. Their ratings are considered the most accurate of all by British bettors, better for wagering purposes than the official ratings produced by the various European Jockey Clubs or the year-end ratings of the International Classifications Committee.

The Timeform rating is a guide to the merit of a horse "arrived at by careful examination of its running against other horses using a scale of weight for distance beaten which ranges around 3 lbs. per length at five furlongs to 2 lbs. per length at a mile to 1 lb. per length at two miles."

The very best horses are rated between 130 and 145, the poorest at 20. Dubai Millennium's top mark before his retirement was 142. Montjeu was at 137 after his win in the King George VI and Queen Elizabeth Diamond Stakes on July 30, 2000.

A good winner of a listed race would earn a Timeform rating of about 110. However, when incorporating Timeform ratings into your handicapping process, do not make the mistake of equating them with Beyer Speed Figures. Timeform ratings are figured on a different scale and use different criteria from Beyer figures. They are best used in comparing one European horse with another.

The State of The Ground

Most American owners attempting to reap the rewards of foreign imports will be looking for horses that have run well on good or good-to-firm ground. A horse whose best foreign form has been on soft ground is not a good American bet until he has proven he can handle a faster surface, whether that surface turns out to be turf or dirt.

"Soft" in Europe is considerably softer than the same course condition in North America, just as "good" is considerably softer in Europe than it is here. So one factor to consider with ex-foreigners is to look for horses who tend to run better on faster ground.

Some horses, however, can run well on both firm and "heavy" ground, but have difficulty on soft or yielding turf. This is because horses that do well in heavy going go right through the mud to the base of the track, which is firm. This is not a hard-and-fast rule, but it is open to consideration.

It is also worth noting that horses that do well on heavy ground (a condition so foreign to America that if it were to appear in this country, all turf races at that track would be off the grass for two weeks) tend to have a big, flat foot, similar to the classic "dirt foot." All in all, it is advisable to take a long look at imports with good heavy-ground form when and if they are tried on dirt.

Undulating, Straight, and Turning Courses

There are very few perfectly level racecourses in Europe. In Britain one can name York, Chester, Haydock, Kempton, Redcar, Southwell (all-weather), and Wolverhampton (all-weather).

In France, the major tracks tend to be a bit less hilly or undulating than British tracks. Maisons-Laffitte, in particular, is almost perfectly level, with turns as sharp as those to be found on typical seven-furlong American turf tracks.

Deauville and its sister track at nearby Clairefontaine are also level, but both have very wide turns, while the first half of the straight mile at Deauville is slightly undulating.

One can make too much of undulations and right-handed or straight courses. If an American-trained horse were to attempt to run at a hilly course such as Epsom or Sandown, or an undulating track such as Newmarket (both the Rowley Mile and the July Course), he would likely run into problems with the rising or falling ground.

But horses who have run well on undulating or hilly European tracks should not have any trouble with level American tracks. By the same token, even if an import has won all of his races on right-handed tracks, the chances are very good he will adapt to left-handed turns. Generally, horses that can turn one way are athletic types who can handle any kind of turn.

Caution, however, might be in order concerning younger imports who have raced exclusively on straight courses, although even these are likely to have had some experience working out on turning courses.

The Start

European newcomers are rarely good gate horses. The early pace of European races, particularly in France and Ireland, can be painfully slow. Even on ground labeled good to firm in France, the first quarter of one-mile races is likely to be run in nothing faster than 28 seconds, so one can imagine how slow these horses are leaving the gate.

Their inability to break alertly should make one think twice about backing any European import first time out at distances of a mile or less, although classy imports can overcome a slow start at any but sprint distances.

Horses that have failed to run well consistently in Europe might be best avoided between six furlongs and a mile until they can show some life at the start.

Time

The old handicapping saw that time only counts in prison still holds true in Europe. Again and again, we see European imports who win races in times six or seven seconds slower than their American equivalents breeze to victory in this country.

However, there are a few points to keep in mind concerning European times. For one thing, all European races are timed from the instant the gate opens. That is, a race at one mile will start and be timed from the mile pole, whereas in America, the timer does not start until horses have sped between 20 and 50 yards after the break.

Another factor is the undulating nature of most European tracks. It takes longer to climb a hill than it does to travel the same distance on level ground, and while horses do pick up speed going downhill, they do not travel these descents at a breakneck pace. Balance must be kept on horses on such courses, especially where the track, as it is at Epsom, can be unbanked on the turn, or banked through a downhill stretch. All of this helps prevent a horse from reaching optimum speed at many points during a race.

And then there is the ground. It is simply impossible to run a quarter-mile in 24 seconds or less on soft or heavy ground. Only a familiarity with the racecourse in question will enable you to interpret times properly.

The Second-Race-Off-the-Plane Theory

One of the most misinformed theories concerning European imports ever devised by American handicappers holds that European shippers perform poorly in their second American starts.

This has a great deal more to do with a horse's new American trainer than it does with any abstract "bounce" theory. Trainers who understand the nature of foreign racing are better able to bring a horse along properly after its arrival here.

A horse who makes his first American start within two weeks of his importation is running largely on the merits of his former trainer, so it is not at all unusual to see him close with a big rush. This is a result of the European style of training where all horses, even front-runners (off those excruciatingly slow paces) are taught to finish strongly.

In America, we ask horses to reach maximum speed within 100 yards after the break. To put it simply, American races are run front to back, while European races are run back to front. If a European import finds itself under the care of a trainer who does not understand this difference and is suddenly thrust into a typical speed-oriented American training regimen, that horse is very likely to back up shortly after arriving here.

There is also the European method of "covering up" a horse, which an astute American trainer will take into account. This is a tactic whereby horses are tucked in behind other horses in work and in races, and taught to accelerate when they are shown daylight—that is, when they are uncovered.

Ex-Europeans that are not covered up early in a race tend to resent being rated when shown daylight and so appear to be rank. Their new trainers and jockeys should be aware of such horses if they expect early success with European imports.

Moreover, if an American trainer does not take into account the fact that European horses spend a good deal more time per day out of their stalls, the hothouse style of American horse housing can take its toll.

All this is why the new trainer of any foreign horse is a rather important factor to consider in handicapping.

Some trainers have a knack with European imports, and the track record to go with it. They include Bobby Frankel, Neil Drysdale, Julio Canani, Christophe Clement, Darrell Vienna, Wally Dollase, Ron McAnally, Bill Mott, Jenine Sahadi, Dick Mandella, and Michael Dickinson.

McAnally and Mandella are also adept with South American imports, while Kiaran McLaughlin does well with his ex-European-by-way-of-Dubai runners. This list is by no means all-inclusive. But in the long run it will pay to stay in touch with the foreigners these trainers receive. In all cases they have a network of knowledgeable bloodstock agents and deep-pocketed owners who make it their business to stay on top of the import game.

Rating the Racecourses

This personal rating of Europe's racecourses was devised after eighteen years of travel and study of European form.

BRITAIN

A	B	C	D
Ascot	Ayr	Beverly	Bath
Goodwood	Haydock	*Chester	Brighton
Newbury	Kempton	Leicester	Carlisle
Newmarket	Lingfield	Nottingham	Catterick
Sandown	Newcastle	Pontefract	Chepstow
York		Redcar	Folkestone
Epsom		Ripon	Hamilton
Doncaster		Salisbury	Musselburgh
		Thirsk	Southwell
		Warwick	Wolverhampton
		Windsor	
		Yarmouth	

*Chester is a Class A track at its three-day classic prep meeting in early May.

FRANCE

A	B	C	D
Longchamp	Bordeaux-Le Bouscat	Craon	The rest
Chantilly	Bordeaux-La Teste	Fontainebleau	
Deauville	Cagnes-sur-Mer	Le Croise-Laroche	
Saint-Cloud	Clairefontaine	Le Lion d'Angers	
Maisons-Laffitte	Compiegne	Nantes	
	Lyon-Parilly		
	Marseille-Borely		
	Toulouse		
	Vichy		

IRELAND

A	B	C	D
The Curragh	Cork	Galway	The rest
Leopardstown		Gowran Park	
		Naas	
		Navan	
		Tipperary	

GERMANY

A	B	C	D
Baden-Baden	Dortmund	Hannover	The rest
Cologne	Frankfurt	Krefeld	
Dusseldorf	Hoppegarten (Berlin)	Bremen	
Hamburg	Mulheim		
Munich	Gelsenkirchen-Horst		

ITALY

A	B	C	D
La Capannelle (Rome)	None	Naples	The rest
San Siro (Milan)		Pisa	
		Turin	
		Varese	

Rating the Races

Not all Group 1 races are created equal. The best races in Britain, France, and Ireland are better than the best in Germany and Italy, and so it goes through each level of group and listed events.

Races in Scandinavia and Spain rate a good deal lower. The best races there are only as good as an Irish listed race. Racing in Austria, Switzerland, Belgium, and the Czech Republic is another full step down the class line.

A	B	C	D	E
British G1	British G2	British G3	British Listed	Irish Listed
French G1	French G2	French G3	French Listed	German Listed
Irish G1	Irish G2	Irish G3	German G3	Italian Listed
	German G1	German G2	Italian G3	
	Italian G1	Italian G2		

There are, however, many notable exceptions in this listing. The Bayerisches Zuchtrennen, which has served as a prep for Dear Doctor's victory in the Arlington Million as well as Timarida's triumph in the Beverly D, is a German Group 1 that truly deserves its ranking, as does the Grosser Preis von Baden. In Italy, the same is true of the Group 1 Premio Roma and the Grand Premio di Milano.

All-Weather Racing

Until 1986, all races in Britain were run on turf. The advent of all-weather racing on a Fibresand track at Lingfield Park signaled a minirevolution in the European sport.

All-weather racing, a charming if unapt euphemism for dirt racing, has never really caught on in Britain. All-weather courses have since been built at Southwell and Wolverhampton in England, but the racing at those three tracks is primarily low-end stuff.

At first, British all-weather tracks were used only in the wintertime, in part as protection from washed-out jump-race meetings. Since the early 1990's, dirt racing has been conducted throughout the year in Britain, as opposed to the turf flat-racing season, which runs from late March to early November.

The quality of British all-weather racing has improved slightly with two listed races, the Winter Derby and the Churchill Stakes (formerly the Wulfrun Stakes) at Lingfield.

But there is hidden gold in them thar all-weather races.

Dirt racing in England has produced American graded-race winners such as Running Stag, River Keen, Hal's Pal, Skimming, Supreme Sound, and Golden Klair, so it is clear that a sharp-eyed horseman—or horseplayer—unencumbered by the jaundiced British eye that disparages all all-weather racing, can find value in the English dirt.

In February 2000, Cagnes-sur-Mer, the Cote d'Azur's wintertime start-up to the French flat-racing season, introduced the first all-weather track in France. The dirt track there is referred to as the *piste du sable*, or "sand course," but it is made up of the same Fibresand composition as the all-weather tracks in England.

Almost immediately, Cagnes-sur-Mer produced a budding dirt star, Speed Jaro, who won a pair of competitive allowance races that winter. After that he was purchased by Blue Field USA Inc. and sent to importmeister Bobby Frankel, for whom he finished second to Gran Premio Carlos Pellegrini winner Asidero in his American debut on turf.

All-weather racing is a largely untapped resource from an American point of view. The ability to single out the horses with true talent at Lingfield, Wolverhampton, Southwell, and Cagnes-sur-Mer is a potential source of riches for any American who cares to delve into the mysteries of all-weather form.

You just may be spotting the next Hal's Pal or Supreme Sound, who paid $17.40 and $12.20, respectively, in their graded-race debuts on dirt. Or Skimming, who popped at 5.90-1 in his American debut on the Santa Anita dirt following a maiden win and an allowance fourth at Wolverhampton and who, four races later, took the Grade 3 San Diego Handicap, then exceeded the expectations of almost everyone when he won the Grade 1 Pacific Classic.

Turf to Dirt

Who can have accounted for the exploits of Cardmania, Lit de Justice, and Elmhurst, mediocre turf horses in France who went on to win the Breeders' Cup Sprint? Or Mazel Trick, a modest French provincial grass specialist who won a pair of Grade 2 dirt races in California?

Or The Deputy, who improved from winning a lowly median auction maiden race at Epsom to become the winner of the Santa Anita Derby? Or Forzando and In Excess, ex-British turf horses who won the Metropolitan Handicap?

Or Santa Anita Handicap winner Urgent Request, Hollywood Gold Cup winners Perrault, Blushing John, and Marquetry, and Pacific Classic victors Missionary Ridge, Tinners Way, and Dare And Go, none of whom had ever won anything better in Europe than a Group 2 turf race?

Two of the reasons are Bobby Frankel and Jenine Sahadi.

Frankel was responsible for Mazel Trick, Missionary Ridge, Marquetry, and Tinners Way, while Sahadi coaxed the necessary improvement out of Elmhurst, Lit de Justice, and The Deputy.

There are no better trainers than those two at the Euro-turf-to-American-dirt switch. If either of them starts running a European import on dirt, it pays to take notice with your wallet.

Key Races/Key Horses

The key-race theory, a popular concept among U.S. handicappers, works just as well when looking at European horses. The trick, of course, is recognizing the key race.

A perfect example of a foreign key race was the first running of the UAE Derby at Nad Al Sheba in Dubai on March 25, 2000. Although the winner, China Visit, failed to distinguish himself afterward, three other horses in that field—Crimplene, Bachir, and Pacino—would amass five Group 1 and two Group 2 victories in the next three months.

It is easy to recognize a Dubai Millennium or a Montjeu in a foreign import's company lines. It is far more difficult to recognize, in the lines of an import that is still eligible for nonwinners of one or two, the name of a horse that subsequently went on to win or place in a group or listed race.

For example, when Green Card made her American debut in an allowance race at The Meadowlands in September 1986, her past performances included a race in France in which she had finished just a length behind subsequent Group 1 Prix Saint-Alary winner Fitnah. Very few knew of Fitnah's form, however, and Green Card was allowed to get away at 8-1. She won easily.

I contend that recognizing this kind of key horse is the single most important element in handicapping foreign imports, but how is one to spot them?

One way is to look for *Daily Racing Form*'s "First-Time Imports" feature on the graded-handicapping pages for Del Mar, Hollywood Park, Santa Anita, Belmont Park, Saratoga, Aqueduct, Keeneland, Churchill Downs, Arlington, and Woodbine, where each new import's chances are assessed. These always include mentions of key races and horses where applicable.

There are no magic formulas to handicapping foreign imports, but there is one thing any horseplayer can do that will pay dividends throughout the rest of his career, and that is to see for himself what is going on in Europe.

Foreign Travel

With upward of 1,000 horses per year being imported to the United States for purposes of racing, and as many as 800 of these coming from Europe, there is no better way to familiarize oneself with European racing than by going there.

Any serious player, especially one who concentrates on Southern California, New York, Kentucky, or Florida, owes it to himself or herself to take a racing vacation in England or France. The benefits of a holiday in England and/or France will pay dividends within weeks after your return home.

For example, 36 of the horses that ran at Royal Ascot's four-day meeting in 1997 had run in the United States by the end of 1999. What's more, dozens of horses that later ran against Royal Ascot's 1997 runners would eventually appear in America. The number of European form lines that are made immediately understandable in American terms from a brief trip to Europe is incalculable.

Here are some dream itineraries, custom made for spending a week each in England and France.

French Derby/French Oaks at Chantilly/Royal Ascot (2nd & 3rd weeks of June)

Glorious Goodwood/1st week of Deauville (Last week of July/1st week of August)

Third Week of Deauville/York August Meeting (3rd & 4th weeks of August)

Ascot's Festival of British Racing/Arc Weekend at Longchamp (Last weekend of September/1st weekend of October

THERE IS only so much that can be gleaned by looking at raw form. If you want to bet European imports with an optimum degree of understanding, two weeks per year in Europe will put you leagues ahead of your competition.

Having done so, the names of certain foreign races and horses will begin to pop off the pages of *Daily Racing Form* as if they were highlighted in red. Your European connection may become the golden road to unlimited devotion.

STICH
ON PEDIGREE
by Lauren Stich

THERE IS A WEALTH of information available to today's Thoroughbred handicapper, but the one area that still puzzles players more than any other is pedigree. Once pedigree handicapping is understood, this incredibly powerful tool will unearth betting opportunities that previously would have been missed.

The three scariest words for a Thoroughbred handicapper are "maiden special weight." They strike fear into every pick-six, pick-three, or tournament player because there are no Beyer

Speed Figures, pace figures, trip notes, and so on for the many first-time starters in these races. Or perhaps the contestants have run before, but are trying a new surface or distance this time.

Maiden special weight races are usually included in the mix on any given day, and bettors who make multiple-race wagers or enter handicapping tournaments must play them. The only reliable handicapping angles are pedigree and, to some degree, trainer patterns. If, instead of dreading the unknown, you can make pedigrees work for you, it will open up a brave new world. Pedigree power is not limited to maiden races, however, and later in this chapter, you will see how applying knowledge of pedigrees in selected races can result in betting coups.

BEFORE YOU can use pedigrees to your advantage, it is necessary to understand their components (sire, dam, damsire) and how they affect racing performance. It has long been my firm belief that, while the sire and the dam are equally important factors in the pedigree, each plays a different role in determining how the racehorse will run.

The male parts of a pedigree (sire and damsire, or broodmare sire) determine the distance and surface where the runner will be most effective. The female parts of a pedigree (dam and her female family, called tail-female) determine racing class. The most important aspect of the pedigree is what this female family has produced, generation after generation. This is the class of the horse.

As every player knows, wrong information is worse than no information. It is utterly frustrating to constantly hear or read that a horse should take to the turf because the dam was either a stakes winner on grass or produced grass winners. The truth is that if the dam was a good runner on the turf, it is most likely due to the fact that her sire was a turf influence. If she produced winners on the turf, it was probably because the stallion she was bred to was also a turf influence.

It is always easier to see something by example, and by breaking down the components of a pedigree, a profile or running style of the horse in question begins to emerge:

CRAFTY COVENTRY (CRAFTY PROSPECTOR–KATE COVENTRY, BY VICEREGAL)
SURFACE: Given that the sire, and especially the sire line, dictates surface and distance preference, Crafty Coventry was a good candidate to possess speed on the dirt. Although his sire, Crafty Prospector (Mr. Prospector), has produced winners on the turf, he has had much more success as a sire of dirt runners.

As the damsire is in the second generation (think of a damsire as a grandparent), his influence is definitely felt, but is not as strong as that of the sire. In this example, Viceregal (Northern Dancer) is a turf influence, but the runner's sire line takes precedence over the damsire's.

DISTANCE: Crafty Prospector is by Mr. Prospector out of an In Reality mare—speed over speed. Not surprisingly, the majority of runners by Crafty Prospector are most effective from five furlongs to $1\frac{1}{16}$ miles. If the damsire of the runner was a stamina influence (such as Secretariat, Al Hattab, or Caucasus) his runners have occasionally been able to stretch out to win at $1\frac{1}{8}$ miles. In this case, Viceregal tends to add speed rather than stamina to the pedigree.

CLASS: We've established that class comes from the dam and her female line (think of it in human terms—mother, mother's mother, mother's grandmother, and so forth), and Kate Coventry had already produced two stakes-winning half-siblings, Kate's Valentine and Talc's Coventry (both by Talc).

PEDIGREE PROFILE: Once the surface and distance preference plus the class of the animal have been ascertained, the result is called a pedigree profile. The pedigree profile will suggest to the player how the horse should run and whether he fits the conditions of the race.

Crafty Coventry made his first start in a maiden race for New York-breds on dirt at seven furlongs. According to his pedigree profile, he was an excellent candidate for the surface and distance. The fact that his dam had previously produced two stakes winners indicated that Crafty Coventry was more than capable of winning a maiden race.

Public handicappers were lukewarm about Crafty Coventry in this spot because they noted that his half-siblings were stakes winners on the grass. They suggested that Crafty Coventry was probably going to be better on turf, and that bettors should wait until he tried that surface. Wrong!

Kate's Valentine and Talc's Coventry preferred turf because their sire, Talc, was a strong turf influence. Talc was a leading sire in New York for many years and was versatile, siring winners on all surfaces, but his strong suit was grass. Thus, Kate's Valentine and Talc's Coventry had a strong profile for turf, and ran to it.

But Crafty Coventry was not by Talc, he was sired by Crafty Prospector, the overwhelming majority of whose runners displayed high speed on dirt.

The result was that Crafty Coventry was not bet as much as he should have been against a suspect field of New York-bred maiden 2-year-olds. He was an overlay at 4-1 and romped to a decisive victory.

Undoubtedly because of his successful half-siblings, Crafty Coventry was tried intermittently on the turf but was never successful on that surface. The same dam produced

Kate's Valentine, Talc's Coventry, and Crafty Coventry, but it was the stallion that dictated the surface and distance where the runner would be most effective.

DUBAI MILLENIUM (SEEKING THE GOLD–COLORADO DANCER, BY SHAREEF DANCER)

Dubai Millenium was an international sensation, a European champion who capped his career with a victory in the Dubai World Cup on dirt. His sire, Seeking the Gold, is a known stamina influence who has been versatile, getting winners on dirt and turf (especially in Japan). Damsire Shareef Dancer has a very strong turf pedigree, with Northern Dancer on top and Sir Ivor on the bottom. So turf and stamina are present in the immediate pedigree, and the class of the dam is unquestionable. Colorado Dancer is one of nine graded stakes winners from her dam, the 1984 Broodmare of the Year, Fall Aspen.

But what kinds of runners would Colorado Dancer produce if bred to a variety of stallions? Here are two hypothetical pedigrees that show how the stallion changes the pedigree profile regarding surface and distance.

CARSON CITY–COLORADO DANCER, BY SHAREEF DANCER

SURFACE: Generally, Carson City's offspring are at home on dirt, but some have succeeded on turf. The reason for this is clear: Carson City is by Mr. Prospector out of a Blushing Groom mare, and the second dam is by Nijinsky II. Mr. Prospector, although known as one of the greatest progenitors of speed on the dirt in this country, has been an extraordinary sire of turf runners as well. Kingmambo, Gone West, Miswaki, Woodman, and Distant View are sons of Mr. Prospector who are superior turf sires. Blushing Groom and Nijinsky II were champions in Europe and their offspring were most effective on turf.

DISTANCE: Carson City was precocious at 2, possessed blinding speed, and had distance limitations. His runners have inherited this speed and, unless crossed with a mare by a very deep source of stamina, usually are most effective from five furlongs to $1^1/16$ miles. In this hypothetical mating, damsire Shareef Dancer helps supply some stamina.

CLASS: As previously written, Colorado Dancer and her entire female family are about as classy as they come. When bred to any top stallion, it is likely that Colorado Dancer will produce a stakes-quality individual.

PEDIGREE PROFILE: A sprinter/miler type who might stretch out on occasion. Should be precocious at 2 and be efficient on all surfaces—dirt, turf, or wet tracks.

Silver Hawk—Colorado Dancer, by Shareef Dancer

SURFACE: Silver Hawk, like all sons of Roberto (for example, Dynaformer, Kris S., Lear Fan, and Red Ransom), is synonymous with turf.

DISTANCE: The Roberto line is one of the best sources of stamina in the United States today. Runners by Silver Hawk usually just get started at one mile, and prefer distances over $1\frac{1}{8}$ miles.

CLASS: See Colorado Dancer, above.

PEDIGREE PROFILE: A slow-maturing runner who would be better with age and distance, and would strictly prefer turf.

Inserting sires such as Salt Lake, Housebuster, Holy Bull, Capote, Caller I.D., Phone Trick, Meadowlake, Bertrando, Cure the Blues, or Jolie's Halo as the covering stallion would likely result in a win-early sprinter/miler on dirt or turf. If A.P. Indy, Kingmambo, Unbridled, Pleasant Colony, Broad Brush, or Lord at War was the covering stallion, the runner would likely mature later, be better as the distances increased, and be effective on any surface.

Of course, breeding has never been an exact science. If it were, everyone would only breed stakes horses. But analyzing pedigrees in this way will prove out more often than not. There are always exceptions to the rule, and horses such as Cigar, John Henry, Holy Bull, Dancing Spree, and Thunder Gulch are prime examples.

Cigar was by Palace Music, a decent racehorse but an undistinguished sire. Since Cigar was from the Northern Dancer line, it was expected that he would prefer turf. Much to the surprise of everyone, including his astute trainer, Bill Mott, Cigar became a different animal on dirt.

John Henry was by an obscure stallion, Ole Bob Bowers, but was as rugged and endearing a racehorse as you will ever see. His pedigree was surely as humble as that of Carry Back, winner of the 1961 Kentucky Derby and Preakness Stakes.

Holy Bull was by a sprinter who sired sprinters. But he had no problems getting $1\frac{1}{8}$ miles and even dug down to hold off Concern in the Travers Stakes at $1\frac{1}{4}$ miles.

Dancing Spree, by Nijinsky II, was expected to be a turf horse, but preferred dirt. He was a versatile individual who not only won the $1\frac{1}{4}$-mile Suburban Handicap but also became a stretch-running sprinter, upsetting the world's best dash specialists in the Breeders' Cup.

Thunder Gulch was by a sprinter/miler (Gulch) but became a champion at 3 when he won the Kentucky Derby, the Belmont, and the Travers. A son of Gulch winning twice at $1\frac{1}{4}$ miles and also at $1\frac{1}{2}$ miles?

These exceptional racehorses were aberrations, albeit delightful ones.

BETTING TURF RACES

In reality, every horse is bred for turf. After all, they were raised on grass and it is their natural surface. In addition, you can find a grass influence in almost every pedigree these days, whether it is in the first, second, or third generation. Of course, some horses are better suited to grass than others. In the very near future, the majority of racehorses will include even more turf influences. In this era of shuttling stallions to either Australia or South America for Southern Hemisphere breeding, American dirt bloodlines are being crossed with Australian and South American turf bloodlines. The result will produce generations of horses that will have more turf influences than ever before.

Where does turf ability come from? In the 1960's, Round Table was the eminent sire of grass horses, along with Intentionally, The Axe II, T.V. Lark, and any stallion imported from Europe, such as Ribot, Sea-Bird, Herbager, and Vaguely Noble. All were extraordinary turf influences whose blood is found in today's leading sires of grass horses.

Ribot's influence continues through Lost Code, His Majesty, Pleasant Colony, and Tom Rolfe. Tom Rolfe, in turn, was the sire of Hoist the Flag, who sired two-time Prix de l'Arc de Triomphe winner Alleged.

Intentionally was a champion sprinter, but his most important contributions were In Reality and Tentam, both brilliant turf influences. The blood of In Reality is best found today through two of his sons, Relaunch and Valid Appeal. In a very short period of time, Bertrando (whose second sire is Relaunch) has become an excellent turf sire.

Herbager sired the hugely successful turf sire Grey Dawn II, while The Axe II sired Al Hattab (damsire of Holy Bull). Stage Door Johnny was a champion on the dirt at 3, but became known as an outstanding turf influence. Sir Gaylord was one of the best horses of his generation on dirt, but two of his best offspring, Habitat and Sir Ivor, were pronounced turf sires, and his grandson Lord Avie is one of the most underrated turf sires.

Other influential turf sire lines include those of Blushing Groom, Never Bend, and Sharpen Up. Blushing Groom's sons at stud include Arazi, Baillamont, Groom Dancer, Mt. Livermore, Nashwan, Rahy, and Rainbow Quest. Never Bend's sons include Riverman, the sire of Irish River, and Mill Reef, the sire of Shirley Heights. Sharpen Up is found in the pedigrees of Conveyor, Diesis, Halling, Husband, Kris, Common Grounds, Selkirk, Sharpo, and Trempolino.

The Caro line has been a solid turf influence with runners such as Cozzene and With Approval. Lord at War was an outstanding turf sire, and his son Patton is his best hope for carrying on this sire line, which included the great Brigadier Gerard.

When Alydar and Affirmed went to off to stud, the smart money was on Alydar to be the better stallion because his female family was so extraordinary. They were both from the same sire line—Alydar was by Raise a Native, while Affirmed was by Exclusive Native, a son of Raise a Native. Alydar did indeed meet those high expectations, and his premature death was a severe loss to the breeding industry. Affirmed got off to a slow start at stud, but once his offspring got a chance to run on turf, here and in Europe, it was a different ball game. His champions included Flawlessly, Bint Pasha, Charlie Barley, Easy to Copy, Peteski, Zoman, One from Heaven, Trusted Partner, Affidavit, Tibullo, and Medi Flash. Most of these horses were champions in Europe.

Affirmed actually got better with age, and over the years he sired Affirmed Success, Mossflower, and Peteski, who were unique in that they were accomplished on both surfaces.

Along with Northern Dancer's, the most influential sire line for turf today is unquestionably that of Roberto. His sire, Hail to Reason, was a champion at 2 in the U.S., but when it comes to turf pedigrees, Roberto rules. Roberto's sons include Dynaformer, Kris S., Lear Fan, Major Impact, Red Ransom, Repriced, Shuailaan, Silver Hawk, and Sunshine Forever.

Over the past three decades, it became evident that any horse with Northern Dancer blood was a prime candidate for turf, even if that runner's sire never raced on the surface. There is no better illustration of this than Danzig.

A brilliant winner of his only three races, all on dirt, Danzig has been an exceptional stallion, transmitting speed to his offspring. As good as his runners have been on dirt—and they have been extraordinary—they have been equally, and arguably more, impressive on turf. In fact, Danzig's sons are much more proficient turf sires than dirt sires.

Although it may be hard to believe now, sons of Danzig were not an immediate success at stud, and there was concern that Danzig was not going to be a "sire of sires" like other sons of Northern Dancer (Nijinsky II, Nureyev, Sadler's Wells). This changed dramatically when runners by Danzig's sons began winning on the turf.

Chief's Crown, a member of Danzig's first crop, had all the tools to be a successful sire, but was an initial disappointment. It was a different story, however, when his offspring hit the grass. Why? Mainly because his sire line (Danzig-Northern Dancer) was grass and his damsire (Secretariat) was also becoming known as a superior turf influence. At the time this was written, a son of Chief's Crown, Grand Lodge, was all the rage in Australia, where his runners were tearing up the turf.

THE HIDDEN-TURF FACTOR

Unquestionably, the most lucrative pedigree-handicapping angle is the "hidden-turf factor." This occurs when a horse is overlooked in a turf race because his or her sire was known as a superior runner on dirt and is not considered a grass influence, but is from a sire line associated with grass.

The well-known stallions Go for Gin, Holy Bull, and Thunder Gulch provide good illustrations of this phenomenon. Aside from being successful racehorses of the mid-1990's, the one thing these three had in common was that their accomplishments on dirt precluded any kind of career on grass. In the same vein, Lemon Drop Kid, who won the Belmont and Travers in 1999 and was named champion older horse the next year, was never tried on the grass because he succeeded so well on dirt (even though he is by turf sire extraordinaire Kingmambo). In the United States, dirt is the preferred surface, and unless horses are strictly bred for turf—that is, unless they are by sires such as Theatrical, Red Ransom, or Nureyev—they generally are not tried on the grass unless they fail to live up to expectations on the dirt.

Although Go for Gin won the 1994 Kentucky Derby, he was beautifully bred for grass. His sire, Cormorant, was also successful on dirt, but he was by His Majesty, a strong grass influence. His Majesty was a son of two-time Prix de l'Arc de Triomphe winner Ribot, who also sired His Majesty's full brother, the brilliant Graustark. If that weren't enough, Go for Gin's dam was by Stage Door Johnny. So, even though Go for Gin raced on dirt, it made sense that his offspring would love turf.

Go for Gin's first crop raced in 1999 and showed some promise on dirt, but really developed at 3 as they matured and stretched out in distance. A runner from his first crop, Hallucinogin (Go for Gin—Impetuous Image, by Mr. Prospector), was ignored by bettors when he made his first start on turf after two dismal efforts on dirt at 2. Sent off at 46-1, Hallucinogin almost wired the field on a soft course and finished fourth, beaten less than two lengths. This form reversal was completely due to the change from dirt to turf. Away seven months, Hallucinogin confirmed his affinity for the grass with a victory in his first start at 3. Bettors were obviously still wary of Hallucinogin, because he returned $16.40.

<table>
<tr><td colspan="2">Hallucinogin</td><td>B. c. 3 (May) KEESEP98 $95,000</td><td></td><td colspan="2">Life 4 1 0 0</td><td>$27,720</td><td>D.Fst 2 0 0 0</td><td>$0 33</td></tr>
<tr><td colspan="2">Own: Centennial Farms</td><td>Sire: Go for Gin (Cormorant) $7,500
Dam: Impetuous Image (Mr. Prospector)</td><td></td><td colspan="2">2000 1 1 0 0</td><td>$25,200</td><td>Wet 0 0 0 0</td><td>$0 —</td></tr>
<tr><td></td><td></td><td>Br: Cox E A Jr (Ky)</td><td>116</td><td colspan="2">1999 3 M 0 0</td><td>$2,520</td><td>Turf 2 1 0 0</td><td>$27,720 83</td></tr>
<tr><td colspan="2">PRADO E S (85 20 15 12 .24) 2000:(697 119 .17)</td><td>Tr: Schulhofer Flint S(13 6 0 2 .46) 2000:(68 17 .25)</td><td></td><td colspan="2">Bel① 2 1 0 0</td><td>$27,720</td><td>Dist① 0 0 0 0</td><td>$0 —</td></tr>
</table>

10May00–5Bel fm 1⅛ ① :512 1:16 1:40 1:52 3↑ Md Sp Wt 42k 83 9 2 2½ 2ʰᵈ 1ʰᵈ 11 Prado E S 115 7.20 68–27 Hallucinogin115¹ A. P. Delta115ⁿᵏ Maestro Brott108²¼ With pace, driving 11
15Oct99–6Bel sf 1⅛ ① :243 :492 1:143 1:48 Md Sp Wt 42k 60 2 1 1ʰᵈ 1½ 2ʰᵈ 42 Bridgmohan S X 118 46.25 50–44 DelMrShow118ⁿᵏ SintJoseph118¹½ RedGmbler118ⁿᵏ Bumped soundly start 10
10Oct99–5Bel fst 1⅛ ⊗ :23 :462 1:121 1:461 Md Sp Wt 42k 29 9 9 11¹⁴ 10¹³ 10¹⁸ 10²⁷¾ Davis R G 118 2.85e 38–32 MandarinMarsh118³¾ TwigN'Berries118⁴ SaturdyPlyer118ʰᵈ No response 14
21Aug99–4Sar fst 6½f :223 :463 1:12 1:184 Md Sp Wt 40k 33 7 10 107 118¼ 10¹² 10¹⁹ Luzzi M J 117 18.60e 61–18 GroupLeader117³¾ KendallPoint117¼ ScoutingReport117½ Lacked a rally 12
WORKS: May30 Bel 4f fst :51 B 18/21 May18 Bel 4f fst :50¹ B 20/31 May5 Bel 4f fst :49³ B 12/31 Apr30 Bel 4f fst :49¹ B 17/27 Apr25 Bel 4f fst :49¹ B 25/72 Apr20 Bel 4f fst :49² B 28/72

Gasperillo Daze (Go for Gin—La Cucina, by Last Tycoon) was really bred for turf on both sides of his pedigree. His damsire, Last Tycoon, was a group-stakes winner in

Europe and he was from the Northern Dancer line. Once again, unfamiliar with the pedigree, and not associating Go for Gin with grass, the betting public ignored Gasperillo Daze and he returned $47.

Holy Bull (Great Above—Sharon Brown, by Al Hattab) is a terrific example of a horse outrunning his modest pedigree. He possessed brilliant speed at 2, and was simply exceptional at 3. When he went to stud, expectations were high. But just what kind of racehorse was he supposed to produce?

His sire, Great Above, was a superior sprinter who was also bred for turf. By grass champion Minnesota Mac, he was out of champion sprinter Ta Wee, a half-sister to 1968 Horse of the Year Dr. Fager. As expected, Great Above was a good sire of sprinters who occasionally won beyond one mile. They also were very effective on turf. In addition, Holy Bull's damsire, Al Hattab (The Axe II) is a superior turf influence as well.

When Holy Bull's offspring began winning across the country on turf, one could only wonder how good he would have been on the grass.

Initially, not many runners by Holy Bull were placed on turf, but when they were, the results were promising (for example, his daughter Confessional). In June 2000 at Belmont Park, Keep It Holy (Holy Bull—Sweet Willa, by Assert) made his turf debut in a maiden special weight race at $1\frac{1}{16}$ miles. Keep It Holy had an absolutely stunning pedigree for grass racing. All the ingredients were there: Not only was there turf ability through Holy Bull, but also, Keep It Holy's damsire was the grass influence Assert. Then there was the class factor: His dam, Sweet Willa, was a full sister to stakes winner Willa On the Move and a half-sister to stakes winners Will's Way, Lady Reiko, stakes-placed Citidancer, and the unraced Ms. Teak Wood, the dam of stakes winner Acceptable. Despite all these factors, Keep It Holy was sent off at 26-1. He won and paid $54.

Keep It Holy
Own: Lael Stables

Gr/ro c. 3 (Apr) FTCFEB99 $160,000		Life 4 1 0 0 $25,200	D.Fst 3 0 0 0 $0 58
Sire: Holy Bull (Great Above) $25,000		2000 3 1 0 0 $25,200	Wet 0 0 0 0 $0 −
Dam: Sweet Willa (Assert*Ire)		1999 1 M 0 0 $0	Turf 1 1 0 0 $25,200 80
Br: Lavin Bloodstock Services (Ky)	L 118		
Tr: Johnson Philip G(1 0 0 0 .00) 2000:(161 24 .15)		Sar① 0 0 0 0 $0	Dist① 0 0 0 0 $0 −

BRIDGMOHAN S X (7 0 0 1 .00) 2000:(664 76 .11)

24Jun00−9Bel fm 1¹⅛ ① :24 :47⁴ 1:12¹ 1:41⁴ 3↑ Md Sp Wt 42k   80 4 2 1ʰᵈ 2½ 1½ 1ⁿᵏ Bridgmohan S X L 116   26.00 83 − 15 KepItHoly116ⁿᵏ *PolishTims*116²½ HighstMountin116ⁿᵒ Vied inside, driving 10
16Jun00−4Bel fst 6f :22 :46 :58⁴ 1:11⁴ 3↑ Md Sp Wt 41k   58 3 1 9⁸ 9⁶¾ 9⁹½ 8⁹ Davis R G L 116   19.30e 70 − 19 Renoir116² Kris B111³¾ Starshooter116½ Steadied on rail turn 13
1Jun00−1Bel fst 6f :23³ :47² :59³ 1:12¹ 3↑ Md Sp Wt 41k   46 1 5 2½ 4²½ 6⁶ 6¹¹ Davis R G 116   12.90 66 − 23 Chief Executive116½ Starshooter116½ Kris B1164½ Bumped backstretch 8
   Previously trained by Motion H Graham
9Dec99−7Lrl fst 6f :22² :46 :58² 1:11 Md Sp Wt 25k   34 6 9 9¹² 9¹³ 9¹⁴ 9¹⁵ Delgado A 120   8.90e 72 − 11 Rajya Sabha120² Stitched Up120¹½ Father Of All Wins120ⁿᵒ Slow start 10
WORKS: Jly25 Sar tr.t 3f fst :37³ B *19/32* Jly18 Bel tr.t 6f fst 1:14³ H *1/2* Jly12 Bel 3f fst :37¹ B *9/16* May30 Bel 3f fst :37¹ B *3/13* May25 Bel tr.t 4f fst :47⁴ H *6/38* May15 Bel tr.t 6f fst 1:15² B *3/7*

As for our third example, Thunder Gulch, it may have been a surprise to see a son of Gulch relish classic distances, but it should not have been a surprise that Thunder Gulch himself soon began to get winners on the turf. Gulch has had good success with his runners on the turf, especially if the damsire was a turf influence. Brave Tender (out of a Northern Dancer mare) won prestigious group events in Japan; Harayir (out of a Shareef Dancer mare) won the 1000 Guineas in England; Torrential (out of a Dr. Fager mare) won the Prix Jean Prat and placed in the American Derby on turf.

Although not many runners from Thunder Gulch's first few crops raced on turf in this country, they won in bunches on the turf in Australia, Europe, and Japan.

This does not imply that Go for Gin, Holy Bull, and Thunder Gulch are strictly turf sires. Their offspring have certainly been successful on dirt as well: Go for Gin sired Jockey Club Gold Cup winner Albert the Great; Holy Bull sired Breeders' Cup Juvenile winner Macho Uno; and Thunder Gulch sired Preakness and Belmont Stakes winner Point Given and Breeders' Cup Distaff winner Spain. But when sons and daughters of these stallions show up on turf, they should not be dismissed because their sires' success came on dirt. If they appear in maiden grass races against runners by high-profile turf sires such as Danzig, Red Ransom, and Theatrical, they are sure to be overlooked. This is where the "hidden-turf" pedigree factor really pays off.

The hidden-turf factor especially applies to new sires. At the time this was written, this list included Afternoon Deelites, Hennessy, Honour and Glory, and Patton.

Afternoon Deelites is by Private Terms out of a Medaille d'Or mare.

Surprisingly, offspring by Private Terms have been effective on grass, even though his own sire, Private Account, was a much better sire of dirt runners. Medaille d'Or supplies abundant turf influence through his sire, Secretariat, and damsire, Northern Dancer.

If any sire has the credentials to become a super turf stallion, it is Hennessy. With the Storm Cat-Storm Bird-Northern Dancer line on top and grass champion Hawaii as the damsire, it is hardly surprising that Hennessy quickly had a winner on turf in Japan.

Honour and Glory has turf written all over him. From the Relaunch-In Reality-Intentionally line, his damsire is Al Nasr, a son of Lyphard (Northern Dancer).

Early in his 3-year-old year in Florida, Patton showed uncommon speed on the dirt. But his pedigree says turf. By the immensely popular and highly successful turf sire Lord at War, Patton is out of a Seattle Slew mare.

Other young sires who fit the hidden-turf angle are A. P. Jet, Cobra King, Demaloot Demashoot, Flying Chevron, Forest Gazelle, Forest Wildcat, Friendly Lover, Golden Gear, Grindstone, Judge T C, Laabity, Lake George, Level Sands, Lit de Justice, Lord Carson, Mahogany Hall, Maria's Mon, Miesque's Son, Mighty Magee, Mister Jolie, Montreal Red, Peaks and Valleys, Ponche, Roar, Sea Salute, Storm of Angels, Torrential, Unbridled's Song, Valid Wager, Wekiva Springs, and Wild Zone.

Two sons of Unbridled, Grindstone and Unbridled's Song, should sire plenty of turf winners if given the chance. Grindstone's damsire is Drone (Sir Gaylord), while Unbridled's Song's damsire is Caro.

Maria's Mon has an exquisite turf pedigree, and while his first crop included 2001 Kentucky Derby winner Monarchos, it will be no surprise to see him sire turf winners as well. He is by Wavering Monarch (a son of exemplary turf sire, Majestic Light) and his damsire is Caro.

All sons of Forty Niner (Mr. Prospector out of a Tom Rolfe mare) have the potential to be good grass sires. Flying Chevron and Roar both have outstanding grass damsires in Herbager and Northern Dancer, respectively.

Cobra King is from the Farma Way-Marfa-Foolish Pleasure sire line and his damsire, Fabled Monarch, is by Le Fabuleux out of a full sister to Round Table. Turf, turf, turf.

BETTING SPRINTS

Just as Northern Dancer, Roberto, and the European stallions are the best sources for turf pedigrees, there are a number of sire lines that are predisposed to speed, starting with the incomparable Mr. Prospector.

Mr. Prospector inherited his blistering speed from his sire, Raise a Native, a foal of 1961 who won all four of his races early in his 2-year-old season. He set a track record for five furlongs at Aqueduct (57 $\frac{4}{5}$ seconds) in an allowance race and then equaled his own record in the Juvenile Stakes. In his next and final start, the Great American Stakes, he blazed 5½ furlongs in a track-record 1:02$\frac{2}{5}$ and was injured in a workout preparing for the Sapling Stakes. Coincidentally, two of the most influential stallions of the past 40 years—Raise a Native and Northern Dancer—were from the same crop.

If you are searching for speed in a pedigree, Mr. Prospector, his sons, and his grandsons are the best place to look. Mr. Prospector, who died in 1999, left behind him hundreds of sons at stud, and some of their sons have become sires as well. His quickest offspring included Carson City, Conquistador Cielo, Crafty Prospector, Distinctive Pro, Naevus, and Northern Prospect, and they have all had stunning success siring sprinter/miler types. End Sweep, a grandson of Mr. Prospector by one of his best runners, Forty Niner, has excelled as a sire of first-time starters. Robyn Dancer and Prospectors Gamble are two other grandsons of Mr. Prospector (through Crafty Prospector) who produce precocious and swift runners.

Mr. Prospector and his brood are hardly the only source of speed.

The In Reality line, primarily through sons and grandsons of both Relaunch and Valid Appeal, has always been associated with speed on any surface. Bertrando, Cee's Tizzy, and Kipper Kelly are ample proof. Bright Launch, Canaveral, Honour and Glory, Judge T C, Mister Jolie, Valid Expectations, and Valid Wager are just starting their stud careers and their runners should have high speed.

Cherokee Run, champion sprinter of 1994, was the leading freshman sire of 1999, when 14 of his 27 starters won, led by champion 2-year-old filly Chilukki. He is an exceptional sire of sprinter/miler types.

The following stallions are categorized as speed sires. They should have early-maturing 2-year-olds and their runners should be most effective from five furlongs to $1\frac{1}{16}$ miles. Although there are times when some of their offspring stretch out to $1\frac{1}{8}$ miles, that is the exception, not the rule.

SPEED SIRES

Afleet	Afternoon Deelites	Air Forbes Won
Alaskan Frost	Allen's Prospect	Alydeed
AmericanStandard	Anet	Apalachee
Apollo	Baldski	Believe It
Bertrando	Bet Big	Bold Forbes
Bold Ruckus	Bold Ruler	Boone's Mill
Boston Harbor	Buckaroo	Caller I.D.
Canaveral	Capote	Carson City
Cherokee Run	Cee's Tizzy	Citidancer
Clever Trick	Concorde's Tune	Confide
Conquistador Cielo	Copelan	Crafty Prospector
Cure the Blues	Cutlass	Demaloot Demashoot
Deposit Ticket	Distinctive Pro	Dixie Brass
Double Negative	D.J. Cat	End Sweep
Falstaff	Favorite Trick	Forest Wildcat
Formal Dinner	For Really	Fortunate Prospect
Friendly Lover	Full Pocket	Gallant Romeo
Geiger Counter	Gilded Time	Glitterman
Habitat	Habitony	High Brite
Hold Your Peace	Holy Bull	Horatius
Housebuster	In Excess	In Reality
Irish Tower	Jolie's Halo	Kipper Kelly
Known Fact	Light the Fuse	Line in the Sand

Lord Carson	Lost Code	Marquetry
Mazel Trick	Medieval Man	Memo
Mercedes Won	Mining	Mister Jolie
Montbrook	Moscow Ballet	Mr. Greeley
Northern Prospect	Notebook	Not For Love
Obligato	Olympio	Out of Place
Phone Trick	Polish Numbers	Ponche
Prospect Bay	Prospectors Gamble	Raja Baba
Rizzi	Robyn Dancer	Salt Lake
Shanekite	Smoke Glacken	Spend a Buck
Storm Boot	Tour d'Or	Tricky Creek
Two Punch	Unreal Zeal	Valid Appeal
Valid Expectations	Valid Wager	Well Decorated
Whitney Tower	Zarbyev	Zuppardo's Prince

BETTING FRESHMAN SIRES

Like the hidden-turf pedigree factor, betting freshman sires is an incredibly lucrative pedigree-handicapping angle. The secret to making money on first-crop stallions is to get on them before they get hot.

The freshman crop of 2000, for example, included recognizable names such as Unbridled's Song, Honour and Glory, and Hennessy. All three figured to be win-early sires, but other first-crop stallions who were overlooked and offered great value included A. P. Jet, Valid Wager, Canaveral, Friendly Lover, Mister Jolie, Ponche, and Storm Creek.

On June 25, 2000, a betting opportunity occurred in the second race at Lone Star Park. The 5½-furlong maiden race featured a full field of 11 2-year-old colts, some of whom were by freshman stallions such as Maria's Mon, Smart Strike, and Miesque's Son. Bettors may have been familiar with Maria's Mon, who was champion 2-year-old colt in 1995 (over Unbridled's Song and Hennessy) and possibly Smart Strike (by Mr. Prospector), who won the 1996 Philip H. Iselin Handicap. But most players in the U.S. probably never heard of Miesque's Son (also by Mr. Prospector). Therein lay the potential for a betting coup. But the fact that he is by Mr. Prospector ought to have alerted bettors that this stallion's runners should at least have speed.

Mr. Miesque (Miesque's Son—Klassy Briefcase, by Medieval Man) had a spectacular pedigree but was ignored by bettors.

To play maiden 2-year-old races—especially those that include horses by first-crop sires—you must know who the stallions are. Further investigation would have revealed that Miesque's Son is a full brother to Kingmambo, one of the world's most exciting young stallions.

Of course, it also helps if you know the dam. Mr. Miesque was doubly attractive because his dam, Klassy Briefcase, was one of the fastest fillies of her generation, setting a Monmouth Park track record at five furlongs on the turf.

2	Mr. Miesque		Dk. b or br c. 2 (Apr) KEEAPR00 $60,000		Life	1	1	0	0	$16,200	D.Fst	1	1	0	0	$16,200	59
			Sire: Miesque's Son (Mr. Prospector) $10,000		2000	1	1	0	0	$16,200	Wet	0	0	0	0	$0	—
Own: Martin Racing Stable & Massey Betty			Dam: Klassy Briefcase (Medieval Man)		1999	0	M	0	0	$0	Turf	0	0	0	0	$0	—
			Br: Elk Manor Farm (Md)	L 121													
LAMBERT C T (357 31 36 45 .09) 2000:(630 55 .09)			Tr: Desormeaux J Keith(80 15 16 11 .19) 2000:(128 24 .19)		LS	1	1	0	0	$16,200	Dist	0	0	0	0	$0	—

25Jun00–2LS fst 5½f :22 :45³ :58² 1:05   Md Sp Wt 27k   59 6 5 87½ 77¼ 44 12¼ Lambert C T   L 118   17.50   89–11   Mr. Miesque118½⅓ Flex Jet118no Won Strike118½   4-w tn, late rally 11
WORKS: Jly18 LS 5f fst 1:00¹ H 2/4 ●Jly11 LS 4f fst :47² H 1/20   Jun20 LS 3f fst :37³ B 12/24   Jun10 LS 5f my 1:02⁴ Hg(d)6/20   May17 LS 4f fst :49³ Bg 10/42   May10 LS 4f fst :50³ B 16/39

Mr. Miesque closed strongly in the stretch and got up to win, paying a nifty $37.

Two days later at Delaware Park, another colt by Miesque's Son made his debut in a 5½-furlong maiden race. San Sebastian was out of the American Standard mare Ice Folly, a half-sister to Sister Act (Saint Ballado), one of the best older fillies or mares of 1999. He showed excellent workouts for his first start, including a half-mile from the gate in 47 seconds, "handily," the best of 64 works at that distance that day. San Sebastian went six wide entering the stretch and closed well to finish third, beaten one length at 6-1.

San Sebastian's next start was at Belmont Park on July 14 in a six-furlong maiden race on the turf. This time, San Sebastian was in deep against a royally bred field that included colts trained by Bill Mott, D. Wayne Lukas, Mark Hennig, Stanley Hough, John Salzman, and Christophe Clement. San Sebastian was dismissed at 15-1. For those who remembered that his sire is a full brother to Kingmambo, this had all the earmarks of a big score.

San Sebastian ran second by a half-length in an eventful race. As soon as the winner, Strategic Partner, crossed the wire, the stewards'-inquiry sign flashed on the board. It took five minutes before the stewards let the results stand. Strategic Partner, a son of the excellent turf sire Kris S. (whose runners include champion Soaring Softly) out of a Majestic Light mare, returned $9.20, while San Sebastian paid $11.60 to place. Irish Lure, the Lukas-trained Lure colt, finished third. The exacta returned $106.50, and the very playable trifecta paid $677.

A POWERFUL HANDICAPPING TOOL

STAR QUEEN *(KINGMAMBO—STARBOARD TACK, BY SEATTLE SLEW)* The power of pedigree handicapping has never been more evident than it was on May 25, 2000, at Churchill Downs. A one-mile maiden race for fillies and mares 3 years old and up featured a full field of 12 with no apparent standouts, with one exception.

Star Queen began her career in France, finishing second on a soft turf course in August 1999. Eight months later, she returned in a six-furlong dirt race and finished last after being bumped at the start. It was basically a non-effort.

Star Queen opened at 20-1 and her odds kept rising. But her pedigree simply could not be overlooked. First of all, she was by Kingmambo. She was also a half-sister to Patience Game, and pedigree-wise, nothing in this race was in the same league. At post time, her odds had skyrocketed to 49-1. Star Queen took the lead around the far turn and drew off to win by 10¾ lengths. She returned $101.20.

With only a two-week rest, she came back in a turf race at 1⅛ miles. Well-placed throughout, she finished an even third, beaten three lengths, this time at even money. Obviously, her connections held her in high esteem, for they sent her to Hollywood Park to contest the Princess Stakes. After a slow, awkward start, she finished fourth, a half-length behind Cash Run at 7-1. Star Queen returned to Kentucky and easily won a grass allowance at 1¹⁄₁₆ miles at 1-2.

2 Star Queen	B. f. 3 (Feb)		Life 3 1 1 0 $25,412	D.Fst 2 1 0 0 $19,530 95
	Sire: Kingmambo (Mr. Prospector) $45,000		2000 2 1 0 0 $19,530	Wet 0 0 0 0 $0 —
Own: Highland Farms Inc	Dam: Starboard Tack (Seattle Slew)		1999 1 M 1 0 $5,882	Turf 1 0 1 0 $5,882 —
	Br: Ross Valley Farm (Md)	L 116⁵		
KUNTZWEILER G (96 6 13 10 .06) 2000:(513 58 .11)	Tr: Salmen Peter W Jr(24 1 2 1 .04) 2000:(97 11 .11)		CD Ⓣ 0 0 0 0 $0	DistⓉ 0 0 0 0 $0 —

25May00–6CD fst 1	:22⁴ :46 1:10⁴ 1:35 3↑ⒻMd Sp Wt 34k	95 8 5 53½ 2² 12½ 10¾ Kuntzweiler G⁵	L 107	49.60 95–05 Star Queen107¹⁰ For Haymarket114½ Jayla122¹	Drew off,hand urging 12
30Apr00– 3CD fst 6f	:21¹ :45 :57³ 1:10¹ 3↑ⒻMd Sp Wt 33k	–0 2 11 9⁹ 11¹⁷ 11²¹11³⁵¼ Hebert T J	L 112 b	16.30 59–10 Kldouny113¹½ AmricnSlw114¹½ Kristi'sSunshin1125¾	Bumped start,outrun 11
Previously trained by Andre Fabre					
8Aug99♦ Deauville(Fr)	sf *1 ⓉRH	ⒻPrix des Marettes-EBF	2⁴ Peslier O	126 *1.20	Wind Silence126⁴ Star Queen126²½ Queen of the Park126¹⁵ 4
	Mdn (FT)29400				Trailed to 2f out,gained 2nd 100y out.Time not taken
WORKS:	Jun3 CDT4f fst :49 B 4/15 May22 CDT3f fst :37² Bg4/7 May16 CDT5f fst 1:02 B 2/8 May9 CDT5f fst 1:02³ B 1/3 Apr26 Kee3f fst :36³ B 5/25 Apr19 Kee6f gd 1:15³ B 1/2				

EARLY COLONY *(PLEASANT COLONY—SHE'S A TALENT, BY MR. PROSPECTOR)* In 1997, trainer Richard Mandella unveiled a 3-year-old colt in a seven-furlong maiden race at Hollywood Park. Early Colony sported a pedigree that couldn't have been any classier, but he was totally ignored in the wagering. Since Pleasant Colony is not particularly known as a good first-time-out sire, bettors might have thought Early Colony needed more distance to be effective.

But there were many signs that Early Colony could win. Pleasant Colony has long been a major source of stamina, and while it is true that his runners tend to mature slowly, his offspring have won at seven furlongs. This is especially true if the damsire was by a brilliant (speed) influence. Early Colony's dam was by the potent Mr. Prospector, and Early Colony was working swiftly in the mornings.

What made Early Colony such an attractive play, however, was his prodigious female family. His dam had already produced stakes winner She's Tops, and his second dam was a half-sister to one of the most prolific mares of the last 30 years, the previously mentioned Fall Aspen. At the time of Early Colony's debut, Fall Aspen had produced eight stakes winners (Timber Country, Princes of Thieves, Fort Wood, Northern Aspen, Hamas, Colorado Dancer, Mazzacano, and Elle Seule). Later she produced her ninth stakes winner, Bianconi, a champion 3-year-old colt in Ireland who became a Kentucky-based stallion. (To underscore the immense quality of this family, Colorado Dancer, as discussed earlier, subsequently produced Dubai Millenium, and She's Tops became the dam of Dixie Union, winner of the 2000 Haskell Invitational.)

A typical Pleasant Colony, Early Colony showed no speed but exploded in the stretch to just get up for the victory. He returned a staggering $74.20 and went on to become a stakes winner on the grass.

ELTISH *(COX'S RIDGE—NIMBLE FEET, BY DANZIG)* In the fall of 1994, Eltish, an English-raced son of Cox's Ridge, arrived in the United States for the Breeders' Cup Juvenile. Eltish had won a pair of group races, the Royal Lodge Stakes and the Lanson Champagne Vintage Stakes, and had finished third to Pennekamp, considered one of Europe's best 2-year-olds, in the prestigious Generous Dewhurst Stakes.

His success on grass was surprising, since Cox's Ridge was one of those rare stallions whose offspring did not really like turf. Occasionally, some of his runners would do well on grass, but they were dramatically more effective on dirt.

In fact, Eltish was a perfect fit for the Breeders' Cup Juvenile. Cox's Ridge had already sired three Breeders' Cup winners—Life's Magic, Twilight Ridge, and Cardmania—and offspring of Cox's Ridge are tailor-made for $1\frac{1}{16}$ miles. There may have been questions about some of the other 2-year-olds going this distance for the first time, but there was absolutely no doubt that Eltish would handle it.

To add to his allure, Eltish came from a storied Christiana Stables female family. His fourth dam, Enchanted Eve, was stakes-placed in the Alabama and Comely Stakes, but became a foundation mare, producing champion handicap mare Tempted, stakes winner Smart, and Witching Hour, the dam of four stakes winners: Salem, Pumpkin

Moonshine, Tingle Stone, and Broom Dance. Broom Dance won the Alabama Stakes, Gazelle Handicap, Bed O' Roses, Post-Deb, and Vagrancy Handicaps, and is the dam of the aforementioned End Sweep.

Enchanted Eve also produced Instant Sin, the third dam of Eltish. Stakes winners from this branch of the family were Contredance, Misgivings, Old Alliance, Shotiche, and Skimble. Nimble Feet, the dam of Eltish, had already produced Souplesse, a listed stakes winner in France. The class of this family was unquestionable. (Nimble Feet subsequently produced stakes winners Forest Gazelle and Light Step and stakes-placed Yamuna.)

Eltish had raced well against the best of his generation in Europe on turf, but since a racehorse's sire dictates surface preference, he was supposed to be much better on dirt. On Breeders' Cup Day, Eltish was dismissed at 16-1 against favorite Timber Country, probably because people assumed that since he came from Europe, he was a turf horse and therefore a shaky proposition on dirt.

Eltish ran a big race and opened a clear lead entering the stretch, but Timber Country came up along the rail and won. Using 8-5 favorite Timber Country with 16-1 Eltish resulted in a very charitable $132 exacta.

Eltish was a shining example of how pedigree handicapping can be a powerful tool for the player.

ANEES (*UNBRIDLED—IVORY IDOL, BY ALYDAR*) In my *Daily Racing Form* column for the 1999 Breeders' Cup, I selected Anees to upset in the Juvenile, because he was the only horse in the race who was really suited to 1 1/16 miles at that time of the year. Not only was Anees bred to get better as the distances increased, but the race also set up for him, since Forest Camp, Dixie Union, Chief Seattle, and High Yield were all speed types who figured to bang heads.

Forest Camp, possessing a sprinter's pedigree (Deputy Minister—La Paz, by Hold Your Peace), was the 5-2 favorite and was the first to fold after leading for six furlongs. Dixie Union had an impossible task from post 12 and never fired. High Yield made a bold four-wide move into the stretch only to come up empty. Chief Seattle actually made what looked like a winning move but was passed in a flash by Anees. Anees opened up on the field so quickly, he looked like a blur on the screen at the finish.

Why Anees paid $60.20 is a mystery—but I didn't complain. Dixie Union and Forest Camp were the most accomplished horses from the West Coast, but they both were speed types on very speed-favoring surfaces in California. In fact, Anees had run an even third to Dixie Union and Forest Camp in the Norfolk Stakes, beaten only five lengths. The Norfolk was the perfect conditioner, setting up Anees to turn the tables at $1\frac{1}{16}$ miles with a better pace scenario.

PEDIGREE HANDICAPPING THE KENTUCKY DERBY

Every year, the same question arises: Who can—or cannot—get the $1\frac{1}{4}$ miles of the Kentucky Derby? Some handicappers turn to Dosage for the answer. Some study the trainers involved. Some merely watch the important Derby preps at $1\frac{1}{8}$ miles. Some use all three criteria.

I liked Strike the Gold to win the 1999 Kentucky Derby because 1) he had the right pedigree for the distance and 2) his racing performance suggested he would be even more effective at $1\frac{1}{4}$ miles than he was at $1\frac{1}{8}$ miles. Yet the critics persisted: His Dosage was so high. I only knew that a colt by Alydar out of a Hatchet Man mare could easily get $1\frac{1}{4}$ miles.

In 1996, few people gave California-bred Cavonnier a chance to win the Derby. But a close look revealed a scintillating pedigree sufficient to win at the Derby distance. Cavonnier was by Batonnier, a son of His Majesty (Ribot) out of the accomplished 2-year-old filly Mira Femme. Cavonnier's dam was Direwarning, a beautifully bred mare by the stamina influence Caveat out of Mazurka, by Northern Dancer.

Mazurka is out of the unraced mare Magic (Buckpasser—Aspidistra, by Better Self), a half-sister to Dr. Fager and Ta Wee. In addition, Magic is the second dam of Unbridled and Cahill Road. Of course, Cavonnier was nipped right on the wire by Grindstone (Unbridled) in a heartbreaking loss.

As YOU can see, pedigree information is a viable and powerful resource for all players. One needn't be an expert on pedigrees to use them as a handicapping tool. Of course, like anything else, the more information, the better. Although it certainly helps to know the dam and her female family (for racing class), the most important aspect of pedigree handicapping for the average player is knowing the sire and sire line. Once you determine the strength of the sire/sire line (speed, stamina, dirt, turf, or off tracks), you will be able to eliminate runners who do not meet the conditions of the race and focus on the real contenders.

Pedigree handicapping is a formidable betting angle, and those who familiarize themselves with pedigree information will be richly rewarded.

WATCHMAKER
ON STAKES RACES
by Mike Watchmaker

WHAT A SIGHT the Churchill Downs backstretch is the Monday morning before the first Saturday in May. There are hordes of media people. There are racing officials. There are hangers-on of dubious distinction. And, oh yes, there are horsemen, who seem to be outnumbered at least 100 to 1.

It is on this Monday morning before the Derby that each year's Derby buzz horse is born. The first question after "How y'all doin'?" is "Who do you like?" Invariably, one Derby prospect's name is traded more than the others, followed by these ominous words: "He's working like a monster." Like the momentum of a runaway train, support for this aspirant then grows well past the point of all reason.

On the Monday morning before the Derby in 1999, the name on almost everyone's lips was Vicar.

Vicar?

I couldn't believe my ears.

Now, Vicar showed a lot of heart winning narrow decisions in the Fountain of Youth and the Florida Derby at Gulfstream, but his third in the Blue Grass, beaten nearly two lengths by Menifee, left me cold. He was on the pace and rode the rail in the Blue Grass, which is always a good thing at Keeneland, but he gave way late. It looked to me like Vicar was a colt who peaked too early in Florida and was on the way to an undeniable decline in form. "He's working like a monster," well-intentioned people insisted.

One year later, the big buzz horse was Captain Steve. The name had changed but everything else remained the same.

I didn't like Captain Steve at all. In his first few starts at 3, he was crushed in the Santa Catalina, was an ineffective third after a perfect trip in the Louisiana Derby, and was again an ineffective third in the Derby prep where he was supposed to fire, the Santa Anita Derby.

In 2001, the buzz was all about Express Tour, the Godolphin horse who had only a single prep race, in Dubai.

So, how did these three big buzz horses do in their Derbies? Vicar wound up 18th, beaten 19 lengths. Captain Steve finished eighth, beaten 14 lengths. And Express Tour ran eighth, beaten 14 lengths.

Of course, there are buzz horses every day at racetracks across America, and some of them actually win. But the Kentucky Derby has its own special set of traps and pitfalls, including the dubious buzz horse.

Racing people start thinking about the Derby the instant the winner of the Breeders' Cup Juvenile crosses the finish line, about six months before the Derby itself. Attention increases with the running of each Derby prep from January through April. Every bit of minutiae is inordinately scrutinized.

Things get really weird in the last week to 10 days before the Derby. By this point, all the preps have been run. The only news now, aside from the occasional injury or defection, arises from the morning workouts. Because there is little else to report, these final Derby works get far more coverage than they deserve, and that creates one of the biggest traps to avoid when it comes to handicapping the Derby: attaching too much importance to the works. It is this phenomenon that creates support for otherwise faulty Derby candidates like Vicar, Captain Steve, and Express Tour.

Why is it that people who normally pay little mind to workouts are suddenly consumed by final-eighth splits for every 60-1 shot who's Derby bound?

Here's a scoop: Unless a horse is physically unable to train, refuses to train, struggles through a six-furlong work in 1:20, or flies through it in 1:09, most of what happens in the mornings leading up to the Derby means nothing. With almost every Derby candidate having had a race within the last four weeks and, with a few isolated exceptions, a minimum of two races on the year, these Derby horses are already fit.

In fact, if you gave Derby trainers a dose of truth serum, they would tell you that in the two weeks before the Derby, they're just trying not to screw their horses up.

Look at the big deal that was made over Fusaichi Pegasus before the 2000 Derby. Two weeks before the race, he acted up on a couple of mornings and it became front-page news because everyone was paying microscopic attention. Trainer Neil Drysdale told anyone who would listen that Fusaichi Pegasus behaved worse at home in California; in addition, the colt's individualism was on display in New York in the pre-race warm-up for the Wood Memorial, and he still won easily. His behavior certainly didn't prevent him from becoming the first successful Derby favorite in 21 years. Perhaps the negative buzz was the reason he paid as much as $6.60.

Another big pitfall to avoid when handicapping is getting caught up in the hoopla of the post-position draw. Now that a one-hour television show has been built around it, the trap has become even deeper.

Around the time of the draw, you always hear a lot of talk about the auxiliary starting gate, used for horses in posts 15 and up. And it's true that trainers who get the first selections for post positions avoid the auxiliary gate. But the truth is, there's nothing wrong with it. Five of the seven Derby winners from 1995 through 2001 (Thunder Gulch, Grindstone, Charismatic, Fusaichi Pegasus, and Monarchos) broke from the auxiliary gate. Charismatic and Menifee actually combined for an auxiliary-gate exacta worth $727.80.

Post positions near the inside aren't as bad as they're made out to be, either. Real Quiet came out of post 3 in a field of 15 when he won the Derby, and Aptitude broke from post 2 when he finished second to Fusaichi Pegasus. And, although both were closers, neither encountered trouble of any significance.

In reality, Derby post position only matters if your horse draws the rail or if he draws the 20 hole. I consider the rail worse than the extreme outside, because the rail horse really has little choice but to go early in order to escape getting shuffled back.

Besides, in just about any race, the most important thing about the post-position draw is not what slot you get, but what kind of horse is breaking next to yours. If your horse is a speed type or a stalker, you would prefer dead closers to be around you. That way, your horse can get right out of the way of those breaking to either side. If your horse is a stretch-runner, you want speed horses breaking next to you so they will quickly get out of your way. That's what's important.

FORTUNATELY, THERE is a simple way to avoid the traps and pitfalls associated with handicapping the Derby, and that is cold, hard analysis. By understanding and recognizing the profile of the modern-day Derby winner, you can identify the legitimate contenders.

Every Derby winner since Apollo in 1882 has had at least one start as a 2-year-old. There is no understating the importance of this. Racing at 2 is critical for physical and mental seasoning, both of which are necessities in the Derby crucible. Fusaichi Pegasus made his only 2-year-old start in December, but you must remember that for him to have been ready for that start, he had to have been in training for months.

It may appear to be a paradox, but history tells us that the Derby runner's 2-year-old racing should not include the Breeders' Cup Juvenile. At the time this was written, the Juvenile had been run 18 times, and none of its winners had won the Derby. Now, perhaps 18 years is not enough time to establish a valid correlation. Eventually the negative Breeders' Cup Juvenile streak will come to an end, just as Fusaichi Pegasus ended the 20-year losing streak of favorites in the Derby. When a Juvenile winner finally does win the Derby, though, it may still prove to be an aberration.

I do believe there is an unmistakable trend at work here. Perhaps it's because 2-year-olds who win the Juvenile peak too early, or because winning at a mile and a sixteenth in late October is a long way from succeeding at a mile and a quarter in May. A review of the winners of the Derby since 1990 suggests that it may be best to avoid running in the Juvenile altogether.

Of the 12 Kentucky Derby winners from 1990 through 2001, only one even ran in the Juvenile: In 1992, Sea Hero was a dull seventh at a little less than 5-2.

Otherwise, recent Derby winners have all, for one reason or another, missed the Breeders' Cup Juvenile.

Monarchos had raced just once, finishing eighth, at the time the 2000 Juvenile was run. Fusaichi Pegasus hadn't started at all when the 1999 Juvenile was run, while Charismatic was still a couple of weeks away from winning a maiden claiming race. Real Quiet, who won a maiden race in his seventh start three weeks before the 1997 Juvenile, didn't make his first graded-stakes attempt until three weeks after that year's Cup.

Silver Charm closed his 2-year-old campaign in mid-September, while Grindstone, winner of the 1996 Derby, made his second and final 2-year-old start on July 1.

Thunder Gulch and Go for Gin ran in Aqueduct's late-season 2-year-old stakes instead of the Breeders' Cup, both winning the Remsen.

Lil E. Tee and Strike the Gold never went beyond the allowance level as 2-year-olds. Unbridled, the 1990 Derby winner, competed in five stakes as a juvenile, but none was graded.

So the 2-year-old profile of the Derby winner shows either a late-developing colt whose spots have been carefully picked by an astute trainer, or a colt who demonstrated real talent, if not brilliance, during an abbreviated campaign.

The 3-year-old profile of a probable Derby winner is, understandably, more finely focused. (I hope you understand that 1999 winner Charismatic, who couldn't finish first in a claiming race as close to the Derby as February and wasn't even favored in that claimer, risks throwing any statistical sample out of whack.)

Every Derby winner from 1990 through 2001 (except Charismatic) had three or four starts going into Louisville, and every one of them except Silver Charm had at least three two-turn preps. Silver Charm had two.

Since 1992, when Beyer Speed Figures became available in *Daily Racing Form* past performances, every Derby winner through 2001, except Charismatic and Sea Hero, had posted a triple-digit number by his first or second start at 3. All of them, except Sea Hero, went to Churchill with at least two triple-digit Beyers at 3, and all of them except Monarchos ran a Beyer figure that was at least in the 90's at 2. The reason this is important is elementary. The average winning Kentucky Derby-winning Beyer from 1992 through 2001 (after eliminating the high and the low, a rule I will use throughout this chapter) was 110. For a 3-year-old to achieve that figure, he has to have shown he was fast in his previous races.

Analysis shows that sharp recent form is essential for success in the Derby. Every Derby winner from 1990 through 2001, except Sea Hero and Thunder Gulch, went into the Derby having hit the board in a Grade 1 or Grade 2 prep. That even includes Charismatic, who won the Grade 2 Lexington before the Derby. Sea Hero and Thunder Gulch both finished relatively close fourths in their last Derby preps.

Where a Derby aspirant comes from is just as important as how he ran. Of the last 12 Derby winners, four emerged from the Blue Grass Stakes, three from the Wood Memorial, two from the Santa Anita Derby, and two from the Arkansas Derby. Charismatic was the only exception, and he finished fourth in the Santa Anita Derby before winning the Lexington.

Finally, an important thing to look for in the successful modern-day Derby candidate is the ability to come from off the pace. Of the 12 Derby winners from 1990 through 2001, only two, Silver Charm and Go for Gin, were speed horses. I define a speed horse as one who was running either first or second, or was within two lengths of the lead in the first call of the result charts. Under these parameters, speed usually wins between 50 and 55 percent of all races on dirt, and 33 percent of races on turf. Since 1990, however, speed has only been successful 17 percent of the time in the Derby. In fact, there hasn't been a front-running Derby winner (one who led at every call) since Winning Colors in 1988.

The key to handicapping the Derby is to avoid overhandicapping. Yes, the Derby is a big deal. But it's still just a race. Focus on the important things, like proper experience, quality of company faced, current form, Beyer figures, the pace setup, likely ability to handle the distance and betting value. And, if people continue to fall in love with horses like Vicar, Captain Steve, and Express Tour, there will always be real betting value. Consider that the average winning mutuel in the Derby from 1990 through 2001 (again, throwing out the high and low) was $23.54.

THE PREAKNESS

The general perception is that the Preakness is a more "normal" race than the Derby. With the field size restricted to 14 and with the hype machine on pause, this perception is correct. The Preakness is about as normal as American classic events get.

When this was written, betting favorites had won three of the 11 Preaknesses from 1990 through 2000, or 27 percent. That's still below the universal strike rate for favorites of 33 percent, but it's a heck of a lot better than favorites have fared in the Derby. And the average winning mutuel in the Preakness through this period, $10.71, is less than half that of the Derby.

There is an obvious explanation. While the Derby is a meeting point for 3-year-olds who have prepped all over the country, and sometimes the world, Preakness contenders primarily emerge from one race, the Derby. Until Red Bullet won the 2000 Preakness, the winners of 16 consecutive Preaknesses all came out of the Derby.

Unfortunately, the way those 16 Preakness winners performed in the Derby wasn't always a good indication of what was to come in Baltimore. Of the 10 Preakness winners in the 1990's, six finished third or better in the Derby, but four finished anywhere from fifth to 16th at Churchill Downs.

Even in the 1980's, of the seven Preakness winners who competed in the Derby, four finished third or better at Churchill Downs, but three others finished anywhere from fifth to 11th.

Red Bullet aside, it doesn't necessarily matter how well a Preakness candidate ran in the Derby; the important thing is that he ran.

Pimlico is a tight-turned track, and the Preakness is a sixteenth of a mile shorter than the Derby, so many believe that it is a race tailor-made for an inside-speed horse. Statistics refute this notion.

Of the 11 Preaknesses from 1990 through 2000, just two were won by speed horses. Only one of those two, Louis Quatorze in 1996, was a front-running winner, and he was the first Preakness winner since Aloma's Ruler in 1982 to lead at every call.

ALTHOUGH THERE is frequently a track bias in favor of rail runners at Pimlico in the days leading up to the Preakness, only two of the 11 Preakness winners from 1990 through 2000 broke from the 1, 2, or 3 hole. They were Tabasco Cat and Prairie Bayou, and they, along with Summer Squall, were the only Preakness winners through the period who spent meaningful time during the race on the rail. Even Louis Quatorze, who led at every call, raced well off the rail. (Now, inside posts certainly do not guarantee a rail trip in the Preakness. Horses with speed from outside posts can gravitate toward the rail, forcing horses from inside posts to get off the rail for racing room.)

While the Preakness is a more formful race than the Derby, you must still focus on where the candidates come from and how they run. In the Preakness, the successful runners come out of the Derby and have the ability to pass horses.

THE BELMONT

You might think that Belmont winners mostly come out of the Kentucky Derby and Preakness. But of the 21 Belmont winners from 1980 through 2000, only nine ran in both the Derby and Preakness. Three ran in the Derby and skipped the Preakness, one came out of the Preakness after passing the Derby, and eight didn't run in either race.

Most of these new shooters have taken the Belmont, and the betting public, a bit by surprise. Only two of the 11 Belmonts from 1990 through 2000 were won by favorites, and the average winning mutuel was $15.81, almost 50 percent higher than the Preakness.

These statistics say a horse can be almost as successful in reaching the Belmont Stakes winner's circle by avoiding both the Derby and Preakness as he can by running in both. When it comes to the Belmont, being fresh is almost as much of an asset as being accomplished. This shows how grueling a series the Triple Crown is and how demanding a race the Belmont is.

Consider the average Belmont-winning Beyer figure from 1992 through 2000. The average winning Beyer for the Kentucky Derby was 110 and for the Preakness was 109.

During this period, both of those races had an average winning Beyer of 109. The Belmont comes five weeks after the Derby and three weeks after the Preakness, and this is the time of year when 3-year-olds tend to display rapid development, which is often beautifully illustrated by Beyer figure patterns. Yet the average winning Beyer for the Belmont—107—is actually lower than those of the first two legs of the Triple Crown.

What is particularly intriguing about the Belmont is the importance of speed. That goes against the grain of the popular perception that the successful candidate for the 1½-mile Belmont is a plodding type who will plug along forever. From 1990 through 2000, speed won only 18 percent of the time in the Derby and Preakness, but during the same period, speed won 36 percent of the time in the Belmont. From 1980 through 1989, speed won half of the 10 Belmonts run.

The reason for this is clear. The pace in the Derby and Preakness is often much faster than in the Belmont. The typical slower pace in the Belmont not only enables horses to carry their speed farther, it also can mute the closing punch of stretch runners. What these numbers do is confirm one of racing's oldest tenets: "The longer the race, the more important the pace."

THE BREEDERS' CUP

Without question, the Breeders' Cup was one of the most important innovations in Thoroughbred racing in the last quarter of the 20th century. From its very first running in 1984, it unalterably changed the face of the game, if for no other reason than it provided an incentive to keep the best horses in training longer. For that, we owe it a debt of gratitude.

The Breeders' Cup now rivals the Kentucky Derby as the high point on the racing calendar. In almost every respect, however, the Breeders' Cup is the polar opposite of the Derby. After months of buildup, the Derby is over in a little more than two minutes. The Breeders' Cup takes nearly five hours to play out. Form at the distance is almost always established among competitors in the Breeders' Cup, but not in the Derby. Generational matchups don't apply to the Derby, but in the Breeders' Cup, 3-year-olds can tackle older horses in six races. Standout horses from other parts of the world are commonplace in the Breeders' Cup, but are still a bit of a novelty in the Derby. The Derby is the only race in America that allows as many as 20 starters, while the size of each Breeders' Cup field is limited to 14. The Derby is a singular point of focus. In the Breeders' Cup, attention is spread over eight races, a whirlwind that can send even the most seasoned horseplayer's head spinning.

For that reason, preparation is essential in handicapping the Breeders' Cup. It is critical to know what type of horse usually wins each Breeders' Cup race. It is important to know that some Breeders' Cup races are more formful than others. It is invaluable to know that Breeders' Cup winners emerge from the same places over and over again.

Consider this: Of the 79 horses who were honored with Eclipse Awards in the 1990's (excluding steeplechase horses), 45 of them, or 57 percent, began their careers at one of the three major tracks in New York (Belmont, Saratoga, and Aqueduct), the three major tracks in Southern California (Santa Anita, Hollywood, and Del Mar), the two major tracks in Kentucky (Keeneland and Churchill Downs), or at Gulfstream Park, the East's leading racing center during the winter.

If you exclude the 19 champions on the turf in the 1990's, 65 percent began their careers at the nation's biggest tracks. If you exclude the 15 Eclipse Award winners during that time who began their careers on foreign soil, 70 percent of the decade's champions made their first starts at the most important tracks in this country.

While it is certainly true that a star horse can emerge from just about anywhere, the facts show that it just doesn't happen often.

It should come as no surprise that most Breeders' Cup winners emerge from the same places that champions do, since the Breeders' Cup has a profound impact on determining champions. Of the 119 Breeders' Cup races run from 1984 through 2000 (excluding the Filly and Mare Turf, which has only been run twice at this writing), 29 percent of all winners last raced in New York, 22 percent in Southern California, 19 percent in Kentucky, and 14 percent in Europe (8 percent in France and 6 percent in England).

A breakout of dirt races and turf races is revealing. In the 85 Breeders' Cup races run on dirt, 31 percent of the winners last ran in New York, 24 percent in Southern California, and 24 percent in Kentucky.

On turf, 38 percent of winners made their last starts in England or France, 27 percent in New York, and 18 percent in Southern California.

Fillies and mares who made their last starts in Kentucky won nine of the 17 Distaffs run from 1984 through 2000. Horses coming out of races in Southern California and New York accounted for 12 of the 17 Sprints. Three of the 17 Classics were won by horses who last ran in the Super Derby at Louisiana Downs, but only one Classic winner came out of a prep race in Kentucky.

Despite the European shippers' good success rate on grass, there is one venue where they haven't done well: Gulfstream Park in warm and humid south Florida.

At the first two Breeders' Cups at Gulfstream in 1989 and 1992, horses who made their last starts in Europe were 0 for 28. Eliminate the dirt starters from the mix, and the futility mark is 0 for 16. Half of those 16 starters went off at 9-1 or less, a quarter of them went off at less than 4-1, one went off at 3-2, and one went off at even money. They certainly did not perform to their odds.

It took Daylami, one of the best horses Europe had seen in years, to finally break the drought at Gulfstream in the 1999 Turf. He improved, if that's the word for it, the record of horses who made their last starts in Europe before competing in a Breeders' Cup at Gulfstream to 1 for 43 overall and 1 for 25 on turf.

Daylami paid $5.20. It's going to take a lot more Daylamis at $5.20 just to get the Europeans back to even at Gulfstream, and horses as good as Daylami don't come along all that often.

Some Breeders' Cup races are, as a rule, more formful than others. The Distaff has the reputation of being the most formful event, but statistics show that this reputation isn't entirely deserved. In the 17 Breeders' Cups through 2000, favorites won the Distaff 47 percent of the time, which is well above the universal average of 33 percent for winning favorites. However, favorites won just as frequently in the Juvenile and Juvenile Fillies.

Focusing just on those Breeders' Cups run from 1990 through 2000, we see that the Distaff, along with the Sprint and the Classic, actually had the *lowest* success rate for favorites—27 percent—while the Juvenile and Juvenile Fillies had the highest at 55 percent.

Looking at the average winning mutuel, an even better indicator of formfulness, the Juvenile, not the Distaff, has had the lowest payoff. The average mutuel for the Juvenile from 1984 through 2000 was $9.01; from 1990 through 2000 it was $8.11. Those are the only single-digit average mutuel payoffs in all the Breeders' Cup races.

Each Breeders' Cup race has its own trends in the type of horse who succeeds.

Race	Average mutuel*	Winning favorites	Speed winners	Average Beyer**
Distaff	$11.60	47 percent	65 percent	110
Juvenile Fillies	$16.81	47 percent	18 percent	94
Mile	$14.45	35 percent	41 percent	112
Sprint	$20.20	24 percent	53 percent	113
Juvenile	$9.01	47 percent	47 percent	100
Turf	$20.39	35 percent	18 percent	112
Classic	$19.15	29 percent	41 percent	116

  *excluding high and low
  ** excluding high and low, 1990-2000

Distaff

One thing that can be counted on in the Distaff is speed. Let's again define speed as horses running either first or second, or within two lengths of the lead, at the first call. Speed horses were 11 for 17 in the Distaffs through 2000 for a strike rate of 65 percent. And it usually takes a quality speed performance to win the Distaff: The average winning Beyer figure from 1990 through 2000 was 110.

Kentucky leads the way as the site of final preps for Distaff winners, and all but one Distaff winner through 2000 emerged from a race in Kentucky, New York (five winners), or Southern California (two winners).

Juvenile Fillies

Favorites do as well in the Juvenile Fillies as any other Breeders' Cup race, but the average mutuel produced in this event is much higher than in its male counterpart, the Juvenile. The average mutuel in all Juvenile Fillies races through 2000 was $16.81.

Through 2000, the Juvenile Fillies was won seven times by a filly who came out of a race in New York, followed by Kentucky at five and Santa Anita at two. However, New York's edge was built up before 1990. From 1990 through 2000, Belmont Park and Keeneland had four Juvenile Fillies winners each.

The Juvenile Fillies has by far the lowest average winning Beyer—94—and it also has the lowest success rate for speed of all Breeders' Cup races on dirt. Speed won only three of the first 17 Juvenile Fillies and all were from 1994 through 1999. The Juvenile Fillies was the only Breeders' Cup race, dirt or turf, that had not been won by a front-runner through the 2000 running.

Mile

The Mile is considered one of the Breeders' Cup's more inscrutable races, but that is not the case. Favorites won 35 percent of Miles through 2000, and from 1990 through 2000, they won at a healthy rate of 46 percent.

The average winning mutuel in Miles through 2000 was $14.45. This was significantly lower than the payoffs in the Sprint, the Turf, and the Classic, and from 1990 through 2000, the Mile's average mutuel was even lower than the Distaff's.

Horses who last started in Europe have had the most success in the Mile, winning seven of the 17 runnings through 2000 (five for England, two for France), with three each for Belmont and Southern California. Since 1990, however, the gap has been closing. From 1990 through 2000, horses who made their last starts in Europe won four Miles (three from England, one from France), while all three Mile winners who came out of races at Belmont did so in the 1990's. The winners of the 1999 and 2000 Miles both came off wins in the Oak Tree Breeders' Cup Mile at Santa Anita.

It is surprising how well speed has done in the Mile. Front-runners won 41 percent of all the Miles through 2000, an unusually high number for turf racing.

Beyer figures say the quality of the Mile winner is equal to that of the horse who wins the much-longer 1½-mile Turf. The average winning Beyer for both races from 1990 through 2000 was 112.

Sprint

More than any other Breeders' Cup race, the Sprint is the spot where you are supposed to take a swing against the favorite. In the 17 runnings of the Sprint through 2000, favorites won at a rate of only 24 percent, the lowest of all the Breeders' Cup events. The average winning mutuel from 1990 through 2000, $20.13, was the highest by far of all the Breeders' Cup races.

Yet, for the most part, the search for the Sprint winner can begin with horses coming out of races in Southern California and end with horses emerging from Belmont Park. In all the Sprints through 2000, seven winners came out of races in Southern California and five from races at Belmont. From 1990 through 2000, the Southern California edge was greater, with six Sprint winners last racing in Southern California and three at Belmont. Only two emerged from anywhere else.

In many years, it seems there is too much early speed in the Sprint, setting it up for closers. But speed wins its fair share in this race. Of all the Sprints through 2000, 53 percent were won by speed. There had been four front-running winners of the Sprint through 2000, tying it with the Distaff as the Breeders' Cup event with the most winners that led at every call.

Juvenile

The Juvenile is the most formful Breeders' Cup race overall.

In regard to speed, the Juvenile is in middle of the Breeders' Cup races; speed won 47 percent of the time.

The winners come from the three spots you would expect—Belmont, Santa Anita and Keeneland—and in almost equal frequency. In all the Juveniles through 2000, the winners of five last raced at Belmont, five last raced at Santa Anita, and four at Keeneland.

Turf

While the Turf has the highest average mutual of all Breeders' Cup races at $20.39, favorites have actually done better than the universal average in this race, winning at a rate of 35 percent through 2000. So favorites who do win the Turf aren't necessarily short-priced, which means that the Turf is as deep a race as people think it is.

It is no surprise that horses who last raced in Europe have done well in the Turf, but horses who made their last starts in New York have also done well. In all the Turfs through 2000, six were won by horses who last started in Europe (four in France, two in England), while horses who last started at either Belmont or Aqueduct also won six. Three were won by horses who last raced at Santa Anita.

It is also no surprise that speed doesn't do well in this 1½-mile test. Only three speed horses were successful in the 17 Turfs through 2000, and Buck's Boy, who wired the field in 1998 at Churchill Downs, was the only front-running winner.

Classic

The best horses in America compete in the Classic—the average winning Beyer from 1990 through 2000 was 116—so it is a bit of a shock to see how susceptible the Classic is to an upset.

Favorites have won only 29 percent of the Classics, and the average winning mutuel is $19.15. This may speak to the depth of the Classic fields, but it also shows that a lot of very popular horses just haven't run all that well in this race.

As a group, the Classic winners are also a little more diverse in geographical terms. Unlike the other Breeders' Cup events on dirt, which are mainly dominated by horses who last started in one of the nation's three major racing centers—New York, Southern California, and Kentucky—the Classic has had winners from almost anywhere.

Only four Classic winners last raced in New York, and four last started at Santa Anita. Three came out of the Super Derby at Louisiana Downs. Only one—Cat Thief, who posted a shocking upset in 1999—last raced in Kentucky.

Speed does fairly well in the Classic, having won 41 percent of the runnings through 2000. Yet for all the high-class speed that has competed in this race, the only front-running winner of the Classic was Black Tie Affair in 1991.

FINALLY, THERE is one other angle to consider in handicapping the Breeders' Cup. That is the home-court advantage. When a Breeders' Cup is run toward the end of a race meet, which mainly happens when the Cup is assigned to Belmont Park or Oak Tree at Santa Anita, horses who competed in prep races earlier in the meet have an advantage. This applies only to dirt races, since the nature of turf courses is far more consistent from track to track. Dirt courses can vary wildly in terms of composition.

Through 2000, there had been 26 Breeders' Cup races run when there was an available prep race over the track, and exactly half of them were won by horses who ran in that prep.

These numbers are even more powerful for the Juvenile and the Juvenile Fillies. That makes sense, too, because 2-year-olds are comparatively unseasoned and generally have not raced over a number of different surfaces. Through 2000, there were 10 Breeders' Cup races run for 2-year-olds with a prep over the track available, and seven were won by horses who came out of those preps.

So, the next time a Breeders' Cup comes at the end of a Belmont or Oak Tree meet, don't say you haven't been warned.

STAKES HANDICAPPING

Handicapping conventional stakes races, even major Grade 1 events, may not necessarily require the specialized information that is so essential when approaching the Triple Crown or the Breeders' Cup. However, stakes races do present their own handicapping challenges, which distinguish them from the run-of-the-mill claiming race.

Factors such as distance, racing surface, pace, final time, speed figures, current form, and fitness are important in every race, but stakes races present another set of issues: Players must also consider the reputations of horses, the "intent" of horses who are prepping for even bigger stakes down the road, and divisional strengths and weaknesses. Matters such as these can make handicapping stakes events more tricky than handicapping the average maiden race.

The following stakes races, which were run in early 2001, presented some of the challenges that are usually found in such races. Let's pretend you and I are at the track, handicapping these events.

The 2001 Santa Anita Handicap

Persssonet (Chi)
Own: Cobra Farm Inc
Green, Gold Cobra On Back, Green
BLANC B (86 6 6 9 .07) 2001:(77 5 .06)

B. g. 6
Sire: Hussonet (Mr. Prospector)
Dam: Percepcion*Chi(Lake Erie*Ire)
Br: Haras de Pirque (Chi)
Tr: Puype Mike(12 1 0 3 .08) 2001:(10 1 .10)

L 110

Life	18	4	6	1	$276,485	98	D.Fst	1	0	0	0	$18,000 97
2001	1	0	0	0	$18,000	97	Wet(307)	0	0	0	0	$0 –
2000	8	2	2	1	$140,450	98	Turf(242)	17	4	6	1	$258,485 98
SA	1	0	0	0	$18,000	97	Dist	0	0	0	0	$0 –

4Feb01-8SA fst 1⅛ :464 1:104 1:353 1:481 4↑ SanAntonioH-G2 **97** 4 78¼ 711 78½ 56 46½ Blanc B LB 112 58.30 87-11 **GuddTor**1151½ **LthlInstrmnt**1163½ **MoonlghtChrgr**1131½ Improved position 8
30Dec00-9SA fm 1⅛ Ⓣ :483 1:124 1:362 1:48 3↑ OClm 100000 **98** 3 55½ 56½ 52¾ 32½ 32½ Take Y LB 119 10.80 86-11 Zanetti1192 *Quianlong*119½ Perssonet119nk Inside to 2nd turn 11
2Dec00-8Hol fm 1½ Ⓣ :491 1:131 2:011 2:254 3↑ HolTurf Cup-G1 **91** 4 711 89½ 87¾ 610 69½ Delahoussaye E LB 126 31.00 80-08 ***Bienamado***1263 Northern Quest126½ Lazy Lode1265 4wd into lane,no bid 8
29Oct00-6SA fm *1½ Ⓣ :502 1:16 2:051 2:274 3↑ C F Burke H-G3 **88** 6 42 53 56 75¼ 66¾ Gomez G K LB 114 8.20 105-06 Timboroa1142½ [DH]Kerrygold116 [DH]ResJudict115¾ Chased btwn,no rally 9
4Sep00-6Dmr gd 1⅜ Ⓣ :474 1:122 1:362 2:123 3↑ Del Mar H-G2 **98** 1 54 63 42½ 31 32½ Gomez G K LB 114 15.20 102 — NorthernQuest1161½ [D]AlvoCrto1151 Prssont1142½ Blockd,stdied past 1/8 8
Placed second through disqualification.
9Aug00-7Dmr fm 1⅜ Ⓣ :494 1:144 1:383 2:151 3↑ [R]Escondido H80k **95** 10 47 44 43 21 21 Gomez G K LB 115 10.60 91-14 Alvo Certo1151 Perssonet1153 Adcat1162½ Came out,willingly 10
7Jly00-2Hol fm 1¼ Ⓣ :51 1:161 1:394 2:024 3↑ OClm 80000N **95** 3 53½ 56 41¼ 3½ 1½ Gomez G K LB 119 16.00 82-18 Perssonet119½ Maxaplenty1211 LegendOfRussi117nk Waited 3/8,rail rally 7
26May00-2Hol fm 1¼ Ⓣ :523 1:162 1:40 2:031 3↑ OClm 62500N **95** 2 1hd 1hd 1hd 2hd 1no Gomez G K LB 118 11.40 80-23 *Perssonet*118no Yaralino1201 Generous Gift118hd Rail,headed,gamely 6
22Apr00-8SA fm 1 Ⓣ :232 :47 1:11 1:353 4↑ OClm 80000N **80** 11 87 64 54½ 97½ 106 McCarron C J LB 118 6.90 75-20 Twilight Affair120no Milk Wood118½ Dolfikar1181 4wd,crowded 1/8 11
2May99-4Hol fm 1¼ Ⓣ :513 1:153 1:391 2:024 3↑ OClm 80000N **92** 7 42½ 3nk 21 32 42 McCarron C J LB 116 *1.10 76-14 Shelter Cove1221 Patriot Love116no Percutant1161 4 wide, outfinished 8
24Mar99-7SA fm 1 Ⓣ :231 :47 1:103 1:351 4↑ Alw 58000N2X **95** 8 79 75½ 83¾ 63½ 2¾ McCarron C J LB 118 *2.50 82-18 Paxos121¾ Perssonet118½ Mantles Star118no 5 wide into stretch 8
Previously trained by Samuel Fuentes
8Nov98♦ Club Hippico(Chi) fm *1½Ⓣ RH 2:27 Gran Premio El Ensayo-G1 Stk 125000 1¼ Albornoz J 123 13.00 Perssonet1231¼ Molto Vivace123nk Val Gardena117½ 16
Impreso 5th,Vasca Furia 7th,Le Grand Duc 8th,Antologica 13th
25Sep98♦ Club Hippico(Chi) fm *1¼Ⓣ RH 1:59 GP Nacional Ricardo Lyon-G1 Stk 60000 43¾ Albornoz J 123 8.00 Le Grand Duc1231 Impreso122¾ Val Gardena1172 12
Antologica 6th
30Aug98♦ Club Hippico(Chi) fm *1 1/16Ⓣ RH 1:402 Polla de Potrillos-G1 Stk 42000 2¾ Rivera A 123 6.00 Nawel123¾ Perssonet123nk Le Grand Duc1232¼ 15
Vindicator 7th
26Jly98♦ Club Hippico(Chi) gd *1 Ⓣ LH 1:371 Allowance Race Alw 6100 42¼ Figueroa M 123 4.00 Nawel123nk Le Grand Duc1231¾ Johnny Tres Mil123nk 8
10Jly98♦ Club Hippico(Chi) fm *1 Ⓣ RH 1:34 Allowance Race Alw 6100 21¾ Figueroa M 117 *1.00 Nawel1171¾ Perssonet1173 Mistic Game1171½ 10
Tavelli (126) 5th
19Jun98♦ Club Hippico(Chi) fm *6f Ⓣ LH 1:091 Allowance Race Alw 6000 2hd Figueroa M 119 - Tavelli119hd Pressonet119½ Edelmiro1194¼ 14
Cayetano Parletti (110) 5th
22May98♦ Club Hippico(Chi) fm *5f Ⓣ Str :573 Maiden Race Maiden 5600 14½ Guzman E 123 *1.00 Perssonet1234½ Koyam1232½ Cayetano Parletti114½ 14

WORKS: Feb24 SA 6f fst 1:114 H *2/19* Feb18 SA 5f fst 1:02 H (d) *6/19* Jan30 SA 5f fst 1:014 H *15/48* Jan21 SA 5f fst 1:00 H *19/82* Dec24 SA 5f fst 1:012 H *43/86*
TRAINER: Dirt(57 .12 $1.36) Routes(32 .06 $1.84) GrdStk(6 .00 $0.00)

Wooden Phone
Own: Durant & Helzer & Helzer
Black, Black And Silver Diamonds, Silver
NAKATANI C S (158 24 30 26 .15) 2001:(135 20 .15)

B. g. 4
Sire: Pick Up the Phone (Phone Trick) $2,000
Dam: Teaksberry Road(High Honors)
Br: T Wynn Jolley (Fla)
Tr: Baffert Bob(110 28 15 10 .25) 2001:(98 24 .24)

L 117

Life	9	3	2	2	$406,136	108	D.Fst	8	3	2	2	$403,136 108
2001	2	1	0	1	$319,776	108	Wet(240*)	1	0	0	0	$3,000 85
2000	5	1	1	1	$65,640	103	Turf(243*)	0	0	0	0	$0 –
SA	6	1	1	2	$361,416	108	Dist	0	0	0	0	$0 –

3Feb01-8SA fst 1⅛ :471 1:102 1:352 1:482 4 Strub-G2 108 3 1½ 2hd 1hd 12½ 12 Nakatani C S LB 117 b 7.20 93-12 Wooden Phone1172 Tiznow1233½ Jimmy Z117¾ Rail duel,clear,drivng 6
13Jan01-8SA fst 1 1/16 :231 :463 1:104 1:42 4 SanFrndoBC-G2 104 5 1½ 1hd 1½ 31 32 Nakatani C S LB 116 b 5.00 92-12 Tiznow1221¼ Wlkslikeduck120¾ WoodenPhone1162 Set pace,outfinished 6
26Dec00-6SA fst 7f :221 :442 1:083 1:213 Malibu-G1 101 1 5 64 52½ 43½ 31½ Nakatani C S LB 116 b 5.80 95-09 Dixie Union1211 Caller One119½ WoodenPhone1161 Came out 1/8,rallied 6
22Nov00-7Hol fst 7f :22 :443 1:092 1:22 3↑ Alw 42000N1X 103 3 4 2½ 11 13 14½ Nakatani C S LB 119 b 6.60 89-19 Wooden Phone1194½ Ceeband1211½ MarqOfZorro119½ Inside,clear,driving 9
11Mar00-3SA fst 1 :222 :462 1:112 1:374 Alw 57000N1X 99 4 45½ 33 2hd 2hd 2no Gomez G K LB 118 b 4.70 82-25 DvidCopperfield118no WoodenPhone1181¾ IndinAffir120no Rail trip,led 1/16 7
19Feb00-3SA fst 1 1/16 :231 :46 1:103 1:423 Alw 54000N1X 85 6 31 11 1½ 44½ 410½ Solis A LB 117 b 7.20 79-20 FusaichiPegasus1173½ Tribunl1193 Toqueville1174 Stalked,led,weakened 7
12Feb00-3SA my 6f :212 :443 :564 1:094 Alw 57500N1X 85 5 5 66 54 44¾ 44½ Flores D R LB 119 3.50 85-13 Echo Eddie1211 Here's Zealous1192 Star Maker1171½ 4 wide into stretch 6
Previously trained by Hatchett James
31Jly99-6Crc fst 6f :221 :46 :582 1:111 Md Sp Wt 24k 97 3 3 21 1hd 16 113½ Homeister R B Jr L 118 *.60 92-14 WoodenPhone11813 WhatBrinstorm118½ OurDiblo1181¾ Kept to pressure 8
17Jly99-3Crc fst 5½f :222 :464 :593 1:061 Md Sp Wt 24k 59 2 5 66½ 54 45 22½ Homeister R B Jr L 118 5.90 90-13 Divine Luck1182½ Wooden Phone118½ Mr. Livingston1182 5 wide, rallied 7
WORKS: ●Feb27 SA tr.t 5f my 1:004 H 1/10 Feb22 SA 6f fst 1:122 H 4/54 Feb11 SA 3f fst :353 B 2/29 Jan29 SA 5f fst 1:002 H 8/116 Jan23 SA 4f fst :472 H 6/49 Jan9 SA 5f fst 1:013 H 17/30
TRAINER: Dirt(639 .23 $1.52) Routes(301 .22 $1.42) GrdStk(114 .22 $1.41)

Beat All
Own: al Maktoum Sheikh Maktoum
Blue, White V-sash, Pale Blue Cap
STEVENS G L (136 27 24 16 .20) 2001:(117 24 .21)

Dk. b or br h. 5
Sire: Dynaformer (Roberto) $30,000
Dam: Spirited Missus(Distinctive)
Br: Allen Joseph (Ky)
Tr: Drysdale Neil(29 8 4 4 .28) 2001:(29 7 .24)

L 113

Life	11	2	3	2	$371,187	100	D.Fst	0	0	0	0	$0 –
2001	1	0	1	0	$15,915	100	Wet(330)	0	0	0	0	$0 –
2000	5	0	1	1	$115,857	–	Turf(295)	11	2	3	2	$371,187 100
SA	0	0	0	0	$0	–	Dist	0	0	0	0	$0 –

18Feb01-3SA fm 1¼ ⓣ :49 1:142 1:38 2:03 4↑ Ⓡ SanMarinoH77k 100 1 44 44 31½ 22½ 21½ Stevens G L LB 121 *.80 77-20 Kerrygold1181½ Beat All1214 Groover1132½ Bid 3wd,2nd best 4
Previously trained by Michael Stoute
23Sep00♦ Ascot(GB) yl 1½ⓣ RH 2:352 3↑ Cumberland Lodge Stakes-G3 Stk 78300 55 Eddery Pat 126 4.00 Mutamam1293 Happy Change126nk King O' The Mana118nk 6
Timeform rating: 108 Behind,4th 4f out,weakened over 1f out.Commander Collins 4th
29Jly00♦ Ascot(GB) gd 1½ⓣ RH 2:30 3↑ King George VI & Queen Eliz St-G1 Stk 1124000 46¼ Darley K 133 33.00 Montjeu1331¾ Fantastic Light1333½ Daliapour1331 7
Timeform rating: 120 Rated in 5th,3rd 2-1/2f out,one-paced to line.Shiva 7th
17Jly00♦ Ayr(GB) fm 1¼ⓣ LH 2:04 3↑ Scottish Classic-G3 Stk 52300 2no Darley K 128 2.75 Endless Hall135no Beat All1283½ Port Vila118½ 7
Timeform rating: 119 Rated in 5th,rallied to duel 150y out,gamely.Island House 5th
21Jun00♦ Ascot(GB) gd 1¼ⓣ RH 2:072 3↑ Prince of Wales's Stakes-G1 Stk 407000 38½ Fallon K 126 66.00 Dubai Millennium1268 Sumitas126½ Beat All1262½ 6
Timeform rating: 118 Dwelt,rated in 5th,angled out 1-1/2f out,3rd 1f out.Sendawar 4th
30May00♦ Sandown(GB) hy 1¼ⓣ RH 2:134 4↑ Brigadier Gerard Stakes-G3 Stk 59800 48¼ Fallon K 122 4.50 Shiva1261¾ Border Arrow1225 Sossus Vlei1221½ 8
Timeform rating: 112 Tracked clear leaders in 3rd,2nd 1f out,faded.Elle Danzig 7th
27Jun99♦ Curragh(Ire) gd 1½ⓣ RH 2:30 Irish Derby-G1 Stk 34575 412 Stevens G L 126 4.00 Montjeu1265 Daliapour1265½ Tchaikovsky1261½ 10
Timeform rating: 111 Tracked in 3rd,2nd 3f out,weakened 2f out.Mutafaweq 5th
5Jun99♦ Epsom(GB) gd 1½ⓣ LH 2:372 Epsom Derby-G1 Stk 1789000 33¼ Stevens G L 126 7.00 Oath1261¾ Daliapour1261½ Beat All126no 16
Timeform rating: 120 Towards rear,progress hfwy,8th 3f out,up for 3rd.Housemaster 4th
30Apr99♦ Newmarket(GB) gd 1¼ⓣ RH 2:014 Newmarket Stakes (Listed) Stk 36400 13 Eddery Pat 120 5.50 Beat All1203 Mukhalif1202½ Silver Robin120½ 9
Timeform rating: 111+ Settled towards rear,rallied to lead over 1f out,drew clear
10Sep98♦ Chepstow(GB) yl 7f ⓣ Str 1:251 Pat Eddery Maiden Stakes(Div1) Maiden 7700 12 Sanders S 126 *1.50 Beat All1262 Thrust1261½ Kondoty126¾ 11
Timeform rating: 90+ Tracked in 5th,roused halfway,led 2f out,ridden out
29Jly98♦ Doncaster(GB) gd 7f ⓣ Str 1:27 Rocket Maiden Stakes Maiden 8900 24 Darley K 126 2.25 Auction House1264 Beat All126nk Initiative126 14
Timeform rating: 83+ Tracked leaders,bid over 1f out,no chance with winner
WORKS: ●Feb24 Hol 7f fst 1:262 H 1/9 Feb9 Hol 5f fst 1:022 H 32/50 Feb3 Hol 6f fst 1:153 H 6/8 Jan28 Hol 5f fst 1:032 H 35/39 Jan21 Hol 4f fst :50 H 35/41 Jan16 Hol 4f fst :502 H 25/32
TRAINER: Turf/Dirt(3 .33 $1.00) Dirt(30 .37 $1.56) Routes(183 .26 $2.04) GrdStk(66 .20 $2.07)

Irisheyesareflying
Own: Dolan Racing St & Graham & Taylor
Gold Multi-colored Emblem On Back
DESORMEAUX K J (169 33 33 26 .20) 2001:(153 28 .18)

B. h. 5
Sire: Flying Continental (Flying Paster) $4,000
Dam: Sharon's Barron(Track Barron)
Br: Fitzpatrick Weston L Mr & Mrs (Cal)
Tr: Dolan John K(37 9 7 5 .24) 2001:(33 10 .30)

L 112

Life	24	5	5	4	$207,756	107	D.Fst	7	3	1	0	$79,905 107
2001	2	2	0	0	$93,600	107	Wet(345*)	6	1	3	1	$62,663 106
2000	7	0	2	3	$42,885	96	Turf(150*)	11	1	1	3	$65,188 94
SA	4	2	0	1	$98,640	107	Dist	0	0	0	0	$0 –

16Feb01-2SA fst 1 :224 :454 1:094 1:353 4↑ OClm 100000N 107 5 2hd 2hd 2hd 12 12 Desormeaux K J LB 119 fn 5.10 93-21 Irisheyesareflying1192 Futural119½ Estio119hd Strong handling 6
27Jan01-7SA wf 6½f ⊗ :22 :443 1:083 1:144 4↑ OClm 80000N 106 3 5 11 1½ 11½ 13½ Desormeaux K J LB 119 fn 19.30 94-10 Irisheyesareflying1193½ BlckSilk1191½ Explicit118no Inside,cleared,driving 9
28Oct00-8SA fm 1 ⓣ :221 :46 1:094 1:342 3↑ Ⓢ CalCupMile H175k 94 7 67½ 76½ 64 42½ 52½ Desormeaux K J LB 118 fn 11.30 84-13 RodToSlew1191½ NtivDsrt122no Fstsspdnbulit117no 4wd move,lost whip 1/8 12
24Aug00-7Dmr fm 1⅜ ⓣ :493 1:15 1:394 2:161 3↑ OClm 62500N 94 4 32½ 32 42 21 2hd Desormeaux K J LB 119 fn 4.90 87-17 SixZero123hd Irisheyesreflying1191¾ PtriotLove123no Pulled,bid,outgamed 6
3Aug00-5Dmr fm 1 1/16 ⓣ :234 :48 1:12 1:43 3↑ Clm 62500 (62.5-55) 85 1 74½ 64½ 84 84¾ 73¾ Espinoza V LB 118 fn 5.60 86-10 ChmpgnePrince1171½ KingClf1181 StormWrck1181 Blocked,steadied 1/8 10
12May00-4Hol fm 5½f ⓣ :22 :443 :564 1:021 4↑ Clm c-(50-45) 88 2 10 97 87½ 62½ 32 Blanc B LB 117 n 4.90 93-05 Gypsisnthplc1131¾ ColonlKlly117nk Irshysrflyng117½ Off bit slow,crowded 10
Claimed from A & S Racing Stables for $50,000, Salih Ahmad S Trainer 2000(as of 05/12): (13 4 2 3 0.31)
26Mar00-3SA fm 1⅛ ⓣ :482 1:124 1:372 1:493 4↑ Ⓢ OClm c-40000 92 4 53½ 56 56 21½ 3nk Espinoza V LB 118 f *2.00 81-18 DixieLaw120no VguelyGllnt118hd Irisheyesreflying1185 Bid btwn,willingly 7
Claimed from Dolan Racing Stable Engel & Friend for $40,000, Dolan John K Trainer 2000(as of 03/26): (27 3 8 6 0.11)
25Feb00-6SA gd 1 :223 :462 1:11 1:361 4 Clm c-(40-35) 87 2 53½ 62¾ 51¾ 42 33 Nakatani C S LB 117 *1.40 87-10 GonCourting1192 DringGnrl1171 Irishysrflying117½ Waited 1/4,tight 1/8 7
Claimed from Cogorno & Sherman for $40,000, Sherman Art Trainer 2000(as of 02/25): (359 62 70 60 0.17)
10Feb00-2BM sly 1 1/16 :232 :463 1:101 1:42 4↑ Clm 50000 (50-45) 96 1 21 31 21 2hd 22½ Baze R A LB 117 4.90 86-20 VoicOfDstiny1172½ Irishysrflying1174 SoringProspct112hd Bobbled break 5
17Dec99-2Hol fst 1 1/16 :231 :47 1:114 1:45 Clm 32000 (32-28) 84 6 3 5 11 1½ 13 2½ Valenzuela P A LB 118 3.50 74-25 BgBdBddy118½ Irshysrflng1182 BfrAndAftr1182½ Rail bid,led,worn down 6
28Nov99-8GG sf 1 1/16 ⓣ :233 :481 1:134 1:473+ 3↑ OClm 40000N 72 1 31½ 42 65 74¾ 109½ Castanon A L LB 117 42.30 61-30 HighNoonMtng115hd Missgon1171 TjShotthDputy116hd Stlkd rail, empty 12
14Nov99-8BM fst 1 1/16 :222 :451 1:092 1:412 Ascot H100k 69 8 67¾ 75 66 714 617 Castanon A L LB 117 22.60 75-17 Mr. Broad Blade1184 Seayabyebye1143 Incitatus1135½ Failed to respond 8
6Sep99-3BM fm 1 1/16 ⓣ :233 :474 1:12 1:422 Alw 38200N1X 92 2 42½ 43 3½ 13½ 1¾ Baze R A LB 118 3.30 94-07 Irshysrflyng118¾ CrsdngPro1183 FormlMtng1184 Strong rail bid, drvng 8
16Aug99-6Dmr fm 1 1/16 ⓣ :233 :472 1:12 1:432 Clm 50000 (50-45) 79 7 56½ 54 42½ 34½ 33½ Gomez G K LB 118 4.70 84-13 Azure Ciel118½ Wild N Golden1163 Irisheyesareflying1183½ Bit tight 1/8 7
22Jly99-6Dmr fst 1 :222 :46 1:103 1:363 3↑ Ⓢ Alw 54000N1X 77 7 63½ 72¾ 76¼ 76¾ 78 Espinoza V LB 115 10.40 81-13 SelectFew116½ PrstigiousChif121no SoulWrrior121½ 4 wide early,no rally 9
2Jly99-7Hol fm 1 1/16 ⓣ :232 :471 1:111 1:412 3↑ Ⓢ Alw 49000N1X 82 9 64¾ 55 54½ 32½ 43 Espinoza V LB 112 30.30 83-16 TheSmokster118½ WalkThatWlk116½ TooHigh1202 Angled in,no late bid 9
31May99-7GG fm 1 ⓣ :233 :474 1:13 1:382 Ⓡ Cal Sire100k 75 5 67 66 42½ 62¾ 65 Lopez A D LB 115 15.90 74-18 Incitatus1161 WalkThatWalk121¾ RdrContct121hd Blckd/14p, chckd 1/8h 8
21May99-5GG fm 1 1/16 ⓣ :234 :49 1:134 1:444+ Alw 42306N1X 79 4 21 2½ 2½ 2hd 42½ Lopez A D LB 118 11.70 81-12 Major Hero1181½ C's Chocolate118¾ Vaca Gold118nk Prssd pace 2w, wknd 9
22Apr99-5GG fst 1 1/16 :23 :48 1:131 1:441 Alw 25000s 80 6 2hd 1hd 11 11 14 Warren R J Jr LB 118 *2.20 81-17 Irshysrflyng1184 PrsdntlPull1181½ RstrdgBrx1181½ Dueled 3-2w, rddn out 8
10Apr99-7GG wf 1 1/16 :224 :462 1:103 1:441 Alw 42024N1X 74 2 73½ 75½ 75 54 44¾ Warren R J Jr LB 118 24.80 76-15 LordStrlng1182 AmrcnShn118¾ WhtAnHonr1182 Saved ground, no rally 10
WORKS: Feb25 SA tr.t 4f my :493 H 2/4 Feb9 SA 5f fst 1:021 H 30/63 Jan21 SA 5f fst 1:002 Hg32/82 Jan16 SA 6f fst 1:164 H 21/22 Jan6 SA 5f fst 1:001 H 9/52 Dec31 SA 5f fst 1:014 H 37/54
TRAINER: Dirt(100 .24 $2.31) Routes(56 .20 $1.49) GrdStk(3 .00 $0.00)

Tiznow

Own: C Straub–Rubens Rev Tr & Cooper M
Hot Pink Royal Blue Dots/cuffs
MCCARRON C J (121 23 17 17 .19) 2001:(111 21 .19)

B. c. 4
Sire: Cee's Tizzy (Relaunch) $5,000
Dam: Cee's Song(Seattle Song)
Br: Cecilia Straub Rubens (Cal)
Tr: Robbins Jay M(14 1 2 1 .07) 2001:(12 1 .08)

L 122

Life	11	6	4	0	$3,644,830	119	D.Fst	11	6	4	0	$3,644,830 119
2001	2	1	1	0	$198,880	108	Wet(345)	0	0	0	0	$0 –
2000	9	5	3	0	$3,445,950	119	Turf(160)	0	0	0	0	$0 –
SA	4	2	1	0	$438,880	119	Dist	3	2	1	0	$2,980,400 116

3Feb01–8SA	fst	1⅛	:471 1:102 1:352 1:482 4	Strub-G2	105 6 3¹ 3nk 4¾ 2²½ 2²	McCarron C J	LB 123	*.30	91–12	**Wooden Phone**117² Tiznow123³½ **Jimmy Z**117¾	Vied 3wd,4wd,2nd best	6
13Jan01–8SA	fst	1 1/16	:231 :463 1:104 1:42 4	SanFrndoBC-G2	108 6 2½ 2hd 2½ 2¹ 1¹¼	McCarron C J	LB 122	*.30	94–12	Tiznow122¹¼ Wlkslikeduck120¾ *WoodnPhon*116²	3wd bid,brushd,gamely	6
4Nov00–10CD	fst	1¼	:472 1:12 1:36 2:003 3↑	BC Classic-G1	116 12 1hd 1hd 1hd 1hd 1nk	McCarron C J	L 122	9.20	107 —	*Tiznow*122nk Gint'sCusewy122³¼ *CptinSteve*122hd	Duel,headed,gamely,drv	13
15Oct00–7SA	fst	1⅛	:47 1:104 1:35 1:471 3↑	GoodwoodBCH-G2	119 7 1¹½ 1¹ 1½ 1hd 1½	McCarron C J	LB 116	*1.20	99–13	*Tiznow*116½ Captain Steve117¹½ Euchre115⁴	Rated, repulsed rival	7
30Sep00–6LaD	fst	1¼	:471 1:102 1:351 1:594	Super Derby-G1	114 4 1hd 1½ 1¹ 1³ 1⁶	McCarron C J	L 124	*.80	103–05	*Tiznow*124⁶ Commendable124¹ Mass Market124⁹	Restrained, ridden out	6
26Aug00–8Dmr	fst	1¼	:452 1:094 1:35 2:011 3↑	PacificClsc-G1	115 4 3² 3³½ 2¹½ 2²½ 2²	McCarron C J	LB 117	4.00	93–14	Skimming124² *Tiznow*117¹¼ Ecton Park124½	Chased,bid, 2nd best	7
23Jly00–6Hol	fst	1⅛	:464 1:103 1:352 1:48	Swaps-G1	107 1 4¹½ 4² 4¹ 2¹½ 2²½	Espinoza V	LB 118 b	2.90	86–11	Captain Steve120²½ Tiznow118¹ Spacelink118²	Pulld,trapped rail 3/8	6
1Jly00–8Hol	fst	1 1/16	:231 :46 1:101 1:421	Affirmed H-G3	103 3 4² 3¹ 3½ 2hd 1nk	Espinoza V	LB 111 b	10.80	89–18	Tiznow111nk *Dixie Union*122² Millencolin117²	Tight rail 7-1/2 & 3/8	6
31May00–4Hol	fst	1 1/16	:233 :462 1:104 1:424 3↑	Md Sp Wt 52k	95 5 2½ 2hd 1² 1⁴½ 1⁸½	Solis A	LB 115 b	*1.30	86–21	*Tiznow*115⁸½ *ColdwterCnyon*116³½ FctulEvidenc115hd	Drew off, ridden out	9
11May00–6Hol	fst	1 1/16	:232 :47 1:12 1:431 3↑	Md Sp Wt 47k	99 3 7³½ 4¹¼ 4² 2¹ 2nk	Solis A	LB 115 b	*2.20	84–15	*SpicyStuff*115nk *Tiznow*115⁴ ColdwterCnyon116½	Crowded strt,waitd 1/4	9
22Apr00–7SA	fst	6f	:212 :441 :563 1:10	Md Sp Wt 47k	82 8 5 6³¾ 8¹⁰ 7⁸¼ 6³	Solis A	B 122 bn	13.80	86–13	Mr.Wondrfl122²½ *ProgrmmdAppl*122no CocontWlly122hd	Steadied near 3/8	10

WORKS: ●Feb22 SA 7f fst 1:234 H *1/7* Feb16 SA 5f fst :593 H *3/89* Jan27 SA 6f my 1:121 H *1/2* Jan6 SA 7f fst 1:263 H *2/3* Dec29 SA 7f fst 1:242 H *1/3* Dec22 SA 6f fst 1:124 H *9/27*

TRAINER: Dirt(66 .17 $1.75) Routes(38 .18 $1.84) GrdStk(8 .63 $6.83)

Nurdlinger

Own: Moreno Robert B
Electric Blue, Blue Rm On White Ball
VALDIVIA J JR (118 13 9 13 .11) 2001:(117 14 .12)

Ch. c. 4
Sire: Order (Damascus) $1,000
Dam: Steff Graf*Brz(Executioner)
Br: Moreno Robert B (Cal)
Tr: Sadler John W(56 9 10 9 .16) 2001:(52 8 .15)

L 110

Life	16	4	2	2	$188,420	96	D.Fst	11	4	1	0	$144,356 96
2001	2	0	0	0	$13,296	96	Wet(275*)	3	0	1	1	$36,480 86
2000	8	2	1	1	$108,600	95	Turf(237)	2	0	0	1	$7,584 75
SA	8	1	1	1	$94,096	96	Dist	0	0	0	0	$0 –

3Feb01–8SA	fst	1⅛	:471 1:102 1:352 1:482 4	Strub-G2	88 2 6⁴½ 6⁸¼ 6⁹¼ 6¹⁰ 5¹¹¾	Baze T C	LB 117	39.50	81–12	**Wooden Phone**117² **Tiznow**123³½ **Jimmy Z**117¾	Angled in, no rally	6
13Jan01–8SA	fst	1 1/16	:231 :463 1:104 1:42 4	SanFrndoBC-G2	96 1 6¹² 6¹⁸ 6¹³ 6⁹ 5⁷	Baze T C	LB 116	30.30	87–12	**Tiznow**122¹¼ Walkslikeduck120¾ ***WoodenPhone***116²	Awkward,slow start	6
26Dec00–5SA	fst	1 1/16	:231 :463 1:11 1:44 3↑	Alw 66080N1X	94 1 8⁷¾ 8¹⁰ 8⁵½ 6¹¾ 1¾	Baze T C	LB 121	7.60	83–23	Nurdlinger121¾ Marq Of Zorro119¹ HouseSpecial119no	Swung out,rallied	8
7Dec00–4Hol	fst	1 1/16	:232 :47 1:112 1:433 3↑	[S]OClm 40000N	95 3 5⁸ 5⁷ 5⁶¾ 4¹¾ 1½	Baze T C5	LB 111	6.80	82–28	*Nurdlinger*111½ DisguysDlimit119¹½ VgulyGllnt119¹	3wd into lane,rallied	6
17Nov00–6Hol	fm	1 1/16 Ⓣ	:234 :473 1:111 1:402 3↑	[S]Alw 43000N1X	75 3 8⁸½ 8⁸½ 8⁹½ 8¹⁰ 8⁸½	Garcia M S	LB 116	15.40	82–10	*Lily'sLad*118nk VguelyGllnt119³½ MeetMeInDixie118nk	Off bit slow,no rally	8
2Nov00–5SA	fst	1	:222 :46 1:104 1:363 3↑	[S]OClm 40000N	82 7 6⁹½ 7⁷¼ 5⁵¾ 4⁷ 4⁷	Garcia M S	LB 116	4.40	81–14	It's AReality118³½ NoApollogee118²½ Halfaleagueonward116¹	Off bit slow	8
20Oct00–3SA	fst	6f	:214 :45 :57 1:093 3↑	[S]OClm 40000N	76 4 7 7¹⁰ 7⁷½ 7⁸½ 6⁷	Nakatani C S	LB 117	*2.30	84–12	ProudLouie118² MeetMeInDixi118¹½ Hlflguonwrd116no	Off slow,no speed	7
11Mar00–8BM	gd	1 1/16	:22 :452 1:10 1:432	ElCmnoRlDby-G3	77 9 13²¹ 13¹⁷ 11¹⁰ 7⁶¼ 6⁸½	Garcia M S	LB 115	7.90	73–20	RmmbrShkh117¹½ TrCnfdnc116³½ CntryCst115no	Lacked needed response	14
12Feb00–1SA	my	1	:223 :454 1:111 1:373	[S]Alw 54000N1X	86 4 4⁸ 3⁹½ 3³½ 3²½ 3¾	Garcia M S	LB 117	1.70	82–17	Misconcption119½ NughtyNcho117nk Nurdlngr117nk	Rallied,drftd out late	5
15Jan00–8GG	wf	1 1/16	:223 :462 1:10 1:423	GldnGateDby-G3	79 5 9¹⁰ 9¹¹ 8⁹¾ 6³¼ 2¹	Garcia M S	LB 120	13.20	88–10	New Advantage120¹ Nurdlinger120nk Shake Loose120¾	Late rally	9
30Dec99–7SA	fst	7f	:222 :444 1:091 1:223	[S]CalBrdrsChmp150k	82 2 9 10¹³ 10¹³ 7⁹½ 5⁵¼	Gomez G K	LB 115	9.50	87–12	GibsonCounty117nk StormyJck122³½ *EchoEddi*115½	Saved ground to lane	10
9Dec99–6Hol	fst	7f	:22 :453 1:111 1:243	Alw 40000s	81 1 8 7⁸¾ 6⁴½ 3½ 1²	Garcia M S	LB 118	*1.70	79–21	Nurdlinger118² AlongCmeGeorge120¹½ *RetsinYr*120¹½	Inside rally stretch	8
30Oct99–6SA	fst	1 1/16	:223 :46 1:11 1:434	[S]Cal Cup Juv125k	81 8 11¹⁴ 11¹² 9¹⁰ 4⁵ 2⁴½	Garcia M S	LB 118	68.90	79–15	Spacelink118⁴½ *Nurdlinger*118¹½ Stormy Jack118²	Off slw,stdied,rallied	11
15Oct99–2SA	fm	1 Ⓣ	:231 :464 1:101 1:34	[R]Pinjara54k	70 3 4⁷ 4⁸ 5¹¹ 5⁹½ 3⁷½	Garcia M S	LB 115	13.80	81–10	PurelyCozzene118⁴ It'sAllInstinct115³½ Nurdlingr115¹½	Bit awkward start	5
23Sep99–11Fpx	fst	1 1/16	:224 :462 1:121 1:451	GatewayGlory50k	61 2 9⁹¼ 5⁷ 6⁴ 5⁵½ 5⁸½	Garcia M S	LB 114	9.50	75–19	Kleofus114²½ Stayton122½ Foxy Sneakers114⁴½	Rail trip, no late bid	10
3Sep99–5Dmr	fst	6f	:221 :46 :591 1:123	[S]Md 32000 (32–28)	55 4 11 9¹³ 8¹⁰ 4⁷½ 1⁵	Garcia M S	LB 118	10.60	77–18	Nurdlinger118⁵ Trif118² Flying Firebirds118¹½	Slw strt,late rush	11

WORKS: Feb28 SA 4f sly :473 H *1/2* Feb21 SA 7f fst 1:273 H *3/6* Feb15 SA 5f gd 1:024 H *46/66* Jan27 SA 6f my 1:144 H *2/2* Jan7 SA 6f fst 1:132 H *6/26* Dec18 Hol 5f fst 1:013 H *11/26*

TRAINER: Dirt(323 .15 $1.78) Routes(86 .14 $1.23) GrdStk(8 .00 $0.00)

Jimmy Z

Own: Moss Mr & Mrs Jerome S
Green Pink Hoop/bar On Sleeves
ESPINOZA V (281 39 34 32 .14) 2001:(248 33 .13)

Dk. b or br g. 4 KEESEP98 $110,000
Sire: Fly So Free (Time for a Change) $7,500
Dam: Secondfromthetop(Fappiano)
Br: Cambus–Kenneth Farm (Ky)
Tr: McAnally Ronald(56 7 12 6 .13) 2001:(46 5 .11)

L 111

Life	14	2	4	4	$186,200	102	D.Fst	10	1	4	4	$157,220 102
2001	1	0	0	1	$60,000	99	Wet(310*)	1	1	0	0	$27,000 87
2000	12	2	4	3	$124,220	102	Turf(210)	3	0	0	0	$1,980 78
SA	8	1	2	4	$129,220	102	Dist	0	0	0	0	$0 –

3Feb01–8SA	fst	1⅛	:471 1:102 1:352 1:482 4	Strub-G2	99 1 5⁴ 5⁷¼ 5⁸¾ 4⁷½ 3⁵½	Pincay L Jr	LB 117	10.10	87–12	**Wooden Phone**117² **Tiznow**123³½ Jimmy Z117¾	Late outside for 3rd	6
30Dec00–5SA	fst	7f	:23 :451 1:092 1:22 3↑	OClm 62500N	98 2 7 7⁹¾ 7¹¹ 7⁵¾ 2¾	Pincay L Jr	LB 118	4.10	94–08	**Tribunal**118¾ Jimmy Z118¹½ No Armistice120nk	Squeezd strt,late foot	7
30Nov00–5Hol	fst	1 1/16	:224 :453 1:102 1:422 3↑	OClm 62500N	95 7 9¹³ 8¹⁰ 6⁵½ 2⁴½ 2³	Stevens G L	LB 117	3.50	85–19	*Freedom Crest*118³ Jimmy Z117¹½ First Journey112⁵	Off slow,2nd best	9
5Nov00–3SA	fst	1	:23 :463 1:102 1:354 3↑	Alw 48000N2X	102 5 5⁴ 4¹¾ 4¹½ 4¹½ 2¹	Stevens G L	LB 116	3.30	91–19	BosqueRedondo116¹ JimmyZ116hd *FredomCrst*118¹½	4 wide,game for 2nd	5
15Oct00–3SA	fst	1 1/16	:233 :474 1:12 1:43 3↑	Alw 48000N2X	95 1 5³ 5²¼ 4¹½ 3¹½ 3¹	Solis A	LB 117	*1.20	87–13	*Dhaffir*120nk Freedom Crest118¾ Jimmy Z117²	Inside, willingly	6
3Sep00–8Dmr	fst	1 1/16	:223 :461 1:104 1:422 3↑	OClm 50000N	100 6 5⁵¾ 4⁴½ 3¹½ 1½ 1⁴	Solis A	LB 114	3.10	91–08	Jimmy Z114⁴ Musical Gambler117no Ceeband116½	3w bid,strong handling	7
5Aug00–7Dmr	fst	1 1/16	:224 :462 1:104 1:43 3↑	Alw 67260N1X	95 8 8¹³ 8¹⁰ 7⁴¾ 4³½ 2¹	Solis A	LB 114	4.20	87–16	Kaiser So Say122¹ *Jimmy Z*114²½ Solarino120²	4wd move,rallied	8
4Jun00–7Hol	fm	1 Ⓣ	:233 :471 1:102 1:343	Alw 51000N1X	69 6 3⁴ 3³ 6⁵ 7⁶¼ 7⁸½	Desormeaux K J	LB 120	4.30	81–08	Morocco120¹ Credit Call118¹ *Pizza N Beer*122nk	3wd,wkened,drftd in	8
10May00–7Hol	fm	1 1/16 Ⓣ	:233 :472 1:11 1:413	Alw 51255N1X	65 2 9⁵¾ 9⁵¼ 11⁷ 10¹⁰ 10¹⁰¼	Solis A	LB 120	3.40	75–10	Heritage Hall120¹½ Credit Call118¹ Turco118½	Tight 7/8,shuffld 5/16	11
1Apr00–4SA	fst	1 1/16	:233 :472 1:12 1:43	Alw 57855N1X	92 3 5⁴½ 6²¾ 6³¼ 5⁵ 3⁴¼	Solis A	LB 118	2.20	84–12	***Tribunal***120¾ Greenbaypacker118³½ Jimmy Z118½	Off rail,late for 3rd	6
11Mar00–3SA	fst	1	:222 :462 1:112 1:374	Alw 57000N1X	96 1 7¹³ 6⁸¼ 5⁴ 4³ 4²	Solis A	B 118	2.30	80–25	DvdCopprfld118no ***WoodnPhon***118¹¾ IndnAffr120no	Inside move,missd 3rd	7
21Feb00–4SA	wf	7f	:222 :452 1:11 1:234	Md Sp Wt 46k	87 2 3 3¹½ 1¹ 1⁶ 1²²	Solis A	B 121	*.40	86–17	Jimmy Z121²² Radix Alis121³½ Dinnerathepalms121¹	Drew off, ridden out	4
15Jan00–7SA	fst	7f	:221 :451 1:10 1:23	Md Sp Wt 45k	85 4 5 4³¼ 4³ 4³ 3¹	Solis A	B 120	2.40	89–09	True Confidence120nk Lytle Creek120¾ *Jimmy Z*120¹½	4 wide turn, rallied	8
18Dec99–8Hol	fm	5½f Ⓣ	:221 :444 :572 1:031	Md Sp Wt 33k	78 3 9 9¹¹ 8¹² 6⁷¾ 4⁴	Solis A	B 120	11.90	84–11	NowVoyger120²½ *DoubleForignr*120½ WhitTopCot120¹	Off slow,late foot	10

WORKS: Feb22 SA 7f fst 1:274 H *6/7* Feb16 SA 5f fst 1:004 H *24/89* Feb11 SA 4f fst :513 H *58/61* Jan27 SA 5f my 1:03 H *15/20* Jan20 SA 7f fst 1:252 H *2/8* Jan14 SA 5f fst 1:02 H *53/83*

TRAINER: Dirt(188 .09 $1.04) Routes(232 .13 $1.62) GrdStk(60 .18 $1.50)

Guided Tour

Own: Fink Morton
Yellow, Brown Hoops And Bars On Sleeves,
MELANCON L (1 1 0 0 1.00) 2001:(96 20 .21)

B. g. 5
Sire: Hansel (Woodman) $7,500
Dam: Dancing Mahmoud(Topsider)
Br: Woodlynn Farm Inc (Ky)
Tr: O'Callaghan Niall M(1 1 0 0 1.00) 2001:(33 5 .15)

L 116

Life	23	9	7	0	$760,033	109	D.Fst	15	7	4	0	$635,385 109
2001	1	1	0	0	$180,000	108	Wet(385*)	2	1	1	0	$95,720 101
2000	14	5	6	0	$516,082	109	Turf(320)	6	1	2	0	$28,928 95
SA	1	1	0	0	$180,000	108	Dist	2	0	1	0	$100,000 106

4Feb01-8SA	fst	1⅛		:464 1:104 1:353 1:481	4↑ SanAntonioH-G2	108	3	31½	21½	2½	1½	11½	Melancon L	LB 115 b	3.40	94-11	GddTor1151½ LthlInstrmnt1163½ MoonlghtChrgr1131½	Rail bid,2wd,gamely	8
30Dec00-9FG	fst	1 1/16		:234 :471 1:121 1:44	3↑ Louisiana H75k	109	5	66	66½	22½	21½	12	Melancon L	L 115 b	2.10	91-09	GuidedTour1152 Vlhol114¾ ConcernedMinister1144¾	3-wide middle move	7
24Nov00-11CD	fst	1⅛		:472 1:113 1:361 1:483	3↑ Clark H-G2	109	1	22	22½	22	21½	24	Melancon L	L 114 b	9.20	89-14	Surfside1134 Guided Tour1141¼ Maysville Slew1131¾	5w trip, 2ndbest	9
4Nov00-10CD	fst	1¼		:472 1:12 1:36 2:003	3↑ BC Classic-G1	94	4	83½	125½	129½	1110	1215	Melancon L	L 126 b	91.90	92 —	Tiznow122nk Giant'sCauseway1223¼ CaptinSteve122hd	Rank,steadied 3/4 pl	13
7Oct00-9Haw	fst	1¼		:484 1:124 1:374 2:03	3↑ HawGoldCupH-G3	106	7	32	43	2½	2½	21	Melancon L	L 113 b	8.40	86-25	DustOnTheBottl1121 GuiddTour113nk GoldnMissil1213½	Gained place late	8
4Sep00-6Tdn	sly	1⅛		:471 1:122 1:381 1:511	3↑ HallFameBCH-G3	101	6	32	33½	2½	12½	15¼	Melancon L	L 116 b	*.50	85-21	Guided Tour1165¼ Sleight1141½ Desert Demon1147	Rallied 3w,much best	6
6Aug00-8WO	fst	1 1/16		:233 :471 1:112 1:42	3↑ SeagramCup132k	105	1	1hd	1hd	2hd	1hd	1½	Boulanger G	L 117 b	*.45	97-03	Guided Tour117½ Air Cool1138¾ Synchronized1112¾	All out inside	5
3Jly00-8CD	fst	1		:221 :442 1:083 1:34	3↑ Alw 62205N4X	106	2	56	44½	31½	11½	13¾	Melancon L	L 122 b	2.60	100-11	Guided Tour1223¾ Coast Of Mane115½ Jadada122hd	4wide, driving	8
8Jun00-9CD	fst	1 1/16		:242 :481 1:123 1:432	3↑ Alw 52400N3X	100	7	43½	31½	31	11½	1½	Melancon L	L 120 b	*2.00	93-07	GuidedTour120½ CoastOfMane1181¾ ReglDom1202	Stalked,4wide,driving	8
4May00-4CD	fst	1 1/16		:243 :482 1:123 1:424	3↑ Alw 52400N3X	100	1	55	55	31	21	2¾	Melancon L	L 120 b	4.70	95-13	VisionAndVers118¾ GuiddTour1204¼ MkYourMrk118nk	4wide bid, 2nd best	6
14Apr00-6Kee	fm	1⅛	Ⓣ	:47 1:112 1:361 1:48	4↑ Alw 65000N3X	89	6	51¾	43	41¾	41¼	53¾	Bailey J D	L 115 b	5.80	89-09	RiverRptor115¾ WillimsNws1151¼ GnrlAvition115½	Stalked,flattened out	10
18Mar00-9OP	fst	1 1/16		:23 :462 1:113 1:431	4↑ Razorback H-G3	100	3	67½	610	56	54½	43	Gonzalez C V	L 111 fb	10.20	85-19	Well Noted112¾ Crimson Classic1151¾ Mr Ross115½	Lacked late bid	7
20Feb00-8FG	fm	*1 1/16	Ⓣ	:242 :492 1:14 1:452	4↑ Alw 34000N3X	95	6	31½	22	21½	22	21½	Martinez W	L 117 b	2.00	91-07	Super Red1171½ Guided Tour117½ Avigator117hd	Close up, game for 2nd	7
24Jan00-9FG	fst	1 1/16	⊗	:244 :483 1:13 1:44	4↑ Alw 34000N3X	99	4	33	34½	33	23½	21½	Martinez W	L 117 b	*1.40	89-22	Power OfHumor1171½ GuidedTour1173½ RoughGuide1174½	Asked, late gain	6
2Jan00-8FG	fm	*1	Ⓣ	:224 :464 1:123 1:372	4↑ Alw 34000N3X	94	2	1013	1011	108	55	24	Martinez W	L 119 b	10.40	95-06	InCseOfFire1224 GuiddTour1191½ RoughGuid1171	Game close mid track	12
16Nov99-8CD	fst	1		:234 :471 1:122 1:37	3↑ Alw 42200N2X	92	6	84½	82½	41½	11	12¼	Melancon L	L 115 b	10.30	85-20	Guided Tour1152¼ Tightlies1151¼ Dead Serious1102½	Split foes,inside,drvg	8
23Oct99-10Haw	fm	1⅛	Ⓣ	:453 1:094 1:35 1:473	3↑ Alw 32155N2X	74	9	77¾	45½	53½	67½	85¾	Razo E Jr	115 b	4.90	91-09	Maneland117no WhichHand114no Snugglin'Man113¾	Close up, steady fade	12
2Oct99-10Haw	fst	1 1/16	⊗	:242 :483 1:131 1:441	3↑ Alw 30888N1X	82	6	63¾	52½	32½	2½	13¼	Guidry M	114 b	*1.20	92-08	Guided Tour1143¼ Sui Generis114nk Watch My Gold1143½	Driving	9
7Aug99-10Haw	sly	1 1/16	⊗	:231 :47 1:122 1:451	3↑ Alw 35464N1X	84	5	96	85¼	41¾	2hd	22¼	Guidry M	114 fb	5.30	85-15	Steel City1162¼ Guided Tour1146 GetTricky1142½	Swung wide second best	10
5Jly99-10EIP	fm	1 1/16	Ⓣ	:233 :462 1:102 1:413	3↑ Md Sp Wt 21k	72	4	43	44½	51¾	21½	1hd	Torres F C	L 113 b	6.90	86-10	Guided Tour113hd Brandish122nk Hello Cielo1131¼	Bump foe start,driving	8

WORKS: Feb22 SA 5f fst 1:02 B 51/77 Feb16 SA 4f fst :522 H 70/70 Feb2 SA 4f fst :511 H 23/26 Jan26 FG 5f fst 1:023 B 8/25 Jan21 FG 5f gd 1:023 B 25/52 Jan14 FG 5f fst 1:03 B 25/41
TRAINER: Dirt(239 .15 $1.63) Routes(204 .14 $1.70) GrdStk(24 .13 $0.88)

Moonlight Charger

Own: Clark Duane B
Green, White Dc Emblem, White Sleeves
BAZE T C (182 28 15 22 .15) 2001:(165 26 .16)

Dk. b or br g. 6
Sire: Alysheba (Alydar) $5,000
Dam: Malibran(Spectacular Bid)
Br: Clark Duane (Ky)
Tr: Sullivan John(10 0 0 2 .00) 2001:(10 0 .00)

L 111

Life	19	4	3	4	$179,368	108	D.Fst	16	3	2	4	$140,368 108
2001	2	0	0	2	$43,680	100	Wet(295)	2	1	1	0	$39,000 105
2000	8	2	1	2	$97,528	108	Turf(300)	1	0	0	0	$0 69
SA	13	4	2	3	$164,548	105	Dist	0	0	0	0	$0 –

4Feb01-8SA	fst	1⅛		:464 1:104 1:353 1:481	4↑ SanAntonioH-G2	100	8	42	32	33	34	35	Baze T C	LB 113	66.00	89-11	GddTor1151½ LthlInstrmnt1163½ MonlghtChrgr1131½	4wd 1st turn,3rd best	8
19Jan01-2SA	fst	1 1/16		:231 :462 1:102 1:423	4↑ OClm 100000N	99	2	23	24	22	31½	32½	Atkinson P	LB 119	9.20	88-21	HighWireAct119hd Tribunl1172½ MoonlightChrgr1198	3wd bid,outfinished	4
13Dec00-3Hol	fst	1 1/16		:241 :472 1:111 1:414	3↑ Alw 53000N3X	77	1	2½	1hd	31½	511	516¾	Delahoussaye E	LB 117	3.90	74-22	FredomCrst119¾ BosquRdondo1162 NwAdvntg1166	Dueled inside, tired	5
11Nov00-7Hol	fst	1 1/16		:231 :461 1:102 1:414	3↑ OClm 100000N	108	1	21	2hd	2hd	1hd	31¾	Delahoussaye E	LB 117	4.80	89-22	LthlInstrumnt1191¾ Zntt117no MoonlghtChrgr1177	Inside,led,outfinished	5
26Oct00-3SA	fst	1		:23 :461 1:10 1:351	3↑ OClm 100000N	85	4	63¾	66	67½	58	510¼	Delahoussaye E	LB 118	4.80	85-05	Dhaffir120nk Estio1201½ Spicy Stuff1181½	Lacked late response	7
6Oct00-7SA	fst	7f		:223 :452 1:091 1:212	3↑ OClm 100000N	92	4	1	33	32½	42½	54½	Atkinson P	LB 118	17.20	93-11	BldeProspector1202½ OutstndingHro113hd Grdy1181	Split foes,no late bid	6
24Mar00-7SA	fst	1 1/16		:232 :47 1:11 1:413	4↑ TokyoCity H76k	102	1	51¾	52½	32	33	33½	Atkinson P	LB 117	5.80	91-13	Luftikus1162 Moore'sFlt1211½ MoonlightChrgr11712	Stalked rail,3rd best	6
20Feb00-4SA	wf	1	⊗	:234 :473 1:113 1:361	4↑ Alw 59740N2X	105	3	21½	21	21½	21	11¼	Atkinson P	LB 120	2.00	90-16	MoonlightCharger1201¼ Mr.Sefrer1161½ Hflinger1161½	Stalked,led, driving	4
28Jan00-7SA	fst	1		:23 :471 1:114 1:364	4↑ OClm 62500N	102	5	2hd	2hd	2hd	1hd	2hd	Atkinson P	LB 120	17.20	87-21	Futural116hd Moonlight Charger1205 Brilliantly1183	Dueled,led,gamely	6
7Jan00-7SA	fst	1 1/16		:23 :463 1:11 1:441	4↑ Alw 54000N1X	87	1	53½	56	42¼	1hd	1nk	Atkinson P	LB 118	12.10	82-14	MoonlightChrger118nk DvonDputy120nk MxpInty116½	4wd bid,led,gamely	9
10Dec99-7Hol	fst	1 1/16		:231 :461 1:102 1:422	3↑ OClm 40000N	83	2	52½	44½	47½	310	213	Atkinson P	LB 118	36.80	75-19	SixBelow11813 MoonlightCharger1181 SaintWynn1161½	Inside to 2nd turn	10
28Oct99-3SA	fst	1⅛		:48 1:121 1:38 1:51	3↑ Alw 40000s	83	6	21	22	2½	11½	12½	Atkinson P	LB 122	5.50	80-25	MoonlightChrgr1222½ CptnHook1181 Hlthlqudtor118hd	Bid,led 1/4,driving	7
2Oct99-10SA	fst	1 1/16		:222 :463 1:121 1:442	3↑ Md 22500 (25-22.5)	76	1	1hd	1hd	12	13	110	Atkinson P	LB 120	7.20	81-19	MoonlghtChrgr12010 AffrToB1208 RoylSunst1201	Inside,drew clear,dvng	10
25Aug99-5Dmr	fst	1		:214 :451 1:101 1:374	3↑ Md 32000 (32-28)	3	3	42½	43	69½	919	942½	Almeida G F	LB 122 b	12.80	40-18	King'sHonor1185 Stbilizr1186 Sydny'sOlympics1181½	Close up, gave way	10
29Jly99-5Dmr	fst	7f		:221 :45 1:094 1:224	3↑ Md 50000 (50-45)	57	3	5	43	44	75¾	711½	Pincay L Jr	LB 123	12.00	77-08	CaseyGriffin1182 Roncesvalles113½ AGoodDncer1232	Inside, weakened	10
18Jly99-10Hol	fm	1	Ⓣ	:224 :46 1:103 1:351	3↑ Md Sp Wt 43k	69	11	46	47½	65	810	811	Sorenson D	LB 123	40.20	76-16	Motto1231 Devil's Tower116no Spice Guy1161¼	Chased, weakened	12
9Apr99-2SA	gd	1 1/16		:23 :473 1:124 1:45	4↑ Md 32000 (32-28)	87	9	2½	2½	2hd	1hd	2hd	Almeida G F	LB 122	27.80	78-22	Anthony'sVl122hd MonlghtChrgr1226½ KntckyBlbrd122nk	Dueled, willingly	9
3Mar99-5SA	fst	6½f		:213 :442 1:092 1:161	4↑ Md Sp Wt 51k	33	8	3	75¼	89¼	814	727	Skelly R V	LB 121	59.40	60-12	Sir Dennis121nk Rapidough121hd Motto1217	Angled in, no factor	9
4Apr98-6SA	fst	6½f		:222 :451 1:091 1:154	Md Sp Wt 38k	22	1	6	65½	49	417	527½	Pincay L Jr	B 120	6.90	62-07	[D]Prado'sCapote115½ ThreeCardWillie12010 RunawyKidd12015	Off slowly	7

WORKS: Feb24 SA 6f fst 1:131 H 6/19 Feb18 SA 5f fst 1:043 H (d) 17/19 Jan15 SA 5f fst 1:001 H 11/83 Jan5 SA 5f fst 1:012 H 15/41 Dec29 SA 4f fst :48 H 10/35 Dec5 SA 5f fst 1:023 H 36/45
TRAINER: Dirt(27 .11 $1.60) Routes(26 .15 $2.08) GrdStk(1 .00 $0.00)

Tribunal

Own: Lewis Beverly J & Robert B
Green, Yellow Hoops/sleeves, Green
FLORES D R (207 33 33 26 .16) 2001:(184 28 .15)

Ch. c. 4 KEEJUL98 $1,800,000
Sire: Deputy Minister (Vice Regent) $150,000
Dam: Six Crowns(Secretariat)
Br: Carl Rosen Associates (Ky)
Tr: Baffert Bob(110 28 15 10 .25) 2001:(98 24 .24)

Blinkers OFF

L 112

Life	9	3	3	0	$159,000	104	D.Fst	9	3	3	0	$159,000 104
2001	2	0	1	0	$42,800	104	Wet(360)	0	0	0	0	$0 –
2000	6	3	2	0	$116,200	100	Turf(280)	0	0	0	0	$0 –
SA	7	3	3	0	$159,000	104	Dist	0	0	0	0	$0 –

3Feb01-8SA	fst	1⅛		:471 1:102 1:352 1:482	4 Strub-G2	98	5	42	41¼	2hd	32½	46¼	Stevens G L	LB 117 b	5.70	87-12	Wooden Phone1172 Tiznow1233½ Jimmy Z117¾	Off slow,bid btwn,wknd	6
19Jan01-2SA	fst	1 1/16		:231 :462 1:102 1:423	4↑ OClm 100000N	104	1	48½	410	45	1½	2hd	Nakatani C S	LB 117 b	*.50	91-21	HighWirAct119hd Trbunl1172½ MoonlghtChrgr1198	Rail trip,led,outgamed	4
30Dec00-5SA	fst	7f		:23 :451 1:092 1:22	3↑ OClm 62500N	100	5	5	31	2½	11½	1¾	Nakatani C S	LB 118 b	3.30	95-08	Tribunal118¾ Jimmy Z1181½ No Armistice120nk	Bobbled strt,led,held	7
1Apr00-4SA	fst	1 1/16		:233 :472 1:12 1:43	Alw 57855N1X	99	1	65	52¼	3nk	2½	1¾	Nakatani C S	LB 120 b	*1.00	88-12	Tribunal120¾ Greenbaypacker1183½ Jimmy Z118½	Rail trip,gamely	6
12Mar00-9FG	fst	1 1/16		:23 :461 1:11 1:431	La Derby-G2	46	8	64	63½	910	1020	1033½	Bailey J D	L 122 b	6.50	61-13	Mighty1222 More Than Ready122½ Captain Steve122hd	Lunged break	10
19Feb00-3SA	fst	1 1/16		:231 :46 1:103 1:423	Alw 54000N1X	97	4	76	77½	33	22	23½	Espinoza V	LB 119 b	2.20	86-20	Fusaichi Pegasus1173½ Tribunal1193 Toqueville1174	Split foes 3/8,2d best	7
23Jan00-6SA	fst	1 1/16		:223 :47 1:113 1:433	Md Sp Wt 47k	94	2	67¼	44	41½	1½	15	Valenzuela P A	LB 120 b	*.90	85-20	Tribunal1205 Hoover Tower120½ Jedi Teddy1203½	Bid btwn,clear,driving	9
1Jan00-9SA	fst	1 1/16		:231 :47 1:113 1:443	Md Sp Wt 47k	88	7	43	52½	31	11	2½	Valenzuela P A	LB 120 b	6.70	79-17	Aptitude120½ Tribunal1203 Hoover Tower1207	Drifted in 1/8,caught	9
11Dec99-6Hol	fst	6½f		:224 :452 1:101 1:163	Md Sp Wt 33k	61	10	3	77½	78½	812	814¾	Valenzuela P A	LB 120 b	*2.20	73-20	DvidCopprfld120nk FuschPgsus1205 Forbodng1201	Angled in turn,no bid	10

WORKS: Feb27 SA tr.t 5f my 1:022 H 5/10 ●Feb22 SA 6f fst 1:12 H 1/54 Feb17 SA 5f fst 1:00 H 13/115 Jan29 SA 5f fst 1:003 H 14/116 Jan15 SA 5f fst 1:00 H 7/83 Jan10 SA 3f fst :352 H 2/40
TRAINER: BlinkOff(401 .23 $1.55) Dirt(639 .23 $1.52) Routes(301 .22 $1.42) GrdStk(114 .22 $1.41)

Jorrocks

Own: Duggan & Equils & Mowrey
Teal, White 'Jem' On Navy Oval Emblem
GOMEZ G K (151 14 23 22 .09) 2001:(137 14 .10)

B. g. 7
Sire: Rubiano (Fappiano) $10,000
Dam: Perla Fina(Gallant Man*GB)
Br: Amstrong Stewart L (Ky)
Tr: Hess R B Jr(63 10 4 6 .16) 2001:(59 9 .15)

Ⓛ 113

Life	39	9	5	4	$118,151	–	D.Fst	6 4 2 0		$34,849	–
2001	4	3	1	0	$37,077	–	Wet(340)	1 1 0 0		$11,988	–
2000	8	2	2	0	$11,870	–	Turf(270)	32 4 3 4		$71,314	–
SA	0	0	0	0	$0	–	Dist	1 0 1 0		$3,665	–

Previously trained by Mick Easterby

1Feb01 ♦ Wolverhmptn(GB) **Timeform rating: 110**	fst 1 1/16	LH 1:493 3↑	Arena Leisure Cndtns Stk(dirt) Alw 15700	15	Quinn J	132	3.00	Jorrocks1325 Hail The Chief1378 Young-Un13211 *Tracked leaders,2nd over 3f out,led 1-1/2f out,drew clear in hand*	12
19Jan01 ♦ Southwell(GB) **Timeform rating: 97**	sly 7f	LH 1:30 4↑	Tote Exacta 1-2 Hcp (dirt) Hcp 18400	1½	Quinn J	135	*2.25	Jorrocks135½ Air Mail1335 Social Contract128¾ *Mid-pack,rail bid 2-1/2f out,blocked,angled out,led 100y out*	16
9Jan01 ♦ Wolverhmptn(GB) **Timeform rating: 97**	fst *1 3/16	LH 2:031 3↑	Ryde Handicap (dirt) Hcp 18300	2nk	Quinn J	133	*.80	Young-Un125nk Jorrocks1336 Hannibal Lad1363 *Rtaed in 6th,rallied into 2nd 1-1/2f out,gamely*	8
1Jan01 ♦ Southwell(GB) **Timeform rating: 95**	fst 1	LH 1:402 4↑	Bet Direct Handicap (dirt) Hcp 18900	15	Quinn J	127	6.00	Jorrocks1275 Culzean135hd Young-Un1254 *Wide twrds rear,angled in for rail bid to lead 1f out,drew clear*	16
8Dec00 ♦ Southwell(GB) **Timeform rating: 83**	fst 1	LH 1:423 3↑	Bet Direct Handicap (dirt) Hcp 8400	11¾	Lucas T	125	*2.50	Jorrocks1251¾ Young-Un1282 Day-Boy1203 *Close up,lacked room 2f out,angled right,led 1f out,drifted left*	11
24Nov00 ♦ Southwell(GB) **Timeform rating: 76**	fst 6f	LH 1:142 3↑	Bet Direct Hcp (Div 1) (dirt) Hcp 7000	2¾	Lucas T	123	4.50	Blakeset135¾ Jorrocks123nk Dahlidya1123½ *Outrun early,bid 2f out,never catching winner*	13
17Nov00 ♦ Southwell(GB) **Timeform rating: 71**	fst 7f	LH 1:292 3↑	Saffie Joseph & Sons Hcp(dirt) Hcp 4100	12	Lucas T	136	14.00	Jorrocks1362 Annie Apple1281¼ High Esteem138nk *Dwelt,outrun early,rallied in traffic to lead 70y out,going away*	15
19Oct00 ♦ Newcastle(GB)	hy 7f	Ⓣ Str 1:391 3↑	Gosforth Park Racing Club Hcp Hcp 3800	1151¼	Darley K	139	*3.00	Oriole1232½ Sand Hawk1292 Ambushed1362½ *Chased leaders,weakened 2-1/2f out*	14
7Oct00 ♦ York(GB)	hy 1⅛	Ⓣ LH 2:044 3↑	Schroders Handicap Hcp 30500	1750¾	Hanagan P5	118	*9.00	Greenaway Bay1151¾ Annadawi1352½ Route Sixty Six1131 *Chased leaders,weakened 3f out*	20
3Sep00 ♦ York(GB) **Timeform rating: 60**	gd 7f	Ⓣ LH 1:261 3↑	Quintin Gilbey Silver Trophy H Hcp 19900	74½	Parkin G	128	8.00	Style Dancer134½ Cusin121hd Bundy128½ *Trailed,progress 3f out,never threatened*	23
29Jly00 ♦ Newcastle(GB) **Timeform rating: 62**	gd 7f	Ⓣ Str 1:254 3↑	Beeswing Handicap Hcp 23900	61¾	Hanagan P7	105	*3.50	Tony Tie138nk Karameg132no Supreme Salutation125½ *Close up,bid with leaders,outfinished*	11
24Jly00 ♦ Beverley(GB) **Timeform rating: 74**	gd 7½f	Ⓣ RH 1:342 3↑	Sailors Families Society Hcp Hcp 10500	2¾	Lucas T	134	4.00	Wilemmgeo106¾ Jorrocks1341½ Kestral1112 *Led to over 1f out,yielded grudgingly*	16
14Oct99 ♦ Redcar(GB) **Timeform rating: 57+**	gd 7f	Ⓣ Str 1:224 3↑	Racing Channel on NTL Handicap Hcp 15500	136½	Lucas T	117	*2.25	Kayo1371¾ Italian Symphony101½ Only For Gold108nk *Tracked leaders,weakening when bumped 1f out*	29
21Sep99 ♦ Beverley(GB) **Timeform rating: 80+**	sf 7½f	Ⓣ RH 1:373 3↑	Brian Merrington Memorial Hcp Hcp 8300	19	Lucas T	122	5.00	Jorrocks1229 Darwell's Folly1382 Tipperary Sunset128¾ *Handily placed in 3rd,wide bid to lead 2f out,easily clear*	16
23Jly99 ♦ Nottingham(GB)	gd *1 70	Ⓣ LH 1:43 3↑	Brackenhurst College Handicap Hcp 8400	1416¼	Roberts M	126	8.00	Adobe1191 Dark Age108½ Melodian1133 *Behind,progress over 3f out,drifted left and weakened 2f out*	16
3Jly99 ♦ Carlisle(GB) **Timeform rating: 52**	gd 1	Ⓣ RH 1:431 3↑	MacMillan Nurses Classified St Alw 5600	56	Parkin G	130	4.50	Arc1303 Time To Wyn1211½ Clarinch Claymore121hd *Led to over 1f out,weakened*	9
15Jun99 ♦ Thirsk(GB)	gd 7f	Ⓣ LH 1:26 3↑	Frankland Handicap Hcp 8400	1212¼	Lucas T	138	10.00	Lunch Party130hd Hakeem1271½ Zoom Up140½ *Pressed pace to halfway,gradually weakened*	12
2Jun99 ♦ Beverley(GB)	gd 7½f	Ⓣ RH 1:373 3↑	Derby Week Handicap Hcp 8600	1325¼	Bardwell G	138	12.00	Tipperary Sunset126¾ Tropical Beach113no Bollin Ethos124¾ *Pressed pace in 3rd,led 3f to 2f out,weakened*	15
8May99 ♦ Beverley(GB) **Timeform rating: 68**	gd 1 1/16	Ⓣ RH 1:50 3↑	Freemen of Beverly Handicap Hcp 11000	713¾	Parkin G	126	25.00	Jedi Knight126no [D]Tipperary Sunset11810 Kass Alhawa126nk *Never far away,weakened 1-1/2f out*	17
20Apr99 ♦ Pontefract(GB)	sf 1	Ⓣ LH 1:534 3↑	Coral Handicap Hcp 18000	1727	Lucas T	134	33.00	Nominator Lad135½ Ca'd'Oro1182 Mawingo124nk *Tracked leders,gradually weakened over 3f out*	19

WORKS: Feb24 SA 5f fst 1:022 H *48/59*
TRAINER: 1stW/Tm(186 .16 $1.61) Dirt(359 .17 $1.85) Routes(157 .13 $1.18) GrdStk(10 .00 $0.00)

Lethal Instrument

Own: Craig Jenny & Sidney H
White, Black Horse Emblem On Back, Blue
PINCAY L JR (246 44 31 34 .18) 2001:(218 37 .17)

B. h. 5
Sire: Gulch (Mr. Prospector) $60,000
Dam: Running Redhead(Storm Bird)
Br: Starstruck Farms (Ky)
Tr: Shirreffs John(27 5 3 3 .19) 2001:(21 4 .19)

L 115

Life	15	5	4	3	$319,700	111	D.Fst	15 5 4 3		$319,700	111
2001	1	0	1	0	$60,000	106	Wet(355)	0 0 0 0		$0	–
2000	9	3	2	2	$161,120	111	Turf(300)	0 0 0 0		$0	–
SA	7	2	2	1	$153,240	107	Dist	0 0 0 0		$0	–

4Feb01-8SA	fst 1⅛	:464 1:104 1:353 1:481 4↑	SanAntonioH-G2	**106**	5	52¼	54½	43½	2½	21½	Nakatani C S	LB 116	4.50	92-11	**GuddTor**1151½ LthlInstrmnt1163½ **MoonlightChrgr**1131½	Inside bid,2nd best	8
28Dec00-7SA	fst 1	:224 :454 1:093 1:352 3↑	[R]Ack Ack75k	**107**	3	42½	54	32	21	11	Nakatani C S	LB 117	*.80e	94-13	LethalInstrument1171 DeputyFlag1206 Dhffir116½	Bid,led past 1/8,dvng	6
3Dec00-8Hol	fst 1⅛	:461 1:10 1:342 1:464 3↑	NativeDivrH-G3	**110**	6	57	55¼	43½	22½	27	Nakatani C S	LB 116	4.00	88-05	Sky Jack1187 *Lethal Instrument*1163½ *Grey Memo*1131½	4wd 3/8,2nd best	8
11Nov00-7Hol	fst 1 1/16	:231 :461 1:102 1:414 3↑	OClm 100000N	**111**	4	54	42	3nk	3½	11¾	Pincay L Jr	LB 119	2.80	91-22	LthlInstrumnt1191¾ *Zntt*117no **MoonlightChrgr**1177	3wd bid,led 1/16,dvng	5
26Oct00-3SA	fst 1	:23 :461 1:10 1:351 3↑	OClm 100000N	**72**	2	51¾	76½	710	712	716¾	Pincay L Jr	LB 120	3.40	78-05	Dhaffir120nk Estio1201½ Spicy Stuff1181½	Saved ground, gave way	7
30Aug00-6Dmr	fst 1	:22 :451 1:094 1:362 3↑	OClm 62500N	**101**	6	54½	56¾	34½	31½	11	Pincay L Jr	LB 117	3.20	93-11	LethlInstrumnt1171 KisrSoSy1191 MilkWood117½	4wd move,led,driving	8
6Jly00-7Hol	fst 1⅛	:471 1:111 1:361 1:491 3↑	OClm 80000N	**99**	5	43½	43½	43	31½	2no	Pincay L Jr	LB 117	*1.10	83-25	*LordStrling*117no *LthlInstrumnt*1171½ MrronGlc1173½	Came out,late surge	6
8Jun00-3Hol	fst 1 1/16	:24 :473 1:114 1:424 3↑	OClm 80000N	**93**	2	33	32	21½	32	36	Pincay L Jr	LB 117	4.20	80-14	Skimming1202 PtienceGme1174 LthlInstrumnt1177	Bid off rail,held 3rd	5
11May00-7Hol	fst 1 1/16	:231 :463 1:111 1:43 3↑	OClm 62500N	**100**	6	31½	52¼	4¾	2hd	31½	Pincay L Jr	LB 117	3.10	84-15	*Euchr*120hd SultrySubstitut1171¼ LthlInstrumnt1176	Bid 4wd,outfinished	7
31Mar00-7SA	fst 7f	:223 :452 1:091 1:213 4↑	Alw 57000N2X	**91**	6	8	65	63¾	53¾	45¼	Pincay L Jr	LB 118	4.10	92-14	*StrightMn*1181½ OutstndingHero118nk PtienceGme1183½	Inside, no late bid	8
30Apr99-2Hol	fst 1 1/16	:234 :473 1:113 1:424	Alw 53000N1X	**93**	2	2½	2hd	2hd	1hd	1nk	Pincay L Jr	LB 119	*.30	86-19	LethlInstrumnt119nk RdEy1176½ KyToSuccss1215½	Dueled,led,held gamely	5
27Mar99-5TP	fst 1⅛	:49 1:13 1:37 1:49	GalleryFurn-G2	**84**	2	31½	41½	51¾	57½	512	McCarron C J	L 121	5.00	78-15	Stephen Got Even1212½ K One King1215 Epic Honor1212½	Off inside, tired	8
6Mar99-1SA	fst 1 1/16	:234 :472 1:11 1:421	Alw 54000N1X	**105**	3	41½	41½	32	31½	2½	Nakatani C S	LB 117	3.90	91-11	StrightMn117½ LethlInstrument1172 Sint'sHonor1197	Stalked,rail rally	6
14Feb99-3SA	fst 1 1/16	:233 :473 1:114 1:42	Alw 56700N1X	**97**	2	55	56	53½	42¾	35	Nakatani C S	LB 117	1.30e	88-11	HighWireAct1171 NoClBrd1214 LthlInstrumnt117½	4wd into lane,no bid	5
16Jan99-6SA	fst 6f	:213 :444 :57 1:092	Md Sp Wt 45k	**98**	2	9	73¾	43	2½	15	Stevens G L	LB 119	4.90	93-05	Lethal Instrument1195 Jab119½ Prince Twining1191½	Steady handling	12

WORKS: ●Feb24 Hol 6f fst 1:124 H *1/14* Feb17 Hol 6f fst 1:134 H *5/19* Jan29 Hol 6f fst 1:163 H *17/21* Jan23 Hol 5f fst 1:014 H *16/30* Jan17 Hol 6f fst 1:12 H *2/10* Jan10 Hol 5f gd 1:014 H *10/46*
TRAINER: Dirt(86 .23 $1.43) Routes(92 .26 $1.99) GrdStk(20 .20 $1.18)

Bienamado
Own: McCaffery & Sangster & Toffan
Gold, Silver Diamond On Back, Silver
SOLIS A (194 23 36 31 .12) 2001:(175 22 .13)

Ch. h. 5
Sire: Bien Bien (Manila)
Dam: Nakterjal*GB(Vitiges*Fr)
Br: John Toffan & Trudy McCaffery (Ky)
Tr: Gonzalez J Paco(13 2 2 0 .15) 2001:(13 2 .15)

L 119

Life	12	6	3	0	$811,009	108	D.Fst	0	0	0	0	$0	–
2001	1	1	0	0	$90,000	107	Wet(298)	0	0	0	0	$0	–
2000	4	3	0	0	$537,070	108	Turf(270*)	12	6	3	0	$811,009	108
SA	0	0	0	0	$0	–	Dist	0	0	0	0	$0	–

20Jan01- 8SA fm 1¼ (T) :503 1:153 1:393 2:023 4↑ SanMarcos-G2 107 3 11½ 11 1hd 1½ 11½ McCarron C J LB 122 *.40 81-19 Bienamado1221½ *Kerrygold*116¾ NorthernQuest1221½ Wide early,game rail 7
2Dec00- 8Hol fm 1½ (T) :491 1:131 2:011 2:254 3↑ HolTurf Cup-G1 108 5 34 21½ 2½ 12 13 McCarron C J LB 126 *1.00 90-08 *Bienamado*1263 NorthernQuest126½ LzyLode1265 Clear,steady handling 8
19Aug00- 9AP yl 1¼ (T) :473 1:114 1:371 2:011 3↑ Arl Million-G1 100 5 56 58 41 42 44¾ Desormeaux K J L 126 *2.90 96-04 Chester House1263¼ Manndar126½ Mula Gula1261 Wide, bid, tired 7
23Jly00- 3Hol fm 1½ (T) :474 1:122 2:003 2:25 3↑ Sunset H-G2 105 1 27 2½ 1hd 11 11½ McCarron C J LB 122 *.20e 94-10 Bienmdo1221½ DeployVenture1151½ SinglEmpir1205½ Led 1/4,game rail lane 5
25Jun00- 9Hol fm 1¼ (T) :463 1:102 1:351 1:584 3↑ [R]Jim Murray H78k 108 7 33 37 1hd 13 17 McCarron C J LB 121 *1.70 102 — *Bienamado*1217 Casino King1171½ Adcat116½ 3wd move,ridden out 8
Previously trained by Foster George
17Oct99- 8WO gd 1½ (T) :491 1:14 2:052 2:321 3↑ CanadianInt-G1 98 7 86½ 57½ 47 45 54 McCarron C J 119 4.20 68-31 Thornfield1261 Fruits Of Love1261 Courteous1261 Mild bid 4 wide 9
Previously trained by Peter Chapple-Hyam
12Sep99♦ Longchamp(Fr) gd *1½(T) RH 2:324 Prix Niel-G2 2hd Hughes R 128 11.00 Montjeu128hd Bienamado1282 First Magnitude1283 4
Timeform rating: 119 Stk 108000 *Led after 4f,drifted left & right stretch,headed near line*
17Aug99♦ York(GB) gd 1½(T) LH 2:29 Great Voltigeur Stakes-G2 21¼ Hughes R 121 5.50 Fantastic Light1211¼ Bienamado1211¼ Glamis1211 7
Timeform rating: 119 Stk 160000 *Trailed,close 7th 4f out,2nd 2f out,held by winner.Mutafaweq 4th*
6Jly99♦ Newmarket(GB) gd 1½(T) RH 2:251 3↑ Princess of Wales's Stakes-G2 58½ Quinn T R 115 14.00 Craigsteel1281 Arctic Owl1311¼ Silver Rhapsody125nk 8
Timeform rating: 106+ Stk 86200 *Rated in 5th,3rd 2f out,weakened 1-1/2f out.Sea Wave 4th,Capri7th*
31Oct98♦ Saint-Cloud(Fr) hy *1¼(T) LH 2:212 Criterium de Saint-Cloud-G1 26 Hughes R 126 *.70 Spadoun1266 Bienamado1263 Cupid1261½ 6
Timeform rating: 103 Stk 122000 *Tracked clear leaders in 3rd,bid 2f out,no chance with winner*
3Oct98♦ Longchamp(Fr) sf *1⅛(T) RH 1:59 Prix de Conde-G3 13 Hughes R 128 *1.90 Bienamado1283 Persianlux1281½ Franky Furbo1282 5
Timeform rating: 111+ Stk 66400 *Tracked in 3rd,rallied between horses to lead 1f out,drew clear*
5Sep98♦ Haydock(GB) gd *140(T) LH 1:421 Stanley Racing Conditions Stks 14↓ Reid J 119 2.00 [DH]Bienamado119[DH]Mixsterthetrixster1244 Crown Of Trees124 3
Timeform rating: 99+ Alw 18000 *Tracked in 3rd,raced greenly,rallied to share lead on line*
WORKS: Feb28 SA tr.t 3f my :381 B *3/4* Feb21 SA 6f fst 1:13 H *3/26* ●Feb15 SA 5f gd :592 H *1/66* Feb8 SA (T) 6f fm 1:13 H (d) *1/1* ●Jan31 SA (T) 5f fm 1:013 H (d) *1/6* Jan15 SA (T) 5f gd 1:04 H (d) *3/6*
TRAINER: Turf/Dirt(8 .50 $5.05) 31-60Days(33 .24 $1.72) Dirt(71 .18 $1.71) Routes(70 .26 $1.69) GrdStk(29 .17 $1.27)

Despite the presence of 2000 Horse of the Year Tiznow, this Santa Anita Handicap has attracted a field of 12 (after the scratch of Nurdlinger), due, no doubt, to the race's prestige and its $1 million purse.

Not surprisingly, there is a lot of deadwood in this dozen, so let's begin by immediately eliminating Perssonet, Jimmy Z, Moonlight Charger, and Jorrocks, all of whom are either too slow to win, according to the Beyer figures, or are clearly overmatched. Secondary eliminations include Irisheyesareflying and Lethal Instrument. Both come into this race in sharp form, but both seem clearly unsuited to the 1¼-mile distance on dirt.

And since the "Big Cap" is a dirt race, as we've just said, let's deal next with turf specialists Bienamado and Beat All. By virtue of his dominant victory in the Hollywood Turf Cup in late 2000 and his victory in the San Marcos in his first start of 2001, Bienamado is the ranking turf horse in the United States. Beat All was third to the brilliant Dubai Millenium in a Group 1 stakes in England in 2000, and he demonstrated that he had adapted to American racing when he ran a decent second in the restricted San Marino Handicap in his first start of 2001. Both Bienamado and Beat All seem to have enough class to win this race, especially Bienamado, and both figure to be comfortable at the distance.

This is the first career attempt on dirt for both Bienamado and Beat All, however, and no matter how well they may have worked on the main track in the mornings, there is no guarantee they will be able to replicate their strong turf form under race conditions. Even so, thanks to Bienamado's accomplishments and the reputation of Beat All's trainer, Neil Drysdale, both are supported at the windows: Bienamado is

6-1 and Beat All is 11-1. Given that they are total question marks on the dirt, and that both will have to answer this question against a reigning Horse of the Year, their prices just aren't good enough. Out they go.

So we're left with four contenders: Tiznow, Wooden Phone, Guided Tour, and Tribunal.

Tiznow, who clinched his Horse of the Year title with a thrilling victory in the 2000 Breeders' Cup Classic, began 2001 well enough with a workmanlike victory in the San Fernando at a distance that was shorter than his best. However, he was upset in the Strub Stakes by Wooden Phone, who ran his finest race to date.

Tribunal was one of trainer Bob Baffert's best hopes for the Kentucky Derby a year ago, but never made it to Churchill because of injury. He also ran in the Strub, finishing fourth after moving prematurely. Guided Tour, meanwhile, is coming off a win in the San Antonio Handicap, an important prep for the Big Cap, in which he earned the same Beyer figure of 108 that Wooden Phone got in the Strub. And, like Wooden Phone, Guided Tour is in career form.

There are two important issues that have to be considered before settling on a selection: the condition of Tiznow, and the track bias at Santa Anita.

At first glance, Tiznow's loss at 1-5 in the Strub could be alarming. It was the third straight race in which his Beyer figure declined, and when jockey Chris McCarron asked him to go on the far turn, he didn't pick it up. Right off the bat, it is not unreasonable to wonder if Tiznow has lost a step. When a high-quality performer loses a step, the fall is much more severe than for an average horse. With an average horse, you can run him for a reduced tag, look for an easier allowance race, or search for a softer stakes spot. When a top horse enters decline, there is nowhere to hide.

Silver Charm illustrates this point well. He was a fine racehorse, winner of two-thirds of the Triple Crown and a Dubai World Cup. He signaled his decline in the 1999 Donn Handicap at Gulfstream, where he was a soundly beaten third as the 4-5 favorite. The excuse was made that drawing the 12 post killed him, but there's a long run to the first turn in $1\frac{1}{8}$-mile races at Gulfstream, and he was no more than two or three wide on the first turn.

The most alarming thing about his performance in the Donn was that Silver Charm was ninth early on, nowhere near the early lead. When a horse like Silver Charm, whose calling card in his best performances was positional speed, suddenly loses that positional speed, it is a sure sign of decline.

Despite sharp workouts for the subsequent Santa Anita Handicap, Silver Charm fell back noticeably through the middle stages of the race and again could do no better than third. He then stopped badly in his defense of the Dubai World Cup, and when he showed no life in the Stephen Foster in his return to these shores, he was retired.

Tiznow's situation for the Big Cap is different from Silver Charm's. He hasn't had stressful, multiseason campaigns and hasn't traveled as extensively. Plus, there is a specific reason Tiznow hasn't run up to his stellar 2000 form. Thanks to his refreshingly candid trainer, Jay Robbins, everyone who follows racing news knows that Tiznow is battling a troublesome quarter crack that has affected his performance in races and compromised his training.

To be sure, Tiznow's quarter-crack problems have not disappeared in between the Strub and the Big Cap, but improved workouts and the fact that the Tiznow people are pressing on with such a valuable piece of horseflesh suggest that the problem has been brought under control.

The other big issue in the Big Cap is track bias. In the three days before the race, and on race day itself, there has been a profound bias toward rail runners on the main track at Santa Anita. Throughout this period, if your horse got to the rail at any point in the race and then stayed there, you were in great shape. If you got to the lead and got to the rail, you were in even better shape.

A bias such as this can have a major impact on the outcomes of even the biggest races. For example, during the 1996 Breeders' Cup at Woodbine, there was a powerful rail bias on the main track. In the Juvenile Fillies, Storm Song raced in the one or two path throughout in her off-the-pace score. She never won again in five subsequent starts; in fact, she never got closer than being beaten 8½ lengths.

In the Classic, Cigar was heavily favored to record a repeat victory. Although he may have declined a bit from his peak, he was still sent off at 3-5. Try as he might—and he was beaten only a nose and a head—Cigar could not overcome a five-wide trip in a 13-horse field racing against that bias.

The rail bias for our Big Cap looks like trouble for Tribunal, because he would have to come from well off the pace and it would be too much to expect him to pick up eight or nine horses while getting clear sailing on the rail. He would have to come off the rail at some point, and that would cost him.

The bias is also trouble for Guided Tour, because regular rider Larry Melancon is coming west for the mount, and you can't bank on him knowing how the track is playing.

Even Tiznow is in trouble with the bias. He isn't going to outrun Wooden Phone for the lead, and although he has the speed to drop in right behind him, Tiznow showed in the Breeders' Cup—and in his first two starts this year—that he prefers to run outside.

And that leaves Wooden Phone. He will go for the lead, and breaking from post 2, the rail is all his. Wooden Phone is better than 6-1. Tiznow, who can't reasonably be expected to be 100 percent even if his quarter-crack troubles are under control, is even money.

NINTH RACE

Santa Anita
MARCH 3, 2001

1¼ MILES. (1.57⁴) 64th Running of THE SANTA ANITA HANDICAP. Grade I. Purse $1,000,000. 4-year-olds and upward. By subscription of $100 each to accompany the nomination, $2,500 to pass the entry box and $7,500 to start with $1,000,000 guaranteed, of which $600,000 to first, $200,000 to second, $120,000 to third, $60,000 to fourth and $20,000 to fifth. The field will be limited. Preference shall be given to the high weights based upon the weight assignments, adjusted for the sex allowance. Total earnings in 2000–2001 will be used in determining the preference of horses with equally assigned weights. No horse shall be assigned more than 126 lbs. Closed Saturday, February 17, 2001 with 27 nominations.

Value of Race: $1,000,000 Winner $600,000; second $200,000; third $120,000; fourth $60,000; fifth $20,000. Mutuel Pool $1,298,411.0 Exacta Pool $695,662.00 Quinella Pool $81,898.00 Trifecta Pool $755,033.00 Superfecta Pool $255,426.00

Last Raced	Horse	M/Eqt.	A.Wt	PP	¼	½	¾	1	Str	Fin	Jockey	Odds $1
3Feb01 8SA²	Tiznow	LB	4 122	5	2½	2½	2½	1hd	12½	15	McCarron C J	1.00
3Feb01 8SA¹	Wooden Phone	LBb	4 117	2	1hd	1½	1hd	2½	2½	2½	Nakatani C S	6.70
3Feb01 8SA⁴	Tribunal	LB	4 116	9	8¹	8½	8½	6hd	4½	3²	Flores D R	22.60
16Feb01 2SA¹	Irisheyesareflying	LBf	5 117	4	3½	32½	31½	31½	3²	41	Desormeaux K J	16.40
4Feb01 8SA¹	Guided Tour	LBb	5 116	7	5²	5²	4hd	41	5hd	51	Melancon L	6.70
3Feb01 8SA³	Jimmy Z	LB	4 111	6	11½	11²	11²	11½	11½	6½	Espinoza V	28.50
4Feb01 8SA³	Moonlight Charger	LB	6 111	8	41	4½	6½	8½	7½	7nk	Baze T C	f-98.80
18Feb01 3SA²	Beat All	LB	5 115	3	7²	6hd	5½	5½	6²½	8³	Stevens G L	11.30
20Jan01 8SA¹	Bienamado	LB	5 119	12	9hd	9hd	9hd	10²	9hd	92½	Solis A	6.10
4Feb01 8SA⁴	Perssonet-CH	LB	6 111	1	10¹	103½	104	9hd	101	101	Blanc B	83.10
4Feb01 8SA²	Lethal Instrument	LB	5 116	11	6²½	7³	7³	7³	8hd	111	Pincay L Jr	21.70
1Feb01 WOL¹	Jorrocks	LB	7 114	10	12	12	12	12	12	12	Gomez G K	65.90

f–Mutuel Field: Moonlight Charger.

OFF AT 4:18 Start Good. Won driving. Track fast.
TIME :23, :46², 1:10³, 1:35⁴, 2:01² (:23.13, :46.41, 1:10.75, 1:35.85, 2:01.55)

$2 Mutuel Prices:				
	5–TIZNOW	4.00	3.20	2.80
	2–WOODEN PHONE		5.40	4.40
	8–TRIBUNAL			8.40

$1 EXACTA 5–2 PAID $10.90 $2 QUINELLA 2–5 PAID $13.00 $1 TRIFECTA 5–2–8 PAID $119.50 $1 SUPERFECTA 5–2–8–4 PAID $1,243.10

B. c, by Cee's Tizzy–Cee's Song, by Seattle Song. Trainer Robbins Jay M. Bred by Cecilia Straub Rubens (Cal).

TIZNOW angled in and dueled outside WOODEN PHONE, forged to the front in hand leaving the second turn, kicked clear into the stretch and proved best under some urging and steady handling. WOODEN PHONE had good early speed and dueled inside the winner on a short advantage, fought back when initially headed nearing the quarter pole, then was no match but second best. TRIBUNAL broke out and bumped a rival, angled in early and saved ground, came out on the second turn and four wide into the stretch and picked up the show. IRISHEYESAREFLYING broke in a bit, stalked the dueling leaders a bit off the rail to the stretch and lacked the needed response. GUIDED TOUR was in a good position off the rail chasing the pace early, continued three deep on the backstretch and second turn, came out a bit into the stretch and could not offer the necessary rally. JIMMY Z between horses early, settled off the inside, came wide into the stretch and improved position. MOONLIGHT CHARGER close up chasing the leaders a bit off the rail, dropped back into and on the second turn and weakened. BEAT ALL broke a bit slowly, settled off the inside, angled in on the backstretch and saved ground to no avail. BIENAMADO bumped and stumbled badly after the start, settled outside and never rallied. PERSSONET (CHI) saved ground off the pace to the second turn, came out a bit on that bend and was not a factor. LETHAL INSTRUMENT bumped between foes at the start, settled off the inside chasing the pace, came five wide into the stretch and weakened. JORROCKS bumped and squeezed badly at the start, angled in and saved ground but was outrun.

Owners— 1, Cooper Michael & Cecilia Straub Rev; 2, Durant Helzer & Helzer; 3, Lewis Robert B & Beverly J; 4, Dolan Racing Stable Graham & Taylor; 5, Fink Morton; 6, Moss Mr & Mrs Jerome S; 7, Clark Duane B; 8, al Maktoum Sheikh Maktoum; 9, McCaffery T Toffan J & Sangster R; 10, Cobra Farm Inc; 11, Craig Sidney H & Jenny; 12, Duggan Equils & Mowrey

Trainers—1, Robbins Jay M; 2, Baffert Bob; 3, Baffert Bob; 4, Dolan John K; 5, O'Callaghan Niall M; 6, McAnally Ronald; 7, Sullivan John; 8, Drysdale Neil; 9, Gonzalez J Paco; 10, Puype Mike; 11, Shirreffs John; 12, Hess R B Jr

Scratched— Nurdlinger (3Feb01 8SA⁵)

$2 Daily Double (6–5) Paid $31.20; Daily Double Pool $82,081.
$1 Pick Three (3–6–5) Paid $82.40; Pick Three Pool $169,276.

I bet Wooden Phone and watched as Tiznow pressed Wooden Phone's lead from the outside, took over at will into the stretch, and drew away to win by five. Wooden Phone, going a distance that was probably a bit too long for him, still held second.

I had the right idea. I just got beat by a monster. Sometimes that happens, and the only thing you can do is tip your hat to the winner. I tipped mine to Tiznow.

The 2001 Blue Grass

More and more, horses running in stakes are really prepping for their main targets, other stakes races down the road. Of course, you see this most frequently in the major preps for the Kentucky Derby.

1 Invisible Ink
Own:Peachtree Stable
Purple; Tan Braces, Tan Bars On Sleeves,
VELAZQUEZ J R (21 3 0 3 .14) 2001:(376 78 .21)

B. c. 3 (Apr) KEESEP99 $105,000
Sire: Thunder Gulch (Gulch) $50,000
Dam: Conquistress(Conquistador Cielo)
Br: Viking Farms Limited (Ky)
Tr: Pletcher Todd A(5 0 1 0 .00) 2001:(136 33 .24)

L 123

Life	6	3	1	1	$178,060	98	D.Fst	4	2	0	1	$144,460	98
2001	3	2	0	1	$142,000	98	Wet(341)	2	1	1	0	$33,600	79
2000	3	1	1	0	$36,060	79	Turf(255*)	0	0	0	0	$0	–
Kee	0	0	0	0	$0	–	Dist	2	1	0	1	$125,200	94

10Mar01-11GP fst 1⅛ :464 1:112 1:37 1:494 Fla Derby-G1 94 2 42 6¼ 5½ 5½ 37 Velazquez J R L122 1.40e 81-13 Monrchos1224½ Outofthebox1222½ InvisibleInk122½ Traffic, check 1/4pole 13
31Jan01-4GP fst 1 1/16 :233 :472 1:113 1:433 Alw 37000N2X 98 1 42½ 31½ 21 21½ 1nk Velazquez J R L122 1.50 90-20 InvisibleInk122nk PercyHope1209 AmricnPrinc1186½ Stdy 1st turn, just up 6
6Jan01-9GP fst 1 1/16 :242 :491 1:133 1:451 Alw 33000N1X 82 4 31½ 51½ 31 2hd 1¾ Velazquez J R L122 *2.00 82-17 *Invisible Ink*122¾ Thunder Blitz1221¼ LateExtra1209¾ Five wide move turn 7
30Nov00-4Aqu my 1⅛ :491 1:152 1:412 1:542 Md Sp Wt 42k 79 1 11 12 1½ 12 11¼ Velazquez J R L119 *1.10 65-31 *InvisibleInk*1191¼ MyTwoSons11913 *LakeAgawam*119no Pace, clear, driving 8
11Nov00-5Aqu sly 1 :233 :474 1:132 1:394 Md Sp Wt 42k 75 8 61¾ 62 41½ 1½ 2¾ Velazquez J R L119 2.85 68-28 OverTheHorizon119¾ *InvisiblInk*119¾ LkAgwm1194½ Game finish outside 10
29Oct00-6Aqu fst 7f :232 :47 1:114 1:243 Md Sp Wt 41k 69 9 1 72¾ 63¾ 37 47¾ Gryder A T 119 10.00 69-23 *EsngAlong*1195½ PyThPnthr1191½ MyTwoSons119¾ Stumbled start, 4 wide 10
WORKS: Apr7 Kee 6f fst 1:152 B *1/2* ●Mar26 Hia 5f fst 1:01 B *1/9* Mar6 Hia 5f fst 1:01 B *3/17* Mar1 Hia 5f fst 1:01 B *2/12* Feb19 Hia 5f fst 1:002 B *5/21* Feb12 Hia 5f fst 1:022 B *15/17*
TRAINER: 31-60Days(155 .17 $1.56) Dirt(577 .18 $1.53) Routes(435 .17 $1.80) GrdStk(92 .17 $1.48)

1a Hero's Tribute
Own:Oxley John C
Gold; Blue Blocks, White Stripes
BAILEY J D (25 7 3 4 .28) 2001:(261 63 .24)

Dk. b or br c. 3 (Mar) KEESEP99 $150,000
Sire: Sea Hero (Polish Navy) $10,000
Dam: Eastern Dawn(Damascus)
Br: Dr & Mrs R Smiser West & Mr & Mrs M Miller (Ky)
Tr: Ward John T Jr(4 2 0 0 .50) 2001:(26 8 .31)

L 123

Life	6	3	1	1	$188,483	101	D.Fst	6	3	1	1	$188,483	101
2001	2	1	0	1	$105,300	101	Wet(310*)	0	0	0	0	$0	–
2000	4	2	1	0	$83,183	91	Turf(210*)	0	0	0	0	$0	–
Kee	1	1	0	0	$33,723	91	Dist	0	0	0	0	$0	–

11Mar01-9FG fst 1 1/16 :232 :461 1:111 1:443 La Derby-G2 90 2 33½ 42 53 51¾ 32¼ Chavez J F L122 2.00 85-12 FiftyStrs1222 **MillnniumWind**122nk Hro'sTribut122hd Steered out, gamely 9
17Feb01-11GP fst 7f :22 :44 1:091 1:221 Alw 38000N2X 101 5 3 2½ 21 11½ 14 Chavez J F L118 2.60 95-15 Hero'sTribute1184 DremRun1222½ ***APVlentin***1183½ Drew away, ridden out 9
4Nov00-2CD fst 1 :214 :434 1:084 1:351 Iroquois-G3 91 7 42½ 54½ 54½ 1hd 2nk Chavez J F L114 6.70 91 – Meetyouthebrig118nk *Hero'sTribute*1143¼ *Kets*112nk 5w,bid,led,outfinished 13
15Oct00-4Kee fst 7f :22 :45 1:101 1:224 Alw 52380N2L 91 1 5 1½ 11½ 11½ 12 Chavez J F L121 *.80 88-11 Hero's Tribute1212 Kazoo1211½ Nicholasville119½ Pace,inside,driving 9
17Sep00-9Bel fst 1 :23 :461 1:113 1:374 Futurity-G1 65 8 4½ 41 85¾ 711 713¾ Chavez J F L122 7.70 62-23 ⒹCity Zip122no Burning Roma1224¾ Scorpion122nk Stumbled badly start 9
19Aug00-2Sar fst 7f :221 :452 1:114 1:252 Md Sp Wt 41k 77 2 8 2hd 22½ 12½ 12 Chavez J F 118 2.90 78-19 Hero'sTribute1182 Volponi1184¾ BrodInitive1183¾ Steadied 1/2 mile pole 9
WORKS: Apr8 CD 5f fst 1:002 B *6/21* ●Apr1 CD 5f sly 1:011 B *1/10* Mar24 GP 5f fst 1:014 B *9/13* Mar4 GP 5f fst 1:041 B *24/25* Feb26 GP 5f fst 1:041 B *24/26* Feb12 GP 5f fst :593 H *3/20*
TRAINER: 31-60Days(34 .18 $0.99) Dirt(115 .21 $1.43) Routes(61 .20 $1.12) GrdStk(27 .15 $0.50)

2 Millennium Wind
Own:Heerensperger David & Jill
White, Red, Yellow And Orange Hoops, Red
PINCAY L JR (—) 2001:(379 61 .16)

Dk. b or br c. 3 (Apr) KEESEP99 $1,200,000
Sire: Cryptoclearance (Fappiano) $20,000
Dam: Bali Babe(Drone)
Br: Parrish Hill Farm (Ky)
Tr: Hofmans David (—) 2001:(33 3 .09)

L 123

Life	4	2	2	0	$304,920	99	D.Fst	4	2	2	0	$304,920	99
2001	2	1	1	0	$214,620	99	Wet(345)	0	0	0	0	$0	–
2000	2	1	1	0	$90,300	99	Turf(210)	0	0	0	0	$0	–
Kee	0	0	0	0	$0	–	Dist	0	0	0	0	$0	–

11Mar01-9FG fst 1 1/16 :232 :461 1:111 1:443 La Derby-G2 91 7 43½ 31½ 1hd 3nk 22 McCarron C J L122 2.20 85-12 Fifty Stars1222 Millennium Wind122nk **Hero's Tribute**122hd 3w both turns 9
21Jan01-7SA fst 1 1/16 :231 :463 1:111 1:421 S Catalina-G2 99 5 33½ 34½ 31 1½ 1½ McCarron C J LB114 *.60 93-13 Millennium Wind114½ Palmeiro1172 Denied1168 3wd bid,led,gamely 6
16Dec00-4Hol fst 1 1/16 :23 :464 1:104 1:421 Hol Fty-G1 99 1 11 1hd 1hd 1hd 21 McCarron C J LB121 3.40 88-15 *PointGivn*1211 *MillnniumWind*1217 GoldnTckt1215 Inside duel,willingly 4
18Nov00-6Hol fst 7f :224 :462 1:111 1:234 Md Sp Wt 37k 90 1 8 74½ 31 11½ 13 McCarron C J LB120 11.70 80-19 Millennium Wind1203 Orientate1202½ Decision1208 Slow into stride,best 8
WORKS: ●Apr10 Kee 5f fst :582 H *1/11* Apr3 Hol 1 fst 1:371 H *1/1* Mar28 Hol 7f fst 1:243 H *1/1* Mar22 Hol 5f fst 1:024 H *15/18* Mar6 FG 6f fst 1:16 B *4/5* ●Feb22 Hol 7f fst 1:24 H *1/10*
TRAINER: 31-60Days(41 .07 $1.56) Dirt(129 .11 $1.44) Routes(80 .13 $1.28) GrdStk(16 .25 $2.65)

3 Dollar Bill
Own:West Gary & Mary
Pink; Black Diamond Belt, Black Diamond
DAY P (15 3 4 1 .20) 2001:(312 49 .16)

B. c. 3 (Mar) KEESEP99 $145,000
Sire: Peaks and Valleys (Mt. Livermore) $10,000
Dam: Saratoga Dame(Saratoga Six)
Br: Mr & Mrs Robert E Courtney (Ky)
Tr: Stewart Dallas(6 0 3 1 .00) 2001:(100 13 .13)

L 123

Life	7	3	2	0	$378,696	102	D.Fst	6	2	2	0	$243,040	102
2001	2	1	0	0	$120,000	102	Wet(383)	1	1	0	0	$135,656	96
2000	5	2	2	0	$258,696	96	Turf(274)	0	0	0	0	$0	–
Kee	1	0	1	0	$90,240	89	Dist	0	0	0	0	$0	–

11Mar01-9FG fst 1 1/16 :232 :461 1:111 1:443 La Derby-G2 90 5 67¾ 65½ 64½ 74¼ 42½ Day P L122 *1.70 85-12 FiftyStrs1222 **MllnnumWnd**122nk **Hro'sTrbut**122hd Clipped heels, stmbled 9
18Feb01-7FG fst 1 1/16 :233 :47 1:111 1:432 Risen Star125k 102 4 44 34½ 35 22½ 12½ McCarron C J L122 *.90 93-22 DollarBill1222½ Gracie'sDancer1142½ Rhy'sSecret122½ 3-w rally, clear late 10
25Nov00-11CD sly 1 1/16 :234 :482 1:134 1:47 KyJockyClub-G2 96 4 54½ 51¾ 42½ 2hd 11¼ Borel C H L113 2.30 75-34 *DollrBill*1131¼ HolidyThunder1136 GiftOfThEgl1134 Angled 5w lane,drvg 6
4Nov00-8CD fst 1 1/16 :232 :464 1:111 1:42 BC Juvenile-G1 79 3 127½ 116 1310 1016 1011½ Migliore R L122 33.20 88 – Macho Uno122no *Point Given*1221½ Street Cry122½ Inside,no factor 14
8Oct00-7Kee fst 1 1/16 :224 :461 1:11 1:43 LaneEndBFty-G2 89 6 1013 910 95 45 23 Migliore R L121 5.20e 87-10 Arabian Light1213 Dollar Bill121hd HolidayThunder121hd 6wide bid, all out 10
4Sep00-6Sar fst 7f :23 :464 1:114 1:243 Md Sp Wt 41k 85 11 1 41½ 31 32½ 1hd Day P L118 *1.60 82-17 Dollar Bill118hd *ThisFleetIsDue*1181 ***APValentine***118hd Fast finish, just up 11
19Aug00-6Sar fst 7f :223 :454 1:112 1:25 Md Sp Wt 41k 78 8 6 73 73¼ 54¼ 2¾ Castillo H Jr L118 5.40e 79-19 *Mongoose*118¾ *Dollar Bill*1182¼ Salty Prince1181 Very greenly, gamely 10
WORKS: Apr8 CD 5f fst 1:003 B *7/21* Apr1 CD 6f sly 1:153 B *1/1* Mar24 CD 5f fst 1:031 B *9/11* ●Mar5 FG 5f fst 1:00 B *1/57* Feb12 FG 5f fst 1:012 B *5/41* Feb4 FG 6f fst 1:14 B *2/9*
TRAINER: 31-60Days(104 .17 $1.83) Dirt(414 .17 $1.58) Routes(168 .15 $2.02) GrdStk(29 .03 $0.23)

4 Bonnie Scot
Own:Kelly William A
Yellow; Green Sash, Yellow Cap.
KUNTZWEILER G (–) 2001:(183 25 .14)

Dk. b or br g. 3 (Apr)
Sire: Lord Avie (Lord Gaylord) $10,000
Dam: Crystal Woods(Woodman)
Br: William A Kelly (Ky)
Tr: Anderson Roger J(1 0 1 0 .00) 2001:(28 6 .21)

L 123

Life	7	4	1	1	$136,997	97	D.Fst	4	2	0	1	$82,977	97
2001	4	3	1	0	$117,740	97	Wet(330)	3	2	1	0	$54,020	91
2000	3	1	0	1	$19,257	70	Turf(350)	0	0	0	0	$0	–
Kee	0	0	0	0	$0	–	Dist	0	0	0	0	$0	–

3Mar01-9TP fst 1 1/16 :224 :454 1:104 1:45 Bataglia Mem99k 86 2 78 69 44½ 1½ 11½ Kuntzweiler G L115b *1.70 86-15 BonnieScot1151½ XCountry112nk DaringPegasus1126½ In close inside 1/4 pl 7
10Feb01-9TP my 1 :222 :46 1:12 1:39 Presidents50k 91 9 814 712 44 2hd 1nk Kuntzweiler G L116b 4.10 80-24 *Bonnie Scot*116nk Big Will1141¼ X Country1142¼ Off inside, driving 9
27Jan01-8TP gd 1 :223 :462 1:122 1:40 Alw 37030NC 83 7 2½ 1hd 12 11½ 21½ Kuntzweiler G L115b *.50 73-32 Halo's Stride1151½ *Bonnie Scot*1153½ Time To Jet1106¾ Off inside, held well 7
3Jan01-7TP fst 1 :223 :454 1:104 1:361 Alw 26100N1X 97 1 2hd 12 18 115 118 Kuntzweiler G L118b *2.30 91-23 Bonnie Scot11818 Big Will1139 *Glory Trail*1152¾ Inside, ridden out 6
15Dec00-2TP sly 1 :23 :472 1:144 1:433 Md Sp Wt 24k 67 8 78¼ 43 2hd 11 15¼ Prather K7 L113b 4.20 54-46 *BonnieScot*1135¼ DavkaDevil12010 PersonalStsh1209 Quick move, driving 10
3Dec00-7TP fst 1 :23 :463 1:12 1:402 Md Sp Wt 24k 40 3 52¼ 52½ 36 412 821¾ D'Amico A J L120b 3.70 48-33 Bracken County1202½ Virtual G1134 Skiffs Tugboat1207 Faded 11
18Nov00-5CD fst 7f :231 :46 1:103 1:232 Md Sp Wt 40k 70 1 8 87¾ 88 44¼ 34½ D'Amico A J L118b 80.20 83-11 Storm Craft1181¼ Table Talk1183¼ Bonnie Scot1182¾ 8w lane,no late gain 9

WORKS: Apr10 Kee 6f fst 1:133 H *1/2* Apr3 Kee 6f sly 1:16 B *1/1*
TRAINER: 31-60Days(16 .25 $2.55) Dirt(141 .13 $1.65) Routes(67 .16 $4.18) GrdStk(1 .00 $0.00)

5 Songandaprayer
Own:Devil Eleven Stable & D J Stable
White; Blue Yoke, Blue Blocks On Sleeves
PRADO E S (–) 2001:(484 68 .14)

B. c. 3 (Mar) FTFFEB00 $1,000,000
Sire: Unbridled's Song (Unbridled) $40,000
Dam: Alizea(Premiership)
Br: Donna M Wormser (Ky)
Tr: Dowd John F (–) 2001:(6 2 .33)

L 123

Life	5	3	0	0	$219,480	101	D.Fst	2	1	0	0	$150,000	101
2001	3	1	0	0	$153,000	101	Wet(362)	3	2	0	0	$69,480	94
2000	2	2	0	0	$66,480	94	Turf(251)	0	0	0	0	$0	–
Kee	0	0	0	0	$0	–	Dist	1	0	0	0	$30,000	88

10Mar01-11GP fst 1⅛ :464 1:112 1:37 1:494 Fla Derby-G1 88 9 52 3½ 3nk 32 510¼ Prado E S L122f 4.80 78-13 Monarchos1224½ Outofthebox1222½ **Invisible Ink**122½ Wide trip, weakened 13
17Feb01-10GP fst 1 1/16 :234 :464 1:104 1:432 FntnOfYouth-G1 101 3 11½ 14 12½ 13 12½ Prado E S L117f 18.00 91-14 Songandaprayer1172½ Outofthebox114¾ City Zip1174½ Inside, driving 11
20Jan01-10GP gd 1 1/16 :222 :454 1:121 1:46 Holy Bull-G3 81 4 2½ 11½ 2hd 41¾ 55 Day P L117f 3.10 73-23 Radical Riley119hd Buckle Down Ben119½ Cee Dee1174 Off rail, tired 8
26Nov00-8Aqu sly 6f :214 :443 :572 1:102 Huntington84k 94 5 — — — — 1nk Gryder A T L116f 10.80 85-22 Songandaprayer116nk Native Heir1182½ *Voodoo*1161 Dense fog, driving 10
15Jun00-5Mth gd 5f :213 :442 :573 Md Sp Wt 26k 78 1 6 12 14 15 1½ Bravo J 118f *.20 92-09 *Songndpryer*118½ *Strbury*11810 UndercoverCper118½ Clear,widened,held 7

WORKS: ●Apr6 Kee 5f fst :592 H *1/33* Mar26 GP 5f fst 1:013 B *5/8* Mar1 GP 7f fst 1:234 H *1/1* Feb9 GP 7f fst 1:263 H *1/2* Jan30 GP 7f fst 1:242 H *1/1*
TRAINER: 31-60Days(17 .06 $1.32) Dirt(164 .21 $2.60) Routes(61 .13 $1.52) GrdStk(7 .29 $6.37)

6 A P Valentine
Own:Ol Memorial Stable & Tabor Michael
Midnight Blue; White Circled Gold Turtle
NAKATANI C S (21 5 4 2 .24) 2001:(222 34 .15)

B. c. 3 (Feb) SARAUG99 $475,000
Sire: A.P. Indy (Seattle Slew) $150,000
Dam: Twenty Eight Carat(Alydar)
Br: W S Kilroy (Ky)
Tr: Zito Nicholas P(5 2 1 0 .40) 2001:(150 34 .23)

L 123

Life	6	3	0	2	$345,670	99	D.Fst	6	3	0	2	$345,670	99
2001	2	1	0	1	$16,560	99	Wet(430*)	0	0	0	0	$0	–
2000	4	2	0	1	$329,110	98	Turf(330)	0	0	0	0	$0	–
Kee	0	0	0	0	$0	–	Dist	0	0	0	0	$0	–

24Mar01-7Hia fst 1 1/16 :231 :453 1:091 1:401 3↑ OClm 150000N 99 2 33½ 38 25 2½ 13¾ Coa E M L112 *.20 116 — A P Valentine1123¾ Six Fifteen1163½ El Ballezano1163½ Ridden out 5
17Feb01-11GP fst 7f :22 :44 1:091 1:221 Alw 38000N2X 87 7 7 85¼ 77 46½ 36½ Day P L118 *1.10 88-15 **Hero's Tribute**1184 Dream Run1222½ *APValentine*1183½ Improved position 9
4Nov00-8CD fst 1 1/16 :232 :464 1:111 1:42 BC Juvenile-G1 59 6 94 83½ 116¾ 1425 1422¾ Chavez J F L122 *2.40 77 — Macho Uno122no *Point Given*1221½ Street Cry122½ Tired,2nd turn 14
14Oct00-9Bel fst 1 1/16 :223 :45 1:092 1:412 Champagne-G1 98 1 92¾ 51¼ 51½ 4½ 11¾ Chavez J F L122 *3.00 90-09 A PValentine1221¾ PointGiven122¾ Yonaguska1221 Through on rail, drvg 10
23Sep00-5Bel fst 7f :224 :46 1:11 1:23 Md Sp Wt 41k 93 5 5 41½ 1hd 15 14¼ Chavez J F L118 *.85 88-13 *A P Valentine*1184¼ *Pure Prize*11812 Bopman118½ Wide move, ridden out 9
4Sep00-6Sar fst 7f :23 :464 1:114 1:243 Md Sp Wt 41k 83 1 10 62½ 42 21½ 31 Chavez J F L118 5.20 81-17 **DollarBill**118hd *ThisFleetIsDue*1181 *APVlentine*118hd 4 wide move, gamely 11

WORKS: ●Apr9 Kee 5f fst 1:00 B *1/17* Apr2 Hia 5f fst 1:022 B *23/30* ●Mar20 Hia 5f sly :591 H *1/4* Mar12 Hia 5f fst 1:013 B *3/13* ●Feb10 Hia 5f fst :59 H *1/24* Feb3 Hia 5f fst 1:024 B *10/15*
TRAINER: Dirt(562 .17 $1.64) Routes(329 .17 $1.63) GrdStk(48 .10 $0.99)

No prep for the 2001 Kentucky Derby came up as deep as the Blue Grass at Keeneland. Of the seven entrants, six are considered legitimate contenders for the Derby. Yet this Blue Grass lacks a critical handicapping component: speed. Speed, or the lack of it, will go a long way toward shaping the outcome of any race. That is especially true on the main track at Keeneland, which naturally tilts in favor of inside speed, and particularly so on big race days like Blue Grass Day, when inside speed is often dominant.

There is only one real speed horse in this Blue Grass—Songandaprayer. After winning both of his starts at 2, he demonstrated he was a horse of substance in his first start at 3, the Holy Bull Stakes. After setting suicidal early fractions and then being hooked on the far turn, he battled all the way to deep stretch before tiring. In the subsequent Fountain of Youth, Songandaprayer capitalized on a situation much like the one that presents itself in the Blue Grass. As the only true speed in the race, he established an easy and uncontested early lead, and parlayed that into a front-running upset victory.

Plotting how this Blue Grass will be run seems easy enough. Songandaprayer will establish a clear early lead, just as he did in the Fountain of Youth, and on the speed-friendly Keeneland surface, he stands a fair chance of making it hold up. As the second-longest shot on the board at 6-1, Songandaprayer is an inspired bet.

The trouble is, there are other factors at play here. Songandaprayer's victory in the Fountain of Youth made him a viable prospect for the Kentucky Derby. But as he is suspect at longer distances, his people had to find out if he could rate off the early lead, and avoid being a target on the front end for other suicidal speed types. Songandaprayer received a first rating lesson in the Florida Derby and was in contention to midstretch before tiring. The question in the Blue Grass is, will Songandaprayer's people give up the huge tactical advantage of an uncontested lead in a Grade 1, $750,000 race in order to give their colt another rating lesson, which might pay dividends in the Kentucky Derby?

The only other colt who can make the early lead is Millennium Wind. He went to the lead once before under similar speedless conditions, when he was a game second to Point Given in the Hollywood Futurity in just his second career start. Moreover, reports in *Daily Racing Form* note that Millennium Wind is in much better condition going into the Blue Grass than he was a month earlier when second in the Louisiana Derby.

The others in the Blue Grass are Dollar Bill, who would have won the Louisiana Derby had he not almost fallen in upper stretch; the entry of Hero's Tribute and Invisible Ink, both of whom received inordinate attention for the slight trouble they encountered in the Louisiana Derby and Florida Derby, respectively; A P Valentine, who hasn't come close to validating his victory in the Champagne Stakes six months earlier; and the overmatched Bonnie Scot.

Let's toss the entry, A P Valentine, and Bonnie Scot. Now, will Songandaprayer go for the lead, or get another rating lesson?

I decided Songandaprayer's people would take the bird in the hand and go for the lead. I restricted my wagers on the Blue Grass to pick threes that also included the Wood Memorial and the Arkansas Derby, and watched as this Blue Grass became one of the ones that got away.

It didn't take long after the gate opened to see that Songandaprayer would decline the early lead at any cost. Sure enough, Millennium Wind willingly accepted it. They went around the track 1-2, and Dollar Bill, who was farther back early than he had to be on paper, finished well to be third. Millennium Wind paid $10.20, the exacta paid $75, and the trifecta paid $277.20.

And I had to pay $4 for a bottle of aspirin.

NINTH RACE
Keeneland
APRIL 14, 2001

1⅛ MILES. (1.46^{4}) 77th Running of THE TOYOTA BLUE GRASS. Grade I. Purse $750,000 Guaranteed. For three year olds. By subscription of $375 each, which should accompany the nomination; $7,500 to enter and start, with $750,000 guaranteed, of which $465,000 to the owner of the winner, $150,000 to second, $75,000 to third, $37,500 to fourth and $22,500 to fifth. Weights: Colts and geldings, 123 lbs.; Fillies, 118 lbs. Starters to be named through the entry box by the usual time of closing. A gold julep cup will be presented to the owner of the winner. A silver julep cup will be presented to the winning trainer and jockey. No supplementary nominations. Closed Tuesday, February 20, 2001 109 with nominations.

Value of Race: $750,000 Winner $465,000; second $150,000; third $75,000; fourth $37,500; fifth $22,500. Mutuel Pool $1,924,646.0 Exacta Pool $1,019,588.0 Trifecta Pool $684,365.00

Last Raced	Horse	M/Eqt.	A.Wt	PP	St	¼	½	¾	Str	Fin	Jockey	Odds $1
11Mar01 ^{9}FG^{2}	Millennium Wind	L	3 123	2	3	1^{1½}	1^{1}	1^{hd}	1^{1½}	1^{5¼}	Pincay L Jr	4.10
10Mar01 ^{11}GP^{5}	Songandaprayer	Lf	3 123	6	1	2^{½}	2^{½}	2^{2½}	2^{2½}	2^{1¾}	Prado E S	6.50
11Mar01 ^{9}FG^{4}	Dollar Bill	L	3 123	4	7	6^{hd}	6^{½}	7	4^{3}	3^{1½}	Day P	*2.20
10Mar01 ^{11}GP^{3}	Invisible Ink	L	3 123	1	4	3^{1½}	3^{1½}	3^{2½}	3^{2}	4^{4½}	Velazquez J R	a-2.20
24Mar01 ^{7}Hia^{1}	A P Valentine	L	3 123	7	6	7	7	6^{hd}	6^{1½}	5^{3½}	Nakatani C S	3.60
3Mar01 ^{9}TP^{1}	Bonnie Scot	Lb	3 123	5	5	5^{3}	5^{5½}	5^{4½}	5^{hd}	6^{1¼}	Kuntzweiler G	39.90
11Mar01 ^{9}FG^{3}	Hero's Tribute	L	3 123	3	2	4^{2}	4^{hd}	4^{hd}	7	7	Bailey J D	a-2.20

***—Actual Betting Favorite.**
a–Coupled: Invisible Ink and Hero's Tribute.

OFF AT 5:36 Start Good. Won driving. Track fast.
TIME :23, :46^{2}, 1:10^{2}, 1:35^{2}, 1:48^{1} (:23.06, :46.52, 1:10.45, 1:35.45, 1:48.32)

$2 Mutuel Prices:			
2–MILLENNIUM WIND	10.20	5.60	4.20
5–SONGANDAPRAYER		7.60	4.80
3–DOLLAR BILL			3.00

$2 EXACTA 2–5 PAID $75.00 $2 TRIFECTA 2–5–3 PAID $277.20

Dk. b. or br. c, (Apr), by Cryptoclearance–Bali Babe, by Drone. Trainer Hofmans David. Bred by Parrish Hill Farm (Ky).

MILLENNIUM WIND moved to the fore inside soon after the start, controlled the pace under careful handling while racing in the two or three path, was earnestly challenged midway on the second turn from the outside by SONGANDAPRAYER, battled that one into submission upon entering the stretch, edged clear, then increased his advantage under intermittent urging. SONGANDAPRAYER went up early to press the winner under light rating, inched after MILLENNIUM WIND on the second turn, gained almost even terms, continued to challenge that one into the stretch, weakened gradually when straightened for the drive and drifted out for a stride leaving the eighth pole when roused with the whip left-handed. DOLLAR BILL, lightly bumped at the start when BONNIE SCOT leaned in, settled inside, was unhurried until the end of the backstretch, was asked a bit, continued inside into the stretch, angled three wide and improved position while not a serious threat. INVISIBLE INK, close up inside from the outset, eased out three wide approaching the second turn, was asked for his best leaving the three-eighths pole, remained prominent until the stretch but was empty the last eighth. A P VALENTINE, five or six wide into the backstretch, edged in around the second turn, continued three wide into the stretch and failed to menace. BONNIE SCOT leaned in at the start bumping lightly with DOLLAR BILL, angled inside early, appeared to be climbing on the backstretch, angled four or five wide into the stretch but flattened out. HERO'S TRIBUTE, taken in hand early to follow the leaders three or four wide, was put to a drive entering the second turn, but tired approaching the stretch.

Owners— 1, Heerensperger David & Jill; 2, Devil Eleven Stable & D J Stable Le; 3, West Gary & Mary; 4, Peachtree Stable; 5, Ol Memorial Stable & Michael Tabor; 6, Kelly William A; 7, Oxley John C

Trainers—1, Hofmans David; 2, Dowd John F; 3, Stewart Dallas; 4, Pletcher Todd A; 5, Zito Nicholas P; 6, Anderson Roger J; 7, Ward John T Jr

$2 Daily Double (8–2) Paid $18.60; Daily Double Pool $90,746.
$2 Pick Three (7–4/8–2) Paid $527.80; Pick Three Pool $126,745.
$1 Pick Four (7–7–4/8–2) Paid $890.60; Pick Four Pool $49,479.

The 2001 Bold Ruler

Earlier on Blue Grass Day, some of the better sprinters in the Northeast got together in an interesting renewal of the Bold Ruler Handicap. As we did with the Santa Anita Handicap, let's try to whittle the field down to the real contenders.

1 Stalwart Member

Own: Goldfarb Sanford & Team Julep St
Black, Gold Yoke/cgs, Gold
ESPINOZA V (—) 2001:(401 51 .13)

Ch. g. 8
Sire: Claramount (Policeman*Fr) $2,500
Dam: Ms. Stalwart(Stalwart)
Br: Wachtel Edwin H (NY)
Tr: Dutrow Richard E Jr(29 8 2 11 .28) 2001:(114 25 .22)

L 117

Life	45	15	5	8	$692,586	112	D.Fst	31	8	3	6	$391,902	108
2001	1	1	0	0	$31,800	108	Wet(355)	12	7	2	1	$296,504	112
2000	10	4	0	2	$199,735	108	Turf(175*)	2	0	0	1	$4,180	87
Aqu	14	4	2	4	$254,726	109	Dist	20	7	2	4	$328,032	112

25Mar01-8Aqu fst 6f :214 :443 :563 1:091 4↑ Alw 53000N$Y 108 1 5 68½ 62¾ 41¼ 1¾ Arroyo N Jr L 120 b *1.80 91-14 StlwrtMember120¾ *UnrlMdnss*1161½ BltimorGry1181½ Clear sailing inside 6
4Nov00-4Aqu fst 7f :222 :45 1:091 1:214 3↑ SportPage H-G3 108 2 6 63¼ 63½ 21½ 11 Arroyo N Jr L 117 b 6.40 91-12 *Stalwart Member*1171 *Istintaj*1172½ Mister Tricky112¾ 4 wide, ridden out 6
Previously trained by Johnson Cleveland
21Oct00-5Bel fst 6f :221 :451 :57 1:092 3↑ [S]Hudson H125k 102 7 5 31 3½ 1½ 1nk Chavez J F L 120 b 4.90 91-12 *StlwrtMmbr*120nk PooskHill1161¼ *Chsin'Wimmn*121hd 3 wide move, driving 9
Previously trained by Dutrow Richard E Jr
23Sep00-9Bel fst 7f :221 :443 1:083 1:213 3↑ Vosburgh-G1 77 9 7 105½ 94¾ 911 915½ Smith M E L 126 b 22.30 80-13 Trippi123½ MoreThanReady1232¼ *OneWyLove*1261 Checked 1/2 mile pole 10
8Sep00-3Bel fst 6f :224 :454 :574 1:094 3↑ Alw 57000N$Y 105 4 5 41 3½ 1hd 13½ Chavez J F L 121 b 3.45 89-17 StlwrtMember1213½ JeniesRob117no OroDMxico1171 Steadied after start 5
14Aug00-7Sar my 6½f :22 :452 1:103 1:173 4↑ Alw 57000N$Y 97 1 6 41½ 31½ 12½ 12½ Chavez J F L 115 b 4.90 86-15 *StlwrtMember*1152½ OroDeMexico1152½ KingRoller122hd Clear path on rail 6
16Jly00-9Bel fst 6½f :222 :452 1:101 1:163 3↑ Clm c-(35-30) 84 6 3 3nk 1½ 2hd 33¾ Chavez J F L 119 fb 3.00 85-13 AncientDncer1192¼ CseDismissd1141½ *StlwrtMmbr*1191 Vied 3 wide, tired 9
Claimed from Wachtel Edwin & Port Sidney L for $35,000, Tesher Howard M Trainer 2000(as of 07/16): (105 14 13 19 0.13)
29Jun00-7Bel fm 1 Ⓣ:23 :453 1:091 1:332 4↑ Clm 50000(60-50) 69 6 31½ 42¼ 41½ 53½ 810½ Rosario H L5 L 111 fb 3.20e 80-17 We Concur1181¼ Extra Genius1181¼ East Of Easy118½ Speed in hand, tired 10
3Jun00-5Bel fm 1 Ⓣ:231 :463 1:102 1:343 4↑ Clm 50000(50-40) 87 3 43½ 41¾ 31½ 22½ 31½ Rosario H L5 L 112 fb 18.00 83-15 OldShanachie1141¼ CloudClub117nk StlwrtMember112¾ Stayed on gamely 9
26Mar00-6Aqu fst 7f :23 :454 1:103 1:23 4↑ Clm 70000(75-65) 59 3 5 1½ 2hd 67 617¼ Smith M E L 115 fb 9.00 68-19 ***LkPontchrtrn***1124 BllyHggrd117¾ HmOnThRdg109½ Bobbled start, tired 6
27Feb00-9Aqu fst 6f ⊡:222 :444 :564 1:092 3↑ [S]H Hughes H83k 89 1 7 3½ 42 53 74½ Gryder A T L 115 fb 5.50 91-11 **Kashatreya**1201 ***SayFloridaSndy***1181¾ PooskHill1181¼ Chased inside, tired 8
21Nov99-7Aqu fst 7f :222 :444 1:093 1:22 3↑ Alw 54000N$Y 73 8 3 1hd 1hd 51¾ 612½ Chavez J F L 122 b 15.30 79-13 *UnrlMdnss*1151¾ WtchmnsWrnng1172¾ RmnGcc115no Bumped start, 3 wide 9
23Oct99-7Bel fst 6f :221 :452 :572 1:093 3↑ [S]Hudson H125k 86 9 6 54¼ 51¾ 75¼ 77¼ Chavez J F L 119 b 3.00 86-19 *Pooska Hill*117¾ Sharcan115¾ Iron Will1151¼ Ducked in start, bumped 9
10Sep99-9Bel my 7f :222 :45 1:091 1:221 3↑ [S]GenDMacArthH54k 101 6 1 12½ 12½ 13½ 12¾ Chavez J F L 116 b 3.05 91-19 StlwrtMember1162¾ FourthAndSix1173½ **Kshtrey**1211½ Set pace, ridden out 6
14Aug99-1Sar sly 7f :222 :452 1:104 1:242 3↑ Clm 40000(40-35) 91 8 2 1hd 12 14½ 11½ Davis R G L 118 b 3.75 83-21 *StlwrtMmbr*1181½ GoldnTnt116¾ SmokSignl116½ Wrapped up under wire 8
1Aug99-6Sar fst 6f :214 :444 :57 1:10 4↑ Alw 52000N1Y 76 2 3 21 55 76½ 710½ Sellers S J L 115 b 28.25 80-12 Rare Rock120nk King Ruckus1184½ Dice Dancer1201 Finished early 7
16Jun99-2Bel fst 6f :222 :444 :564 1:092 4↑ Clm 45000(45-35) 94 1 2 11 1hd 2½ 22¾ Gryder A T L 117 b 10.00 91-13 Adverse1192¾ StlwrtMember117nk *GoldenTnt*1153½ Hard-ridden, held place 7
12May99-6Bel fst 6½f :221 :434 1:083 1:15 4↑ Clm 75000(75-70) 55 7 3 3½ 43½ 713 723 Gryder A T L 117 b 8.80 74-11 Baltimore Gray1179¾ *Able Red*117¾ Simud114nk Chased outside, tired 7
7Apr99-3Aqu fst 6f :22 :45 :57 1:091 4↑ Clm 100000(100-75) 80 1 4 32½ 43½ 53¼ 58 Smith A E5 L 114 b 2.70 84-16 Johnny Legit117no Brutally Frank1111¾ Premium1161 Chased rail, no rally 5
28Feb99-8Aqu sly 6f ⊡:222 :45 :571 1:101 3↑ [S]HolliHughesH53k 92 2 4 2½ 21 22½ 43½ Espinoza J L L 117 b *1.15 87-16 **Kashatreya**116½ Thepromonroe115nk Dr J1162¾ Chased pace, no punch 5

WORKS: Apr11 **Aqu 4f fst :48 B** *3/17* ●Mar21 **Aqu 4f fst :48 B** *1/8* ●**Mar15 Aqu 5f fst 1:01 B** *1/9* Mar8 **Aqu ⊡ 5f gd 1:022 B** *2/2* Mar1 **Aqu ⊡ 5f fst 1:03 B** *5/6* Feb24 **Aqu ⊡ 4f fst :512 B** *8/11*
TRAINER: Dirt(351 .25 $1.67) Sprint(235 .25 $1.64) GrdStk(8 .13 $1.85)

1a Lake Pontchartrain

Own: Goldfarb Sanford
Black, Gold Yoke/cgs, Gold
ESPINOZA V (—) 2001:(401 51 .13)

B. g. 6
Sire: Salt Lake (Deputy Minister) $20,000
Dam: Peppermint Lane(Alydar)
Br: Overbrook Farm (Ky)
Tr: Dutrow Richard E Jr(29 8 2 11 .28) 2001:(114 25 .22)

L 113

Life	25	9	3	7	$337,903	109	D.Fst	18	5	2	6	$193,100	109
2001	3	0	2	1	$32,403	109	Wet(350)	7	4	1	1	$144,803	104
2000	5	2	0	2	$78,820	96	Turf(220)	0	0	0	0	$0	–
Aqu	8	3	1	2	$116,006	109	Dist	16	5	3	3	$208,240	108

17Mar01-8Aqu fst 7f :22 :44 1:081 1:211 3↑ Toboggan H107k 109 2 5 68½ 66½ 41 3½ Arroyo N Jr L 113 b 4.40 93-17 PpngTom118½ **SyFlordSndy**117hd LkPontchrtrn1133½ Game finish outside 6
16Feb01-8Aqu fst 6f ⊡:231 :454 :571 1:09 4↑ Alw 52000N$Y 108 1 4 33½ 31½ 31 2½ Castellano J J L 116 b *1.35 99-12 BltmorGry116½ LkPontchrtrn1163¾ *Bbby'sBckr*1164 Game finish outside 5
18Jan01-8Aqu fst 6f ⊡:223 :451 :57 1:084 4↑ Alw 51000C 104 7 3 74¾ 62¾ 22 22 Arroyo N Jr L 123 b 4.70 99-08 *PpingTom*1172 LkPontchrtrin1231½ UnrlMdnss1203 Game finish outside 8
23Dec00-8Aqu fst 6f ⊡:223 :454 :573 1:094 3↑ Gravesend H-G3 96 6 11 1112 107 75¼ 33¼ Arroyo N Jr L 116 b 7.60 90-13 ***SyFlordSndy***1161¾ *LbrtyGold*1151½ LkPntchrtrn1161¾ Rallied into lane, clsd 11
29Nov00-8Aqu gd 6f :214 :443 :563 1:093 3↑ Alw 52000N$Y 89 4 10 1010 107 63½ 1¾ Arroyo N Jr L 119 b *1.15e 89-15 LkPntchrtrn119¾ ***SyFlrdSnd***118hd Blncthbdgt1191 Traffic, bumped, drive 10
26Mar00-6Aqu fst 7f :23 :454 1:103 1:23 4↑ Clm 75000(75-65) 96 5 2 64½ 41¼ 1½ 14 Arroyo N5 L 112 b *1.40 85-19 *LkPontchrtrn*1124 BllyHggrd117¾ HmOnThRdg109½ 4 wide trip, driving 6
29Jan00-9Aqu fst 6f ⊡:23 :46 :574 1:094 3↑ Paumonk H81k 92 1 5 65¼ 63¾ 56½ 45¼ Castillo H Jr L 114 b 6.40 88-14 Falkenburg1151½ Brushed On113nk He's A Charm1133½ 3 wide, mild rally 7
12Jan00-8Aqu fst 6f ⊡:23 :462 :583 1:11 4↑ Alw 57000N$Y 96 4 3 51¼ 3½ 41 31¾ Castillo H Jr L 119 b *2.25 85-24 Malted1141¼ BrutallyFrank114½ LakePontchrtrin119nk 3 wide, good finish 7
26Dec99-7Aqu fst 6f ⊡:224 :453 :571 1:092 3↑ Gravesend H-G3 91 6 5 41¼ 3½ 54½ 57 Bridgmohan S X L 113 b 8.70 88-15 CowboyCop1155¼ *BrushedOn*112nk UnrelMdnss116½ Chased 4 wide, no bid 9
Awarded fourth purse money
25Nov99-9Aqu sly 6f :223 :453 :57 1:09 3↑ Fall Hwgt H-G2 96 6 1 63¾ 63½ 56½ 57¾ Smith M E L 127 b *2.40 85-18 *Richter Scale*1345¾ *Aristotle*130¾ Bought In Dixie128nk Swung 5 wide turn 7
11Nov99-8Aqu fst 6½f :223 :454 1:094 1:16 3↑ Alw 57000N$Y 105 5 2 1½ 1hd 2hd 31½ Prado E S L 118 b *2.55 89-20 Honorifico118½ Laredo1211 LakePontchartrin1181½ Speed inside, gamely 6
20Oct99-3Bel sly 6f :221 :45 :571 1:094 3↑ Alw 51000N$Y 104 2 4 41½ 2hd 2hd 13¼ Velazquez J R L 115 b 1.45 92-17 LkPontchrtrin1153¼ BoughtInDixi1191¼ Lumbrmn1171½ Spilt rivals, driving 5
10Jan99-8Aqu my 6f ⊡:224 :46 :574 1:101 4↑ Handicap56k 96 5 5 53¼ 21 22 31½ Diego I L 113 b 3.45 89-14 AbleRed1141¼ *EstmdFrind*116nk *LkPontchrtrin*1137¼ Bid outside, flattened 5
29Nov98-3Aqu fst 6½f :222 :45 1:09 1:152 3↑ Alw 44000N$Y 101 1 7 1hd 3nk 2hd 1nk Diego I7 L 111 b 4.30 94-13 LakePontchrtrin111nk Simud1183½ *RpidRobyn*120¾ Speed ins, came again 7
11Nov98-6Aqu wf 6f :22 :443 :563 1:091 3↑ Alw 44000N3X 100 1 7 1½ 21 21½ 21¾ Bridgmohan S X L 117 b 2.65 91-12 Simud1101¾ *Lake Pontchartrain*117¾ SunnySide1083¾ Pace, dug in gamely 8
3Nov98-5Aqu fst 6f :231 :464 :583 1:104 Clm 75000(75-65) 64 2 6 42½ 65 69¼ 58¾ Arguello F A Jr L 119 b *1.15 76-19 BrushdOn113½ LglLnd1134¼ [DH]ShimmrMQuck117 Steady turn, no threat 7
7Oct98-7Bel fst 7f :223 :462 1:104 1:232 3↑ Alw 44000N3X 92 4 5 11 1hd 2½ 33 Bridgmohan S X5 L 114 b 4.00 82-25 RmpntLion1161 LodedGun1172 LkePontchrtrin1142 Set pressured pace 6
17Sep98-7Bel fst 6f :232 :462 :582 1:11 Clm 75000(75-65) 87 1 4 31 2hd 1hd 13¾ Nakatani C S L 117 b *.80 86-16 LkePontchrtrin1173¾ LeglLnd1134½ ThundrBow115¾ 3w move, ridden out 5
27Aug98-6Sar fst 6f :223 :462 :583 1:111 Clm c-(60-50) 86 1 6 31½ 41½ 2½ 1½ Day P L 117 b *.80 85-19 *LkPontchrtrin*117½ ThundrBow1171½ Pbo'sPl1133 Awaited room rail turn 7
Claimed from Overbrook Farm for $60,000, Lukas D Wayne Trainer 1998(as of 08/27): (440 79 63 49 0.18)
1Aug98-4Sar fst 7f :222 :452 1:094 1:221 3↑ Alw 41000N3X 87 5 2 2hd 1hd 41½ 48½ Day P L 117 b 7.90 85-12 Dice Dancer1112½ **Kashatreya**1166 Mr Bert113no Bumped, in tight str 7

WORKS: Apr11 **Aqu 4f fst :484 B** *6/17* Mar11 **Aqu ⊡ 4f fst :503 B** *12/18* Mar3 **Aqu ⊡ 4f fst :503 B** *3/3* Feb11 **Aqu ⊡ 5f fst 1:031 B** *4/8* Jan17 **Aqu ⊡ 3f fst :373 B** *1/2*
TRAINER: Dirt(351 .25 $1.67) Sprint(235 .25 $1.64) GrdStk(8 .13 $1.85)

1x Prince Monty

Own: Goldfarb Sanford & Laneve Nicholas
Black, Gold Yoke/cgs, Gold
LOPEZ C C (62 8 15 5 .13) 2001:(281 42 .15)

Ch. g. 5
Sire: Montbrook (Buckaroo) $7,500
Dam: Princess Ro Ro(Secret Prince)
Br: Stock Mike & Terrill William J (NY)
Tr: Dutrow Richard E Jr(29 8 2 11 .28) 2001:(114 25 .22)

L 111

Life	19	6	1	2	$180,037	97	D.Fst	14	6	0	2	$170,837	97
2001	3	1	0	1	$33,495	97	Wet(284)	4	0	1	0	$9,200	88
2000	8	1	1	0	$32,300	88	Turf(195*)	1	0	0	0	$0	65
Aqu	6	3	0	1	$92,012	90	Dist	12	5	0	1	$137,505	97

11Mar01-8Aqu fst 6f ▪:23 :454 :581 1:11 4+ Alw 45000N2X 97 2 3 1hd 1½ 1½ 1½ Lopez C C L 116 b *1.70 90-19 Prince Monty116½ Sir Ghost1164½ Natural1183¼ Pace, clear, held on 5
15Jan01-7Aqu gd 6f ▪:224 :454 :58 1:11 4+ Alw 45000N2X 84 5 1 1½ 11 2hd 42 Lopez C C L 116 b *.80e 88-12 Dancer's Wish1161½ Royal Ruby120nk Two Tour116½ Set pace, gave way 7
12Jan01-4Aqu fst 6f ▪:223 :452 :571 1:10 4+ Clm 45000 (45-35) 91 1 4 32 32 32 3½ Velasquez C L 118 b 3.60 94-10 Concorde Light118½ Riker113hd Prince Monty1181 3 wide, game finish 8
29Nov00-9Aqu gd 6f :214 :441 :561 1:092 3+ Clm c-(35-30) 88 7 2 1½ 1½ 1½ 4½ Rojas R I L 121 b 7.40 89-15 Ancient Dancer121nk Wolf Boy119½ Ordained119nk Drifted deep stretch 12
Claimed from Bianculli Ralph & Malafronte Joseph for $35,000, Gullo Gary P Trainer 2000(as of 11/29): (262 26 33 27 0.10)
28Oct00-7Aqu fst 7f :223 :452 1:104 1:243 3+ Alw 43000N1X 83 5 2 1½ 15 1½ 1no Ebina M L 119 b 21.00 77-23 Prince Monty119no Graze1171½ Belle's Tiger1211 Well clear, held on 10
30Sep00-4Bel gd 1 Ⓣ:233 :481 1:13 1:382 4+ Clm 40000 (40-35) 65 4 12 11 1½ 83¾ 1011½ Leon F L 118 b 26.50 55-27 WeConcur118½ DesignerProspct1161¾ Notority117½ Steadied while tiring 10
Previously trained by Ferraro M Anthony
17Apr00-9FL gd 4½f :223 :462 :53 3+ ⓈAlw 15000N3 59 7 3 1hd 3½ 52¼ Davila M A Jr L 116 b *1.20 86-15 Red Hunt116no Lifes Work116hd Highcat1161¼ Steadied stretch 8
4Apr00-8FL sly 4½f :22 :454 :522 3+ ⓈAlw 20800NC 72 5 5 21 22 22¾ Davila M A Jr L 116 b *1.05 88-14 Mom'sLittleGuy1172¾ PrincMonty116nk GoChndlr116nk Chased, held place 6
Previously trained by Gullo Gary P
27Feb00-9Aqu fst 6f ▪:222 :444 :564 1:092 3+ ⓈH Hughes H83k 73 2 5 1hd 1hd 42½ 810¾ Castillo H Jr L 114 b 18.80 84-11 Kashatreya1201 Say FloridaSandy1181¾ PooskaHill1181¼ Vied inside, tired 8
23Jan00-8Aqu fst 11/16 ▪:23 :464 1:113 1:443 4+ Alw 48000N3X 78 5 1½ 13 11 31 712¾ Castillo H Jr L 117 b 25.75 73-23 NotSoFst119½ Notesybingrn1192½ TicklMRd114hd Brushed, dueled, faded 9
5Jan00-8Aqu fst 6f ▪:23 :46 :58 1:10 4+ Alw 47000N3X 73 2 7 1½ 2½ 33 712¼ Castillo H Jr L 119 11.90 80-18 Falkenburg122hd Greek Tycoon1178 Medford115¾ Rushed inside, tired 7
18Dec99-2Aqu fst 6f ▪:23 :46 :581 1:104 Clm 70000 (70-60) 93 2 4 11 12 14½ 13 Castillo H Jr L 119 *1.55 88-16 PrinceMonty1193 SilverMgistrte1191¾ NightCllr117¾ Pace, clear, driving 8
4Dec99-7Aqu fst 6f ▪:23 :453 :571 1:091 3+ Alw 47000N3X 83 2 5 1hd 41 54 69½ Castillo H Jr L 116 6.60 87-11 Aristotle1114¾ Sense Of Duty116hd Driver1211¼ Vied inside, tired 7
17Nov99-7Aqu fst 6f :221 :452 :573 1:103 3+ ⓈAlw 45000N2X 90 1 6 1½ 1½ 16 13 Castillo H Jr L 115 *1.40 85-20 Prince Monty1153 Lambourne1174¾ Star Plot117no Wrapped up late 8
20May99-9Bel fst 6f :221 :45 :564 1:092 3+ ⓈAlw 44000N2X 77 3 4 32 41½ 42¾ 53½ Migliore R L 114 2.90 90-03 PooskaHill118no SilkBroker1131½ DotsPlesure122nk Chased between,faded 8
1May99-9Aqu fst 1 :233 :463 1:101 1:35 Withers-G2 73 2 5½ 5¾ 52½ 86½ 812 Douglas R R L 116 25.25 81-08 SuccessfulAppel120½ BestOfLuck1164½ TresurIslnd116½ Inside trip, tired 8
10Apr99-9Aqu fst 7f :222 :45 1:094 1:224 Bay Shore-G3 81 3 4 31½ 41 32 33 Douglas R R L 116 9.90 85-07 Perfect Score118hd Royal Ruby1143 PrinceMonty1162 Game finish inside 8
25Mar99-9Aqu fst 6f :222 :461 :58 1:101 ⓈAlw 42000N1X 84 9 3 2½ 1½ 13 16½ Douglas R R L 116 2.30 87-14 PrinceMonty1166½ Houstand116no Can'tBCught121nk With something left 9
19Dec98-2Aqu fst 6f ▪:232 :471 :594 1:13 ⓈMd Sp Wt 38k 61 10 3 2½ 2½ 1½ 13½ Douglas R R L 119 *1.20 77-16 Prince Monty1193½ Olive Flu1192 Full Support119no Steady urging 12

WORKS: Apr5 Aqu 5f fst 1:001 B 2/5 Mar27 Aqu 4f fst :481 H 1/2 Mar10 Aqu▪ 3f fst :383 B 4/5 ●Mar2 Aqu▪ 4f fst :474 B 1/7 ●Feb24 Aqu▪ 4f fst :47 H 1/11 Feb8 Aqu▪ 4f fst :511 B 6/9
TRAINER: 31-60Days(90 .22 $1.61) Dirt(351 .25 $1.67) Sprint(235 .25 $1.64) GrdStk(8 .13 $1.85)

2 Max's Pal

Own: Dweck Raymond
Violet White Ball
CHAVEZ J F (4 0 1 1 .00) 2001:(434 93 .21)

Ch. c. 4 OBSMAR99 $120,000
Sire: Marquetry (Conquistador Cielo) $15,000
Dam: Singin Up a Storm(Storm Cat)
Br: Parrish Hill Farm (Ky)
Tr: Perkins Ben W Jr(13 4 2 1 .31) 2001:(74 14 .19)

L 116

Life	14	10	1	0	$525,420	109	D.Fst	12	9	1	0	$506,970	109
2000	10	8	1	0	$485,070	109	Wet(325)	1	1	0	0	$18,000	78
1999	4	2	0	0	$40,350	78	Turf(295)	1	0	0	0	$450	64
Aqu	1	0	0	0	$0	83	Dist	11	9	1	0	$407,570	109

7Oct00-3Med fst 6f :22 :444 :564 1:094 BergenCounty100k 98 5 1 22 21½ 1hd 1no Wilson R L 124 *.60 90-15 Max's Pal124no Trounce113¾ Stormin Oedy1192½ Dueled all out,lasted 5
2Sep00-8Mth fst 6f :211 :433 :561 1:091 Rumson75k 103 1 6 42 32½ 1hd 11½ Wilson R L 121 *.80 95-12 Mx'sPl1211½ StorminOedy1182½ Governor'sPride1153½ Clear, mild pressure 7
15Jly00-10Lrl fst 6f :221 :443 :561 1:08 Montpelier75k 109 1 2 31 21½ 21 2nk Wilson R L 122 *.90 102-10 ⒹDisco Rico119nk Max's Pal1226¾ Stormin Oedy1191¾ 3wd,std'd late,game 5
Placed first through disqualification.
24Jun00-9Mth fst 6f :211 :432 :553 1:09 JerseyShrBC-G3 98 5 2 3nk 21 21½ 2nk Wilson R L 122 *1.50 96-09 Disco Rico115nk Max's Pal1222½ Stormin Oedy1175 Close up, gamely 6
3Jun00-7Del fst 6f :213 :444 :572 1:101 Legal Light75k 103 6 3 21½ 2½ 2½ 1¾ Wilson R L 122 *2.40 92-14 Max's Pal122¾ Disco Rico117¾ Stormin Oedy1225½ Long drive, prevailed 8
13May00-9Pim fst 6f :223 :45 :573 1:101 Hrsch Jacobs75k 98 5 3 53½ 53½ 2½ 1nk Wilson R L 119 4.30 95-10 Max'sPal119nk UltimateWarrior1191¾ StorminOedy119nk 2-path 1/8,driving 8
19Mar00-9Aqu fst 1 :224 :453 1:093 1:341 Gotham-G3 83 9 3nk 4¾ 2½ 5¾ 78¾ Beckner D V L 123 17.50 88-11 RedBullet113½ Aptitude1134 PerformingMagic114¾ Chased 3 wide, tired 9
26Feb00-9Aqu fst 6f ▪:23 :46 :574 1:103 BestTurn82k 86 3 4 1hd 1½ 11½ 11 Beckner D V L 122 *1.60 89-14 Mx'sPl1221 AppelingDnger113¾ MnorProspct115nk Vied outside, driving 7
23Jan00-6Aqu fst 6f ▪:232 :464 :59 1:113 FCapossela81k 90 5 2 1hd 1½ 13 12 Beckner D V L 117 *1.55 84-19 Max's Pal1172 Citizen1152½ Rich Down1153½ Drew clear, driving 6
2Jan00-3Aqu fst 6f ▪:223 :454 :58 1:104 Alw 45000N2X 89 4 3 21½ 1½ 1hd 1nk Beckner D V L 117 2.95 88-17 Max'sPl117nk GngstRp1191¾ ChiefJStrongbow1171½ Gamely inside, driving 5
10Oct99-7Med gd 5f Ⓣ:213 :453 :583 Morven45k 64 4 4 32 32 34½ 53½ Rivera L Jr L 117 4.50 81-16 Brilliant Deniro117¾ Rumsononthriver111½ D'part114½ No punch 11
19Sep99-8Del fst 6f :213 :444 :58 1:113 Dover75k 69 4 2 2hd 2hd 1hd 41½ Diaz L F L 115 *1.30 84-12 LghtnngPcs1171 ABCMmmGd115hd AllOrThCt115no Pace, faded final 1/8 7
27Aug99-8Mth gd 6f :213 :443 :57 1:102 Alw 30000N1X 78 5 1 1hd 1hd 11 11½ Diaz L F L 118 8.70 90-14 Max's Pal1181½ Gadir120¾ Zemped1141 Dueled, game effort 6
4Aug99-1Del fst 5f :22 :461 :591 Md Sp Wt 29k 59 4 2 2½ 1hd 1½ 1no Diaz L F L 118 *1.90 89-11 Max's Pal118no Tuscan Chief1181½ Trentino118¾ Short lead all out 7

WORKS: Apr6 Aqu 4f fst :49 B 4/13 ●Mar29 Aqu 5f fst :59 Hg 1/11 Mar24 Aqu 5f fst 1:04 B 20/27 ●Mar16 Aqu 5f fst 1:023 B 1/4 Mar11 Aqu▪ 5f fst 1:041 Bg 11/12 Mar3 Aqu▪ 4f fst :492 B 2/3
TRAINER: +180Days(15 .27 $1.92) Dirt(304 .23 $1.75) Sprint(221 .24 $1.78) GrdStk(20 .20 $1.90)

3 Kashatreya

Own: Cohn Seymour
Purple/white Blocks White Sleeves
PEZUA J M (35 4 5 6 .11) 2001:(90 14 .16)

Ch. g. 7
Sire: Daring Groom (Blushing Groom*Fr) $2,000
Dam: Douce Carotte(Caro*Ire)
Br: Cohn Seymour (NY)
Tr: Hertler John O(11 3 1 1 .27) 2001:(42 5 .12)

L 113

Life	38	9	6	5	$505,848	105	D.Fst	29	8	5	3	$442,829	105
2001	3	0	1	1	$28,051	99	Wet(350)	8	1	1	2	$63,019	101
2000	7	2	0	1	$135,295	101	Turf(175*)	1	0	0	0	$0	75
Aqu	12	3	1	2	$186,973	100	Dist	19	6	2	4	$359,464	105

17Mar01-8Aqu fst 7f :22 :44 1:081 1:211 3+ Toboggan H107k 90 4 4 47 43½ 51½ 59 Pezua J M L 114 28.75 85-17 PpingTom118½ SyFloridSndy117hd LkPontchrtrn1133½ Rail run turn, tired 6
18Feb01-8Aqu fst 6f ▪:224 :452 :57 1:092 3+ ⓈHol Hughes H79k 99 1 5 56 51¾ 32½ 22¾ Pezua J M L 119 6.00 95-10 SayFloridSndy1232¾ Kshtrey1191¾ Entepreneur116½ Inside move, gamely 5
27Jan01-9Aqu fst 6f ▪:222 :45 :563 1:09 3+ Paumonok H80k 96 5 5 54 43 33½ 33¾ Pezua J M L 116 10.50 96-06 Lexicon1191½ Say Florida Sandy1192½ Kashatreya1161½ Inside run turn 6
23Dec00-8Aqu fst 6f ▪:223 :454 :573 1:094 3+ Gravesend H-G3 90 7 10 96 94 65 55½ Castillo H Jr L 118 6.30 88-13 SyFlrdSndy1161¾ LbrtyGld1151½ LkPntchrtrn1161¾ Pinched early,steadied 11
23Nov00-9Aqu fst 6f :221 :454 :581 1:11 3+ Fall Hwgt H-G2 92 4 7 85½ 72 3nk 1¾ Vergara O L 131 8.60 82-24 Kashtrey131¾ ExcitingStory1311 OroDeMexico130no Split rivals, driving 8
9Nov00-8Aqu fst 6f :224 :46 :572 1:091 3+ Handicap61k 98 4 5 53½ 2hd 2½ 41½ Vergara O L 116 16.80 90-15 BrutllyFrnk122¾ Lumbermn115½ DoubleScren114no 4 wide move, gamely 5
10Jun00-8Bel fst 6f :224 :46 :58 1:101 3+ TrueNorth H-G2 90 2 6 52¾ 52½ 72½ 77¼ Vergara O L 114 18.60 80-13 Intidab1171 Brutally Frank1191¾ Oro DeMexico1131 Between rivals, tired 7
7May00-8Aqu fst 7f :222 :45 1:09 1:213 3+ Carter H-G1 96 1 2 64 62 73 75 Vergara O L 114 14.50e 87-18 BrtllyFrnk116hd WstrnEprssn113½ AffrmdSccss1221½ 3 wide between foes 7
15Apr00-7Aqu gd 6f :212 :44 :56 1:083 3+ BoldRuler H-G3 100 7 7 68¾ 54½ 34½ 34½ Vergara O L 115 12.60 89-12 Brutally Frank115hd Kelly Kip1214½ Kashatreya1151¾ Inside run turn 7
27Feb00-9Aqu fst 6f ▪:222 :444 :564 1:092 3+ ⓈH Hughes H83k 101 3 8 65 53 1½ 11 Vergara O L 120 *2.55 95-11 Kashatreya1201 SyFloridSndy1181¾ PooskHill1181¼ Stumbled st, lost iron 8
25Nov99-9Aqu sly 6f :223 :453 :57 1:09 3+ Fall Hwgt H-G2 98 1 5 52½ 53 43½ 46¾ Pezua J M L 127 9.00 86-18 Richter Scale1345¾ Aristotle130¾ Bought·In Dixie128nk Checked rail turn 7
10Sep99-9Bel my 7f :222 :45 1:091 1:221 3+ ⓈGenDMacArthH54k 87 5 2 69½ 56½ 34 36¼ Gryder A T L 121 5.80 85-19 StlwrtMember1162¾ FourthAndSix1173½ Kshtry1211½ 3 wide run turn,faded 6
11Aug99-9Sar fst 6f :224 :452 :57 1:09 3+ A Phenomn H-G2 92 3 3 75½ 63¾ 75 710½ Samyn J L L 111 48.25 85-12 Intidab1131½ Artax1172¾ Yes It's True117¾ Steadied repeatedly 7
4Jly99-8Bel fst 7f :223 :444 1:08 1:203 3+ Tom Fool H-G2 84 4 5 56½ 57 58 513½ Samyn J L L 112 12.50 86-08 Crafty Friend116¾ Affirmed Success1195 Artax117hd Inside, no response 5
5Jun99-8Bel fst 6f :212 :442 :564 1:093 3+ TrueNorthH-G2 105 3 9 812 74¾ 5¾ 1¾ Samyn J L L 110 26.50 93-10 Kashatreya110¾ Artax119¾ The Trader's Echo1111 Determinedly outside 9
19May99-8Bel sly 6½f :222 :451 1:09 1:152 3+ Alw 46000N3X 78 7 5 73½ 43 49½ 612½ Bailey J D L 120 2.35 82-07 Master O Foxhounds122½ Intidab1186¾ Iron Will1223 5 wide, no rally 10
24Apr99-6Aqu fst 6f :223 :451 :57 1:092 4+ Alw 57000C 92 4 5 63¾ 53 43½ 31½ Pezua J M L 117 2.70 89-14 OroDeMexico117no KingRuckus1171½ Kshtry117¾ Steadied stretch,game 7
28Feb99-8Aqu sly 6f ▪:222 :45 :571 1:101 3+ ⓈHolliHughesH53k 101 4 2 54 52¾ 32½ 1½ Pezua J M L 116 3.90 91-16 Kashatreya116½ Thepromonroe115nk Dr J1162¾ Dug in, along late 5
31Jan99-8Aqu fst 6f ▪:231 :46 :574 1:094 4+ Alw 44000N3X 105 4 6 74½ 62½ 2½ 1¾ Pezua J M L 120 3.35 93-19 Kashatreya120¾ Mr.Buffum118nk Copeln'sPche1092½ Steadied,split rivals 9
26Dec98-8Aqu fst 6f ▪:224 :46 :581 1:11 3+ GravesendH-G3 92 1 8 64½ 31½ 32½ 53 Douglas R R L 114 25.00 84-21 SFlrdSnd117nk EstmdFrnd114nk HmOnThRd1171½ Inside move, weakened 8

WORKS: ●Apr6 Bel tr.t 4f fst :47 B 1/35 Mar12 Bel tr.t 4f fst :491 B 20/66 Mar4 Bel tr.t 4f fst :484 H 5/72 Feb13 Bel tr.t 4f fst :484 B 8/26 Feb8 Bel tr.t 4f fst :49 B 11/42 Jan23 Bel tr.t 3f fst :37 B 2/17
TRAINER: Dirt(187 .11 $1.55) Sprint(144 .12 $1.67) GrdStk(10 .10 $1.92)

4 Delaware Township

Own:New Farm
Purple, Black Collar/diamond, Black
WILSON R (3 2 0 0 .67) 2001:(148 34 .23)

Ch. h. 5
Sire: Notebook (Well Decorated) $15,000
Dam: Sunny Mimosa(Sunny North)
Br: Bono Mr & Mrs Harry (Fla)
Tr: Perkins Ben W Jr(13 4 2 1 .31) 2001:(74 14 .19)

L 117

Life	14	7	2	1	$410,110	116	D.Fst	13	7	2	1	$402,610 116
2001	2	0	1	0	$49,000	105	Wet(400)	1	0	0	0	$7,500 67
2000	8	4	1	1	$287,010	116	Turf(215)	0	0	0	0	$0 –
Aqu	0	0	0	0	$0	–	Dist	7	4	0	1	$248,010 116

19Feb01- 9Lrl fst 7f :222 :443 1:092 1:22 3↑ Gen GeorgeH-G2 **105** 3 5 43¼ 43¾ 2½ 23½ Bravo J L 120 2.20 93 – 16 *PeepingTom*1143½ DlwrTownship1202¾ *DiscoRico*1171¾ 3-4w,rzd 3/8,willing 7
15Jan01- 9GP fst 6f :213 :442 :564 1:093 3↑ MrProspectH-G3 **99** 6 9 84 73¾ 41¾ 42½ Day P L 116 *1.40 89 – 14 *Istintaj*1162 Miners Gamble115nk Smokin Pete115hd Finished willingly 13
4Nov00- 6CD fst 6f :204 :432 :551 1:073 3↑ BC Sprint-G1 **94** 14 9 109¼ 119½ 1110 107½ Sellers S J L 126 14.10 99 — *KonGold*126½ HonestLdy123½ BetOnSunshine1262 Wide early,no factor 14
14Oct00- 7Bel fst 6f :213 :442 :561 1:082 3↑ ForestHllsH-G2 **110** 1 2 32 1hd 11½ 11½ Day P L 114 2.80 96 – 10 DelawareTownship1141½ Bevo1144 ValintHlory1132¾ 3 wide move, driving 7
23Sep00- 9Bel fst 7f :221 :443 1:083 1:213 3↑ Vosburgh-G1 **103** 6 10 42 31 22½ 43¾ Bravo J L 126 b 10.30 91 – 13 Trippi123½ MoreThanReady1232¼ *OneWyLove*1261 Sluggish start, inside 10
27Aug00- 8Mth fst 6f :212 :433 :553 1:074 3↑ Longfellow75k **116** 2 7 2hd 1hd 14 17 Bravo J L 113 b 2.80 102 – 11 DlwrTownshp1137 🄳LoddGn1192 ***SyFlrdSndy***122¾ Aggressive hand ride 8
22Jly00- 9Mth fst 1 :24 :474 1:121 1:371 3↑ SalvatoreH-G3 **104** 2 11½ 1½ 1hd 1hd 21¼ Bravo J L 112 b 4.50 87 – 12 LvItToBzr1201¼ *DlwrTwnshp*1125 PrmDrctv1141¾ Broke thru gate,gamely 5
30Jun00- 9Mth fst 6f :221 :452 :573 1:102 3↑ OClm 50000(50-45)N **102** 4 1 1½ 12 13½ 15½ Bravo J L 120 b *.20 89 – 24 DlwrTownshp1205½ PonrSprt1185 WlknrndMny1165½ Widened, ridden out 4
1Jun00- 8Mth fst 6f :22 :442 :562 1:084 3↑ OClm 50000(50-45)N **96** 5 3 3½ 42½ 32 32 Velasquez C L 120 *1.40 95 – 12 Mckendree1182 *ProudestBull*118no *DelwrTownship*1204¾ Outside, gaining 7
13May00- 4Pim fst 6f :234 :462 :581 1:102 3↑ OClm 35000(35-30)N **96** 6 7 2hd 1hd 12½ 12 Wilson R L 119 *1.20 94 – 10 DlrTnshp1192 TlghtPrnc1192 FrtyEghtHrs115nk Brk slow,sent wd,drvng 7
Previously trained by Perkins Benjamin W
5Sep98-12Crc sly 7f :221 :454 1:123 1:261 🅂Fla Stallion125k **67** 6 7 61¾ 2½ 31½ 48¼ Toribio A R 118 *.60 70 – 18 SlyRajab1183¾ GradeOne1181 *TenPoundTest*1183½ Drew even,nothing left 9
Affirmed division Previously trained by Perkins Ben W Jr
2Aug98- 8Mth fst 5½f :214 :45 :572 1:034 Tyro50k **87** 4 3 44 55½ 34 2hd Toribio A R 118 *.60 98 – 10 🄳Heroofthegame116hd DelawareTownship1183 PersonlNote1163¼ Missed 6
Placed first through disqualification.Previously trained by Perkins Benjamin W
19Jun98- 6Bel fst 5½f :221 :46 :58 1:042 Alw 37000N2L **80** 1 2 32½ 2½ 12½ 16 Toribio A R 116 *.65 93 – 10 *Delaware Township*1166 Robin Goodfellow1162¾ Waller1162¼ Kept to task 5
20May98- 1Del fst 4½f :23 :472 :532 Md Sp Wt 24k **73** 6 4 1hd 12½ 19½ Toribio A R 118 *.40 92 – 19 *DlwrTownshp*1189½ LttlMornngDw1184½ GlttrngStr1183¼ Green, ridden out 6

WORKS: Apr11 Aqu 3f fst :364 B *5/13* ●Apr2 Bel tr.t 5f gd :594 H *1/26* Mar24 Bel tr.t 5f fst 1:004 B *2/35* Mar15 Bel tr.t 5f fst 1:013 B *5/24* ●Feb15 Lrl 4f fst :473 H *1/23* Feb9 GP 5f fst 1:002 B *7/29*
TRAINER: 31-60Days(71 .30 $2.44) Dirt(304 .23 $1.75) Sprint(221 .24 $1.78) GrdStk(20 .20 $1.90)

5 Say Florida Sandy

Own:Rotella John
Hot Pink, Lime Green Diamond Hoop, Pink
BRAVO J (75 14 13 16 .19) 2001:(343 70 .20)

Dk. b or br h. 7
Sire: Personal Flag (Private Account) $8,500
Dam: Lolli Lucka Lolli(Sweet Candy*Ven)
Br: Bacon Sanford (NY)
Tr: Serey Juan(43 13 7 5 .30) 2001:(147 42 .29)

L 117

Life	69	24	12	8	$1,282,406	110	D.Fst	59	24	10	6	$1,229,552 110
2001	5	2	2	0	$125,281	109	Wet(310)	9	0	2	2	$52,854 109
2000	15	5	5	1	$366,787	107	Turf(250*)	1	0	0	0	$0 36
Aqu	16	4	4	3	$244,888	110	Dist	47	19	9	5	$1,017,299 110

7Apr01- 8Aqu fst 1 :23 :452 1:081 1:333 3↑ WestchestrH-G3 **95** 1 2hd 3nk 31½ 32½ 56¼ Bravo J L 116 f *1.70 93 – 04 Ct'sAtHome1142½ LittleHns1131¼ MilwukBrw1171 Altered course stretch 6
17Mar01- 8Aqu fst 7f :22 :44 1:081 1:211 3↑ Toboggan H107k **109** 6 1 32½ 32 2½ 2½ Bravo J L 117 f 3.50 93 – 17 PpingTom118½ SyFloridSndy117hd **LkPontchrtrin**1133½ Led between calls 6
18Feb01- 8Aqu fst 6f ⊡ :224 :452 :57 1:092 3↑ 🅂Hol Hughes H79k **106** 3 2 3½ 2hd 11½ 12¾ Bravo J L 123 f *.70 98 – 10 SayFloridSndy1232¾ **Kshtrey**1191¾ Entepreneur116½ Split foes, ridden out 5
27Jan01- 9Aqu fst 6f ⊡ :222 :45 :563 1:09 3↑ Paumonok H80k **102** 2 4 42 22½ 23 21½ Bravo J L 119 f *1.55 98 – 06 Lexicon1191½ *SayFloridaSandy*1192¼ **Kashatreya**1161¼ Game finish outside 6
6Jan01- 7Aqu fst 6f ⊡ :222 :451 :571 1:094 4↑ Handicap61k **107** 4 6 55 3½ 1hd 11½ Bravo J L 121 f *.90e 93 – 17 SyFlordSndy1211½ Bbby'sBckr1171½ UnrlMdnss1141¼ 3 wide move, driving 7
23Dec00- 8Aqu fst 6f ⊡ :223 :454 :573 1:094 3↑ Gravesend H-G3 **104** 5 7 72 52¾ 12½ 11¾ Bravo J L 116 f 6.70 93 – 13 *SyFlrdSndy*1161¾ *LbrtGld*1151½ **LkPntchrtrn**1161¾ Bumped,bid,kept to drv 11
29Nov00- 8Aqu gd 6f :214 :443 :563 1:093 3↑ Alw 52000N$Y **87** 9 8 61¾ 63¾ 53 2¾ Rosario H L5 L 118 f 3.00 88 – 15 **LkPntchrtrn**119¾ *SyFlrdSndy*118hd Blncthbdgt1191 Game finish outside 10
4Nov00- 4Aqu fst 7f :222 :45 1:091 1:214 3↑ SportPage H-G3 **99** 3 1 52¼ 41¼ 62¾ 44¼ Bravo J L 117 f 4.00 87 – 12 ***StlwrtMember***1171 *Istintj*1172½ MisterTricky112¾ Between foes, no rally 6
21Oct00- 5Bel fst 6f :221 :451 :57 1:092 3↑ 🅂Hudson H125k **98** 9 9 51½ 51¾ 62 41½ Bridgmohan S X L 123 f 2.40 89 – 12 ***StlwrtMembr***120nk PooskHill1161¼ *Chsin'Wimmin*121hd 4 wide, good finish 9
7Oct00- 7Del fst 6f :222 :46 :584 1:114 3↑ Wilmington H100k **103** 2 3 2½ 3nk 31½ 2½ Bridgmohan S X L 121 f *2.00 83 – 24 JustCallMeCrl119½ SyFloridSndy1211½ *Bobby'sBuckroo*1151¾ Best of rest 7
8Sep00- 8Bel fst 7f :224 :461 1:102 1:23 3↑ 🅂GenDMacArthH83k **105** 5 1 2½ 2hd 12 11¼ Bridgmohan S X L 122 f 4.30 88 – 17 SyFlrdSndy1221¼ HrtsAtRsk1161 Chsn'Wmmn122½ When roused, driving 8
27Aug00- 8Mth fst 6f :212 :433 :553 1:074 3↑ Longfellow75k **92** 3 6 63¼ 57 57½ 39 Lopez C C L 122 f 3.00 93 – 11 **DlwrTownshp**1137 🄳LddGn1192 *SyFlrdSndy*122¾ Not good enough lane 8
Placed second through disqualification.
29Jly00- 9Pha fst 6f :212 :433 :553 1:074 3↑ Pha BCH-G3 **100** 4 4 53¾ 65 54 23 Lopez C C L 117 f 5.30 98 – 11 IronPunch1143 SayFloridSndy117¾ JustCllMeCrl118no Late run, 2nd best 7
2Jly00- 8Mth fst 6f :213 :441 :564 1:10 3↑ Shrewsbury75k **107** 1 6 31 42½ 31 11¾ Bravo J L 119 f *2.20 91 – 17 SyFlordSndy1191¾ *MyJff'sMomb*1131¾ *HldyMsc*1171¼ Eased out turn, drvg 7
27May00- 9Mth fst 6f :222 :452 :574 1:101 3↑ Alw 42000N$Y **93** 2 5 41 42¾ 41¼ 3½ Elliott S L 122 f 1.80 89 – 14 ChngngOthgrd115½ MyJff'sMomb115no *SyFlrdSndy*1222¾ Inside, willingly 6
30Apr00- 7Del fst 6f :222 :452 :574 1:102 3↑ Damitrius75k **104** 3 4 51¾ 41¾ 2hd 11¾ Bridgmohan S X L 119 f *.90 91 – 13 SyFlordSndy1191¾ Monk'sFlcon115nk Bobby'sBckro114no Drifted, driving 6
31Mar00- 8Aqu fst 6f :224 :453 :572 1:092 4↑ Handicap61k **103** 6 2 21 21 1hd 1nk Bridgmohan S X L 116 f 3.10 90 – 19 *SyFloridSndy*116nk *DoubleScren*114nk SwpWll1156¼ Speed outside, driving 7
27Feb00- 9Aqu fst 6f ⊡ :222 :444 :564 1:092 3↑ 🅂H Hughes H83k **98** 7 3 42½ 31½ 2½ 21 Bridgmohan S X L 118 f 3.15 94 – 11 **Kashatreya**1201 *SyFloridSndy*1181¾ PooskHill1181¼ Speed 3 wide, gamely 8
Previously trained by Dowd John F
29Jan00- 9Aqu fst 6f ⊡ :23 :46 :574 1:094 3↑ Paumonk H81k **92** 4 6 53¾ 31½ 45 55½ Bridgmohan S X L 113 f 14.80 87 – 14 Falkenburg1151½ Brushed On113nk He'sACharm1133½ Chased 3 wide, no bid 7
9Jan00- 8Aqu fst 170 ⊡ :24 :473 1:112 1:411 4↑ Alw 59000N$Y **87** 1 63 63¾ 51½ 59 67½ Lopez C C L 114 f 3.60e 87 – 18 BillyHaggard114nk *CarryMyColors*1141 Laredo1141¾ Stumbled badly start 8
Awarded fifth purse money

WORKS: ●Mar4 Aqu ⊡ 3f fst :36 B *1/11* Feb11 Aqu ⊡ 3f fst :381 B *3/3*
TRAINER: 1-7Days(24 .38 $2.81) Route/Sprint(36 .19 $2.01) Dirt(527 .24 $1.82) Sprint(362 .24 $1.78) GrdStk(10 .10 $1.54)

6 Shadow Caster

Own:Gatsas Stables
White, Blue Ball, Blue
MIGLIORE R (43 12 11 4 .28) 2001:(294 51 .17)

Ch. h. 5
Sire: Future Storm (Storm Cat) $5,000
Dam: Just Dance(Duck Dance)
Br: Hobeau Farm (Fla)
Tr: Terranova John P II(8 2 3 0 .25) 2001:(38 6 .16)

L 115

Life	32	8	5	6	$420,667	114	D.Fst	25	7	4	4	$394,717 114
2001	1	0	0	0	$6,438	101	Wet(320)	5	1	1	2	$25,550 92
2000	11	4	2	2	$247,450	114	Turf(300)	2	0	0	0	$400 63
Aqu	3	0	1	0	$19,230	101	Dist	18	5	4	3	$208,649 100

17Mar01- 8Aqu fst 7f :22 :44 1:081 1:211 3↑ Toboggan H107k **101** 1 2 1hd 1½ 31 44 Chavez J F L 116 b 5.60 90 – 17 PpngTom118½ **SyFlordSndy**117hd **LkPontchrtrn**1133½ Set pace, weakened 6
4Nov00- 6CD fst 6f :204 :432 :551 1:073 3↑ BC Sprint-G1 **89** 4 1 31½ 42¼ 109¾ 139½ Chavez J F L 126 b 50.90 98 — *Kona Gold*126½ Honest Lady123½ Bet On Sunshine1262 Pressed,4w,tired 14
14Oct00- 7Bel fst 6f :213 :442 :561 1:082 3↑ ForestHllsH-G2 **76** 4 4 42½ 52¾ 67 513 Chavez J F L 116 b 6.10 83 – 10 **DelawareTownship**1141½ Bevo1144 ValintHlory1132¾ Bumped start, 4 wide 7
30Aug00- 9Sar fst 6½f :213 :441 1:082 1:15 3↑ Forego H-G2 **114** 9 2 31½ 2hd 2½ 11 Chavez J F L 113 b 50.75 99 – 07 ShadowCster1131 Intidb118no SuccessfulAppel119nk Game effort, driving 10
28Jly00- 3Sar fst 6f :222 :45 :57 1:092 4↑ Alw 56000C **100** 4 1 1hd 2½ 1½ 1½ Bailey J D L 116 b 4.00 98 – 07 *Shadow Caster*116½ Oro DeMexico1185 Erlton116¾ Speed inside, driving 5
Previously trained by Assimakopoulos C
26Jun00- 8Rkm fst 6f :222 :452 :574 1:103 3↑ Alw 16660N$Y **98** 6 2 11½ 12½ 12 15 Hampshire J F Jr LB 116 b *.50 96 – 16 *Shadow Caster*1165 Diggin' For Fun118¾ CoArt1168¼ Well off rail, driving 6
3Jun00-11Suf fst 6f :214 :45 :571 1:10 3↑ JB Moseley H186k **98** 4 3 21 32 33½ 32¾ Bridgmohan S X LB 110 b 54.80 90 – 17 KingRoller116¾ Blncethebudget1132 *ShdowCstr*1102¼ Blocked rail bkstr 9
20May00-12Suf gd 6f :214 :444 :573 1:10 3↑ Wm Almy Jr25k **92** 5 1 1½ 12 11 22 Molinari E LB 119 b 3.40 91 – 10 Makin Progress1192 Shadow Caster119¾ *Prolanzier*1221 Faltered 7
6May00-10Suf fst 6f :213 :451 :581 1:111 4↑ Alw 16660N$Y **82** 5 2 1hd 13 11 41 Hampshire J F Jr LB 122 b *.80 86 – 20 MisterJiggs113¾ FrontCover116nk WarthawkBoy117hd Ran out turn, tired 6
12Apr00- 8Suf fst 6f :221 :46 :583 1:114 4↑ Alw 16660N$Y **96** 6 2 11½ 14 15½ 13¾ Hampshire J F Jr LB 114 b *.80e 84 – 20 Shadow Caster1143¾ Kay's Guy1142½ Warthawk Boy1173 Ridden out 7
27Mar00- 8Suf fst 6f :22 :461 :591 1:124 4↑ Alw 16660N$Y **87** 2 3 1½ 1½ 1hd 2¾ Vega H LB 114 b *1.30 78 – 32 Copper Canyon122¾ *Shadow Caster*1141½ Front Cover1172 Faltered 8
13Mar00- 8Suf gd 6f :221 :46 :584 1:114 4↑ Alw 16660N$Y **83** 6 1 11 13 12½ 32¾ Vega H LB 114 b *1.40e 81 – 24 *Copper Canyon*114¾ *Makin Progress*1172 Shadow Caster1143¼ Weakened 7
24Sep99- 4Med yl 5f ⓣ :213 :444 :57 3↑ Alw 40000NC **63** 10 4 51¾ 65¼ 107½ 1110 Bridgmohan S X L 112 b 7.90 82 – 12 I Claudius116½ Rudirudy1221 Seigneurial116½ Three wide trip 12
15Aug99- 9Rkm gd 1$\frac{1}{16}$ ⊗ :231 :464 1:12 1:452 K McHughMemH25k — 4 — — — — — Vega H LB 120 b *.70 — 16 Whr'sTylor1183½ Kng'sClok1168¾ Brb'sGromSkp1146 Stum st, lost jockey 7
6Aug99- 8Sar fst 6f :221 :451 :573 1:101 Amsterdam-G3 **91** 3 2 2hd 1hd 3½ 64¼ Chavez J F L 117 b 30.50 86 – 15 SuccessfulAppel1221¼ LionHerted114¾ SilverSson1191½ Vied inside, tired 9
3Jly99- 9Mth sf 1$\frac{1}{16}$ ⓣ :243 :482 1:123 1:45 LamplightrH75k **38** 5 1½ 2½ 42 712 727 Elliott S L 114 b 18.30 55 – 18 PhiBetaDoc1164½ GreenFee111½ *NorthEastBound*116hd Showed brief lead 7
19Jun99- 8FL fst 6f :221 :444 :564 1:084 3↑ FL Brds Cup-G3 **81** 2 2 3½ 32 37 311¼ Panell D L 106 b 5.70 86 – 13 Good And Tough1197¾ Crucible1133½ Shadow Caster106 Tired 3
29May99-11Suf fst 6f :214 :451 :573 1:094 3↑ JB Moseley H235k **98** 5 1 31 42½ 43½ 45¾ Baez R LB 114 b 30.90 88 – 13 *GoodAndTough*1161 *RunJohnny*1161 *WirMCollct*1143¾ 4 wide, weakened 7
24Apr99- 8Suf fst 1 :234 :472 1:13 1:41 Faneuil Hall25k **82** 1 1½ 11½ 16 19 18 Baez R LB 122 b *.60 85 – 26 Shadow Caster1228 *Heffy*1172¾ Chance Spender1193¾ Rail, easily 8
21Mar99- 9Aqu fst 1 :221 :443 1:092 1:343 Gotham-G3 **44** 6 43 31 64 109¾ 1031½ Luzzi M J L 118 b 134.75 63 – 15 Badge1207½ *Apremont*120¾ Robin Goodfellow1136 Chased on rail, tired 11

WORKS: Apr9 Bel tr.t 4f fst :494 B *17/30* Apr3 Bel tr.t 4f fst :492 B *20/64* Mar28 Bel tr.t 3f fst :361 B *2/25* Mar11 GP 5f fst 1:011 B *4/14* Mar1 GP 5f fst 1:004 B *4/25* Feb24 GP 4f fst :483 B *7/42*
TRAINER: Dirt(105 .18 $2.74) Sprint(78 .18 $3.16) GrdStk(15 .07 $6.90)

Max's Pal is a paragon of consistency in New Jersey and the mid-Atlantic tracks, and though he's been away since October, he won his debut and has won after every layoff line that appears in his past performances. But he has never beaten the level of competition he faces in this spot, and to ask him to do so while also coming off a layoff is asking too much. He's out, and so is Kashatreya, whose recent Beyer figures are just too slow and who doesn't seem to be in form, either.

Trainer Richard Dutrow Jr. has done amazing things with his claims in New York. But Lake Pontchartrain has had trouble closing the deal lately—he's on a four-race losing streak—and Prince Monty would have to improve even on the improvement he has already shown for Dutrow. No thanks.

Shadow Caster finished well behind Say Florida Sandy and Lake Pontchartrain in his first start in 2001, and it is conceivable he can benefit from that outing and improve second time back. On the other hand, since his huge upset of the Forego Handicap in August 2000, he has done little to suggest that was anything more than a fluke. And Shadow Caster is essentially a speed type. With Prince Monty surely aiming for the front end, and Max's Pal likely to show enhanced speed being fresh, Shadow Caster figures to be a victim of the pace from his inside post.

That leaves Delaware Township and Say Florida Sandy.

Delaware Township showed a lot of ability in 2000, especially in the Forest Hills Handicap at Belmont Park, which earned a nice 110 Beyer. In fact, he was a popular dark horse prospect for the Breeders' Cup Sprint at Churchill Downs, at least until the post-position draw, when he drew the 14 hole. He is cutting back to his preferred six-furlong distance in the Bold Ruler after a good try when second in the seven-furlong General George Handicap in his previous start. But his loss in the Mr. Prospector Handicap at Gulfstream in his first start of 2001 is cause for pause.

Sure, Delaware Township finished ahead of nine opponents when fourth in the Mr. Prospector, but he was the 7-5 favorite in that race and he actually lost ground in the final furlong. The winner of the Mr. Prospector, Istintaj, proved to be the most accomplished sprinter in Florida that winter. However, Istintaj was only an upper-level allowance performer the previous year in New York, and he was subsequently trounced when sent to Dubai for the rich Golden Shaheen sprint on the Dubai World Cup undercard. In other words, the sprinters in Florida during the winter of 2001 may not have been up to usual standards. Delaware Township should have run better than he did in the Mr. Prospector.

Say Florida Sandy comes into the Bold Ruler off a tired fifth as the 8-5 favorite in the Westchester Handicap. On the face of it, that race was ugly, but it really wasn't. The Westchester was at a mile, which is farther than Say Florida Sandy wants to go.

In fact, at the Bold Ruler distance, he is an impressive 19 for 47. At all other distances he is only 5 for 22.

Moreover, two starts back, Say Florida Sandy gave Peeping Tom, who whipped Delaware Township in the General George, all he could handle in the Toboggan Handicap, actually taking the lead in deep stretch before bowing by a half-length. And the Toboggan, at seven furlongs, was also a bit longer than Say Florida Sandy prefers.

Say Florida Sandy's ability to close fits the anticipated pace scenario, and the fact that he is running back in just a week is also very encouraging, since his trainer, Juan Serey, bats a heady .380 and sports a gaudy $2.81 return on investment with horses he runs back within a week. The icing on the cake is that Say Florida Sandy is 4-1, while Delaware Township is the 3-2 favorite.

EIGHTH RACE
Aqueduct
APRIL 14, 2001

6 FURLONGS. (1.07²) 26th Running of THE BOLD RULER HANDICAP. Grade III. Purse $100,000. (Up to $19,400 NYSBFOA). A HANDICAP FOR THREE YEAR OLDS AND UPWARD. By subscription of $100 each, which should accompany the nomination; $500 to pass the entry box; $500 to start, with $100,000 added. The added money and all fees to be divided 60% to the winner, 20% to second, 11% to third, 6% to fourth and 3% to fifth. Trophies will be presented to the winning owner, trainer and jockey. Closed Saturday, March 31, 2001 with 17 Nominations.

Value of Race: $109,200 Winner $65,520; second $21,840; third $12,012; fourth $6,552; fifth $3,276. Mutuel Pool $715,899.00 Exacta Pool $553,920.00 Trifecta Pool $347,732.00

Last Raced	Horse	M/Eqt. A.Wt	PP	St	¼	½	Str	Fin	Jockey	Odds $1
7Apr01 ⁸Aqu⁵	Say Florida Sandy	Lf 7 117	5	5	5²	3ʰᵈ	12½	11½	Bravo J	4.20
19Feb01 ⁹Lrl²	Delaware Township	L 5 117	3	2	41½	5½	3ʰᵈ	22½	Wilson R	1.55
17Mar01 ⁸Aqu³	Lake Pontchartrain	Lb 6 113	4	7	7	7	5ʰᵈ	3¾	Espinoza V	a-3.95
17Mar01 ⁸Aqu⁵	Kashatreya	L 7 113	2	4	6⁵	61½	2ʰᵈ	42½	Pezua J M	18.00
7Oct00 ³Med¹	Max's Pal	L 4 116	1	3	1ʰᵈ	1ʰᵈ	4ʰᵈ	5ⁿᵏ	Chavez J F	3.35
17Mar01 ⁸Aqu⁴	Shadow Caster	Lb 5 115	7	6	3½	4½	6⁶	6¹⁶	Migliore R	7.80
11Mar01 ⁸Aqu¹	Prince Monty	Lb 5 114	6	1	22½	2ʰᵈ	7	7	Lopez C C	a-3.95

a–Coupled: Lake Pontchartrain and Prince Monty.

OFF AT 4:14 Start Good. Won driving. Track fast.
TIME :21⁴, :45, :56⁴, 1:08³ (:21.99, :45.13, :56.98, 1:08.67)

$2 Mutuel Prices:

5–SAY FLORIDA SANDY	10.40	4.10	2.50
4–DELAWARE TOWNSHIP		3.00	2.20
1A–LAKE PONTCHARTRAIN (a–entry)			2.30

$2 EXACTA 5–4 PAID $36.00 $2 TRIFECTA 5–4–1 PAID $87.00

Dk. b. or br. h, by Personal Flag–Lolli Lucka Lolli, by Sweet Candy*Ven. Trainer Serey Juan. Bred by Bacon Sanford (NY).

SAY FLORIDA SANDY was unhurried outside early on, rallied four wide on the turn, drew clear when roused and was kept to a drive to the wire. DELAWARE TOWNSHIP raced close up inside, was sent up into traffic entering the stretch, bumping soundly with SHADOW CASTER, was taken up then finished gamely but could not get to the winner. LAKE PONTCHARTRAIN was outrun early as stable mate PRINCE MONTY argued the pace, came wide into the stretch and finished gamely outside. KASHATREYA was outrun early, put in a good run along the inside into the stretch and lacked a solid finishing kick. MAX'S PAL contested the pace along the inside and tired in the final furlong. SHADOW CASTER raced close up outside, rallied three wide nearing the stretch, was bumped soundly as DELAWARE TOWNSHIP attempted to bull his way through turning for home and tired. PRINCE MONTY contested the pace from the outside and tired in the stretch.

Owners— 1, Rotella John; 2, New Farm; 3, Goldfarb Sanford; 4, Cohn Seymour; 5, Dweck Raymond; 6, Gatsas Stables; 7, Goldfarb Sanford & Laneve Nicholas

Trainers—1, Serey Juan; 2, Perkins Ben W Jr; 3, Dutrow Richard E Jr; 4, Hertler John O; 5, Perkins Ben W Jr; 6, Terranova John P II; 7, Dutrow Richard E Jr

Scratched— Stalwart Member (25Mar01 ⁸AQU¹)

$2 Pick Three (7–1–5) Paid $228.50; Pick Three Pool $95,354. $2 Pick Six (7–7–9–7–1–5) 6 Correct Paid $2,684.00; Pick Six Pool $85,916. $2 Pick Six (7–7–9–7–1–5) 5 Correct Paid $49.40

I bet Say Florida Sandy to win and singled him in rolling pick threes, and watched happily as he rallied into a hot pace to take the lead turning for home, then went on to score.

Now, I should note that Delaware Township ran into a wall of horses at the same time Say Florida Sandy was sweeping to the lead. A case could be made that Delaware Township might have been best. But I'm not going to apologize if I got lucky, because all horseplayers need a bit of that.

Boy, if someone could write a book on how to be lucky at the track, what a best-seller that would be!

ABOUT THE AUTHORS

 **ANDREW BEYER** is the author of the all-time best-selling handicapping book, *Picking Winners,* and the popular *My $50,000 Year at the Races, The Winning Horseplayer,* and *Beyer on Speed.* A columnist for the *Washington Post,* Beyer is the creator of the Beyer Speed Figures, the industry standard for measuring racehorse performance, which appear exclusively in *Daily Racing Form.* He lives in Washington, D.C.

 **TOM BROHAMER** is the author of the classic *Modern Pace Handicapping* and is widely recognized as the leading pace analyst in this country. In addition to playing the races professionally, Brohamer lectures about racing throughout Southern California. He lives in Palm Desert, California.

STEVEN CRIST is the CEO, editor, and publisher of *Daily Racing Form*. Crist was formerly the turf writer for *The New York Times*, editor-in-chief of *The Racing Times*, and a vice president of the New York Racing Association. He is known in racetrack circles as the King of the Pick Six. Crist is also the author of *Offtrack* and *The Horse Traders*. He lives in Hempstead, New York.

STEVE DAVIDOWITZ is the author of the handicapping classic *Betting Thoroughbreds*. Davidowitz writes a regular column for *The HorsePlayer Magazine* and an Internet feature for Track Master. Davidowitz is also the editor of *The American Racing Manual,* the annual racing yearbook and almanac published by *Daily Racing Form*. He lives in Stamford, Connecticut.

DAVE LITFIN is the New York handicapper for *Daily Racing Form* and the author of *Dave Litfin's Expert Handicapping* as well as *Real-Life Handicapping*. Besides his daily analysis, Litfin writes a weekly column on handicapping. Before joining *Daily Racing Form*, Litfin was a handicapper for New York's *Daily News*. He lives in Centereach, New York.

JAMES QUINN is the author of many successful handicapping titles, including the recently revised edition of *The Handicapper's Condition Book*. Quinn is recognized as the leading authority on identifying the class of horses, and conducts handicapping seminars throughout Southern California. Quinn has also written the lead articles on the Kentucky Derby and the Breeders' Cup Classic for *The HorsePlayer Magazine*. He lives in Arcadia, California.

ALAN SHUBACK is the European racing writer for *Daily Racing Form* and is one of this country's foremost experts on European racing. At *The Racing Times*, Shuback developed the two-line format for past performances of imports that has become the industry standard and a great benefit to handicappers. Shuback has reported on major races throughout the world. He lives in New York City.

LAUREN STICH writes about pedigree analysis and breeding for *Daily Racing Form*. Stich has worked for *The Morning Telegraph*, *The Racing Times*, and has freelanced on television and for *American Turf Monthly*. Stich also is a Thoroughbred breeder, bloodstock agent, and consultant at Thoroughbred auctions. She lives in Las Vegas, Nevada.

MIKE WATCHMAKER is the national handicapper for *Daily Racing Form*. He helps shape handicapping policy for the paper and improve the data in the past performances. Watchmaker, a former handicapper at *The Racing Times* and New York Racing Association linemaker, also ranks the leaders in each racing division throughout the year and writes regular columns on major events of Thoroughbred racing. He lives in Hicksville, New York.